中国统计出版社
China Statistics Press

（京）新登字 041 号

图书在版编目(CIP)数据

’99 今日中国：汉英对照 / 翟立功主编
－北京：中国统计出版社，1999
ISBN 7-5037-2680-6
I.’9…
II. 翟…
III. 经济建设－成就－中国－英、汉
IV.F12

中国版本图书馆 CIP 数据核字(1999)第 43994 号

中国统计出版社出版
（北京西城三里河月坛南街 75 号　100826）
Published by China Statistics Press
75 Yuetan Nanjie, Sanlihe
Beijing 100826, P.R. China
新　华　书　店　经　销
北京大路策划咨询有限公司设计制作
深圳中轻包装印刷有限公司印刷
889 × 1194 毫米　16 开本　34.5 印张　80 万字
1999 年 11 月第 1 版　1999 年 11 月第 1 次印刷
定价：460 元

《'99 今日中国》编辑委员会

顾　　问：赵启正

编 委 会

主　编：翟立功

副主编：赵少华　谢鸿光　李　军　巨奎林

编　委：（按姓氏笔画排序）

马思敏　王天昊　王庆存　王纪德　王志宏
王瑞明　冯乃林　巨奎林　田雪平　刘　科
刘运朋　任振良　李　军　宋康乐　汪长海
严建辉　张黎明　邸胜军　陈东辉　林大茂
周强武　赵　雯　赵少华　项　威　钟守洋
骆如敏　夏卫东　徐南山　章国荣　谢鸿光
翟立功

总策划：姜永华

编 辑 部

总编辑：刘　科

副总编：朱维盛　陈越月

编辑部成员：（按姓氏笔画排序）

王立群　叶礼奇　张　冰　陈悟朝　倪春海
倪燕尧　魏相臣

China Today ’99 Editorial Committee

序　　言

《’99今日中国》正式出版了。本书详细介绍中国经济总体发展趋势及各地区经济状况、中国高科技工业园区情况，是一部反映新中国建国50年成就的重要文献。

中华人民共和国刚刚度过了50年华诞。对于绵延五千多年的中华文明而言，50年只是弹指一挥间。然而，在这50年中，中国发生了翻天覆地的变化，面貌焕然一新。在中国共产党的领导下，掌握了自己命运的中国各族人民，团结奋斗，艰苦创业，取得了社会主义建设的巨大成就。国内生产总值实际增长了29倍，各项社会事业蓬勃发展，社会主义文明和法制建设以及精神文明建设取得了显著进步，12亿人口基本解决了温饱问题，普遍过上了丰衣足食的生活。半个世纪前贫穷积弱的旧中国已一去不复返，中华民族不仅站起来了，而且正在和平与发展的道路上阔步前进。

新中国成长的过程中，改革开放以来的20年，是中国经济发展生机最旺盛、综合国力增长最快、人民得到实惠最多的时期。这一时期，国内生产总值年均增长速度由改革开放之前26年间的6.1%，提高到9.6%；粮食产量由1978年的3亿多吨提高到1998年的5亿吨以上；主要工业产品成倍增长，技术水平明显提高。根本原因是，在邓小平理论指引下，中国坚持以经济建设为中心，推进改革，扩大开放，勇于探索，确立了社会主义市场经济体制框架，找到了建设有中国特色社会主义的康庄大道。这不仅开创了中华民族伟大复兴的新纪元，而且为今后进一步的繁荣和发展提供了根本保证。

中国人民坚信，再经过50年的奋斗，到下世纪中叶新中国成立100周年时，中国将基本实现现代化，成为一个富强民主文明的社会主义国家。

《’99今日中国》编委会

PREFACE

China Today '99 is now available to our readers. An important document recording the achievements of New China over the past five decades, this book contains a detailed introduction to the developmental trends of the Chinese economy as a whole, as well as the situations in various parts of China and development of the high-tech development zones.

China celebrated its 50th anniversary this October 1st. Compared with 5,000 years of Chinese civilization, 50 years seems a very short span of time. However, China has undergone earth-shaking changes in the last five decades and is now presenting a totally new face to the world. Under the leadership of the Communist Party of China, the Chinese people have taken their fate into their own hands, united, and worked hard to obtain great achievements in socialist construction. China's gross domestic product has increased by 29 times over the past five decades. Social undertakings have flourished. Socialist ethics, culture, and law have made remarkable headway. Most of the 1.2 billion Chinese now have access to sufficient food and clothing. Old China, characterized by poverty and weakness, has become a distant memory. The Chinese nation has not only stood up, but is striding forward along a course of peace and development.

The past 20 years have witnessed the fastest growth of China's comprehensive national strength and the greatest improvements in living standards. During this period, China's average annual GDP growth rate rose from 6.1 percent of the 26 years prior to the reform and opening to 9.6 percent. Grain output increased from 300 million tons in 1978 to 500 million tons, and the output of major industrial products doubled and redoubled, while the technical level of these products was also been greatly upgraded. Following Deng Xiaoping Theory, China has shifted its focus to economic construction, pushing forward the reform and opening and taking bold experimental measures. China has successfully established the framework of a socialist market economic system and has maneuvered the correct path of building socialism with Chinese characteristics. This has not only ushered in a renaissance era for the Chinese nation, but has also laid a solid foundation for further prosperity and development.

The Chinese people believe, through the next 50 years of concerted efforts, their nation will realize modernization in time to celebrate the 100th anniversary of the PRC in 2049. At that time, China will surely emerge as a prosperous, strong, democratic and culturally advanced modern socialist country.

China Today '99 **Editorial Committee**

目　　　录

CONTENTS

发　展　篇　DEVELOPMENT

改革开放篇　REFORM AND OPENING

地　区　篇　ADMINISTRATIVE AREAS

中国科技工业园篇 CHINA'S SCIENCE AND TECHNOLOGY INDUSTRIAL PARKS

资 料 篇 DATABASE

发　展　篇

DEVELOPMENT

发　展　篇

DEVELOPMENT

经济发展综述

Overview: National Economic Development

1949年10月1日，一个庄严的声音响彻世界：中华人民共和国成立了！中国人民从此站起来了！如今，50年过去了，昔日贫穷落后的旧中国已经彻底成为历史，中华大地发生了巨大的变化。50年来，全国各族人民汇集在共和国的旗帜下，万众一心，艰苦奋斗，奋发图强。以毛泽东为核心的第一代领导集体带领人民构筑起社会主义的宏伟大厦，以邓小平为核心的第二代领导集体带领人民走上改革开放的富裕之路，以江泽民为核心的第三代领导集体带领人民沿着建设有中国特色社会主义道路开拓前进、创造新的辉煌。新中国的50年，是中华民族不断探索、不断奋进的50年，是中国人民改天换地、扬眉吐气的50年，是中华人民共和国独立自主、繁荣昌盛的50年。

50年的辉煌成就

50年来，在中国共产党的正确领导下，全国

各族人民用自己勤劳的双手和生生不息的拼搏精神，不断克服前进中的各种艰难困苦，创造了令人瞩目的东方奇迹。短短的50年间，祖国面貌一新，综合国力显著增强，各项建设事业蓬勃发展，对外交往日益密切，人民生活水平大大提高。

一、综合经济实力显著增强，提前实现了“翻两番”的战略目标

建国以来，中国先后制定了一系列国民经济发展战略目标，特别是进入改革开放以后，邓小平站在历史的高度，从国情出发，提出了中国经济发展分“三步走”的伟大战略步骤：第一步，从1981年至1990年国民生产总值翻一番，解决人民的温饱问题；第二步，从1991年到本世纪末国民生产总值再翻一番，人民生活达到小康；第三步，到下世纪中叶，人均国民生产总值达到中等发达国家水平，人民生活比较富裕，基本实现现代化。为实现这些战略目标，全国人民励精图治、艰苦奋斗，取得了一个又一个胜利，在1987年提前3年实现第一步翻一番目标的基础上，到1995年，又提前5年实现了第二步再翻一番的目标。50年来，中国综合经济实力明显增强。1952年国内生产总值为679亿元，1998年达79396亿元，扣除价格因素，年平均增长7.7%，大大高于同期世界年平均增长3%左右的水平。经济的快速增长大大缩小了中国与发达国家的差距。据世界银行估算，1997年中国的经济总量已跃居世界第7位，排在美国、日本、德国、法国、英国和意大利之后。

许多重要工农业产品的产量已跃居世界前列。解放初期，中国钢产量居世界第26位，原油居27位，发电量居第25位，与中国幅员辽阔、人口众多的泱泱大国形象极不相称。经过50年大规模的经济建设，主要农产品中，谷物、肉类、棉花、花生、油菜籽、水果等的产品产量已跃升为世界第一位，茶叶、大豆、甘蔗居第三位。主要工业产品中，钢、煤、水泥、化肥、电视机产量居第一位，发电量、化学纤维居第二位，糖、原油产量分别居第四、五位。其他主要产品产量的位次也明显前移。

经济结构趋于优化。解放初期，中国基本处于自给自足的自然经济阶段，工业、商业、交通运输业极不发达，服务业十分落后，产业结构畸形发展。1952年中国第一产业占国内生产总值的比重高达50.5%，第二、三产业分别仅占20.9%和28.6%。50年来，在农业得到大力加强的基础上，随着工业、金融、科技、文教、信息、咨询和社会服务等第三产业的迅猛发展，中国三次产业结构显现出农业比重不断趋于下降和二、三产业比重逐渐提升的合理化演进过程，符合世界范围产业结构的演化规律。截止1998年，一、二、三产业占国民生产总值的比重分别为18.4%、48.7%和32.9%，与1952年相比，第一产业比重下降32.1个百分点，第二产业比重提高27.8个百分点，第三产业比重提高4.3个百分点，产业结构的不断改善，使一度制约中国经济发展的一些瓶颈产业，如原材料、燃料动力、交通运输等的紧张状况基本缓解。

科学技术发展迅猛，生产力水平大为提高。新中国成立50年来，中国科技队伍不断发展壮大，科研领域不断拓展，科研活动硕果累累，60年代“两弹”的研制成功和牛胰岛素的人工合成；70年代人造卫星的成功发射；80年代北京正负电子对撞机对撞成功、籼型杂交水稻的培育、水下导弹成功的发射、亿次“银河”巨型计算机的研制成功；90年代“银河—Ⅲ”百亿次计算机的成功研制、5兆瓦低温核供应反应堆的投入使用、纳米电子学超高密度信息存储研究取得突破性进展、单克隆抗体技术用于临床治疗等等，一串串闪亮的科技火花，标志着中国在原子能技术、生物技术、高能物理、航天技术、信息技术、自动化技术、新材料技术等许多“高、精、尖”领域已经跨进世界先进行列。

二、第一、二、三产业全面发展，买方市场初步形成

农业生产稳步发展。中国是一个古老的农业大国，解放前的近百年间，由于受帝国主义和封建主义的双重压迫，农业生产水平十分低下。新中国成立以来，特别是中共十一届三中全会以来，农村通过变革生产关系，实行家庭承包责任制、改革农产品购销体制、调整农产品收购价格等一系列重要的政策措施，极大地激发了广大农民的生产积极性，促进了农村经济全面发展。农业增加值由1952年的342.9亿元增加到1998年的14600亿元，扣除价格因素，增长3.5倍，平均每年增长3.3%。农产品产量有了很大的提高。1998年，粮食产量达49000万吨，比1949年增长3.3倍，人均产量比1949年增长1倍；棉花产量达450万吨，增长9.1倍，人均产量增长3倍；油料产量达2314万吨，比1949年增长8.0倍，人均产量增长2.9倍；水产品产量达3906万吨，比1949年增长85.8倍，人均产量增长36.6倍；1997年猪牛羊肉产量达4090万吨，比1949年增长17.6倍，人均产量增长7.7倍。中国用占世界10%的耕地成功解决了占世界22%人口的温饱问题，对世界粮食安全和世界经济发展作出了巨大贡献。

工业经济快速增长。50年来，中国工业发展经历了由优先发展重工业到农轻重并举，由发展纺织、煤炭、机械、钢铁等传统产业向改造传统产业、开发石油、化工、电子、航天航空、生物材料、原子能等新兴产业转化；由主要聚集在东部少数地区向全国各地迅速扩展的发展过程。工业增加值由1952年的119.8亿元增加至1998年的33430亿元，扣除价格因素，增长157.7倍，平均每年增长11.6%。随着工业基础建设的加强，生产能力的不断扩张，主要工业产品产量快速增长。1998年与1949年相比，纱产量由32.7万吨增加到542万吨，增长15.6倍；布由18.9亿米增加到241亿米，增长11.8倍；糖由20万吨增加到826万吨，增长40.3倍；原煤由0.32亿吨增长到12.5亿吨，增长38倍。电视机、电冰箱、照相机、洗衣机、计算机、空调器等一大批新兴电子产品产量也呈迅猛扩张之势：彩色电视机由1980年的3.2万台增加到1998年的3497万台，电冰箱由1957年的0.16万台左右增加到1998年的1060万台；洗衣机由1978年的0.04万台增加到1998年的1207万台；房间空调器由1978年的0.02万台增加到1998年的1157万台。

第三产业长足发展，对经济发展的保障和支持能力大为增强。运输邮电业增加值由1952年的29亿元增加到1998年的5029亿元，扣除物价因素，实际增长42.5倍，平均每年增长8.6%。在交通运输方面，货运量由1949年的1.61亿吨增至1998年的126.44亿吨，增长78倍，其中，公路运量增长最快，为121.6倍，铁路运量增长27.8倍，水运增长42.1倍，管道运输增长57.4倍。客运量由1949年的1.37亿人增至1998年的137.73亿人，相当于平均每人旅行11次，比1949年的0.25次提高了43倍。沿海主要港口货物吞吐量大大增强，由1952年的1440万吨增至1998年的92237万吨，增长63倍。邮件处理手段逐步机械化，邮政综合计算机网的建设已经取得了明显成效。邮电通信业的大力发展，使人们一般交流和贸易交流的方式已由改革之初的以信件、电话、电报为主要方式发展为包括移动电话、传真、传呼、电子邮件(e-mail)、数据传输等多种先进快捷的交流方式。金融保险业增加值由1952年的11亿元增加到1996年的4017亿元，扣除价格因素，实际增长68.3倍，年均增长10.1%。与此同时，各种新兴服务业应运而生，社区服务网络逐步形成，大大方便了人民群众的生活。

三、基础设施明显改善，经济发展后劲进一步增强

1950-1998年中国共完成固定资产投资

177993亿元，其中基本建设完成投资72125亿元，更新改造完成投资32516亿元，投产建成基本建设项目130多万个，其中大中型项目约6200个。各行各业的基础设施和装备得到极大的发展和改善，积累了雄厚的“家底”，不仅大大促进了各时期经济的增长，而且为下阶段经济的进一步发展以及实现第三步战略目标打下了良好的基础。

在工业方面，彻底改变了旧中国基础薄弱、技术落后、部门残缺不全、分布极不合理的状况，建立了门类比较齐全、布局比较合理、独立的工业体系，生产能力大为增强。石油生产摘掉了“中国贫油”的帽子，建立了大庆、华北、胜利、克拉玛依、塔里木以及渤海、南海等一大批大型和特大型油田，原油生产量由1949年的12万吨扩大到1998年的1.61亿吨。钢铁生产雄居世界首位，建立了首钢、武钢、攀钢、宝钢、鞍钢等一大批骨干钢铁企业，年产钢量由1949年的15.8万吨扩大到1998年的11559万吨，增长了731倍。汽车生产从无到有，迅速扩张，先后建立了一汽、二汽、上海大众、湖北神龙等一批具有一定规模的现代汽车企业，汽车年产量由1955年的100辆左右迅猛扩展到1998年的163万辆，年生产能力已达到200万辆。结束了长期困扰中国缺电、少电的历史，建立了葛洲坝水电站、漫湾水电站、隔河岩水电站、庄于电厂、石调口二电厂以及秦山和大亚湾核电站等一大批水电、火电、核电厂，正在建设中的三峡水利枢纽工程、黄河小浪底、二滩水电站等特大型工程也将于近年建成发电。发电量由1949年的43亿千瓦小时增长到1998年的11670亿千瓦小时，增长270倍，此外，煤炭、水泥以及电子、通讯、船舶等的生产能力也大大增强。工业整体技术水平大为提高。50年来，采取自主创新和技术引进相结合的方式填补了许多国内空白，一批标志着国家工业实力的工业产业从无到有，从小到大，迅速发展壮大。现代冶金设备、采矿设备制造业，大型电力设备制造业，飞机、汽车制造业，大型精密机床制造业，高级合金和重要有色金属冶炼业，石油化学工业，有机合成材料制造业，航空航天工业，电子计算机工业，船舶工业等等的建立，都标志着中国工业技术水平已达到了相当的高度。

在农田水利方面，大力发展农村水利事业，农田灌溉条件大大改善。全国灌溉面积已由1952年的1996万公顷扩大到1997年5124万公顷。建成了大量的防洪、排涝、灌溉、发电等工程设施。到1997年底，全国兴建大中型水库8.5万座，总蓄水容量4583亿立方米。农业生产条件大大改善，逐步走上机械化、水利化、电气化的道路。1997年与1952年相比，农业机械总动力由18万千瓦增加到42016万千瓦；农用大中型拖拉机由1307台增加到689051台；农用载重汽车由280辆增加到875571辆。耕、种、排、灌、收割、运输实行一条龙机械化操作的面积逐年增加。

在交通运输方面，已基本形成以铁路为骨干，公路、水运、民用航空和管道组成的综合运输网。铁路营业里程由1949年的2.18万公里增至1998年的5.76万公里，增长1.6倍，先后建成了包兰、兰新、宝成、成昆、湘黔、湘赣、浙赣、京九等重要铁路干线，形成了纵横交错的铁路交通干线网，除西藏外，全国其他省、自治区、直辖市都已通了铁路，广大内陆地区交通闭塞、经济文化落后的状况有了明显的改观。公路里程由1949年的8.07万公里增至1998年的127.9万公里，增长14.8倍，公路等级明显提高，路况大为改善，建成了京津塘、沈大、沪杭甬、广深等一大批高速公路，还有许多正在建设中。内河航道经过疏浚，通航条件大大改善，通航里程由1949年的7.36万公里增长到1998年的11.03万公里。民用航空是中国发展最快的运输方式，到1998年为止，民用航空开通了1122条国际国内航线，构成了四通八达的蓝天运输网；管道运输伴随石油工业的成长迅速发展，输油(气)管道里程由1958年的200

公里增加到1998年的2.31万公里。

在邮电通讯方面，已建成包括光纤、数字微波、程控交换、移动通信等覆盖全国、通达世界的公用电信网，并建成了业务种类齐全、网点密布的公用邮政网。全国邮路和农村投递线路总长度由1949年的70.6万公里增加到1998年的621.5万公里，增加7.8倍。目前，全国已有77.6%的乡镇设有邮电局，通电话乡镇的比重达92.9%，进入长话自动网的乡镇比重达87.5%。电话网规模容量迅速扩大。电话交换机容量已由1952年的47万门猛升至1998年的1.38亿门。网路规模在世界上排名迅速上升至世界第二位。移动通讯、数据通信从无到有，迅猛发展。1998年中国的移动通信用户已达2386万户，固定电话和移动电话总用户已突破1亿户大关，数据通信网络也初具规模，1998年中国电信数据通信总用户已达到156万户，其中，计算机互联网(CHINA-NET)用户达到68万户，中国公众多媒体用户达到52.5万户。

四、城乡居民生活水平显著提高，基本实现了从贫困到小康的历史性跨越

50年来，伴随着中国经济的迅猛发展，综合国力的显著增强，城乡居民生活也连续上了几个大的台阶，总体上经历了消除贫困、解决温饱、迈向小康三个大的过程，消费水平、消费结构和消费环境都发生了明显变化，全国居民实际消费水平由1952年的每人每年80元，提高到1998年的每人每年2973元。城乡居民储蓄存款由1952年的8.6亿元增加到1998年的53408亿元，消费结构基本改变了多少年来以吃、穿等生存资料为主的单一格局，住、用、行和文化娱乐等享受和发展方面的消费支出明显提高。建国之初，城镇居民用于吃和穿的开支占到全部生活费支出的80%，农村居民更是高达90%以上。到1998年，生活费支出中城镇居民用于吃和穿的支出比重已下降为55.6%，农村居民下降为59.6%。城市煤气、液化气普及率由1957年的1.5%提高到1998年的78.8%。居民生活的舒适程度大大提高。居民家庭对现代化的耐用消费品的拥有，从无到有，从少到多，且普及程度迅速提高，大大提高了城乡居民的生活水平。人们对消费品的购买从50-70年代的百元级“老四件”（自行车、手表、缝纫机、收音机），80年代千元级的“新六件”（电视机、洗衣机、录音机、电冰箱、电风扇、照相机）到90年代万元级、十万元级的电脑、小汽车、商品房，消费档次大大提高。目前，“老四件”早已在农村普及、“新六件”在多数城镇也已接近饱和，人们对万元级商品的需求正处于资金积累和逐步增加消费的阶段。到1998年底，城镇居民家庭平均每百户耐用消费品拥有量：彩色电视机105台、电冰箱76台、洗衣机91台、照相机36台。农村居民家庭每百户耐用消费品拥有量：自行车137辆、电冰箱9台、彩色电视机33台、洗衣机23台。

五、对外经济关系日趋密切，在世界贸易中的地位日益增强

50年来，中国对外贸易经历了从仅对前苏联和东欧等周边国家进行贸易到逐步扩展为包括日本、欧盟、美国等在内的220多个国家和地区的发展过程。对外贸易规模不断扩大，在世界贸易中的地位不断提高。对外贸易总额由1952年的19.4亿美元增至1998年的3239亿美元，增长166倍，年均增长速度高达11.8%。进出口总额在世界贸易中的排名已由1978年的第32位上升到第11位，其中，出口总额在世界出口贸易中的排名居第9位，中国已成为世界上举足轻重的贸易大国。外汇储备由改革开放之初的21.5亿美元增加到1998年的1450亿美元，居世界第二位。出口商品结构不断改善。1952年，农副产品等初级产品出口所占比重高达83.4%，1998年，机电产品、轻纺产品等高附加值的工业制成品比重高达88.8%，初级产品的比重则下降为11.2%。

利用外资规模不断扩大。建国之初，由于受到西方国家的经济封锁，中国利用外资渠道单一，规模小，主要依靠前苏联向中国提供低息贷款。随着中国经济的发展，特别是从1978年开始实行改革开放政策以来，利用外资工作得到迅速发展，不仅规模大、项目多，而且形式多样。1978-1998年，中国实际利用外资总额累计达4069亿美元，外商投资在农业、工业、交通、饮食娱乐业等部门兴办了一大批企业和设施；外商投资还进入了邮电业、商品零售业、金融保险业等领域。20年间共批准外商直接投资项目30多万个。外商投资的平均规模由80年代初的122万美元增加到1998年的263万美元。

迈向更加辉煌的21世纪

新中国50年之际，也是中国即将迈入新世纪之时。展望下世纪，中国共产党的第十五次代表大会为中国勾画经济发展的宏伟蓝图：第一个十年实现国民生产总值比2000年翻一番，使人民的小康生活更加宽裕，形成比较完善的社会主义市场经济体制；再经过10年的努力，到建党100年时，使国民经济更加发展，各项制度更加完善；到世纪中叶建国100年时，基本实现现代化，建成富强民主文明的社会主义国家。

这一目标的确立是建立在中国过去50年经济发展经验总结及未来中国经济发展现实条件的基础上的。从国际形势看，尽管短期内国际局势有许多不确定因素，但长期来看，全球化和多极化是人类社会发展的大趋势，争取较长时期的国际和平环境是可能的。从国内形势看，中国在经济发展空间、物质基础和资金供应方面仍具有快速发展的潜力和动因，首先是人均收入水平偏低，城乡、地区、产业结构发展不平衡为经济增长提供了空间；其次是经济快速增长的物质基础较为充足。建国后尤其是近20年来中国已形成可观的综合国力，劳动力供应充足，农业稳定发展，能源、交通、通信等“瓶颈”制约状况大为缓解；再次是经济快速增长有资金的保证，国内的资金积累、高储蓄率仍将是主要资金渠道，中国的巨大市场也将吸引越来越多的外资。更为重要的是，中国有已被实践证明是正确的建设有中国特色社会主义基本理论和路线的指导，有建国50年来建设社会主义正反两方面的经验教训。这些都将为实现中共十五大提出的宏伟战略蓝图提供强大的思想政治保证。

同时，人们也应该看到，中国在前进道路上还存在许多困难和挑战：国民经济整体素质不高，结构不合理现象严重；地区发展差距较大；农村人口比重大，劳动力素质低；城乡之间、地区之间、各收入阶层间居民收入差距扩大，城乡部分群众生活比较困难；人均资源短缺与环境污染比较严重，环境保护和可持续发展面临严峻挑战等。重视和不断解决这些问题，是推动中国经济持续发展的动力。

站在世纪之交的门槛，回顾过去，中国人无不为取得的辉煌成就而自豪，无不为祖国的日益昌盛而骄傲；展望未来，人们对建设一个更加强大的中国充满信心，21世纪将是中国改变落后面貌，实现民族腾飞的世纪。中国人民相信，在邓小平理论伟大旗帜指引下，在中国共产党坚强领导下，经过全国各族人民同心协力，顽强拼搏，一定能够战胜前进路上的各种困难，将建设有中国特色社会主义的伟大事业推向更加辉煌灿烂的明天。

On October 1, 1949, a solemn voice announced to the world: “The People’s Republic of China is now founded, and the Chinese people have stood up.” Now, 50 years have passed, great changes have taken place, and the old,

backward China no longer exists.

For the past 50 years, all nationalities of the country, united with one heart under the banner of the People's Republic of China, have worked strenuously for the prosperity of the country. The first generation of leadership, with Chairman Mao Zedong at the core, led the people to establish the great mansion of socialism, and the second generation of leadership, with Deng Xiaoping at the core, directed the people to get on the track of reform, opening up and prosperity; and the third generation of leadership, with Jiang Zemin at the core, led the people to embark on the socialist market economy path with Chinese characteristics, and created new prosperity. The past 50 years were ones of continuous searching and hard work; 50 years of changing the world and pride; and 50 years of independence and prosperity in the history of the People's Republic of China.

Remarkable Achievements in the Past 50 Years

Under the leadership of the Communist Party of China, the Chinese people have surmounted numerous difficulties and made marvelous achievements with their own hands and their conrageous spirit. China has taken on a new look as its comprehensive national power has been strengthened, with all industries devloping vigorously, foreign relations expanded and people's living standards improved greatly.

I. Comprehensive Economic Power Promoted and Strategic Target of "Quadrupling GNP" Achieved Ahead of Schedule

Ever since the establishment of the PRC, the Chinese government has set a series of strategic targets for national economic development. After the introduction of the policy of reform and opening, Deng Xiaoping proceeded from China's actual conditions and proposed the great strategic "Three Steps" of economic development. Step 1, to double China's GNP of 1981 by the year 1990 with the chief aim of providing adequate food and clothing for the Chinese people. Step 2, to double the GNP once again so that the Chinese people would enjoy a fairly comfortable life by the end of this century. Step 3, to increase the per capita

GNP to the level of a medium-developed country by the middle of the next century and achieve modernization. In order to achieve these targets, the Chinese people have exerted great efforts, worked hard and tirelessly, and achieved one success after another. In 1987, the target of the first step was achieved 3 years ahead of schedule, and in 1995, the target of the second step was achieved 5 years ahead of schedule.

China's comprehensive strengh as a nation has been greatly improved since the founding of the PRC. The GNP was 67.9 billion yuan RMB in 1952, and was 7939.6 billion yuan RMB in 1998, representing a yearly increase of 7.7% at constant prices, much higher than the world average of 3% in the same period. This rapid economic growth greatly narrowed the gap between China and tthe deveoped countries. A World Bank estimate in 1997 showed that China's GNP in that year ranked 7th in the world, after the United States, Japan, Germany, France, the United Kingdom and Italy.

China's output of many important industrial and agricultural products ranks first in the world. In the early years after Liberation, China's output of steel ranked 26th in the world, crude oil 27th, and energy production 25th, which hardly fitted China's status as one of the largest and most populous countries in the world. After 50 years of economic construction, China's output of grain, meat, peanut, rapeseed and fruit leapt to become the first in the world, while the output of other major agricultural products such as tea, beans and sugarcane ranked third in the world. As for major industrial products, the output of steel, coal, cement, fertilitzer, cotton, textiles and TV sets ranked first in the world, energy production and synthetic fibers third, sugar forth and crude oil fifth. The output of other major products have also improved their rankings.

The economic structure has been optimized. In the early years after Liberation, China had a self-supporting and self-sufficient resource-based economy. Its industrial structure was irregular, with underdeveloped manufacturing, commerce, transportation and service industries. In 1952, the output of primary industry accounted for 50.5% of the GNP, while secondry industry and tertiary industry accounted for 20.9% and 28.6% respectively. Over 50 years of development, the manufacturing and tertiary industries including finance, science and technology, education and culture, information, advisory and social services, grew rapidly and vigorously on the basis of a greatly strengthened agricultural sector. The proportion of agricultural production decreased, while the proportion of secondary and tertiary industries gradually increased, which is rational and in line with the evolutionary laws of industrialization. By the end of 1998, primary, secondary and tertiary industries accounted for 18.4%, 48.7% and 32.9% of the GNP respectively. Compared with 1952, the proportion of primary industry decreased by 32.1 percentage points, that of secondary industry increased by 27.8 percentage points, and that of tertiary industry increased by 4.3 percentage points. The optimization of the industrial structure eased the stress on provisions of raw materials, energy sources and transportation, which had once constrained the economic development of China.

With the rapid development of science and technology, productivity has been greatly promoted. In the past 50 years, China's growing S&T forces expanded exploration in various fields and scored one achievement after another. In the fields of nuclear technology, bio-technology, high-energy physics, aerospace, information, automation and new materials, China ranks as one of the most developed countries with the successful development of the "two bombs" (the nuclear bomb and hydrogen bomb) and synthetic bovine insulin in the 1960s, the launch of a man-made satellite in the 1970s, the hybridization of indica rice, the launch of a sub-surface missile, and the development of

the "Galaxy" hundred-million-megabyte super-computer in the 1980s, the development of the "Galaxy-III" ten-billion-megabyte the application of the 5MW nuclear heating reactor, the breakthrough in the study on nanometer electronic super-high intensity information memory, the application of the 5MW nuclear heating reactor, the breakthrough in, and the application of single cloned antigen to clinical treatment in the 1990s.

II. With the Harmonious Development of Primary, Secondary and Tertiary Industries, a Buyers' Market Has Taken Initial Shape in China

Agriculture has been steadily developing. China is a large agricultural country with a long history. However, its agricultural production level remained low for nearly a hundred years before Liberation due to the dual oppressive forces of imperialism and feudalism. After the establishment of the PRC, and especially after the 3rd plenary session of the 11th CPC National Congress in 1978, the farmers' enthusiasm was aroused, and the overall development of the rural economy achieved through a series of measures and policies to reform productive relations including the household contract responsibility system, agriproducts purchase-market system reforms, and the adjustment of the purchase price of agri-products. As a result, the value added of agriculture grew by 3.5 times from 34.29 billion yuan RMB in 1952 to 1,460 billion yuan RMB in 1998, representing a yearly increase of 3.3%, allowing for inflation. Agricultural output rose greatly as well. Grain output reached 490 million tons in 1998, increasing by 3.3 times compared with that of 1949, or 100% in terms of per capita output. The output of cotton reached 4.5 million tons, increasing by 9.1 times, or 3 times per capita. In 1997, the output of oil-producing crops reached 23.14 million tons, increasing by 8.0 times or 2.9 times per capita. Aquatic products reached 39.06 million tons, increasing by 85.8 times or 36.6 times per capita. The output of meat reached 40.90 million tons, increasing by 17.6 times or 7.7 times per capita. China has made great contributions to the food security and economic development of the world by providing adequate food and clothing to 22% of the world's population with only 10% of the world's arable land.

Industry is growing rapidly. The past 50 years have witnessed great changes in China's industry, the emphasis of which shifted from heavy industry to the balanced development of agriculture, heavy industry and light industry. Traditional industries such as textiles, coal, machinery and steel have given way to the emerging industries, including petroleum, chemicals, electronics, space, aviation, biogenenics and nuclear energy. The location of these industries has been expanding from the eastern coastal region to all over the country. The output of industry increased 157.7 times from 11.98 billion yuan RMB in 1952 to 3343.0 billion yuan RMB in 1998, allowing for changes in prices, representing an annual growth rate of 11.6%. The output of major industrial products has been rising swiftly with the strengthening of the industrial infrastructure and the expansion of production capacities. The output of yarn increased from 327,000 tons in 1949 to 5.42 million tons in 1998, up 15.6 times; the output of cotton cloth went from 1.89 billion meters to 24.1 billion meters, up 11.8-fold; sugar from 200,000 tons to 8.26 million tons, up 40.3 times; raw coal from 32 million tons to 1250 million tons, up 38 folds. The production of new electronic products like TV sets, refrigerators, cameras, washing machines, computers and air-conditioners also is booming. The production of TVsets increased from 32 thousand in 1980 to 34.97 million in 1998, refrigerators from 1,600 in 1957 to 10.60 million in 1998, washing machines from 400 in 1978 to 12.07 million in 1998, household air-conditioners from 200 in 1978 to 11.57 million in 1998.

Tertiary industry made rapid progress, providing better support and security for economic development. The value added in the sectors of transportation and posts and telecommunications increased by 42.5 times from 2.9 billion yuan RMB in 1952 to 502.9 billion yuan RMB in 1998, allowing for changes in prices, representing an annual growth rate of 8.6%. Freight transportation volume increased from 161 million tons in 1949 to 12.644 billion tons in 1998, up 78-fold. Among this, the volume of road transportation increased by 121.6 times, rail transportation by 27.8 times, water transportation by 42.1 times, and pipeline transportation by 57.4 times. The volume of passenger traffic increased from 137 million persons (0.25 trips per person) in 1949 to 13.773 billion persons (11 trips per person) in 1998, up 43 times. The handling capacity of major coastal ports jumped from 14.4 million tons in 1952 to 922.37 million tons in 1998, up 63 times. Mechanization of mail handling has been accomplished and a comprehensive computerized postal network has resulted in greater efficiency. Modern and rapid means of communication such as mobile phones, fax, pagers, e-mail and data transmission have replaced traditional means, including mail, telephone and telegraph, which earlier dominated people's daily communications and business transactions. The value added in the sectors of finance and insurance increased by 68.3 times from 1.1 billion yuan RMB in 1952 to 401.7 billion yuan RMB in 1996, with an annual growth rate of 10.1%. People have benefited greatly from the emerging services and community service networks.

III. Distinctly Improved Infrastructure and Momentous Economic Development

From 1950 to 1998, China's total investment in fixed assets mounted to 17799.3 billion yuan RMB. Among this, investment of 7212.5 billion yuan on capital construction and 3251.6 billion yuan on epuipment renewal and improvement was accomplished. A total of 1.3 million capital construction projects were completed, 6,200 of which are large or medium sized. The considerable development of basic facilities and equipment in all sectors has provided adequate resources for rapid economic development in different phases and laid a solid foundation for further economic development and the achievement of the strategic target of the Third Step.

In terms of industry, the incomplete and irrationally allocated industrial sector with a weak basis and outdated technology has been replaced by an independent industrial system with a full range, rational layout and strengthened productive capacities. With the establishment of huge oilfields, including the Daqing, North China, Shengli, Karamay, Tarim, Bohai and Huanghai fields, China ceased to be a country poor in oil. The output of crude oil increased from 120,000 tons in 1949 to 161 million tons in 1998. Iron and steel complexes were established in Beijing, Wuhan, Panzhihua, Baoshan and Anshan. The output of steel increased by 731 times, from 158,000 tons in 1949 to 115.59 million tons in 1998, ranking top in the world. A large number of modern automobile enterprises with scale production capacity such as the First Automobile Plant, the Second Automobile Plant, Shanghai Volkswagen and Hubei Citroen were established one after another and the manufacturing of motor vehicles expanded rapidly. The annual production increased from 100 in 1955 to 1.63 million in 1998. At present, China's annual automobile production capacity has reached 2 million. With the establishment of hydro, thermal and nuclear power plants, such as the Gezhouba, Manwan and Geheyan Hydropower plants, Zhuangyu and Shidiaokou power plants, and the Qinshan and Daya Bay nuclear power plants, the problem of electricity shortage in China has been resolved. Super projects, including the Three Gorges Water Control Project, the Xiaolangdi Project on the Yellow River and the Ertan Hydropower Plant are to be completed and connected to the

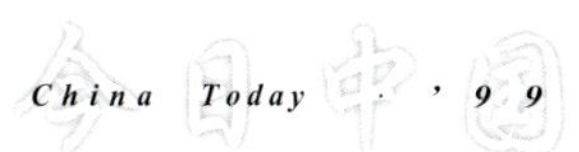

grid in the near future. The volume of power generation has increased by 270 times from 4,300 MWh in 1949 to 1,167,000 MWh in 1998. The production capacity of coal, cement, electronics, telecommunications, shipbuilding, etc. has also greatly risen. In the past 50 years, the overall technological level of industry had risen continuously, and through independent development and technology introduction, industries that symbolize the national strength grew out of nothing and expanded from small to large. The productive capacity of modern metallurgical equipment, mining equipment, large electrical equipment, aircraft, automobiles, large precision machinery and organic synthetic materials, as well as the emergence of aviation, aerospace, computer and shipbuilding industries, show that industrial technology in China has reached a high level.

The government has exerted great efforts in rural water-control works which have greaty improved the irrigation conditions of farmland. The irrigated area of the whole country expanded from 19.96 million hectares in 1952 to 51,24 million hectares in 1997. A large number of flood-control, drainage and irrigation projects, and hydropower plants have been established. By the end of 1997, a total of 85,000 large and medium-sized reservoirs had been built, with a total retaining capacity of 458.3 billion cubic meters. Agricultural production conditions have been highly improved, and mechanization and electrification have been highly improved and mechanization and electrification have been accomplished. From 1952 to 1997, the total power of agricultural machinery increased from 0.18 MW to 420.16 MW; large and medium-sized agricultural tractors from 1,307 to 68,9051; and agricultural trucks from 280 to 875,571. Mechanized farming, with coordinated cultivation, irrigation and reaping is expanding year by year.

In the transportation sector, a comprehensive network has taken shape with railways as the backbone, linking highways, waterways, aviation and pipelines. The total mileage of railways increased 1.6 times from 21,800 km in 1949 to 57,600 km in 1998. Trunk railway lines from Baoji to Lanzhou, from Lanzhou to Xinjiang, from Baoshan to Chengdu, from Chengdu to Kunming, from Hunan to Guizhou, from Hunan to Jiangxi, from Zhejiang to Jiangxi and from Beijing to Kowloon have been built, forming a crisscross railway transportation network. Railways are accessible in all provinces, municipalities and autonomous regions throughout the country, with the exception of Tibet, greatly improved the situation of the hinterland which was inaccessible and underdeveloped in the past. The length of highways increased by 14.8 times from 80,700 km in 1949 to 1.279 million km in 1998. Highway quality has also been much improved. The Beijing-Tianjin-Tanggu, Shenyang-Dalian, Shanghai-Hangzhou-Ningbo and Guangzhou-Shenzhen superhighways have been built, and many others are under construction. The transport condition of the inland rivers has been improved by dredging, and the mileage increased from 73,600 km in 1949 to 110,300 km in 1998. By the end of 1998, altogether 1,122 domestic and international airlines had been established to form a crisscrossing aviation network, making civil aviation the transport means with the highest growth rate in China. With the growth of the petroleum industry, pipelines also developed rapidly. The pipeline length grew from 200 km in 1958 to 23,100 km in 1998.

In postal and telecommunications service, a public telecommunications network covering the whole country and reaching the world has been established, including such means as optical fiber, digital microwave, mobile communication and programmed switchboard exchange system, and the public postal network is in good shape with conveniently located service stations and a full range of services. The total postal routes in China rose from 706,00 km in 1994 to 6,215,000 km in 1998, representing a 7.8-fold increase. At present, 77.6% of all townships have their own postal offices, and 92.9% are accessible by telephones, and 87.5% are connected to the auto long-distance direct-dialing network. The scale and capacity of the telephone network is growing rapidly. The telephone switchboard capacity increased from 0.47 million lines to 138 million lines. China's telephone network scale has leapt forward and ranks second in the world, immediately after the U.S. and Japan. Mobile and digital telecommunications, developed from nothing, is expanding briskly. In 1998, the number of phone users reached 100 million, among which 23.86 million were mobile phone users, while the total number of digital telecommunications users reached 1.56 million, including 680,000 internet users and 525,000 public multimedia users.

IV. Urban and Rural Residents Leap From Poverty to Prosperity

In the past 50 years, with the brisk development of the national economy and the strengthening of the comprehensive national power, China experienced three stages from poverty elimination, providing the people with adequate food and clothing to prosperity. The level, structure and circumstances of consumption have changed greatly. The residents'per capita consumption increased from 80 yuan RMB in 1952 to 2,973 yuan RMB in 1998. The saving of the urban and rural residents grew from 0.86 billion yuan RMB in 1952 to 5,340.8 billion yuan RMB in 1998. The unitary consumption structure dominated bu basic needs such as food and clothing has been altered, and housing, transportation and entertainment expenditures have climbed dramatically. Urban residents'expenditures on food and clothing as a proportion of their total living expenses decreased from 80% in the early years after the founding of the PRC to 55.6% in 1998, and that of the rural residents from 90% to 59.6%. The gas useage rate in the urban area increased from 1.5% in 1957 to 78.8% in 1998. With more and more modern durable consumer goods available, the people's living standards have improved gradually. The popular "four durable goods" (bicycle, watch, sewing machine and camera) in the 1950s-1970s gave way to the "new six goods" (TV set, washing machine, cassette recorder, refrigerator, electric fan and radio) in the 1980s, and then the computer, car and house in the 1990s. By now, the "four durable goods"are widely spread in rural areas, the "new six pieces" have saturated most cities and towns, and the consumption of high-value commodities has been increasing. In 1998, every 100 urban families had 105 TV sets, 76 refrigerators, 91 washing machines and 36 cameras, and every 100 rural families had 137 bicycles, 9 refrigerators, 33 color TV sets and 23 washing machines.

V. China's Rising Status in International Trade and Strengthened Foreign Economic Relations

In the past 50 years, China's foreign trade partners expanded from neighboring countries, including the former Soviet Union and Eastern European countries, to more than 220 countries and regions, including Japan, the EU and the US. With the foreign trade scale expanding continuously, China's status in international trade has risen accordingly. The total volume of foreign trade jumped from $1.94 billion in 1952 to $323.9 billion in 1998, up 166 times, or 11.8% per year. China's total import and export volume ranked 32nd in the world in 1978, and is presently 11th in terms of imports and 9th in exports, making it an important trading force in the world. China's foreign exchange reserve ranks 2nd in the world, leaping from $2.15 billion in the early years after the introduction of the policy of reform and opening-up to $145 billion in 1998. The export commodity structure has also been improved. In 1952, the proportion of primary products such as agricultural and by-products in the total export volume was 83.4%. Then the figure decreased to 11.2% in 1998, while the proportion of high-value-added

industrial products including electronics, machinery and textiles mounted to 88.8%.

The scale of foreign investment utilization is expanding. During the early years after the establishment of the PRC, China largely relied on the former Sovie Union for low-interest loans as a result of the economic blockade enforced by the Western countries. Since the introduction of the policy of reform and opening in 1978, the utilization of foreign fund has been growing speedily in large scale and diversified form. From 1978 to 1998, the utilized investment totaled $406.9 billion. A large number of enterprises and facilities in the sectors of agriculture, industry, transport, restaurants and entertainment have been established with foreign investmen. Foreign funds have also been utilized in posts and telecommunications, retail, finance and insurance. In the past 20 years, altogether 300,000 foreign direct investment projects have been approved. The foreign investment scale on average increased from $1.22 million in the early 1980s to $2.63 million in 1998.

Striding Toward a More Brilllant New Century

The 50th anniversary of the establishhment of the P.R.C. marks the turning of the century. In the grand blueprint for economic development in next century, the 15th CPC Congress decided: to double the GNP of 2000 by 2010 and form a mature socialist market system; to further develop the national economy and improve institutions with another decade of efforts; to accomplish moderniza-

北京西站
BEIJING WEST RAILWAY STATION

tion and make China a strong and democratic socialist country by the middle of the next century when we celebrate the 100th anniversary of the establishment of the P.R.C. This blueprint is based on China's 50 years of experience and its practical conditions of economic development. From the international perspective, globalization and multi-polarization is the trend of long-term social develoment of mankind, and it is possible to achieve a peaceful international environment, though at present factors of instabilities still exist. From the domestic perspective, China still has the potential for rapid development owing to its material base and capital supply. Firstly, its low per capita income and unbalanced rural and urban development will tap economic growth. Secondly, since the founding of the PRC, and especially since the introduction of the policy of reform and opening, China has gained considerable comprehensive national power. The sufficient manpower, stable development of agriculture, and the ease of the "bottle-necked" situation in the sectors of energy, transport and communications serve as a strong material basis for rapid economic growth. Thirdly, accumulated capital and savings still serve as the major capital channel, and China's huge market is attracting more and more foreign investment, which provides assurance for rapid economic growth. Under the guidance of the theory of establishing Chinese socialism which has been proven in practice and with the experience and lessons gained in 50 years of practice, we will bring the goals proposed by the 15th CPC Congress into being.

At the same time, we should be aware of the difficulties and challenges before us, such as the poor quality of economic development, irrational economic structure, uneven development across the country, low quality of labour, disparity of incomes, shortage of per capita resources, environmental pollution, and so on. The resolution of these problems will promote the sustainable development of our national economy.

Reviewing the past at the turn of the century, we cannot but be proud of achievements we have scored and the prosperity of our country. And looking forward to the future, we have confidence in building a more powerful China. The 21st century will witness China discarding underdevelopment and rising in the world. We are convinced that under the guidance of Deng Xiaoping Theory and the leadership of the Communist Party of China, with the joint efforts of all ethnic groups of the whole country, we will assuredly overcome the difficulties on the road ahead and carry on our great cause of establishing Chinese socialism.

城乡居民生活丰富多彩

The Colorful Lives of the People in Both Urban and Rural Areas

从贫困走向小康的城镇居民

建国50年来，中国经济取得令人瞩目的发展，人民生活向前跨越了一大步。回顾50年来城镇居民生活的发展变化，经历了一个从脱离贫困，解决温饱到迈向小康的历程。

一、城镇居民收入增长50年变迁

建国50年来城镇居民生活变化大体分为两个阶段：1979年以前30年为一个阶段；改革后20年为第二阶段。前30年中居民生活发展几起几落，改善甚微。中共十一届三中全会的召开为中国经济发展带来转机，从此国民经济高速发展，人民生活水平迅速提高。

——改革前30年城镇居民收入水平几起几落的发展状况。

1.解放前：饥寒交迫，民不聊生。解放前夕，旧中国的经济已处于崩溃边缘，连年战争留下满目疮痍，生产力遭到严重破坏，市场萧条，物价飞涨，失业现象严重，广大劳动人民在生存线上挣扎，翘首盼解放。据1948年3月24日《新民报》报道，1948年的1000万元仅折合1937年的27元。由于物价飞涨，广大劳动人民连最低的生活都难以维持。据统计，1948年秋，仅北京市的赤贫户和次贫户共68000户、人口246000人，约占全市人口的24%。

2.解放初：发展生产，争取温饱。1949年火热辉煌的金秋，中国人民当家作了主人，当时大部分人的生活仅维持在最低的生存水平上。据当时保留下来的统计资料表明，1949年城镇居民人均年现金收入还不足100元。面对这样的局面，中国共产党和人民政府采取了一系列措施医治战争创伤，恢复和发展生产，稳定物价，安排就业，以安定人民生活。广大人民也以主人翁的精神和热情，投入到新中国的建设中去，为新中国的发展奠定了最初的物质基础。到1952年人均现金收入增加到156元，比1949年增长56.8%。

"一五"期间（1953-1957年），面对人口众多而生产力低下的现实，国家采取了广就业、低工资的政策，使人人有饭吃的理想在一种较低层次上成为现实。这在发展生产、稳定民心上起到了很大的作用，人们对救民于水火的共产党充满了热爱和感激，对自己当家作主充满了自豪和热情，这种精神所焕发出的创造力和劳动热情是难以估量的。因此，"一五"时期被称为是建国后中国经济建设的第一个"黄金时代"。1957年城镇居民人均现金收入达到254元，比1952年增长62.8%，扣除物价因素实际增长48.5%，平均年递增8.2%。

3.改革前：政治运动不断，国民经济和人民生活徘徊不前。由于种种历史和现实的原因，中国没有冷静下来把全部精力投入到扎扎实实的经济建设中，1958年的"大跃进"、1966-1976年的"文化大革命"使人民生活几起几落，在温饱线上徘徊20年之久。人们不会忘记，1959年开始的三年自然灾害，使各种食品和轻工业品严重短缺，不少地区不得不减少居民的粮食定量，增加凭票、凭证、限量供应各种食品、轻工业品的范围，人民生活陷入困境。正是在这个时期，整个世界发生了突飞猛进的变化，相形之下，中国经济以及人民生活与世界发达国家的差距越拉越大。

新建住宅小区
New Uptown

到了十年动乱结束后的1978年，城镇居民人均可支配收入343元，比1957年增长35.4%，扣除物价上升因素，21年里城镇居民收入水平实际增长18.5%，平均每年递增仅0.8%。中国改革开放的总设计师邓小平曾说过："我们奋斗了几十年，就是为了消灭贫困。"但是人民生活直到1978年中共十一届三中全会召开之后才开始有了真正的转机。

——改革后20年国民经济持续发展，居民收入迅速增加。改革20年是中国经济发展最快、城镇居民收入增长最多的20年。调查资料表明，城镇居民人均可支配收入从1978年的343元增加到1998年的5425元，扣除物价因素，20年实际增长2.2倍，平均年递增6%。为城镇居民生活水平从生存到温饱再向小康发展的历史性跨越奠定了坚实的基础。

1. 城镇居民就业面扩大，就业者负担人数减少。1949 年全国城镇总人口仅有 0.6 亿人，城镇就业人数为 1533 万人，平均每一就业者负担人数为 3.76 人；1997 年城镇总人口增加到 3.7 亿人，增长 5 倍，就业人数增加到 2 亿人，增长 12 倍，平均每一就业者负担人数降低到 1.83 人，负担系数减少一半。

改革开放之前，特别是 50-60 年代，城镇居民平均每户家庭人口多达 4-5 人，平均每户就业人口 1957 年为 1.33 人，1964 年为 1.56 人，就业面还不足 30%。自 80 年代以后，家庭规模逐年缩小，1998 年平均每户家庭人口仅为 3.16 人，就业面提高到 57%。

2. 就业渠道拓宽，收入来源增多。随着国家经济的发展，城镇就业人口的增加，城镇居民就业渠道不断拓宽，解放初期的 1949 年城镇就业者中职工人数为 809 万人，个体劳动者为 724 万人。随着年代的推移，城镇个体经济逐年萎缩，到 1978 年全国城镇个体劳动者仅有 15 万人，城镇就业者中绝大多数为国有和集体职工，就业形式极为单一。改革开放为城镇经济注入活力，就业渠道逐年增多，外资、私营、合资等各种经济类型单位从无到有，个体劳动者也越来越多，在城镇就业者中比重逐年增长，据统计，1988 年城镇就业者中其他各种经济类型单位职工 99 万人，个体劳动者 648 万人，二者合计占城镇就业总人口的 5.2%。到 1997 年其他各种经济类型单位职工猛增到 1861 万人，个体劳动者增加到 1919 万人，二者占城镇就业总人口的比重提高到 18.7%。

就业渠道的拓宽使城镇居民收入来源逐渐增多，1981 年城镇居民收入中 91% 来自国有集体职工的工资和福利补贴，其他方面的收入不足 1/10。1998 年国有集体职工的工资性收入占全部收入的比重下降到 66.9%，比 1981 年下降 24 个百分点。

改革开放改变了人们的就业观念，城镇居民从事第二职业等劳动收入明显增多，1998 年家庭人口平均每人收入 174 元，比 1981 年增长 28 倍，占全部家庭收入的 3.2%。

改革开放使居民投资意识不断增强，财产性收入增长迅速。随着企业股份制的推行，股票债券等有价证券发行量的增加，城镇居民的金融活动日趋活跃。1998 年城镇居民人均财产性收入 133 元，占全部收入的 2.4%。

城镇居民收入增加更为突出地反映在银行存款的变化上。改革前 30 年全国居民存款余额从 1952 年的 8.6 亿元增长到 1978 年的 210.6 亿元。从 1978 年起居民储蓄存款余额呈几何级数增长：1978 年到 1986 年 8 年中存款余额增长 10 倍，达到 2237.6 亿元；又过 8 年 1994 年增加到 21518.8 亿元，16 年增长 100 倍；4 年以后，1998 年居民储蓄存款余额又增到 53407 亿元，比 1978 年增长 254 倍。

二、贫困—温饱—小康，城镇居民消费变化三部曲

——为温饱奋斗的改革前 30 年。改革前 30 年，城镇居民消费发展几经波折、起起落落。解放初期新中国从战争的废墟中崛起，特别是“一五”时期，随着经济建设的恢复发展，人民生活水平有了很大提高。但 1958 年“大跃进”又将中国经济带入低谷，紧接着三年困难时期，人民生活明显下降。“文革”前期国家经济刚刚复苏，长达十年的“文化大革命”又把中国经济推向崩溃的边缘，人民生活水平停滞不前。回顾这 30 年人民生活发展历程，风雨坎坷，改善甚微。

调查资料表明，1957 年城镇居民人均消费支出 222 元，其中食品消费 130 元，衣着消费 27 元，两项合计占消费支出的 70%，其他方面的消费不足 30%；1964 年人均消费支出 221 元，扣除价格因素比 1957 年减少 10.4%，其中食品消费 131 元，

衣着消费24元，两项合计比重没有变化；1978年人均消费支出311元，扣除价格因素比1957年增长22.6%，其中食品消费179元，衣着消费42元，两项合计比重为71%，与前20年相比变化很小。改革前30年城镇居民大部分消费都用在衣食温饱方面。

前30年中城镇居民消费的特点是限量供应型。绝大多数生活消费品都凭票凭证定量供应，居民家庭消费变化事实上与收入关系不大，只能反映当时的市场供应状况。

——迈向小康的改革20年。改革20年城镇居民生活消费水平的提高与前30年形成明显的反差，改革前努力了30年的温饱问题在“六五”期间（1981-1985年）短短几年中得到彻底的解决。城镇居民生活消费摆脱了票证的限制，真正达到丰衣足食的温饱阶段，从此开始向小康目标迈进。

1. 从限量供应到品种齐全讲究营养的食品消费。据联合国粮农组织提出的用恩格尔系数判定生活发展阶段的一般标准：60%以上为贫困；50-60%为温饱；40-60%为小康；40%以下为富裕。改革前30年以及改革初期城镇居民恩格尔系数都在57%以上，保持在刚刚脱贫仍在温饱最低线上徘徊的水平。直到“六五”期间，国家经济得到发展，市场供应日趋繁荣，人民收入水平大幅度提高，城镇居民消费逐步取消了票证限制，恩格尔系数略有回升以后，1985年迅速下降到53.3%，彻底解决了温饱问题，开始了迈向小康目标的历程。

进入90年代，城镇居民恩格尔系数逐年下降，1994年首次跌落50%的大关之后继续下降，1998年达到44.5%，用这一指标衡量，目前中国城镇居民总体生活消费已达到小康水平。

50年来，城镇居民食品消费的变化从数量品种的增加逐步向质量营养的改善发展。改革前城镇居民食品消费极为单调，据调查，1957年人均食品消费支出130元，其中购买粮食支出51元，占食品消费的39%，肉禽蛋鱼虾26元，占20%，烟酒茶9元，占7%，其余34%为全年购买蔬菜调料水果等其他食品的消费；1981年粮食消费占食品的比重下降到22.8%，比1957年减少16个百分点，肉禽蛋鱼虾26.9%，增加7个百分点，其他食品41.3%，增加7个百分点；1998年城镇居民人均食品消费1927元，其中粮食消费支出227元，占食品消费的比重为11.8%，比1957年减少27个百分点，肉禽蛋鱼虾640元，占33.2%，增加13个百分点，烟酒茶消费185元，占9.6%，蔬菜消费197元，占10.2%，干鲜瓜果类消费121元，占6.3%，在外用餐227元，占11.8%，糖果糕点牛奶等其他食品消费330元，占17.1%。

主要食品消费量的变化也较为明显，粮食消费量逐年减少，肉禽蛋鱼等动物性食品的消费量逐年增加。1998年城镇居民人均购买粮食86.7公斤，比1957年减少48.1%；购买肉禽蛋鱼虾49.5公斤，比1957年增长1.5倍；其他食品的消费量也有较大增加：人均购买食用植物油7.6公斤，比1957年增长81%；购买鲜瓜果54.8公斤，比1981年（1957年无调查数字，下同）增长1.6倍；购买鲜奶6.2公斤，增长51.2%。

2. 从遮体御寒到美化生活体现个性的衣着消费。改革前城镇居民衣着消费极为单一，“新三年、旧三年，缝缝补补又三年”是当时社会提倡的风气。据调查，1957年平均每人购买成衣0.7件，购买各种布料7.3米，大约可做不足一条被子（当时的被褥基本上是买布来做）；1964年人均购买成衣1件，购买各种布料4米。当时中国人的着装是统一的单调，追求美被作为一种腐朽的资产阶级思想来批判，不分年龄性别统一的式样，蓝黑绿呆滞沉闷的色彩，也反映出人们当时单调的生活。改革开放改变了人们的思想观念，色彩缤纷各种款式的服装为城镇居民生活增添了亮丽的色彩。1981年城镇居民人均购买服装2.5件，比

1957年增长2.6倍，衣料7米，与1957年持平；1998年人均购买服装5.8件，同比增长7.3倍，购买衣料1.4米，同比有所减少，另外购买纺织装饰品4元，床上用品（床单被罩等）20元，反映出城镇居民衣着消费中社会化服务程度增强，自己动手缝制衣物的比重越来越小。

3. 从“老四件”、“新四件”到现代四大件的用品消费。城镇居民生活变化又较为显著的反映在家庭耐用消费品更新换代上，改革前人们追求的是“三转一扭”的“老四件”，即自行车、缝纫机、手表和收音机；改革初期又转向以彩电、洗衣机、电冰箱、录音机等为主要代表的“新四件”；目前电话、空调、家用电脑、轿车等新的消费品又逐渐进入城镇居民家庭。据调查，1981年城镇居民家庭平均每百户拥有彩电0.6台，洗衣机6台，电冰箱0.2台，录音机13台，刚刚开始进入萌芽期；到1988年彩电拥有量增加到44台，洗衣机增加到73台，电冰箱增加到28台，录音机增加到64台，进入发展期；到1998年城镇居民家庭平均每百户拥有彩电105台，比1988年增长1.4倍；洗衣机91台，同比增长24.7%，电冰箱76台，增长1.7倍，已基本达到饱和期。而新一代的消费品又取而代之，1998年城镇居民家庭平均每百户拥有空调器20台，家用电脑4台，家用轿车0.25台，还有63.8%的家庭装有电话。

4. 从分得开住得下到设备齐全风格各异的住房消费。温饱问题解决以后，人们开始关注衣食以外的消费，住房是一项最重要也是最难解决的问题。“小康不小康，关键看住房”，这是前几年较为流行的一句口号，正说明改善住房条件的难度所在。50年来各级政府为改善城镇居民的住房问题做出了极大的努力。

解放前城镇居民每间瓦房或土房住3-5人的家庭占总户数70%以上，而且房租贵得惊人。解放以后虽然逐年有所改观，但主要力量用在解决温饱问题上，人民对住房的需求并不很高，分得开住得下就满足。改革开放以后，人民生活逐年提高，住房设施需要相应配套，各种家具、耐用消费品需要空间放置，各种电器需要足够的电容量，洗衣机需要上下水管道等等，人们对住房条件不再满足于过去的简单需求。改善居民住房问题成为各级政府领导的重要工作之一。据调查，1981年城镇居民家庭中人均居住面积8平方米以上的家庭仅有13.5%，1988年上升到48.1%，1998年又扩大到76.8%。而无房户、人均4平方米以下的拥挤户和大儿大女合居一室的不方便户1981年高达37.5%，1988年下降到14.9%，1998年仅有0.9%。居住条件的改善更为明显，截止到1998年末，有68.3%的城镇居民家庭住上了单元配套住房，74%的家庭居室内有厕所或浴室，72.6%的家庭使用煤气或液化石油气，41.1%的家庭有可取暖的空调或暖气设备，63.8%的家庭安装了电话，38.1%的家庭住房归自己所有，还有23.9%的家庭已购买了现有住房的部分产权。

住房条件的改善增加了城镇居民的住房消费支出。1981年城镇居民人均住房消费21元，其中水电燃料费14元，分别占消费支出的4.6%和3.1%；1998年人均住房消费支出增加到408元，水电燃料费增加到235元，分别比1981年增长18.4倍和15.8倍，消费比重分别增加到9.4%和5.4%。水电燃料等消费数量逐年增长，1998年城镇居民人均消费自来水31.2吨，比1992年（1992年以前由于消费比重小，没有分细项调查，下同）增长39.9%；电228.3度，增长1.1倍；液化石油气15.5公斤，增长56.5%；管道煤气29.3立方米，增长48%。

5. 从封闭自守向信息开放网络时代发展的交通通信消费。随着经济的快速发展，人民生活节奏的加快，现代化的交通通信迅速进入居民消费中。1981年城镇居民家庭人均交通通信支出仅6.6元，其中交通支出6.12元，通信支出（事实上只是邮电费）0.48元。1998年猛增到257元，增长38倍，其中交通支出115元，增长17.8倍；通信

中国农村新貌
A New Look in Rural China

支出142元，增长近300倍。相比之下，通信支出的增长更为迅猛。据调查，1998年城镇居民平均每百户购买电话7.1个，BP机2.3个；截止到1998年末城镇居民有63.8%的家庭拥有电话，另外平均每百户家庭拥有3.3个移动电话，3.8台家用电脑；全年人均电讯费支出109元，城镇居民生活消费正在向现代化的信息网络时代发展。

农民生活大大提高

一、收入快速增加，为生活水平提高奠定了坚实基础

中华人民共和国的建立，结束了进入近代以来的中国农村经济长期停滞乃至倒退的颓局，农业生产迅速增长，农民收入迅速提高。1949-1998年，农村居民人均纯收入由44元提高到2162元，提高48倍。

在这具有历史性变动的50年中，特别是1978年中共十一届三中全会后，农村率先推行的以家庭联产承包责任制为主要内容的经济体制改革，为农村居民收入持续快速增长带来新的契机，1998年农村居民人均纯收入达到2162元，短短20年收入翻了4番，比1978年的134元增加2028元。收入增加额是1949-1978年29年增加额的22.5倍。这期间，农村居民名义纯收入增长了15倍，年平均增长14.9%；扣除物价因素后的实际纯收入增长3.4倍，年平均增长6.3%。如今，中国农村居民整体生活已摆脱贫困，温饱有余，并正向着小康生活乃至更高层次的富裕生活迈进。

建国50年，尤其是改革以来的20年，农村居民收入来源逐步多元化。但在前30年，农村居民从集体所得的工分收入是最主要的来源，通常占70%以上。1978年后，农村居民收入来源主要发生了三大变化：一是收入由以集体为主转变为家庭经营为主。农村居民全年纯收入中的集体收入份额由1978年的66%以上下降到1985年后的不足10%，与此同时，农村居民家庭经营纯收入份额则由1978年的27%提高到81%以上。二是第一产业收入由以粮食生产为主转变为农、林、牧、副、渔多种经营。1978年改革初，农村居民生产结构主要是以单一搞饭吃的粮食生产为主，粮食收入是农村居民收入的主要来源，而1998年，农民全年总收入中，粮食收入份额只占27%，同期，其他除粮食收入外的农、林、牧、副、渔多种经营份额则占到37%。三是从事二、三产业的非农收入增长迅速，并逐步成为农村居民收入增加的重要来源。1998年，农村居民生产性纯收入中，从事第一产业的生产所得收入比重为60.7%，比1978年的91.5%下降30.8个百分点，从事二三产业的生产所得收入比重为39.3%，比1978年提高30.8个百分点。

随着农村社会化、商品化进程的逐步加快，改变了过去较长时期以来的中国农村经济的自给、半自给状况及以农为主的单一生产结构，农村居民的实物收入为主状况逐步被货币收入的迅速提高所替代。1978年，农村居民出售农副产品收入人均仅为27元，占总收入的17.6%；人均全部货币纯收入为56元，在全年纯收入中，货币收入率只占41.9%。到1998年，随着农村商品经济在广度和深度上以及数量和质量上的不断拓展和提高，农村居民商品交换活动增加，收入形态逐渐货币化。一方面，1998年农民全年出售产品收入提高到1029元，比1978年增长38倍，占总收入的比重提高到34%，提高了16.4个百分点；另一方面，纯收入中，货币纯收入额达到1400多元，增长24倍，货币收入率提高到67%以上。这种变化标志着中国农村居民已经走出了传统的自给自足经济的圈子，步入了商品经济发展的轨道。

二、消费质量提高，整体生活稳步迈向小康

1949-1998年，农村居民生活整体水平显著提高。人均生活消费支出1998年达到1590元，比1949年提高37.8倍，年均增长7.8%。其中，1978年农村经济体制改革后农村居民生活消费变化更为明显，农村居民人均生活消费支出由1978年的116元增加到1998年的1590元，增加1474元，增长12.7倍，年平均增加74元，年递增14%；扣除物价因素，实际增长也达3倍以上，每年实际递增达到6%，高于前29年年均消费增长3.7%的速度。

在农村居民生活消费方方面面的巨大变化中，人均食品消费总支出由1954年的41元增加到1998年的850元，增长19.7倍；衣着支出由8元增加到98元，增长11.3倍；居住支出由5元增加到240元，增长47倍；用品、服务类及其他支出由10元增加到403元，增长39倍。

农村居民生活消费结构序列则由满足基本生存需要的“一吃二穿三住”变化为其他更高层次的享受性支出大幅度提高。消费结构也明显表现出生存资料比重减少，发展和享受资料比重提高的趋势。1954年，生活消费结构序列为基本生存型的吃、穿、住、用及其他，其中吃的比重高达69%；穿占13%；居住占9%；用品及其他占9%。到1984年，以农村居民的恩格尔系数降到60%以下为标志，消费结构序列越过了一个质的界线，农村居民整体生活跨入温饱阶段。吃、穿比重较大幅度下降，居住、文化娱乐用品、服务性支出及其他比重有较多增加。这期间，农村居民生活消费支出中吃的比重虽然仍位居第一，但所占份额已下降到59.1%；居住为第二位，占17.4%；文化娱乐用品、服务性及其他支出为第三位，占13.1%；穿着位次后移，占10.4%。1998年，随着农村居民整体生活水平的进一步提高，农村居民消费构成中满足基本生活需要的吃、穿、住份额继续下降，生活消费结构序列进一步升级优化为

吃占53.4%；文化娱乐用品、服务性支出及其他支出提高为25.3%；居住占15.1%，穿为6.2%。如今，全国已有95%以上的农村居民过上了温饱有余的生活，有25%左右的农户已经过上了小康生活。

这些年来，农村居民生活的自给性消费明显下降，对市场的依赖性逐渐增强是其消费水平提高的另一个重要表现。1978-1998年，全国每一农村居民的货币性生活消费支出额由48元达到1128元，增长了23.5倍，货币性生活消费支出占生活消费支出总额的比重由1978年的41%提高到1998年的70.7%，提高了近30个百分点。其中，农村居民人均用于购买食物的现金支出额由19元增加到429元，增长21.6倍；食品的货币性支出占全部食品支出额的比重由24.1%提高到50.5%，提高了26.4个百分点；居住的货币性支出为199元，货币支出率达到83.2%，比1978年提高31.9个百分点；其他穿、用、家庭设备用品及服务支出、医疗保健、交通通讯等项的商品化程度则已基本达到饱和。

如果说，建国后的前30年，农村居民生活曾经历过曲折的发展过程，则后20年，以中共十一届三中全会为标志，中国农村居民生活的划时代巨变具体表现在如下6大方面：

——食品质量明显提高。农村居民食物消费质量普遍提高。主要表现在：彻底摆脱了过去较长一段时期的消费品不足而转变为讲究吃好、档次提高、营养丰富三大变化上。一是食物消费在吃饱的基础上转化为吃好。人均主食支出占食品支出的比重由1978年高达65.3%下降到1998年的35.5%，下降了29.8个百分点。同期，人均副食支出占食品支出的份额则由1978年的31.4%上升到1998年的42.9%；二是食物消费细粮增加，粗粮减少。1998年与1978年比较，农村居民人均粮食消费总量虽然仅增加了1.6公斤，但其中细粮消费数量由123公斤增加到209公斤，细粮消费比重由49.4%提高到83.9%；粗粮消费则由125公斤减少到40.5公斤，减少了67.6%。三是营养状况显著改善，营养丰富的油脂类和享受性食物成倍增长。1998年，农村居民人均消费的油脂类食物比1978年增长了2.1倍；肉禽类食物增长了1.6倍；蛋类增长了4倍；水产品增长了3.3倍。热量摄入达到了营养部门要求标准；同时热量中来源于淀粉类食物的比重下降，来源于水产品、禽蛋产品等高蛋白食物及其他精制食品的比重上升。

——穿着更加舒适高档。衣着是人们对物质生活和精神生活的共同需要。农村居民衣着消费的突出变化是对原布的购买量逐步下降，对成衣的购买量逐步增加，并越来越讲究穿着的款式、花色、质量、舒适和装饰，有的还趋于高档化。1998年农村居民人均衣着支出达到98元，比1978年增长5.6倍；人均购买各种布料1.97米，比1978年减少64.1%；人均购买成衣服装1件，比1983年增长了1.2倍。

——居住状况极大变化。较长一段时间，农村居民住房条件较差，房屋比较简陋，土坯墙的草顶、瓦顶房居多。如今，排排砖瓦房甚至一幢幢新颖、别致的楼房拔地而起，成为改革后农村最直观、最明显的变化。1998年，农村居民人均居住支出240元，比1978年高出19.1倍。平均每户年末使用住房面积由1978年的8.1平方米增加到1998年的23.7平方米，增长1.9倍。人均住房面积中，砖木结构和钢筋混凝土结构住房面积1998年达到17.88平方米，占75.4%，比1981年的48.6%提高了26.8个百分点；新建房屋每平方米价值，1985年只有40元，1998年提高到227元，提高了4.7倍。目前，在较为富裕地区，相当多农民家庭的住房及内部装饰正向着现代化生活方式发展。

——家庭耐用品成倍增加。农村居民购买耐用品数量成倍增加，是这些年农村居民生活水平显著提高的又一重要标志。1965年平均每百户农民家庭拥有自行车7.6辆，收音机2台，钟表10

台，缝纫机2.6架。到1998年，这些过去农村居民家庭渴望的老四大件（自行车、缝纫机、钟表、收音机）等耐用品的拥有已基本饱和，而其他新型的家用电器则迅速增长。1998年末，平均每百个农村住户年末拥有电视机96台，其中彩色电视机33台，拥有收录机32台、电风扇112台、洗衣机23台，一些农户还购买了录像机、照像机、电冰箱，甚至空调、电脑也已进入部分富裕农民家庭。

——精神生活日益充实。建国以来，随着农村社会经济的逐步繁荣，农村居民在物质生活丰富的同时，精神生活也日益丰富多彩。如今，不仅电视机获得了相当的普及，很多农户也意识到知识和信息的重要性，对文化教育的投入增多。到1998年，农村居民人均文教娱乐用品及服务支出159元，占生活消费的10%；同时，由于农村基础设施的改善及社会经济生活的逐步一体化，农村居民交通通讯支出增加，1998年人均该项支出达到61元，占生活消费的3.8%；随着收入的提高，农村居民亦开始更多的关注自己的身心健康，过去大病小治，小病不治的现象有了较大改变，1998年，农村居民人均医疗保健支出达到68元，占4.3%。

——生存环境极大改善。生存环境或社区环境对一个地区经济的发展具有重要影响。过去较长时间，农村社会发育程度普遍较低，社区环境比较落后，1978年后，随着国家和地区对各种基础设施投入力度的加大，为农村居民生活质量的提高起到了重要的作用，农村居民在改善自身生活质量的同时，生活条件、生存环境也逐步改善。到1998年，全国农村有95%以上的行政村通了公路，70%左右的行政村通了电话，70%以上的行政村用上了安全卫生水，95%以上的行政村通了电。农村交通、邮电、电力事业的发展，改善了农村生活、生产条件，加快了落后地区的脱贫步伐，更方便了城乡经济、文化交流，为农村经济的持续稳定发展奠定了坚实的基础。

Urban Residents: From Poverty to a Fairly Well-Off Life

In the past 50 years, since the founding of the People's Republic, China has witnessed an attention-catching economic development, and the livelihood of the Chinese people has made big strides. The lives of the Chinese people both in urban and rural areas have gone from shaking off poverty to being adequately fed and clothed and to being better off.

I. The Change of Income of Urban Residents over the Past 50 Years

The change in the lives of the urban residents over the past 50 years since 1949, when New China was established, can be roughly divided into two stages. The first stage is the 30 years before 1979, and the second stage, the 20 years since 1979, when China initiated its reform. The development in the lives of the urban residents experienced ups and downs in the first stage, with only an insignificant improvement. The convocation of the Third Plenary Session of the 11th CPC Central Committee in December 1978 marked a favorable turn in the development of China's national economy. Since then, the national economy has developed at high speed, and people's livelihood has improved rapidly.

— The Ups and Downs in the Development of the Urban Residents' Income in the 30 Years Prior to China's Reform

1. Before Liberation: People suffering hunger and cold in the urban areas. On the eve of Liberation, old China's economy was on the verge of bankruptcy. Scenes of devas-

tation from years of wars met the eye everywhere. Productivity was seriously damaged, the market was desolate and depressed with prices skyrocketing, and unemployment was omnipresent. The broad masses of the laboring people, struggling for existence, looked forward to the nation's liberation. According to a report printed in *Hsin Min Pao* on March 24, 1948, ten million yuan that year had the purchasing power of 27 yuan in 1937. The skyrocketing prices made it hard for the laboring people to maintain even the lowest living standards. According to statistics, in the fall of 1948, there were 246,000 people in 683,000 families, 24 percent of the total population of Beijing, living in extreme or secondary poverty.

2. The early days of Liberation: Developing production to have enough to eat and wear. In the fall of 1949, the Chinese people became masters of their destiny. At that time, most of the urban residents could earn only the most meager of livings. The average annual cash income was less than 100 yuan per urban resident. The Party and government adopted a series of measures to heal the wounds of war, to restore and develop production, to keep prices stable, to provide employment, and to ensure a stable life for the people. People in the urban areas, in the spirit and enthusiasm of masters of their country, plunged into construction, laying a foundation for the development of New China. By 1952, the annual cash income per urban resident had gone up to 156 yuan, an increase of 56.8 percent over that of 1949.

During the period of the First Five-Year Plan (1952-1957), in the face of China's large population and low productivity, the Party and government implemented a policy of extensive employment and low income and realized at a low level the idea that everyone had food, which played a marked role in developing production and setting people's minds at ease. The people cherished a sentiment of love and gratitude to the Chinese Communist Party, which had pulled them out of the abyss of misery. Filled with enthusiasm and pride of being masters of their own destiny, they aroused in themselves an immeasurable creative power and an enthusiasm for work. The period of the First Five-Year Plan was called the First Golden Time for China's economic construction after the founding of the People's Republic of China. In 1957, the annual cash income per urban resident reached 254 yuan, 62.8 percent more than the figure of 1952. The actual increase was 48.5 percent after allowing for price rises, averaging a yearly increase of 8.2 percent.

3. Prior to China's Reform: The rise of one political movement after another made the national economy and the people's lives remain stagnant. Because of historical and realistic reasons, the Chinese people failed to be cool-headed and could not plunge themselves into economic construction in a down-to-earth manner. The Great Leap Forward of 1958 and then the ten years of the Great Cultural Revolution from 1966 to 1976 made the people experience ups and downs in their lives and linger about on the subsistence line for 20 years. In the three years of "natural" calamities, there was a critical shortage of food and light industrial products, forcing quite a few regions to reduce the monthly quota of food grain for the urban residents and enlarge the scope of foodstuffs and light industrial products that were supplied by vouchers or certificates or by a limited quota.

During the same period, astonishing changes took place in the rest of the world. The gap between China's economy and that of the developed countries became wider and wider.

In 1978, when the chaos brought about by the "ten-year cultural revolution" came to an end, the average per-capita disposable income for city dwellers was 343 yuan, an increase of 35.4 percent over that of 1957. After deducting the factor of price rises, the actual increase over 21 years was a mere 18.5 percent, an average increase of 0.8

percent per year. Deng Xiaoping, the chief architect of China's reform and opening up said, "The purpose of our struggle over the past several decades was to eliminate poverty." People's lives began to turn for the better in a real manner only after the Third Plenary Session of the 11th CPC Central Committee.

— The National Economy Has Achieved a Sustained Development and the Income of Urban Residents Increased Rapidly in the 20 Years Since China Initiated the Reform

The past 20 years of reform have been the period in which China's national economy has made the most rapid development and the income of the urban residents has increased the most. Statistics show that the average per-capita disposable income for urban residents increased from 343 yuan in 1978 to 5,425 yuan in 1998, representing an increase of 2.3 times within 20 years, or an annual increase of 6 percent, after deducting the factor of price rises. The increase of the annual income laid a solid foundation for a historic leap of the urban residents' livelihood from the former struggle for survival to having enough food and clothing and to being comfortable well-off.

1. Job openings for urban dwellers expanded and the number of people depending on others for a living declined. In 1949, the year the whole country was liberated, there were only 60 million urban dwellers in China, of whom 15.33 million had jobs, averaging 3.76 persons supported by every job holder. In 1997, the number of urban dwellers was 370 million, an increase of five times over the figure of 1949, while the job holders were 200 million, an increase of 12 times. The number of dependents on every job holders was 1.83 persons.

In the years before reform began in China, especially the 1950s and 1960s, the family size averaged four to five people. The average number of job holders in one family was 1.33 in 1957 and 1.56 in 1964, both figures less than 30 percent of the family members. The family size diminished after the 1980s. In 1998, the average number of members in an urban family were 3.16, 57 percent of whom had jobs.

2. The scope of employment was widened and the sources of income increased. The development of the national economy created more job opportunities for the urban residents and constantly broadened the scope of employment. Of the job holders in 1949, 8.09 million were employees working in government institutions or state-and privately-owned enterprises and 7.24 million were individual laborers working on their own. As time passed, the individual economy diminished in China's urban areas. By 1978, there remained only 150,000 urban individual laborers, while most of the working people were employees of state- and collective-owned establishments, presenting a unitary picture of employment. The reform and opening policy inserted fresh energy into China's urban economy. The scope of employment widened year by year. Foreign-owned, cooperative, and privately-owned enterprises and firms of other economic forms began to be established. The number of individual laborers kept increasing, accounting for a growing proportion in the total number of urban employees. Statistics showed that there were 990,000 people working in other than state- and collective-owned enterprises and 6.48 million individual laborers in urban China in 1988, making up of 5.2 percent of the total urban employees that year. In 1997, however, the number of employees in other than state- and collective-owned enterprises went up to 18.61 million and the number of individual laborers increased to 19.19 million, combining to constitute 18.7 percent of the total number of employees in the urban areas.

The widening of the scope of employment has increased the sources of income for the urban residents. In 1981, 91 percent of the income of the urban residents came from wages and welfare subsidies of employees working in state- and collective-owned enterprises, and less than one-tenth percent of their income was from other sources. In 1998,

the income from wages or salaries of the state- and collective-owned employees accounted for 66.9 percent of the total income of urban residents, a decrease of 24 percent from the figure of 1981.

The implementation of the reform and opening policy changed people's conception of employment. There was a marked increase in the income of urban residents by engaging in a second occupation. In 1998, the yearly per-capita income from the second occupation was 174 yuan, 28 times more than that of 1981, accounting for 3.2 percent of a family's income.

The implementation of the reform and opening policy helped heighten the consciousness of investment of city dwellers, whose income from property investment rapidly increased. There appeared increasingly invigorating financial activities among urban residents with the establishment of the share-holding system and the issuance of stocks, bonds, and negotiable securities. In 1998, the per-capita income from property investment averaged 133 yuan in urban China, making up of 2.4 percent of the total per-capita income.

The amount deposited in banks also reflected the income increase of urban residents. In 1952, there was 860 million yuan of bank savings. The figure increased to 21.06 billion in 1978. However, the bank savings increased by tenfold within eight years from 1978 to 1986, reaching 223.76 billion. In 1994, another eight years later, the figure stood at 2,151.88 billion. The savings of urban residents increased a hundredfold in 16 years from 1978 to 1994. Four years later, in 1998, the figure shot up to 5,340.7

billion, or 254 times of that of 1978.

II. The Three Stages of Change in Urban Residents' Consumption

— 30 Years' Efforts to Solve the Problem of Food and Clothing Before the Reform.

In the 30 years prior to China's reform, the consumption by urban residents showed a checked pattern. In the early days of the People's Republic, especially during the period of the First Five-Year Plan, people's livelihoods improved markedly with the restoration and development of the economic construction. The Great Leap Forward of 1958, which pulled China's economy down into a low ebb, was followed by three consecutive years of difficulties in the national economy (1960 to 1962), in which the people's livelihoods dropped drastically. The national economy recovered before the Cultural Revolution started in 1966. The ten years of the Cultural Revolution pushed China's economy to the verge of collapse, and people's livelihoods remained unimproved.

Statistics showed that the nonproductive expenditure per urban resident in 1957 was 222 yuan, including 130 yuan on food and 27 yuan on clothing. The money paid for food and clothing made up 70 percent of the per-capita nonproductive expenses. In 1964, the nonproductive expenditure per urban resident was 221 yuan, a drop of 10.4 percent as compared with that of 1957 after deducting the factor of price rises. The amount paid for food was 131 yuan, and that for clothing, 24 yuan. The proportion of expenses for food and clothing in the total nonproductive expenditure remained the same as that of 1957. In 1978, the nonproductive expenditure per urban resident was 311 yuan, an increase of 22.6 over the figure of 1957 after deducting the factor of price rises. Of the total per-capita expenditure, 179 yuan was on food, and 42 yuan, on clothing. The combined expenditures on food and clothing accounted for 71 percent of the total yearly per-capita expenditure, only a slight change from the past 20 years.

In the 30 years before the reform was initiated, the majority of consumer goods for daily use were supplied in limited quota by vouchers and certificates in the urban areas. There was not much correspondence between the change of urban families' consumption and their income. The change only reflected a picture of supply on the market.

— The 20 Years of Reform Toward Being Fairly Well-Off

There was a sharp contrast in the consumption level of urban residents between the 30 years prior to the reform and the 20 years after the reform began. The problem of enough food and clothing that China had tried to find a solution for 30 years before the reform was completely solved in a few years during the period of the Sixth Five-Year Plan (1981-1985). Urban residents freed themselves from the restriction in the supply of consumer goods for daily use, achieved the stage of ample food and clothing, and marched toward the goal of being well-off.

1. From the Supply of Food on Ration to the Consumption of Various Nutrient Foods. The UN Food and Agricultural Organization suggested that the Engel Coefficient be used as the standard in judging the stages of the development of people's lives: a coefficient above 60 percent means poverty; between 50 to 60 percent, sufficient food and clothing; between 40 and 50 percent, well-off; and below 40 percent, prosperous. The Engel Coefficient of urban residents' livelihood in the 30 years before the reform and in the early years of the reform was over 57 percent, meaning that China's urban residents had freed themselves from poverty but lingered at the lowest level of having enough food and clothing. During the period of the Sixth Five-Year Plan, the national economy achieved development, people's incomes increased by a large margin,

vouchers and certificates used in the supply of consumer goods for daily use were abolished, and the Engel Coefficient dropped again. In 1985, the coefficient dropped quickly to 53.3. People in the urban areas have completely solved the problem of enough food and clothing and are on the road to achieve the goal of being well-off by the year 2000.

The Engel Coefficient continued to drop in the 1990s. In 1994, it was below 50 percent for the first time in Chinese history. In 1998, it was 44.5 percent, indicating that the livelihood of urban residents as a whole had already reached the level of being well-off.

In the past 50 years, the food consumption of urban residents has changed from the increase of the quantities and varieties of food to the improvement of food quality and nutrition. Before the reform started, the food consumption of urban residents was dull. According to statistics, the 1957 yearly expenditure on food was 130 yuan per capita in the urban areas, including 51 yuan on grain, or 39 percent of the total; 26 yuan on meat, poultry, eggs, fish, and shrimp, or 20 percent of the total, nine yuan on cigarettes, tea, and alcohol, or seven percent of the total; and 34 percent on vegetables, fruit, seasonings, and other foodstuffs. In 1981, the proportion of grain in food consumption dropped to 22.8 percent, six percent lower than that of 1957; that of meat, poultry, eggs, fish, and shrimp consumption, 26.9 percent, an increase 6.9 percent over that of 1957; and that of vegetables, fruit, and other foodstuffs, 41 percent, an increase of seven percent. In 1998, the per-capita expenditure on food was 1,927 yuan, including 227 yuan on grain and accounting for 11.8 percent of the total food expenses, 27 percent lower than that of 1957; that on meat, poultry, fish, and shrimp was 640 yuan, accounting for 33.2 percent of the total food consumption, or an increase of 13 percent over that of 1957; that on cigarettes, tea, and alcohol was 185 yuan, or 9.6 percent of the total food consumption; that on vegetables was 197 yuan, or 10.2 percent; that on dried and fresh fruit was 121 yuan, or 6.3 percent; that on eating out was 227 yuan, or 11.8 percent; that on sweets, pastries, and milk was 330 yuan, or 17.1 percent of the total.

There was a marked change in the quantities of consumption of principal foodstuffs. The amount of grain consumed was on the decline, and the consumption of meat, poultry, eggs, fish, and shrimp was on the increase year by year. In 1998, urban residents purchased an average of 86.7 kilograms of grain per capita, a decrease of 48.1 percent below from 1957, and 49.5 kilograms of meat, poultry, eggs, fish, and shrimp, an increase of 1.5 times over that of 1957. There was a remarkable increase of the amount of other foodstuffs consumed. In 1998, the amount of edible oil purchased per urban resident was 7.6 kilograms, an increase of 81 percent over the figure of 1957. The amount of fresh fruit purchased per person was 54.8 kilograms, an increase of 1.6 times over that of 1981, and the amount of fresh milk purchased was 6.2 kilograms, an increase of 51.2 percent over the 1981 figure (no statistics was available for 1957).

2. Clothing Consumption from the Purpose of Body Coverage and Warmth to the Purpose of Beautifying Lives and Showing Individual Characteristics.

Before China's reform, urban residents worn dull clothes. At that time, there prevailed a custom in society that "A suit can be worn for three years when it is new, another three years before it is worn out, and three more years after it is mended." According to statistics, urban residents in China bought an average of 0.7 items of clothing per-capita plus 7.3 meters of cloth, not enough to make a quilt (quilts and cotton-padded mattresses were basically made by the families themselves at that time), in 1957. In 1964, the per-capita purchase of clothes averaged one item of clothing and four meters of cloth. Attempts to seek beauty were considered a manifestation of bourgeois ideas and criticized accordingly. Men and women, old and young, all wore blue, black, or green suits of dull style. This also reflected the dull lives people led at that time. People's ideology began to change when the reform was implemented. Colorful clothes of varied style added bright color to people's lives. In 1981, urban residents bought an average of 2.5 items of clothing per capita, an increase of 2.6 times of that of 1957 and seven meters of cloth, the same as that of 1957. In 1998, urban residents bought an average of 5.8 items of clothing per person, an increase of 7.3 times over that of 1957 and 1.4 meters of cloth, a decrease when compared with the 1957 figure. They also bought four yuan worth of textile ornaments and 20 yuan worth of bedding (bed and quilt covers). The above figures show that clothes sewn by urban residents themselves have decreased.

3. From the "Old Big Four" and the "New Big Four" to the Modern Four Pieces. The replacement of durable household goods reflected another remarkable change of the life of urban residents. Before China's reform, urban residents pursued possession of a bicycle, a sewing machine, a wrist watch, and a radio, known as the "old big four pieces". In the early days of the reform, their pursuit turned to a color television set, a washing machine, a refrigerator, and a radio-cassette-recorder, referred to as the "new big four pieces". At present, a telephone, an air conditioner, a home computer, and an automobile, the "modern four pieces", began to enter the home of urban residents. A survey showed that, in 1981, there were 0.6 television sets, six washing machines, 0.2 refrigerators, and 13 radio-cassette-recorders in every 100 households in urban China. By 1988, the number of color television sets went up to 44; washing machines, 73; refrigerators, 28; and radio-cassette-recorders, 64. In 1998, there were 105 color television sets in every 100 households in the urban areas, an increase of 1.4 times over that of 1988; 91 washing machines, an increase of 24.7 percent; and 76 refrigerators, an increase of 1.7 times, basically reaching the level of saturation. The pursuit of the new big four pieces began to be replaced by the modern four pieces. In 1998, there were 20 air conditioners in every 100 households of urban residents, four home computers, and 0.25 cars. Telephones found their way into 63.8 percent of the urban households.

4. From Having Enough Space to Live to Living with Various Facilities. After acquiring sufficient food and clothing, people turned their attention to other items. Housing is one of the most important and most difficult problems to be tackled. "What counts is the housing condition of the people in judging if their livelihood has reached the stage of being well-off." These words, then often on the lips of urban residents a few years ago, explain the difficulty of improving housing conditions. In the past 50 years, great efforts have been taken by government at various levels to improve housing for urban residents. Before Liberation, more than 70 percent of the urban households had three to five family members sharing one tile-roofed or earthen room. The rent was astonishingly high. After Liberation, people's housing conditions improved year by year, but the government concentrated its effort on producing enough food and clothing for its people. At that time, the people did not ask for much, and they were satisfied if there was sufficient space to live and if the parents and grown-up children could live in separate rooms. People's livelihood has improved yearly with the implementation of the reform and opening policy. Not content with previous housing conditions, people demanded auxiliary housing facilities, spaces for furniture and other durable household consumer goods, sufficient power for electric appliances, and water supply and drainage pipes for connecting washing machines. The improvement of urban housing became one of the achievements of government leaders. Statistics show that 13.5 percent of the urban households averaged a per-person living space of more than

eight square meters in 1981. The percentage rose to 48.1 in 1988 and to 76.8 in 1998. In 1981, some 37.5 percent of urban households had no housing, had a per-person living space of less than four square meters, or the parents shared the same room with their grown-up children. This percentage dropped to 14.9 in 1988 and to 0.9 in 1998. There was a marked improvement in the living conditions for urban residents. By the end of 1998, some 68.3 percent of urban residents lived in apartments, 71 percent of the households had their own toilets and bathrooms, 72.6 percent of the households cooked with gas or liquefied petroleum, 41.1 percent of the households had air conditioning or heating systems, 63.8 percent of the households had telephones, 38 percent of the households owned their apartments or houses, and 23 percent of them purchased part of the ownership of their apartments or houses.

With the improvement in housing conditions, the expenses on housing for urban residents increased. In 1981, the per-person housing expenses of urban residents were 21 yuan, including 14 yuan for water, electricity, and cooking fuel, accounting for 4.6 and 3.1 percent of the total per-capita nonproductive expenditures respectively. In 1998, the per-person housing expenses was 408 yuan, including 235 yuan for water, electricity, and cooking fuel, an increase of 18.4 times and 15.8 times over the 1981 figures, or accounting for 9.4 percent and 5.4 percent of the per-person nonproductive expenditures. In 1998, the consumption of water for each urban resident was 31.2 tons; electricity, 228.3 KWh; liquefied petroleum gas, 15.5 kilograms; pipeline gas, 29.3 cubic meters; an increase of 39.9 percent, 1.1 times, 56.6 percent, and 48 percent over the figures of 1992 (there were no breakdowns available for the years before 1992 because the consumption of the listed items was insignificant).

5. The Development of Transport and Communications from a Closed, Conservative State to an Information Network Era. With the rapid development of the national economy and the acceleration of the tempo of people's life, modern transport and communications have quickly entered people's life. In 1981, the per capita expenditure on transport and communications in the urban areas was 6.6 yuan, of which 6.12 yuan was transportation cost and 0.48 yuan was paid for communications (mainly for post fees). In 1998, the per-person expenditure on transport and communications shot up to 257 yuan, an increase of 38 times over 1981, of which 115 yuan was paid for transportation, an increase of 17.8 times, and 142 yuan was on communications, an increase of nearly 300 times. Statistics show that every 100 urban households purchased 7.1 telephones and 2.3 beepers in 1998. By the end of 1998, some 63.8 percent of the urban households had telephones, and there were 3.3 mobile telephones and 3.8 home computers in every 100 households. The money paid for communications rose to 109 yuan per-person that year. The consumption of urban residents is now geared toward a modern information network era.

Great Improvement of Farmer's Life

I. Income Increase–a Solid Foundation for a Better Life

With the founding of the People's Republic of China, the stagnating and declining situation of rural economy in the Chinese contemporary history ended. The agricultural production has developed rapidly and the farmers' income has grown at a high speed. From 1949 to 1998, the average net income for rural residents has grown from 44 yuan per person to 2,162 yuan, an increase of 48 times.

In the 50 years of historic changes, especially after the Third Plenary Session of the 11th Central Committee of the Communist Party of China, a reform of economic system first took place in the rural area. The rural household contract responsibility system with remuneration linked to output as its main purpose provided a new opportunity for the continuous rapid growth of rural residents' income. The average net income per person for rural residents reached 2,162 yuan in 1998, 4 times that of 1978, and the increased amount of 1998 was 22.5 times of that from 1949 to 1978. The net income of rural residents has been multiplied by 15 times statistically, 14.9% annually on the average, while their real income has increased by 3.4 times, a 6.3% increase annually, after deducting the inflation rate factor. Indeed, the Chinese rural residents have already been lifted out of poverty and live with sufficient food and clothing, advancing toward a relatively comfortable life or even better one.

Since 1949, especially in the past 20 years' reform, the source of income for rural residents has become diversified gradually. However, in the previous 30 years, the work points gained from the collective farms were the main source of income, which was usually the source for more than 70% of their income. Since 1978, three main changes have taken place in rural residents' source of income: 1). The source of income has shifted from collective economy to family run economy. The proportion of the collective income in the rural residents' net income declined from 66% in 1978 to less than 10% in 1985; meanwhile, the proportion of the income from family run business rose from 27% in 1978 to more than 81%.2). The source of income has shifted from the primary industry of grain production to a multimanagement of farming, forestry, animal husbandry, sideline production and fishery. In 1978, the year the reform began, the rural residents' production was mainly that of grain, which was the main source of income. In 1998, the income from grain production is only 27% of the total annual income; at the same time, the income from farming (except for grain), forestry, animal husbandry, sideline production and fishery is 37% of the total income. 3). The nonagricultural income from the secondary and tertiary industries has been growing rapidly, which becomes the main source of rural residents' income. In 1998, of the net income from production, 60.7% was from the primary industry production, 30.8% lower than 91.5% of 1978, while 39.3% of the net income was from the secondary and the tertiary industry production, 30.8% higher than that of 1978.

With the socialization in the rural areas, the gradual commercialization has changed the situation of Chinese rural economy, which used to be self-sufficient or semi-self-sufficient with the single production structure of farming; the income in money has replaced the income in kind. In 1978, the average income of rural residents was only 27 yuan from selling agricultural and sideline products, which was 17.6% of the total income. In 1978, the income from sideline production was 27 yuan per person, 17.6% of the total income; the total money income was only 57 yuan per person, which was only 41.9% of the annual net income. As the rural commodity economy develops in width and depth, quality and quantity, the commodity trade has been strengthened, and the money income has gradually become the main form of income. On one hand, in 1998, the income from selling agricultural products increased to 1,029 yuan, 38 times higher than that of 1978, which accounted for 34% of the total income, increasing by 16.4%. On the other hand, money income reached more than 1,400 yuan, increasing 24 times. The proportion of money income rose to more than 67% of the total net income. This change symbolizes that Chinese rural residents have gone beyond the traditional self-sufficient economy, and stepped into the track of the development of a commodity economy.

II. Improvement of Living Standard

From 1949 to 1998, the overall livelihood of rural residents has improved remarkably. The living expense per person reached 1,590 yuan in 1998, 37.8 times that of 1949, increasing by 7.8% annually. During the period, the change of living expense for rural residents after the reform of the rural economy system is even more apparent. The rural residents' living expense increased from 116 yuan per person in 1978 to 1,590 yuan in 1998, an increase of 1,474 yuan, up 13.7 times, or an annual increase of 74 yuan or an annual increase rate of 14%. Offsetting the inflation rate, the actual growth was still more than 3 times and reached 6% annually, higher than the average 3.7% increase rate of living expense in the previous 29 years.

Great changes have taken place in every aspect of rural residents' life. The total expense for food per person increased from 41 yuan in 1954 to 850 yuan in 1998, an increase of 19.9 times. The expense for clothing has increased from 8 yuan to 98 yuan, or an increase of 11.3 times. The expense for commodities of daily use and service and other expense increased from 10 yuan to 403 yuan, an increase of 39 times.

The rural residents consumption structure has changed from satisfying the basic needs, "food first, clothing second and housing third", to a large enhancement in the expense for enjoyment at higher levels. The consumption structure evidently demonstrates that the proportion of survival materials has declined greatly, and the proportion of materials for development and enjoyment has enlarged. In 1954, the consumption structure included food, clothing, housing, commodities of daily use and other items. Among these, the proportion of food was as high as 69%, clothing 13%, housing 9%, and daily commodities and other items 9%. In 1984, as the Engel Coefficient dropped below 60%, the consumption structure undertook such a quality change that rural residents as a whole began to lead a life with sufficient food and clothing. The proportion of the expense for food and clothing declined dramatically, while that for housing, entertainment and service increased greatly. During this period, the proportion of the expense for food in rural residents' living expense was still the largest, but it declined to 59.1%. The proportion of the expense for housing was the second largest, accounting for 17.4%; the proportion of the expense for entertainment, service and other items was the third, 13.1%; the proportion of the expense for clothing has declined 10.4%. In 1998, as the living standard in rural areas further developed, the proportion of the basic needs—food, clothing and housing—declined continuously in the structure of the rural residents' consumption. Their consumption structure changed: food accounted for 53.4% in the total expense, entertainment, service and other items 25.3%, housing 15.1%, and clothing 6.2%. At present, 95% of the rural residents in China lead a life with more then sufficient food and clothing, and 25% of rural families lead a relatively comfortable life.

In recent years, self-sufficient consumption has declined in rural residents' life, and their life has become more and more dependent on market, an another indication of the improvement of consumption level. From 1978 to 1998, the annual money consumption of rural residents increased from 41 yuan per person to 1,128 yuan, an increase of 23.5 times. The proportion of money consumption in the total expense rose from 41% in 1978 to 70.7% in 1998, increasing nearly 30 percentage.

Among this, the rural residents' money expense for food increased from 19 yuan to 429 yuan, an increase of 21.6 times. The proportion of the money expense for food in the total expense for food rose from 24.1% to 50.5%, increasing by 26.4 %. The money expense for housing was 199 yuan, 83.2% of the total expense for housing, 31.9% higher than that of 1978. The degree of commercialization was almost 100% in the areas of clothing, commodities for daily use, household facilities, service, medical treatment and health care, transportation, and communications.

In the first 30 years since the founding of the People's Republic of China, the development of rural resident livelihood experienced twists and turns. However, with the Third Plenary Session of the 11th CPC Central Committee at the end of 1978 as a milestone, the past 20 years witnessed epoch-making changes in Chinese rural residents' life, which can be specified in the following six aspects:

—The quality of food has improved evidently. The overall improvement of rural residents' food consumption is mainly shown in the following areas: People have completely got rid of the life without sufficient food, and begun to pay attention to the taste of food, to raising the quality of food, and to enriching the nutrition of diet. First, after rural residents have enough food, they begin to improve their diet. The proportion of the expense for staple food in the total expense for food declined from 65.3% in 1978 to 35.5% in 1998, declining by 29.8 %. At the same time, the proportion of the expense for non-staple food per person rose from 31.4% in 1978 to 42.9% in 1998. Secondly, the consumption of wheat flour and rice increased while that of coarse food grain has decreased. A comparison of 1978 and 1998 indicates that, although the total grain consumption of each rural resident only increased 1.6 kilograms, the consumption of wheat flour and rice increased from 123 kilograms to 209 kilograms, and the proportion of wheat flour and rice increased from 49.4% to 83.9% in the total food consumption. On the other hand, the consumption of coarse food grain decreased from 125 kilograms to 40.5 kilograms, dropping by 67.6%. Thirdly, the nutrition of the diet improved markedly, nutritious cooking oil and other luxury food increased several times. Comparing to the situation in 1978, the consumption of cooking oil by each rural resident increased by 2.1 times in 1998; that of meat and poultry by 1.6 times; that of eggs by 4 times; that of aquatic products by 3.3 times. The amount of calories taken in reached the standard set by the nutrition authorities; meanwhile, less calories were taken from starchy food, and more from high protein food such as aquatic products, poultry, eggs and other refined food.

—Clothing has become more comfortable and high-grade. Clothing is a common need in people's material and spiritual lives. The marked change in rural residents' consumption of clothing is that less and less cloth was purchased, while more and more ready made clothes were bought, and the rural residents paid more and more attention to the style, color, quality, comfort and ornamentation of their clothes, some even bought high-grade clothing. In 1998, the rural residents' expense for clothing per person reached 98 yuan, 5.6 times of that in 1978; the per person purchase of cloth was 1.97 meters, a drop by 64.1% when conpared with that of 1978; and the per person purchase of ready-made clothes was one piece, an increase of 1.2 times over that of 1983.

—Living conditions have improved greatly. Rural residents' living conditions were poor for quite a long time. Their houses used to be simple and crude, which sun-dried mud bricked walls and a straw or tiled roof. At present, rows of brick and tile-roofed houses and even blocks of story buildings with a novel design have been built, an evident change of the rural areas after the reform. In 1998, the rural residents' expense on housing per person was 240 yuan, 19.1 times more than that in 1978. The per household living space increased from 8.1 square meters in 1978 to 23.7 square meters in 1998, increasing by 1.9 times. The value of newly built houses was 40 yuan per square meter in 1985, and the figure went up to 227 yuan in 1998, increasing by 4.7 times. At present, in some better-off areas, quite a number of rural residents' houses and the internal decorations are modern oriented.

—Household durables have been doubled or redoubled. The quantity of durables purchased by rural residents has increased several times, another significant indication of the improved living standard of rural residents. In 1965, there were only 7.6 bicycles, 2 radios, 10 watches and clocks

and 2.6 sewing machines in every one hundred rural households. By 1998, the demand for these major articles by rural families reached saturation. The demand for other household electrical appliances grew rapidly. By the end of 1998, there were 96 television sets, including 33 color ones, 32 tape recorders, 112 electric fans and 23 washing machines in every one hundred rural families. Some of the families purchased video recorders, cameras, refrigerators, and even air-conditioners and computers.

— Spiritual life became enriched colorful. Since 1949, as the rural economy prospers gradually, the material life for rural residents has become more and more colorful. At present, television sets have become popular, and many rural families have realized the importance of knowledge and information, and invested more in culture and education. By 1998, the rural residents' expense per person on culture, education, entertainment and service was 159 yuan, 10% of the total living expense; at the same time, due to the improvement of basic facilities in the rural areas and the gradual integration of social economic life, the rural residents' expense on transportation and communications increased. In 1998, the expense on transportation and communications per person reached 61 yuan, 3.8% of the total living expense. As the income increases, rural residents have shown more concern for their physical and mental health. The cases of underestimating serious diseases and neglecting less serious ones have been greatly reduced. In 1998, the rural residents' expense per person on medical treatment and health care was 68 yuan, 4.3% of the total living expense.

—Living environment has improved enormously. Living environment or community environment can influence the development of regional economy. For quite a long time in the past, the rural society was not developed, and the community environment was backward. Since 1978, the strengthening of investment in infrastructure construction has played an important role in improving the quality of life of the rural residents. Meanwhile, the liveing conditions and living environment for the rural residents have improved gradually. By 1998, more than 95% of the administrative villages in the rural areas were connected by roads; about 70% of the administrative villages had access to telephones and clean water supply; more than 95% of the administrative villages had electricity supply. With the development of transportation, post, telecommunication and electricity in the rural areas, the livelihood and production conditions in the rural areas improved; the pace of overcoming poverty was accelerated in the backward areas; the exchange of economy and culture between the urban and rural areas laid a solid foundation for a sustained, stable development of the rural economy.

教育科技事业的发展

Great Achievements in Education and Science

教育事业取得巨大成就

中华人民共和国的教育事业，是在经济落后、文化教育很不发达的基础上发展起来的。经过50年的努力，教育事业取得了巨大的成就。

旧中国的教育事业非常落后。全国人口中80%以上是文盲，学龄儿童入学率只有20%左右。在各级各类学校中，受外国控制的教会学校和私立学校占很大比重。学校分布极不合理，高等学校和中等专业学校多数集中在大中城市和沿海一些省份，中、小学也是大多设在城镇，内地、边远地区和少数民族地区的教育事业更加落后。全国各级各类学校学生仅占全国人口的5%左右，图书资料、教学设备十分缺乏，教材亦陈旧落后。国民党统治时期的1912-1948年的36年中，高等学校毕业生仅有21.08万人，而且学科专业结构极不合理。

新中国成立后，确立了社会主义教育方向，

对旧的教育制度进行了根本性的改造，各级各类教育事业得到了迅速发展。1998年在校学生数与解放前最高年（高等学校为1947年，中、小学为1946年，下同）相比，普通高等学校增长了21.99倍，普通中等学校增长了40.11倍，学龄儿童入学率达到99.3%，幼儿教育和各级成人教育也有了很大发展。

到1965年，普通高等学校数比解放前最高年增长1.1倍，在校学生比解放前最高年增长3.3倍；普通中等学校在校生比解放前最高年增长6.6倍；小学在校生比解放前最高年增长了3.9倍；学龄儿童入学率达到85%。成人教育也有较大发展。

1949年到1965年，普通高等学校共为国家培养研究生1.6万人，本专科毕业生155万人；通过业余、函授教育培养了20万本专科毕业生。普通中等专业学校培养了295万毕业生；农业、职业中学和普通中学共培养了2000多万劳动后备力量，对中国的各项建设事业作出了重要贡献。

1966年到1976年，中国的教育事业受到严重挫折，直到1976年10月“文化大革命”结束，特别是中共十一届三中全会后，中国的教育事业才取得了飞速发展。

一、普通高等教育得到了迅速发展

为了尽快使专门人才的培养适应国民经济和社会发展的需要，普通高等学校采取多层次，多形式办学，挖掘了高等学校的办学潜力、创办了短期职业大学，扩大了招生规模，调动了社会各方面培养人才的积极性。1977年普通高等学校恢复招生考试后，当年招收学生仅27.3万人；1998年达到108.36万人，是1977年的3.9倍，平均每年增长6.8%。在校生规模从62.5万人增加到340.88万人，是1977年的5.45倍，平均每年增长8.5%。在普通高等教育高速增长的同时，成人高等教育也取得了较大发展。招生人数从1980年的20.4万人增加到1998年的100.14万人，平均每年增长约9.3%，在校人数从49.7万人增加到282.22万人，平均每年增长约10.3%。1997年与1977年相比，高等教育毛入学率从1.4%提高到9.17%，每万人口中拥有的大学生人数从235人增加到482人。

为了适应经济和社会发展对更高层次专门人才的需求，研究生的培养能力显著增强。研究生培养单位由1981年的593个，增加到1998年的736个；1981年研究生招生人数和在校生人数分别为0.9万人和1.9万人，到1998年研究生招生人数和在校生人数分别达到了7.25万人和19.89万人，保持了较高的增长速度。

二、中等教育迅速发展，扭转了长期以来中等教育结构形式单一的格局

根据中央决定，确定了从中学阶段学生开始分流的原则。初中毕业生一部分升入普通高中，一部分接受高中阶段的职业技术教育；高中毕业生一部分升入全日制普通高等学校，一部分接受高等职业技术教育。充分发掘了中等专业学校和技术学校的办学潜力，扩大了招生规模，并且有计划地将一批普通高中改办为职业高中，同时在普通高中增设职业班，多种形式发展职业技术教育。1980年普通高中阶段教育（包括普通高中、职业高中、普通中专）共有学校3.77万所，招生人数和在校生人数分别为460.9万人和1139.5万人；高中阶段职业教育（包括职业高中、普通中专）招生77.5万人，在校生169.7万人，分别占整个高中阶段招生和在校生的16.8%和14.89%；到1998年普通高中阶段教育（包括普通高中、职业高中、普通中专和技工学校）共有学校3.11万所，招生人数和在校生人数分别达782.46万人和2083.47万人。普通高中阶段职业教育招生422.91万人，在校生1145.47万人，分别占整个高中阶段招生和在校生的54.05%和54.98%。彻底扭转了长期以来中等教育结构形式单一的格局。

三、普及义务教育、扫除青壮年文盲，全民教育普及程度提高

实现基本普及义务教育、基本扫除青壮年文盲，是提高整个中华民族素质、实现社会主义现代化、推进社会全面进步的奠基工程，是实现“科教兴国”战略的根本举措。国家致力于提高全民教育普及程度，把“两基”确定为中国教育发展的重中之重。1986年《中华人民共和国义务教育法》颁布，1988年国务院发布了《扫除文盲工作条例》，开始在全国有计划有步骤地实施九年义务教育和开展扫除文盲工作。经过几年的努力，“两基”工作取得重大进展。到1998年，全国小学学龄儿童入学率从1978年的94%提高到98.9%，初中毛入学率从66.4%提高到87.3%。全国73%的人口地区普及了九年义务教育，“普九”验收的县（市、区）总数达到2242个，北京、天津、上海、广东、江苏、浙江等9个省市已实现“两基”。全国青壮年文盲率已从1982年的22.56%下降到1998年的5.5%，2/3的县（市）非文盲率达到95%以上。全民族的文化水平得到了较大的提高。

在实施“普九”的同时，中国中小学师资队伍也得到了充实和加强。中小学专任教师中达到规定学历要求的人数，初中由1978年的9.8%提高到1998年的83.4%，小学由1978年的47.1%提高到1998年的94.6%。中小学教师职务聘任制度和教师专业合格证书制度的实施，促进了教师业务水平的提高。

四、盲聋哑、残疾人和弱智儿童教育有了一定发展

1998年全国共有盲聋聋哑学校1535所，比1978年增加了1243所，招生数和在校生数分别为4.91万人和35.84万人，分别是1978年0.59万人和3.1万人的8.32倍和11.56倍。在普通学校随班就读的残疾儿童招生数占特殊教育招生总数的比重已提高到59.7%，在校生的比重达到67.8%。

幼儿教育越来越受到重视和关心。1998年全国有幼儿园18.14万所，比1978年增加1.74万所，幼儿园在园幼儿（包括学前班）达2403.03万人，比1978年的787.7万人增长了3.05倍。为了对学龄前儿童进行丰富多彩的教育，在部分幼儿园开设了艺术班、美术班、英语班等，深受社会和家长的欢迎。

五、成人教育蓬勃发展，成为整个教育事业的重要组成部分

改革开放以来，成人教育采取多种多样的办学形式，利用各种各样的教学手段，使其得到较大的发展。1986年国务院批转国家教委制定的《关于改革和发展成人教育的决定》，成人教育的重点转向了岗位培训，同时突破了单一的培养规格和办学模式，实行了毕业证书、单科合格证书和专业证书三种证书制度，向多功能、多规格发展。同时，为适应经济建设的需要，成人高等和中等专业学校及时开设了许多短线专业，缓解了人才的供求矛盾，促进了各项事业的均衡发展。

1998年全国成人高等学校为962所，另有900多所普通高校举办了函授、夜大学，成人高等教育在校本专科学生达到282.22万人，是1980年49.75万人的5.67倍。成人中、初等教育也得到了迅猛发展，1998年全国约有7200万人参加了各种类型的成人中、初等学校学习。

从1981年起，自学考试经过试点已全面展开。1981年，高等教育自学考试只开考15个专业，到1998年，高等教育自学考试已开考426个专业，本专科毕业生约197.6万人。高等和中等教育自学考试制度的建立，为中国成人教育的发展又开拓了一条新的途径。

利用远距离视听手段进行教学的方式进一步扩大了成人教育的实施范围。1986年7月，“中国电视教育”正式开通，1986年10月1日卫星电视

频道正式播出。据统计，中国教育电视台十多年来共播出各类教育教学节目10万多小时，取得了巨大的社会效益。通过中国教育电视台播出的电视课程，中央广播电视大学已培养毕业生近200余万人；2000多万人接受继续教育与岗位培训；200多万中小学教师和校长收看各类继续教育课程和校长培训讲座。中国燎原广播电视学校为上亿农民送去了实用技术和致富信息，为农民脱贫致富，发展经济发挥了重要作用。

六、对外教育交流空前活跃，效果明显

改革开放以来，为学习、借鉴外国先进的科学技术和管理经验，促进高层次人才的培养，中国政府制定了出国留学工作的一系列方针、政策。1978年至1997年底，中国派往100多个国家的出国留学生达29.2万人。其中：国家公派4.7万人；单位公派9.15万人；自费15.34万人。学成回国的留学生达9.85万人。在派出留学生的同时，中国还接受了大量外国留学生。1978年至1997年底，中国已接受了来自世界160多个国家和地区的25.8万名外国留学生来华学习。其中享受中国政府奖学金的外国留学生达6.4万名，享受非中国政府奖学金的外国留学生19.4万名。1997年，共接受160多个国家的4.3万余名来华留学生，其中享受中国政府奖学金的4600余人。另外，中国政府同联合国有关组织和世界银行等国际组织以及众多国家进行了多种形式的教育合作与交流，中国政府与118个国家签订了119个政府协议，参加和举办国际学术会议，组团考察，派出访问学者，聘请外国专家、教师来华任教或短期讲学。中国教育界同各国教育界，学术界建立了广泛的联系，活跃了学术空气，增进了相互的了解和友谊。

七、科学研究成果显著

改革开放以来，高等学校在推动科技面向经济、发展科学技术和培养高级专门人才方面，作出了重要的贡献。在人文社会科学领域，1997年高等学校的研究机构共17160个，社科活动人员20.6万人，发表学术论文92691篇，出版专著5697部，鉴定成果1504项。在理、工、农、医学科领域，1997年高等学校设立科研机构1627个，每年从事科研的教师和研究生14万人。高等学校科学研究在国家科学研究事业中发挥了重要的作用：一是为国民经济建设和发展高新技术解决了一大批带有全局性的重大关键技术难题，承担了大批科技任务。1997年高等学校重大科技成果约占全国总数的33.6%；二是建成了一批国家级科学研究基地，为科技发展和科技人才培养奠定了良好的研究基础。全国高等学校已建成了100个国家重点实验室，共有固定研究人员2700人，客座研究人员11800人；三是在国内、国外刊物上收录的高等学校科学研究论文，占全国总数的比重分别达56.2%和60.2%；四是高等学校的科技成果转让也取得成果。1997年签订技术转让合同4248份，实际收到转让费3.86亿元。

经过50年的努力，中国培养出了一支德才兼备的知识分子队伍，极大地提高了全民族的科学文化水平。从1949年至1998年，全国普通高等学校本专科毕业生达1300多万人，研究生50多万人；中等专业学校毕业生1800多万人；成人高等学校（包括自学考试）和成人中等专业学校毕业生计2800多万人。以上高、中等专业人才共计6000多万人，为中国社会主义现代化建设输送了大量专业人才。此外还培养了近四亿具有中学文化水平的劳动者。根据1997年1‰人口抽样调查推算的数字与1964年人口普查数字相比，全国每10万人口中拥有各种文化程度的人数大大提高。大学文化程度的由495人提高到2737人，高中文化程度的由1570人提高到10382人，初中文化程度的由5572人提高到32064人，小学文化程度的由33730人提高到40663人，全民族的教育文化水平有了显著提高。

经过 50 年的努力，建立了一支适应教育事业发展的教职工队伍和科学研究队伍。1998 年，全国普通学校和成人学校共计有教职工 1580.32 万人，其中专任教师有 1206.14 万人。全国普通高等学校和成人高等学校有教职工 123.35 万人，其中专任教师 50.39 万人；普通中等学校和成人中等学校有教职工 673.05 万人，其中专任教师 476.92 万人；小学和成人初等学校有教职工 668.16 万人，其中专任教师 591.29 万人；幼儿园有教职工 115.76 万人，其中专任教师 87.54 万人。素质逐步提高的教师队伍确保了教学工作的正常开展和教学水平的不断提高。

科技事业取得长足发展

一、奠定基础，统筹规划

1. 搞好科研机构布局，延揽培养科技人才

新中国成立时，全国科学技术人员不超过 5 万人，其中专门从事科学研究工作的人员不足 500 人，专门的科研机构只有 30 多个。1949 年 11 月，在旧中国中央研究院和北平研究院的基础上成立了中国科学院，之后各部门、各地区也相继成立了一批科研机构。一批在国外工作、学习的知识分子纷纷回到祖国，大批社会闲置专业技术人员被招考录用，同时国家教育事业的大发展，使中国的科技人才迅速增加，科技力量快速增长。1955 年，全国科研机构已发展到 840 个。到“文革”前，全国科研机构已增加到 1600 多个，形成了中科院、高校、产业部门、国防部门和地方科研机构五方面组成的科技大军。

2. 制定科技发展规划，开拓新兴科技领域

1956 年，中国第一个科学技术发展长远规划——《1956 年至 1967 年全国科学技术发展远景规划》诞生。规划的主要任务提前五年完成，从而建立和发展了中国的原子能、电子学、半导体、自动化、计算机技术、喷气和火箭技术等一批新兴科学技术领域，促进了一系列新兴工业部门的诞生和发展，对中国科技体系的形成起了决定性作用。经过短短几年的努力，中国科技事业发生了很大变化，到 1962 年，全国科研机构已发展到 1296 家，专业从事研究工作的科技人员近 20 万，均是规划伊始时的 3 倍。之后，中国在 1962 年又制定了《1963 年至 1972 年科学技术发展规划》，规划确定了重点科研项目 374 项，3205 个中心问题和 15000 个研究课题。这一规划对指导中国科技事业的持续发展起到了重要的历史作用。

二、开拓进取，发展壮大

1. 科技队伍稳步壮大

中共十一届三中全会以后，中国的科技人力资源得到迅速的恢复和发展，1998 年末，国有企事业单位拥有的专业技术人员已达 2091.3 万人，是 1978 年的 4.8 倍，平均每年增加 82.8 万人，是改革前平均增加 15.1 万人的 5.5 倍。平均每万职

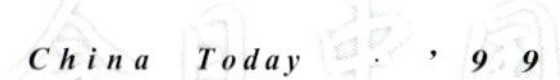

工中专业技术人员大幅度增长，从1978年的593人提高到2374.2人。

在科技人力资源迅速增长的同时，一支具有一定规模和水平的科技人才队伍逐步形成。90年代以来，科学家工程师占从事科技活动人员的比重一直保持在56-60%之间，科技队伍的素质稳步提高。到1998年，全国从事科技活动人员已达281.4万人，其中科学家工程师149万人，均比1991年增长23.1%和12.8%。

2. 科研和技术开发机构较快发展

至1998年中国已有县以上国有独立研究与开发机构5578个，从事科技活动人员58.8万人，其中科学家工程师36.3万人，比1987年增加了1.5万人，增长2.6%；科学家和工程师所占比重为61.7%，比10年前的47.8%增加了13.9个百分点。科研活动人员素质显著提高。

高等院校科研队伍是中国科技战线上一支活跃的力量，在科技事业中发挥着重要作用。1998年，中国高校办理、工、农、医专业研究与开发机构1487个，其中自然科学270个，占18.2%；工程科学641个，占43.1%；医学372个，占25%；农学204个，占13.7%。有科技活动人员28万人，比1991年增长9.1%，占全部教学人员的比重为68.8%，比1991年提高了8.7个百分点。

企业是中国现代化建设的重要支柱。到1998年，全国大中型工业企业共办有技术开发机构10926个，比1988年增加了1倍；机构中从事技术开发的人员达41.1万人，比1988年增加近14万人，增长了50.5%；其中科学家和工程师24万人，占58.4%，比1988年的41.6%增加了16.8个百分点。

3. 增加科技经费投入，增强科技发展后劲

随着国家经济实力不断增强，中国科技经费投入稳步增加。1998年全国科技经费支出总额达1128.5亿元，是1991年的2.9倍；全国人均科技经费支出额由1991年的33.5元提高到90.4元；全年研究与实验发展（R&D）经费支出551.1亿元，是1991年的3.5倍。改革开放以来国家财政对科技事业的投入以平均每年11.5%的速度递增，1998年财政对科技的拨款已达466.5亿元，是1978年52.9亿元的8.8倍。其中科学事业费151.3亿元，占32.4%；科技三项费210亿元，占45%；科研基建费47.3亿元，占10.1%。科学事业费和科研基建费分别是1978年的3.3倍和7.1倍。作为科技投入主体的中国大中型工业企业用于技术开发的经费支出较快增加。1998年中国大中型工业企业技术开发经费支出达到478.7亿元，是1988年的4.1倍。

三、科技计划顺利实施，科技活动广泛开展

1. 面向经济建设主战场的科技工作成效显著

“科技攻关计划”始于1982年，其宗旨是集中全国主要科技力量，对在国民经济和社会发展中遇到的重大科学技术问题进行联合攻关。其中仅“八五”期间（1991-1995）就安排了180个国民经济急需解决的重大科技攻关项目，5年间投入资金总额90多亿元，获科技成果6万多项（其中有35%达到了国际水平），累计取得直接经济效益超过600亿元。

“星火计划”是引导农村经济走上依靠科技进步的发展轨道和提高农民素质的一项计划。至1998年底，“星火计划”已累计完成项目4.5万项。1998年实施项目1753项，当年落实资金121.3亿元，新增产值333.4亿元；“星火计划”的实施，已成为“科技兴农”的重要途径。

为提高企业的市场竞争和技术创新能力，形成有利于自主创新的企业技术进步机制，国家于1996年开始启动“国家技术创新工程”，并已取得进展。1998年国家安排了528项重点技术创新项目，组织实施了1420项国家级重点新产品试产，完成了15项重大技术装备的研制及鉴定验收。

2. 发展高新技术及其产业，推动经济增长

为跟踪世界高科技发展前沿，自1986年起国家开始实施高技术研究发展计划（“863”计划）。经过“七五”（1986-1990）的入轨和“八五”（1991-1995）的攻坚，至1995年底，计划已取得研究成果1200项，其中有540项达到国际水平，获国家级奖73项，获国内外专利244项。“九五”（1996-2000）的前两年又取得268项科研成果，其中达到国际领先水平的21项，国际先进水平125项，两者占成果总数的54.5%。“863”计划的顺利实施，为中国高技术发展起到重要的推动作用。

为引导和推动高技术成果商品化、产业化和国际化，尽快建立起中国的高新技术产业，1988年，国家开始实施“火炬计划”。至1998年，国家级高技术开发区已从1991年的27个发展为53个，区内高新技术企业由2587家迅速发展到16097家，从业人员由13.8万人猛增到174万人；1998年实现技工贸总收入4839.6亿元，总产值4333.6亿元，出口创汇85.3亿美元，分别是1991年的55.4倍、60.9倍和12.1倍。

3. 发展基础研究，赶超世界水平

基础研究是科学技术事业持续发展的根基。1997年全国用于基础研究的经费支出37亿元，是1991年的5倍；全国投入基础研究人员7.1万人，比1991年增长16.4%。

为支持基础研究，1984-1997年间，国家累计投资18.1亿元建成了150多个重点实验室。据统计，1997年国家重点实验室中，每月有固定人员4340人，客座人员14633人；当年承担科研项目5871项，筹集经费4.9亿元；全年取得获奖成果达347项，发表论文12221篇；当年毕业研究生2862人。为进一步提高中国基础研究水平，稳定基础研究队伍，1986年国家自然科学基金会成立，为中国基础研究的稳步发展发挥了重要的作用。至1998年，基金会共累计资助项目5万项，资助经费约45亿元。从1991年起，中国开始实施旨在进一步加强基础研究工作的开展。几年来该计划共实施项目213项，累计落实资金3.9亿元；1998项目发表论文497余篇，其中有1975余篇发表在国际刊物上。

四、科技产出丰硕，成果举世瞩目

早在文革之前，中国已开发了一批尖端技术，取得了以“两弹一星”、人工合成牛胰岛素结晶为代表的一批科技成果。改革开放以来，中国科技成果更是硕果累累，繁花似锦。1978-1997年，中国成功发射了45颗卫星，其中返还式卫星的成功发射使中国成为继美国和原苏联之后第三个掌握卫星回收技术的国家。1981年成功地用一枚运载火箭发射了三颗卫星，成为继原苏联、美、法之后第四个掌握“一箭多星”技术的国家。此外，中国成功地完成了水下导弹发射；攻克了高温气冷堆、快中子增殖反应堆等关键技术；北京正负电子对撞机对撞成功；5兆瓦低温核供应反应堆、大亚湾核电站投入使用；原子级操纵技术和原子级加工技术居世界前列；在世界上首先培育成转基因杂交水稻；纳米电子学超高密度信息存储研究获突破性进展；“银河－Ⅲ”百亿次计算机研制成功；6000米自制水下机器人完成洋底调查任务；乙型肝炎基因工程疫苗、单克隆抗体技术用于临床治疗。这些成果的取得，标志着中国在原子能技术、空间技术、高能物理、生物技术、计算机技术、信息技术等方面，已达到和接近国际先进水平。

据统计，1981年以来中国共取得重大科技成果46.5万项，其中有近20%的成果达到了国际先进水平。1979-1998年获国家发明奖2903项，国家科技进步奖7297项。

为鼓励和保护发明创造，促进技术交流和经济发展，1985年《中华人民共和国专利法》正式实施。1985-1998年，中国专利局累计受理国内

外专利申请86万件，授权专利43万件，其中1998年受理申请专利12.2万件，授权专利6.8万件。据对120个国家、地区（组织）的排序，中国当年的发明专利申请量和授权量分别居第21位和第24位。

近年来，中国科技人员在国内外发表的论文数逐年增加。1997年，中国科技人员在国内科技期刊发表科技论文121512篇，比1989年的86419篇增长40.1%。同时，中国科技人员发表的国际科技论文也有大幅度增长，据统计，1997年中国科技人员在国际上发表的期刊论文35311篇，是1989年的2.9倍，按论文数量排序，中国已从1989年的第15位跃居到第9位。

五、国际合作日益广泛，科技交流空前活跃

改革开放以来，中国科技工作逐步摆脱了封闭局面，实施了全方位的对外开放政策，科学技术合作与交流日益广泛和活跃起来。迄今，中国已先后同150个国家和地区建立了科技合作关系，同近百个国家和地区缔结了政府科技合作或经济技术合作协定。以民间形式开展的国际科技合作与交流更为活跃。中国科协及其所属团体共参加了244个国际科技组织，有293人次的科学工作者在国际科技组织中担任执委会（理事会）执委（理事）以上职务；281人次担任国际组织专业委员会领导职务；中国科学院有253名科学家在国际科学组织中担任职务，国家自然科学基金会已与36个国家科学基金组织签定了合作协议和备忘录。1998年中国官方和民间对外科技合作与交流项目达2.2万项，人员往来7万人次，分别是改革开放之初的20.6倍和12.4倍。近5年来，共引进国外专家超过40万人，派出培训的各类技术管理人员约20万人。国际合作与交流的扩大，推动了中国技术及技术产品的出口。1998年中国签定技术引进合作6254项，成交金额163.8亿美元，是1991年的17.5倍和4.7倍；1998年签定技术出口合同2500项，成交金额66.9亿美元，是1991年的5.4倍和5.2倍。国际科技合作与交流的广泛开展，对加快中国科学技术水平的提高和促进国民经济的发展都起到了积极的推动作用。

Great Achievements in Education

The education in the People's Republic of China grows out of its poor economic and educational foundation. Through the past 50 years' hard work, great achievements have been gained in education.

Before 1949, education was extraordinarily backward. Over 80% of Chinese population were illiterate, only about 20% of the children of school age were enrolled at schools. Among different kinds of schools, large proportions of them were private schools and missionary schools controlled by foreign countries. The location of schools was not balanced. Most universities, colleges and technical secondary schools were located in big cities and coastal provinces, and most primary and middle schools were in cities and towns. The education was even more backward in inland and remote areas and areas inhabited by minority nationalities. The students at schools only accounted for about 5% of the total Chinese population. Books, reference materials and educational equipment were very limited and the textbooks were obsolete and backward. During the 36-year reign of Kuomintang from 1912 to 1948, there were only 210,800 people graduated from universities and colleges, and the design of majors was not scientific.

Since 1949, the socialist education goals have been established. The old education system has been reformed fundamentally and education at various levels and of different types has gained rapid progress. In comparison with the years of the largest amount of students at school before 1949 (1947 for universities and colleges, 1946 for primary and middle schools), the number of students at universities and colleges increased by 21.99 times and those at middle schools by 40.11 times in 1998. Meanwhile, 99.3% of the children at school age were enrolled in schools, while pre-school education and adult education at different levels made great progress.

In 1965, the number of universities and colleges increased by 1.1 times, in comparison with the best year before 1949, while the number of university students increased by 3.3 times; that of students at middle schools by 6.6 times, and that of students at primary schools by 3.9 times. 85% of children at school age were enrolled in school, and adult education also made big progress.

From 1949 to 1965, higher educational institutions turned out 16,000 postgraduates and 1.55 million undergraduates for the country. Another 200,000 graduated through spare-time education and correspondence education. The senior secondary schools trained 2.95 million students, and the agricultural, vocational schools and junior secondary schools trained more than 20 million people for the labour market, making a great contribution to the construction of the country.

From 1966 to 1976, China's education has suffered serious frustration. Until the end of "cultural revolution" in 1976, especially after the Third Plenary Session of the 11th CPC National Congress in 1978, a rapid development has been gained in China's education.

I. Rapid Improvement of Higher Education

In order to meet the need of national economic and social development, universities and colleges have been growing in various forms and at different levels and have exploited their potentials. By running short-term vocational universities and expanding enrolment, enthusiasm of education in various social organizations has been stimulated. Upon the restoration of the college entrance examination in 1977, some 273,000 students got enrolled. In 1998, the enrolment reached 1,083,600, 3.9 times that of 1977, with an annual increase of 6.8%. The number of students at school increased from 625,000 to 3,408,800, 5.45 times that of 1977, with an annual increase of 8.5%. When formal higher education has developed rapidly, adult higher education has gained a big progress. The enrolment increased from 204,000 in 1980 to 1,001,400 in 1998, with an annual increase of 9.3%. The students at school increased from 497,000 to 2,822,200, an increase of about 10.3% annually. In comparison with 1977, the 1997 rate of enrolment in higher education has increased from 1.4% to 9.17%; the number of college students in every 10,000 people increased from 235 to 482 persons.

In order to meet the demand for high-level professionals in the economic and social development, the capacity for training postgraduates has expanded evidently. The number of units for postgraduates training increased from 593 in 1981 to 736 in 1998. In 1981, the numbers of postgraduates enrolled and those already at school were 9,000 and 19,000 respectively; In 1998, the numbers of postgraduates enrolled and at school reached 72,500 and 198,900 respectively, still maintaining a high growth rate.

II. Diversification of Secondary Education Through Its Rapid Development

According to the central government's decision on the distribution of secondary school students, some graduates from junior high schools go to senior high schools for further study, while some others go to vocational secondary schools. Some graduates from senior high schools go to universities and colleges for full-time study, while some others go to study at colleges for professional training. The vocational and technical schools' potential for running

schools, therefore, has been exploited thoroughly, and their enrolment has been expanded. In addition, some regular middle schools have been converted into vocational schools with careful planning, meanwhile, vocational classes have been arranged in regular middle schools, so that the vocational and technical education can develop in multi-forms. In 1980, there were 37,700 schools for secondary education (including regular high schools, vocational senior high and junior high schools) with the enrolment and the number of students at school reaching 4.609 million and 11.395 million respectively. The vocational high schools recruited 775,000 and the number of students at schools was 1.697 million, accounting for 16.8% and 14.89% of the overall high school students and the number of students at school respectively. In 1998, there were 31,100 high schools (including regular high schools, vocational high schools, technical secondary schools and polytechnic schools), with the enrolment and the number of students at school reaching 7,824,600 and 20,834,700 respectively. The enrolment of vocational high schools is 4,229,100, and the number of students at school is 11,454,700, 54.05% and 54.98% of the overall high school enrolment and the number of students at school respectively. This shows that the singular structure of secondary education has thoroughly changed.

III. Popularization of Compulsory Education and Elimination of Adult Illiteracy for the Improvement of the National Education Level

Achieving compulsory education and eliminating adult illiteracy is a foundation for improving the whole nation's quality, realizing the socialist modernization, promoting the overall social advance and the essential move for the implementation of the strategy "revitalizing China through science and education". The government has devoted to promoting the education level of the whole nation with universalizing compulsory education and eliminating adult illiteracy as the focus of educational development. In 1986, "Law on Compulsory Education" was promulgated and in 1988 "Regulation on Eliminating Illiteracy" was released, initiating the universalizing of the nine-year compulsory education and the elimination of illiteracy in a planned and strategic way. After several years of effort, great progress has been made in these two fields. The rate of school-age children attending primary school increased from 94% in 1978 to 98.9% in 1998. The rate for attending junior high schools increased from 66.4% to 87.3%. The nine-year compulsory education has been universalized in the area where 73% of the population inhabit. The education has been universalized in as many as 2,242 counties, and the universalizing of compulsory education has been basically realized in nine provinces and big cities including Guangdong, Jiangsu and Zhejiang provinces, Beijing, Tianjin and Shanghai cities. The rate of adult illiteracy in China dropped from 22.56% in 1982 to 5.5% in 1998. In 2/3 of the counties, the rate for illiteracy is lower than 5%. The education level of the whole nation has been upgraded.

With the implementation of "the nine-year compulsory education policy", teachers at primary and secondary schools have gained improvement both in quality and quantity. The rate of the full-time teachers at secondary schools with a required education background increased from 9.8% in 1978 to 83.4% in 1998 and those at primary schools increased from 47.1% in 1978 to 94.6% in 1998. The implementation of the appointment system and teaching certificate system has promoted the teachers' quality.

IV. Development of the Education for the Disabled

There were 1,535 schools for the blind and the deaf in 1998, 1,243 more than that in 1978. The enrolment and the number of students at school were 49,100 and 358,400, 8.32 times the figure of 5,900 in 1978 and 11.56 times the figure of 31,000 in 1978 respectively. The ratio between disabled children enrolled at regular schools and those at special schools reached 59.7% and the proportion of students at school reached 67.8%.

Pre-school education has been given more and more attention and concern. There were 181,400 kindergartens in China in 1998, 17,400 more than that in 1978. There are 24,030,300 children in kindergartens (including preschool classes), increasing by 3.05 times from 7.877 million in 1978. In order to diversify pre-school education, some kindergartens offer classes such as English, arts, painting and so on, which are warmly welcomed by society and parents.

V. Adult Education—an Important Component of Education

Since the reform and opening up to the outside world, different ways of running schools and various teaching methods have been utilized in adult education, which has promoted big development in adult education. In 1986, the State Council passed "Decisions on the Reform and Development of Adult Education" formulated by the State Education Commission. The focus of adult education has shifted to on-the-job training, and the singular training format and way of running schools have been reformed. Three-certificate system (degree certificates, single subject certificates and specialized major certificates) has been further improved towards the direction of multifunction and multi-format. At the same time, in order to meet the need of economic construction, higher education and vocational schools for adults have provided courses for the specialties that are badly needed, which alleviated the conflict between supply and demand of personnel and accelerated the balanced development of various areas.

In 1998, there were 962 universities and colleges for adult education and there are another more than 900 universities and colleges that run correspondent courses and evening schools. There were 2,822,200 adult students at school for higher education, 5.67 times the 497,500 students in 1980. Adult education at elementary and secondary levels has also gained a rapid progress. There were about 72 million adults receiving elementary and secondary education at schools of different kinds.

After several experiments at selected points, examinations of higher education for the self-taught have been fully performed since 1981. In 1981, only 15 majors could provide examinations for the self-taught people. Now it grows to 426 majors with 1,976,000 graduates. The establishment of examination system for the self-taught adult secondary and higher education has paved another way for the development of adult education in China.

The utilization of distant audiovisual technology has further promoted the implementation range of adult education. In July 1986, the program "China Television Education" was officially launched and on October 1, 1986, the satellite television channel began to broadcast. According to the statistics, the Television Education Station has broadcast 100,000 hours of various education programs, resulting in a significant social benefit. Through the television courses broadcast by China Television Education Station, Central Television and Radio University has trained more than Two million students. More than 20 million people have received the continuing education and on-the-job training. Two million school principals and teachers have taken various continuing education courses and attended the lectures in the principal training programs. China Liaoyuan Radio and Television School has provided 100 million farmers with practical skills and information on acquiring wealth, which plays an important role in getting rid of poverty and developing economy.

VI. Positive and Productive International Educational Exchange

In order to learn the advanced science and technology

and management experience from foreign countries and improve the training of competent personnel at advanced level, the government has formulated a series of policies on study abroad since the implementation of the reform and opening up policies. From 1978 to the end of 1997, 292,000 Chinese were sent abroad, among whom 47,000 were sent by the government, 91,500 by various organizations, and 153,400 on their own expenses. Now 98,500 of them have returned to China after finishing their study. China also received a large number of foreign students. From 1978 to the end of 1997, some 258,000 foreign students from more than 160 countries and regions have studied in China, among which 64,000 on the governmental scholarship and 258,000 on nongovernmental scholarship. In 1997, there were 43,000 students from about 160 countries studying in China, with more than 4,600 of them receiving the governmental scholarship.

In addition, the Chinese government has established cooperative and exchange educational programs in various forms with the United Nations, the World Bank and other international organizations or countries. The Chinese government has signed 119 governmental agreements with 118 countries and held or participated in international symposiums, organized group investigations, exchanged visiting scholars, invited foreign experts to teach or give lectures in China. The Chinese educational institutions have established extensive relations with their counterparts in other countries, which activated the academic atmosphere and deepened the mutual understanding and friendship.

VII. Remarkable Achievements in Scientific Research

Since the reform and opening up to the outside world, universities and colleges have made significant contributions in developing economy-oriented science and technology and training advanced personnel in special areas. In the field of humanities and social sciences, there were 17,160 research institutions in universities and colleges in 1997 with 206,000 research faculty members. They have published 92,691 research papers and 5,697 monographs, provided appraisal for 1,504 items of scientific achievements. In the fields of agriculture, medicine, and science and technology, there were 1,627 scientific research organizations in universities and colleges with 140,000 professors and graduate students doing research. The scientific research in universities and colleges plays an important role in the national scientific research. Firstly, it has solved many technological problems of overall significance for the economic development of the nation and the development of new technology, and undertaken many items of scientific research. Secondly, the establishment of scientific research bases at national level has been serving as a good research foundation for developing science and technology and training personnel. A hundred national key laboratories have been established in universities and colleges with 2,700 research staff and 11,800 visiting scholars. Thirdly, research papers published by faculties from universities and colleges on domestic and foreign periodicals account for 56.2% and 60.2% of the total respectively. Finally, universities and colleges have gained achievements in science and technology. In 1997, there were 4,248 contracts signed on technology transfer, valued at RMB 386 million yuan.

After 50 years' hard work, China has trained a group of intellectuals with both ability and integrity, which has greatly raised the scientific level of the whole nation. From 1949 to 1998, there were 13 million undergraduates and 500,000 postgraduates in universities and colleges, 18 million from secondary vocational schools, and 28 million adults receiving university or secondary vocational school education (including the national self-taught examination). More than 60 million people have become competent labor force for the construction of modernization in China. In addition, there are about 400 million people having received secondary school education. The comparison between the 1‰ population sample survey in 1997 and the population census in 1964 shows that the education level of every 100,000 people improved significantly in 1997. The number of people with higher education increased from 495 to 2,737, those with senior high school education from 1,570 to 10,382, those with junior high school education from 5,572 to 32,064, and those with primary school education from 33,730 to 40,663. The education level of the whole nation has gained a remarkable improvement.

After 50 years' effort, a significant number of teaching and administrative staff and researchers have been trained for educational development. In 1998, there were 15,803,200 teaching and administrative staff working at regular and adult schools with 12,061,400 full-time teachers. There were 1,233,500 teaching and administrative staff working at regular and continuing higher education institutes with 503,900 full-time teachers. There were 6,730,500 teaching and administrative staff working at regular and adult secondary schools with 4,769,200 full-time teachers. There were 6,681,600 teaching and administrative staff working for basic education and basic education for adults with 5,912,900 full-time teachers. There were 1,157,600 teaching and administrative staff working in kindergartens with 875,400 full-time teachers. The steady improvement of teachers' quality has assured the success of current teaching and the continuous improvement of teaching.

Rapid Development of Science and Technology

I. Foundation Construction and Overall Planning

1. Construction of Scientific Research Institutions and Recruitment of Scientific and Technological Personnel

When New China was founded in 1949, there were no more than 50,000 scientists and technicians in China. Among them, only 500 were engaged in scientific research in just over 30 research institutions across the country. In November 1949, the Chinese Academy of Sciences was established by merging the old Central Research Academy of China and Beijing Research Institute. Since then, the central and local government departments have set up various research institutions. Many intellectuals working and studying abroad returned to their motherland for their contribution, and various kinds of technicians and professionals were recruited from society. These measures, together with the rapid growth of the national education, have greatly increased the number of scientific and technological personnel and thus the scientific and technological level. By 1955, there were 840 scientific and technological research institutions nationwide, which reached 1,600 by 1965, when the "cultural revolution" started. There were five major groups for scientific and technological research in this area: the Chinese Academy of Sciences, the universities, those under the central government departments, the defence departments and the local institutions.

2. Drawing Up the Scientific Development Plan and Opening Up the New Areas

The year of 1956 saw the birth of China's first long-term plan for scientific and technological development—the Long-Term National Program for Scientific and Technological Development during 1956 and 1967. The major tasks of the program were completed five years earlier. Some new scientific areas such as atomic energy, electronics, semiconductors, automation, computer sciences, jet and satellite technology were established and developed and so were the new industrial departments. All these played a decisive role in the formation of China's scientific and technological system. In a few years, China's scientific and technological industry underwent great changes, and there were 1,296 research institutions and 200,000 research personnel by 1962, three times as many as in the first year of the program. Later in 1962, China promulgated the Scientific and Technological Development Program for 1963 to 1972, which prioritized 374 key programs, 3,205 projects and 15,000 research topics. This program was of great historical importance to the sustained growth of our science and technology.

II. Further Progress and Growth

1. Steady Increase of Scientific and Technological Personnel

Since China adopted the reform and open policy 20 years ago, its scientific and technological personnel resources have been recovered and developed rapidly, with 20.913 million scientific and technical personnel working in the state organizations by the end of 1998, 4.8 times that of 1978. This represents an annual increase of 828,000 personnel on the average, 5.5 times as many as the average annual increase of 151,000 personnel before 1978, when China impelemented the reform and open-up policies. As a result, the number of professionals and technicians per 10,000 staff rose dramatically, from 593 in 1978 to 2,374.2 in 1998.

With the increase of the scientific personnel resources, the expertise level of the Chinese scientists has also improved much. Since the 1990s, the scientists and engineers have accounted for 56-60% of the personnel engaged in scientific and technological activities. The scientific and technological workers numbered 2.814 million in 1998, including 1.49 million scientists and engineers. That represents a 23.1% and 12.8% increase over the year of 1991.

2. Rapid Development of Scientific and Technological Institutions

By 1998, China boasted of 5,578 state-owned research and development institutions at the county level or above, staffed by 588,000 scientific and technological personnel. Of them, scientists and engineers numbered 363,000, accounting for 61.7% of the total, as against 47.8% of 1978.

The higher education institutions are another active contingent in China's scientific and technological front. In 1998, the Chinese universities had 1,487 research and development institutions. Of them, there were 270 or 18.2% for natural sciences, 641 or 43.1% for engineering, 372 or 25% for medical research, and 204 or 13.7% for agriculture. There were 268,000 related personnel, up 9.1% over 1991. They accounted for 68.8% of the total teaching staff, up 8.7% over 1991.

Enterprises are the pillar in China's modernization construction. The national large and medium-sized enterprises have set up 10,926 R&D departments, twice that of 1988, with 411,000 people engaged in R&D, up 50.5% over 1988. Of them, 240,000 are scientists and engineers, accounting for 58.4% of the total, 16.8% higher than that of 1988.

3. Increase of Capital Input in Science and Technology Development

With the steady improvement of the national economic strength, China's input of capital in science and technology has increased. The total input for 1998 reached 112.85 billion yuan, 2.9 times that of 1991. The per-capita science and technology input has grown from 33.5 yuan in 1991 to 90.4 yuan in 1998. The input in R&D for 1998 was RMB 55.11 billion yuan, 3.5 times that of 1991. Since China adopted the reform and open policies in 1978, the state's fiscal allocation to the science and technology sector has increased at an average annual rate of 11.5% . In 1998, the fiscal allocation to this sector reached 46.65 billion yuan, 8.8 times that of 1978. Of the input, 15.13 billion yuan went to basic science research, accounting for 32.4%, 3.3 times that of 1978, 21 billion yuan to applied scientific research, accounting for 45% or 7.1 times that of 1978, and 4.73 billion yuan to science-related infrastructure construction, accounting for 10.1%. As one of the main forces in scientific input, China's large and medium-sized enterprises have increased their capital investment in R&D rapidly, RMB 47.87 billion yuan in 1998, 4.1 times that of 1988.

III. Smooth Implementation of Science Programs and Broad Development of Scientific and Technological Activities

1.Economic Development-Oriented Scientific Achievements

Strategic Science and Technology Program started in 1982. Its aim is to gather the national scientific strength to solve the major scientific problems encountered in the national economic and social development. From 1991 to 1995, 180 strategic projects were planned concerning the solution of the key economic issues. The total investment for the five years is over 9 billion yuan, with over 60,000 scientific and technological achievements (35% of which have reached the international level). The aggregated economic returns are over 60 billion yuan.

The star program is another one which aims to develop the agricultural economy with the support of scientific progress and improve the farmers' quality. By the end of 1998, the star program has completed 45,000 projects in all. The year of 1997 implemented 1,753 projects with real input of 12.13 billion yuan and an additional output of 33.34 billion yuan. The implementation of the star program has been an important means for "the development of agriculture by science and technology".

In order to raise the competitiveness and innovation capabilities of the companies and cultivate their own technological advance mechanism, the state introduced the National Technical Innovation Program in 1996 and has made much progress since then. In 1997, the state organized the implementation of 528 technical innovation projects and the trial production of 1,420 national-level new products. Meanwhile, it has 15 hi-tech equipment projects developed and examined.

2. Promotion of Economic Growth Through the Development of Hi-Tech Industries

China began to implement hi-tech R&D Development Program (863 Program) since 1986 with the purpose of catching up the hi-tech development of the world. By the end of 1995, i.e., through ten years hard work, the program has made 1,200 research achievements, of which, 540 were of international level, 73 received the national awards and 244 were patented. Some 268 scientific research achievements were made during 1996-1997. Of them, 21 reached the world-leading level and 125 of the world level. They accounted for 54.5 % of the projects. The successful implementation of the 863 Program has played a significant role in promoting hi-tech development in China.

In order to promote the commercialization, industrialization and internationalization of hi-tech research achievements and to establish its own hi-tech industries, China began to carry out the Torch Program in 1988. By 1998, the national hi-tech development areas have grown from 27 in 1991 to 53 in 1997, with their hi-tech enterprises growing from 2,587 to 16,097 and employees from 13,800 to 1.74 million. The 1998 output from the hi-tech development areas is 483.96 billion yuan, with industrial output at 433.36 billion yuan, exports at US$ 8.53 billion, 55.4 times, 60.9 times and 12.1 times those of 1991 respectively.

3. Development of Basic Researches to Catch up with the World Level

Basic research is the foundation for the steady growth of science and technology. In 1997, China's expenditure on basic research was 3.7 billion yuan, 5 times that of 1991. The national input of human resources was 71,000 persons/year, up 16.4% against 1991.

In order to support the basic research, the state has invested 1.81 billion yuan in the establishment of 150 key laboratories during 1984 and 1997. According to the statis-

tics, there were 4,340 permanent staff and 14,633 temporary staff working in the national key laboratories in 1997. In that year, 5,871 research projects were undertaken, 490 million yuan were obtained as research fund, 347 project achievements were awarded, and 12,221 research essays were published. Also 2,862 postgraduates finished their studies from universities. In 1986, the National Natural Science Fund was established with the aim to raise China's basic research level. The Fund input RMB 4.5 billion in total in service super developmeny during 1986 and 1998 and funded 50,000 projects. Since 1991, China has launched the "Climbing Program" in order to promote its basic research level. In the past few years, 213 projects have been implemented with input of RMB 390 million yuan and over 4,970 research essays have been published, including 1975 in international publications, under this program.

IV. Remarkable Scientific and Technological Achievements

As early as in 1965, China developed various hi-tech products characterized by the atomic bomb, the hydrogen bomb and the satellite as well as the synthetic crystalline bovine insulin. Since China adopted reform and open-door policies, our scientific and technological achievements are even more remarkable. During 1978 and 1997, China has successfully launched 45 satellites. Its satellite-recovering technology has made China the third country capable of this technology in the world, after the United States and the former Soviet Union. In 1981, China succeeded in launching three satellites in one carrier rocket and became the fourth country of the world which masters this technology, after the former Soviet Union, the United States and France. Meanwhile, China successfully launched missiles from underwater, overcame the technical problems concerning high temperature air cooling reactor and fast neutron breeder reactor. Such technologies as 5 megawatt low temperature nuclear supply reactor, Dayawan nuclear power station, atomic manoeuvre technology and atomic process technology, transgenic hybrid rice, etc., are all of the world level. We have also made breakthroughs in high-density information storage research, and we have successfully developed Milky Way—III high speed computer, carried out the 6,000 meters deep-sea research by our own-developed underwater robot. All those have marked China's world level in atomic energy, space technology, high-energy physics, biotechnology, computer sciences, information technology, etc.

According to the statistics, China has made 46,500 research achievements since 1981, with about 20% are of the advanced world level. During 1979 and 1998, 2,903 achievements have got National Invention Award, and 7,297 for the National Advanced Science and Technology Award.

In 1985, the Patent Law of the People's Republic of China was promulgated with the purpose of encouraging invention and promoting technological exchanges and economic growth. The China Patent Office has accepted 860,000 patent applications from both home and abroad and approved 430,000 during 1985 and 1998, including the acceptance of 122,000 applications and approvals of 68,000 for 1997 only. Of the 120 countries and regions, China came out the 21st and 24th in terms of the number of applications and approvals.

In the past years, Chinese scientists have turned out more research papers each year. They had 121,512 papers publicized at home for 1997, 40.1% more than in 1989. Meanwhile their publications in international journals have also risen greatly, 35,311 papers for 1997, 2.9 times those of 1989. Ranking by the number of papers published, China has jumped from No.15 in 1989 to No. 9 in 1997.

V. More International Cooperation and Exchanges

Since China adopted reform and open policies, its scientific and technological sector has implemented the same policy accordingly. There have been increasing cooperation and exchanges with foreign countries in this sector. Now China established cooperative relations with 150 countries and regions and signed governmental science and technology cooperation or economic and technological cooperation agreements with nearly 100 countries and regions. The non-governmental cooperation and exchanges are even more active. The Chinese Science Association and its subsidiaries have joined 244 international organizations, 293 Chinese scientists have taken the position of councillors in the international scientific and technological organizations at different periods, and 281 have taken the leadership positions in such organizations. For example, 253 scientists from the Chinese Academy of Sciences have taken positions in such organizations. The National Natural Science Fund has signed cooperative agreements and memorandums with 36 counterparts from other countries. In 1998, there were 22,000 scientific and technological cooperation and exchange projects between China and foreign countries on a government or non-government basis, with 107,000 personnel exchanges, 20.6 times and 12.4 times that of 1978. In the past five years, China has introduced over 400,000 foreign experts and sent nearly 200,000 personnel abroad for study. The international cooperation and exchanges have promoted export of China's technology and its products. In 1998, China signed 2,500 technical export contracts, valued at US$ 6.69 billion, 5.4 times and 5.2 times those of 1991 respectively. As for imports, China has signed 5,984 technical import contracts in 1997, totalling US$ 15.92 billion, 16.7 times and 4.6 times those of 1991 respectively. China's foreign cooperation and exchange have played an important role in raising China's science and technology level as well as promoted the national economic growth.

改革开放篇

REFORM AND OPENING

改 革 开 放 篇

REFORM AND OPENING

中国国际地位和影响的提高

The Rise of China's International Status

改革开放20年的中国外交

1999年，当世界即将进入21世纪时，中国迎来了它改革开放的第20个年头。20年来，中国的现代化建设事业获得了举世公认的发展，在外交领域亦取得了令人瞩目的成就。随着综合国力的不断增强，中国的国际地位日益提高，已成为国际舞台上一支举足轻重的力量，发挥着越来越重要的作用。现在，中国正以崭新的面貌屹立于世界民族之林，中国与世界的关系越来越密切，“让世界走近中国，让中国走进世界”正在化为现实。

改革开放20年来，中国外交成就的取得，无疑与外交政策的战略性调整密切相关，而外交政策的调整是邓小平理论的重要组成部分。70年代中后期，世界形势开始发生实质变化，以邓小平为首的中国领导人敏锐地察觉到了这种变化，紧紧把握新的时代特征，实现了外交指导思想的重大转变，为改革开放后中国外交打开新局面奠定了基础。邓小平先生认真分析了风云变幻的国际形势，深刻地指出，当今世界正处于大变动的历史时期，多极化是不可逆转的世界潮流。在今后一个较长时期内，虽然战争的危险依然存在，但新的世界战争的爆发并非完全不可避免，只要世界爱好和平的人民共同努力，争取和平的国际环境是可能的。1985年，他进一步指出，“现在世界上真正的大问题，带全球性的战略问题，一个是和平问题，一个是经济问题或者说发展问题”，从而科学地揭示了当今时代的主题和特征，成为新

时期中国独立自主的和平外交路线的思想基础。以此为指导，在以江泽民为核心的中央领导下，中国开展了全方位的外交活动，为改革开放事业创造了和平的国际环境，开拓了广阔的国际活动空间。

在原有独立自主的和平外交思想的基础上，中国进一步发展了自己的外交理论，赋予独立自主新的涵义。在对外关系中，中国不同任何国家结盟，不依附于任何大国或大国集团，在处理重大国际问题时，不屈从于任何大国的压力，而是从中国人民和世界人民的根本利益出发，根据事情本身的是非曲直，独立自主地决定自己的态度。邓小平先生指出："我们坚持独立自主的和平外交政策，不参加任何集团，同谁都交朋友，谁搞霸权主义我们就反对谁，谁侵略别人我们就反对谁。我们讲公道话，办公道事。"中国还将独立自主原则创造性地应用于党际关系领域，作为中国共产党发展同其他政党关系的准则，中国提出，在处理党与党之间的关系时，不应有大小、强弱之分，而应按照独立自主、完全平等、互相尊重、互不干涉内部事务的原则，本着求同存异的精神通过平等协商加以解决。

在邓小平外交思想的指导下，中国外交工作不断开创新局面。

中国同亚洲、非洲、拉丁美洲的发展中国家建立和发展了"全天候"的友好合作关系。在反对霸权主义和强权政治，争取建立公正、合理的国际政治经济新秩序的国际斗争中，双方密切配合，结下了深厚的友谊。在经济领域，中国加强了与其他发展中国家之间的南南合作，努力按照"平等互利、讲求实效、形式多样、共同发展"的原则探索新的合作途径。中国特别注意发展与周边国家的睦邻友好关系，在解决历史遗留问题、勘定边境线、推动经贸合作等方面取得重大进展。对于一些历史遗留问题、边界问题等，中国本着平等的原则，力求通过协商同有关国家达成一致意见，或在搁置争议的前提下进行共同开发，为合理解决争端创造和谐有利的气氛，以最终消除争端。这种用和平方式解决领土争端的全新思路，这种灵活务实的做法，对世界和平作出了重大贡献。

中苏实现关系正常化，中俄关系继续发展。自60年代中苏关系恶化以来，中苏关系一直处于僵冷、对峙状态。进入80年代，随着国际形势的变化，中苏都开始战略调整，希望改善相互关系。1989年，中国与苏联本着"结束过去、开辟未来"的精神，实现了关系正常化。1991年苏联解体后，中国继续发展了同俄罗斯及其它独联体国家的友好关系。1996年，中国与俄罗斯确立了建立面向21世纪的"战略协作伙伴关系"的发展方向，标志两国关系进入了一个新的历史发展阶段。

中国改善了同西方主要发达国家的关系。1979年元旦，中美双方在经过长达8年的艰苦谈判后，正式建立外交关系。同年1月，邓小平副总理访美，实现了新中国高级领导人对美国的第一次正式访问，为新时期中美进行战略对话打开了大门。20年来，中美关系历经风雨，在曲折中不断向前发展。虽然这期间中美关系曾几次面临严峻考验，如80年代初的售台武器问题，1989年的政治风波，1996年的台湾海峡危机等，但双方从大局出发，最终还是使中美关系回到了健康发展轨道上来。通过接触，双方共同认识到：作为世界大国，中美有着众多的共同利益，发展彼此间的友好合作关系将对双方都有利。经过中美两国的共同努力，中美关系已步入了一个新的发展阶段。1997年江泽民主席访美和1998年克林顿总统访华，两国确立了努力建立"建设性战略伙伴关系"的发展方向，实现了历史性的突破，中美关系正逐步走向成熟。当然人们也看到了中美关系，除合作的一面，还有不断发生摩擦的一面，如1999年5月以美国为首的北约轰炸中国驻南斯拉夫使馆便是一例。

在对美关系不断改善的同时，中国与日本、西欧的关系也得到了恢复和发展。作为亚洲的近邻，中日两国在1972年实现邦交正常化的基础上，1978年又缔结了《中日和平友好条约》。1982至1983年，两国领导人通过互访，确立了“和平友好、平等互利、相互依赖、长期稳定”的四项原则。1992年，江泽民总书记访日和明仁天皇访华，及1998年江泽民主席再次访日和1999年小渊首相访华，确立并巩固了中日“致力于和平与发展的友好合作伙伴关系”，有力地促进了中日关系继续沿着健康稳定的方向发展。在对欧关系方面，中欧关系经历了80年代末的一段曲折后，已进入了全面改善与发展的新时期，双方正在努力建立一种“全面合作伙伴关系”。双方高层互访频繁，政治和经贸交流势头强劲，合作水平不断提高。

这一时期，中欧关系中一个特别重要的方面是，中国通过与英国及葡萄牙的和平谈判，分别签署了关于香港和澳门问题的联合声明，确认中国将分别于1997年7月1日和1999年12月20日恢复对香港和澳门行使主权，解决了双边关系中的两个重大遗留问题，也使中国的和平统一大业又向前迈进了一大步。1997年7月1日，五星红旗在香港会展中心冉冉升起，标志着香港重新回到祖国怀抱，中国从此洗雪百年国耻。两年来，中国中央政府严格按照一国两制、港人治港的原则，同香港特区政府保持了良好的关系，打消了一些国家的疑虑，获得了广泛的国际信任。今年12月20日，中国将恢复对澳门行使主权，同样实行一国两制和澳人治澳的原则，这无疑将进一步加强中国的国际影响和良好的国际形象。

中国作为联合国安理会的一个常任理事国和最大的发展中国家，积极参与联合国等国际组织的活动，在维护国际和平与安全、促进人类进步与发展方面的国际事务中发挥着独特的积极作用。中国坚定不移地维护国家主权和领土完整，坚决反对国际反华势力在国际组织中制造“两个中国”、“一中一台”、让台湾“重返”联合国的图谋。在日内瓦联合国人权委员会会议上，中国与其他主持正义的国家一道，八次挫败了美国等西方国家提出的反华提案，打击了西方反华势力的嚣张气焰，维护了联合国宪章的宗旨和原则。积极的对外交往无疑为中国的改革开放和经济建设创造了一个良好的外部环境。20年来，中国经济迅速增长，综合国力显著增强。目前，中国已同220多个国家和地区开展了经贸往来。中国的经济总量已跃居世界第七位。中国的进出口总额已从1979年的206亿美元提高到1998年的3240亿美元，在世界排名从第32位跃居第11位。中国的外商投资企业已从1980年的第一家，增加到1998年底的30多万家，合同外资金额5700多亿美元，实际利用外资总额2656亿美元。中国在境外投资开设企业5000多家，遍及世界139个国家和地区。迄今，中国已连续6年成为利用外资最多的发展中国家，并仅次于美国居全球第二。外汇储备从1978年的1.67亿美元增至1998年底的1450亿美元，稳居世界第二位，在1998年亚洲金融风暴发生后，中国的人民币汇率一直保持稳定。国际社会和舆论普遍认为：中国已成为稳定亚洲经济乃至世界经济的重要力量。

20年来，在坚持和平共处五项原则的基础上，中国通过加强同发展中国家的外交、睦邻外交、大国外交、全球和地区的多边外交、首脑外交、党际外交、民间外交等多种形式的外交活动，发展了同几乎所有国家的友好合作关系。目前，中国已同160多个国家建立了正式外交关系，中国提出的一系列外交和国际准则正日益为国际社会认同，中国作为负责任的大国地位进一步得到确认。如今，国际舆论用“中国的外交处于建国以来的最好时期”对中国外交予以高度评价，这无疑正是改革开放20年来中国外交的真实写照。

中国与国际组织

建立和发展与国际组织的关系是中国外交工作的重要组成部分。70年代初，中国恢复了在联合国的合法席位，并先后加入了与联合国相关的国际组织以及其他一些国际组织。中国在国际组织中既坚持原则又积极参与，赢得了广泛赞誉。

一、历史的回顾

建国50年来，中国和国际组织关系的发展走过了一个曲折的路程。

1. 新中国成立至1978年

1949年10月，中华人民共和国成立伊始，就着手与世界各国及团体发展友好合作关系，但由于帝国主义的长期封锁和阻挠，新中国和国际组织的交往仅于1971年恢复在联合国合法席位后开始和增多。在这一阶段，中国政府根据当时的外交政策和两个超级大国争霸世界、国际形势动荡不定的特点，主要是与联合国等国际政治组织发生联系，与经济、贸易、文化方面的国际组织联系相对较少。

中国是联合国的创始会员国，但是，70年代以前，联合国在美国的操纵下，中国在联合国的合法地位被台湾当局占据，新中国长期被排斥在联合国外。直到1971年联合国第26届大会在世界爱好和平国家和人民的支持和声援下，新中国在联合国的合法权利才得以恢复。中国人民的这一伟大胜利宣告了美国孤立新中国的政策彻底失败。此后，中国不仅与包括西方国家在内的一大批国家实现了关系正常化，而且和许多国际组织相继建立和恢复了友好关系。

中国在联合国的地位恢复不久，就在一系列重大国际问题上鲜明地表明了主持正义、反对强权、反对侵略、维护联合国宪章宗旨和原则、维护各国的独立与主权以及国际安全的立场。这一立场赢得了国际社会广泛的支持，中国的威望也日益提高。1978年12月到1979年12月，亚洲地区相继发生了柬埔寨受侵和阿富汗受侵的事件，出现了两个新的热点，中国自始至终坚定、鲜明地反对任何霸权行为，这对正在为反对大国干涉中小国家而斗争的国家来说无疑是一个鼓舞。

2. 改革开放以来的新时期

1978年底中共十一届三中全会确立了改革、开放的政策，中国的对外政策和同国际组织的关系有了新的发展。中国不仅扩大了和国际政治组织的联系，而且还和世界经济、金融、贸易、教育、文化和科学技术等组织建立了联系，以及积极参与和支持联合国维护和平与安全活动。

中国自1980年2月开始，参加裁军谈判会议，并于1983年派出专职裁军大使常驻日内瓦。1984年1月，中国成为国际原子能机构的正式成员，并很快成为指定理事国。1986年起，中国参加了联合国裁谈会的禁止核试验、防止核战争、防止外空军备竞赛、禁止化学武器等重要议题的审议工作。

中国逐步主动、全面地介入联合国各个领域及相关国际组织的工作。首先，中国与国际贸易机构积极发展关系。国际贸易领域的主要机构，一是联合国贸易和发展会议，主要负责审议与贸易和发展有关的国际经济问题，重点是商品价格。二是关税及贸易总协定（现为世界贸易组织），主要主持历次国际多边贸易谈判。中国和联合国贸易和发展会议的关系建立比较早，自1972年开始，中国参加了联合国贸易和发展会议的历次会议。1980年11月，中国在贸易和发展会议共同基金协定上签字，随后参加了黄麻、天然橡胶、木材、锡四个单项协定，在该组织中起了积极的作用。中国是关税及贸易总协定的创始国之一。70年代中国未和该组织发展过联系。1981年7月，中国以观察员身份列席了总协定纺织品委员会关于第三个国际纺织品贸易协议的谈判会议。1986年9月，中国代表列席了关税及贸易总协定部长级会议，支持进行第八轮多边贸易谈判，并取得全面参加这一轮多边贸易谈判的资格。至1999年8月，中国加入世贸组织的谈判已取得了突破性进展。

中国积极参加国际粮食、农业组织的活动。属于联合国系统的农业组织主要有三个，即联合国粮食及农业组织、世界粮食计划署、国际农业发展基金会等。中国和这些组织都建立了实质性联系。1979年中国正式参加了世界粮食计划署，次年8月该署派出驻华代表，1980年10月中国与该组织签订了向中国提供援助的基本协定。中国与国际农发基金会的合作关系也很好，而且富有成效。

中国还是联合国开发计划署、人口活动基金、儿童基金会、人权委员会、社会发展委员会、麻醉品委员会、妇女地位委员会、难民事务高级专员公署、预防犯罪和刑事司法委员会等机构的成员，在联合国几十个机构中发挥积极作用。

中国在非联合国系统的国际组织中的作用也有了很大发展，尤其是积极参与亚太区域组织的经济技术合作与交流。1991年，中国正式加入了亚太经合组织（APEC）。此后，中国元首每年都参加该组织领导人非正式会议。针对APEC组织各成员的实际情况，中国领导人积极倡导APEC组织应有其独特的运行方式，即“APEC方式”：充分尊重各成员的多样性，承认成员之间的发展水平和发展阶段的差异及其带来的不同利益与需求；强调灵活性、渐进性和开放性；遵循平等互利、协商一致、求同存异、自主自愿的原则；实行单边行动与集体行动相结合。中国倡导的“APEC方式”受到了APEC组织和国际舆论的高度评价和重视。针对该组织尤其是西方成员极力推动的亚太地区贸易投资自由化政策，中国坚持认为经济技术合作和贸易投资自由化是APEC的两大支柱，两者相辅相成，相互促进。在1998年的APEC领导人非正式会晤中，由中国国家主席江泽民提议的《走向21世纪的科技产业合作议程》和《技能开发行动计划》获得一致通过，标志着中国在该组织中所发挥的积极的、建设性作用得以加强并取得了成效。此外，中国于1986年被太平洋经济合作理事会接纳为正式成员，参加了此组织所有专题组的活动。中国还于1994年成为太平洋盆地经济理事会的成员，中国经过与该组织长达八年艰苦谈判后，才排除干扰（台湾问题），实现了与该组织关系正常化。

到1998年底，中国已经加入了近千个国际组织，签署了200多个国际公约。

二、中国在国际组织中的原则立场

1. 坚持独立自主的外交原则

中国在联合国等国际组织活动中，是独立的一方，不属于任何集团，也不依附于世界任何一方。中国一贯坚持独立自主的和平外交方针，不搞大国沙文主义，反对侵略战争和霸权主义，主持国际正义。中国是根据事情的是非曲直以及中国人民和世界人民的根本利益，而不是依附某个大国或者某个集团的利益决定自己的立场和政策。因此，中国在国际社会和国际组织中的地位日益提高。

2. 坚持和平共处五项原则

在如何发挥联合国等国际组织的作用上，中国和西方一些国家的观点是不同的。西方一些国家认为，当前建立的国际政治经济新秩序应该由西方一国或西方几个大国主宰，他们甚至提出了“主权过时论”、“人权无国界论”以及其他干涉别国内政的理论。西方一些国家的这种理论不会给世界带来和平与安全，而只能为一些国家干涉别国内政制造借口，造成国际局势的动荡。和平共处五项原则是与以上种种理论针锋相对的，今天，它仍然具有强大的生命力。中国在对外交往上不仅继承，而且发展和完善这些原则。过去，中国坚持和平共处五项原则，得到世界广大爱好和平人民的支持，今后中国仍然把它作为中国外交政策和中国参与国际组织活动的基石。

3. 和广大发展中国家一起共同维护发展中国家的权益

中国是一个发展中国家。共同的遭遇和共同的命运把中国和广大发展中国家紧密联系在一起。本世纪60年代以后，一大批殖民地和半殖民地国家独立了，它们在联合国等国际组织中，已经占了绝大多数。在36届联大以前，这些国家已经占联合国会员国总数的2/3，在联合国内成为一支举足轻重的政治力量。中国在联合国内和广大发展中国家密切配合，互相支持，不仅提高了自身的地位，同时也进一步推动了世界的和平与发展。

4. "互惠互利"、"有给有取"，为发展中国经济利益服务

改革开放20年来，中国的对外关系进行了适当的调整，克服了过去那种"只给不取"的方针，广泛地参与到国际社会中去，参加了以联合国系统的多边经济技术合作。在"互惠互利"、"有给有取"的原则指导下，中国既向联合国发展系统及其他国际组织提供了捐款，也接受国际组织的各项发展援助。

三、中国与国际组织的互惠合作关系

自1971年中国在联合国合法席位恢复以来，中国的多边外交日趋活跃，不仅相继加入了众多的国际组织，而且中国一些民间组织也在逐步发展与国际非政府组织的关系。

一方面，中国积极履行加入多边国际机构所应承担的各项财政义务。中国每年从中央财政预算中拨专款用以缴纳国际组织会费、捐款、维和摊款、股金等各项支出。随着经济的不断发展，中国将会对国际社会作出更大的贡献。1998年，中央财政直接用于缴纳会费、捐款及相关支出的国际组织有近500个，共支出近1亿美元（不包括对世界银行、国际货币基金组织、亚洲开发银行、非洲开发银行等国际金融组织的支出）。在这项支出中，认缴联合国及其相关机构的各种费用占大部分比例。同时，自1973年起，中国还每年向联合国系统和其他一些国际组织提供一定数额的自愿捐款，至1998年底，共捐款近2亿美元和1亿多元人民币（不包括对世界银行、国际货币基金组织，亚洲开发银行、非洲开发银行等国际金融组织的支出）。近年来，随着中国对外开放的深入和国际地位的提高，中国还参加了不少区域性多边合作基金。至1998年年底，中国加入或设立的基金有：亚欧合作基金、亚欧会议信托基金、中国东盟合作基金、东盟基金、中国APEC科技产业合作基金等。特别是中国去年对外宣布设立的中国APEC科技产业合作基金（基金规模暂定为1000万美元，）受到国际社会的广泛关注。这是中国首次在一个国际组织内单方面设立的专项基金，包括中国在内的所有APEC成员都可以从中获益，其意义是十分深远的。

另一方面，中国在这些领域的财政支出扩大了中国在国际事务中的影响，同时也为中国从这些国际组织争取更多的无偿援助起到了积极作用。据不完全统计，从1979年到1997年底，中国共接受联合国世界粮食计划署、联合国儿童活动基金、开发计划署、人口活动基金、工业发展组织、粮农组织、全球环保基金等机构的无偿援助近20多亿美元（包括现金、实物和技术援助），受援项目涉及能源、交通、邮电、农林牧渔、教育、文化、卫生、环境保护以及救灾等领域，为中国的经济发展和现代化建设起到了一定的积极作用。中国从国际金融机构获得的优惠贷款及相关援助也推动了中国的经济发展。（1）国际农发基金会：中国从1981年获得国际农发基金会第一笔贷款以来，至今已获得14笔贷款，贷款协议金额达3.5亿美元，项目涉及中国15个省区，推动了中国农业扶贫工作的发展；（2）亚洲开发银行：

截止1998年年底，亚洲开发银行共批准对中国的贷款项目和技援项目达379个，总金额近85亿美元；(3) 世界银行：至1999年6月底，世行对华贷款金额达320亿美元，215个项目，贷款领域涉及国民经济各个方面。

四、结束语

中国是世界上最大的发展中国家，是联合国安理会常任理事国，在维护世界和平，促进世界发展的事业中负有重要责任。在人类即将进入21世纪之际，中国将继续坚持改革开放的方针，加快经济发展的步伐，不断加强和联合国等国际组织的密切合作，为国际社会作出更大的贡献。

中国的对外援助

向发展中国家政府提供援助是中国政府应尽的国际主义义务。中国对外提供援助是为了帮助受援国发展民族经济，维护国家主权，捍卫民族独立，促进中国和广大发展中国家的友好和经贸关系。多年来，中国政府一直按照1964年周恩来总理访问非洲时宣布的《中国对外经济技术援助的八项原则》，向发展中国家提供力所能及的援助。近年，随着国际经济形势的变化，为使有限的援外资金发挥更大的效益，在遵循援外八项原则的基础上，对援外方式进行了改革。同时，对发展中国家欠中国政府的经援债务政策也进行了适当的调整。

一、中国政府对外援助基本情况

中国政府自1950年开始对外提供经济援助。截至1998年底，已签订无息贷款（低息）及无偿援款协议金额848亿元人民币（币别下同），政府贴息优惠贷款援助协议金额62亿元。受中国政府援助的国家达134个。在援助款项下，中国政府向受援国政府提供了成套项目援助、一般物资援助、技术援助、项目合资合作援助等。

自1954年开始提供成套项目援助，至1998年底，承建成套项目1887个，已建成1554个。自1963年至1998年底，中国政府先后向63个国家派遣了医疗队，派出人数累计16000余人次。

二、中国政府对外援助方式

目前，中国的对外援助主要采取政府贴息优惠贷款方式、援外项目合资合作方式和无偿援助方式。

1. 政府贴息优惠贷款援助

政府贴息优惠贷款（下称优惠贷款）是中国政府指定的金融机构对外提供的具有政府援助性质、含有赠予成份的中、长期低息贷款。优惠贷款的利率与中国人民银行公布的基准利率间的利息差额，由政府财政援外经费贴息。优惠贷款是中国政府在1995年对援外方式进行改革时，确定的一种新的援外方式。目的是通过政府援外资金与金融机构资金的结合，扩大中国对外援助规模和资金来源，推动双方企业在投资、设备、技术等方面的合作。

中国对外经济贸易合作部是优惠贷款援助的主管机构。中国进出口银行是中国政府指定的对外提供优惠贷款的承贷机构。

优惠贷款主要用于中国企业与受援国企业合资合作建设、经营的生产性项目，或提供中国生产的成套设备、机电产品出口等。贷款期限一般掌握在10-15年左右。贷款利率3-5%，成套设备和机电产品贷款利率为2%。截至1998年底，已实施优惠贷款项目43个。

2. 援外项目合资合作

援外项目合资合作是在中国政府与受援国政府原则协议的范围内，双方政府给予政策和资金支持，中国企业同受援国企业以合资经营、合作经营的方式实施的项目。援外项目合资合作的目的是：促进双方企业在管理、技术上长期合作，培养受援国企业管理人才，帮助受援国增加收入和就业，从而提高援助的效益。中国外经贸部是援外项目合资合作的主管机构。

援外合资合作项目分为三种形式：一是中国政府援建项目中已建成的生产性或其它具备合资合作条件的项目，由受援国企业经营转为双方企业合资、合作经营；二是中国政府对外新承担的生产性或其它具备合资合作条件的项目，受援国企业以中国援款作为资本，中国企业再按双方企业商定的股权比例投入资金，项目由双方合资建设和经营；三是受援国政府和中国政府签订原则协议，在政策或资金上给予扶持，双方企业直接合资合作。

3. 无偿援助

中国政府对第三世界某些经济特别困难的国家提供无偿援助。无偿援助主要用于帮助受援国建设中、小型生产性项目、社会福利项目、提供一般物资援助和技术援助。

项目援助是由中国政府负责项目的考察、设计，提供全部或部分成套设备、建筑材料，派人组织或指导施工、安装和试生产，并在项目建设过程中全面提供技术援助。在项目选择上，根据受援国的需要和中国的可能，以经济效益好、投资少、收效快的中小型项目为主。

物资援助是由中国政府向受援国提供生产资料及生活必需品，解决生产建设和人民生活的急需。这种方式主要用于帮助遭受严重自然灾害的经济特别困难的国家恢复和发展生产，克服人民生活方面的紧急困难。

技术援助是指除了在项目建设过程中全面提供技术援助外，中国政府还根据受援国的需要，在项目建成移交后，继续派遣专家进行生产技术指导或帮助经营管理。派遣医疗队和在中国境内举办针对发展中国家学员的专业技术培训班也是技术援助的重要方式。

三、中国政府对受援国经援债务的政策

中国与发展中国家的债务问题，主要是中国对受援国提供经援无息贷款或低息贷款形成的官方债务。

过去中国对受援国的经援债务，一直采取不逼债（可延期）的政策。1997年，中国政府根据国际政治经济形势的变化，对世界银行和国际货币基金组织确定的重债贫困国欠中国政府的经援债务问题宣布：中国是人均收入较低的发展中国家，是净债务国；中国对发展中国家的援助是朋友间的帮助，是为发展受援国的民族经济，不带任何附加条件。中国政府愿意对减轻重债贫困国的债务负担作出自己的努力，按照个案处理的原则，通过双边渠道减免一些重债贫困国的债务。

China's Foreign Affairs in the Last 20 Years

In 1999, as the world greets the 21st century, China welcomes its 20th year of reform and opening to the outside world. China's drive to modernization has won international acclaim for its progress, while in the realm of foreign affairs it has scored striking successes. With the ceaseless strengthening of the nation and its daily rise in international standing, China has become a decisive power, playing an increasingly important role in world affairs. Now China, with a brand-new look, stands tall among the community of nations of the world, and relations between China and the rest of the world are becoming ever closer. "Letting the world approach China, and letting China enter the world" is becoming a reality as each day dawns.

The achievements that China has made in the past 20 years since the beginning of reform and opening to the outside world are, beyond doubt, closely related to China's strategic foreign policy; and the readjustment of China's foreign policy has been an important component of Deng Xiaoping theory. In the mid to late 1970s, substantive changes took place in the international arena. China's leadership, guided by Deng Xiaoping, were sharply conscious of such changes, fully grasped the distinctive characteristics of the era, and realized important changes in the precepts governing foreign affairs, thereby laying down a basis for China to develop new vistas in its foreign affairs after reform and opening to the outside world. After accurately analyzing a tractable international situation, Deng Xiaoping pointed out with profound consequences: The world today is in a historical period heralding great changes, and multi-polarization is a worldwide tide that cannot be reversed. For a long time to come, the danger of war will continue to exist, but the outbreak of a new world war is not completely unavoidable. So long as peace-loving people in the world make a joint effort, it is possible for us to achieve a peaceful world. In 1985, Deng Xiaoping pointed out: "The key issues of global strategy in the world today are peace, and economic problems or development." He thus elucidated in a scientific way the themes and characteristics of the era today. His tenets have become the ideological basis for China's independent and peaceful foreign policy during the recent period. Under the guidance of Deng Xiaoping theory and the leadership of the Central Committee of the Communist Party of China (CPC) with Jiang Zemin at its core, China has initiated comprehensive diplomatic activity, created a peaceful international environment for China's reform and opening, and widened the space for international relations.

On the basis of its original independent and peaceful ideas governing international relations, China has further developed its theory of foreign affairs, and instilled new significance to the notion of independence. Regarding the external affairs, China shall not form alliance with any other country, nor depend on any big nation or any big nation bloc. In handling important international issues, China shall not submit to pressure from any big nation; and shall decide its own attitude independently, proceeding from the fundamental interests of the Chinese people and the people of other countries, and in the light of the rights and wrongs of the issue. Deng Xiaoping pointed out: "We adhere to an independent and peaceful foreign policy. We shall not join any blocs, and shall make friends with everyone. We shall oppose anyone who upholds hegemonism, and anyone who invades others. We speak fairly and act fairly." In addition, China has upheld the principle of independence and self-initiative in relations between the Communist Party of China and parties of other countries, and the Communist Party of China takes these principles as the norm for developing relations with other parties. In handling these relations between parties, China proposes to act according to the principle of independence and self-initiative, complete equality, mutual respect, and noninterference in each other's internal affairs, without regard to the size or strength of the parties concerned; as well, problems shall be solved in the spirit of seeking common ground on major issues while reserving the right to differ on minor points and through equal consultation.

Under the guidance of Deng Xiaoping's diplomatic thinking, China's work on foreign affairs has constantly proposed new initiatives.

China has established and developed "all-weather" friendship and cooperation relations with developing countries in Asia, Africa and Latin America. In the struggle against hegemonism and power politics, and in striving for the founding of a new justice and rational international political and economic situation, both sides have cooperated closely and established deep friendships. In the economic field, China has strengthened South-South Cooperation with other developing countries, and worked hard to probe new channels for cooperation in accordance with the principle of "equality and mutual benefit, striving for efficiency, diversity and common development". China has paid particular attention to developing good neighborly relations with surrounding countries, and has made great progress in solving the issues left over by history, determining boundary lines after surveys and promoting economic and trade cooperation. As to issues left unresolved by history and boundary questions, China has tried its best to reach agreement with the countries concerned through consultation, or has engaged in common development on the basis of laying aside contentious issues so as to create a harmonious and favorable atmosphere for resolving the disputes reasonably and ultimately eliminating them. This fresh new approach to solving territorial disputes through peaceful means and these flexible and practicable methods have made great contributions to world peace.

After relations between China and the former Soviet Union were normalized, those between China and Russia have continued to develop. After worsening in the mid-1960s, relations between China and the former Soviet Union remained cool, inflexible and confrontational. After 1980, along with changes in the international situation, both China and the former Soviet Union began to readjust their strategies, hoping to improve relations. In 1989, in the spirit of "putting an end to the past and opening up the way to the future", relations between the two countries normalized. After the dissolution of the Soviet Union, China has continued to develop friendly relations with Russia and other countries of the Commonwealth of Independent States. In 1996 China and Russia established an ongoing policy orientation towards "strategic, cooperative partnerships" geared to the 21st century, signifying that relations between these two countries have entered a new historical stage of development.

China has improved relations with leading developed countries in the West. On New Year's Day in 1979, after eight-years of intense negotiations, the People' s Republic of China and the United States formally established diplomatic relations. In January of the same year, Vice-premier Deng Xiaoping paid a visit to the United States, thus realizing the first formal visit of a top leader of New China to the United States, and the opening for strategic talks between China and the United States in the new period. In the past 20 years relations between China and the United States have constantly advanced despite many ups and downs. During this period, relations between these two countries were strained by several severe confrontations, such as around the US selling of weaponry to Taiwan in the early 1980s, the events at Tiananmen in 1989 and the crisis in the Taiwan Straits in 1996. The two governments took the whole situation into consideration and finally brought healthy relations between China and the United States back on track. Through continuous contact, both sides have realized that as two big countries in the world, China and the United States have numerous common interests, and developing friendly cooperation between them will be favorable to both sides. Thanks to the efforts of the two countries, relations between China and the United States have entered a new stage of development. Through President Jiang Zemin's visit to the United States in 1997 and President Clinton's visit to China in 1998, the two countries have established an ongoing policy orientation of striving to establish "constructive strategic partnerships," thus making a historic breakthrough. Relations between China and the United States are becoming more mature. However, people have also witnessed not only the acts of cooperation between China and the United States, but also the conflicts that occur now and then. For instance the North Atlantic Treaty Organization's (NATO) bombing of the Chinese embassy in Yugoslavia in May 1999.

Meanwhile relations between China and Japan, as well

as between China and Western Europe, have been restored and are developing. As close neighbors in Asia, China and Japan, on the basis of the normalization of relations between the two countries in 1972, signed the Sino-Japanese Peace and Friendship Treaty in 1978. The leaders of the two countries, through exchange visits in 1982 and 1983, established the four principles of "peace and friendship, equality and mutual benefit, mutual reliance and long-term stability". Through General Secretary Jiang Zemin's visit to Japan, and Emperor Akihito's visit to China in 1992, and President Jiang Zemin's return visit to Japan and Prime Minister Obuchi's visit to China in 1999, the two countries have established and consolidated "friendly cooperative partnerships devoted to peace and development", thus taking powerful steps to promote Sino-Japanese relations and develop a healthy and stable policy orientation. Relations between China and Europe have entered a new period of overall improvement and development after some setbacks in the 1980s. Both sides are working hard to establish "comprehensive cooperative partnerships". Leaders on both sides have frequently exchanged visits; political, economic and trade exchanges between the two sides are vigorous; and the level of cooperation has constantly improved.

During this period the most important events in relations between China and Europe were: China signing of a joint declaration with Britain on the issue of Hong Kong, and another joint declaration with Portugal on the issue of Macao. These two joint declarations have confirmed the resumption of sovereignty by China over Hong Kong on July 1, 1997 and over Macao on December 20, 1999, thus resolving two important historically unresolved issues on bilateral relations and enabling China to make a big step forward toward the peaceful reunification of the country. On July 1, 1997, the rise of the five-star red flag at the Hong Kong Convention Center marked Hong Kong's return to its motherland, with China thereby wiping out 100 years of national humiliation. In the past two years the central government of China has maintained good relations with the government of the Hong Kong Special Administrative Region in strict accordance with the principles of "one country, two systems", "administration of Hong Kong by the Hong Kong people", thus dispelling some countries' misgivings and gaining extensive international trust. On December 20 of this year, China will resume the exercise of sovereignty over Macao, and the principles of "one country, two systems" and "administration of Macao by Macao people" will also be adopted. It should undoubtedly further strengthen China's international influence and its international image.

As a permanent member of the Security Council of the United Nations and the largest developing country in the world, China has actively participated in activities organized by the United Nations and other international organizations, and is playing a unique and positive role in safeguarding international peace and security. China unswervingly defends its sovereignty and territorial integrity as a nation, and resolutely opposes international intrigue by anti-China forces in trying to create "two Chinas", or "one China, one Taiwan", or to allow Taiwan's "return" to the United Nations. At the UN Human Rights Commission meetings held in Geneva, China, together with other countries supporting justice, frustrated the anti-China proposals put forward by the United States and other Western countries on eight occasions, thus countering the arrogance of Western anti-China forces and safeguarding the aims and principles of the United Nations Charter.

Active foreign exchanges have, beyond any doubt, created a favorable external environment for China's reform and opening to the outside world as well as economic construction. In the past 20 years China's economy has grown rapidly, and its overall power as a nation has been remarkably strengthened. Now, China has economic and trade ties with more than 220 countries and regions in the world. The size of China's economy ranks seventh in the world. China's import and export volume increased from US$ 20.6 billion in 1979 to US$ 324 billion in 1998, leaping from 32nd place in the world to 11th place. In 1980 the first enterprise with foreign investment was set up in China, while by the end of 1998 there were more than 300,000 foreign-funded enterprises in China, involving contracted foreign capital totaling more than US$ 570 billion, with US$ 265.6 billion actually utilized. China has initiated more than 5,000 enterprises outside Chinese territory, in 139 countries and regions. Until now China has led developing countries in utilizing the most foreign capital for five years in succession, ranking second in the world in total foreign investment, second only to the United States. China's foreign exchange reserves increased from US$ 167 million in 1978 to US$ 145 billion at the end of 1998, also ranking second in the world. In 1998, after the Asian financial storm broke, the exchange rate of the Renminbi maintained its stability. The international community and public opinion have generally affirmed that China has become an important force in stabilizing the Asian economy as well as the world economy.

In the last 20 years, on the basis of adhering to the Five Principles of Peaceful Coexistence and through various forms of foreign relations, such as diplomatic relations with developing countries, good-neighbor diplomacy, big nation diplomacy, global and regional bilateral diplomacy, state leadership diplomacy, diplomacy among parties and nongovernmental diplomacy, China has developed relations of friendship and cooperation with almost all countries. At present: China has established formal diplomatic relations with more than 160 countries; a series of diplomatic and international norms are being recognized by the international community with each passing day; and the position of China, as a responsible large country, has been further confirmed. Now the international community and public opinion speak highly of China's foreign affairs, saying "China's foreign affairs are now at their best since the founding of New China". It is undoubtedly a reasonable assessment of China's foreign affairs in the last 20 years of reform and opening to the outside world.

China and International Organizations

Establishing and developing relations with international organizations is an important component of China's diplomatic activities. In the early 1970s China once again took its rightful seat at the United Nations. Since then, China has joined international organizations related to the United Nations as well as other international organizations. China has won widespread praise in these international organizations for upholding their principles and actively participating in various activities.

I. Historical Retrospection

In the past 50 years since the founding of the People's Republic of China, relations between China and international organizations have withstood a tortuous course.

1. From the Founding of New China to 1978

As soon as the People's Republic of China was founded, China started to develop relations of friendship and cooperation with other countries and international organizations in the world. However, due to a long-term blockade and obstruction, New China did not have much contact with international organizations until 1971 for new China's legitimate rights in the United Nations to be restored. During this period the Chinese government was in contact mainly with international organizations affiliated to the United Nations, and had much less contact with international economic, trade and cultural organizations.

China is a founding member of the United Nations. Yet, before the 1970s, when the United Nations was under the control of the United States, China's legitimate position in the United Nations was denied for quite a long time. It took until 1971 for New China's legitimate rights in the United Nations to be restored at the 26th UN General Assembly, through the support of peace-loving countries and people around the world. This great victory of the Chinese people proclaimed the thorough defeat of the United States' policy of isolating New China. Since then, China has not only normalized relations with a large number of countries including Western countries, but has also established and resumed friendly relations with many international organizations.

Soon after the resumption of China's position in the United Nations, China clearly expressed its stand in supporting justice, opposing power and aggression, safeguarding the UN Charter and principles, safeguarding the independence and sovereignty of each country and international security, through a succession of important international issues. This stand won widespread support from the international community, and China's reputation improved daily. Between December 1978 and December 1979, two new hot spots erupted in Asia — Kampuchea and Afghanistan were invaded. China has always resolutely and clearly opposed any hegemonic action. This is undoubtedly an inspiration to countries who have waged struggles to oppose large countries from interfering with medium-sized and small countries.

2. A New Period After the Initiation of Reform and Opening to the Outside World

Since the initiation of the policy of reform and opening to the outside world at the Third Plenary Session of the 11th National Congress of the Communist Party of China (CPC) held at the end of 1978, China has made new progress in its foreign policy and its relations with international organizations. China has not only expanded contact with international political organizations, but also established contact with economic, financial, educational, cultural, and scientific and technological organizations in the world.

Since February 1980, China has participated in disarmament talks, and in 1983 China sent a full-time disarmament ambassador to be stationed in Geneva. In January 1984, China became a formal member of the International Atomic Energy Commission, and soon afterwards, a defined council member state. Since 1986, China has participated in United Nations disarmament talks, and taken part in the examination of some important topics under discussion, such as a nuclear tests ban, nuclear war prevention, arms races prevention, and a ban on chemical weapons.

China has gradually participated more and more in the work of all sectors of the United Nations and relevant international organizations, of its own accord and in a comprehensive manner. First of all, China has actively developed relations with international trade bodies. The main international trade bodies include: Firstly, the UN Trade and Development Conference which is in charge of examining international economic issues related to trade and development, with the price of commodities as its focal point. Secondly, the General Agreement on Tariff and Trade (GATT, now the World Trade Organization), which is mainly in charge of international multilateral trade talks. China established relations with the UN Conference on Trade and Development (UNCTAD) very early, and since 1972 China has participated in all its meetings. In November 1980, China signed the Common Fund Agreement of the UN Trade and Development Conference, and then participated in four single-commodity agreements on jute, natural rubber, timber and tin, thus playing an active role in the organization. Although China was a founding member state of GATT, in the 1970s China did not have any contact with

GATT. In July 1981, as a nonvoting delegate in an observer capacity, China attended the Negotiations Conference on the Third International Textiles Trade Agreement held by the GATT Textiles Committee. In September 1986, a Chinese nonvoting delegate attended the GATT Ministerial-level Conference, and obtained the right to attend the current round of bilateral trade talks. Until August 1999, talks on China joining the World Trade Organization (WTO) had achieved a breakthrough.

China has actively participated in activities sponsored by international grain and agricultural organizations. There are three such organizations belonging to the United Nations–the Food and Agriculture Organization (FAO), the World Food Program, and the International Agriculture Development Fund. China established firm relations with these organizations. In 1979, China formally joined the World Food Program, and in the following year the Program sent representatives to China; and in October 1980, China signed a basic agreement for providing aid to China through this Program. Cooperative relations between China and the International Agricultural Development Fund are strong and have achieved remarkable success.

China is also a member of the UN Conference on Trade and Development, the UN Fund for Population Activities, the UN Children's Fund, the UN Human Rights Commission, the UN Social Development Commission, the UN Narcotics Commission, the UN Status of Women Commission, the UN High Commission for Refugees, UN Crime Prevention and Criminal Judiciary Commission, among others. China plays an active role in the several dozen bodies of the United Nations.

China's role in the other international organizations has also been greatly enhanced. In particular, China actively participates in economic and technological cooperation and exchanges organized in the Asian-Pacific region. In 1991, China formally joined APEC. From that time onwards, China's head of state has taken part every year in informal APEC meetings of leaders. In accordance with the actual conditions of all the members of APEC, China's leadership has advocated that APEC should have its own unique operational form, i.e., an "APEC Form": Fully respecting the diversity of all members, acknowledging the different levels and stages of development among members and the different interests and demands caused by these differences; stressing flexibility, gradual progress and openness; and combining unilateral actions with collective action. The "APEC Form" advocated by China has been highly supported by APEC and international public opinion. As APEC constituents, especially Western members, have spared no effort in promoting trade and investment liberalization policies in the Asian-Pacific region, China insists that economic and technological cooperation and trade and investment liberalization are the twin main pillars of APEC, which complement and mutually promote each other. During the informal APEC meeting of leaders in 1998, the Cooperation Agenda for Scientific and Technological Industry in the 21st Century and the Action Plan for the Development of Technical Capability put forward by President Jiang Zemin were adopted unanimously, highlighting the fact that the active and constructive role China plays in the organization has been strengthened and has achieved success. In addition, in 1986, China was admitted as a formal member of the Pacific Economic Cooperation Council (PECC), and has participated in the activities of the Special Topic Group of the PECC. In 1994, China became a member of the Pacific Basin Economic Council (PBEC). After eight years of intense negotiations with PBEC, China finally removed the main obstruction (the Taiwan Issue) and normalized relations with the Council.

By the end of 1998, China had joined nearly thousand international organizations, and signed more than 200 international conventions.

II. China's Principles and Positions in International Organizations

1. Adherence to an Independent Principle in Foreign Affairs

In international activities organized by the United Nations and other international organizations, China is an independent player; it does not belong to any bloc, nor attaches itself to any side in the world. China always adheres to its own independent and peaceful foreign policy, does not adopt big-nation chauvinism, opposes aggressive wars and hegemonism, and supports international justice. China bases its own policy positions on whether a matter is right or wrong, and in the interest of the Chinese people as well as of the people of other countries, rather than in the interests of a certain big nation or bloc. Hence China's position in international society and international organizations advances with each passing day.

2. Upholding the Five Principles of Peaceful Coexistence

China's viewpoint on the role of the United Nations and other international organizations is different from that of Western countries. Some Western countries maintain that the current new international political and economic order should be dominated by one or several large Western countries. They even put forward theories like "sovereignty is out-of-date", and there are "no national boundaries for human rights", and other theories that interfere with other countries' internal affairs. These theories put forward by some Western countries can only serve to invent excuses for certain countries to interfere with other countries' internal affairs, rather than bring peace and security to the world, thus resulting in global turmoil. The Five Principles of Peaceful Coexistence are diametrically opposed to the aforementioned theories; and today they still have strong vitality. China has not only carried forward, but also developed and perfected these principles in foreign affairs. In past years China's upholding of the Five Principles for Peaceful Coexistence has won support from the broad masses of peace-loving people in the world. In the future China will still build, on this foundation stone, its foreign policy and its policy towards international organizations.

3. Developing Countries Unite to Safeguard Their Own Interests

China is a developing country. Common experiences and destiny have linked China closely with the developing countries. Since the 1960s, a large number of colonial and semi-colonial countries have won their independence. In international organizations, including the United Nations, they make up the overwhelming majority. Before the 36th UN General Assembly, these countries accounted for two-thirds of the total member states of the United Nations. Now they have become a significant political force in the United Nations. China's close coordination with developing countries, and the exchange of support with them in the United Nations, have not only improved its own status, but also pushed forward world peace and development.

4. The Principles of "Mutual Benefit" and "Giving and Receiving" Serve China's Economic Interests

In the past 20 years, since initiating its policy of reform and opening to the outside world, China has appropriately readjusted its foreign relations, overcome its former policy of "only giving, without receiving", thrown itself into international society, and participated in multilateral economic and technological cooperation under the United Nations system. Under the guidance of the principles of "mutual benefit" and "giving and receiving", China has contributed funds to the UN development system and other international organizations, and received various forms of development aid from international organizations.

III. Mutually Beneficial Cooperation Between China and International Organizations

Since China's resumption of its rightful place in the

United Nations in 1971, bilateral diplomacy has become an everyday activity. China has joined a large number of international organizations, and some Chinese non-governmental organizations have developed relations with international non-governmental organizations.

On the one hand, China actively performs various financial obligations as a member of a bilateral international body. Every year China allocates special funds from its central financial budget to pay membership dues, monetary donations, its share of peacekeeping expenses, share capital and other necessities. Along with the constant development of China's economy, China is making a greater contribution to the international community. In 1998, central finance paid membership dues, monetary donations and relevant expenses to nearly 500 international organizations, totaling nearly US$100 million (excluding expenditure to the World Bank, International Monetary Fund, Asian Development Bank, African Development Bank and other international financial organizations). Various fees that China must pay to the United Nations and relevant bodies make up the most part of such expenditure. In addition, from 1973 has China provided a certain amount of monetary donations to the United Nations system and other international organizations of its own accord. By the end of 1998, China had donated altogether nearly US$ 200 million and more than 100 million RMB yuan (excluding expenditure to the World Bank, International Monetary Fund ,Asian Development Bank, African Development Bank and other international financial organizations). In recent years, along with the deepening of China's reform and opening to the outside world and the improvement of its international position, China has joined many regional bilateral cooperation funds. By the end of 1998, China joined or set up the following funds: the Asia-Europe Cooperation Fund, the Asia-Europe Conference Trust Fund, the China ASEAN Cooperation Fund, the ASEAN Fund, the China APEC Scientific and Technological Industrial Cooperation Fund, and others. The proclamation of the China APEC Scientific and Technological Industrial Cooperation Fund, especially, received a great deal of attention from the international community the size of the Fund being currently pegged at US$ 10 million. This is the first special fund set up by China itself in an international organizations; and all APEC members, including China, will benefit from it. Hence it has profound significance.

As well, China's financial expenditures in these areas have extended China's influence in international affairs, and played an important role in drawing free aid from these organizations for China. According to incomplete statistics, from 1979 to the end of 1997 China drew more than US$ 2 billion of free aid from the UN World Food Program, the UN Children's Activity Fund, the UN Development Program, the Population Activity Fund, the Industrial Development Organization, the Food and Agriculture Organization, and the Global Environmental Protection Fund, with projects involving energy, communications, post and telecommunications, agriculture, forestry, animal husbandry and fisheries, education, culture, public health, environmental protection and disaster relief. These grants have played an active role in China's economic development and modernization drive. Preferential loans and related aid drawn from international financial institutions have also promoted China's economic development.(1) International Agricultural Development Fund (IADF): Since China's first loan from the IADF in 1981, China has obtained 14 loans, the agreed capital of the loans totaling US$ 350 million, with projects spread throughout 15 provinces and autonomous regions in China, thus promoting China's poverty alleviation work. (2) Asian Development Bank (ADB): By the end of 1998, the ADB had approved 379 loans and technological aid projects, involving a total of US$ 8.5 billion. (3) International Bank for Reconstruction and Development (IBRD-the World Bank): By the end of June, the World Bank had granted US$ 32 billion to China, involving 215 projects covering various sectors of the national economy.

IV. Conclusion

China is the largest developing country in the world, and a permanent member of the Security Council of the United Nations. China therefore has important responsibilities for safeguarding world peace, and promoting the world development. As humanity greets the 21st century, China will continue to adhere to its policy of reform and opening to the outside world, speed up economic development, constantly strengthen close cooperation with the United Nations and other international bodies, and make greater contributions to the international community.

China's Foreign Aid

Providing aid to developing countries is an international duty of the Chinese government. China provides aid to other countries, aimed at helping recipient countries to develop their national economy, safeguard their sovereignty, defend national independence, and promote friendly, economic and trade relations with other developing countries. For many years the Chinese government has always offered as much aid as it can to developing countries in accordance with China's Eight Principles of Foreign Economic and Technological Aid as declared by Premier Zhou Enlai during his visit to Africa in 1964. In recent years, along with the changes in the international economic situation, China, on the basis of the Eight Principles, has reformed its approach to foreign aid so as to make its limited foreign-aid disbursements produce greater mutual economic benefits. At the same time, China has made adjustments where appropriate of its policy on economic-aid-related debts owed by developing countries.

I. Basic Conditions for Foreign Aid

The Chinese government started to provide foreign aid in 1950. By the end of 1998, the interest-free (low-interest) loans and grant agreements signed by China involved 84.8 billion RMB yuan (the same below for the type of currency), and government discount preferential loans and aid agreements involved 6.2 billion RMB yuan. Altogether 134 countries received aid from the Chinese government. Under the aid fund, the Chinese government provided complete sets of projects which included ordinary material aid, technological aid, joint-ventures and cooperative aid.

From 1954 China started to provide aid in terms of complete sets of projects. By the end of 1998 China had undertaken 1,887 comprehensive packages, of which 1,554 have been completed. From 1963 to the end of 1998, the Chinese government sent medical teams to 63 countries, involving a total of over 16,000 personnel.

II. Forms of Foreign Aid

At present China mainly adopts the government subsidized preferential loan method, the foreign aid in the form of cooperative joint ventures, and the free-aid form.

1. Government Subsidized Preferential Loans

Government subsidized preferential loans (hereinafter referred to as "preferential loan") are medium-term and long-term low-interest loans, offered by those financial institutions designated by the Chinese government, in the nature of government-to-government aid and grants. The difference in the interest rate of a preferential loan and the standard interest rate issued by the People's Bank of China is made up by the government's foreign-aid funds. Preferential loans are a new form of foreign-aid decided upon by the Chinese government in 1995 when China reformed its foreign-aid policy. The purpose of such loans is to expand the scale and capital resources of China's foreign aid, and to promote cooperation between enterprises on both sides, on investment, equipment and technology through the combination of the government's foreign-aid capital and the capital of financial institutions.

China's Ministry of Foreign Trade and Economic Cooperation is responsible for preferential loan aid, and the China Import and Export Bank has been designated by the Chinese government to provide preferential loans to foreign countries.

Preferential loans are mainly used in production projects constructed or operated by a Chinese enterprise and an enterprise of a recipient country in the form of a cooperative joint venture, or in providing complete sets of Chinese-produced equipment or electromechanical products. In general the loan terms range from 10 to 15 years, with the interest rates for joint ventures ranging between 3 to 5 percent, and for complete sets of equipment, 2 percent. By the end of 1998, China had offered 43 preferential loan projects.

2. Foreign Aid in the Form of Cooperative Joint Ventures

A foreign-aid project in the form of a cooperative joint venture is a project implemented by a Chinese enterprise and an enterprise of the recipient country, as defined by the principle agreement signed by both governments, and supported by both countries in terms of policy and capital. The purpose of such cooperative joint-venture projects are: promotion of long-term cooperation between both enterprises in management and technology, assistance in training managerial personnel and in increasing income and employment in the recipient country, thus raising the economic benefits of the aid. The Ministry of Foreign Economy and Trade of China is responsible for foreign-aid projects in the form of cooperative joint ventures.

There are three types of cooperative joint-venture foreign-aid projects: First, government-aided construction projects, completed production projects or other projects for founding cooperative joint ventures. Second, a projection project or a project qualified for founding a cooperative joint venture newly undertaken by the Chinese government, which may be constructed and operated with joint investments, when an enterprise in a recipient country invests Chinese government funds as an investment and a Chinese enterprise makes an investment in proportions decided through consultation. Third, when the Chinese government offers aid in terms of policy and capital according to a principle agreement signed by both governments, with enterprises from both sides directly involved in a cooperative joint venture.

3. Grants

The Chinese government offers grants to some Third World countries in severe economic difficulty. Grants is mainly used to help recipient countries construct medium-sized and small production and social-welfare projects, and provide general material and technological aid.

A Chinese aid project refers to a project where Chinese government is in charge of its investigation and design, provides all or part of complete sets of equipment and construction materials, sends personnel to organize or guide construction, installation and production on a trial basis, and offers comprehensive technological aid during the construction of the project. In selecting projects, China will, in accordance with the needs of a recipient country and China's ability, mainly select medium-sized and small projects with minimal investment and favorable short-term economic returns.

Material aid refers to the means of production and basic necessities of life provided by China to recipient countries to meet urgent requirements for production, construction and people's livelihood. Through material aid, China will mainly help countries in severe economic difficulty to restore and develop production, and provide emergency relief after serious natural disasters.

Technological aid refers to aid provided by China in a comprehensive way during construction, and where, in accordance with the requirements of the recipient country, the Chinese government continues to send experts to offer productive and technological guidance or help with management and operation of a project after its completion and transfer to the recipient country. Sending medical teams, and running specialized technological training classes within Chinese territory, in keeping with the needs of developing countries, are other important ways in which China provides technological aid.

III. Policy on Debts Owed by Recipient Countries

Debts owed to China by developing countries mainly involve official debts resulting from the provision of economic aid through interest-free or low-interest loans.

In the past, with respect to debts owed by developing countries to China, China adopted the policy of not pressing for payment of debts (payment deferral). In 1997, in accordance with changes in the international political and economic situation, the Chinese government made a declaration on economic aid granted by the Chinese government to poverty-stricken countries with heavy debts, as designated by the World Bank and the International Monetary Organization; China is a developing country with a fairly low per capita income, and a net debtor nation; aid provided by China to developing countries is seen as help among friends so as to help develop the national economy of recipient countries. The Chinese government is willing to make efforts to reduce the debt burden of poverty-stricken countries with heavy debts. In accordance with the principle of handling every case individually and through bilateral channels, China will reduce and exempt some of the debts of poverty-stricken countries with heavy debts.

中国对外开放与合作

China's Opening Up and International Cooperation

中国对外开放基本情况

1978年底中共十一届三中全会以前，由于国际、国内种种环境变化原因，中国对外经济交往经历了50年代被迫对苏联的“一边倒”、60年代前期被迫过分强调自力更生、60年代后期不自觉进入“闭关锁国”状态、70年代与西方国家普遍建立外交关系的4个阶段。

但中国还未开始真正意义上的对外开放，甚至在唐山大地震后，中国还拒绝接受各种国际援助。是中国共产党第十一届中央委员会第三次会议，实事求是，解放思想，才为中国走上改革开

港口之晨
The Morning of the Port

放之路指明了方向。

一、建立对外开放“窗口”，逐步扩大开放地域

中国的对外开放从建立经济特区“窗口”开始。1979年经中共中央、国务院决定，在深圳、珠海、汕头和厦门试办特区，并在1980年改为“经济特区”；以后经七届人大一次会议决定，又设立了海南省并在全省建立经济特区。经中共中央、国务院决定，1984年大连、天津、秦皇岛、青岛、烟台、上海、南通、连云港、宁波、温州、福州、广州、湛江、北海等14个沿海港口城市在对外开放中获得经济特区的部分优惠政策；天津港、大连的大窑湾、上海的外高桥、江苏的张家港、宁波的北仑港、福建的马尾、厦门的象屿、青岛、广州、汕头、海口、深圳的福田和沙头角等13地建立了保税区；1985年长江三角洲、珠江三角洲和闽东南三角地区开辟为沿海经济开放区，后又开辟了环渤海经济开放区；1988年140个市、县，包括杭州、南京、沈阳3个省会城市划入开放区；1990年上海市在浦东实行经济技术开发区和某些经济特区的政策；1991年继1988年批准北京市后，再批准全国21个国家高新技术产业开发区；1992年又批准海南省开放建设洋浦经济开放区，以后还批准建设了苏州工业园区；当年还以上海浦东为龙头，开放重庆、岳阳、武汉、九江、芜湖等5个沿江城市，同时开放哈尔滨、长春、呼和浩特、石家庄等4个边境、沿海地区的省会城市以及太原、合肥、南昌、郑州、长沙、成都、贵阳、西安、兰州、西宁、银川等11个内陆省会城市，以后几年又相继开放了一大批较符合条件的内陆市县，此外，中国还陆续开放了一大批旅游城市。

现在，中国的对外开放地域已从经济特区扩大到沿海开放城市，进而逐步扩大到沿边、沿江地带直至内陆省会城市、地区，从而初步形成由沿海到内地、从东部到中部、西部的全方位、多层次的对外开放格局。

二、大力引进和利用外资，充分利用两种资源和市场

对外开放的主要内容之一就是大力引进和利用外资，包括引进国外人才、先进技术和设备及管理经验，在利用外资方面，中国大力借用国际组织和友好国家政府的优惠低息贷款，并在近期国际市场上成功发行了一些债券，但主要还是借用国际商业贷款。中国利用外资，主要是吸收外商直接投资。从1980年批准第一批3家外商投资企业以来，中国不断下放设立外商投资企业的批准权，到1998年底，中国已累计批准外商投资企业32万多家，在外商投资企业中的中方从业人员已达1750万人。自1993年以来，中国已连续6年成为利用外商直接投资最多的发展中国家，在全世界排名也仅次于美国。从1979年到1998年，中国共借用国外资金1271.3亿美元，实际引进外商直接投资2656亿美元，并通过其他形式利用外商其它投资147亿美元。此外，中国还尽可能地对国外，如澳大利亚、南美沿海国家、美国、德国、俄罗斯、独联体国家及东欧国家，进行一些必要的投资，以充分利用中国的资源、技术和经验，发展海外市场。

中国加大了引进国外人才的步伐。目前每年外国专业技术人员来华入境的人次数已占外国人来华入境总人次数的6%以上。同时，对外开放也提高了中国的国际形象，引来众多的外国留学生。中国累计已接受培训了152个国家和地区的留学生25万人。

中国打开了国民出国的大门。出国留学的人数越来越多，方式越来越多样，层次也越来越高。大批学成归来的中国学子目前已在中国的社会主义建设中担纲挑梁，成为骨干。

对外开放促进了中国科技、教育、文化事业的蓬勃发展，也促进了中国扩大对外文化交流及其走上商品化、市场化的道路。中国已积极成功地举办了许多国际会议和运动会，包括世界妇女代表大会和世界博览会，向国际社会宣传、展现了中国改革开放后的崭新面貌。中国已与135个国家和地区建立了科技合作关系，与154个国家和地区建立了教育文化交流和合作关系，签订了95份政府间科技合作协议，加入了75个国际学术组织，向103个国家和地区派遣了近30万留学人员。

三、树立大经贸思想，发展外经贸往来

发展对外贸易是中国对外经贸往来的重点，也是对外开放的重要目标，改革开放以来，中国不断深化外经贸体制改革，并采取了许多开放措施，促进外贸发展。通过下放外贸经营权，目前中国已有专业外贸企业9000多家，获得外贸自营权的生产企业和科研院所近万家，已开业的拥有自营进出口权的外商投资企业15万多家。1999年初已两次批准共61家私营生产企业的外贸经营权，外贸公司对外开放合资经营的试点工作也已经开始。

在扩大对外贸易中逐步确定的市场多元化战略、以质取胜战略和优先发展机电产品战略及以进带出策略，目前已取得初步成功。中国的贸易伙伴已从1978年的几十个发展到现在的227个，遍及世界各地。中国从事对外经济合作的企业已从改革开放初的几家发展到目前上千家企业组成的门类齐全、有相当强国际竞争力的队伍，业务范围已遍及180多个国家和地区。

由于大力改革开放，中国对外经贸往来发展引人注目。1978年，中国的商品外贸总额仅206.4亿美元，列世界第27位，1988年、1994年、1997年则分别突破1000亿、2000亿、3000亿美元。1992年，中国已占世界商品出口贸易额的第11位和商品进口贸易额的第12位，而1998年则分别上升到第9和第10位。中国的服务贸易虽起步较晚，且总体规模至今还不大，但发展较快，年均增速达15.4%，快于世界增长水平。1998年，中国对外经济合作完成营业额首次超过100亿美元，达101.3亿美元。自1995年起援外方式向合资、合作方式转变，目前已取得实质性进展，已实施优惠贷款项目51个。中国对外援助的国家达到115个，援建的成套项目达到1548个。

对外开放使中国经济加快融入世界经济全球一体化的进程，提高了中国参与国际分工和交换的能力和水平，使中国的经济外向性加强，对外依存度大幅提高。中国对外贸易额占国内生产总值的比重从1978年的9.8%上升到1998年的33.7%，其中出口占18.9%，进口占14.9%；外商在华直接投资存量与中国国内生产总值的比例从1985年的不足1.6%上升到1997年的24.4%；1997年中国的外债余额与当年的国家财政收入的比例达125%，与国家外汇储备的比例也达94%。

四、制定“一国两制”方针，发展两岸四地往来

对外改革开放，除了要对外国开放，还要充分利用华人的力量。香港、澳门、台湾与大陆的统一，是全世界华人的共同心愿。80年代中国政府制定的“一国两制”方针，对香港、澳门作出了主权完整不容谈判、资本主义制度可以长期保持不变的决定，并宣布适用于台湾。1997年7月1日，香港顺利实现回归，1999年12月20日，澳门也将回归，为台湾与大陆的统一提供了成功的经验。

改革开放中，中国大陆大力发展与香港、澳门、台湾的经贸往来，使两岸四地的交流合作日益密切。相互经贸关系的发展，对促进中国的和平统一有重要意义。中国大陆对香港的贸易额仅次于对日本、美国的贸易额；在香港的进口额和转口出口额中均一直占第一位；在世界范围对外投资萎缩的1998年，吸收香港的实际直接投资仍

然占当年全国吸收总额的41.2%；港澳同胞每年往返大陆人次都在几千万以上；对澳门的贸易额1998年达8.7亿美元，比上年增长13.8%；台湾已成为大陆的第五大贸易伙伴和第二大进口市场及吸引境外资金的第二大来源地，而大陆也已成为台湾的第二大出口市场。目前大陆和台湾已分别设立了海协会和海基会，两岸正向实现正常直接“通商、通邮、通航”而努力。

1998年，大陆对港、澳、台三地的贸易额合计为667.8亿美元，占当年中国外贸总额的20.6%；吸收港、澳、台胞实际对大陆的直接和其它投资额合计为228.9亿美元，占当年中国吸收外商实际投资总额的48.1%；港、澳、台胞来大陆的人次数合计为5625万，占当年中国接待国际旅游总人次的88.6%。

中国在对外开放中，还十分重视海外华人的作用。中国允许“来去自由”和海外华人投资享受外商投资同等待遇等政策使他们放心、安心。目前每年回国的华侨都在10万人次以上，1998年达到12.1万人次，比上年增长21.9%。

五、加快与国际经济接轨步伐，不断扩大对外开放的领域

中国不断加强涉外经济法律、规定的制定和透明度，以保证对外开放进程不断，增强国际社会对中国的信任。由对外贸易经济合作部负责不定期对外发布的文告，成为完整公布中国最新涉外经济政策的窗口，使对外贸易和外商来华投资有法可依。中国还逐步加入了一大批国际公约和条约，与89个国家签订了双边“保护投资协议”，与160多个国家签订了“贸易议定”。中国不遗余力地打击走私、盗版等违法经济活动，公正审判涉外经济案件，维护国内外当事人的合法权益，为扩大开放、吸引外资创造了良好的外部环境。在美、欧地区发达国家对中国出口商品实行反倾销的情况下，中国政府加强了组织应诉和调查，并开始运用反倾销手段保护民族幼稚工业。在公布反倾销法的基础上，1998年，中国已首次成功对国外的新闻纸倾销进行了反倾销立案调查。

中国在计划经济下的出口补贴做法、多重汇率并行、对内分贸易和非贸易汇率、对外分官方和调剂汇率的做法、人民币和外汇券同时流通的做法等等，在改革开放中均先后被停止执行，传统的进口高关税政策也被彻底改变。目前中国的进口关税税率总水平已降到16.7%，到2005年，将降到10%，更加接近国际水平。

中国坚持不与任何国家结盟，但积极参加国际性、地区性经济合作活动。90年代中国还加入了亚洲及太平洋经济合作组织，参加了亚欧会议，并成为东盟对话国之一。中国国家领导人多次参加亚太经合组织的最高领导人会议，阐述中国的主张。江泽民主席在1993年出席第一次领导人非正式会议时，正式提出建立国际经济新秩序的主张，1997年出席第五次领导人非正式会议时正式提出了《走向21世纪的科技产业合作议程》的倡议，在1998年第七次领导人非正式会议上被正式通过。江主席在第八次会议上，还提出了促进国际金融稳定发展和推动建立国际金融新秩序的三点主张。

中国作为发展中国家，尽管受到这两年亚洲金融危机和世界金融动荡的很大影响，特别是出口贸易严重受挫，但却以大国负责任的态度，始终公开宣布并一直保持人民币的不贬值，还参与了国际社会对泰国、印度尼西亚的金融贷款援助，为稳定世界金融秩序作出了重大贡献。

中国从80年代起就为恢复在关税和贸易总协定中的地位、进而为加入世界贸易组织而努力，作出了极大让步，只是由于以美国为首的西方发达国家要价太高，超出中国作为发展中国家的地位所应尽的义务过多，而迟迟未能实现。但中国把对外开放作为基本国策的决心不会改变。中国正在进一步开放经济领域，特别是服务领域

的国内市场，市场准入、国民待遇等国际通行准则将在中国逐步、全面、彻底地得到执行。

国际金融危机已提醒中国，在全球经济一体化的加快过程中，中国要扩大改革开放，也要保护国民经济不受国际经济的不良影响冲击而顺利发展。中国必将在继续扩大对外开放过程中，加强经济立法，不断完善政府宏观管理体制，保证改革开放的健康、顺利发展。

中国利用外资的回顾与展望

利用外资是对外开放基本国策的重要内容。改革开放以来，中国利用外资成绩卓著，有力地促进了国民经济持续、快速、健康发展。

一、20年来，中国利用外商直接投资工作情况

20年来，中国吸收外商投资的历程大致分为四个阶段：

1.1979-1985年是起步阶段。1978年，中国政府作出了把工作重点转到以经济建设为中心的轨道上来。开辟了社会主义现代化建设的新时期。作为对外开放重要内容的利用外资开始起步。1979年，随着中国第一部利用外资法律《中华人民共和国中外合资经营企业法》的出台，1980年第一批外商投资企业宣告成立。到1985年底，中国累计实际使用外资60多亿美元，年均吸收外商投资10亿美元。

2.1986-1991年是完善法律体系、打开局面的阶段。为进一步打开吸收外商投资的局面，在总结前6年利用外资经验的基础上，1986年中国政府颁布了《关于鼓励外商投资的规定》，随后制定了一系列配套法规并采取了相应鼓励措施。这一阶段，中国投资环境得到很大改善，利用外资步伐开始加快，累计实际使用外资190亿美元，年均31亿美元，是上阶段的3倍多。

3.1992-1997年是高速发展阶段。1992年邓小平南巡讲话和中共十四大召开极大地解放了人们的思想，促进了生产力的发展。随着国民经济的快速发展，中国吸收外资步入高速发展期。1992年当年中国新批合同外资金额为前13年的1.11倍，实际使用外商投资为前13年总和的50%。1993年当年新批合同外资金额1114.36亿美元，为1992年的1.92倍，创历史最高水平，实际使用外资金额比1992年增长2.5倍。自1993年起中国已连续6年成为世界上仅次于美国的第二大吸收外资的国家。在使用外资规模大幅度增长的同时，外商投资产业结构也得到很大改善，在继续保持以制造业为主的前提下，农业、基础设施等领域利用外资的比重有了较大幅度的提高，外商投资已从初期的以一般加工工业为主扩展到基础产业、基础设施和高新技术领域。世界排名前500名的跨国公司已有300多家在中国投资设立了企业，越来越多的跨国公司将中国作为其投资的重点区域，资金技术密集型大型项目和基础设施项目大幅度增加。外商投资方式趋向多样化，投资领域进一步扩大，绝大多数服务业领域已开始有条件地对外开放。在中国沿海地区外商投资迅速增长的同时，中国内陆地区吸收外商投资也有了较快的发展。这一阶段中国累计实际使用外资1968亿美元，年均吸收外商投资328亿美元，是前13年的8倍。

4. 从1998年开始中国吸收外资进入结构调整、稳定发展的新阶段。1997年底中国政府召开了全国利用外资工作会议，总结了20年来中国吸收外资的经验，提出了进一步扩大对外开放，提高利用外资水平的要求。在继续保持吸收外资相当规模的同时，吸收外资工作将与国民经济整体发展更紧密地结合，更加注重改善吸收外资的产业、地区结构，对中国产业结构调整和技术进步做出更多的贡献。

经过20年的努力，中国对外开放、利用外资

取得了举世瞩目的成就。截止到1998年底，中国共批准设立外商投资企业324167家，实际利用外资金额达2656亿美元。1998年，外商实际投入金额占中国当年全社会固定资产投资总额的13.11%，创造的工业产值占全国工业总产值的22%，进出口总额占全国进出口总额的48.7%，实现税收占全国工商税收的12.5%。

利用外资极大地促进了国民经济发展和社会进步。其主要作用是：弥补了中国国内建设资金的不足，引进了大量先进、适用技术和管理经验，创造了更多的就业机会，培养了大批人才，增加了国家税收和外汇收入，加速了对外经济贸易发展，提高了中国经济的国际竞争力，促进了思想解放和观念更新，推动了社会主义市场经济体制改革和法律体系建设的进程，提高了中国的国际地位。总之，利用外资有利于发展生产力，有利于增强国家的综合国力，有利于提高人民的生活水平。

二、中国鼓励引导外商投资的基本政策

纵观世界上经济发展中国家在投资引导上的基本做法，一是将鼓励外商投资纳入国家鼓励投资的总体政策之中，国家对来源于不同渠道的各种投资制定相同的政策，只要是国家鼓励投资的领域，内外资机会均等；二是将产业政策和地区政策作为国家鼓励投资政策的基本依据，紧紧围绕产业、地区政策目标制定具体的优惠政策和配套措施；三是为鼓励投资者向国家支持的产业或地区投资，国家给投资者提供以税收减免为主的优惠待遇。

1. 坚持依法管理，保护投资者的合法权益

社会主义市场经济是法制经济，为实现对外商投资企业依法管理，依法实施检查监督，保护投资者的合法权益，中国政府健全和完善了有关外商投资企业的法律、法规和规章制度，努力做到有法可依，有章可循，管理有据。

外商投资企业作为国际资本流动的产物，它是由中外双方或者外国一方投资创办的，并且一开始就按照市场经济的规则来运作，中国政府积极地、有选择地吸收、借鉴和采纳国际上一些通行的、行之有效的做法来管理外商投资企业，使企业的经营管理活动尽可能地符合国际惯例。同时，由于设立在中国境内外商投资企业是中国的法人，中方国有资产还参与了一部分企业的投资，企业的经营管理活动也要受整个社会生产力发展水平和国家现行经济管理体制的制约，如果全盘照搬国际惯例而不结合中国现阶段的实际，非但不可取，而且事实上也是难以行得通的。因此，在管理过程中对国际惯例有所取舍，对其中一些适合中国国情的做法尽可能地借鉴吸收和消化创新。

外商投资企业享有国家法律、法规所赋予的各项权利，包括在人、财、物、产、供、销等方面的自主权，以及国家给予的各项政策优惠。中国政府尊重企业的自主权，放手让企业在国家法律、法规规定的范围内独立自主地开展经营活动，支持、帮助企业发展生产，扩大经营，提高效益，保护其合法经营的权利和投资利益。同时，企业也有依法经营，依法纳税，严格按合同办事，并自觉接受管理和监督的义务。中国政府依法对外商投资企业实施必要的检查和监督，规范企业行为，维护正常的经营秩序，确保企业健康顺利发展。

2. 积极、合理、有效地利用外资

“积极、合理、有效”是现阶段中国利用外资的基本方针。所谓“积极”就是指在利用外资的指导思想上、战略上要积极，利用外资是发展国家生产力、加速现代化建设的重大举措，应该大胆地去实践。所谓“合理”指的是利用外资的具体工作要审慎，不能急于求成，要根据各个不同时期、不同行业、不同地区的不同情况，考虑国内综合配套能力和经济承受能力，把握好利用外

资的规模和速度，合理地引导外资投向，优化外资投资结构，不断提高利用外资的质量和水平。所谓“有效”是指要善于引进和利用外资。要尽量把引进的外资投向发展国民经济的“刀刃”上，多举办技术含量高的项目，使外资与国民经济发展规划有机结合起来。外资的引进应符合中国的发展战略和产业政策；在此基础上，努力做好吸收、消化工作。

3. 为鼓励投资者向国家支持的产业和地区投资，国家给投资者提供以税收减免为主的优惠待遇

中国政府为吸引外资向国家支持的产业和地区倾斜，对外商投资企业给予以企业所得税为主的不同幅度的各种税收减免和优惠政策。

中国政府为外商投资企业所得税优惠政策包括企业所得税减免和企业再投资退所得税两个内容。

（1）企业所得税减免。中国政府的企业所得税减免政策对设在经济特区的外商投资企业和设在经济技术开发区的生产性外商投资企业，减按15%的税率征收企业所得税；对设在经济特区、经济技术开发区、沿海经济开放区所在城市的老市区的生产性外商投资企业，减按24%的税率征收企业所得税。

中国政府对生产性且经营期限在10年以上的外商投资企业，从其获利年度起，两年免征、三年减半征收企业所得税。对从事港口、码头建设的中外合资经营企业按15%的税率征收企业所得税。经营期限在15年以上的，从其获利年度起，5年免征，5年减半征收企业所得税。

对从事农业、林业、牧业的外商投资企业和设在经济不发达的边远地区的外商投资企业依照生产性外商投资企业和从事港口、码头建设的中外合资经营企业规定享受减税、免税待遇期满后，企业申请并经批准，在以后10年内给予按应纳税额减征15-30%企业所得税的税收优惠。

中国政府对产品出口型外商投资企业，在依照税法规定免征减征期满后，凡当年出口产品产值达到产品产值的70%以上的，可继续减半征收。但对已按15%的税率缴纳所得税的产品出口型企业，符合上述条件的，减按10%的税率征收企业所得税；对先进技术型外商投资企业，在依照税法规定免征减征期满后，仍为先进技术型企业的，可给予延长三年减半征收企业所得税优惠。

（2）再投资退所得税。再投资退所得税是指外商投资企业的外国投资者，将从企业取得的利润直接再投资于该企业，增加注册资本，或者作为资本投资开办其他外商投资企业，经营期不少于5年的，经投资者申请，中国税务机关批准，退还其再投资部分已缴纳所得税的40%的税款。

三、中国今后利用外资的政策导向

进一步扩大对外开放，提高利用外资水平，是中国政府今后利用外资的基本方针。明确强调继续把吸收外商直接投资作为利用外资的重点，并将采取如下政策导向措施：

1. 积极引导外资投向，进一步优化外商投资的产业结构。根据国家的产业政策，适应产业结构调整和升级的要求，重点鼓励外资投向农业、高新技术产业、基础工业、基础设施、环保产业、出口创汇型产业，积极引导外资投向传统产业和老工业基地的技术改造，充分发挥比较优势，继续发展符合产业政策的劳动密集型项目。

2. 进一步扩大外商投资领域。进一步开放竞争性产业，扩大石油化工、建筑业等利用外资的规模。有步骤地推进服务贸易的开放，结合中国加入世贸组织的谈判，在现有零售、银行、保险业试点的基础上，对矿业资源、旅游、外贸、电讯等行业抓紧研究合资、合作开发问题。

3. 逐步对外商投资企业实行国民待遇。国民待遇是国际交往的一条基本原则。改革开放以来，为吸收外商投资，中国政府在进出口权、用

人自主权、分配制度和税收等方面，对外商投资企业采取了许多超国民待遇的投资鼓励措施，实践证明，这些优惠政策措施对吸引外商投资，引进先进技术发挥了重要作用。但随着改革开放的不断深入和社会主义市场经济体制的逐步建立，这些政策措施与国际通行规则和市场经济公平竞争原则的矛盾日益突出，它使内资企业在激烈的市场竞争中处于十分不利的地位，对外商投资企业实行国民待遇已成为各种所有制企业的共同呼声。与此同时，改革开放以来中国涉外税收制度几度改革的经验表明，统一内外资企业的税收政策不会降低中国对外国投资者的吸引力，也不会减少国家的财政收入。相反，它有利于为各类企业创造一个平等竞争的外部环境，从而在更高层次和水平上吸引外国投资。这就要求各级政府和部门必须转变观念，改变过去那种主要依靠减税让利等优惠政策吸引外资的思路，逐步取消不平等的税收减免政策，使吸引外资逐步从政策优惠向市场导向转变，由倾斜政策逐步向国民待遇转变，通过主要依靠创造优越的投资环境，健全的法制和高效的管理，以及有吸引力的市场，而不是靠政策优惠来吸引外资。

4. 进一步鼓励外资投向中西部地区。继续发挥东部地区对外开放、利用外资的优势，支持东部地区积极发展资金、技术密集型产业和出口型产业。继续办好经济特区、上海浦东新区、苏州工业园区以及各类国家级经济和技术开发区。同时，国家将进一步鼓励外资投向中西部地区，继续扩大中西部地区的对外开放。中国政府将鼓励沿海地区外商投资企业到中西部地区再投资，外商投资比例超过25%的项目，视同外商投资企业；同时将进一步提高国际金融组织和外国政府优惠贷款用于中西部地区项目的比重。经国家有关部门批准，中西部确有优势产业项目可列入鼓励类外商投资项目，享受进口自用设备免征关税和进口环节增值税等优惠，对限制类和限定外商股权比例项目的设立条件和市场开放程度，可适当放宽；国家将优先安排一批农业、水利、交通、能源、原材料和环保项目在中西部吸收外资，并加大对项目配套资金及相关措施的支持；鼓励中西部军转民企业和国有大中型企业利用外资进行技术改造。

5. 多渠道多方式吸收外商投资，实施利用外资多元化战略。今后要在继续鼓励港澳台、东南亚投资的基础上，扩大北美、日本的投资，重点做好对欧盟的招商引资。中国政府将积极进行新的外商投资方式的试点。鼓励国有大中型企业采取多种方式利用外资进行资产重组，盘活存量资产。继续积极发展加工贸易和补偿贸易，允许国有小型企业和集体企业对外出售，允许私营企业吸收外资。

在合资方式方面，要继续做好合资、独资、合作工作，做好BOT项目融资，对发行股票要积极稳妥地进行，逐步扩大规模。对转让基础设施的经营权（收益权），要抓紧规范管理，抓紧试点。

6. 大胆引进和积极引导跨国公司投资。目前国外中小企业投资是中国利用外资的重点，今后要根据跨国公司的特点，推进与它们的合作。继续实行以市场换技术的方针，进一步开放国内市场，通过与跨国公司的合作，尤其是有重点地扶持中国大型企业与之合作，引进适用的技术、资金、管理经验及营销方式。鼓励与跨国公司合作建立研究开发中心，增强技术消化和创新能力，带动相关企业和产业共同发展。

7. 对于符合贷款原则的外商投资企业，给予必要的信贷支持。通过国有资产存量重组，发行股票债券和建立投资基金等多种方式，帮助合资中方有效利用资本市场筹措资金，解决好合资中方股金来源问题。

8. 大力改善投资环境，依法加强对外商投资企业的管理。在进一步改善投资硬环境的同时，下大力气改善投资软环境，使整个利用外资工作进一步提高水平。当前重点抓好以下几项工作：加强涉外经济法制建设，抓紧修订现行的利用外资基本法律法规，加快BOT管理法规的出台；坚决制止对外商投资企业一切形式的乱检查、乱收费、乱摊派、乱罚款，切实保障外商投资企业经营管理自主权，维护投资各方的合法权益不受侵犯；依法保护劳动者正当权益，提高政府部门的办事效率；结合深化投融资体制改革，改进外资项目的审批方法，简化审批程序；加快建设统一开放、竞争有序的市场环境，对外商投资企业实行国民待遇；严厉打击走私、伪冒、骗税、逃套汇、侵犯知识产权等非法行为；依法加强监督管理，完善对外商投资企业的联合年检工作。

发展中的中国旅游业

旅游业是当代世界发展最快、前景最广阔、规模最大的新型产业之一，也是关联带动功能很强的经济产业。旅游业的发展水平是一个国家和地区经济发展、社会进步和人民生活质量的重要标志之一。中国旅游业经过20多年的发展，取得了令人瞩目的成绩，旅游业总收入由1978年的22.5亿元上升到1998年的3438亿元，年均增长25%。1998年，中国旅游业克服金融危机等不利因素的影响，继续保持增长势头，比1997年增长10.2%，增幅高于国民经济的增长速度，占GDP比重达到4.2%，显示了旅游业发展的强大生命力。

中国是旅游资源非常丰富的国家，古老的长城、秀丽的桂林山水、秦始皇兵马俑以及神秘的东方文化等深深吸引着无数中外游客。到目前为止，列入国家级风景名胜区的有119处，国家级自然保护区94处，国家级旅游度假区12处，国家级森林公园309处，国家历史文化名城99处，国家优秀旅游城市54个，列入联合国自然和文化遗产名录的有21处。如此众多的旅游资源，为中国旅游业发展提供了得天独厚的条件。

中国政府十分重视旅游业发展，并采取了积极的政策。一是建立了旅游发展基金，主要用于旅游宣传促销、人员培训等；二是加大了旅游景区的基础设施投入，改善了旅游环境。1978—1998年，中国旅游业利用社会资金的总体规模超过3700亿元人民币；三是加快了重点旅游项目的开发建设。1998年中国在435个旅游项目中精选推出了中国旅游业发展的第一批优先发展项目43个；四是中国政府已把旅游业确定为国民经济新的增长点，为旅游业的发展创造了良好的宏观环境。

中国加大旅游宣传力度，开展了一系列旅游主题活动。在'93山水风光游、'94文物古迹游、'95民俗风情游、'96度假休闲游、'97中国旅游年、'98华夏城乡游、'99生态环境游中，吸引了海内外的众多游客，全面展示了中国丰富多彩的旅游产品体系。

中国加强与世界旅游界合作，促进了旅游业的对外开放。1998年中国组织了大型展销活动17次、促销团队9个、邀请海外旅行商和记者48批；举办'98中国国际旅游交易会，云集38个国家和地区的1300多个旅游机构和企业，成为亚太地区规模最大、档次较高的国际旅游交易会；在美国最大的广播电视网CNN上连续近百次的电视广告，在美国最大的商城举办中国旅游节等活动，直接面向公众促销；加强与主要客源国和国际旅游组织交往，多次会见WTO负责人，出席亚太旅行协会第47届年会，与有关国家签署了旅游合作协定，全面介绍和宣传中国旅游业的发展变化，加强官方与民间两个渠道的旅游合作关系，进一步扩大了中国旅游业的国际影响。

中国旅游业的发展，对国民经济产生了重要作用。一是促进了产业结构调整。目前，中国已有24个省、区、市把旅游业作为重点产业和支柱产业来发展，云南、陕西、浙江等省旅游业总产出已占当地国民生产总值的5%以上，北京、上海已达到13%。二是促进了社会消费。目前中国人民实现小康生活水平的已达到75.61%，人们对旅游的需求逐渐增多。1998年，中国国内旅游总人数达6.94亿人次，而农民占4.445亿人次，为总人次的64%，充分说明了旅游需求在各部分人群中的社会广泛性。三是提供了就业机会。到1997年底，中国仅国际旅游业直接和间接从业人员就达816万人，其中北京市1997年旅游业直接和间接就业人数50.2万人，占该市第三产业和全市劳动就业人数的14%和8%。据中国科学院国情研究第二号报告称，预计到2000年，中国仅旅游业一项一年就可以吸收2000万个劳动力。四是增加了外汇收入。1989-1998年的10年期间，中国旅游外汇收入年均增长率为23.7%，大大高于同期世界旅游外汇收入8.05%的年平均增长率。1998年中国国际旅游总收入126.02亿美元，比上年增长4.37%，旅游创汇在世界各国的排位由第八位提升至第七位。五是培植了财源。旅游资源丰富、旅游业发达地区，旅游业创造的税收占当地财政收入的比重越来越大，例如福建武夷山市财政收入60%来自旅游业；1991-1995年期间，浙江舟山市仅直接来自旅游业的税收就达4000多万元。

中国旅游业经过20年的发展，在国际市场上已具有相当的地位和竞争优势；国内旅游消费的现实需求性强，市场基础广阔，能够增加和刺激最终消费；旅游业的关联带动作用显著，能够促进经济和社会的繁荣；旅游业吸纳就业量大，有利于缓解就业压力；旅游资源的独特性和不可替代性，可以使中国的资源得到更加合理有效的利用，特别是拥有丰富旅游资源的中西部地区，通过旅游开发，促进区域经济的均衡和协调发展。

中国政府高度重视旅游业的可持续发展，注重资源的有效保护和合理开发，正在调整和重新制定旅游业2001-2005年的“十五”规划。中国旅游业正在成为国民经济新的支柱产业。

合资企业生产车间
Workshop of a joint Venture

Brief Review of China's Opening to the Outside World

The period from 1949, when New China was founded, to 1978, when the Third Plenary Session of the 11th Central Committee of CPC was held, saw the country experiencing four different stages of development regarding foreign relations and in particular foreign trade and economic exchanges, due to the adoption of different government policies based on varying international conditions.

In the 1950s, the former Soviet Union became the leading and, sometimes, the only country in the world with which China tried to maintain full relations in all fields. After the extremely close Sino-Soviet relations were replaced by an ideological split-up and lasting cold war, China became suspicious of all foreign influences and emphasized self-reliance in all aspects of life the early 1960s, virtually closing its doors to the outside world by the late 1960s. The door was reopened in the late 1970s, finally enabling the country to return to the international community. Actually, China did not adopt an genuine opening-up policy until 1978. For example, when the catastrophic earthquake happened in Tangshan city in Hebei Province in 1976, the Chinese government refused to accept any international assistance. It was the Third Plenary Session of the 11th Central Committee of CPC that put China's opening-up drive well on track by emphasizing the principle of "seeking truth from fact" and "emancipating the mind."

I. Opening "Windows" to the Outside and Gradually Expanding Foreign Relations

The establishment of the economic development zones in the southeast coastal areas was designed to open some "windows" to seek direct contact with the outside world, and had the effect of forming bridgeheads for the advancement of China's opening-up movement.

In 1979, the Central Committee of the CPC and the State Council determined that four special zones (Shenzhen, Zhuhai and Shantou in Guangdong Province and Xiamen in Fujian Province) be opened to direct foreign investment and cooperation. The following year, the four opened places were formally named special economic zones (SEZ). Soon after, the First Session of the Seventh National People's Congress approved that the whole province of Hainan be an economic development zone. In 1984, Dalian, Tianjin, Qinhuangdao, Qingdao, Yantai, Shanghai, Nantong, Lianyungang, Ningbo, Wenzhou, Fuzhou, Guangzhou, Zhanjiang and Beihai, all of which are port cities, were approved by the Central Committee of CPC and State Council to enjoy some preferential policies that were specially designed for SEZs. In the following years, bonded zones began mushrooming in many places such as the Tianjin Port, Dayaowan in Dalian, Waigaoqiao in Shanghai, Zhangjiagang in Jiangsu Province, Beilun Port in Ningbo, Mawei Port in Fuzhou, Xiangyu in Xiamen, Qingdao, Guangzhou, Shantou, and Futian and Shatoujiao in Shenzhen.

In 1985, the Yangtze Delta, the Pearl River Delta and a large region in southeast Fujian Province were designated to be economically opened-up areas, and they were soon followed by an even larger region rimming the Bohai Sea. In 1988, the central government decided that 140 cities and counties including Hangzhou, Nanjing and Shenyang, the three provincial capitals, should be on the list of economically opened areas. In 1990, the famous Pudong Economic and Technical Development Zone was established in Shanghai. In 1991, 21 state-level high- and new-technology industrial development zones were established throughout the country, following the first one in Beijing, which was approved in 1988. In 1992, Yangpu in Hainan Province was opened to foreign investment and cooperation, followed soon by the Suzhou Industrial Park in Jiangsu Province. In order to speed up the development of the regions along the Yangtze River, Chongqing, Yueyang, Wuhan, Jiujiang and Wuhu were opened that year, with Shanghai, which had already been opened, being their spearhead. During this period, Harbin, Changchun, Huhhot, Shijiazhuang, the capital cities of four provinces, either on the border or on the coast, were opened. In the inland regions, 11 provincial capital cities were also opened, including Taiyuan, Hefei, Nanchang, Zhengzhou, Changsha, Chengdu, Guiyang, Xi'an, Lanzhou, Xining and Yinchuan. Besides, a number of cities which are scenic spots were also opened one after another.

During the past 20 years, the opening-up movement has grown from just a few SEZs to cover almost all the coastal and inland areas, having the effect of completely opening China to the outside world.

II. Attracting Foreign Capital and Investment

Attracting and making good use of foreign investment is an important element of China's opening-up policy. However, China is also eagerly in need of talents, advanced technology and management from foreign countries. While seeking foreign investment, China paid more attention to maintaining close contacts with the international organizations and foreign governments with which China has enjoyed friendly relations. It was via these organizations and governments that China acquired low-interest loans with favorable terms. In recent years, China successfully issued bonds on the international market. Nevertheless, the main channels through which China has obtained its desperately-needed capital are commercial loans.

Foreign direct investment has always been the main source through which China absorbs foreign capital. In 1980, the government approved the first group of foreign-invested enterprises put into operation in China, which numbered only three. By the end of 1998, over 320,000 foreign-invested enterprises were in operations in China, creating employment for 17.5 million Chinese. In the past six years, China has been the No.1 developing country in the world in attracting foreign direct investment, and it has ranked the second among all the developing and developed countries in this respect, only after the United States.

During the period from 1979 to 1998, China borrowed a total of US$ 127.13 billion of foreign capital, attracted direct investment worth US$ 265.6 billion, and attracted and used foreign investment through various other sources which totaled US$ 14.7 billion. Besides, China encourages its companies and enterprises to invest overseas in order to make full use of Chinese natural resources, technology, experiences, to develop overseas market. At present, most of the Chinese investment overseas is concentrated in Australia, the coastal countries in South America, the United States, Germany, Russia, the Commonwealth of Independent countries and eastern European countries.

China has spared no effort to attract talents from the overseas market. Currently foreign professionals account for 6 percent or more of the total number of foreigners visiting China every year. In addition, as the opening-up policy of China helps to create a good image of the country, about 250,000 foreign students from 125 countries have come to China to study during this period.

A more liberal policy has also been adopted to allow more and more Chinese to study overseas. At present, a great number of Chinese students are studying abroad, majoring in various fields, while a great many have returned to China, playing active roles in China's modernization drive.

The opening-up policy has resulted in a boom in China's scientific, technological, educational and cultural development. It has also enabled China to become part of the international cultural market. In recent years, China has successfully held and organized a number of international conferences and sports meetings, including such important events as the Fourth UN Conference on Women and the World Fairs. By providing a venue for these international meetings, China has advertised its economic and social progress to the world. So far, China has established cooperative relations in science and technology with 135 countries; it has established cooperative relations and exchanges in education and culture with 154 countries; it signed 95 government-to-government agreements in scientific and technological cooperation; it is a member state of 75 international academic organizations; and it had sent about 300,000 people to study in 103 countries.

III. Promoting the Fully-Dimensional Development of Foreign Trade

Since China began implementing the new policies of reform and opening up, a number of measures have been adopted in its foreign trade sector's institutional reform thus promoting a fully-dimensional development of it. In recent years, more and more enterprises and companies have been granted the right to engage in foreign trade. For example, 61 private enterprises were granted the right in the early half of 1999. As a result, the companies specially engaged in foreign trade number more than 9,000 throughout the country and those enterprises which have just been granted the right to engage in foreign trade number over 150,000. Some pilot schemes have also been conducted in several provinces, opening Chinese foreign-trade companies to foreign investment and cooperation.

China has had a strategy for developing foreign trade, which emphasizes the seeking of a larger market share by exporting diversified goods, improving competitiveness by producing and providing quality goods, and giving priority to developing electronic and machinery products for export. Now the development of China's foreign trade based on this strategy has born fruit. The number of China's trading partners has increased to 227 from just a few dozen 20 years ago. Now, nearly a thousand Chinese companies are engaged in economic cooperation in a large market covering 180 countries and regions, making China a competitive force in this regard.

Due to the acceleration of the reform and opening-up drive, significant progress has been made in the development of China's foreign trade since the early 1980s. In 1978, the foreign trade volume of China in commodities was only US$ 20.64 billion, ranking 27nd in the world, which rose to over US$ 100 billion, US$ 200 billion and US$ 300 billion respectively in 1988, 1994 and 1997. By 1992, China ranked 11th in the world in the export of commodities and 12th in import of commodities, rising respectively to ninth and 10th in 1998. Though China was rather late in developing the export of labor, the sector has seen rapid development, with its annual growth rate being 15.4 percent, faster than the world average. In 1998, China's economic cooperation had a turnover of US$ 10.13 billion, a historical breakthrough. China has also changed its practice from merely providing foreign assistance to other countries to a new way by which China helps foreign countries by investing in local projects or running businesses cooperatively. Up to now, China has provided foreign assistance for 115 countries, implementing 51 projects with favorable terms and equipment for 1,548 projects.

The policy of reform and opening up has enabled China to join the international competitiveness more actively. In the past 20 years, China's ability to participate in international division and exchange and its dependence on foreign trade and cooperations has enhanced to a great extent. In 1998, the foreign trade volume accounted for 33.7 percent (including 18.4 percent from export and 14.9 percent from import) of China's GDP, a sharp increase from 9.8 percent in 1978. In 1997, 24.4 percent of China's GDP was contributed by direct foreign investment, also a sharp contrast with 1.6 percent in 1985. In 1997, the ratio of the surplus of China's foreign debt with state revenue was 1.25:1, and with foreign exchange reserve was 0.94:1.

IV. Adopting "One Country, Two Systems" Policy and Promoting the Exchange of "Two Banks and Four Regions"

It is a dream shared by every Chinese person in the world that the reunification of the Chinese mainland, Hong Kong, Macao and Taiwan is achieved one day. The Chinese government began carrying out the policy of "one country, two systems" in the 1980s, dealing with the issues relating to Hong Kong, Macao and Taiwan. According to the policy, the sovereignty of Hong Kong and Macao is not negotiable and the two regions are allowed to maintain the capitalist system for a long time to come after returning to the motherland. On July 1, 1997, Hong Kong became a special administrative region of China smoothly, and Macao will be returning to the motherland in the same way on December 20, 1999. The reunification of the mainland China with Taiwan will also be realized one day.

During past 20 years, mainland China enhanced its economic and trade exchanges with Hong Kong, Macao and Taiwan, which contributed greatly to the cause of China's peaceful reunification. Hong Kong is mainland China's third largest trading partner, after only Japan and the United States. In 1998, the trade volume between mainland China and Macao stood at US$ 870 million, representing an increase of 13.8 percent over 1997. Mainland China has always been Hong Kong's largest trading partner in term of imports and exports trade. 1998 was a bad year witnessing global stagnation of investment. However, direct investment in mainland China by Hong Kong investors was still active, accounting for 41.2 percent of the total investment in the mainland that year. Each year several millions of Hong Kong residents shuttle between Hong Kong and the mainland. Taiwan has also close trading relations with the mainland, being the fifth largest overseas trading partner of the mainland, the second largest overseas market of the mainland's exporting goods, and the second biggest source from which the mainland absorbs overseas capital. In the mean time, the mainland has become the second largest market for Taiwan's exports. At present, the Straits Exchange Foundation (SEF) on the Taiwan side and the Association for Relations Across the Taiwan Straits (ARATS) on the mainland are working actively as a bridge linking the two sides closer, and in particular promoting the "three direct links" of trade, mail and air and shipping services across the Taiwan Straits.

In 1998, the trade volume of the mainland with Hong Kong, Macao and Taiwan stood at US$ 66.78 billion, accounting for 20.6 percent of the mainland's total trade volume that year. The combined direct investment from the three regions in the mainland reached US$ 22.89 billion, accounting for 48.1 percent of the total overseas investment in the mainland that year. About 56.25 million people from the three regions visited the mainland in 1998, accounting for 88.6 percent of the total overseas visitors.

The Chinese government encourages overseas Chinese to play an active role in helping China's modernization drive. It has introduced a new regulation that gives everyone the freedom to enter and leave China any time at their wills. The Chinese living overseas are allowed to enjoy the same preferential policies with foreign investors in investing on the mainland. In the last couple of years, the mainland received about 100,000 overseas Chinese each year, the figure being 121,000 last year, representing an increase of 21.9 percent over 1997.

V. Joining International Practice at a Faster Pace

The Chinese government has undertaken a series of active measures to improve China's institutional structure so as to speed up the pace of joining the international practice in trade and economic cooperation. Transparency in legislation and policy making relating to foreign trade and foreign-related affairs has been improved to a great extent. The Ministry of Foreign Trade and Economic Cooperation (MOFTEC) issues its new policies to both domestic and overseas media, letting everybody know clearly the up-to-date official information in this regard. Now China has been a signatory state of a number of international conventions and agreements, signing bilateral agreements on the protection of investment with 89 countries and trade agreements with 160 countries.

In the judicial field, much attention has been paid to combating smuggling, pirated publications and other economic crimes. A number of court proceedings in relation to these kinds of cases were opened to the public and media reporting. Given the situation in recent years that some Western countries take antidumping measures against Chinese exporting goods, the Chinese government has enhanced its efforts in response to these accusations while conducting necessary investigations into the allegations. The Chinese side has also adopted antidumping measures to protect the embryonic national industries. Based on the Chinese Anti-Dumping Law, the Chinese government successfully brought the case to court that foreign-made newsprint was dumping into China in 1998.

Some old policies and practices that China adopted for a long time during the period when the planned economic system dominated the country have been nullified one by one in recent years. These old practices included government subsidies for exports, the adoption of various interest rates for different sectors, RMB and FEC in circulation at the same time and so forth. China traditionally imposed high tariffs, and the foreign trade policy has also recently been abolished. At present, the general level of China's tariff barrier has been lowered to 16.7 percent, further lowering to 10 percent by 2005 to become closer to the international level, according to the government plan.

China is a nonaligned country, but it actively participates in regional and international cooperation in relation to economy and trade. Since the early 1990s, China has joined APEC and attended European-Asian Conferences, and it has begun dialogue with ASEAN countries. Chinese President Jiang Zemin has attended APEC summit meetings several times, formally expounding the Chinese points of view toward the new order of international economy. He proposed the Cooperative Protocol on Science, Technology and Industry Toward the 21st Century at the fifth informal meeting of the APEC leaders in 1997, which was ratified in 1998 at its seventh meeting. At the eighth informal meeting of APEC leaders, President Jiang expounded China's three proposals on maintaining the stable development of international finance and establishing the new order of international finance.

China is a developing country and it has inevitably suffered from the recent Asian financial crisis and the volatility of international financial market as a result of it. The foreign trade sector of China is the first victim to bear the cost. However, China has taken a responsible attitude toward the global difficulties, preventing the devaluation of RMB amid the torrent of currency values plummeting in Asia. China has also joined other countries in providing financial assistance to Thailand and Indonesia, making a great contribution to the stability of global financial order.

China has spared no effort in returning the GATT since the 1980s, always making great concessions for this purpose. But China has not reached the goal yet, because the US-led Western group is extremely particular with what China should do as a WTO member, which is apparently far beyond the ability of China, a developing country. Despite this setback, China will never change its determination to keep reforming and opening up to the outside world.

China is gradually opening more sectors and a larger domestic market to foreign investors and enterprises.

The recent Asian financial crisis is an important event alarming China as to how its national economy should be well protected given the acceleration of the globalization trend in economy. In order to speed up its economic development while joining the international practice at a faster pace, China will improve legislation in economic and trade fields, and reform the government institutions in economic macro-control so as to guarantee the modernization drive will advance healthily and smoothly.

China's Utilization of Foreign Capital: the Past and the Future

Utilizing foreign capital is an important aspect of China's national policy of opening to the outside world. Since the initiation of reform and opening to the outside world, China has achieved significant success in utilizing foreign capital, thus powerfully promoting the sustained, rapid and healthy development of the national economy.

I. 20 Years of Substantial Direct Foreign Investment

China's absorption of foreign investment in the past 20 years can be generally divided into four stages:

1. The preliminary stage (1979-1985): In 1978, the Chinese government made a decision to place economic construction at the center of its work, thus ushering in the new period of constructing socialist modernization. This was the beginning of the utilization of foreign capital, a crucial aspect of opening to the outside world. In 1979, the Law of the People's Republic of China on Chinese-Foreign Joint Ventures, China's first law on utilizing foreign capital, was promulgated; as well, in 1980 the first group of foreign-invested enterprises were set up in China. By the end of 1985, China had utilized more than US$6 billion of foreign capital in total, with the average annual foreign capital absorbed by China eventually reaching US$1 billion.

2. The stage of perfecting the legal system and opening up new prospects (1986-1991): To further absorb foreign capital, the Chinese government, on the basis of its experiences of utilizing foreign capital in the previous six years, promulgated the Regulations on Encouraging Foreign Investment in 1986, and worked out a series of supporting regulations and implemented corresponding measures. During this stage, China's investment environment greatly improved, the pace of utilizing foreign capital speeded up, and China actually utilized US$19 billion of foreign capital, or US$3.1 billion a year on average, more than three times that of the previous stage.

3. The stage of high-speed development (1992-1997): Speeches made by Deng Xiaoping during his tour of southern China in 1992 and the decisions of the 14th Central Committee of the Communist Party of China liberated people's thinking, and promoted the development of productive forces. Along with the rapid development of the national economy, China entered a period of high-speed development, absorbing foreign capital. In 1992, newly approved contracts involved a large amount of foreign capital, 1.11 times the total amount of the previous 13 years, and the foreign capital China actually utilized made up 50 percent of the total amount of the previous 13 years. In 1993, newly approved contracts involved a total of US$ 111.436 billion, or 1.92 times the 1992 figure, the highest in history, and the foreign capital actually utilized was 3.5 times the 1992 figure. After 1993, China became the second-ranked country in absorbing foreign capital in the world for six years running, only surpassed by the United States. When the foreign capital utilized by China increased by a large margin, the structure of foreign-invested industries greatly improved. On the premise that foreign capital is

primarily invested in manufacturing, foreign investment in agriculture, infrastructure facilities and other sectors also encouraged by China has increased by a large margin. Foreign capital is now invested not only in the processing industry, but also in basic industries, infrastructure, and the new and high-tech sectors. More than 300 of the top 500 transnational corporations in the world have set up enterprises in China, as transnationals increasingly make China their key region for investment, and the number of large capital-intensive and technology-intensive projects as well as infrastructure projects has risen greatly. Diverse strategies have been adopted by foreign investors to foster investment, as the field for investment has further expanded; and the greater part of the service sector has been provisionally opened to the outside world. While foreign investment has increased rapidly in China's coastal areas, China's inland areas have also made great progress in absorbing foreign capital. At this stage China actually utilized US$ 196.8 billion in foreign capital, absorbing US$ 32.8 billion of foreign capital a year on average, 8 times the total of the previous 13 years.

4. The new stage of structural adjustment and the stable development of foreign capital absorption since 1998: At the National Working Session on Utilizing Foreign Capital held at the end of 1997, the Chinese government summed up the experiences of absorbing foreign capital in the past 20 years, and put further provisions forward for opening wider to the outside world and improving the level of foreign capital utilization. While continuing to absorb foreign capital, China should integrate the absorption of foreign capital with the development of the national economy as a whole, and attach greater importance to improving industrial and regional structures with foreign investment, thus making greater contributions to the readjustment of China's industrial structure and technological progress.

Thanks to the efforts of the past 20 years, China has achieved world-renown progress in its opening to the outside world and utilization of foreign capital. By the end of 1998, China had approved the establishment of 324,167 foreign-invested enterprises, and had actually utilized US$ 265.6 billion in foreign capital. In 1998, the capital actually invested by foreign business made up 13.11 percent of China's total investment in the fixed assets of the whole society; the industrial output value created by foreign-funded enterprises was 22 percent of the nation's total; their total import and export volume was 48.7 percent; and their tax revenue, 12.5 percent of the total.

Utilizing foreign capital has greatly promoted national economic development and social progress. Its main roles are: Making up for China's insufficient capital for domestic construction, importing a large amount of advanced, practical, technical and managerial experiences, creating more employment opportunities, increasing the state's tax revenue and foreign-exchange earnings, accelerating foreign economic and trade development, strengthening the Chinese economy's international competitiveness, promoting the liberation of thinking and new ideas, stimulating the reform of the socialist market economic system and the construction of the legal system, and raising China's international status. In short, utilizing foreign capital is favorable to the development of productive forces, the comprehensive strengthening of the nation and the improvement of the people's standard of living.

II. The Basic Policy to Foster and Guide Foreign Investment

Economically advanced countries in the world adopt certain basic methods for guiding investment. First, they include policy for encouraging foreign investment within the country's overall policy for attracting investors. They have worked out the same policy for varied investments from diverse channels, and offer equal opportunity for domestic and foreign capital in those sectors where investment is to be encouraged. Second, they make industrial and regional policy the fundamental basis for state policy encouraging investment, and have worked out concrete preferential policies and supporting measures in close accordance with the objectives of their industrial and regional policies. Third, to encourage investment in industry or a region which the state supports, preferential treatment such as a reduction in and exemption from taxes is usually offered to investors by the state.

1. Adherence to Law in Protecting the Rights and Interests of Investors

The socialist market economy is an economy based on law. To manage foreign-invested enterprises, and examine and supervise them according to law, and protect investors' legitimate rights and interests, the Chinese government has broadened laws, regulations and rules, and does its best to ensure that laws are adhered to and regulations observed as the basis for proper management.

When international capital is floated, a foreign-invested enterprise is set up as a joint venture with a Chinese enterprise, or as a foreign enterprise itself; and is operated according to the rules governing the market economy. The Chinese government has, in whole or in part, absorbed, learned and adopted internationally accepted and effective methods to manage foreign-invested enterprises so as to make their operation and management conform to international practice as much as possible. Foreign-funded enterprises are located within Chinese territory, as such they are firm legal entities in China, and China's state-owned assets have been contributed as investments to some enterprises. The operation and management of foreign-funded enterprise are bound by the development level of the productive forces of the whole society and the existing system of operation and management within the country. Indiscriminate imitation of international practices at this stage without considering realities in China is not only undesirable, but impracticable. Efficient management requires accepting good points and rejecting bad points, and learning, absorbing and digesting useful internationally accepted practices as much as possible.

Foreign-invested enterprises enjoy various rights granted by the state laws and regulations, including autonomy over employment, finance, materials, production, supply and marketing, as well as the numerous preferential policies offered by the government. The Chinese government respects the autonomy of enterprises, gives them a free hand to initiate operations independently within their sphere as prescribed by state laws and regulations, supports and helps them to develop production, expand operations and improve economic returns, and safeguards their legitimate rights of operation and investment interests. Meanwhile, enterprises shall perform the duties of operation and remit taxes according to law, observe contract obligations, and conscientiously accept management and supervision. The Chinese government shall implement necessary examination of and supervision over foreign-invested enterprises according to law, standardize their actions, safeguard the normal operation of enterprises, and guarantee their healthy and smooth development.

2. Active, Reasonable and Effective Utilization of Foreign Capital

"Active, rational and effective" are China's basic principles for utilizing foreign capital at the present stage. "Active" refers to being active in the guiding philosophy and strategy for utilizing foreign capital; making use of such capital as an important measure in developing the country's productive forces, and speeding up the modernization drive. "Rational" refers to being prudent when handling the actual utilization of foreign capital. One should not be over-anxious for quick results, but should, in accordance with different conditions of different periods, industries and regions, take into account comprehensive domestic supportability and economic sustainability, regulate the scale and speed of foreign capital utilization, rationally guide foreign investment, optimize the structure of foreign investment, and constantly improve the quality and level of foreign capital utilization. "Effective" refers to adeptness at attracting and utilizing foreign capital. China should try its best to use foreign investment in the development of the national economy, and carry out more high-tech-related projects so as to make foreign capital coutributing to the development of the national economy. The import of foreign capital should conform with China's development strategy and industrial policy, and it is on this basis that China should absorb and digest foreign capital.

3. Tax Reductions, Exemptions and Incentives

To encourage foreign investment in industry and in regions that the state encourages faster development, the Chinese government offers foreign-funded enterprises a reduction in and exemption from various kinds of taxes.

Preferential policies on the income tax of foreign-invested enterprises by the Chinese government involve an enterprise income tax and an refunded income tax on their reinvestment.

(1) Reduction of and exemption from enterprise income tax. According to the preferential policies on the reduction of and exemption from income tax offered by the Chinese government, foreign-funded enterprises in the special economic zones, and foreign-funded production enterprises in the economic and technological development zones shall pay their enterprise income tax at a reduced rate of 15 percent; and foreign-funded production enterprises in the old city areas of the cities where special economic zones, economic and technological development zones and coastal economic development zones are located shall pay enterprise income tax at a reduced rate of 24 percent.

The Chinese government specifies that foreign-funded production enterprises scheduled to operate for a period of 10 years or more shall be exempted from income tax in their first two profit-making years and allowed a 50 percent reduction of income tax in the following three years. Chinese-foreign joint ventures engaged in the construction of ports and piers shall pay their income tax at a rate of 15 percent. A foreign-funded enterprise scheduled to operate for a period of 15 years or more shall be exempted from income tax in the first five profit-making years, and allowed a 50 percent reduction of income tax in the following five years.

Foreign-funded enterprises engaged in agriculture, forestry and animal husbandry, and those in remote, economically underdeveloped regions shall enjoy a reduction in and exemption from income tax in the same way as foreign-invested production enterprises and the Chinese-foreign joint ventures engaged in the construction of ports and wharves, and shall be allowed a 15 to 30 percent reduction in income tax for another 10 years following the expiration of the period for exemption and reductions upon approval of the application submitted by the foreign-invested enterprises.

If the output value of export products of a foreign-funded enterprise exceeds 70 percent of its total output value in the current year, it shall be allowed a 50 percent reduction of income tax upon the expiration of the period for exemption and reductions. If an enterprise whose products are for export and which has paid its income tax at a rate of 15 percent conforms to the above-mentioned conditions, it shall pay its income tax at a reduced rate of 10 percent. If a technologically advanced enterprise remains as such upon the expiration of the period for exemption and reductions, it shall be allowed a 50 percent reduction of the enterprise income tax for another three years.

(2) Refunding income tax for reinvestment means when a foreign investor of a foreign-funded enterprise reinvests

his or her profit obtained from the enterprise to increase registered capital, or takes it as an investment for another foreign-funded enterprise scheduled to operate for a period of not less than five years, he or she shall, upon approval by the tax authorities of an application filed by the investor, be refunded 40 percent of the income tax already paid on the reinvested portion.

III. Policy for Future Utilization of Foreign Capital

Opening wider to the outside world and increasing the level of foreign capital utilization are the Chinese government's basic principles for utilizing foreign capital. China has clearly stressed that it shall continue to put emphasis on the absorption of direct foreign investments while utilizing foreign capital, and shall adopt the following policy-guided measures:

1. Active Guidance of Foreign Investment and Further Optimization of Industrial Structure

In accordance with industrial policy, and the requirements for the readjustment and upgrade of the industrial structure, China will mainly encourage foreign investors to make investments in agriculture, new industries and high-tech industries, basic industries, infrastructure, environmental protection, export-oriented enterprises, along with the technological innovation of traditional industries and old industrial bases, and while bringing into full play their comparative advantages, continue to develop labor-intensive projects in conformity with industrial policy.

2. Further Expansion of Foreign Investment

China will further open competitive industries, expand foreign investments in petrochemical, construction and other industries, promote the opening of the service industry, and accelerate research into the formation of joint ventures and cooperative enterprises in mineral resources, tourism, foreign trade and telecommunications, as discussed in the talks on China's entering the World Trade Organization, and on the basis of the pilot projects in the retail, banking and insurance industries.

3. Gradual Extension of National Treatment to Foreign-funded Enterprises

National treatment is a basic principle in international exchange. Since the initiation of reform and opening to the outside world, the Chinese government, in order to absorb foreign investment, has adopted incentives that are more favorable than national treatment in terms of import and export rights, employment autonomy, the distribution system and taxation for foreign-funded enterprises. Practice has proven that these preferential measures have played an important role in absorbing foreign investments and importing advanced technologies. Along with the constant deepening of reform and opening to the outside world and the gradual building of the socialist market economic system, the contradictions between these policy measures and international practice and the fair competition principle of the market economy are becoming sharper, and have placed domestic-funded enterprises in a very unfavorable position in the fierce competition for market share. Foreign-funded enterprises enjoying national treatment has become the wide concern of enterprises of various ownership. Meanwhile the experiences of the several reforms of China's foreign tax system, after the adoption of the policy of reform and opening to the outside world, show that the adoption of a unified taxation policy for domestic and foreign enterprises will not reduce China's attractiveness to foreign investors, nor decrease the state's financial revenues. On the contrary, it will favor the creation of fair external environment for various kinds of enterprises, thus absorbing foreign investment at a higher level. Hence it requires that governments and departments at all levels shift viewpoints, by changing their former thinking on absorbing foreign capital through preferential policies of reducing taxes and conceding profits, and gradually abolishing the inequitable policies on the reduction of and exemption from taxes. This will result in a gradual shift from guidance by preferential policy to market guidance, and from preferential policy to national treatment in absorbing foreign capital, as well as absorbing foreign capital mainly through a favorable environment, a sound legal system, highly efficient management and attractive market conditions, rather than through preferential policies.

4. To Foster Greater Foreign Investment in Central and Western China

The policy making will continue to bring into full play its Eastern region's advantages in opening up and utilizing foreign capital, support it to actively develop capital- and technology-intensive industries and export-oriented industries, and continue the efficient administration of the special economic zones, Shanghai Pudong New Area, Suzhou Industrial Park Area and the various national economic and technological development zones. At the same time, the Chinese government will further encourage foreign investment in central and western China, opening these regions wider to the outside world. The Chinese government will encourage foreign investment in the coastal areas to reinvest in central and western areas, where a project whose foreign investment exceeds 25 percent of its total investment shall be regarded as a foreign-invested enterprise; and will further raise the proportion of the preferential loans offered by international financial institutions and foreign governments to central and western China. With the approval of the relevant departments of the State, superior industrial projects in central and western China could be listed as favored foreign-invested projects and enjoy preferential treatment, such as exemption from Customs duties, on imported equipment for use by these projects themselves, as well as value-added taxes in import, the restrictions over the conditions for the founding of strictly controlled projects and projects with the limited proportion of foreign stocks, and the restrictions over the market opening of them will be appropriately relaxed. The Chinese government will give priority to a number of agricultural, water conservancy, communications, energy, raw and processed materials and environmental protection projects in central and western China to absorb foreign capital, and strengthen these projects in terms of supporting capital and relevant measures, to encourage military enterprises that have been transferred into civil enterprises, and to help state-owned large and medium-sized enterprises begin technological innovation with foreign capital.

5. Implementing a Diversified Strategy to Absorb and Utilize Foreign Investment

In the future, China will absorb more investment from North America and Japan and lay stress on attracting business and importing foreign capital from the European Union. The Chinese government will actively start experiments with new forms of foreign investment, encourage state-owned large and medium-sized enterprises to reorganize their assets by using foreign capital in order to enliven these stock assets, actively develop processing and compensation trades, allow state-owned small enterprises and collective enterprises to be sold and permit privately owned enterprises to absorb foreign capital.

China should continue to run Chinese-foreign joint ventures, solely owned foreign enterprises and Chinese-foreign cooperative enterprises well, efficiently handle BOT project financing, actively and steadily issue stocks, gradually expand the scale of such investment, and pay great attention to the standardized management and experiments in transferring the operation rights (profit-making rights) of infrastructure facilities.

6. Boldly Introducing and Actively Guiding Investment by Transnational Companies

At present China absorbs foreign capital mainly from

foreign medium-sized and small enterprises. In the future, China should promote cooperation with transnational companies in accordance with their characteristics. China will continue to adopt the principle of exchanging technology with the market, further open the domestic market, and import applicable technology, capital and management skills, as well as operation and sales forms through cooperation with transnational companies, especially supporting China's large enterprises to cooperate with them. China will encourage the establishment of research and development centers in cooperation with transnational companies, strengthen the abilities of technological assimilation and innovation, and foster the common development of relevant enterprises and industries.

7. Offer Necessary Credit Support to Foreign-Invested Enterprises Conforming to the Loan Principle

It will help the Chinese side in foreign joint ventures in China to effectively make use of the capital market to collect capital through reorganizing state-owned assets, issuing stocks, and establishing investment funds and other forms, thus solving their fund resources.

8. Greatly Improving the Investment Environment and Strengthen Management of Foreign-invested Enterprises According to Law

While further improving the outside investment environment, China will spare no effort to improve the policy environment so as to further optimize the utilization of foreign capital. At present China will lay stress on greatly strengthening the building of the legal system, paying close attention to revising the existing laws and regulations on utilizing foreign capital, speeding up the formulation of BOT administration regulations; resolutely stopping all forms of unauthorized collection of funds from, and unjustified financial levies and fines on foreign-invested enterprises, truly protecting foreign-funded enterprises' autonomy in operation and management, and safeguarding legitimate rights and interests of investors so as not to infringe upon them; protecting workers' just rights and interests according to the law, and raising the work efficiency of government departments; improving and simplifying the process of examination and approval of foreign-funded projects in connection with deepening investment and financing systems; speeding up the building of a unified, open, competitive and orderly market environment, offering national treatment to foreign-funded enterprises; sternly cracking down on smuggling, counterfeiting, tax evasion and currency arbitrage, infringements on intellectual property rights and other illegal acts; strengthening supervision and administration according to the law, and perfecting the joint annual examination of foreign-invested enterprises.

Development of China's Tourism

Tourism is one of the new industries that have developed on the largest scale, with the brightest future, in the world today. It is also a sector of the economy which can spur the development of other industries. The level of development of tourism in a country or region is an important indicator of economic development, social progress and quality of life. Thanks to the efforts of the past 20 years, China's tourism has made world-renowned achievements. The total income from tourism increased from 2.25 billion yuan in 1978 to 343.8 billion yuan in 1998, with an average annual growth rate of 25 percent. In 1998, China's tourism overcame various unfavorable factors, including the financial crisis, growing by 10.2 percent over 1997, higher than the growth rate of the national economy, making up 4.2 percent of the GDP, thus demonstrating its strong vitality.

China is a country rich in tourist attractions. The ancient Great Wall, scenic Guilin, the Terra-cotta Horses and Warriors excavated from sites near Emperor Qin Shihuang's tomb, as well as its ancient and mysterious oriental culture, have all attracted numerous Chinese and foreign tourists. So far, China boasts 119 national level scenic areas and show place, 94 national level nature reserves, 12 national tourist resorts, 309 national level forest park, 99 famous historical and cultural cities at the national level, and 54 national outstanding tourism cities, including 21 UN natural and cultural heritage sites. A great number of tourist attractions in China provide great potential for the development of the country's tourism industry.

The Chinese government has attached great importance to the development of tourism, and has adopted several proactive policies. First, China has set up tourism development funds, which are mainly used to promote tourism and tourist products, and to train personnel. Second, China has strengthened investment in the infrastructure necessary for tourism and scenic sites, and improved the tourism environment. From 1978-1998 Chinese tourism utilized more than 370 billion yuan in social capital. Third, China has attached great importance to the development and construction of key tourist projects. In 1998, from 435 tourism projects, China selected 43 giving them priority in development. Fourth, the Chinese government has taken tourism as a new factor contributing to the development of the national economy, thus creating a favorable macro environment for the development of tourism.

China has also strengthened the promotion of tourism by launching a series of activities with special themes, i.e., the '93 Landscape and Scenic Tour, the '94 Historical Sites Tour, the '95 Folk Customs Tour, the '96 Holiday Tour, the '97 China Tourism Year, the '98 China City and Countryside Tour and the '99 Ecotour, which have all attracted a large number of domestic and foreign tourists and displayed China's rich and varied tourist attractions in an comprehensive way.

China has reinforced cooperation with tourist groups around the world, thus promoting its rich culture to the outside world. In 1998, China organized 17 large sale exhibitions, and 9 sale teams, and invited 48 groups of foreign tourism industry people and correspondents; held the '98 China International Tourism Fair, which gathered more than 1,300 tourist organizations and enterprises from 38 countries and regions, still the largest and best international tourism fair in the Asian-Pacific region; an advertisement on China's tourism was televised nearly 100 times through CNN, the largest broadcasting and TV network of the United States to directly promote China's tourism; China strengthened contacts with its main tourist-originating countries, met responsible officials of the WTO, attended the 47th Annual Meeting of the Asian-Pacific Tourism Association, signed tourism cooperation agreements with relevant countries, introduced changes in and promoted the development of China's tourism, intensified governmental and non-governmental tourism cooperation, and further extended the influence of China's tourism in the world.

The development of China's tourism has played an important role in the national economy. First, it has promoted the improvement of the industrial structure. At present, 24 provinces, autonomous regions and municipalities in China take tourism as their key and pillar industry. The total tourism output of Yunnan, Shaanxi and Zhejiang provinces makes up more than 5 percent of their respective GNPs; that of Beijing and Shanghai, 13 percent. Second, it has promoted social consumption. Now 75.61 percent of the Chinese people have a high quality of life, and people's demands for tourism are increasing. In 1998, Chinese people traveling within China totaled 694 million people/times, 64 percent, or 444.5 million people/times of whom were farmers. This fully indicates that the demand for tourism is extensive among this important section of the Chinese population. Third, tourism has increased employment. By the end of 1997, the international tourism industry of China directly and indirectly employed 8.16 million people, of whom Beijing's tourism industry absorbed 502,000 in 1997, making up 14 percent of the total employed in tertiary industries in Beijing, and 8 percent of the total employed in the municipality. The 2nd Report on the Study of State Conditions made by the Chinese Academy of Sciences predicts that by the year 2000 China's tourism industry will employ 20 million workers a year. Fourth, tourism has increased foreign-exchange earnings.

During the ten years from 1989 to 1998, the average annual growth rate of foreign-exchange earnings brought in by China's tourism industry was 23.7 percent, much higher than the world average which was 8.05 percent. In 1998, the total foreign exchange earnings of the China International Travel Service alone reached US$ 12.602 billion , an increase of 4.37 percent over the previous year, ranking seventh in the world, up one rank from the previous year. Fifth, tourism has cultivated financial resources. In areas with famous tourist attractions and advanced tourism, the proportion of tax revenue generated by tourism is becoming larger and larger. For instance, 60 percent of the financial revenues of Wuyishan City, Fujian Province, came from tourism; and from 1991 and 1995, taxes paid by the tourism industry of Zhoushan City, Zhejiang Province, reached more than 40 million yuan.

Thanks to the efforts of the past 20 years, China's tourism industry occupies a dominant position and cultivates competitive advantages in the international market; domestic demands for tourism are strong, promising a broad basic market, which will increase and stimulate overall consumption; tourism will promote economic and social prosperity; tourism needs to employ a large number of people, helping to alleviate employment pressures; and the uniqueness and irreplaceable nature of tourist attractions should lead to the rational and effective utilization of these national resources, thus promoting the balanced, harmony deve lopment of the regional economies, particular for the middle-west regional economies with abundant tourist resources.

Chinese government has attached high importance to the sustainable development of tourism, paid attention to the rational and effective utilization of the resouces. Now, Chinese government is adjusting and framing again the Tenth Five-Year Plan (2001-2005) of Chinese tourism. Chinese tourism is becoming a new mainstay of national economy.

中国投资体制的改革与投资环境的改善

China's Reform of the Investment System and Improvements in the Investment Environment

建国50年来，固定资产投资对国民经济的发展起到了极其重要的作用，体现在巩固国防建设，壮大经济实力，提高人民生活水平，推进技术进步和社会主义市场经济的建设等各个方面。当然，在探索中前进，也付出了代价。回顾过去，中国的固定资产投资建设大体经历了从无到有的创业阶段、起伏不定的发展阶段和改革开放后的突飞猛进阶段。

投资体制的改革

新中国建国初期开始建立的计划管理体制和1978年底中共十一届三中全会之后的投资体制，是伴随着国民经济和社会事业的发展，在反复探索和实践过程中，不断地得到改革和发展的。建国以来的50年里，大致经历了五个阶段：

一、高度集中的投资计划体制的形成时期（从1949年新中国成立到1957年）

这一时期，制定了《基本建设工作的暂行办法》，建立了计划管理机构，成立了专门为基本建设服务的中国人民建设银行，发布了《基本建设工程设计和预算文件审核批准暂行办法》以及基本建设工程设计任务书审查批准暂行办法，成立了建委，形成了高度集中的投资决策管理体制。这个时期以中央集中管理为特点，对基本建设经济、技术、计划、施工、财务和物资等方面进行统一的宏观调控，在解放初期面临的百废待兴的局面下，对于有效地集中全国人力和有限的财力、物力，开始有计划、有秩序地组织大规模的建设起了重要的作用，并为迅速地建立计划管理体系奠定了良好的基础。

二、集中、下放、再集中的不断变化与艰难曲折发展时期（1958-1979年）

1958年由于人民公社、大跃进运动的开始，为发挥地方投资积极性，随即开始了集中体制的第一次权力下放，投资则在1958年膨胀的基础上，1959年进一步膨胀，到1960年开始"调整、项固、充实、提高"，1961年在无法支撑高投资的情况下，两次调减投资计划，1962年开始了投资决策权力的第一次回收；从1963-1968年投资体制经历了一段相对稳定时期；1969年随着国有企业管理权限下放地方，投资的决策权也相应下放，受此影响，随后的两年又出现了投资规模的膨胀；从1972年提出要加强基本建设管理，投资管理权限有所上收，直至1979年，投资决策管理体制经历了一个相对稳定时期，体制上没有大的变化，投资除1978年头脑发热，大规模引进成套设备和技术，引发膨胀外，其他时候相对平稳。这一时期，由于国家工作重心以阶级斗争为主，决策中的失误比较多，付出了很大的代价。综上所述大致上有三个比较大的起伏变化：1958-1965年，围绕"权限下放"与"集中管理"进行探索和调整，由"下放"到"上收"；1966-1978年，"文化大革命"开始到粉碎"四人帮"前，全国基本建设工作受到挫折，遭到破坏，经济秩序混乱；1978年到中共的十一届三中全会召开之后，基本上属于恢复被"文化大革命"破坏了的建设领域秩序的时期。

三、投资体制改革初步启动时期（1980-1987年）

随着农村经济体制改革不断深入，投资体制改革也开始起步，简政放权、缩小指令性计划范围和建设实施市场化是这一时期改革的基本特点。经过几年的酝酿和在基本建设的某些环节进行改革试点的基础上，1984年，国家把改革基本建设管理体制，大力提高投资效益，作为经济体制改革的一个重要方面提到日程上来，同年中共

中国人民银行
People's Bank of China

十二届三中全会颁布了《中共中央关于经济体制改革的决定》，进一步明确了改革的方向、性质、任务和方针政策，对正在开展的建筑业和投资管理体制的改革起了决定性的推动作用，从而拉开了中国投资体制改革的序幕。经过几年的改革和实践，在以下几方面进行了一系列的改革，并取得了一定成效。

1. 实行“分灶吃饭”财政包干体制，改变建国以来由中央集中“统收统支”的财政分配体制，出现中央政府和地方政府两级利益主体，包括投资决策权在内的两级管理体制得到初步划分。随着国有企业实行经营承包制、乡镇企业的崛起和三资企业的出现，以往政府作为单一投资主体的局面开始被打破。

2. 在中央财政预算内对基建拨款实行“拨改贷”，使地方财政利用机动财力和预算外收入扩大基建投入，国内银行逐年扩大固定资产的投资贷款业务，开征国家能源交通重点建设基金和建筑税，企业利用自身积累的资金和折旧基金扩大投入，发行重点建设债券和企业债券，吸收国际金融组织和外国政府贷款，外商直接投资涌入等，使建设资金渠道迅速拓展，有偿使用的范围不断扩大。

3. 改进投资计划管理体制，开始编制全社会固定资产投资计划，对全社会的固定资产投资活动进行分类计划和指导，下放了固定资产投资项目的审批权限，简化了项目审批程序，进一步扩大了地方政府和企业的投资决策自主权。

4. 借鉴国际上先进的技术经济评价方法，重新规范建设项目前期工作的程序、内容和深度，将可行性研究执行及评估工作正式纳入项目决策程序。

5. 在建设施工领域里全面推行建设项目投资包干责任制，对勘察设计单位则推行技术经济承包责任制，并推进建筑材料和设备供应单位实现企业化经营，试行建筑安装工程招标投标和工程承包制，在建设实施领域里率先引入了市场竞争机制。

四、投资体制改革进一步深入时期（1988-1991年）

这一时期既是治理整顿时期，又是投资体制改革比较活跃的时期。建设领域盲目铺摊子、重复建设和投资膨胀的现象依然相当严重；在重点建设上，仍然没有改变中央包揽过多的局面，中央掌握的投资与承担的重点任务不相适应；而预算外投资受部门与地方利益的驱使，大量地投向一般加工工业和非生产性的楼堂馆所等的建设，以至于能源、原材料和运力不足的矛盾难以解决；在投资安排上，仍然主要采取行政办法，投资效益难以保证，针对这一系列问题，在总结前一阶段改革经验教训的基础上，1988年国务院颁发了《关于投资管理体制近期改革方案》，把投资体制的改革引向深入。1989年又颁发了《关于当前产业政策要点》，明确了国民经济各个领域中支持和限制的重点，加强了对投资结构的调整。这一阶段改革的主要内容是：

1. 对重大的长期的建设投资实行分层次管理，加重地方的重点建设责任。在这个方针指导下，面向全国的重要的建设工程，由中央或中央为主承担；区域性的重点建设工程和一般性的建设工程，由地方承担。并具体地划分了中央投资或以中央为主投资项目、地方投资项目的具体范围，采取了一些切实可行的经济办法，实行谁投资谁受益的原则，调动了地方兴办重点建设项目的积极性。

2. 扩大企业的投资决策权，使企业成为一般建设的投资主体，也是第一次有了投资决策权。企业第一次从旧体制的束缚中解放出来，在服从国家中长期计划、行业规划和国家法规的前提下，有权自主地筹措资金和物资；有权自主地把本企业的生产发展基金、折旧基金和其它自有资金捆起来使用；有权自主地选定投资方式和建设方案，进行可行性研究，委托评估，开展各项前期工作；有权自主地支配应得的投资收益。

3. 建立基本建设基金制，保证重点建设有稳定的资金来源。1982年国家在编制基本建设年度计划时，在基本建设项目中选择了一批基础工业和基础设施以及一些重大社会发展项目，按合理工期组织建设。这些重点建设项目，关系到国民经济发展后劲和国家财政的稳定增长，但投资大、建设周期长，为了保证重点建设有稳定来源，建立了中央基本建设基金，极大地促进了一批基础工业和基础设施以及一些重大社会发展项目的建成投产。

4. 成立投资公司，用经济办法对投资进行管理。为了塑造国家级投资主体，使其逐渐具有投资经营者的身份，保证国有资金的有效使用，1988年中央一级成立能源、交通、原材料、机电轻纺、农业、林业六个国家专业投资公司，负责经营、管理本行业中央投资的经营性固定资产投资项目。作为中央一级的投资经营企业，投资公司具有控股公司的职能，又承担国家政策性投资的职能。通过独立核算，用经济办法进行管理，逐步将建设工作中的行政关系改变为经济合同关系。

5. 制定正确的产业政策，明确国民经济各个领域中支持和限制的重点，加强对投资结构调整。改革后，投资规模迅速扩大，同时，在产业结构中也出现了较为严重的问题：农业、能源、原材料和交通运输等基础产业显得十分薄弱；一般加工工业生产能力过大，高水平的加工能力不足；出口产品结构层次低；产业的地区分布不够合理，企业组织结构分散，生产集中度差，专业化水平低等，既影响资源的合理配置和利用，又妨碍经济的稳定发展和宏观经济效益的提高。为此，制定了正确的产业政策，明确国民经济各个领域中支持和限制的重点，开始对投资结构进行调整。

五、投资体制改革攻坚时期（1992年至今）

以邓小平1992年南巡讲话为契机，中国进入了加快改革开放、加快经济建设的新的历史时期，也是经济增长速度最快、波动幅度最小的时期。作为事关改革与发展重要推动力和核心的投资问题及其体制改革，也再一次引起全国的极大关注。按照1992年中共十四大提出的建立社会主义市场经济体制改革的总目标，在全面深入分析研究14年投资体制改革的历史进程及经验教训的基础上，比较完整地提出了深化投资体制改革的方案及其实施步骤。远期方案的总体框架包括界定企业的产权关系、完善政府投资的管理与经营体制、划分各类投资主体的社会分工和建立投资间接调控体系等方面；投资体制近期改革的重点确定为：规范和强化国有单位投资主体的约束机制、改进与完善政府和企业的投融资体制、建立和健全政府对投资的间接调控体系。这一阶段的改革内容包括：

1. 健全以产业政策为基础的宏观调控体系，改进投资计划管理体制。根据市场、经济和社会发展趋势，制定近期和中长期的国家产业政策、技术政策和装备政策。对符合产业政策并达到规模经济的投资项目，国家在各个方面给予支持编制。投资计划的重点逐步从年度投资工作量计划转为年度投资资金计划，从资金源头入手对投资总量进行调控。

2. 明确投资主体分工，改革投融资方式。适应企业转机建制，特别是现代企业制度建立的要求，明确企业是一般生产性项目投资的基本主体。根据项目的行业特点及经济效益、社会效益和市场需求等情况，将投资项目划分为竞争性项目、基础性项目和公益性项目三大类。明确竞争性项目以企业为基本投资主体，投资活动推向市场，由企业通过市场筹资、建设和经营。基础性项目主要由中央及各级地方政府集中必要的财力、物力进行投资，并吸收企业和外商参与投资。公益性项目主要由各级政府运用财政资金安排建设，同时鼓励企业、个人投资兴办社会事业项目。

3. 组建国家开发银行，实现商业性投资贷款和政策性投资贷款相分离。以利于国家加强和改善投资宏观调控，在资金上保证国家重点建设的顺利实施。

4. 实行项目法人责任制和固定资产投资项目资本金制度，开始建立和规范投资主体的风险约束机制。

改革开放以来，投资领域发生了巨大的变化，表现为如下几个特点：

（1）投资主体多元化。1978 年以前，在高度集中的计划经济条件下，国家充当投资的唯一主体，政府统揽项目的决策权，企业仅仅是依附于各级政府的建设单位，没有任何投资的决策权、经营权。1980 年，在全社会固定资产投资中，国有单位在建项目总投资所占比重高达 95.5%，集体经济与个人投资在建项目总投资仅占不足 5%；在当年完成投资中，国有经济占全社会固定资产投资额的 87.9%。1984 年之后，国有经济投资主体的比例相对降低，非国有投资主体的比例逐步提高。国有经济投资主体的投资比例由 80 年代初的 81.9% 下降到 90 年代的 65% 左右。10 年降低了 16.9 个百分点，而非国有经济的比例由 18.1% 提高到 35% 左右。1998 年在全社会固定资产投资额中各种经济成份投资所占比例为：国有经济 54.1%、集体经济 14.8%、股份制经济 6.9%、联营经济 0.2%、港澳台经济 4.7%、外商经济 5.8%、个体经济 13.2%。多元化的投资主体已基本形成。

（2）投资资金多源化。在传统的投资体制下，国家不仅在投资主体上占据垄断地位，投资资金的使用方向也由中央政府的主管部门严格控制，充分地体现政府的意志。因而投资的资金来源单一，使用集中。1979 年以后，中国开始推进财政分配体制的改革，传统的统收统支被财政“分灶吃饭”和“基数包干”的改革所取代。中央银行预算内资金相当一部分改为“拨改贷”资金，地方部门以及企业筹集资金，支配资金的空间也大大扩展。1981-1988 年，国家预算内投资的年均增长速度只有 5.9%，而国内贷款的年均增长速度达 33.3%，自筹及其他投资的年均增长也保持了 22.7% 的速度，此后，国家进一步放宽了项目的计划管理权限，确定了吸引和利用外资的政策等。1981 年全社会利用外资的投资额仅为 36.36 亿元，1997 年则达到 2893.08 亿元，增长 78.6 倍，平均每年增长 31.5%。中国投资资金的来源构成发生了巨大变化，投资资金多源化的特点已十分显著。到 1997 年，在全社会固定资产投资额中：国家预算内投资 3%、国内贷款 19%、利用外资 11%、自筹资金 55%、其他投资 12%。

（3）投资决策分权化。随着项目审批权限的下放，投资的决策权也不再统一集中。从 80 年代开始，到 1992 年，政府对不违反产业政策的项目，又给予了企业自由决策权，至此，投资决策权开始由高度集中向相对分散化过渡，改革投资计划管理，扩大地方投资审批权，对自筹资金的指标适度控制等等措施的实行，使得地方政府开始具有了规定范围内的投资决策权，出现了中央政府、地方政府、各种经济类型的企业等多元投资主体并存的格局。各投资主体地位的差异，促使国家投资在实现宏观发展战略目标的同时，兼顾到投资的经营目标，地方投资在追逐政绩目标的同时，兼顾到社会福利，缓和就业压力的目标；企业投资则在比较利益导向下，在盈利、福利、政绩、就业竞争力等多目标中进行选择，出现投资目标多重化，投资决策分散化的格局。投资主体多元化和投资资金来源多源化的发展进程，从另外的角度也证实投资决策权力分散化。1981 年固定资产投资的资金来源中国家预算内拨款 269.76 亿元，占当年全社会固定资产投资 961.01 亿元的

28.1%，而1998年国家投资比重则降低到4.2%。相应国内贷款的比重由12.7%升至19.5%，利用外资由3.8%升至9.2%，自筹及其他投资由55.4%升至68.2%。由此看出由国家决策的投资越来越小，地方和企业自主经营的项目越来越多，投资决策分散程度加大。

（4）投资管理间接化。随着分散的投资格局逐步形成，市场在长期资源的配置方面发挥了越来越重要的作用。国家计划直接分配投资配置资源的职能越来越少，而主要依靠财政、金融等宏观经济政策对市场进行引导，再由市场来引导分散的企业投资。宏观调控与旧体制下的计划管理相比，难度和复杂性加大。基于这些深刻的变革，政府对宏观投资的管理方式，从依靠行政命令直接控制企业投资行为，开始转变为通过各项经济政策引导市场，进而间接影响企业投资行为；从依靠国家计划指标和项目审批等手段直接控制投资总规模和投资结构，转变为主要通过经济、技术及政策等手段间接调控投资总规模和投资结构，实现政府对社会投资管理方式的转变。

投资环境的改善

新中国成立以后，百业待兴，经济基础十分薄弱。1949年到1952年，在实行巩固国防、稳定物价和全面恢复、重点建设的经济总方针下，很快地治愈了战争创伤，并开始了部分重点建设。1950-1952年全国完成固定资产投资78亿元，中国建设的第一批能源项目，如鹤岗、辽源、阜新等几个煤矿，抚顺、小丰满电厂扩建，以及鞍钢、抚顺铝厂等原材料工业项目的改建都陆续开始进行。

“一五”时期，1953-1957年累计完成固定资产投资612亿元，年平均增长36.7%，这一时期以“156”项工程为重点，建成一批为国家工业化必需的冶金、汽车、机械、煤炭、石油、电力、电信、化学及国防等基础工业项目。国民经济的各种比例关系基本协调，生产与建设健康发展，人民生活明显改善。其中1956年建设规模搞得过大，当年全民所有制单位完成固定资产投资比上年增长52.8%，占国家财力的比重高达52.1%，导致物资紧张，只好增加进口，压缩固定资产投资。

“二五”时期，1958-1962年累计完成固定资产投资1307亿元，比“一五”时期增长一倍，年平均增长18.8%。在急于求成的“左”的错误思想指导下，脱离中国国情，违背经济发展的规律，盲目推行“大跃进”。1958年固定资产投资279亿元，比上年增长84.5%，其后两年继续扩大，1960年达到416亿元。1958年至1960年，固定资产投资占国家财力的比重高达60%以上，再加上自然灾害，农业大幅度减产，轻工业生产倒退，重工业仍继续调整发展，造成国民经济比例严重失调，整个国民经济处于十分艰难的境地。1961年中共八届九中全会确定对国民经济实行“调整、巩固、充实、提高”的八字方针，建设领域压缩投资规模，1961年固定资产投资减少到156亿元，削减62.5%，1962年继续压缩到87亿元，才使积累与消费比例严重失调有所缓解。

1963至1965年为经济调整时期，累计完成固定资产投资500亿元，仅相当1960年一年的投资，年平均增长36%，建设规模从大步后退到逐步回升，到1965年，固定资产投资达到217亿元，才恢复到1957年的水平。工农业失调状况有较大改善，积累与消费的比例也趋向正常，与此同时，开始建设一些新兴的电子、原子能、合成化学及日用塑料等工业，为国民经济继续发展打下了良好的基础。

“三五”时期，1966-1970年累计完成固定资产投资1209亿元，年平均增长3.6%，是各个计划时期增长速度最低的。1966年开始的“文化大革命”使正常的建设秩序被打乱，投资减少，1967年只有188亿元，比上年减少26.3%，1968年又减少到151亿元，投资效果也连年下降，1967年至1969年的固定资产交付使用率不到60%。

“四五”时期，1971-1975年累计完成固定资产投资2276亿元，年平均增长7.2%。在提出“备战备荒”的口号以后，开始了“三线”建设为主的大规模投资活动，投资骤增，消费与积累比例再度失调。1975年经过整顿后不久，经济状况有所好转。

“五五”时期，1976-1980年累计完成固定资产投资3186亿元，年平均增长5.3%。1976年粉碎“四人帮”后，又提出一些不切实际的奋斗目标，投资规模再度膨胀，给国民经济带来很大的冲击。1978年，中共十一届三中全会确立了改革开放方针以后，建设领域执行“调整、改革、整顿、提高”的方针，在合理安排建设规模、调整投资结构、加强重点建设方面做了大量工作，投资体制改革也做了积极探索和实践，并取得阶段性成果。

“六五”时期，1981-1985年全社会累计完成固定资产投资7998亿元，年平均增长19.4%。80年代，全国把工作重点转移到社会主义现代化建设上来，1982年中共十二大确定，把农业、能源和交通、教育、科学作为经济发展的战略重点。这时以电力建设为中心，开展了包括山西、安徽、内蒙古西部等煤炭基地，大秦铁路和秦皇岛港煤码头运煤大通道，上海宝钢一期工程为主要内容的大规模建设，加快了中国经济发展的步伐，为今后国民经济发展奠定了坚实的基础。

“七五”时期，1986-1990年全社会累计完成固定资产投资20594亿元，平均每年增长16.5%。各年增长率分别为18.7%、20.6%、23.5%、-8%和4.5%。投资总量在改革调整中经历了“增长、滑坡、回升”的波动过程，尤其是1989年因投资下降而导致市场疲软。1988年中共十三届三中全会决定进行治理经济环境、整顿经济秩序的工作，投资领域在坚持控制总量的同时，继续调整结构，压缩了一批楼堂馆所和一批高消费、低水平、重复生产的加工工业，基础产业有所加强。投资主体与投资渠道多元化趋势有了进一步发展。重点建设成就显著，5年累计完成投资1967亿元，平均每年增长33.4%。

“八五”时期，1991-1995年全社会累计完成固定资产投资63808亿元，年平均增长速度达36.9%。特别是在1992年邓小平南巡讲话和中共十四大精神指引下，加快固定资产投资领域的开发与建设，并取得了巨大的成就。这一时期是中国各个五年计划中重点建设搞得最好、成就最大的时期。能源和铁路运输的紧张状况得到缓解。国家还逐步加大了对机械电子、汽车、石化等支柱产业的投资。重点建设了上海、茂名、吉化30万吨乙烯、无锡微电子工程等项目。还在大江大河大湖治理、增加有效灌溉面积、建设大型生态防护林体系、重要农产品商品生产基地和支农工业方面进行了重点建设。

“九五”时期，1996-2000年前3年全社会累计完成固定资产投资76261亿元，年平均增长12.4%，这一时期主要开展了以铁路、高速公路、电站、通信设施等大规模基础设施建设，加工工业项目的建设已经大幅度减少。

50年来特别是近20年来，随着中国包括投资体制改革在内的各项改革的不断深化，固定资产投资在不断促进中国社会与经济稳步快速发展中，发挥了巨大的作用。1950-1998年共完成固定资产投资177993亿元，其中基本建设完成投资72125亿元，更新改造投资32516亿元。建成投产基本建设项目130万个，其中大中型项目约6200个，竣工各类房屋建筑面积232亿多平方米。

一、壮大了国家的经济实力

工业建设方面：通过50年大规模经济建设，中国建立起了工业品种繁多，门类齐全的工业生产体系，有的在产量上居世界前列，有的在技术上居于世界领先地位，为中国社会主义市场经济的建立、完善和发展提供了重要的物质基础。

1949年新中国成立后，从无到有，建立起中国的石油开采业、石油化工业，先后有一批特大和大型油田如大庆、华北、胜利、克拉玛依、塔里木、渤海以及南海油田等，原油产量居世界第五位，达1.6亿吨，形成了石油天然气集团总公司、石化集团总公司为主的石化加工体系。中国的钢产量从建国初期的60万吨达到目前一亿多吨，拥有世界产量最大的钢铁生产体系，以首钢、武钢、攀钢、宝钢、鞍钢等现代化的钢铁企业为代表，再加上一大批中小型钢铁企业，年产量已连续几年居世界第一位。一汽、二汽、上海大众、湖北神龙汽车等一批现代化汽车企业的建成投产，使得中国1998年汽车年产量达163万辆，生产能力达到240万辆。中国的发电机组容量共约2.5亿千瓦，年发电量11670亿千瓦小时，居世界第二位，仅次于美国。先后有葛州坝水电站、漫湾水电站、隔河岩水电站、庄于电厂、石洞口二电厂等重点项目建成投产；秦山和大亚湾核电站的建成，结束了中国大陆无核电的历史，标志着中国核电建设已取得重大突破；正在建设的三峡水利枢纽工程是世界上最大的水电站，目前已顺利实现大江截流，二期工程已经开始，它将成为一项具有防洪、发电、航运等巨大的经济和社会效益的跨世纪工程；黄河小浪底、二滩水电站等也将于近年建成发电。新增煤炭开采能力近8亿吨，煤炭产量最高达13亿吨，多年稳居世界第一位，建立了山西、内蒙古、黑龙江等煤炭基地。一大批水泥生产企业的水泥产量达到5.36亿吨，连续多年居世界第一位。建立了大批棉纺织和化学纺织企业，中国棉布和化学纤维的产量长期居世界第一位。除了基础产业和传统产业得到迅猛发展以外，特别是电子等新兴产业也象雨后春笋般地蓬勃发展起来，中国先后建成了一大批新型电子企业，电视机产量多年居世界第一位，电冰箱、空调器、洗衣机等电器产品产量也居世界前列，1998年全国生产微型电子计算机291万部。

农田水利建设方面：到1997年底全国兴修了大中小型水库8.5万座，水库总蓄水量4583亿立方米。建成灌区5579处，有效灌溉面积2249.5万公顷，治理水土流失面积7224.1万公顷，治碱面积661.2万公顷，堤防保护耕地面积3414.6万公顷，对抵御自然灾害起了重要作用。

交通运输邮电方面：到1998年底铁路营业里程5.76万公里，比解放初期2.2万公里增加3.56万公里，每年平均新增710公里。电气化里程达1.3万公里。先后建成重要铁路干线如包兰、兰新、宝成、成昆、湘黔、湘赣、浙赣线等，形成了五纵四横的铁路交通干线网。1997年建成投产的京九铁路，成为中国铁路建设史上规模最大、投资最多、一次性建成里程最长的铁路干线，全长2553公里，跨越9省市和98个市县。到1998年底全国公路里程达127.85万公里，比解放初增加119.55万公里，每年增加2.39万公里，已建成高速公路8733公里，主要有京津塘、沈大、沪杭甬、广深等，还有一大批高速公路正在建设。沿海主要港口货物吞吐量达9亿多吨，比1950年的872万吨增长了上百倍。上海港扩建成为逾亿吨大港，跨入世界领先行列。随着对外贸易的开展，不仅对原有的港口进行了大规模的改建和扩建，还开辟了防城、北仑、石臼、秦皇岛等新港区。民航事业也有了长足发展，新建、扩建和改建了143个民用机场。邮电新建、扩建了以北京为中心联接广大城乡的通信设施，建成局用交换机容量1.38亿门，电话机拥有量达1.3亿部，移动通信设备2386万部，建成了全世界第二大移动通信网。

二、提高了国民经济的技术装备水平

建国以来，尤其是改革开放以来，中国工业的技术水平和成套设备水平不断提高。在利用外资引进成套设备的同时，也引进了国外的先进技术、先进设备和管理经验，通过消化吸收，提高创新，大大提高了国产化水平。例如，上海宝山钢铁厂二期即达到600万吨钢的生产能力，三期提高到1000万吨钢以上，成为中国新建规模最大的现代化大型联合钢铁企业；著名的贵溪冶炼厂则是中国第一座年产20万吨铜的大型现代化的铜冶炼厂；山西化肥厂是中国现代化大型氮磷复合肥料基地；江苏仪征化纤公司生产工艺具有世界水平，最终缩聚生产能力达到了每天100吨，这在世界上也是少有的；北京正负电子对撞机属于高科技物理领域的项目，是中国自行设计，利用国产设备建造成功的第一台调整高速加速器和大型粒子探测仪；南沿海光缆、京太西兰乌光缆、京沈哈光缆等长途通信光缆工程，广泛使用了光纤通信、微波通信、卫星通信和程控交换技术等多种现代化通信手段；在民航建设中，3条航路实现高空二次雷达覆盖管制，在80个机场配置了91套仪表着陆系统，在120个机场和导航点安装了全向信标和测距设备，使航空技术水平得到极大提高。

三、调整了不合理的产业结构

改革开放前，针对重工业基础薄弱的状况，以重工业为重点进行了大规模的基本建设，使中国的产业结构发生了显著变化。1978年工业总产值占社会总产值的比重上升到61.9%，在工业总产值中，重工业产值比重由建国初期的26.5%上升到56.9%，基本形成了一个独立的比较完整的工业体系。

1979年以后，针对过去在经济建设中过分突出重工业，忽视了轻工业和人民生活方面的建设，以及重工业中能源、原材料工业和交通运输邮电业比较薄弱等问题，进一步调整了投资结构。近20年国有单位用于轻工业建设的投资6567亿元，将前26年轻重工业之比1:9改变为1:4.7。国有单位用于能源建设投资16289亿元，年平均增长速度为21%；交通运输业投资11137亿元，年平均增长22%；邮电通信业投资4216亿元，年平均增长38%，大大超过其他行业的平均发展速度。通过调整投资方向，国民经济的薄弱环节得到一定的加强。

四、改善了人民的物质和文化生活条件，改变了城市面貌

改革开放以来，对住宅、文教卫生、城市公用设施等方面进行了大量投资。1979年至1997年，住宅建设投资达32417亿元，占全社会固定资产投资的23%。建成住宅建筑面积161亿平方米，城市人均居住面积从1978年的3.6平方米增加到1998年的9.3平方米；农村人均居住面积从1978年的8.1平方米增加到1998年的23.7平方米。城市公用设施也有很大发展。到1998年全国城市自来水普及率为96%，城市用气普及率达78.8%，1998年电话普及率10.6%，城市每百人拥有电话30部。

Since the founding of the People's Republic of China 50 years ago, investment in fixed assets has played an extremely important role in consolidating the national defense, expanding the economic strength, improving people's livelihood, and promoting the progress of science and technology and the construction of the socialist market economy –in short, in the development of the national economy as a whole. Of course, prices were paid in the wake of advancement while exploring ways to develop investment in fixed assets. The development of China's investment in fixed assets in the past 50 years has gone through a pioneering stage, then a stage of development with ups and downs, and finally a stage of remarkable progress after the reform and opening policy was initiated.

The Reform of the Investment System

The planning and management system established in the early days of New China and the investment system that appeared after the convocation of the Third Plenary Session of the 11th Central Committee of the Chinese Communist Party at the end of 1978 have seen constant reforms and development through repeated explorations and practices, following the development of the national economy and other socialist undertakings. In the past 50 years, the development of the planning and management system and the investment system can be divided into five stages:

I. The formation of a highly-centralized investment and planning system that lasted from October 1949, when New China was founded, to 1957

During this period, the government drew up *The Provisional Measures for the Work of Capital Construction;* set up planning and management institutions and the Chinese People's Bank of Construction specializing in serving capital construction; and issued *The Provincial Measures for the Examination and Approval of Documents on the Design and Budget of Capital Construction Projects* as well as provisional methods for the examination and approval of letters of task for the design of projects.

The government also established the State Construction Commission, forming a highly-centralized investment decision-making and management system characterized by a centralized management by the central authorities. The system played an important role in exercising a unified macro control over economy, technology, planning, project construction, finance, and materials concerning basic facility projects and in amassing in an effective way the nation's manpower and limited financial and material resources to start a large-scale construction in a planned, orderly manner in the early days of Liberation when many things in China were waiting to be done. The system also laid a solid foundation for a quick establishment of the planning and management system.

II. The centralization, transfer of power to lower levels, and re-centralization in the period of development with constant changes and twists and turns from 1958 to 1979

In 1958, The people's communes were set up and the Great Leap Forward started. To give free rein to local initiatives in investment, the power of the centralized investment system was delegated to the lower levels for the first time. In 1959, investment further expanded on the basis of the expansion in 1958, which forced the central government to adopt measures of adjustment, consolidation, substantiation, and enhancement.

In 1961, seeing that there was no way to continue propping up high investments, the central government twice cut down its investment plan, and in 1962, began to take back its power of investment decision-making once delegated to the lower levels. The investment system remained comparatively stable from 1963 to 1968. In 1969, the power of decision-making in investment was transferred to the lower levels together with the power of management of State-owned enterprises, which was followed by another two years of expansion of investment scale.

In 1972, the central government strengthened its management of capital construction and retrieved part of the delegated power over investment management. China's investment management system experienced a stable period from 1972 to 1979, except in 1978, when large-scale introduction of foreign equipment and technology triggered another round of bloated investment. In this period, the State centered its focus of work on class struggle. There were many mistakes in decision-making for which the nation paid a high price. In short, there were three big ups and downs. The years from 1958 to 1965 were a period of exploration and readjustment of the power transfer to the lower levels and centralized management over the investment system. From 1966 to 1978, the whole nation was plunged into the ten-year Cultural Revolution, and then the "gang of four" was crushed. In this period, capital construction in the country as a whole suffered damage and setbacks, and the economic order was in chaos. The years after the convocation of the Third Plenary Session of the 11th CPC Central Committee in 1978 were a period of restoration of the order in the construction field disrupted by the Cultural Revolution.

III. The years from 1980 to 1987 marked the initial period of the reform of the investment system

With the deepening of the reform of the economic system in rural China, the reform of the investment system began and was characterized by streamlining administration, instituting decentralization, reducing the scope of mandatory plans, and establishing an investment market. In 1984, based on several years' deliberation and experiments of the reform of some links in capital construction, the State began working on the reform of the management system of capital construction and the enhancement of investment results as an important aspect of economic reform. In the same year, the Third Plenary Session of the12th CPC Central Committee issued *A Decision of the CPC Central Committee on Economic Reform.* The decision further expounded the direction, nature, tasks, policies, and principles of the reform, gave impetus to the reform then being carried out in the building industry and the system of investment management, and ushered in the reform of China's investment system.

Over the past several years, reforms have been conducted and achievements made in the following aspects:

1. The implementation of "serving different diners from different pots," namely a contract system in which the central government and the local governments were responsible for their own finances, thus changing the system practiced since the founding of New China, in which the central government was responsible for both revenue and expenditure. A two-level management system of the central and local governments, including investment decision-making, was established. The situation in which the government acted as the unitary main body of investment was broken in the course of the practice of the contract system in the State-owned enterprises and the rise of rural industry and the three types of foreign-funded enterprises.

2. The allocation of funds for capital construction within the central financial budgets changed to loans. The channel of fund raising for capital construction and the scope of compensable use of the capital construction funds

were broadened with the expansion of the investment in capital construction by the local governments using their stand-by financial resources and extrabudgetary income; the year-by-year increase of investment in fixed assets loans and the collection of the construction-fund tax and construction tax on the State's major energy and communications projects by domestic banks; the construction of projects by enterprises using their own accumulation and depreciation funds; the issue of major project construction bonds and enterprise bonds; the loans from international financial institutions and foreign governments; and the inflow of funds from foreign investors.

3. Improving the system of investment planning and management, drawing up a plan of investment in fixed assets for the whole society, planning and giving instructions to investment in fixed assets activities carried out by the whole society according to their classifications, delegating the power to examine and approve the projects of fixed investment, simplifying the procedures of examination and approval, and further extending the power of the local governments and enterprises to make their own decisions on investment.

4. Using advanced international methods of technological and economic appraisals to re-standardize the procedures of the work and the content and degree of depth of projects before construction started and including the conduct of feasibility studies and appraisals in the procedure of decision- making on projects.

5. Implementing in an all-round way the responsibility system in project construction and the responsibility system of technological and economic results in project survey and designing, promoting business management in construction materials and equipment supply, experimenting with public bidding and tendering in project installation and the contract system in project construction, and introducing the mechanism of market competition into the building construction industry.

IV. The investment system was carried out in a deep-going way from 1988 to 1991

This period was characterized by the reorganization and improvement of the investment system and the active implementation of reform. There were still the serious problems of rash launching of new projects, construction of duplicate projects, and investment expansion. In the construction of major projects, the situation in which the central government took on too many things remained unchanged, and there existed a disharmony between the amount of investment under the control of the central government and the tasks it shouldered for the construction of major projects. Prompted by the interests of different departments and regions, a huge amount of extrabudgetary investment was made in the construction of ordinary processing enterprises as well as office buildings, auditoriums, hotels, and guest houses.

It was difficult to solve the shortages of energy and raw materials and the insufficiency of transport capacity The arrangement of investment was mainly through administrative means, making it hard to guarantee investment results. In 1988, in view of the existing problems and the experiences and lessons learned in the reform, the State Council promulgated *An Immediate-Term Plan for the Reform of the System of Investment Management,* pushing a deeper implementation of the reform of the investment system. In 1989, the State Council issued *The Gist of the Current Industrial Policies,* clearly delineating which fields in the national economy should be supported or restricted and strengthening the readjustment of the investment structures. From 1988 to 1991, reform was mainly carried out in the following ways:

1. The implementation of investment management of major long-term projects at different administrative levels

and increasing the weight of responsibilities on local governments for the construction of major projects. The central government was completely responsible or accepted most of the responsibility for important projects constructed in the interest of the whole nation. Local authorities were in charge of the construction of regional projects, major and ordinary. A specific scope was worked out for the projects the central government invested in or acted as the main investor for and those invested in by local authorities. Practical and effective economic measures were adopted for practicing the principle of letting the investors receive benefits, thus arousing the enthusiasm of the local governments for investing in major projects.

2. Increasing the right of enterprises to make decisions on investment and making them the main investors in ordinary projects. For the first time, the enterprises freed themselves from the shackles of the old system, and they had the right to raise funds and materials; to combine the use of production development funds, depreciation funds, and other money they had; to choose the methods of investment and the plans of construction; to carry out feasibility studies, appraisals on commission, and pre-construction work; and to dispose of investment returns due to them on the condition that they follow the State's medium- and long-term plans, programs of various trades, and State laws and regulations.

3. The establishment of the system of capital construction fund to ensure that major construction projects had stable financial sources. In 1982, when drawing up the annual plan for the projects of capital construction, the State selected a batch of basic-industrial and basic-facility projects and major projects for social development and organized their construction according to a rational time limit. These projects had a bearing on the development of the national economy and the steady growth of the State revenue, but they required large investments and a long construction time. To guarantee a stable source of funds for the major projects, a central basic-facility construction fund was established, thus markedly promoting the construction and commissioning of a number of basic-industrial and basic-facility projects and major projects for social development.

4. The founding of investment companies to manage investment by economic means. In 1988, to form a State-level investment main body, enable it to obtain the status of an investment operator, and ensure an effective use of State-owned funds, six central-level special companies were set up to be responsible for the operation and management of the investment projects funded by the central governments in the fields of energy, communications, raw materials, electric machinery, textiles, light industry, agriculture, and forestry. These central-level special investment companies had the function of proprietary companies and operated State investments that were permitted by policy. They conducted management by such economic means as independent accounting, trying to gradually change the administrative relations in the construction industry to relations of economic contracts.

5. The formulation of correct industrial policies, making clear which key points in the fields of the national economy should be supported or restricted and strengthening the readjustment of the investment structures. After the reform was implemented in China, the scale of investment expanded rapidly. Meanwhile, serious problems appeared in the industrial structure. The basic industrial sectors, such as agriculture, energy, raw materials, communications, and transportation, were very weak. The ordinary processing industries had a production capacity that exceeded the demand but lacked high-level processing capability. The products exported were low-grade. There was an irrational regional distribution of the industry, a dispersed organizational structure of enterprises, a poor con-

centration of production, and a low grade of specialization, affecting the rational allocation and utilization of resources and hindering a stable economic development and the enhancement of macro economic results.

V. The years from 1992 onward have marked a period for the reform of investment system

Following the publication of the speeches Deng Xiaoping made during his inspection tour of South China in 1992, China entered a new historic era in which the reform and opening policy and the economic construction have been carried out in an accelerated way. This period also marks the fastest economic growth with the minimal fluctuation of any period. The question of investment and the reform of the investment system, and the driving power and core of the reform and development caught the attention of the whole nation. In accordance with the general target put forward by the 1992 14th CPC National Congress, namely, the establishment of a socialist market economic system, and based on the analysis of the reform of the investment system during the previous 14 years and the summary of the experiences and lessons in the reform, a complete plan and a series of specific steps to deepen the reform of the investment system was worked out. The long-term plan includes clearly demarcating the property right of enterprises, perfecting the system of managing and operating government investment, dividing the work of the main investment bodies, and establishing an indirect system for regulating investment. The most pressing needs of the immediate-term reform of the investment system are to standardize and step up the mechanism of constraint for the State-owned main investment bodies, to improve the government and enterprise investment and fund-raising systems, and to establish and improve a system for the government's indirect regulation over investment. In the years since 1992, the reform has been, and is to be, carried out in the following ways:

1. Improving the macro regulation system on the basis of the industrial policies and the management system of investment plans, drawing up the State's immediate- and long-term industrial, technological, and equipment policies in line with the trend of development of the market, the economy, and the society. The State gives various kinds of support to investment projects that conform to the industrial policy and are up to the economy of scale. The stress on investment plans should gradually shift from the plan of the annual amount of invested work to the plan of the annual invested capital, starting with the source of capital, to regulate the total amount of investment.

2. It was clearly defined the division of the work of main investment bodies and the reform of the means of investment and fund-raising. To meet the demands of the change of operational mechanism of enterprises and the establishment of enterprise system, especially the establishment of modern enterprise system, it was made clear that enterprises are the basic investment bodies of ordinary production projects. The investment projects are divided into three categories-competitive, basic, and public welfare-according to their characteristics, the economic and social results, and the demands of the market. It was also made clear that enterprises are the basic investment bodies of competitive items, and enterprises conduct fund-raising, construction, and management through the market.

The basic projects are mainly invested in by the central and local governments by pooling necessary financial and material resources and attracting investments by enterprises and foreign investors. The construction of projects for public welfare is mainly carried out by governments at various levels with local funds. Enterprises and individuals are encouraged to invest in the development of social undertakings.

3. Setting up the State Development Bank and sepa-

上海南浦大桥
The Nanpu Bridge in Shanghai

rating commercial investment and loans from policy-permitted investment and loans so that the State may strengthen and improve its macro regulation over investment and ensure a smooth construction of the State's major projects.

4. Implementing the responsibility system of legal persons in project construction and the capital system in the investment projects and establishing and standardizing the mechanism of risk-taking restraint for the main investment bodies.

Since the implementation of the reform and opening policy, the tremendous changes that have taken place in the field of investment are as follows:

(1) The multiplication of main investment bodies. Before 1978, under the highly centralized planned economy, the State took on the decision-making on all projects as the sole main investment body. The enterprises that attached themselves to the government at various levels were only work units to carry out project construction. They had neither the power to make decisions nor the right to operate projects. In 1980, the investment by State-owned units in the projects then under construction made up 95.5 percent of the total investment in fixed assets by the whole society, and the investment in the above said projects by the collective-owned economy and by individuals accounted for less than five percent. The State-owned economy ac-

counted for 87.9 percent of the total investment in fixed assets completed by the whole society in the same year.

After 1984, the State-owned economy as the main investment body dropped its proportion of the investment in fixed assets by the whole society while the proportion by the non-State-owned economy increased. The proportion of investment by the State-owned economy dropped from 81.9 percent in the early 1980s to 65 percent in the 1990s, and the proportion of investment by the non-State-owned economy went up from 18.1 to about 35 percent in the corresponding period. In 1998, the proportions of the investment in fixed assets by various economic elements were 54.1 percent by the State-owned economy, 14.8 percent by the collective-owned economy, 6.9 percent by the share-holding economy, 0.2 percent by the jointly-operated economy, 4.7 percent by companies from Hong Kong, Macao, and Taiwan, 5.8 percent by foreign firms, and 13.2 percent by individuals. The multiple investment bodies basically took shape.

(2) Multiple sources of investment funds. Under the old investment system, the State held a monopoly position as the main investment body and the central government exercised strict control over the use of the investment funds. As a result, there was a unitary source and a centralized use of investment funds. After 1979, China began to reform its financial allocation system, and the traditional unified control over State revenues and expenditures was replaced by "serving meals to different diners from different pots," namely, the system of dividing revenues and expenditures between the central and local governments and holding each responsible for its basic quota of finance. A considerable amount within the budget at the central bank was changed from allocated funds into loans. There was a bigger flexibility for the local departments and enterprises in the matter of raising or disposing of funds by themselves.

From 1981 to 1988, the annual increase of investment within the State budget was 5.9 percent, the annual increase of loans reached 33.3 percent, and the annual increase of self-raised and other investment remained at 22.7 percent. The State further relaxed its control over project planning and management and defined the policy on the introduction and utilization of foreign funds.

In 1981, the amount of foreign funds used in China was 3.636 billion yuan. The figure rose to 289.308 billion yuan in 1997, 79.6 times that of 1981, or a yearly increase of 31.5 percent. There was a great change in the source of investment funds. By 1997, of the fixed investment by the whole society, three percent was from funds within the State budget, 19 percent came from domestic loans, 11 percent was from foreign fund, 55 percent was from self-raised fund, and 12 percent was from other investments.

(3) Decentralized investment decision-making. With the transfer of the power of project examination and approval to the lower levels, there was no more unitary centralized decision-making on investment. From the 1980s to 1992, the central government entrusted the enterprises with the authority to make decisions themselves on projects not in violation of industrial policy. Up to then, the investment decision-making began to transit from high-centralization to comparative decentralization. The reform of investment planning and management, the expansion of local power of project examination and approval, and the practice of a moderate control over the quota of self-raised funds enabled local governments to make decisions on investment within a stipulated scope.

There appeared a coexistence of multiple investment bodies-the central government, the local governments, and various economic enterprises. The difference of the positions of investment bodies spurred the central government to realize the objective of a macro development strategy in investment while giving consideration to the investment operations objective, spurred the local governments to pursue an objective of achievements while taking into account the social welfare and the objective of easing employment pressure, and spurred the enterprises to choose between profit, welfare, achievements, competitive power of employment, and other objectives.

The result was the appearance of multiple investment objectives and decentralized investment decision-making. The process of the development of multiple investment bodies and multiple sources of investment funds confirmed from another angle the decentralization of investment decision-making. Of the 1981 investment in fixed assets, 26.976 billion yuan was allocated from funds within the State budget, accounting for 28.1 percent of the total investment in fixed assets that year in China. The percentage dropped to 4.2 percent in 1998.

Meanwhile the proportion of domestic loans in the yearly investment in fixed assets rose from 12.7 percent in 1981 to 19.5 percent in 1998, that of foreign funds from 3.8 percent to 9.2 percent, and that of self-raised and other funds from 55.4 percent to 68.2 percent. The projects invested in by the State diminished, the projects operated by the local governments and enterprises increased, and the degree of decentralization in investment decision-making became higher.

(4) Indirect management of investment. With the formation of a decentralized investment setup, the market played an increasingly important role in the allocation of long-term investment resources. The State became weaker in its function of directly allocating the resources of investment according to the State plan. Under this system, the State guides the market by means of financial and other macro economic policies and the market then guides the investment by enterprises. Macro regulation is more difficult and more complicated than the planned management that was practiced under the old system. Based on the above-mentioned deep reforms, the mode of macro management exercised by the central government over the investment activities of enterprises began to change from direct control by issuing administrative orders to guiding the market and then indirectly influencing the investment activities of enterprises with economic policies, from direct control over the scale and structure of investment through issuing the quota of the State plan and the procedure of project examination and approval to indirect control over the scale and structure of investment by means of economic, technological, and policy measures.

Investment Environment Improved

After the founding of New China, its economic basis was very weak, and much remained to be done. From 1949 to 1952, under the general economic principle of consolidating national defense, stabilizing prices and all-round restoration with stress on key projects, the Chinese people quickly healed the wounds of wars, and began construction of some key projects. From 1950-1952, China fulfilled investment in fixed assets of 7.8 billion yuan. Several coal mines in Hegang, Liaoyuan and Fuxin, as well as power plants in Fushun and Xiaofengman, were expanded. In addition, Anshan Iron and Steel Works, Fushun Aluminum Factory and other raw materials industrial projects were reconstructed.

The First Five-Year Plan (1953-1957) achieved accumulated investment in fixed assets of 61.2 billion yuan, with an annual average growth rate of 36.7 percent. It highlighted 156 projects badly needed by State industrialization in the fields of metallurgy, automobile, machinery, coal, petroleum, power, telecommunications and chemical industry and national defense. The proportional relationship of various economic sectors was basically coordinated; production and construction developed healthily; and people's living standards improved significantly. But 1956 saw the overdevelopment of construction scale. That year, investment in fixed assets by units of public ownership was 52.8 percent over the previous year, accounting for 52.1 percent of the state financial resources. This situation resulted in the shortage of materials and goods, increased imports and the reduction in fixed assets investment.

The Second Five-Year Plan period (1958-1962) fulfilled investment in fixed assets of 130.7 billion yuan, double that of the previous five years, with an annual average growth rate of 18.8 percent. Guided by the wrong ideology of "Left" deviationism that was divorced from the country's actual conditions and went against the rule of economic development, the "great leap forward" was blindly launched. Investment in fixed assets in 1958 amounted to 27.9 billion yuan, 84.5 percent higher than the previous year. The situation lasted two years, with the figure in 1960 reaching 41.6 billion yuan. Between 1958 and 1960, the proportion of fixed assets investment from the state financial resources was as high as 60 percent. Moreover, China suffered serious natural calamities which led to a big drop in agricultural output and the retrogression of light industry, but heavy industry continued to develop amidst readjustment. The whole national economy was in a very difficult position. In 1961, the Ninth Plenary Session of the Eighth Central Committee put forward the eight-character principle of "readjustment, consolidation, filling out and raising standards." The investment scale in fixed assets in 1961 was reduced to 15.6 billion yuan, a decrease of 62.5 percent, and that in 1962 was cut to 8.7 billion yuan, easing somewhat the imbalance between accumulation and consumption.

The 1963-1965 period was the one of economic readjustment. Accumulated investment in fixed assets amounted to 50 billion yuan, or equivalent to the investment in 1960, with an annual average growth rate of 4.6 percent. The scale of construction began rising again from falling back. By 1965, investment in fixed assets amounted to 21.7 billion yuan, returning to the 1957 level. The imbalance between industry and agriculture improved considerably, and the disproportion between accumulation and consumption tended to be normal. Meanwhile, some new industries related to electronics, atomic energy, synthesized chemicals and daily plastics, appeared, laying a good foundation for economic development.

The Third Five-Year Plan (1966-1970) fulfilled investment in fixed assets of 120.9 billion yuan, with annual average growth of 3.6 percent, representing the lowest growth rate compared with other five-year plan periods. The "cultural revolution," which started in 1966, brought chaos to normal construction, and investment was reduced. In 1967, it stood at only 18.8 billion yuan, 26.3 percent less than the previous year. In 1968, it fell further to 15.1 billion yuan. From 1967 to 1969, the rate of fixed assets available for use was less than 60 percent.

The Fourth Five-Year Plan (1971-1975) achieved investment in fixed assets of 227.6 billion yuan, with an annual average growth rate of 7.2 percent. After putting forward the slogan of "being prepared against war and being prepared against natural disasters", large-scale investment was concentrated on construction of the "third line" (remote regions away from coastal areas). This resulted in the sharp increase of investment. Consumption and accumulation was again out of proportion. After rectification, 1975 saw a favorable turn of the economic situation.

The Fifth Five-Year Plan (1976-1980) saw investment in fixed assets of 318.6 billion yuan, with annual average growth rate of 5.3 percent. After the "Gang of Four" was smashed in 1976, some unrealistic objectives were put forward again, which led to investment scale swelling, and the normal development of the national economy being adversely affected. Soon after the Third Plenary Session of 11th Party Central Committee decided to launch the reform and opening program in 1978, the central government carried out the principle of "readjustment, reform, rectification and enhancement" in the field of construction. Much work was done in proper arrangement of construction scale, readjustment investment structure and strengthening key project construction. Active exploration and practice were also made in reform of investment system, and many achievements were made.

The Sixth Five-Year Plan (1981-1985) witnessed investment in fixed assets of 799.8 billion yuan with annual average growth rate of 19.4 percent. During the 1980s, the focus of the work was shifted to construction of socialist modernization. In 1982, the 12th National Party Congress set agriculture, energy, communications, education and science as the strategic focus of the national economy. Centering on power construction, China launched large-scale construction of coal bases in Shanxi, Anhui and western Inner Mongolia, the Datong-Qinhuangdao railway and the Qinhuangdao coal port, and the first-phase of Shanghai Baoshan Steel and Iron Company, laying a solid foundation for future development of the national economy.

The Seventh Five-Year Plan (1986-1990) achieved investment in fixed assets of 2059.4 billion yuan, with annual average growth rate of 16.5 percent. The growth rate of each year in the period was 18.7 percent, 20.6 percent, 23.5 percent, -8 percent and 4.5 percent respectively. The total amount of investment fluctuated—growth, drop and rise again. Particularly in 1989, the market was weakened after the drop of investment. In 1988, the Third Plenary Session of the 13th Central Committee decided to rectify the economic order. While persisting in the control of the total amount of investment, China continued to readjust its economic structure, with stress on cutting down luxury building projects incompatible with state financial resources, as well as projects consuming high levels of energy and with a low production level, along with redundant projects. As a result, basic industries were strengthened. Meanwhile, the trend of diversifying investors and channels were further developed. Remarkable achievements were made in major investment fields. In the five years, the investment totaled 196.7 billion yuan, with annual average growth rate of 33.4 percent.

During the Eighth Five-Year Plan (1991-1995), particularly in 1992, guided by the speeches of Deng Xiaoping during his tour to south China and the spirit of 14th National Party Congress, China quickened the pace of development and construction in the field of investment in fixed assets with remarkable achievements greater than any other five-year plan periods. The whole society fulfilled investment in fixed assets of 6,380.8 billion yuan, with annual average growth rate of 36.9 percent. Energy shortages and railway transport bottlenecks were reduced. The state gradually made more investment in pillar industries including machinery, electronics, automobiles and petrochemical sectors. Key projects were 300,000-ton ethylene works in Shanghai, Maomin and Jihua, and Wuxi micro-electronics factory. Besides, efforts were made to harness rivers and lakes, increase effective irrigated areas and build large-scale biological shelter-forests. Investments were also pooled to build agricultural produce production bases and farm-supporting industries.

The Ninth Five-Year Plan spans 1996 to 2000. In the first three years, the whole society fulfilled investment in fixed assets of 7,626.1 billion yuan, with annual average growth rate of 12.4 percent. Construction focused on railways, expressways, power stations, telecommunications facilities. Processing industrial projects were reduced by a big margin.

In the past 50 years, particularly in the past 20 years, along with the deepening of various reform measures including the investment system, investment in fixed assets has played a significant role in promotion of social and economic development. Between 1950-1998, China fulfilled investment of 17,799.3 billion yuan, of which, 7,212.5 billion yuan went to the investment in capital construction, and 3,251.6 billion yuan to upgrading and transformation projects. Some 1.3 million capital construction projects were completed, of which 6,200 were large and medium-sized projects, with total floor space of 23.2 billion square meters in different kinds of factory buildings.

I. Strengthening the national economy

Industrial construction: after 50 years of large-scale economic construction, China has established a complete industrial system, producing a wide range of industrial products. Some products lead in the world in their output and some take leading positions technically in the world, providing an important material basis for the establishment, perfection and development of the socialist market economy.

After the founding of New China in 1949, China established oil exploration and petrochemical industries. A number of extra-large and large oil fields, including Daqing, Huabei, Shengli, Karamay, Tarim, Bohai and Hainan oilfields, have emerged. Annual crude oil output is now 160 million tons, ranking fifth in the world, forming an oil-gas incorporation and a petrochemical processing system headed by the petrochemical group company.

China's steel output has jumped from 600,000 tons in earlier stage of New China to more than 100 million tons so far. It now boasts the world's largest production capacity, represented by Shoudu, Wuhan, Panzhihua, Baoshan and Anshan modern steel companies, accompanied by a large number of medium-sized and small steel companies. The total steel output has ranked first in the world for several years.

After the founding of a group of modern automobile enterprises, including China's No.1 and No.2 motor vehicle plants, Shanghai Volkswagen, Hubei Citroen Fukang, China's motor vehicle output in 1998 reached 1.63 million, with production capacity hitting 2.4 million. China's generator capacity totaled 250 million kw, with annual generated energy reaching 1167 billion kwh, ranking second in the world next to the United States. A number of key power projects, such as Gezhouba Hydropower Station, Manwan Hydropower Station, Geheyan Hydropower Station, Zhuangyu Power Station and Shidongkou No.2 Power Station, have been completed and gone into operation. The completion of Qinshan and Daya Bay nuclear power stations indicated China has made major breakthroughs in its nuclear power construction. The Three Gorges Key Water Control Project, which is under construction, is the largest hydropower station in the world. It has been successful in damming the river so far, and the second phase of the project has started. It will become a cross-century project that will produce tremendous economic and social results through its functions of flood prevention, generating energy and navigation. The Xiaolangdi Hydropower Station and Ertan Hydropower Station are near completion. China has increased its coal mining capacity by 800 million tons due to completion of a number of coal bases in Shanxi, Inner Mongolia and Heilongjiang, and it has had annual maximum coal production of 1.3 billion tons, taking first place in the world for many years. China now has a large number of cement producing enterprises, with total output reaching 536 million tons, first in the world for many years. Due to completion of a large number of cotton textile and chemical fiber enterprises, China's cotton cloth and chemical fiber output has long ranked first in the world. Apart from the rapid development of basic industries and traditional industries, many newly rising industries such as electronics have sprung up like bamboo shots after a spring rain. China now has many electronic enterprises, with TV set output ranking first in the world for many years. Refrigerators, air conditioners, washing machines and other household appliances have reached the forefront. In 1998, a total of 2.91 million micro-computers were produced.

In the field of construction of farmland and water conservation, China had 85,000 large, medium-sized and small reservoirs by the end of 1997, with the total reservoir storage amounting to 458.3 billion cubic meters. It has built 5,579 irrigated regions, thus bringing 22.495 million hectares under irrigation. Efforts were also made to reduce soil erosion by 72.241 million hectares and improve alkaline land of 6.61 million hectares. So far, 34.146 million hectares of cultivated areas have been protected by embankments, effectively withstanding natural calamities.

In the field of communications, transportation, post and telecommunications, by the end of 1998, the length of railway lines opened to traffic came to 57,600 km, 35,600 km more than the figure of 22,000 km at the early stage of New China, with annual average growth of 710 km. Electrified railway lines reached 13,000 km. Major railway trunks were completed, including Baotou-Lanzhou, Lanzhou-Urumqi, Baoji-Chengdu, Chengdu-Kunming, Hunan-Guizhou, Hunan-Jiangxi and Hangzhou-Nanchang lines, thus forming a well-developed railway trunk network. The Beijing-Kowloon Railway was completed in 1997, stretching 2,553 km and spanning nine provinces and municipalities, including 98 cities and counties, making it the longest trunk line with largest scale and investment in the history of railway construction. By the end of 1998, the length of highways in use reached 1.279 million km, increasing by 1.196 million km compared with the figure in the early days of New China, with an annual average increase of 23,900 km. The completed expressways, with a total length of 8,733 km, include Beijing-Tianjin-Tanggu, Shenyang-Dalian, Shanghai-Hangzhou-Ningbo and Guangzhou-Shenzhen expressways. In addition, a large number of expressways are under construction. The total cargo volume handled by major coastal ports reached more than 900 million tons, more than 100 times greater than the figure of 8.72 million tons in 1950. Shanghai Port has developed into one of world's largest ports, with annual cargo handling capacity of more than 100 million tons. With the development of foreign trade, efforts have been made to rebuild and expand existing ports on a large scale, in addition to building new port areas in Fangcheng, Beilun, Shijiu and Qinhuangdao. Considerable progress has also made in civil aviation undertakings, which is marked by 143 civil airports built, enlarged, and renovated. Telecommunication facilities with Beijing as center have been completed, linking all cities and the countryside throughout the country. The volume of switchboards used in telephone offices amounted to 138 million lines. The volume of telephone sets numbered 130 million, and mobile telephones reached 23.86 million, forming the second largest mobile telecommunications network in the world.

II. Enhancing the Technological and Equipment Levels of National Economy

Since the founding of New China in 1949, particularly since the reform and opening program launched in 1978, China's industrial technological and complete equipment levels have been steadily improved. While importing complete sets of equipment using foreign capital, China has also imported foreign advanced technologies, equipment and management techniques. Through digesting, absorbing foreign technologies, and further making technological renovation and creation, domestic industrial technological level has been greatly enhanced. For example, Shanghai Baoshan Iron and Steel Works realized a production capacity of 6 million in its second phase, and 10 million in its third phase, becoming a modern integrated complex, the largest of the kind in China. Guixi Smelter is China's first large-scale modern copper smelter with annual production capacity of

国际精品总汇

200,000 tons. Shanxi Chemical Fertilizer Factory is another large-scale nitrogenous-phosphate compound fertilizer production base in China. Jiangsu Yizheng Chemical Fiber Co. owns technological processes of world advanced level, with daily condensation polymerization capacity of 100 tons, with which only a few of companies in the world can match. Beijing positive-negative electronic collider is a self-designed high-tech physical project using domestically-made equipment. It is China's first large accelerator regulating high speed and exploring particles. Optical fiber, micro-wave and satellite telecommunication systems are widely used, such as the optical cable laid along China's southern coastal line, the Beijing-Taiyuan-Xi'an-Lanzhou-Urumqi optical cable and the Beijing-Shenyang-Harbin optical cable. In civil aviation construction, three air routes are under high-altitude conic radar control, 80 airports are equipped with instruments for landing, and 120 airports and radio navigation spots are installed with all-directional beacon lights and distance-measuring equipment. As a result, the technological level has been greatly raised.

III. Irrational Industrial Structure Readjusted

Before the launching of reform and opening program, China conducted large-scale capital construction, with the focus on heavy industry to change the backward situation. Remarkable changes have taken place in the industrial structure. In 1978, the proportion of total industrial output value in the total output value went up to 61.9 percent. The proportion of heavy industry output value in the total industrial output value rose from 26.5 percent in the early stage of New China to 56.9 percent, basically forming a fairly complete and independent industrial system.

After 1979, China further readjusted the investment structure in view of the situation of over-emphasizing heavy industry in economic construction in the past and over-looking light industry and people's living standards, as well as the weak links related to energy, raw materials, communications and transportation, post and telecommunications. Over the past 20 years, state-owned units invested 656.7 billion yuan in light industry construction, bringing the ratio of 1:9 between light and heavy industries 26 years ago up to 1:4.7. state-owned units invested 1,628.9 billion yuan in energy construction, with annual average growth rate of 21 percent; 1,113.7 billion yuan in communications and transportation, with annual average growth rate of 22 percent; 421.6 billion yuan in post and telecommunications, with an annual average growth rate of 38 percent, far above the average growth of other sectors. Through readjusting investment direction, the weak links in the national economy have been strengthened to a certain degree.

IV. People's Material and Cultural Living Conditions Improved, and Urban Outlook Changed

Since the reform and opening program, a great deal of investment has been pooled for housing, culture, education, public facilities. From 1979 to 1997, housing construction investment reached 3,241.7 billion yuan, accounting for 23 percent of the total fixed assets investment. The total completed housing space reached 16.1 billion square meters. The per-capita housing space in cities increased from 3.6 square meters in 1978 to 9.3 square meters in 1998, while per-capita housing space in the countryside rose from 8.1 square meters in 1978 to 23.7 square meters. Urban public facilities also made progress considerably. By 1998, the popularization rate of tape water in cities throughout the country stood at 96 percent, that of gas reached 78.8 percent. In 1998, the telephone installation rate was 10.6 percent, averaging 30 sets for every 100 urban citizens.

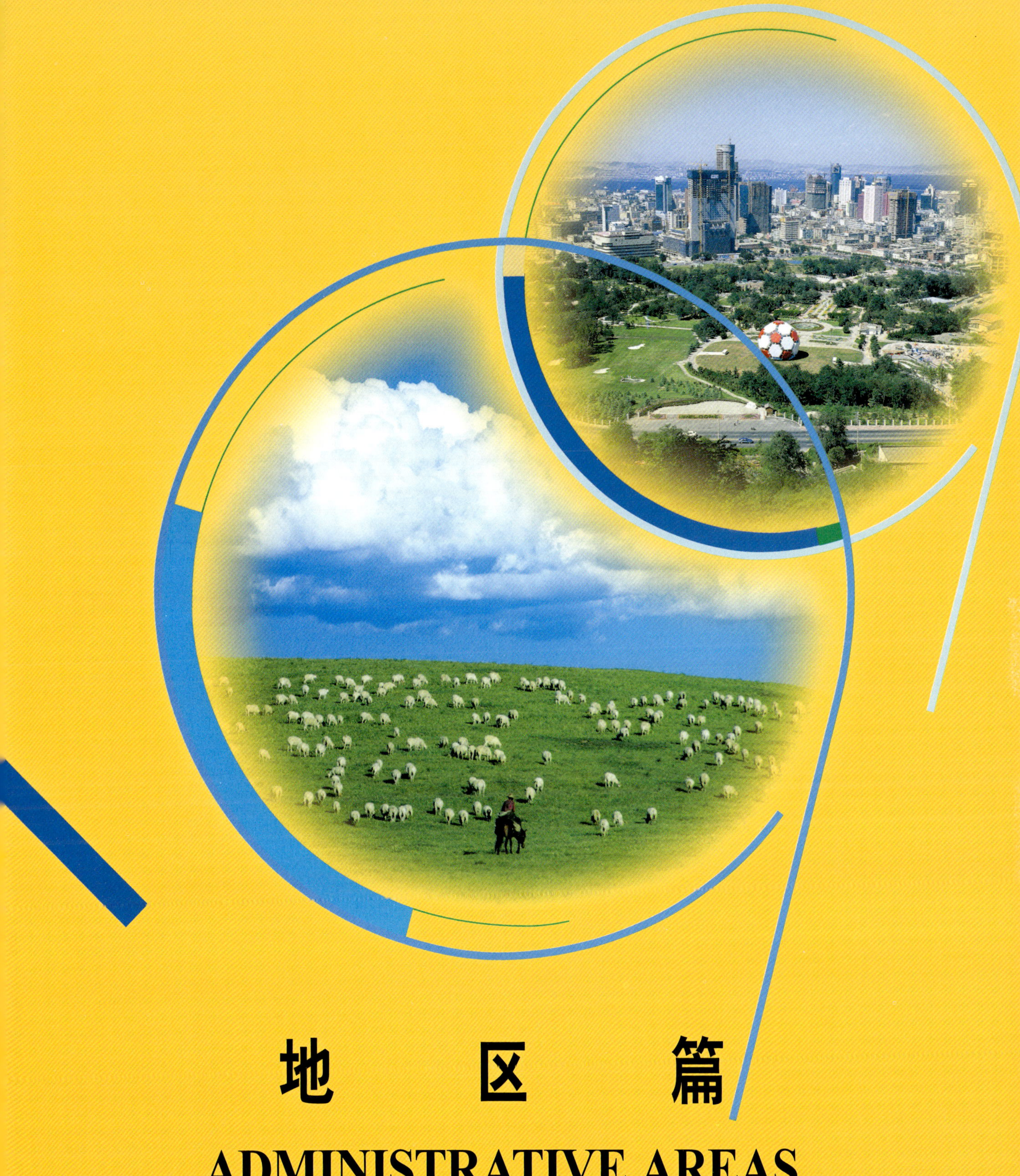

地　　区　　篇

ADMINISTRATIVE AREAS

地　区　篇

ADMINISTRATIVE AREAS

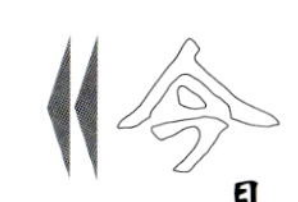

古老而又充满活力的北京

Beijing: Ancient Yet Full of Vigor

一、 经济发展情况

北京是中华人民共和国的首都，全国的政治中心、文化中心和国际交往中心，是中央人民政府的直辖市，是世界历史文化名城。现辖十二区六县，总面积16808平方公里，其中市区面积735平方公里。人口1091.5万，流动人口平均每天300万以上。北京市的综合经济实力在全国各大城市中仅次于上海，已形成了以高新技术、汽车、电子等技术密集型支柱产业为核心、综合配套能力较强的工业体系和功能日臻完善的第三产业体系。北京是全国最大的科技和文化中心。现有国家级科研机构400多所，拥有包括北京大学、清华大学等著名学府在内的高等院校70多所，每年向社会输送10余万名高素质人才。到1998年末，全市拥有各类专业技术人员132.2万人。

建国50年以来，北京这座有3000年悠久历史的古老城市，在社会和经济发展的各方面实现了巨大飞跃。特别是中共十一届三中全会以来，北京市坚决贯彻对内搞活经济、对外实行开放的经济建设方针，取得了令人瞩目的成就。到1998年，北京市国内生产总值达到2011.3亿元，按可比价格计算，比1978年增长5.5倍，平均每年增长9.8%；人均国内生产总值已达1.8万元，按可比价格计算，相当于1978年的4.3倍。在全市人民的共同努力下，北京市国内生产总值提前5年、人均国内生产总值提前2年实现了比1980年翻两番的奋斗目标。同时，北京的经济结构调整也取得了明显的进展。在全市的经济总量中，一、二、三产业之间的比例关系由1978年的5.2∶71.1∶23.7转变为1998年的4.3∶39.1∶56.6，经济结构得到了优化，第三产业成为带动经济增长的主要力量。北京市商业十分发达，形成了多种经营方式、多种流通体制的新格局。到1998年末，社会商品零售额1195.21亿元，比1978年增长26倍，年平均增长17.93%。商业网点总数达到24.13万个，销售额超亿元的商业企业达105家。利用外资大幅度增加，对外贸易迅速增长。1987年至1998年，北京累计签订利用外资协议项目1.4万个，协议利用外资267.7亿美元，实际利用外资152.1亿美元。1998年末，全球最大500家跨国公司已有151家在京投资。三资企业规模不断扩大，平均规模由1990年的107.8万美元扩大到1998年的958.5万美元。外资投向已从一般的加工工业延伸到基础工业和基础设施领域。1979年至1998年，累计出口总额为244.1亿美元，年平均增长10.59%。出口商品结构改善，机电产品出口比重增加。

二、投资环境

为了吸引外资，促进改革开放的深入发展，北京在保护古都风貌的基础上，进行了空前规模的城市建设，相继建成一批增强首都功能的交通、通讯、能源、市政和环境保护等重点工程，城乡面貌发生明显变化，成为全国城市基础设施现代化水平较高的城市之一。北京作为中国的交通枢纽，形成了空路、水路、陆路四通八达的交通网络。北京已开通国际航线69条，通往世界36个国家和地区的56个大城市；除台湾省外，从北京到中国各省、自治区、直辖市及主要城市都有班机往返。客运、货运列车通往除西藏自治区和台湾省外各省、自治区首府及主要城市，从北京发出的国际列车可通过蒙古、俄罗斯、匈牙利等国到达罗马尼亚。从北京到中国北方最大的港口——新港，走京津高速公路大约只需两小时。北京市内交通向多元化、立体化发展。截止到1998年，北京已拥有高速公路176公里，一、二级公路1330公里，永久性公路桥梁2223座和公路隧道45座，全市平均每平方公里拥有公路0.81公里，公路密度居全国之首。北京已经成为中国与世界各国邮政、通讯的主要枢纽。到1998年底，全市交换机容量达686万门，移动电话用户达到116.7万户，国内直拨电话可达2094个城市，国际直拨电话可达200多个国家和地区。同时，电子信箱、电视会议、传真存储转发及公众信息网迅猛发展。全年用电总量为276.2亿千瓦小时。全市集中供热采暖面积突破3800万平方米。全年售水量75968万吨。城市环境质量不断改善，城市绿化覆盖率达到34.9%。北京是中国人民银行和全国各大金融及保险机构总部所在地，已被列入金融对外开放试点城市，对国际金融资本和国际金融机构有着很强的吸引力。到1998年底，外国金融机构和组织在京的代表机构达225家（为非营业机构），占全国的40%；14家外资银行在京设立了分行。北京拥有涉外宾馆、饭店已达到308家，共有客房7万间，其中五星级饭店16家。

三、发展前景

近期发展目标是：

实现经济体制从传统计划经济体制向社会主义市场经济体制的转变，实现经济增长方式从粗放型向集约型转变，大力发展适合首都特点的经济。在1999-2000年的二年内，全面完成现代化建设第二步战略部署，实现国内生产总值年均递增9%，城乡居民人均收入年均递增3-5%，科技进步对经济增长的贡献率达到50%。

远期发展目标是：

进一步增强和完善全国政治中心和文化中心的功能，建设现代化国际城市，成为全国文化教育和科学技术最发达、道德风尚和民主法制建设最好的城市；发展以高新技术产业为先导、第三产业发达、产业结构合理、高效益高素质的适合首都特点的经济；人民生活在实现小康的基础上，向更加宽裕的水平迈进；各项社会事业全面发展，人口素质进一步提高，社会秩序和社会风气明显好转，环境状况进一步改观，城市管理水平明显提高。到2010年，全市国内生产总值比2000年翻一番，形成比较完善的社会主义市场经济体制，经济科技综合实力和社会发展程度，达到并在某些方面超过中等发达国家首都城市的水平，为在21世纪中叶把北京建设成为现代化国际

城市奠定基础。

重点发展领域:

根据北京市“九五”计划和2010年发展目标，全市将加强城市基础设施建设和着重发展高科技产业。高新技术及其产业是北京的优势和希望所在，是首都经济新的核心，今后要重点加以扶植，逐步形成以信息产业为龙头，以商品化、产业化和国际化为目标，以电子信息、生物工程和新医药、光机电一体化、新材料等新兴产业为主导的高新技术产业群。同时，积极利用高新技术改造传统产业，全面提升产业的技术水平，加快国民经济信息化进程。北京将继续大力发展第三产业，并保持其高于其它产业的增长速度，逐步建立起服务首都、面向全国和世界、结构优化、功能完善、布局合理的第三产业体系。

I. Basic Facts About Beijing Economic Development

Beijing is the capital of the People's Republic of China and a municipality directly under the jurisdiction of the Central People's Government, while serving as the national political and cultural and international exchange center and enjoying a reputation as an ancient cultural city. Beijing has a total of 16,808 square kilometers, 735 square kilometers of which is the city proper, and has 10.915 million permanent residents. There is a floating population of 3 million each day. Beijing is divided into 12 districts and 6 counties. In terms of comprehensive economic strength, Beijing is the second greatest among all Chinese cities, next to Shanghai. The city has set up a relatively complete industrial system, with high-tech, auto and electronic sectors playing important roles, and has gradually built its tertiary industry. Beijing is the largest national center of science, technology and culture and is also home to more than 400 state-level research institutes. There are 70 schools of higher learning in the city, including the prestigious Beijing and Qinghua universities, and these produce well over 100,000 graduates every year. At the end of 1998, the city had 1.322 million school-trained technical specialists.

Since 50 years ago, Beijing, an ancient city with a history of 3,000 years, has made overall progress in social and economic development. Especially during the resent two decades, guided by the policy "reform, open, invigorate", Beijing's economy has undergone a series of brilliant achievements. In 1998, the city generated 201.13 billion yuan in GDP, 6.5 times more than in 1978 at comparable prices, an annual average increase of 9.8 percent; the city's per capita GDP amounted to 18,000 yuan, 5.3 times that of 1978 at comparable prices, achieving the goal of quadrupling that of 1980 two years ahead of schedule. Meanwhile, the city's economic structural adjustment progressed obviously. The proportion of primary, secondary and tertiary industries to the city's economic development changed from 5.2 percent, 71.1 percent and 23.7 percent in 1978 to 4.3 percent, 39.1 percent and 56.6 percent in 1998. The tertiary industry took the lead in the city's economic growth. Beijing has a well-developed commercial system based on diversified forms of operation and varied channels of commodity circulation.By the end of 1998, retail sales of social consumer goods had amounted to 119.52 billion yuan, 26 times the figure in 1978, an annual average increase of 17.93 percent. The number of retail sales units had grown to 241,300 units. Some 105 retail sellers each had an annual sales volume exceeding 100 million yuan. Foreign trade expanded swiftly and foreign capital has been greatly used. From 1987 to 1998, the number of projects introducing foreign investment amounted 14,000. These involved US$26.77 billion in contract investment and the actual use of foreign investment amounting to US$15.21

billion yuan. By the end of 1998, 151 of the 500 largest transnational corporations in the world had invested in Beijing. The scale of foreign-funded enterprises was expanded. These absorbed foreign capital from US$1.078 million on average in 1990 to US$9.585 million in 1998. The field of foreign investment has been adjusted from processing industry to basic industry and basic infrastructure construction. From 1979 to 1998, the aggregate gross export amount to US$24.41 billion, and the average annual rate of growth was 10.59 percent. The export proportion of mechanical and electrical products rose and the composition of exported products was further optimized.

II. Investment Environment of Beijing

In order to introduce foreign capital and deepen the reform, Beijing has carried out unprecedentedly large scale urban infrastructure construction, on the basis of protecting the style and features of this ancient city. A bulk of important projects in transportation, telecommunications, energy, public utilities and environmental protection have strengthened the capital's performance. Both urban and suburban areas have put on a clear new face and Beijing boasts one of the best urban infrastructure facilities systems in China. As a hub of national communications, Beijing has formulated a network of air, water and land routes, extending in all directions. The city boasts 69 international air routes, linking 56 cities in 36 countries and territories. There are domestic air routes, reaching all provinces and autonomous regions and their main cities except Taiwan Province. Passenger and freight trains link the capitals of all province, autonomous regions and chief cities except Tibet and Taiwan. International trains from Beijing can reach Romania via Mongolia, Russia, and Hungary. In relation to waterways, it takes only about 2 hours by the Beijing-Tianjin-Tanggu Expressway to get to Xingang—the biggest sea port in northern China—from Beijing. The Internal transportation of Beijing has developed toward three-dimension plurality. By the end of 1998, the total length of expressways and first and second grade roads reached 176 kilometers and 1,330 kilometers respectively. Beijing had 2,223 highway bridges and 45 highway tunnels. Beijing is rated as first in China with an average 0.81 kilometers of roads per square kilometer of its land area. Beijing has become an international postal and telecommunications center, where direct dialing is possible to 2,094 cities in China and to more than 200 countries and regions throughout the world. The city's capacity of switchboards amounted to 6.86 million gates and the number of subscribers of mobile telephones came to 1.167 million by the end of 1998. Furthermore, electronic mail, television conferencing, fax storage and retransmission, as well as a public information network have developed swiftly and vigorously. By the end of 1998, the annual total amount of power consumption was 27.62 billion kilowatt-hours and the annual total amount of water sold was 759.68 million tons. The city's concentrated heat-supply area exceeded 38 million square meters. Environmental quality has constantly improved. Some 34.9 percent of the urban area is now covered with greenery. Beijing is home to the headquarters of the People's Bank of China and financial organizations and insurance companies. Now that it is open, Beijing has become all the more attractive to international capital. At the end of 1998, there were 225 representative offices of foreign banks and financial organizations in Beijing. The figure accounted for 40 percent of the national total, and 14 foreign-funded banks had branches operating in Beijing. Beijing now has 308 star-class hotels with 70,000 standard rooms, including 16 five-star hotels.

III. Prospects of Development

Long Term Target:

The city shall oblige itself to perfect and improve the performance of its functions as the national political and

cultural center, and strive to develop into a modern international metropolis rated as the best in China in the development of science and technology and the most successful in building social and ethical standards, democracy and rule by law. Work shall be done to develop a local economic system suited to the specific conditions of the Chinese capital and an economic system led by new and high-tech industries, based on a well-developed tertiary sector, and featuring a rational industrial structure and good economic performance. The people will first become well-to-do and, after that, their life will continue to improve. Social undertakings will develop in an all-round manner, and the quality of the local population will improve, as will the order and general mood of society. The environment will be significantly better, as will be urban management. By the year 2010, the city's GDP will have grown to double that of 2000. The city should complete the task of building a market-oriented economy and become as good in economy, science and technology as capitals of the countries with an average level of development while outstripping them in some aspects. All this will prepare Beijing to eventually become a modern international metropolis by the mid-21st century.

Short Term Target:

The city should realize the change from a traditional planned economy system to a socialist market-oriented economy system and vigorously develop the economy fit for capital performance. From 1999 to 2000, the city should have attained all the targets set for the second phase of the city's modernization and achieved an annual average increase of 9 percent in GDP, the incomes of urban and rural resident should increase at an annual average rate of 3-5 percent, and scientific and technological progress should be responsible for 50 percent of the economic growth.

Key Areas for Foreign Investment:

According to municipal planning for social economic development in the 1996-2000 period and through to 2010, the city will intensify the construction of infrastructure facilities and call for priority in high-tech development. The development of high and new technologies is a major content of the economy of the capital city. High-tech enterprises, with key target industries included, such as electronics and information, biological engineering, new pharmaceuticals, integrated optical, machinery and electronic products and new materials, have gradually been formulated. High-tech enterprises are moving towards the right tracks of industrialization, internationalization and commercialization. Meanwhile, the traditional industries should be renovated and upgraded by high-tech applications. The city should accelerate informationlization of the national economy. The city should continue to vigorously develop the tertiary industry and maintain a higher growth rate than among other industries. A tertiary industrial system, serving the capital, facing China and the world, with perfect performance and rational structure has been formulated.

走向现代化的新天津

New Tianjin: Stepping Towards Modernization

天津是中国四大直辖市之一，是中国北方最大的沿海开放城市，现辖18个区县，全市总面积11919平方公里，人口905.09万。天津工业基础雄厚，门类齐全，综合配套能力强，轻重工业均比较发达。近年来形成了以汽车和机械设备，微电子和通讯设备，海洋化工和石油化工，优质钢管和优质钢材为重点的四大支柱产业。天津第三产业比较发达，以贸易、金融、交通通讯、房地产为主的第三产业有了长足的发展，天津作为北方商贸金融中心的作用日益显现出来。天津科技教育也比较发达，有独立科研机构158所，专业技术人员57.08万，高等院校20所。

新中国成立后，特别是经过20年的改革开放和发展，天津发生了巨大变化，开创了建国以来经济发展的最好时期。1998年国内生产总值达到1336.38亿元，比1978年增长5倍，年平均增长9.3%，人均国内生产总值由1978年的1160元提高到1998年的14808元。1998年社会消费品零售总

天津新港
Tianjing New Port

额达到587.12亿元，平均每年增长17%。外向型经济取得突破性的发展。1979-1998年，天津累计与外商签订合同12413个，协议外资金额231.26亿美元，实际利用外资173.50亿美元。外贸出口大幅度增长，1998年达到54.99亿美元，比1978年增长5.6倍，平均每年增长9.9%。

天津是中国大陆投资环境最好的地区之一，有六个方面的比较优势。一是地理区位优势。天津地处环渤海地区中心位置，腹地辽阔，进出自如。二是交通设施配套。以天津港为枢纽，海、陆、空三位一体的大交通框架已经形成。三是科技人才密集。天津技术人才众多，熟练劳动者队伍庞大，能够满足经济大发展的需要。四是土地资源丰富。尚有120平方公里滩涂荒地可供开发，这是世界大城市中少有的优越条件。五是金融产业发达。国际金融功能迅速扩展，货币、证券、外汇、黄金、期货市场比较齐备。六是市场发育完善。天津作为北方传统的商品集散地，市场规模较大，运作规范，开放度高。外贸机构、中介服务、保税仓储加工和运输相互配套，服务快速高效。天津又是中国社会治安最好的地区之一。总之，天津是投资者举办实业，开发经营、施展抱负的理想场所。可以佐证的是，美国摩托罗拉在天津投资累计已达12亿美元，获取的利润比包括其在美国本土的世界各地分公司都多。可口可乐、奥的斯、美孚、大通、本田、雅马哈、NEC、丰田、诺和诺德、扎努西、汉高、拜耳、三星及中国香港的一大批跨国公司在天津踊跃投资，也都取得了一流的经营成果，获利丰厚。

最近，天津被中国政府定位为环渤海地区经济中心，要努力建成为现代化港口城市和中国北方重要的经济中心。在跨世纪的发展过程中，天津将更加开放，以更加积极的姿态走向世界。发展目标是：到2010年，努力把天津建设成为现代化港口城市和中国北方重要的经济中心，成为中国率先基本实现现代化的地区之一。

今后天津鼓励和吸引外资的重点领域是：

——滨海新区的招商引资与基础设施建设。目前已经做了大量的前期投入和多方面的准备工作，正在成为中国北方大量吸纳国际资本和先进技术的热点和富有活力的经济新区。

——大规模的成片危陋平房改造。这将为城市发展空间提供更大的扩展，为加快建设金融中心区、商务中心区、大力发展服务产业准备了充分的条件。

——国有大中型企业嫁接改造调整。当前，天津正在利用多种形式，大力组建跨国、跨地区、跨行业的大型企业集团

——投资建设一批高新技术产业。天津是中国科技人才最密集的地区之一，有60多万科技人员，在200万人的产业大军中，有一支技艺素质较高的高级技工队伍。对于有利于高新技术产业发展的外商投资，天津将给予政策上的更大优惠。

所有这些，都为海外投资者提供了难得的商机和广阔的舞台。欢迎一切有识之士来天津投资开发、观光旅游、探亲访友。天津的大门永远向朋友们敞开！

Tianjin is one of the four municipalities directly under the Central Government and one of the largest opening coastal cities of northern China. There are 18 districts and counties under the jurisdiction of Tianjin. The total land area is 11,919 sq. km and the population is 9.0509 million. The city's industry has a strong basis, complete categories and comprehensive accessory capabilities. The light and heavy industries are all developed. In recent years, it has formed four mainstay industries, which cover the fields of automobile & mechinery equipment, micro-electron & communication equipment, sea chemical & petroleum chemical,

and high quality steel tube & steel products. The tertiary industry is developing quite well. Commerce trade, banking, transportation, telecommunications, and real estate are all making remarkable progress. The function of Tianjin as a commercial & banking center is even more obviously. The science and education are also developing well. There are 158 scientific research institutions, 570,800 technical personnel and 20 general universities.

Since the founding of the People's Republic of China, especially, with the reform and opening in the past two decades, Tianjin has changed tremendously and started to enter the best development period. In 1998, the gross domestic product (GDP) was 133.638 billion yuan, increased five times over 1978, and the annnual average increase rate was 9.3 percent. The per capita GDP grew from 1,160 yuan in 1978 to 14,808 yuan in 1998. Total retail sales of consumer goods was 58.712 billion yuan in 1998, and the annual average increase rate was 17 percent. The opening to the outside world made breakthroughs. From 1979 to 1998, the number of signed foreign investment projects was 12,413; the total investment of foreign capital was US$23.126 billion; the actual use of foreign capital was US$17.35 billion. Exports increased rapidly, with a value of US$5.499 billion in 1998, increasing 5.6 times over 1978, and the annual average increase rate was 9.9 percent.

Tianjin is one of the best investment regions of China. There are six superiorities. First, it has a superior geographical position. Tianjin is located at the central position of the Bohai Coastal Region, having extensive hinterland and convenient traffic. Second, it has accessory transportation facilities. A transportation system of sea, land and air has been formed, which takes Tianjin Port as its hub. Third, it boasts large numbers of scientific personnel and skilled workers who can satisfy the needs of economic development. Fourth, it owns abundant land resources. There is 120 square km of uncultivated land that can be developed. No other large city has such superiority. Fifth, it has a developed banking industry and its international banking function has quickly enlarged. It is equipped with many financial markets, such as currency, securities, foreign exchange, gold and futures. Sixth, its markets have developed comprehensively. Tianjin is the traditional center in northern China to concentrate & deliver goods. These markets have a large scale and standard business and are open to the outside. They are equipped with foreign trade facilities, brokeraging, warehouse processing, and transportation are high speed and highly efficient. Tianjin is also one of the best public security regions. In short, Tianjin is a satisfying region for investors mising to develop and manage business. For example, the total investment of Motorola reached US$1.2 billion in Tianjin, and the profit of Tianjin Motorola is more than that of other branches in the world. Many famous companies actively invested in Tianjin and have gained rich benefits, including Coca Cola, OTIS, Mobil, DaTong, Honda, Yamaha, NEC,TOYOTA, Novo Nordisk, ZANUSST, Henkel, Baeyar, and Samsung as well as other Hong Kong multinationals.

Recently, Tianjin was defined as the economic center of the Bohai Coastal Region and a modernized port city and the important economic center of orthern China by the State Council. Looking forward to the coming century, Tianjin will continue to open to the outside world and step to the world actively. Tianjin's development goal is that Tianjin will be a modernized port city, an important economic center of northern China, and a modernized city in the year of 2010.

The major fields of Tianjin for drawing foreign capital:

The New Seaside Region is drawing foreign capital and basic facility's construction. We have invested in the first stage and made some preparation. New Seaside Region is becoming the new hot and dynamic economic region of northern China in drawing international capital and advanced technology.

—Urban renewal is a major task. This will enlarge the development space of the city, prepare abundant conditions to quicken the construction of banking and business and develop the service industries.

— State-owned large & medium-sized enterprises will be reformed and adjusted. Tianjin is establishing multinational, multi-regional, multi-trade enterprise groups in various forms.

— Through investing in and constructing hi-tech industries, Tianjin is becoming a scientific talent concentrated region and now has more than 600,000 scientific personnel. There are many high quality and high-grade technical workers among the city's 2 million workers. Tianjin will give more favourable policies for investors to invest in hi-tech industries.

All these fields will provide the rare chance for investor abroad. We welcome all of you to invest, tour and visit your relatives & friends in Tianjin. The door of Tianjin will be open for friends forever.

今日河北

Hebei Today

河北是中国北方的一个重要沿海省份。全省总面积18.8万平方公里，人口6569万，海岸线长487公里，有11个省辖市。改革开放以来，特别是进入90年代以后，河北经济迅速发展，全省国内生产总值年均递增13.7%，连续8年超过全国平均增长水平。在跨世纪的发展中，河北已经具备更快更好发展的基础。

一、区位优势明显，市场空间广阔

河北位于中国华北腹地，内环京津，外环渤海，属国家重点规划发展的京津冀经济圈。京、津的资金、技术、信息等生产要素可以为河北所用，京、津的许多产业可以直接转移到河北。同时，河北又是京津所需商品物资和能源的最大供应地。这一区域市场极为广阔，拥有1.2亿人口的消费群体，市场容量在全国占有很大份额。目前该地区正在成为中国新的经济增长带，必将为各国客商来这里投资并获取好的收益提供难得的机遇。

二、交通通信发达，运输联络便捷

河北处在首都北京连结全国各地的交通枢纽地带，铁路和公路货物周转量分别居全国第1位和第2位。境内有京广、京沪、京九、京哈、京包、石太等15条国家干线铁路通过，于去年11月开工建设的跨世纪工程——朔黄铁路将与京广、京沪、京九等干线相互交叉，在河北形成纵横交错、高密度的铁路运输系统；公路密布如网，有京石、石安、石太、京津塘等17条国家干线公路，1998年高速公路通车里程达5.7万多公里。自北向南有秦皇岛港、京塘港和正在建设的黄骅港3个较大的出海口岸；省会石家庄大型民航机场已实现国际通航；全省电话交换机总容量621.11万门，各市县均实现了程控直拨。发达便捷的交通通信条件，把河北与世界各国和地区紧密联系在一起，极大地促进了国际交流与合作。

三、产业基础雄厚，经济实力较强

1998年，全省国内生产总值达4256亿元，比上年增长10.7%，经济总量居全国第6位。河北除具有雄厚的农业、能源、原材料、交通通信基础设施和基础产业外，工业门类较多，具有很好的发展条件。1998年，全省国有及年销售收入500万元非国有工业企业7597家，其中大中型企业1146家，已形成了包括化工、医药、建材、冶金、机械、纺织、轻工等产业的资源加工型经济结构，许多行业和产品在全国占有重要地位。其中，建材工业中的卫生陶瓷、平板玻璃产量居全国第1位和第2位；能源工业中的原煤、原油产量和发电量分别居全国第6、7、4位；冶金工业中的钢和生铁产量居全国第5位和第3位；化学、医药工业在全国占优势地位，其中位于省会石家庄市的华北制药厂集团是全国最大的抗菌素生产基地，青霉素产量居世界第2位。河北作为环京津、环渤海经济大省，其优势越来越被海内外投资者所认知，正在成为投资热点地区。

四、自然资源丰富，开发潜力巨大

河北自然资源禀赋甚好，是全国矿资源大

省。炼焦煤、化工灰岩、铁矿石、水泥灰岩储量分别在全国居第1、第2、第3、第4位，石油和天然气也有相当储量。河北省是中国旅游资源丰富的地区之一，自然和人文景观资源总量与陕西省并列全国第一，其中有已列入世界文化遗产的承德避暑山庄、全国著名的沿海避暑胜地北戴河、万里长城之首山海关、清东陵和清西陵等旅游景区，这些风景名胜每年都吸引大批中外游客前来旅游观光。

五、对外开放发展势头强劲

经过多年的开放与发展，河北省初步形成了以环渤海地区为前沿，以中心城市为依托，以各类开发区为窗口，以铁路、公路干线为纽带，外资、外贸、外经并举的全方位、多层次、大开放格局。目前，河北省已与世界175个国家和地区建立了经贸关系。到1998年底，全省实际利用外资累计达90.6亿美元。建成投产"三资"企业2728家，年外贸出口达43.06亿美元。为进一步扩大对外开放、吸引外资，河北在改善投资硬环境的同时，也着力强化软环境建设，已初步建立起一整套维护外商和外商投资企业合法权益、有利于外商投资企业生产经营的政策、制度和规章，实现了对外商投资的依法管理。省和11个省辖市都设立了利用外资审批、管理、服务机构，成立了外商投资企业管理服务中心、外商投资企业合法权益保护中心和侵犯外商合法权益举报中心，为海外客商的生产、经营提供优质高效的服务，依法保护投资者的合法权益。

按照《河北省国民经济发展"九五"计划和2010年远景目标纲要》，到2010年，河北省将建立起比较完善的社会主义市场经济体制，国内生产总值比2000年再翻一番，力争翻一番半，主要经济指标进入全国前10位，建成经济强省。为了实现这一跨世纪的宏伟目标，河北将以更加积极的姿态走向世界，加快"两环开放带动"战略的

金山岭长城
The Jinshanling Section of the Great Wall

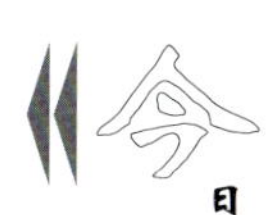

实施，促进产业产品结构的优化和新经济增长点的形成，进一步拓宽利用外资领域，吸引更多的国际产业资本和金融资本，并鼓励能够发挥河北省比较优势的对外投资，切实加强与世界各国和地区的经济技术合作。

今后一个时期，河北吸引外商投资的重点：一是加强农业、电力、原材料和交通通信等基础产业和基础设施建设；二是壮大和提高化工（医药）、机械、冶金、建筑（建材）、食品等支柱产业；三是改造和提高纺织、轻工等传统产业；四是积极培育和加快发展电子、信息、新材料、生物工程等先导产业；另外，第三产业中的住房、商贸设施、旅游资源开发和法律、审计、会计等社会服务体系建设也将积极寻求对外合作。

Hebei is an important coastal province in the north of China. It covers 188,000 square km and has a population of 65.69 million. Hebei has 11 cities directly under its jurisdiction. In the 1990s, the opening policy has brought Hebei rapid economic development with its GDP increasing 13.7 percent annually, above the national average level for 8 years in succession. A better and quicker foundation has been set up in the trans-century development.

I. Geographical Advantage and a Huge Market

Hebei is situated in the central part of northern China a round the Bohai Sea and surrounded by Beijing and Tianjing. Together with the two municipalities, the Jing (Beijing)-Jin (Tianjin)-Ji (Hebei) economic area is formed and is the major development area in the national development plan. So the essential factors of production from Beijing and Tianjin, such as funds, trained personnel, technologies and information, are available to Hebei Province, and many of their industries can be directly shifted to Hebei; on the other hand, Hebei is an important supplier of commodities, raw materials and energy resources needed by the two municipalities. 120 million consumers make up a huge market, taking a large share in the whole nation. The area is becoming a new economic increase zone in the country and will provide a great chance for foreign investors to gain desirable benefits.

II. Good Transportation and Communication Facilities

Hebei is a hub of transportation joining Beijing with other parts of the country. The total rail freight traffic ranks 1st and highway freight traffic 2nd place in the country. There are 15 national railways running through Hebei, such as the Beijing-Guangzhou, Beijing-Shanghai, Beijing-Kowloon, Beijing-Harbin, Beijing-Baotou and Shijiazhuang-Taiyuan railways. The trans-century Shuozhou-Huanghua Railways, which began its construction in November of 1997, will cross the Beijing-Guangzhou, Bejing-Shanghai, Beijing-Kowloon railways, forming a dense network of railways transportation. There are 17 national highways extending across the province, such as the Jing-Shi (Beijing-Shijiazhuang), Shi-An(Shijiazhuang-Anyang), Shi-Tai (Shijiazhuang-Taiyuan), and Jing-Jin-Tang (Beijing-Tianjin-Tanggu) highways. The total length of highways in use came to 57,000 kilometers in 1998. The Qinhuangdao Port, Jingtang Port and Huanghua Port, which is under construction, are the major seaports along the coastline. Shijiazhuang Airport in the capital city has opened international route; the telephone exchange capacity has reached 6.211 million lines and domestic and international direct dialing services have become available in all the cities and counties. Such well-developed, easy transportation and communication facilities bring Hebei closer to the other countries in the world and are of great benefit to international exchange and cooperation.

III. A Strong Industrial Foundation and Great Comprehensive Strength

In 1998, the provincial GDP reached 425.6 billion yuan, increasing by 10.7 percent over the last year, ranking 6th in terms of the total economic amount. Not only is it well-based frastructure and basic industry, such as agriculture, energy resources, raw material, transportation and communication, Hebei also has a wide spectrum of industry and it has laid a good foundation for future development. In 1998 State-owned enterprises and non-state-owned enterprises with annually selling incomes of 5 million yuan reached 7,597, of which the number of large and medium-sized State-owned enterprises came to 1,146. These formed a resource processing structure, including chemical, pharmacy, building materials, metallurgy, machinery, textiles and light industry. Many of the industries and their products sharing important places in the country, in which the outputs of sanitary porcelain and plane glass share 1st and 2nd place; the outputs of the raw coal, crude oil and the electric energy production rank 6th, 7th and 4th respectively in the energy industry, the outputs of the steel and iron rank 5th and 3rd place in the metallurgy industry. The chemical and pharmaceutical industries occupy a prominent position in the nation. The North China Pharmaceutical Plant, located in the provincial capital Shijiazhuang, is the largest antibiotics production base in the country, with its output of penicillin ranking 2nd in the world. As an economic power around the Bohai Sea and surround Beijing and Tianjin, Hebei's advantages are being recognized by investors from home and abroad, and it is becoming the focus of investment.

IV. Rich Natural Resources and Profound Potential for Further Exploration

Hebei was rich in mineral resources. The deposits of coking coal, chemical limestone, iron ore and cement limestone rank 1st, 2nd, 3rd, and 4th. Hebei also has richest tourism resources, sharing 1st place with Shaanxi Province in terms of natural and historical landscapes. Some are listed as World Culture Heritage Sites such as the Chengde Imperial Summer Villa. The nationaly famous summer retreat along the coast are the Beidaihe Summer Resort, Shanhaiguan Pass-the start of the Great Wall, the Eastern Imperial Tombs and the Western Imperial Tombs of the Qing Dynasty. These sceneries attract a great number of tourists from home and abroad every year.

V. Strong Impetus in the Development of International Economic Cooperation

As a result of many years development based on the area around the Bohai Sea as the forward position, depending on the major cities as the "back-up", using the development zones as the "windows", and taking the mainland routes as the links, an all-round opening structure integrated with foreign economic cooperation has gradually taken shape in Hebei Province. Hebei has established economic and trade relations with 175 countries and regions. By the end of 1998, the total foreign funds used in the province reached US$9.06 billion , 2,728 foreign-funded enterprises had begun operations, and the total export value had reached US$4.306 billion. To attract more foreign funds, Hebei is opening wider to the outside world and making great efforts in soft environment construction while improving the hard environment. A complete set of polices, rules and regulations has been established not only to protect the legal rights of overseas investors and foreign-funded enterprises, but also to contribute to their operation and production, so that legitimate administration of foreign investment is ensured. To provide the best services to overseas investors in their production and business operation and to protect their legitimate rights, three centers (namely the Management and Service Center, the Legal Rights and

邯郸钢铁集团公司夜景

Night Scene of Handan Iron & Steel Complex

Interests Protection Center and the Legal Rights Violations Reporting Center for Foreign-Funded Enterprises) have been set up at the provincial level, as well as at the municipal level in 11 cities.

In conformity with the "9th Five-Year Plan" and the "Program of Developing Projection Towards the Year 2010", Hebei will set up a more complete socialist market economic system and double its 2000 GDP value, even trying its best to triple its 2000 GDP value by 2010. In order to become an economically powerful province, the major economic indicators will be pushed to among the nation's top 10. To realize the grand trans-century projection, Hebei will cooperate with the world more actively, quicken the pace of development and opening to the outside world, promote industries and product upgrades so as to gain new economic strength. The fields attracting foreign funds will become wider, so as to attract more international capital and finanucing; in the meaning time, we will promote international economic and technical cooperation.

In the coming period, the focus of drawing foreign funds will be:

1. Intensifying the basic industries and infrastructure, such as agriculture, power, raw materials, transportation, and communication;

2. Increasing and upgrading the major industries, such as chemicals (pharmaceuticals), machinery, metallurgy, construction (building material), and food;

3. Reforming and upgrading traditional industries, such as textiles and light industries;

4. Fostering and accelerating the development of leading industries, such as electronics, information, new materials, and genetic engineering. In addition, social services in the tertiary industries are also a key sector for foreign investment, such as residential apartments, shopping facilities, and tourism, as well as law agents, auditing and accounting.

山西——奋力创建中西部发展示范区

Shanxi: Striving to Guide the Midwest

一、经济概况

山西因地处太行山西侧而得名，是中华民族的发祥地之一，属古晋国崛兴之地，故简称“晋”。山西处于中国东部经济发达地区和中西部欠发达地区连接部的特殊位置，对加快中西部发展起着示范、引导、辐射、带动效应和承东启西的作用。现辖5个地区、6个省辖市和119个县、市(县级)、区，省会为太原市。全省总面积15.63万平方公里，人口3172万，其中市镇人口1043万。山西工业门类比较齐全，拥有40个工业大类中的38个，已形成以重工业为主体，以煤炭、电力、冶金、机械、化工为支柱的比较完整的工业体系，是全国重要的能源、原材料基地，原煤、洗精煤、焦炭、生铁、氧化铝产量居全国第一。山西矿产资源丰富，煤、铝土、耐火粘土、铁矾土、珍珠岩、镓、沸石等的储量居全国首位。山西旅游资源得天独厚，佛教圣地五台山、大同云岗石窟、黄河壶口瀑布驰名中外。

建国50年来，特别是中共十一届三中全会以来，山西省坚定不移地深化改革，扩大开放，促进发展，社会经济面貌发生了巨大变化，提前4年顺利实现了“翻两番”的战略目标。1998年国内生产总值1601.1亿元，比1978年增长4.59倍，年平均增长8.98%；粮食产量两次突破100亿公斤大关，1998年达到108亿公斤，创历史最高水平；社会消费品零售总额547.6亿元，比1978年增长15.94倍，年平均增长15.20%。对外经济贸易与合作在基础差、起步晚的情况下，取得了突破性的进展。1984-1998年，山西累计协议利用外资30亿美元，外商实际投资9亿美元。外贸出口大幅度增长，1978年以来累计出口总额105亿美元，1998年达到14.5亿美元，是1978年的近200倍。目前山西共有外商投资企业1279个，出口创汇额接近全省出口总额的10%。

二、投资环境

改革开放以来特别是进入90年代，山西省狠抓交通、通信、能源、市政等基础设施建设，大力发展第三产业，投资环境得到了有效改善。铁路营业里程达到2511公里，形成了以太原为中心的贯通省境的铁路网，省会太原可直通全国19个主要城市。公路网络四通八达，已建成太原—旧关、太原—原平两条高速公路，实现了县县通邮路、乡乡通公路和村村通机动车的“三通”目标。航空航线达到28条，形成了以太原为中心辐射全国的空中运输网，可直通全国29个城市。山西电信事业发展迅速，1998年全省公用电话交换机总容量已达到208万门，全部市县电话用户都可以直拨国内、国际长途，市内电话机数达130万户。同时，还有移动电话、传呼机、磁卡电话等。山西金融业发展也很快，金融机构和网点大量增加，主要金融机构的日常业务已实现电子化。衣、食、住、行十分方便，涉外宾馆、饭店近几年得到长足发展，设施先进，环境优雅，公共交通四通八达，出租车仅省城太原就有近万辆，商业网点众多，购物环境得到极大改善。随着万家寨引黄工程的建成，山西供水紧张的状况将得到极大缓解。招商引资越来越受到政府和社会各界的重

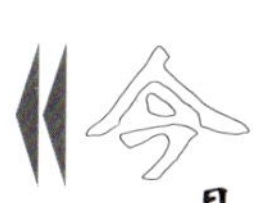

视，两年一度的“山西国际经济贸易洽淡会”和每年一度的“山西商品交易会”越办越好。

三、发展前景

改革开放以来，山西作为中西部内陆省份，与东部发达地区形成了较大的差距。中共十四届五中全会和全国人大八届四次会议通过的“九五”计划及2010年远景目标纲要，明确提出要加快中西部地区发展，逐步缩小地区差距。山西将以建设中西部内陆经济发展示范区为目标，抓住环渤海地区经济发展的机遇，充分发挥区域优势，加快产业在地区间重组、转移和升级，不断提高资源配置的整体效益。

近期发展目标：继续深化改革，扩大开放，逐步与世界经济接轨；大力加强农业、基础设施和优势产业，搞好能源重化工基地综合开发；适应市场需求变化，依靠科技进步，从调整产品结构入手，培育多元化支柱产业。全面提高经济的整体素质和社会文明程度，逐步缩小同发达地区的差距，综合经济实力和人民生活争取达到全国平均水平。

远期发展目标：到2010年，建立健全的社会主义市场经济体制；全方位扩大对外开放，与世界经济全面接轨；实现能源重化工结构重组和升级，初步完成农村工业化、工业现代化、农村城镇化、市场国际化的产业革命任务，实现经济与社会、环境可持续发展，综合经济实力和人民生活水平力争赶上全国中等水平和中西部地区的先进水平。

四、鼓励投资的重点领域

建设中西部内陆经济示范区，实现兴晋富民的宏伟目标，既需要三千万三晋儿女长期不懈的努力，也离不开世界各国的资金、技术、管理、人才和信息支持。山西将按照“积极、合理、有效”的原则，进一步改善投资环境，简化办事程序，提高办事效率，提高外商投资的质量和效益。今后山西鼓励和吸收外商投资的重点领域是：

1. 建设一批经济建设急需的基础设施和基础产业项目。包括农业、水利、能源、交通等行业，重点是黄土高原水土保持、优质高效农业、水利设施、能源综合利用及环境保护、高等级公路等方面的项目。

2. 对一批传统的一般工业项目进行技术改

万家寨水利枢纽工程
Wanjiazhai Key Water Control Engineering

造，形成规模大、市场覆盖面广的名、优、新、特产品。包括轻纺、烟草、医药、机电、冶金、化学、建材等行业，重点是特种钢、铝及铝材、建筑用钢材、焦炭及焦化（煤化工）、重型汽车、煤炭机械、高标号水泥、化学纤维等领域。

3. 建立一批能迅速转化为生产力的高新技术产业。重点发展方向是材料科学和新材料技术、光电子科学和光机电一体化技术、生物技术、微电子科学和电子信息技术、医药科学和生物医学工程等。

I. General Survey

Shanxi is named for its location to the west of the Taihang Mountains. This region was among the birthplaces of the Chinese nation. In ancient times, the state of Jin rose from the fertile soil of Shanxi. For this reason, the region has also been given the name "Jin". Shanxi occupies a special position linking the economically-developing eastern regions with the undeveloped midwestern regions, therefore playing the roles of demonstrator, guide, disseminator, impetus, and link in the accelerated development of the Midwest. Shanxi Province includes five prefectures, 6 cities and 119 counties or county-level cities and districts under its jurisdiction. Taiyuan is the capital of the province. Covering an area of 156,300 square kilometers, the province has a population of 31.72 million. Among these, the urban population is 10.43 million. The province has established a fairly complete industrial system, including 38 out of the 40 industrial sectors. Coal, electrical power, metallurgy, machine-building and chemicals serve as the pillars of the provincial economy. Shanxi is also one of China's important energy and raw materials bases, with the outputs of raw coal, washed coal, coking coal, pig iron, and aluminum oxide each ranking first in China. It is endowed with rich natural resources, with the reserves of coal, bauxite, refractory clay, iron alumina, pearlite and gallium also ranking first in China. In addition, Shanxi has rich tourism resources, including Wutai Mountain, which is a sacred Buddhist peak, the Yungang Grottoes at Datong, and the waterfalls at Hukou. These are just some of the internationally-famous tourist attractions found in the province.

Since the founding of New China in 1949, especially since the Third Plenary Session of the 11th Central Committee in 1978, tremendous social and economic changes have taken place in Shanxi due to the firm implementation of the reform and opening program. The province has fulfilled the goal of quadrupling its regional output four years ahead of the schedule. Its gross regional output in 1998 reached 160.11 billion yuan, 5.5 times the figure in 1978, representing an annual average growth of 8.98 percent. Grain output topped 10 million tonnes in each of the last two years, with a record high of 10.8 million tonnes in 1998. Total commodity retail sales reached 54.76 billion yuan, 16.94 times the figure in 1978. This reflects an average annual growth rate of 15.20 percent. Shanxi's foreign trade and economic cooperation has made breakthrough progress despite a poor original foundation and a late start. Between 1984 and 1998, the total contracted foreign capital in Shanxi reached US$3 billion, with realized foreign investment hitting US$900 million. Foreign exports increased considerably. Since 1978, the accumulated exports totalled US$10.5 billion, and the volume of exports in 1998 stood at US$1.45 billion, approximately 200 times the figure in 1978. To date, some 1,279 foreign-funded enterprises have begun operations in Shanxi, accounting for 10 percent of the province's total foreign exchange earnings.

II. Investment Environment

Since the reform and opening program was launched in

1978, especially during the 1990s, great efforts have been made to construct transportation, telecommunications and urban infrastructure facilities and to develop tertiary industries. As a result, the investment environment has been effectively improved. Rail tracks in use reached 2,511 kilometers, forming a railway network with Taiyuan as the center, linking the province directly with 19 major cities throughout the country. Its highways radiate in all directions. Two expressways from the capital to Jiuguang and Yuanping have been completed. A postal network now covers all counties, and a road network radiates to all towns and villages. Twenty-eight air routes converge on Taiyuan, linking Shanxi with the rest of the country. Recent years have also witnessed the rapid development of telecommunications in the province. In 1998, the total capacity of public telephone switchboards reached 2.08 million lines. Telephone services in all cities and counties became program-controlled. The number of urban telephone users reached 1.3 million. At the same time, cellular telephones, personal pagers, and magnetic card phone services have become available in Shanxi. Rapid development has also been seen in the financial sector, which is shown in the considerable increase of financial institutions and branch offices. These financial institutions are using the latest computer technology to link customers with global financial networks. Visitors to Shanxi will find convenience in shopping, accommodations and transportation. Over the past few years, foreign-oriented hotels and restaurants have grown in number. They are equipped with advanced facilities and are beautifully decorated. In Taiyuan alone, there are some 10,000 taxis in operation. Numerous retail branches have greatly improved the shopping environment. With the completion of the Wanjiazhai Yellow River Diversion Project, the shortages of water will be greatly eased. Inviting foreign capital and business people has drawn more and more concern from the government and all walks of life. The bi-annual Shanxi International Economic and Trade Talks and the annual Shanxi Commodities Fair have become increasingly brisk year after year.

III. Prospects for Development

Since 1979, Shanxi, as an inland province in the midwestern region, has experienced a major development gap when compared with the rapidly advancing eastern regions. The Outline of the Ninth Five-Year Plan for National Social and Economic Development and Long-Range Objects Through the Year 2010, which was passed at the Fifth Plenary Session of the 14th Central Committee, clearly defined the tasks of speeding up development in the midwestern region and gradually narrowing the regional gap. Shanxi set the goal of building itself into a guiding zone in the economic development of the midwestern region. It will firmly grasp the opportunity for development of the Bohai-Ring areas, fully display regional advantages, speed up regional industrial reorganizing, transferring and upgrading, and continuously raise the economic results in resource allocation.

The short-term targets are:

Continuously deepening the reform, opening wider to the outside world, and gradually bringing Shanxi into the orbit of the global economy; Vigorously strengthening agriculture, infrastructure facilities and already comparatively strong industries, with a focus on the comprehensive development of energy, chemicals, and heavy industries; Conforming to market demands and changes, relying on scientific and technological progress to readjust the product mix and fostering diversity in the pillar industries, and raising overall economic quality and promoting cultural and ethical progress, gradually narrowing the gap with the developed regions, and striving to raise comprehensive economic strength and living standards to match or exceed the nation's average level.

The long-term targets are:

By 2010, establishing a sound socialist market economy, opening wider in all directions to the outside world, and completing the integration with the global economy; Realizing the reorganization and upgrading of energy, chemicals, and heavy industries and initially fulfilling rural industrialization, industrial modernization, rural urbanization, and market internationalization; Fulfilling sustainable social and environmental development, bringing the comprehensive economic strength and living standards up to the nation's average level or the advanced level in the midwestern region.

IV. Encouraging Investment in Major Areas

The effort to realize its grand target for becoming an inland guide for the midwestern region, invigorating Shanxi and raising living standards calls for the unremitting efforts of 30 million Shanxi citizens for a long period to come. The effort also requires the support of various countries in terms of funds, technologies, management, talented people and information. In accordance with the principle of "active, rational and effective," further efforts will be made to improve the investment environment, simplify procedures, raise work efficiency, and enhance the quality and economic results of foreign investment. Shanxi will encourage and absorb foreign investment in the following areas:

1.Constructing a batch of infrastructure facilities and basic industrial projects badly needed for economic construction. These will involve agriculture, water conservation, energy and transportation, with a focus on projects related to water and soil conservation on the Loess Plateau, high quality and highly effective agriculture, water conservation facilities, the multi-purpose utilization of energy, environmental protection and high-grade highways.

2. Technical upgrading of a batch of ordinary industrial projects in traditional industries to form scale production of famous, excellent, new and special products. These will cover the light, textile, cigarette, medicines, machinery and electricity, metallurgy, chemicals and building materials sectors, specially in the areas of special rolled steel, aluminum and its products, rolled steel for construction, coke and coking chemistry, heavy-duty truck manufacture, coal machinery, high-grade cement, and chemical fibers.

3. Building a batch of high-tech industries that can quickly transform the productive force, with a focus on the development of materials sciences and new materials technologies, photoelectric sciences and photo-mechanical electronic integrated technologies, biological technologies, micro-electronics, electronic information technology, pharmaceutical sciences and bio-medical projects.

迎泽大街
Yingze Street

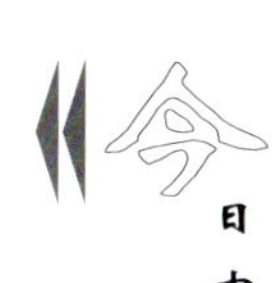

阔步前进中的内蒙古自治区

The Development of the Inner Mongolia Autonomous Region

内蒙古自治区成立于1947年5月1日，是中国最早成立的第一个少数民族自治区，也是中国北方对外开放的重要窗口。北与蒙古国、俄罗斯交界，国境线长4200公里，地跨东北、华北、西北，相邻八省区，全区土地面积118.3万平方公里，现辖4个直辖市和8个盟，下设101个旗、县、市、区，自治区首府设在呼和浩特市。1998年末，全区总人口2344.88万人，由49个民族组成，其中蒙古族392.86万人。

一、经济发展情况

内蒙古自治区地域辽阔，资源丰富，素有“东林西铁，南粮北牧，遍地矿藏”之美称，开发潜力巨大。目前，内蒙古已成为全国重要的农牧业、能源和原材料生产基地，特别是随着改革开放的不断深入和社会主义市场经济体制的建立，内蒙古国民经济和社会发展取得了举世瞩目的成就，在中国的地位也不断提高，尤其是涌现出一批闻名国内外的名牌产品，冠以鄂尔多斯品牌的羊绒系列服装被国家工商局评为中国驰名商标，成为全国5个少数民族自治区唯一的驰名品牌；基础设施面貌焕然一新，取得了历史性的突破，投资环境得到明显改善。科技教育事业不断发展壮大，目前，全区有各类专业技术人员近50万，近14万人获得高、中级专业技术职称资格，全区各类科技机构324家，自然科学学会和研究会92个，高等院校18所，共设置10个学科201个专业种类，高校科研机构52个。特别是改革开放20年以来，内蒙古经济社会以超过前30年的规模和速度前进，1998年全区国内生产总值1192.29亿元。比1947年增长59.2倍，比1978年增长5.6倍；人均国内生产总值5069元，比1947年增长13.4倍，比1978年增长4倍；财政收入131.2亿元，比1947年增长14.6万倍，比1978年增长18倍；粮食总产量157.54亿公斤，比1947年增长7.5倍，比1978年增长2.2倍；工业增加值399.42亿元，比1974年增长344倍，比1978年增长5倍；外贸进出口总额13.86亿美元，比1947年增长125倍，比1978年增长85.6倍；社会消费品零售总额400.9亿元，比1947年增长482倍，比1978年增长11.9倍。国民经济的快速发展，使城乡人民生活水平也显著提高。

二、投资环境

为加快对外开放步伐，内蒙古自治区下大力气加强基础产业、基础设施和中蒙、中俄边境口岸建设，出台了一系列鼓励外商及港澳台商投资的优惠政策，特别是进入90年代以后，内蒙古的交通、通迅和城市建设得到长足发展。目前，交通运输十分便捷，形成了铁路、公路、民航为骨干的运输网络，近10年来对区内7个民航机场进行了扩建，通往国内外航线20余条；建成了旗县以上的无线寻呼网、移动电话网、分组交换网、数字数据网，旗县以上地区实现了国际、国内直拨通话。城市规模不断扩大，功能日益完善。现设城市20座，呼和浩特市是自治区政治、经济和文化中心，“草原钢城”包头市是中国少数民族地区最大的工业城市和国家的冶金、稀土及重型汽车生产基地。

内蒙古开通了公路、铁路、水运、航空一、二类口岸18个，其中二连浩特、满洲里铁路、公路，呼和浩特、海拉尔航空及黑山头、室韦水路等一类口岸11个。中俄两国政府共同协商建立的边境地区跨国贸易区，中俄满洲里—后贝加尔斯克互市贸易区，设有商贸金融、保税仓储、出口加工、服务游乐等功能设施；包头稀土高新技术产业开发区是国家级高新技术产业开发区，现进入开发区独资、合资企业达30家；自治区级开发区有呼

和浩特金川开发区、如意经济技术开发区、临河经济技术开发区和赤峰平庄经济开发试验区。截至1998年底全区工商部门注册的“三资”企业达977家，目前内蒙古有外经贸公司200多家，同世界上80多个国家和地区建立了贸易和经济合作关系，出口商品达680余种。

内蒙古自治区人民政府下设对外开放办公室，综合、协调全区对外开放、对外经济协作工作，并且设立了内蒙古自治区对外招商引资服务中心、外商投资项目审批综合服务中心和外商投诉咨询服务中心等外商投资管理中介机构，专门从事招商引资有关的各项工作。内蒙古涉外服务功能显著提高，全区现有涉外旅行社21家，涉外宾馆、酒店200余家，其中三星级酒店12家，中国银行内蒙古分行及其所属分支机构与260余家海外分行、港澳联行及国外代理银行建立了直接代理关系。

三、发展前景

内蒙古自治区是国家经济战略布局中重要的能源、原材料生产基地，处于“承东启西”的重要战略地位。经过半个世纪的艰苦奋斗，内蒙古经济社会面貌发生了巨大变化，这片神奇的宝地开发潜力巨大，在未来的发展中更加充满了希望和魅力。

近期发展目标：到2000年，内蒙古总体目标是基本实现小康和初步建立起社会主义市场经济体制。围绕这一总目标，通过强化农牧业基础地位，进一步搞好科技教育，加强基础设施建设，培育壮大支柱产业和优势产业以及大力培育新的经济增长点等措施，实现预期目标，保持国民经济持续、快速、健康发展，1996-2000年预期经济增长目标为年均递增10%，不断提高经济运行质量和效益；大力发展外向型经济；保持固定资产投资的适度增长；努力实现财政收入和城乡人民生活水平的提高；促进市场繁荣，抑制通货膨胀；促进社会事业全面发展。

远期发展目标：到2010年内蒙古经济和社会发展要以显著提高国民经济整体效益为核心，继续推进经济增长方式的转变，逐步实现劳动密集型和资金密集型产业向技术与知识密集型产业转变，到2010年国民生产总值比2000年翻一番，人民的小康生活水平明显提高，形成比较完善的社会主义市场经济体制，实现经济和社会可持续发展。

四、投资的重点领域

内蒙古自治区为充分发挥资源优势，发展特色经济，促进企业技术进步、名优产品扩张和产业结构优化升级，提高经济运行质量和效益，制定了《内蒙古自治区当前产业发展序列》。鼓励投资的重点领域是：以农畜产品为原料的加工工业，煤炭、电力和天然气为主的能源工业，冶金工业，以重型汽车为主的机械装备工业，化学工业、建材工业和森林工业等；农牧业生产基地建设，农牧林水基础设施，交通、邮电建设，城市公用事业，安居工程和经济适用商品住宅建设等；加速发展以稀土、生物制药和以机电一体化为主的高新技术产业领域。特别是对于在自治区境内国家级和自治区级经济技术开发区内建设的国外、区外投资项目，将享受更加优惠的政策和政府提供的全方位优质服务。

Founded on May 1, 1947, the Inner Mongolia Autonomous Region was the first autonomous region established in China. It has been an important window to northern China during the period of reform and opening. Neighboring Mongolia and Russia to the north, it has 4,200 kilometers of borders. Its territory, 1.183 million square kilometers, makes up parts of northeastern, northern and northwestern China and borders 8 provinces and regions. Under its jurisdiction are four cities and 8 Banner leagues (an administrative division at the county level), counties, towns and districts. Huhhot is the region's capital. By the end of 1998, its population had reached 23,448,800. Among the 49 ethnic groups that form the population, there are

3,928,600 Mongolians,18,626,400 Han and 893,800 others.

I. Economic Development

The Inner Mongolia Autonomous Region boasts a vast territory with abundant resources. It is well known for its verdant forests in the east, iron mines in the west, grain fields in the south and animal husbandry in the north. Abundant in mineral resources, it has great potential for development. Inner Mongolia has become a national production base in agriculture, animal husbandry, energy and raw materials. It has achieved great success in its economic and social development and occupies an increasingly important position in China. What merits attention is the emergence of a set of brandname products well known both in China and abroad, such as Erdus cashmere sweaters, which were selected as a famous national brand by the State Administration for Industry and Commerce, the only one from the five autonomous regions in China. As infrastructural facilities have undergone a historical breakthrough and taken on a new look, the environment for investment has improved remarkably. Science and technology have developed dynamically. Now, there are nearly 500,000 professionals and technicians in the autonomous region, and nearly 140,000 have been conferred advanced and intermediate titles for their qualifications in different fields. The autonomous region has 324 scientific and technical institutions, 92 research institutes in natural sciences, 18 universities and colleges, with 10 branches of learning and 201 specialties, and 52 research centers. Since the Third Plenary Session of the Eleventh CPC Central Committee, the reform and opening policies have pushed forward social and economic development at a speed and scale quicker and larger than that of the previous 30 years. The 1998 GDP of the region reached 119.229 billion yuan, an increase of 59.2 times that of 1947 and 5.6 times that of 1978; the GDP per capita in 1998 was 5,069 yuan, an increase of 13.4 and 4 times that of 1947 and 1978 respectively; the total revenues that year were 13.12 billion yuan, an increase of 146,000 and 18 times over that in 1947 and 1978; the gross grain output was 15.754 billion kilograms, an increase of 7.5 and 2.2 times compared with 1947 and 1978; the total added output value of industry was 39.942 billion yuan, an increase of 344 and 5 times that of 1947 and 1978; the total volume of imports and exports reached US$1.386 billion, an increase of 125 times and 85.6 times that of 1947 and 1978; the general volume of retail sales of consumer goods was 40.09 billion yuan, an increase of 482 times and 11.9 times that of 1947 and 1978. The fast development of the regional economy has remarkably improved the living standards of the people.

II. Environment for Investment

To quicken the pace of reform and opening to the outside world, the Inner Mongolia Autonomous Region has made great efforts to strengthen industry, infrastructural facilities and the construction of ports bordering Mongolia and Russia. A series of preferential policies aimed at encouraging foreign investment and investment from Hong Kong, Macao and Taiwan has been launched. Entering the 1990s, transportation, telecommunications and urban construction have been well planned and developed from a long-term perspective. Now, a network of transportation, comprising railway, highways and aviation, provides excellent service to customers thanks to the past ten years of efforts in the renovation and expansion of seven airports in the region and the operation of over 20 new airlines. Wireless paging networks, mobile phone networks, telephone switchboards and digital and database networks have been constructed above the county level, and domestic and international long distance calling service is now available at the county level. The scale of cities has been growing with ser-

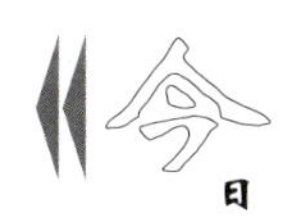

vices improving with each passing day. Among the 20 cities in the region, Huhhot is the political, economic and cultural center, while Baotou, nicknamed "Iron City on the Grasslands", is the largest industrial city in China's minority areas and the base of metallurgy, rare-earth and heavy vehicle production in China.

Inner Mongolia has opened 18 trading points of first and second rank, of which 11 are first rank, such as Erlianhot and the Manchurian highway and railway terminals, Huhhot and Hailar Airport, and the Heishantou and Shiwei ports. The Sino-Russian trading zone, established on a cooperative basis between China and Russia, functions as a trading and financial center, a free-trade zone, a depot, a processing center for export goods and a service and entertainment center. The Baotou Rare-earth High-tech Industrial Development Zone is a state-level high-tech development zone, and 30 foreign enterprises and joint ventures are now operating there. Development zones at the regional level include Huhhot's Jinchuan Development Zone and Ruyi Economic and Technological Development Zone, Linhe's Economic and Technological Development Zone and Chifeng's Pingzhuang Economic Development Experimental Zone. By the end of 1998, 977 foreign enterprises and joint ventures had registered with the administratives departments for industry and commerce. Today, more than 200 companies in Inner Mongolia have established trade and economic cooperative relations with over 80 countries and regions in the world, and 680-plus kinds of goods have been exported.

The people's government of the Inner Mongolia Autonomous Region has set up an Opening-up Office in charge of coordinating and balancing the work of opening to the outside world and foreign joint venture projects. And administration and service centers have also been set up to attract foreign investment, to help foreign investment projects get approval and to provide legal services to foreign businesses. In the region, there are now 21 travel agencies and 200-odd hotels (12 three-star hotels) granted with the right to serve foreigners. The headquarters of the Bank of China in Inner Mongolia and its branch offices have established direct relations with 260-odd international branches and with foreign banks in Hong Kong, Macao and around the world.

III. Prospects for Development

The Inner Mongolia Autonomous Region is an important production base of energy and raw materials on the strategic map of China's economic development because it connects China's relatively developed east coast and developing western hinterland. After a half century of efforts, the economy of the region has taken great steps forward, with enormous potential for future development. It is a land of treasure, hope and attraction.

Short-term development goals: The general goal is to realize the blueprint of a high standard of living and build a socialist market economic system by the year 2000. To reach the goal, the government has adopted measures such as improving the status of agriculture and animal husbandry, further promoting scientific and technological education, enhancing infrastructural construction, expanding and strengthening mainstay industries and going all out to support new areas of economic growth so as to keep the regional economy developing at a steady, healthy speed. The target annual growth rate for between 1996-2000 is 10 percent. The government has also focused on the work of developing an export-oriented economy, maintaining an appropriate investment growth in fixed assets, making strenuous efforts to improve revenue and the living standards of the people, propelling the prosperity of the market, curbing inflation and promoting the full development of socialism.

Long-term goals: In the first decade of the next century, the autonomous government will concentrate its efforts on the marked improvement of the region's economy as a whole. It will continue to better the structure of its economy, gradually changing from labor-intensive industries to capital-, technology- and knowledge-intensive industries. By the year 2010, the GNP is targeted to double that of 2000 and the living standards of the people should see a marked improvement. A mature socialist market economic system will be established with the potential for further social and economic development.

IV. Key Fields for Investment

To fully use its resources to develop an economy with local characteristics, make technological advancements in enterprises, gain a greater market share with its brandname products, balance and better its industrial structure, and develop the economy in a healthy and efficient way, the Inner Mongolia Autonomous Region has worked out "Ranking of Priority Industries for Development in the Inner Mongolia Autonomous Region". Key fields it encourages investment in include: agricultural and animal products processing, coal, power and natural gas production, metallurgy, machine building with heavy vehicles as the core, chemicals, construction materials and forestry industries, construction of farming and animal husbandry bases, infrastructural construction for farming, animal husbandry, forestry and water conservancy, transportation, post and telecommunications, public facilities in cities, housing, and high-tech industrial fields based on rare earth, bio-medicine, and mechanical and electrical industries. To further encourage investment in state and regional economic and technological developing zones, foreign-investment projects and domestic out-of-province-investment projects enjoy preferential policies and a quality services package provided by the government of the autonomous region.

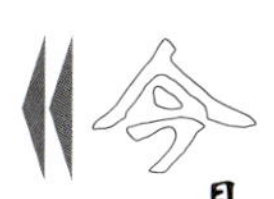

辽宁——老工业基地焕发青春

Liaoning: The Old Industrial Base Regains Its Vitality

一、经济发展

辽宁省是中国北方的工业基地和沿海对外开放地区。现辖14个地级市，土地总面积14.75万平方公里，总人口4157万。辽宁是新中国成立后建立起来的重要工业基地，有一批有代表性的国有大中型企业。布局较为合理，体系完整，门类齐全，基础雄厚。科技实力比较雄厚，科研机构门类齐全，学科基本配套，攻克关键技术和开发能力较强，并拥有一批装备着国际先进测试手段的国家级实验基地，构成了领域广泛的科研体系。

建国50年来，辽宁省社会经济面貌发生了巨大的变化，特别是改革开放20年来，辽宁省开创了建国以来经济和社会发展的最好时期。老工业基地正焕发青春，国民经济持续增长。1998年，国内生产总值3881.7亿元，比1978年增长4.3倍，年平均增长8.7%；社会消费品零售总额1568.7亿元，比1978年增长21倍，年平均增长16.7%。国民经济实力大大增强。1998年人均国内生产总值9415元，年平均增长7.7%。外向型经济发展取得可喜成绩，1979-1998年，辽宁省共签订利用外资项目20137个，合同利用外资375.9亿美元，实际利用外资186.4亿美元，外资投向包括冶金、机械、化工、电子、交通等行业。目前辽宁省有投产开业的“三资企业”7505家，企业经营良好。外贸出口大幅度增长，1978年以来，累计出口总额达1103亿美元，年平均增长10%。

二、投资环境

为了加速发展外向型经济，辽宁省努力改善投资环境，加快交通、能源、基础设施建设，大力发展第三产业，投资环境日臻完善。

1. 地理位置优越。辽宁省是中国东北地区唯一的沿海省份，是东北经济区通向世界的海路进出口门户，是连接东北经济区和环渤海经济区乃至中国内陆广大地区的结合部。

2. 自然资源丰富。现已发现的矿藏资源有115种，已开发的矿藏有69种，矿藏资源品种齐全；土地类型多，水、土、光、气温组合条件好，不仅野生动物、植物资源丰富，也为农、林、牧、副、渔业发展提供了良好的条件；由于濒临黄海、渤海两个海域，海洋资源和旅游资源十分丰富，具有巨大的开发潜力。

3. 交通运输便利。已经形成了以港口为门户，以铁路为动脉，以公路干线为骨架，民用航空和管道运输相配合的纵横交错的立体运输网络。铁路密度居全国第一；公路通车里程已超过4万公里；大连、营口、丹东、锦州等五个对外港口，主要生产性泊位142个，万吨级泊位46个；沈阳和大连的航空港已开辟了通达日本、香港、韩国、俄罗斯的航线；全省各市县都开通了国内国际直拨程控电话。全省本地网电话交换机总容量已达678万门，电话普及率达到16.8部／百人。

4. 综合科技实力较强。有各类科研与技术开发机构1133个，高等学校61所，企事业单位各类专业技术人员182万，民营科技企业已发展到6100家，具备较强的消化吸收国外先进技术独立开发新产品的能力。

三、发展前景

面对充满机遇而又富有挑战的新世纪，辽宁已经确立了迈向21世纪的长远发展战略目标："九五"期间提前实现第二步战略目标，下世纪前10年为实现第三步战略目标打好基础，塑造老工业基地新形象。

近期发展目标：重点搞活国有经济和国有大中型企业，建立现代企业制度，建立、健全市场体系和社会保障体制，初步建立社会主义市场经济体制框架；把转变经济增长方式贯穿到国民经济各个领域、各个环节，提高国民经济整体素质和经济效益；对外开放向着宽领域、纵深化、高水平发展，加速与国际经济接轨；全面实现现代化建设的第二步战略目标。

远期发展目标：形成比较完善的社会主义市场经济体制，逐步完成经济增长方式的转变；产业结构进一步优化，三次产业协调发展；建成新型原材料工业基地、重大成套装备基地、高新技术产业化基地；社会生产力、综合经济实力和人民生活水平再上一个新台阶。

四、投资重点

辽宁省到本世纪末要抓好机械、冶金、电子、化工、纺织、轻工、农业和基础设施等重点行业的利用外资。

1. 机械工业。机械工业利用外资要以跟踪发展高新技术、主攻重大成套设备，发展工程机械、汽车等两个带动性大的行业。

2. 电子工业。采用高新技术，开展电子产品的开发与应用，以及为现代化生产配套的高新技术产品，重点搞好五大工程，即计算机及其应用工程、通讯工程，电力电子工程，电视、音响工程；金卡工程，带动全省电子工业发展。

3. 冶金工业。通过对现有骨干企业的技术发

沈阳—大连高速公路
Shenyang-Dalian Expressway

展，加速冶金工业技术装备更新；重点发展板管带材、复合材，实现产品升级换代；搞好产品的深加工，增加附加值。

4. 石油化工工业。充分利用辽宁省石油资源和煤炭资源，吸收外资发展有机化工材料和合成材料。

5. 建材工业。利用外资加快技术改造步伐，发展节能和综合利用产品、新型建筑材料、高技术无机非金属新材料。

6. 医药工业。重点引进目前国内尚不能生产的药品，以及国际上先进的制剂技术，发展化学新药。

7. 轻工业。以重点工业优势为依托，优先发展新型日化、工程塑料、电光源三个新兴行业，发展食品、包装、五金三个行业。

8. 纺织工业。以国内外市场为导向，调整产品结构、原料结构，以高技术、高附加值的服装和辅料为龙头，进行系列改造。

9. 高新技术产业。利用外资重点发展工业机器人产业化、计算机产业、新材料产业、现代通信产业、电力电子产业、智能控制及仪表产业、机电一体化产业、现代生物技术产业、精细化工产业、高效节能、环保产业十大高新技术产业。

10. 基础设施建设。大力发展电力工业。重点抓好电厂的利用外资，尽快使项目建成投产。积极发展交通、港口建设。重点抓好沈阳至山海关、沈阳至四平高速公路及桃仙机场扩建工程。搞好城市环境保护和治理。积极利用国外资金，搞好以沈、大、鞍、抚、本等大中城市为中心的城市环境治理。邮电通信业，抓好市话和长途交换网建设。

11. 农业。利用外资对农业资源进行深加工，改变出口结构，提高单位产量和出口创汇值，发展高效创汇农业。

I. Development Situation of Economy

Liaoning Province is an industrial base and open coastal area, covering an area of 147,500 square kilometres with a population of 41.57 million. It has 14 prefecture-level cities under its jurisdiction. As an important industrial base since the founding of the PRC, Liaoning has a group of large- and medium-sized State-owned enterprises, which have rational distribution, integral system, complete categories and tremedous strength. It also has a group of national experimental bases equipped with the latest and most advanced testing methods. As a result, Liaoning has a comprehensive science and technology research system.

Since the founding of New China in 1949, the economy and society of Liaoning have made great changes. This is especially true of the period since 1978. Because of the adoption of reform and opening program, Liaoning has gained a lot of opportunities to develop its economy, and its economy is increasing steadily. Its economy is stronger and stronger. Liaoning's GDP reached 388.17 billion yuan in 1998, 4.3 times over that of 1978, with an annual growth rate of 8.7 percent. Its total retail commodities sales, coming to 156.87 billion yuan, were 21 times over 1978, with an annual increase rate of 16.7 percent. At the same time, Liaoning's per capita GDP reached 9,415 yuan, with an average growth rate of 7.7 percent every year.

After 20 years of reform and opening, Liaoning's internationally-oriented economy has made considerable progress. The total volume of exports came to US$110.3 billion, with an annual growth rate of 10%. On the other hand, from 1979 to 1998, 20,137 projects utilizing foreign investment were signed. The total contracted value amounted to US$37.59 billion, among which, US$18.64 billion was actually used. The foreign capital focused on industries of metallurgy, machinery, chemistry, electronics and transportation. At present, there are 7,505 joint-venture enterprises registered in Liaoning.

II. Investment Environment

Liaoning is the only province of northeastern China that has a coastline. As a result, it has become a window for northeastern areas and a connection of the northeastern economic zone, Bohai economic zone, and inland provinces. It is abundant in natural resources. There are 115 kinds of varified mineral resources, of which 69 kinds have been exploited. Moreover, boasting its good condition of the natural environment and abounding with marine and tourism resources, there is enormous potential for Liaoning to develop industries of farming, forestry, animal husbandry, fishery and tourism.

However, Liaoning is putting more efforts into improving the investment environment. It has strengthened the development of tertiary industries and the construction of transportation, energy and other infrastructure facilities. These efforts have resulted in notable improvement in various service facilities. In 1998, the length of highways opened to traffic in the province reached over 40,000 kilometres, and the highway density took the lead in China. The coastal open ports, including Dalian, Yingkou, Dandong and Jinzhou, boasted 142 berths, of which 46 are deep-water berths capable of handling 10,000-dwt cargo vessels. The airport at Liaoning operates routes to Japan, Hong Kong, Korea and Russia. The capacity of telephone switchboards reached 6.78 million units. The number of phones per 100 population is 16.8 units.

Liaoning has 1,133 science and technology research institutions in various fields and 61 universities or colleges of higher leaning. The enterprises, possessing 1.82 million professional technicians, have the capability to absorb advanced foreign techniques and develop new products.

III. Prospects for Development

Facing the new century full of opportunities and challenges, Liaoning has made short-term development targets and long-term targets. The short-term targets are enlivening the state-owned enterprises, initially establishing the basic framework for a socialist market economic system, opening the markets of Liaoning wider and deeper, promoting the economy's efficiency, and realizing the second strategic target of modernization construction.

The long-term targets are establishing a perfect socialist market system, optimizing the industrial structure, readjusting the development of the industries, and establishing new raw material bases and new hi-tech industrial bases.

IV. Key Fields for Investment

In the next few years, Liaoning will encourage the development of industries related to machinery, metallurgy, electronics, texiles and agriculture. Additional emphasis will be placed on projects to develop the raw materials industry, petrochemistry industry, building materials industry, medicine industry, light industry and high new technology industry. Moreover, it is favorable to invest in infrastructure facilities. Besides the construction of the eletricity industry, transportation and ports, the construction of highway, airport, telecommunications and environmental protection industries longs for investment.

走向新世纪的吉林

Jilin: Marching Toward the New Century

吉林省地处东北中部，人口2603.23万。全省有朝、满、蒙、回、锡伯等43个少数民族，占全省总人口的10.21%。

吉林省土地总面积为18.74万平方公里，其中山地占36%，平原占30%，丘陵占5.8%，台地及其他占28.2%。土地资源比较丰富，农业用地占21.1%，林业用地占48.6%，牧业用地占8.1%，渔业用地占3.4%，其他用地占18.8%。全省水资源主要集中于松花江、鸭绿江、牡丹江、辽河、嫩江6大水系，总水域面积为64万公顷，江河水面为37.3万公顷。森林资源十分丰富，东部长白山区是全国林业基地之一，19万公顷的长白山自然保护区原始森林保护完好，是中国重要的林木及野生资源储藏库和举世瞩目的旅游胜地，植物多达870余种，可食用植物200多种，拥有的动物资源达1100多种。1980年列入联合国生物保护圈。矿产资源比较丰富，全省已探明矿种74种，占全国探明含量矿种的44.6%，主要矿种为铁、铜、铅、锌、硼、石英砂、石油、钼、煤炭、油页岩、煤等，全省矿产储量居全国前5位的有22种，居前10位的有43种。

建国50年来，吉林省发生了巨大的变化，国民经济快速增长。

改革开放20年中，吉林省综合实力显著增强。到1998年，全省国内生产总值达1564.42亿元，比1978年增长5.5倍，年均递增9.8%。人均国内生产总值由1978年的381元增加到1998年的5937元。产业结构不断优化，合理调整各产业在国民经济中的比例关系。第三产业迅速发展，三次产业增加值在经济总量中的比重发生了较大变化，由1978年的29.3：52.4：18.3转变为26.5：37.7：35.8，第三产业比重明显上升，经济走上了持续稳定发展的轨道。进入90年代后，吉林省把发展对外贸易和外向型经济作为突破口，1998年全省进出口总额16.53亿美元，其中出口7.49亿美元。全省共有4个国家级开发区和12个省级开发区，增大了对外商投资的吸引力，到1998年全省实际利用外资5.78亿美元，外商直接投资达4.09亿美元。

改革开放的20年是吉林省投资规模最大，成效最为显著的20年。20年间，全社会固定资产投

吉林树挂
Rim-fog Trees in Jilin

资累计完成3100亿元，是前29年的14倍，建成投产和交付使用的基本建设，更新改造项目2.9万个，新增固定资产3000亿元。各级政府和企业多方筹集资金，加强对生产基础的技术改造和科技应用的投入力度，相继建成了一批新工艺和新生产线，开展了技术改造、技术开发、产品和设备的更新换代及高科技领域的生产应用研究，在生物工程、电子信息、新材料及光电一体化等高新技术领域取得了可喜的成就，高新技术产值已占工业总产值的10%左右。20年来，吉林省交通邮电事业发生了历史性的巨大变化，20年间全省交通运输邮电通讯业累计完成投资236亿元，年均增长21.4%，全省公路通车里程增加到2.5万公里，平均每年递增0.47%。客运量年平均增长14.98%。货运量年平均递增11.05%。1978全省仅有1个民用机场，到1997年底，全省拥有民用机场3个，民航共开辟航线43条，国际航线3条，可与国内30个大中城市及香港、俄罗斯、日本、韩国等地区和国家通航。1997年全省邮电业务总量完成37.5亿元，比1978年增长96.4倍，连续15年超过国民经济发展速度。

经济的发展，同时促进了城乡居民收入的增加和生活水平的提高。1998年底，全省农民人均纯收入为2383.60元，与1978年相比，人均收入增长12.1倍，年均递增13.7%；城镇居民的可支配收入也由1983年的451.31元增加到1998年的4206.60元，年均递增16.0%。科教事业蓬勃发展，目前全省已初步建成门类比较齐全、配套、科技和经济相结合的科研体系。普通高等学校1998年达41所；在校学生11.79万人；文化艺术事业、卫生事业和体育事业都取得了令人瞩目的成就。

目前，吉林省各族人民全面实施科教兴省、开放带动和县域突破三大战略，以经济效益为中心，继续推进改革开放，突出结构调整和市场开拓，把扩大内需作为促进经济增长的主要措施，重点发展效益农业，搞好国企改革和脱困，推进技术创新，加快县域经济发展，保持社会稳定，实现国民经济持续、快速健康发展和社会全面进步。

Located in the center of northeastern China, Jilin Province has a population of 26.0323 million. It is home to 43 ethnic minorities, such as Korea, Manchu, Mongolia, Hui and Xibo, making up 10.21 percent of the total population.

Of its total area of 187,400 square kilometers, mountains make up 36 percent, plains 30 percent, hills 5.8 percent and plateaus and others 28.2 percent. Jilin Province is rich in land resources, with land for agricultural use accounting for 21.1 percent, forestry 48.6 percent, animal husbandry 8.1 percent, fisheries 3.4 percent, and other uses 18.8 percent. Its water resources mainly consist of six water systems, including the Songhua, Yalu, Mudan, Liaohe and Nengjiang rivers, with a total water area of 640,000 hectares. The water area of the rivers is 373,000 hectares. It is rich in forestry resources, the Changbai Mountains in the east are one of the nation's major forest bases. The primitive forest in the Changbai Mountains Nature Reserve, which covers an area of 190,000 hectares, has been well preserved. It is an important storehouse of trees and natural resources, as well as a world-renowned tourist attraction. It is home to more than 870 species of plants, including over 200 species of edible plants, and more than 1,100 species of animals. In 1980, it was included in the UN Man and Biosphere project. Jilin has abundant mineral resources. It has 74 kinds of proven mineral resources, making up 44.6 percent of the total China has verified, including iron, copper, lead, zinc, boron, quartz sand, molybdenum, oil shale, petroleum and coal. Of these, deposits of 22 kinds are among the nation's top five, and 43 varieties are among

the top 10.

In the past 50 years since the founding of New China, tremendous changes have taken place in Jilin Province.

Since the adoption of the policy of reform and opening to the outside world, the comprehensive strength of Jilin Province has been remarkably strengthened.

In 1998, GDP reached 156.442 billion yuan, or 6.6 times that of 1978, with an average annual growth rate of 9.8 percent. The per capita GDP increased from 381 yuan in 1978 to 5,937 yuan in 1998. In the last 20 years, Jilin Province has constantly optimized its industrial structure and readjusted the proportions of various industries in the national economy. A great change has taken place in the proportions of the primary, secondary and tertiary industries in the total economic volume, changing from 29.3 : 52.4 : 18.3 in 1978 to 26.5 : 37.7 : 35.8. Jilin's economy has developed in a sustained way. Since 1990, it has taken foreign trade and the export-oriented economy as its breakthrough point. In 1998, its total import and export volume reached US$1.653 billion, including US$749 million in exports. Jilin has four national development zones and 12 provincial-level development zones, which have attracted much foreign capital. By 1998 the province had utilized US$578 million, and direct investment by foreign businesses had reached US$409 million.

In the 20 years since the initiation of reform and opening to the outside world, Jilin Province has made the largest investments and achieved the greatest successes. During these 20 years, it has invested 310 billion yuan in social fixed assets, 14 times the total figure of the 29 years before the reform and opening to the outside world. It has completed 29,000 capital construction projects and renewal and transformation projects; and its fixed assets have increased by 300 billion yuan. Governments at all levels and enterprises have collected funds by various ways to strengthen the technological transformation of production and the application of science and technology; a group of new techniques and production lines have been formed one after another. They have started technological transformation and development, renewed products and equipment, and engaged in research into the application of high technologies. Encouraging achievements have been made in the new- and high-tech fields of biological projects, electronic information, new materials and the integration of light and electricity. The output value of new and high technologies makes up about 10 percent of the total industrial output value.

Historical changes have taken place in Jilin's transportation, post and telecommunications. In the past 20 years, 23.6 billion yuan has been invested in transportation, post and telecommunications, with an average annual growth rate of 21.4 percent. Highways open to traffic have increased to 25,000 kilometers, with an average annual growth rate of 0.47 percent. The annual turnover of passenger transportations increased by 14.98 percent on average; the annual turnover of freight transportation by 11.05 percent. In 1978, Jilin had only one airport. At the end of 1997, it had three civilian airports used by 43 airlines, including three international ones. Regular flights link Jilin with 30 large and medium-sized cities of China, as well as with Hong Kong, Russia, Japan, the Republic of Korea and other countries and regions. In 1997, its post and telecommunications business volume reached 3.75 billion yuan, or 97.4 times the 1978 figure. Its average annual growth rate has exceeded that of the national economy for 15 years in succession.

The economic development has increased urban and rural incomes and improved living standards. At the end of 1998, the rural net income came to 2,383.6 yuan, or an increase of 13.1 times the 1978 figure, with an average annual growth rate of 13.7 percent. Urban disposable incomes increased from 451.31 yuan in 1983 to 4,206.6 yuan in 1998, with an average annual growth rate of 16.0 percent.

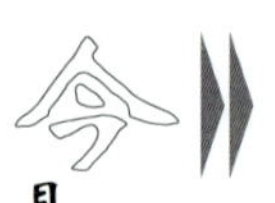

长白山
Changbai Mountain

Science and education undertakings have developed vigorously. Now, the province has a scientific research system with various categories, featuring the integration of science, technology and economy. The number of institutions of higher learning increased to 41 in 1998; and the number of college students grew to 117,900 in 1998. Eye-catching achievements have been made in culture, art, public health and sports.

The people of all ethnic groups in Jilin are implementing the three major strategies of developing Jilin with science and education, accelerating the economic development through opening to the outside world and making breakthroughs in the areas under the jurisdiction of the counties by continually promoting reform and opening to the outside world with economic benefits as the center, stressing the structural readjustment and the opening up of the market, promoting the economic growth through the expansion of domestic demand, putting emphasis on the development of beneficial agricultural, reforming the state-owned enterprises and helping them get rid of poverty, promoting technological innovations, speeding up the economic development of the areas under the jurisdiction of the counties, and maintaining social stability so as to realize the sustained and rapid development of the national economy and the all-round social progress.

黑龙江——中国对外开放的北大门

Heilongjiang: Chinaís Northern Gate

一、经济发展

黑龙江省系由境内最大的河流黑龙江而得名。全省现辖13个地级市，土地总面积45.4万平方公里，占全国大陆面积的4.7%，居全国第6位；总人口3773万，其中市镇人口占54%。黑龙江省是中国重要的煤炭、石油、木材、机械和商品粮基地，曾为全国的经济发展作出了重要的贡献。改革开放20年来，全省在发展、改造传统工业的同时，还形成了汽车、石化、电子、食品和医药等新型支柱产业。

建国50年来，特别是近20年来，是黑龙江省经济发展最快的时期。1998年，全省实现国内生产总值2833亿元，年平均增长6.8%，其中近20年年平均增速为7.5%，比前30年年平均增长速度加快1.2个百分点。1998年全省人均国内生产总值7557元，比1978年增长2.5倍，年均增长6.5%。社会消费品零售额949.7亿元，比1978年增长2.6倍，年平均增长6.6%。对外贸易领域扩大，利用外资成倍增长。1998年全省进出总额达到38.1亿美元，比1978年增长84倍，年均增长24.85%。1979-1998年，累计签订利用外资项目5961项，合同利用外资金额69.6亿美元，实际利用外资41.5亿美元。目前全省有“三资企业”4000多家，已有112个国家和地区同黑龙江省保持经济贸易关系和进出口业务。

二、投资环境

1.独特的地理位置。黑龙江省与俄罗斯有3045公里的边境线，是亚洲及太平洋地区通向欧洲大陆的重要通道，绥芬河、黑河、同江等口岸城市是沟通独联体、东欧各国经济贸易往来的窗口和桥梁，目前黑龙江有一类开放口岸25个。

2.丰富的自然资源。黑龙江处于世界著名的三大黑土带之一，盛产大豆、小麦、玉米、马铃薯、水稻等粮食作物以及甜菜、亚麻、烤烟等经济作物，是全国主要的商品粮基地之一。黑龙江是全国十大草原之一，适于发展畜牧业，其中松嫩草场是世界三大羊草地之一。黑龙江森林面积、森林总蓄积和木材产量均居全国首位。全省境内江河湖泊众多，有黑龙江、乌苏里江、松花江、嫩江和绥芬河五大水系，水资源丰富。已发现的矿产达131种，石油、石墨、矽线石等10种矿产储量居全国之首，煤炭储量居东北三省第一位。黑龙江自然风光秀美，山水景色粗犷，冰雪景观绚丽，野生动物珍奇，文化古迹独特，夏季是避暑的胜地，冬季是冰雪的乐园，有多姿多彩的旅游资源。

3.发达的交通通信环境。交通运输已经形成陆、水、空和地下管道运输并行的综合运输网。目前，全省拥有哈长、滨绥、滨洲等60条铁路干线、支线和联络线，是全国铁路密度较高的地区之一。航空运输业迅速发展，民用航空开通国内国际航线66条，哈尔滨太平国际机场是全国著名的大机场之一，可以起降目前世界上最先进的民航客机。黑龙江水系是中国通航的三大水系之一，全省共有港口、码头331个，有16个水运港口对外开放。邮电通信能力大为提高，形成了以光缆网为主体、以微波网为辅助，多传输路径的现代化通信格局，基本实现了乡以上的交换程控化和传输数字化，全省每百人拥有电话机8部，电话普及率13%，移动电话111.1万户，计算机网络用户1.1万户。

4.较强的综合科技实力。全省有科研与技术开发机构884个，各类专业技术人员128万，在基础理论、应用研究和技术开发方面取得了10多万项科学技术成果，得到了明显的经济效益。

三、发展前景

黑龙江确立了面向21世纪的发展目标：1996-2000年力争人均国内生产总值翻两番，初步建立社会主义市场经济体制，人民生活达到小康水平；到2010年，全省国内生产总值再翻一番，形成比较完善的社会主义市场经济体制，实现社会的全面进步。

近期目标：大力推进产业结构调整与升级，

三次产业的比重由目前的19：53：28调整为15：53：32；实施对工业结构的战略性调整，加快培植支柱产业，汽车、化工、食品、电子、医药等五大支柱产业产值占全省工业总产值的比重由目前的26%提高到38-43%；广泛采用先进技术装备社会各部门，加快国民经济的信息化进程；大力发展科技教育，促进科技与经济的结合，培养各级各类人才，普遍提高劳动者素质；促进区域经济协调发展。

远期目标：产业结构实现高级化，三次产业比重调整到10：50：40。基础产业和基础设施同国民经济和社会发展基本相适应。资金和技术密集型产业占主导地位。经济的外向度大大提高，服务高效、功能完善的第三产业体系基本形成。科技进步对经济增长的贡献率达到50%以上，部分领域科学技术达到国际先进水平。总人口控制在4234万以内，人民生活达到90年代初中等发达国家水平。

四、投资重点

今后一个时期，黑龙江省利用外资将以农业综合开发和农副产品精深加工、大中型企业技术改造、基础设施建设以及发展高新技术产业和乡镇企业为重点，重点培植汽车、化工、食品、电子和医药五大支柱产业。

1. 优先发展基础产业

(1)以粮食为主的农业和相应的深加工工业。

(2)以能源、交通为主的基础设施和基础产业建设。

2. 重点发展主导产业

(1)电子工业。

(2)机械工业。发展电站成套设备、大重型机械设备、子午胎、工量具、中小轴承生产基地。

(3)以石油化工为主的化学工业。

(4)汽车工业。

3. 充分发挥资源优势，发展轻纺、食品、医药、建材、冶金和以旅游服务业为主的第三产业等行业

(1)轻纺工业。

(2)食品工业。

(3)医药工业。

(4)建材工业。

(5)冶金工业。

(6)扩大对第三产业的投资。

Heilongjiang Province was named after the Heilongjiang River, the largest river running across the province. Under the jurisdiction of the provincial government are 13 cities of prefectural level, occupying a land of 454,000 square kilometres. Heilongjiang is the sixth largest province and its area accounts for 4.7 percent of the total mainland of China. It has a population of 37.73 million, 54 percent of which are urban residents. Heilongjiang is famous for having abundant natural resources, therefore it is one of China's production bases for coal, petroleum, timber, grain and machines. During the last 20 years since the new policy of reform and opening was initiated, Heilongjiang has developed its own pillar industries, such as car manufacturing, petro-chemicals, electronics, food and pharmaceuticals.

I. Economic Development

Big progress has been made in Heilongjiang's economic construction since 1949. The last 20 years in particular have witnessed a rapid economic growth. In 1998, the province realized a GDP of 283.3 billion yuan. From 1978 to 1998, the GDP increased by an average of 7.5 percent a year. In 1998, the per capita GDP reached 7,557 yuan, representing an increase of 2.5 times compared to 1978, with an annual increase of 6.5 percent. The total sales of commodities was 94.97 billion yuan, about 2.6 times more than that in 1978, and with an annual increase of 6.6 percent.

Heilongjiang is situated in the central section of northeastern Asia, an ideal place to conduct foreign trade with adjacent countries. In 1998, the province realized a foreign trade volume of US$3.81 billion, about 84 times that of 20 years ago, and with an annual increase of 24.85 percent. During the period from 1979 to 1998, 5,961 foreign-funded projects were signed between foreign investors and the province, with the total capital by contract being US$6.96 billion and actual use of the capital being US$4.15 billion. Now the number of foreign-invested enterprises in Heilongjiang is over 4,000, and the province maintains stable foreign trade relations with 112 countries and regions.

II. Investment Environment

The province has a border with Russia stretching for 3,045 kilometres, and it thus is a pivotal place to link the Asian-Pacific region with Europe. The province has opened 25 ports so far, including the large ones in Suifenhe, Heihe and Tongjiang, through which the busy traders between China and the Commonwealth of Independent States or Eastern European countries shuttle back and forth.

Heilongjiang is located in one of the largest black-earth regions in the world, favorable for the growth of soya beans, wheat, corn, potatoes, paddy rice, sugar beets, flax, and flue-cured tobacco. This makes Heilongjiang one of the important bases in China for the production of grain for commercial purposes. Animal husbandry has developed in the province as it is home to a vast stretch of grassland. Its Songnen Grassland is believed to be one of three quality pastures in the world that are ideal for sheep.

The land of Heilongjiang is densely covered by forest, with more forest cover than any other province and more timber output. The province has rich resources in water since it is crossed by five large river systems: the Heilongjiang River, the Wusuli River, the Songhua River, the Nenjiang River and the Suifen River. Up to now 131 minerals have been discovered in the province, and it ranks first of all the provinces in 10 mineral reserves including graphite. It has the richest deposits of coal in northeastern China.

Heilongjiang is blessed with natural charm and countless historical and cultural relics. It is a perfect place to spend summer holidays and a paradise for winter sports enthusiasts.

A developed transportation sector includes 60 railway trunk lines. Taiping International Airport in Harbin is a large and modern-equipped airport, accommodating the most advanced airplanes in the world. By now 66 air routes link the province with many domestic and overseas cities. The provinces have several water routes served by 331 ports and docks and 16 of these are open to foreign businesses and clients. Its telecommunications network has been modernized in recent years, with all the facilities at the township level or higher now being programmed-controlled or digitally operated. There are eight phones for every 100 residents in the province, 1.111 million users of mobile phones and 11,000 people connected to the Internet.

There are 884 scientific research institutes in the province, staffed by 1.28 million people. They are mainly devoted to basic research and the development of applied technology. Their efforts have resulted in over 100,000 technical achievements which have brought in huge economic profits for Heilongjiang.

III. What the Future Holds

A development plan has been created for Heilongjiang in the 21st century. According to it, by end of 2000, the province's per capita GDP will quadruple that of 1995; a socialist market system will have basically taking form; and the local people will enjoy a better standard of living. By the year 2010, the province's GDP will double again and a well-established market system is expected, promoting

大庆石化
Daqing Petrochemistry Plant

overall social progress.

According to the short-term development plan, the province's industrial structure will be readjusted and upgraded. Now the proportion of the primary, secondary and tertiary industries is 19:53:28 and the ratio will be adjusted to 15:53:32. Priority will be given to developing such sectors as car manufacturing, the chemical industry, food, electronics and the pharmaceutical industry, which are the five pillars in the province. The total output of these sectors will be increased to account for 38-43 percent of the province's total industrial output from 26 percent at the present time. In order to achieve this goal, more advanced technology and equipment will be employed, and every department will have quicker access to up-to-date information. Scientific research and education will be greatly improved so as to foster more talents necessary for the province's economic and social development while upgrading the quality of the local population.

According to the long-term plan, the proportion of primary, secondary and tertiary industries will be further adjusted to 10:50:40 and basic industries and infrastructure will be highly developed to adequately support the province's comprehensive economic take-off. Some capital or technology-intensive industries will play a leading role in the province's economic development, and the foreign-oriented sectors will be expanded to a great extent. A modern, highly efficient tertiary industry is expected to take form. Scientific and technological research will develop rapidly, contributing 50 percent or more to the province's economic growth. The total population in Heilongjiang will be controlled at 42.34 million or less, and living standards will reach the level of the semi-developed countries in the early 1990s.

IV. Main Points To Attract Investment

In the coming years Heilongjiang will attract foreign investment mainly for the development of agriculture, fine-processing of agricultural products, technical innovation in large or medium-sized enterprises, infrastructure construction, high and new-technology, and township enterprises. The five pillar industries will remain the hot points for the government to encourage rapid development .

The basic industries will be given priority. While developing grain-based agriculture and fine-processing of agricultural products, the province will reclaim more wasteland and improve the low-yield farmland and grassland.

In the development of energy and infrastructure, a number of projects relating to large-scale power plants, hydropower plants and thermal-supply engineering will be constructed.

The leading sectors which should develop fast in the province are:

— Electronics industry.

— Mechanical industry.

— Chemicals industry centered on petro-chemical production.

— Auto industry.

By taking full advantage of local natural resources, Heilongjiang will accelerate the development of textiles, food, pharmaceuticals, building materials, metallurgy, tourism and other tertiary industries.

— Textiles and other light industries.

— Food industry.

— Pharmaceuticals.

— Building materials.

— Metallurgy industry.

— Investment in tertiary industries will be expanded.

上海——璀璨的东方明珠

Shanghai: A Bright Pearl of the East

一、经济发展

上海是中国重要的经济中心城市、交通枢纽和对外贸易口岸，也是中国科学技术、文化教育事业的重要基地之一。现辖16个区、4个县，总面积6340.5平方公里。至1998年末，全市户籍人口1306.58万人，占全国总人口1%，其中市区人口1070.62万。

建国50年来，上海经济建设取得了巨大成就。特别是改革开放以来，上海人民走出了一条具有中国特色、体现时代特征、符合上海特点的发展新路。尤其是90年代以后，上海国民生产总值连续7年保持10%以上的增长率，1998年上海国内生产总值达到3688亿元，平均每年增长9.1%；人均国内生产总值2.82万元，按当年汇率计算，已突破3400美元，相当于中等发达国家水平；1998年，上海完成财政收入1146亿元，平均每年增长9.3%；工业总产值5897亿元，比1952年增长90倍，平均每年增长10.3%，社会消费品零售总额1471亿元，平均每年增长9.9%；1979-1998年，全市累计签订外商直接投资合同项目18984个，合同金额349亿美元，实际吸收外资金额247亿美元。其中合同金额在1000万美元以上的大项目占全部外商直接投资金额的比重达68.9%，世界最大的100家工业性跨国公司已有59家落户上海。1998年，上海完成外贸进出口总额260.46亿美元，平均每年增长12.3%，其中出口总额163.28亿美元，平均每年增长11.3%。

二、投资环境

建国50年来，上海累计用于城市基础设施投资2461亿元，其中，改革开放20年间，累计用于城市基础设施投资2401亿元，平均每年增长24.7%。相继建成了一大批具有标志性意义的重大城市基础设施工程项目，如南浦大桥、杨浦大桥、徐浦大桥、奉浦大桥、内环线高架道路、南北高架道路、地铁一号线、延安东路隧道复线、合流污水治理一期工程、沪宁高速公路上海段等。

上海铁路运输在全国铁路运输中起着举足轻重的作用。1998年上海铁路完成货物运输量3430万吨，完成旅客发送量2760万人次，上海铁路新客站每天进发列车可达73对。上海港是中国最大的港口，也是著名的综合性国际中转港口。现拥

有港口码头泊位135个，其中万吨级泊位67个。1998年，港口货物吞吐量已达1.64亿吨，完成集装箱吞吐量306.63万国际标准箱，在国际集装箱港口运输业中位居第11位。上海的远洋运输业与200多个国家和地区的500多个港口、600多家船公司建立了海上贸易往来业务。上海虹桥国际机场是中国三大国际航空港之一，与国内外102个城市通航，每天进出港飞机300多架次，其中国际和地区航班60多架次。1998年上海航空港旅客发送量695万人次。上海的公路运输四通八达，已形成了辐射15个省市的公路客运网络，从上海始发的省际班线达476条，跨省市零担班线130多条，可直达1288个市、县、镇。1998年，公路运输旅客发送量1922万人次，货物运输量2.64亿吨。上海市内交通网络日臻完善，交通管理手段先进。至1998年末，上海实有公交线路1098条，公交运营车辆1.53万辆，全年运客达24.88亿人次，平均每天客运量682万人次。上海的出租汽车服务业发展迅速，1998年末共有运营出租汽车4.1万辆。

上海邮电通信事业发展迅速，公众通信能力大大增强。至1998年末，上海电话交换机总容量已达618万门，全市电话用户达431万户。目前上海长途电话已实现了全球通，可达世界各地。同时上海先后推出了无线寻呼、移动电话、用户传真、电子邮件、会议电视、可视电话、多媒体信息服务等50余种新业务，还开通了南沿海光缆、中日海底光缆，国际通信能力大大增强。1998年末，上海与97个国家（地区）建立了邮件直达关系，国际特快专递业务通达200多个国家和地区，与34个国家和地区建立直达邮路。

上海金融业历来比较发达，金融领域对外开放逐步扩大。至1998年底，上海持有经营金融业务许可证的各级各类中外资金融机构达2450家，其中营业性外资金融机构62家，分别来自20多个国家（地区），成为全国外资金融机构数量和种类最多的城市。目前，有19家外资银行分别已获准迁址浦东经营人民币业务，一个以中国人民银行为中央银行，国有商业银行为主体，多种金融机构并存的金融体系已基本形成。

目前，上海有星级宾馆126家，其中五星级宾馆7家。1998年，上海共接待了来自世界各地177个国家和地区的旅游者152.71万人次，其中，外国人117.55万人次。

1990年，中共中央、国务院正式宣布开发开放浦东，9年来，浦东开发开放取得重大进展。1998年，浦东新区国内生产总值708.85亿元，比1990年翻了两番多，平均每年增长21.3%，国内生产总值占全市比重由1990年的8.1%上升至1998年的19.2%。为改善投资环境，浦东开发坚持城市基础设施建设先行的原则，9年间共完成城市基础设施投资620亿元，占同期新区固定资产投资总额的26.8%。浦东新区优越的地理位置和日益改善的投资环境吸引着大批海内外投资商，浦东这片热土成了国内外客商的投资热点。至1998年底累计，浦东新区已签订外商投资项目5472项，合同外资177亿美元。其中1000万美元以上的大项目达449项，著名跨国公司进入浦东有88家，共投资149个项目。

三、发展前景

面对充满机遇而又富有挑战的新世纪，上海确定了迈向21世纪的长远发展战略目标：到2010年，上海基本建成国际经济、金融、贸易中心之一，浦东新区基本建成具有世界一流水平的外向型、多功能、现代化的新区，崛起成为新的国际经济中心城市。

具体要达到以下几个方面：

基本形成世界大都市的经济规模和综合实力。到2010年，国内生产总值和第三产业的结构比例接近或达到发达国家经济中心城市的水平。

城市空间布局合理优化。

城市基础设施基本实现现代化。

全面参与国际分工和国际经济循环。

形成社会主义市场经济运行机制。

经济、社会与环境协调发展。

上海第九个五年计划（1996-2000 年）主要预期指标：国内生产总值年均增长 10-12%；工业总产值年均增长 14%；农业总产值年均增长 3.5%；到 2000 年，全市外贸进出口总额达 380 亿美元，其中出口总额 200 亿美元；到 2000 年，社会消费品零售总额 1950 亿元；“九五”期间，协议吸收外资 375 亿美元，实际吸收外资 240 亿美元；职工工资和农民纯收入扣除物价因素年均增长 3-5%；市区人均居住面积达到 10 平方米，住房成套率达到 70%，民用煤气普及率达到 90%；到 2000 年，三、二、一产业结构比例为 45∶53∶2；科技进步对经济增长的贡献率达到 50%；普通高校、专科在校生达到 16.4 万人；上海专业人才总量达到 171 万人，每万人口中，专业人才达到 1224 人，每万劳动者中，专业人才达到 2200 人；上海居民平均期望寿命达到 76.5 岁。

四、鼓励投资的重点领域

上海将进一步改善投资环境，以吸引海内外客商的投资。为鼓励外商来沪投资，上海在执行国家公布的有关鼓励外商投资的政策法规的同时，还制定了以下鼓励外商投资的项目。主要有：

1. 国家急需的交通、能源、重要原材料工业和农业技术开发项目；

2. 适应国际市场需求，拓展国外新市场，促进上海现有企业技术改造，提高产品档次，扩大出口创汇项目；

3. 引进先进技术，改进产品性能，节约能源、原材料，提高企业技术经济效益，填补国内生产空白，并适应市场需求的新设备、新材料项目；

4. 合理综合利用资源和再生资源的新技术、新设计项目；

5. 适应国际、国内市场需求需要的高新技术产业项目；

6. 鼓励外商在浦东外高桥保税区投资开办进出口贸易企业、国际转口贸易企业和为国际贸易服务的加工、包装、仓储、运输企业；

7. 鼓励外商按上海和浦东新区统一规划，带项目投资开发成片土地，特别鼓励外商投资改造老市区的棚户简屋区，以及能带动其他项目的项目。

I. Economic Development

Shanghai is an important economic center, a hub of communications and a foreign trade port of China, as well as one of the country's scientific, technological, cultural and educational bases. It has jurisdiction over 16 districts and four counties, with a total area of 6,340.5 square kilometers. At the end of 1998, the population was 13.0658 million, accounting for one percent of the national total. There were 10.7062 million urban residents.

In the past 50 years since the founding of New China, Shanghai has made tremendous achievements in economic construction. Especially since the adoption of the policy of reform and opening to the outside world, the people of Shanghai have opened up a new development path with Chinese and era characteristics. Beginning in 1990, the growth rate of Shanghai's GNP was more than 10 percent for seven years in succession. In 1998, GDP reached 368.8 billion yuan, with an average annual growth rate of 9.1 percent; and per capita GDP stood at 28,200 yuan, or more than US$3,300 calculated according to the year's exchange rate, equivalent to the level of medium-advanced countries. In 1998, Shanghai achieved 114.6 billion yuan in financial income, with an average annual growth rate of 9.3 percent.

Its total industrial output value reached 589.7 billion yuan, with an average annual growth rate of 10.3 percent. The social retail sales volume of consumer goods totaled 147.1 billion yuan, with an average annual growth rate of 9.9 percent. Between 1979 and 1998, 18,984 projects with direct foreign investment were signed, involving US$34.9 billion, with US$24.7 billion actually used. Of the total foreign-invested projects, large ones involving an investment of more than US$10 million made up 68.9 percent; 59 of the world top industrial trans-national enterprises have settled down in Shanghai. In 1998, the import and export volume totaled US$26.046 billion, with an average annual growth rate of 12.3 percent, of which the total export volume was US$16.328 billion while the average annual growth rate was 11.3 percent.

II. Investment Environment

Since the founding of New China, Shanghai has invested 246.1 billion yuan in urban infrastructure facilities, including investment of 240.1 billion yuan made in the past 20 years since the initiation of the policy of reform and opening to the outside world, with an average annual growth rate of 24.7 percent. A large number of important infrastructure projects have been set up, such as the Nanpu, Yanpu, Xupu and Fengpu bridges, the inner-ring elevated highway, the south-north overhead highway, the No.1 subway route, the multiple tracking of the tunnel in the East Yan'an Road, the first phase of the sewage treatment project, and the Shanghai Section of the Shanghai-Nanjing Expressway. Shanghai has taken on an entirely new look.

Shanghai's railway transport network plays a significant role in the national system. In 1998, the Shanghai railway station handled 34.3 million tonnes of freight and 27.6 million passengers; and every day 73 pairs of trains used the new railway station. Shanghai is the largest port in China, as well as a famous comprehensive international transfer port. Now, the port has 135 berths, including 67 10,000-dwt berths. In 1998, it handled 164 million tonnes of freight, and 3.0663 million international standard containers, a number which ranks 11th in the world. Shanghai's ocean-going transportation has established contacts with over 500 ports and some 600 shipping companies of more than 200 countries and regions. Shanghai Hongqiao International Airport is one of the three major international airports in China. There are now regular flights to 102 domestic and foreign cities, and more than 300 planes take off or land every day, including some 60 international flights. In 1998, the airport handled 6.95 million passengers. Shanghai's highways radiate in all directions, and a highway passenger transport network radiating to 15 provinces and municipalities has been formed. There are more than 130 trans-provincial bus lines, reaching 1,288 cities, counties and towns in China. In 1998 the highway passenger traffic was 19.22 million, and the highway freight traffic reached 264 million tons. The urban traffic network of Shanghai has been improved with each passing day, with advanced traffic management means. At the end of 1998, Shanghai had 1,098 public traffic routes, and 15,300 public buses and other vehicles. In 1998, they carried 2.488 billion people, transporting 6.82 million passengers a day on average. Shanghai's taxi service has developed rapidly. At the end of 1998 it had 41,000 taxis.

Shanghai's post and telecommunications have developed rapidly, and its public telecommunication ability has been greatly strengthened. At the end of 1998, the total telephone exchange capacity reached 6.18 million circuits, and 4.31 million households had telephones installed. Through DDD and IDD, people in Shanghai can make phone calls to all parts of the world. With the promotion of some 50 new means, such as pagers, mobile telephones, facsimile, E-mail, teleconferencing, picture-phones, multimedia information service, the southern coastal optical cable and the Sino-Japan submarine cable, Shanghai has greatly strengthened its international telecommunications capability. At the end of 1998, it established mail direct-sealing relations with 97 countries and regions; its international express mail service reaches more than 200 countries and regions, and direct postal routes were established with 34 countries and regions.

Shanghai is advanced in finance. In recent years, it has opened its financial fields wider to the outside world. At the end of 1998, it had 2,450 financial institutions with both Chinese and foreign investment, and had licensed 62 foreign-funded financial institutions from more than 20 countries and regions, ranking first in China in the number and variety of foreign-funded financial institutions. At present, 19 foreign-funded banks have been approved to move to Pudong to engage in Renminbi business. A financial system with the People's Bank of China as the central bank, the state-owned commercial banks as the mainstay, and the co-existence of various kinds of financial institutions has basically formed.

Shanghai has 126 star-rated hotels, including seven five-star ones. In 1998, Shanghai received 1.5271 million tourists from 177 countries and regions, of whom 1.1755 million were foreigners.

In 1990, the Party Central Committee and the State Council formally proclaimed that Pudong should be opened up and developed. In the past nine years, it has made great progress. In 1998, the GDP of the Pudong New Area was 70.885 billion yuan, or more than quadruple the 1990 figure, with an average annual growth rate of 21.3 percent. The proportion of Pudong's GDP in Shanghai's total GDP increased from 8.1 percent in 1990 to 19.2 percent in 1998. To improve the investment environment, the Pudong New Area has adhered to putting the construction of urban infrastructure facilities first. In the past nine years, Pudong has invested 62 billion yuan in urban infrastructure facilities, making up 26.8 percent of the Pudong New Area's total investment in fixed assets. Thanks to its favorable location and improved investment environment, Pudong has attracted a large number of domestic and foreign investors, and has become an investment hot spot for domestic and foreign business people. By the end of 1998, it had signed 5,472 agreements for foreign-invested projects, involving US$17.7 billion . Of these, large projects each involving more than US$10 million numbered 449. Altogether, 88 trans-national companies have settled in Pudong and have invested in 149 projects.

III. The Development Prospects

To welcome the new century full of opportunities and challenges, Shanghai has decided its long-range development strategic objectives:

By 2010, Shanghai will become one of the international economic, financial and trade centers; the Pudong New Area will be turned into a first-class export-oriented, multifunctional and modernized city in its own right. Shanghai will be a new international economic metropolis.

The following objectives have been set:

Shanghai will basically form the economic scale and comprehensive strength of a world metropolis. By 2010, its GDP and the proportion occupied by tertiary industry will be close to, or will reach the level of, the economic capitals of advanced countries.

Outlay will be reasonable and optimized.

The urban infrastructure facilities will be basically modernized.

Shanghai will participate in international division of labor and international economic circulation.

The socialist market economic operation mechanisms will be formed.

The development of the economy, society and environment will be coordinated.

上海船厂
Shanghai Shipyard

Shanghai's targets during the Ninth Five-Year Plan (1996-2000) are: Average annual growth rate of the GDP of 10-12 percent; total industrial output value of 14 percent; and total agricultural output value of 3.5 percent. By 2000, Shanghai's total import and export volume will be US$38 billion, including exports of US$20 billion. By 2000, the social retail sales volume of consumer goods will be 195 billion yuan. During the Ninth Five-Year Plan, contracted foreign capital will be US$37.5 billion, with US$24 billion actually absorbed. The wages of staff and workers and peasants' net income will increase by 3-5 percent annually on average after allowing for inflation. The living area per urban resident will reach 10 square meters, and apartments will make up 70 percent of total housing. Ninety percent of urban households will use gas. By 2000, the ratio of tertiary, secondary and primary industries will be 45:53:2; and the contributing rate of scientific and technological progress to economic growth will reach 50 percent. Students at the institutions of higher learning and the colleges for professional training will number 164,000; and the professional personnel of Shanghai will stand at 1.71 million. There will be 1,224 professional personnel per 10,000 people, and 2,200 professional personnel per 10,000 laborers. It is expected the lifespan of Shanghai residents will be 76.5 years on average.

IV. The Key Fields in Which Investment Is Encouraged

Shanghai will further improve the investment environment so as to absorb domestic and foreign investment, and

encourage foreign business people to make further investment. While implementing the state policies and regulations on encouraging foreign investment, Shanghai has worked out the following projects where it is encouraged:

1. Communications, energy and important raw and processed materials industries and agricultural technological development projects urgently needed by the state;

2. Projects that meet the needs of the international market, help open up new foreign markets, promote the technological transformation of the existing enterprises in Shanghai, raise the grades of products and increase foreign earnings through product exports;

3. New equipment and new materials projects that import advanced technologies, improve the functions of products, save energy, raw and processed materials, help raise enterprises' technological and economic benefits, fill in the gaps in domestic production, and meet the needs of the market;

4. New-tech and new-design projects that utilize natural resources and regenerative resources in a reasonable and comprehensive way;

5. New- and high-tech industrial projects that suit the demands of the international and domestic markets;

6. Establishment of import and export trade enterprises, international entrepot trade enterprises and processing, packing, storing and transportation enterprises which serve international trade in the Waigaoqiao Free Trade Zone in Pudong;

7. Investments in the development of large tracts of land, especially in the transformation of the shanty towns in the old city area of Shanghai, and projects that can accelerate the development of other projects.

走向辉煌的江苏

Jiangsu: On the Road to Glory

一、经济发展情况

1. 经济地理

江苏是中国开发较早的地区之一，位于中国大陆东部沿海的中心，扼长江入海门户。平均气温 13.5 摄氏度，年降水量 800–1200 毫米，无霜期达 200–240 天，气候湿润，四季分明。江苏东临太平洋，拥有 1000 多公里的海岸线，周边有上海、浙江、安徽、山东三省一市环绕。长江、淮河、京杭大运河纵横全省，长江水运连接中国腹地。这里平原辽阔，河湖众多，百草丰茂，世称“鱼米之乡”。全省现有土地面积 10.26 万平方公里，平原面积占 69%，居住着 7182.5 万勤劳善良的人民。

江苏现设南京、镇江、常州、无锡、苏州、扬州、南通、徐州、连云港、盐城、淮阴、宿迁和泰州 13 个省辖市，下设 64 个县及县级市。江苏北部的滩涂开发、粮棉种植全国闻名。南部的机械工业、电子工业、化工工业、汽车工业及轻纺、旅游业构筑起座座明星城市。

2. 50 年经济、社会发展情况

——综合实力日益雄厚。1998 年，全省国内生产总值 7199.95 亿元，较 1952 年递增 8.3%。在占全国 1% 的土地上，创造出占全国 9% 的 GDP，居全国第二位。

——比例结构趋向合理。三次产业在 GDP 的比重由 1952 年的 52.7：17.6：29.7 变为 1998 年的 14.2：50.5：35.3。经过调整，全省经济结构朝经济规模化、产业高度化、经营国际化、区域协调化转变。

——经济体制迅速转轨。从商品经济发展较快的实际出发，江苏较早开始了以市场经济为改革取向的探索，大力推进由计划经济向市场经济的转轨。

——对外开拓成果丰硕。1998 年全省外贸依存度为 30.4%、实际利用外资相当于全社会固定资产投资的 22.8%，大力推动了“经济国际化”战略的实施。

——国内贸易繁荣兴旺。1998 年，全省消费品零售总额 2238.01 亿元，为 1978 年的 26 倍，整个市场货源充足，价格便宜，购销两旺。

——社会事业兴旺发达。全省科技教育、文化艺术、新闻出版、广播影视、体育卫生各项社会事业都蓬勃发展，繁荣兴旺。

——人民生活显著提高。在经济发展的基础上，城乡人民生活显著改善，全省基本实现小康，苏南及沿江部分地区达到较为富裕程度。

二、投资环境

多年来，江苏努力营造良好的投资环境，先后有连云港、南通港、张家港、南京港、镇江港、江阴港、扬州港、太仓港、常熟港、高港对外开放。无锡、常州、南通、连云港、盐城、徐州等机场开辟了通往全国各主要城市的航班，南京空港也已开通 50 条国内航线，并拥有直达香港、澳门的航班，还将开辟数条直达世界主要城市的航班，进一步拉近江苏与世界的距离。京沪、陇海铁路贯穿全省，其中陇海铁路西接俄罗斯，直达荷兰鹿特丹，人称“欧亚大陆桥”，连云港被誉为“东方桥头堡”，江苏正步入陆桥经济时代。在道

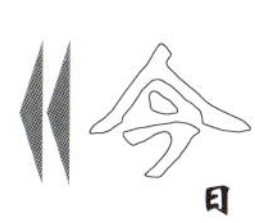

路建设上，江苏省构筑起稠密的公路网，通过沪宁高速公路，从省会南京到中国最大的城市上海只需3小时。目前，数条高速公路和横跨长江的公路大桥正在建设之中。在江苏，人们通过高效、便捷的空中、陆地和海上交通与全国及世界各地进行交往。

江苏省通信事业发展迅速，通信规模容量、装备水平、通信能力及通信网的自动化、数字化程度等均已跨上一个新的台阶，通信能力和通信业务总量都位居全国第二。省内已形成以光缆为主体，以数字微波为辅助的长途传输干线网；规模最大、功能最多的省级无线寻呼系统已覆盖江苏省所有市、县，移动通信亦已覆盖全省。电话声讯服务等新技术、新业务正在逐步推广应用。有线、无线的通信网络使全省进入了信息高速公路传送的时代，巨大的通信网络沟通着全国乃至世界。

沿海、沿江、沿公路、沿铁路而建的城市群落给江苏经济发展提供了中国其他区域无法比拟的便利条件，和谐、稠密、高素质的人口以及良好的基础设施支持了众多企业的发展。近年来，越来越多的外国投资企业落户江苏，国际著名的

跨国公司如摩托罗拉、奔驰、飞利浦、爱立信、巴斯夫、三菱、三井等也纷纷在江苏设立了分支机构和合资企业。

三、发展前景

江苏今后经济、社会发展的战略部署是：到2010年，全省基本实现现代化，人均国内生产总值在“九五”实现第三个翻番的基础上再翻一番半，达到世界中等发达国家的水平。在建设有中国特色社会主义道路上进一步开拓前进；形成基本同国际接轨的比较完善的社会主义市场经济运行机制；产业结构和生产力布局趋于合理，工业、农业和科学技术基本实现现代化，第三产业较为发达，基础设施完善配套；全民受教育程度和劳动者素质基本适应现代化建设的需要；人民生活由小康走向富裕，生活环境有明显改善，逐步实现共同富裕和城乡一体化。努力把江苏省建设成为经济繁荣、科教发达、生活富裕、法制健全、社会文明的省份。

四、鼓励投资的重点领域

农牧渔业：特种蔬菜、花卉工业化生产，粮棉油果新品、优良畜种培育，珍贵鱼类养殖。纺织业：高档特种棉毛织物、化纤混纺织物后整理，超细、阻燃、防静电等特种纤维。医药业：抗生素高产菌种，抗肿瘤、心血管药，激素，缓释剂，靶向剂及其它新剂型项目，医药器械。化学工业：化肥，高效低毒经济新农药，有机化工原料，合成材料，精细化工，橡胶制品。石油加工业：轻油裂解装置和后加工石油化工生产装置。电子工业：新一代通信产品，广播电视产品，计算机及外部设备，电子测量仪器及应用产品，电子元器件产品，基础材料及专用设备。建材工业：4000T/日、525标米以上大型水泥厂，高档屋面建材，高纯度水晶粉提纯，建筑节能技术。机械工业：数检系统，柔性加工中小机床，改装汽车及汽车零配件，内燃机，精密轴承模具。轻工业：日用机械，家用电器，电光源，日用硅酸盐，精密电子仪器。新技术产业：机器人，氮化硅及精密陶瓷，生物技术产品，同位素，激光技术。交通运输业：港口建设，公路、运河桥梁及设施。

I. Economy

1. Economic Development and Geographic Location

Jiangsu was one of the earliest areas to develop in China. It is located centrally on the eastern coastline of China where the Yangtze River flows into the sea. The average temperature here is 13.5 degrees centigrade; the annual rainfall is 800-1200 millimeters and the frost-free period lasts 200-240 days a year. Facing the Pacific Ocean in the east, the province has a coastline of 1,000-odd kilometers and connects with the city of Shanghai and provinces of Zhejiang, Anhui and Shandong. The Yangtze River, the Huaihe River and the Beijing-Hangzhou Canal pass through its territory, providing convenient transportation to provinces in China's hinterland. Being a province of vast plains, crisscrossing rivers and verdant vegetation, it is famed as a “Land of Fish and Rice”. On an area of 102,600 square kilometers, of which 69 percent are plains, lives a population of 71.825 million.

Under its jurisdiction are the 13 provincial cities of Nanjing, Zhenjiang, Changzhou, Wuxi, Suzhou, Yangzhou, Nantong, Xuzhou, Lianyungang, Yancheng, Huaiyin, Suqian and Taizhou, and 64 counties and towns at the county level. The wilderness in northern Jiangsu has been cultivated and developed into a well-known national grain and cotton production area. In the south, the rapid development of industries such as machines, electronics, chemicals, automobiles, textiles and tourism has brought many a town prosperity and renown.

2. Social and Economic Development in the Past 50 Years

— Overall strength enhanced. In 1998, the gross domestic product of the province was 719.995 billion yuan, with an annual growth rate of 8.3 percent between 1952-1998. On land taking up only 1 percent of China's territory, 9 percent of the country's GDP in 1998 was produced, ranking second nationwide.

— Proportion and structure rationalized. The proportion of the primary, secondary and tertiary industries in GDP changed from 52.7:17.6:29.7 in 1952 to 14.2:50.5:35.3 in 1998. The economy of the province has been heading towards large-scale production, high-tech production, the adoption of international administrative practices and regional balance of industries.

— Economic system changed. Due to the rapid development of the commodity economy, Jiangsu earlier made reforms in its economic system, going all out to accelerate the transformation from a planned economy to a market economy.

— Achievements in foreign trade. In 1998, the province drew foreign capital equaling 22.8 percent of the gross fixed investment in the province, largely promoting the strategy of "economic globalization."

— Flourishing domestic market. In 1998, the overall volume of retail sales of consumer goods in the province reached RMB 223.801 billion yuan, 26 times that of 1978. The market is robust with an ample supply of cheap goods.

— Well-developed society. Science, technology, culture, arts, publishing, radio, film and television, sports and sanitation facilities have all developed in a healthy and steady way.

— Living standards improved. With economic development, living conditions have improved remarkably. People are now leading comfortable lives, and in southern Jiangsu and the coastal areas some even lead a well-off life.

II. Environment for Investment

Over the years, Jiangsu Province has been making efforts to create a good environment for investment. Consecutively, ports like Lianyungang, Nantong, Zhangjiagang, Nanjing, Zhenjiang, Jiangyin, Yangzhou, Taicang, Changshu and Gaogang have opened to foreign trade. New airports like Wuxi, Changzhou, Nantong, Lianyungang, Yancheng, Xuzhou have started new flights to major cities in the country. Nanjing Airport has over 50 domestic flights and flights to Hong Kong and Macao. International flights will begin to shorten the distance between the province and the world. Rail lines between Beijing-Shanghai and Lanzhou-Lianyungang cut through the territory. The latter extends outside China to Rotterdam in the Netherlands and is known as the "Eurasian Continental Bridge" while Lianyungang is famed as the "Bridge Head in the East." Jiangsu Province also has a well-developed network of highways. It is only a three-hour drive from Nanjing, the provincial capital, to Shanghai, the largest city in China, by way of the Shanghai-Nanjing Highway. At present, several highways and bridges spanning the Yangtze River are under construction. People in Jiangsu today are able to contact with the world quickly thanks to the efficiency and convenience of air, land and sea transportation.

Telecommunications in Jiangsu have developed quickly with high capacity, quality equipment, communication capacities and automatic and digital networks, with business capacity and volume ranking second in the country. A network of telecommunication arteries has been set up, using optical cable and digital microwave. A paging network, the largest, multifunctional one at the provincial level in China, and a mobile phone network now cover all of the province's territory. Other new technologies and services are being spread for practical use. Cable and wireless telecommunication networks have brought the province into the information super highway era and closer to other parts of China and the world.

Cities and towns built along the coast, rivers, highways and railways play an important role in the development of the local economy. The convenient transportation they enjoy becomes an envy of other provinces. Dense habitations and a well-educated population, as well as good infrastructural facilities, have supported the development of many enterprises. In recent years, more and more foreign enterprises have set up joint ventures in Jiangsu, such as the world-famous companies like Motorola, Mercedes-Benz, Philips, Ericsson, and Mitsubishi.

江苏华西村
Huaxi Village in Jiangsu

III. Prospects for Development

The Ninth Provincial Congress of the Party worked out a strategic plan for the further economic and social development of the province. By the year 2010, the province is to realize the goal of modernization, and the per capita GDP is to equal that of a moderately developed country. The province plans to make further explorations into socialism with Chinese characteristics, adopt international practices to improve the socialist market economy, rationalize industrial and labor force structures, realize basic agricultural, industrial and scientific and technological modernization, develop tertiary industries to a new stage with well-organized infrastructural facilities, improve the education of the population to meet the needs of building modernization, improve living conditions, and eliminate the differences between rich and poor, rural and urban. In brief, through the efforts of its people, Jiangsu will become a province with a prosperous economy, advanced science and technology, high living standards, and a mature legal system.

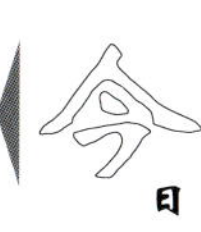

IV. Key Fields for Investment

Agriculture, animal husbandry, fishing: modernization of special vegetable and flower production, new strains of grain, canola, and fruit, animal breeding, and rare fish aquiculture. Textiles: high-quality special cotton and woolen fabrics, processing of polyester and cotton-polyester fabrics, super-fine fibers, fire-resistant fibers, and static-electric-resistant fibers. Medicine: high-yield bacteria breeding for producing antibiotics, medicines for cancer, cardiovascular diseases and disorders, hormones, moderators, and other new-type medicines and medical equipment. Chemistry: chemical fertilizer, high-efficiency and low-toxic pesticides, raw materials for organic chemical industry, synthetic materials, refined chemical industry, and rubber products. Oil processing industries: light oil splitting decomposition equipment and post-processing petrochemical production equipment. Electronics: new telecommunication products, radios and television products, computer and accessories, electronic survey instruments and applied products, electronic parts and components, basic materials and special equipment. Building materials: large-scale plants that can produce over 4,000 tonnes daily of cement graded 525 and above, high-quality materials for building surfaces, and crystalline powder purifying and energy-saving technology. Machinery: digital checking systems, small- and middle-sized machine tools for flexible processing, automobile refitting and molds for autoparts and components, internal combustion engines and precision bearings. Light industries: household appliances, household electrical appliances, household silicate, and precision electronic instruments. High-tech industries: robots, silicon nitride, fine pottery and porcelain, bio-products, isotope and laser technology. Transportation: construction of ports, highways, bridges and facilities.

向基本实现现代化迈进的浙江

Zhejiang: Striding Towards Modernization

一、经济发展概况

浙江地处中国东南沿海，长江三角洲南翼，北与中国最大的城市上海相邻。现辖10个地级市和1个地区。陆域面积10.18万平方公里；海岸线总长6486公里，居中国首位。人口4456万。全省山青水秀，物产丰饶，人杰地灵，素有“鱼米之乡、丝茶之府、文物之邦、旅游胜地”的美誉。

建国50年来，浙江面貌发生了巨大的变化，尤其是中共十一届三中全会以来，浙江抓住特定的机遇，坚定不移地放手发展社会主义市场经济，取得了令人瞩目的成就。1998年，全省国内生产总值达到4988亿元，比1949年增长83倍，其中1979年至1998年年平均增长13.5%，是全国经济增长最快的省份之一；人均国内生产总值由1949年的72元提高到1998年的11247元。目前浙江经济总量和人均国内生产总值均居全国第4位。经济结构发生了深刻变化，实现了由落后的农业省向先进的工业化社会的历史性跃进。在国内生产总值中，第一、二、三产业比例，由建国初期的68.5：8.0：23.5，变为1998年的12.4：54.3：33.3。外向型经济发展成效显著。1979年至1998年，全省累计出口总额700亿美元，签订利用外资项目1.59万个，协议利用外资金额278亿美元，实际利用外资135亿美元。科技教育、文化卫生和人民生活都有很大进步。现有高等院校32所，各类专业科技人员77万。1998年，城镇居民人均可支配收入7837元，农村居民人均纯收入3815元，分别居全国31个省市区的第4位和第3位。

二、投资环境

长期以来尤其是进入90年代之后，浙江致力于基础设施建设和涉外经济管理与服务，投资环境明显改善。浙江海、陆、空运十分便利。现有万吨级以上泊位41座，与世界上70多个国家和地区的400多个港口有运输往来。宁波港是中国四大中枢港之一，1998年货物吞吐量达8709万吨，居中国内地第2位。铁路有沪杭、浙赣、杭甬三条复线和杭宣、金温两条平线。公路网四通八达，继沪杭甬高速公路全线通车后，省内多条高速公路正在加紧建设，部分路段已通车。浙江现有杭州、宁波、温州、黄岩、义乌、衢州、舟山7个民用航空机场，开通国内外航线160余条。杭州萧山国际机场建设已经启动。邮政电信事业发展迅速。全省各市(地)都已建成长途自动电话交换网，可直拨214个国家和地区；电话机总容量和移动电话总容量分别居全国各省市区的第4位和第3位。供电、供水充足。现有电力装机容量1434万千瓦。到1998年底，全省有金融机构12000万家，其中外资和中外合资银行4家。全省有涉外饭店380家，其中星级饭店、宾馆175家。同时，一个确保外商合法投资权益的法律、政策环境已经基本形成，投资服务体系日趋完善。

三、发展前景

世纪之交的浙江，已经制定了提前基本实现全省现代化奋斗目标。这就是：到2005年争取有近1/3的市县基本实现现代化，到2010年争取有近2/3的市县基本实现现代化，到2020年全省基本实现现代化，即基本达到或接近当时世界中等发达国家的发展水平。

近期发展目标是：今后5年，经济增长速度高于全国平均水平，经济总量和综合实力继续处于全国前列，经济结构战略性调整取得重大进展，主要产业的技术层次、经济效益与竞争能力进一步提高；初步建立并逐步完善社会主义市场经济体制，初步形成与国际惯例接轨的外向型经济运作方式；社会文明程度与经济发展水平相协调，人民的思想道德和科学文化素质进一步提高，多数地区人民生活从小康走向更加富裕，脱贫地区实现小康，城市化进程加快，城市对经济社会发展的促进作用明显增强。

四、鼓励投资的重点领域

浙江鼓励外商按国家公布的《外商投资产业指导目录》进行广泛投资。根据浙江产业结构现状和调整要求，今后鼓励和吸收外商投资的重点领域是：

1. 农林水利、交通、电力建设和电网改造、城市基础设施建设项目。

2. 依托浙江沿海深水港口和现有企业，利用国内外资源和省内非金属矿产，发展石油化工、合成材料、新型建筑材料、金属冶炼和压延加工等上水平、上规模的原材料项目。

3. 加快机械、电子、化工、医药四个主导产业的培育，加速棉纺、丝绸、水泥三个行业整体改造，提高加工深度和技术水平，节约能源和原材料，扩大出口的项目。

4. 适应国内外市场需要的电子信息、生物与医药、机电一体化、新材料等高新技术产业的项目。

5. 综合利用资源和再生资源以及利用防治环境污染的新技术、新设备的生产项目。

6. 提高农副产品加工深度的新技术项目和出口创汇农业项目。

I. Economic Development

Zhejiang Province is located on China's southeastern coast, south of the Yangtze River Delta. Adjacent to the north is Shanghai, China's largest city. Zhejiang is divided into 10 cities and 1 prefecture at the provincial level, with a total area of 101,800 sq.km, and a coastline of 6,486 km,

浙江省经济技术开发区
Zhejiang Economic & Technological Development Zone

the longest in China. The total population of the province is 44.56 million.The province is noted for its picturesque scenery, and the abundance of its products has made it widely known as a "Land of Fish and Rice". It is also noted for its silk and tea, as well as for its numerous historical and cultural sites of interest to scholar and tourists alike.

Great changes have taken place in Zhejiang Province since the founding of the People's Republic of China in 1949. The reform and opening have been a great impetus to Zhejiang's overall development. The people throughout the province took hold of the opportunity and firmly developed the socialist market economy. Dramatic changes were seen in various social undertakings. Zhejiang's GDP in 1998 was 498.8 billion yuan, an increase of 83 times over 1949. Of this amount, the average annual growth rate from 1979 to 1998 was 13.5 percent, standing out as one of the few economically vibrant areas in China. Per capita GDP rose from 72 yuan in 1949 to 11,247 yuan in 1998. At present, both Zhejiang's GDP and per capita GDP rank fourth in China. Great changes have taken place in economic structure. Zhejiang's economy has realized an enormous leap forward from the backward agricultural province to the advanced industrial province. Of the gross domestic product, the proportion among primary, secondary and tertiary industries had been adjusted from 68.5:8.0:23.5 during the initial post-liberation period to 12.4:54.3:33.3 in 1998. Zhejiang made great achievements in export-oriented economy. By the end of 1998,its total value of exports was US$70 billion. There were 15,900 foreign-invested contracts signed,amounting to foreign investment US$27.8 billion, of which US$13.5 billion was actually utilized. Rapid development was scored in science, education, culture, public health and people's life. By the end of 1998, Zhejiang had altogether 32 institutions of higher learning, producing 770,000 professionals and technicians of all specialization. In 1998, the annual per capita disposable income of urban households was 7,837 yuan. The annual per capita net income of rural households was 3,815 yuan, ranking 4th and 3rd respectively among all the provinces in China.

II. Investment Environment

For some time, especially in the 1990s, Zhejiang has devoted itself to infrastructure development and foreign-related economic management and services. Obvious improvement was achieved in these aspects of the environment. Zhejiang has flourishing highway, railway and airway networks. There were 41 berths of 10,000-dwt capacity and above. Shipping lanes stretch from these harbors to more than 400 ports in over 70 countries and regions worldwide.Beilun Port in Ningbo is one of China's four top transfer harbors.In 1998, the volume of freight handled by Ningbo Harbor reached 87.09 million tonnes, ranking second in China.Zhejiang's main railway lines are the Shanghai-Hangzhou, Hangzhou-Jiangxi and Hangzhou-Ningbo multi-track and the Hangzhou-Xuancheng and Jinhua-Wenzhou railroads. Highways in the province radiate in all directions. Following the completion of the Shanghai-Hangzhou-Ningbo expressway, the province is pushing ahead with the construction of other expressways. Some expressways have been opened to traffic. Zhejianng has seven airports at Hangzhou, Ningbo, Wenzhou, Huangyan, Yiwu, Quzhou and Zhoushan and operates over 160 domestic and international air routes. Construction of the Xiaoshan International Airport in Hangzhou has already started. Posts and telecommunications are forging rapidly ahead.Automatic long-distance dialing exchanges have been installed in every city and prefecture. International long distance program-controlled exchanges link 214 countries and regions abroad. The users of telephones and mobile phones rank fourth and third respectively among all the provinces in China. There is now a sufficient supply of electricity and water. The total installed electricity capac-

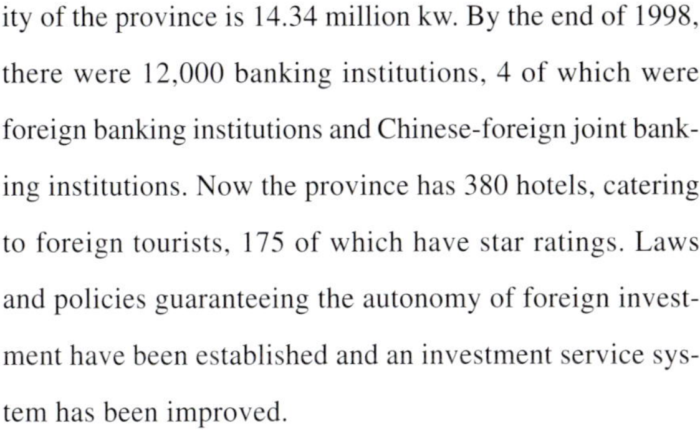

ity of the province is 14.34 million kw. By the end of 1998, there were 12,000 banking institutions, 4 of which were foreign banking institutions and Chinese-foreign joint banking institutions. Now the province has 380 hotels, catering to foreign tourists, 175 of which have star ratings. Laws and policies guaranteeing the autonomy of foreign investment have been established and an investment service system has been improved.

III. Development Targets

At the turning point to the 21st century, Zhejiang has worked out a strategic plan to basically accomplish modernization ahead of schedule. The plan is, by the year 2005, to basically accomplish the modernization in nearly one-third of the cities and countries; by 2010, in nearly two thirds; and by 2020, in the whole province. That is, the province will basically come up to the standards of a moderately-developed country.

Zhejiang's development targets in the near future are:

The economy will increase faster than the nation's average level in the next five years, and its economic standing and comprehensive strength will continue to lead the country. The strategic adjustment in economic structrue will make rapid progress.The technological level, economic benefit and competitive ability will make bigger strides forward. A socialist market economy system will be basically set up and gradually improved. The province will basically establish an operation system meeting international standards. The social civilization level will coordinate with the economic development level, and the people's ideology and moral concepts and the level of science and education will be further improved. Well-to-do families in most areas will become richer, and poverty released areas will become well-off. The course of urbanization will be quickened, and cities' ability to promote economic and social development will be strengthened.

IV. Focal Point of Future Investment

Zhejiang will encourage foreign business, who comply with "the Guiding Catalogue of Foreign Investment in Industries" published by China, to invest in every aspect. According to Zhejiang's present industrial structure conditions and adjustment demand, the focal point of future investment will be:

1.The construction projects of agriculture, forestry, water conservancy, electricity, power network transformation, and urban infrastructure.

2.Raw materials projects to develop petroleum and chemical industry, synthetic materials, modern building materials, metals smelting and pressing, depending on harbor resources advantages and present enterprises, using resources at home and abroad and provincial non-metal minerals.

3.The projects to accelerate the rearing of the four major industries of machinery, electronics, chemicals and pharmaceuticals, to speed up the overall transformation of the three industries of cotton spinning, silk and cement, to increase processing depth and technical competence, to economize in raw materials and energy, to enlarge exports.

4.The projects of high and new technical industries such as electronic information, organisms and pharmaceuticals, mechanical and electrical integration, and new materials, to meet the needs of market at home and abroad.

5.The productive projects of new technology and equipment to comprehensively use resources and regenerated resources, and to guard against environmental pollution.

6.The new technical projects to enhance processing depth in agricultural products and the agricultural projects to earn foreign exchange through exports.

奋进中的安徽

Anhui: Advancing with Economic Development

一、经济发展情况

安徽省简称"皖"，地处中国东南部，是临江近海的内陆省份。现辖13个省辖市、4个地区、9个县级市和56个县；总人口6152万，土地面积13.96万平方公里，分别占全国的5%和1.5%。安徽是中国矿产资源大省，已发现各类矿产135种，其中煤、铁、铜、硫、磷等储量居全国前列；是全国重要的粮棉油畜牧水产生产基地，正常年景粮食总产量在2500万吨以上，粮食、油料、水产品产量都在全国前10位之内；是重要的能源、原材料生产基地，拥有一批现代化原材料工业基地和能源供应基地；是新崛起的轻工业大省，目前已形成了家电、烟酒、日用化工为支柱的轻工业生产体系；是科技实力比较雄厚的省份，全省有各类专业技术人员91万，拥有各类研究开发机构861个，高等院校34所，省会合肥是中国四大科教基地之一；是旅游资源丰富的省份，名山秀水遍布境内，黄山有着"国之瑰宝、世界奇观"的美誉，九华山是中国四大佛教名山之一，齐云山是中国四大道教名山之一，巢湖、太平湖风景名胜区也驰名遐迩。

新中国成立50年来，特别是改革开放20年来，安徽取得了经济建设和社会各项事业的全面发展。1998年，全省实现国内生产总值2805亿元，比1978年增长6.8倍，年均增长10.8%；人均国内生产总值4576元，增长5倍，年均增长9.4%；国内生产总值提前6年、人均国内生产总值提前5年实现在1980年基础上翻两番的战略目标。1998年与1978年相比，安徽财政收入年均增长13.1%；城乡居民收入年递增幅度均达15%以上。外向型经济发展取得了可喜成绩，目前已形成多层次、全方位的对外开放格局。1980-1998年，全省累计签订利用外资协议额68.6亿美元，实际利用外资50.3亿美元，外资投向遍及工业、农业、商业、服务业等各行各业；1998年全省外贸进出口总额31.2亿美元，比1978年增长293倍，年均增长32.9%，占国内生产总值的比重由1985年的3.5%提高到9.2%。

二、投资环境

改革开放以来，安徽着力加大基础设施和基础产业投资力度，全方位改善投资和发展的软硬环境，已建成包括公路、铁路、航空、水运在内的综合运输体系，基本形成现代化通信网络主体框架。

目前，安徽铁路正线延展里程达3080公里，密度居华东之首，仅近几年即新建成铁路5条，大型铁路枢纽3个。公路通车里程达3.9万多公里，其中高速公路294公里。在航空方面，已建成合肥、黄山、安庆、芜湖等6座开通民航班机的机场，其中合肥、黄山机场被国家批准为对外航空口岸。水运也很发达，境内的长江、淮河、新安江三大水系提供内河航道6000多公里，并与许多国家和地区开通了远洋航线。芜湖、铜陵、安庆、马鞍山、池州港均对外开放。铜陵长江大桥已经建成；本世纪末中国规模最大、科技含量最高的芜湖长江公铁两用大桥正在建设之中，2000年将投入使用。

安徽邮电通讯建设也位居全国前列，是全国第三个实现所有市县通讯数字化的省份，所有县以上城市（镇）均已开通程控电话，实现了电话交换程控化、长途传输数字化，可直拨国内1600个城市和国外180个国家和地区。1997年正式建成模拟和数字两大移动电话网络，邮电数字移动电话网覆盖全省。

三、鼓励投资的重点领域

为贯彻实施“外向带动”战略，积极、合理、有效地利用外资，安徽制定了一系列投资政策，重点鼓励外商对下列项目的投资：一是应用农业新技术、发展生态农业、农业综合开发、增加农产品出口创汇和贫困地区农业开发项目；二是能源、交通、水利等基础设施和重要原材料工业项目；三是用高新技术、先进技术，改进产品性能、节约能源和原材料，生产适应市场需求而国内、省内生产能力不足的新设备、新材料；四是适应国际市场需求，能够扩大产品外销的项目；五是综合利用资源和再生资源及采用保护环境的新技术、新设备产业；六是第三产业中广告、信息咨询、会计师事务所等中介服务机构等。对于鼓励类外商投资项目，除可依照国家和省有关规定享受优惠待遇外，对从事投资额大、回收期长的农业、能源、交通等基础设施建设与经营的，经批准可扩大相关经营范围。

四、经济发展前景

《安徽省国民经济和社会发展“九五”计划和2010年远景目标纲要》全面系统规划了安徽经济发展的美好前景。

近期发展目标是：经济增长率高于全国平均水平；基本消除贫困现象，人民生活达到小康；加快现代企业制度建设，初步建立社会主义市场经济体制；大力推进工业化、城镇化和农业现代化，为安徽由农业大省向农业强省、资源大省向加工业大省、人口大省向经济大省的跨越奠定良好的物质技术基础。

远期发展目标是：到2010年实现人均国内生产总值在2000年基础上再翻一番，人均国内生产总值超过全国平均水平；人民的小康生活更加宽裕；形成比较完善的社会主义市场经济体制；综合省力跨入全国先进行列，并向下个世纪中叶实现第三步战略目标迈出坚实的步伐。

I. General Survey of Economic Development

Anhui Province, known for short as Wan, is an inland province in southeast part of China. Today, it has jurisdiction over 13 cities, 4 prefectures, 9 county-level cities and 56 counties. With a population of 61.52 million, it covers an area of 139,600 square km, accounting for 5 percent and 1.5 percent of the country's total respectively.

Blessed with abundant mineral resources, the province has discovered 135 different mineral products. Of them, the reserves of coal, iron, bronze, sulphur and phosphorous rank first in the country. It is an important base for grain, cotton, oil, animal husbandry and aquatic products. The annual output of grain exceeds 25 million tons, and those of grain, oil-bearing crops and aquatic products rank among the top 10 nationally.

It is also an important base for processing energy resources and raw materials, and is now emerging as an important center of light industry. The latter is based on the pillar industries of household electrical appliances, cigarette production, wine and daily necessities turned out by the chemical industry. With solid scientific and technological strength, Anhui has 910,000 professional technicians, 861 various research and development establishments, and 34 institutions of higher learning.

Hefei, the provincial capital, is well known as one of the four educational bases of science and technology in China.

The province boasts famous mountains and clear rivers. For example, the Huangshan Mountain has a good reputation as the "soul of the country" and as a "world wonder". Jiuhua Mountain is rated as one of the famed four Buddhist Mountains in China; and the Qiyun Mountain one of the famous four Taoist Mountains. Other scenic spots such as Chaohu Lake and Taiping Lake are also well known far and widely.

For five decades since the founding of New China, especially since the Third Plenary Session of the 11th Central Committee, the Anhui people have been working hard to push forward the reform and opening up with intelligence and wisdom under the leadership of the provincial Party Committee and government. The result of this is huge achievement in economic construction, and an all-round development in various social undertakings.

In 1998, its GDP was 280.5 billion yuan, an increase of 7.8 times over 1978, or an annual average growth of 10.8 percent. The average per-capita GDP was 4,576 yuan, a 5-fold gain, or an annual average increase of 9.4 percent. Its GDP was realized six years ahead of schedule, while that for the average per-capita GDP met the strategic target of quadrupling the 1980 figure five years in advance.

Compared with 1978, the annual average growth of the province's revenue in 1998 was 13.1 percent. The scope of the annual income growth for urban and rural residents progressively increased by over 15 percent. Today, a remarkable achievement has been made in the exported-oriented economic development, which has paved the way for the emergence of an all-round, multi-layer open structure.

Between 1980-98, utilization of foreign funds through

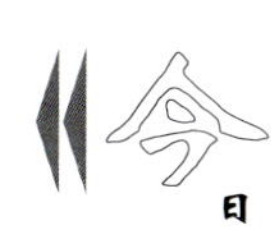

negotiated agreements totaled US$6.86 billion, with paid-in capital of US$5.03 billion. The overseas investment involved various sectors including industry, agriculture, commerce and services.

The volume of local imports and exports in 1998 was US$3.12 billion, an increase of 293 times over 1978, or an annual growth of 32.9 percent. The proportion related to its GDP increased from 3.5 percent in 1985 to 9.2 percent.

China. Over the past few years, five new railway lines were built, forming three large hubs. Highways now total 39,000 km, including 294 km of expressway.

In the field of air transport, six airports handling civilian scheduled flights have been opened in Hefei, Huangshan, Anqing and Wuhu. Of them, Hefei and Huangshan airports were rated as suitable for handling international traffic.

The province has witnessed rapid development in

合肥五里墩立交桥
Wulidun Overpass in Hefei

II. Environment Available for Investment

Since the reform and opening-up policy was carried out in 1978, the local authorities have redoubled their efforts to increase investment earmarked for the construction of infrastructure facilities and basic industry, improving the soft climate for investment and development. A comprehensive transportation system including highways, railway lines, air and water transport have been formed, basically creating a modern communications network.

At present, the mileage of railways in the province has stretched to 3,080 km, with its density ranking first in east

water transport. The Yangtze, Huaihe and Xin'anjiang rivers can offer more than 6,000 km of waterways within the area, opening many shipping routes linked to a great many countries and regions.

Some harbors including Wuhu, Tongling, Anqing, Ma'anshan and Chizhou have already opened to the world, and the Tongling Bridge spanning the Yangtze River has been completed. At present, the Wuhu Yangtze River Bridge for automobiles and trains is expected to be put into use by 2000.

The construction of post and telecommunications facilities in the province ranks first in the country. Anhui is also the third province to realize digital communications services in cities and counties. Program-controlled telephones have already been opened to all cities and towns, allowing direct links with 1,600 cities within the country, as well as 180 countries and regions.

III. Major Areas of Investment

In order to enthusiastically utilize foreign capital in an effective and rational way, the local government has worked out a series of investment policies to implement the strategy for facilitating economic development in inland areas through aid from the economically developed coastal areas. It has decided to encourage overseas investors to invest in the following projects:

1. Projects to develop applied technologies for farming and ecological agriculture; the projects for comprehensive development of agriculture, increase of foreign exchange from exports of agricultural products, and agricultural development projects in poverty-stricken areas;

2. Projects related to infrastructure facilities in energy, communications and water conservancy; and important raw materials projects;

3. Projects to use new- and hi-tech technology to improve the function of products and save energy resources and raw materials; the projects to produce new equipment and new materials that are in short supply in the province or in the country so as to meet the needs of the market;

4. Projects to expand product export in line with the requirements of the international market;

5. Projects comprehensively utilizing resources and renewable resources, as well as the industries adopting new technology and new equipment for environmental protection;

6. Intermediary service establishments offering advertising, information consulting and certified accounting services.

Projects belonging to the category of encouragement by the state, especially those engaging in agriculture with a great influx of investment and a long recovery period, or those involving in construction and management of energy, communications and other infrastructure facilities, are allowed to expand their management scope with the approval of departments concerned, in addition to enjoying preferential treatment worked out by the State and the province.

IV. Prospects for Economic Development

The Outline of the Ninth Five-Year Plan for National Economic and Social Development and the Long-Term Objectives Through the Year 2010 of Anhui Province augurs a bright future for local economic development in an all-round way.

The short-term targets for development are: to raise growth rate higher than the nation's average level; basically eliminate poverty to bring people's living standards up to the comparatively well-off level; accelerate the construction of a modern enterprise system; initially establish a socialist market economic system; propel industrialization, rural urbanization and agricultural modernization. This will lay a solid material and technological foundation for Anhui to build itself from an agricultural province into one with powerful agricultural economy, merely a resource-rich province into one with important industrial sectors, and a populous province into one with strong economic strength.

The long-term targets for development are: by 2010, to double the average per-capita GDP in 2000, higher than the average national level; make the people's comparatively well-off living standards more wealthy; establish a much-improved socialist market economy system; strive to enter the rank of the country's advanced provinces in its economy; and make solid strides toward the third strategic goal for the mid-21st century.

迈向21世纪的福建

Fujian: Striding Forward into the 21st Century

一、发展情况

福建省地处中国东南沿海，位于台湾海峡西岸，邻近港澳，面对台湾。全省土地面积12.14万平方公里，人口3299万，现辖8个地级市、1个地区，84个县(市、区)。福建依山靠海，旅游资源十分丰富，名胜古迹众多，武夷山和湄洲岛被列为国家级旅游度假区。福建省是中国重点侨乡，旅居世界各地的华侨和华人超过800万。福建省是中国率先实行改革开放的省份之一，是中国的综合改革试验区，全省经国家批准对外开放区达4.32万平方公里，占全省面积的35.6%。

建国50年来，福建国民经济和社会发展取得了举世瞩目的成就。特别是改革开放20年来，福建进入了全面发展的崭新阶段，经济持续快速增长，综合实力明显增强。1998年，全省实现国内生产总值3330.18亿元，比1978年增长11.9倍，年均增长13.6%；人均国内生产总值10200元，比1978年增长8.6倍，年均增长12.0%；1998年全省预算内财政收入281.42亿元，比1978年增长了17.6倍，年均增长15.7%。对外开放不断扩大，外向型经济取得了可喜的成绩。全省已初步形成了经济特区、沿海开放城市、经济技术开发区、台商投资区、保税区、高科技园区、综合改革试验区等多层次、多方位的对外开放格局。1978年以来，全省累计利用外商直接投资263.16亿美元，其中1998年40.12亿美元，外商投资领域已涉及轻工、纺织、服装、电子、机械、化工、冶金、建材、农林水产、交通、能源、房地产、金融及旅游服务等行业。累计出口总值738.83亿美元，其中，1998年外贸出口120.73亿美元，比1978年增长62.5倍，年均增长23.1%。

二、投资环境

改革开放以来，福建加快了基础设施建设步伐，调整投资结构，重点加强了交通、邮电通信、能源、城市市政等基础设施建设，明显地改善了投资环境，有力地促进了全省经济发展。公路四通八达，公路总里程4.8万公里。境内有五条国道，泉厦高速公路已建成通车，福泉高速公路1999年也将建成。铁路有鹰厦、外福、漳泉肖、横南线，

运输里程1068公里。福建有福州、厦门、晋江、武夷山等机场，开辟航线119条，可通国内主要城市和东南亚及港澳地区。在水路运输方面，形成了以福州、厦门、湄洲湾为主的沿海港口体系，开辟了254条国内外航线，通往日本、朝鲜、俄罗斯、南斯拉夫和东南亚等国家和地区的126个港口。全省共有涉外宾馆、饭店120多家，床位3万多张，其中星级饭店143家，包括五星级饭店4家，具备年接待海外旅游者200万人次的能力。福建邮电通信在全国居领先水平，全省城乡电话交换机总容量突破547万门，长途自动交换机容量达到19.7万终端，移动通信系统覆盖各市县及沿海发达乡镇。城乡电话用户达347.5万户，移动电话用户达142.2万户；城乡电话普及率达到16.56部／百人，其中，城市电话普及率达到53.95部／百人，移动电话普及率达4.31部／百人。福建同国际金融机构合作日趋密切，全省有外资和中外合资金融机构28家，全省金融机构已与海外4400多家银行建立了代理或业务往来关系。福建城市基础设施日益配套完善，供水、供电充足。拥有华东最大的水电站(水口水电站)和福州华能、厦门嵩屿等大型火电厂。

三、发展前景

近期发展目标：到2000年，国民经济综合实力进入全国前列，实现人均国内生产总值比1980年翻三番；人民生活全面实现小康目标；初步建立健全社会主义市场经济体制，初步建立与国际惯例相衔接的对外经济体制，初步形成健全的社会发展体系。

远期发展目标：到2010年，福建经济建设，人民生活再上一个大台阶。国内生产总值在1996年实现比1980年翻三番的基础上再争取翻两番，跻身全国十大强省行列，人民生活接近或达到当时中等收入国家和地区的水平。形成比较健全和完善的社会主义市场经济体制和运行机制，国民经济的整体素质显著提高，实现经济和社会可持续发展。

四、鼓励外商投资的重点领域

为进一步提高福建对外开放和经济发展的水平，福建省人民政府颁布了《福建省进一步鼓励外商投资的若干规定》，鼓励外商投资以下重点领域，可享受税收优惠政策、减免收费项目、以及享受优惠的地价。对外商投资企业实行国民待遇。

1. 外商投资石油化工、机械电子、建筑建材、林产业、水产业、轻纺业等支柱产业和重点产业的骨干重点企业。

2. 外商投资开发农业、牧业等项目。

3. 外商投资港口码头、电力等基础设施项目。

4. 外商投资经营高新技术企业。

5. 鼓励外商投资兴建普通住宅等项目。

6. 鼓励外商投资福建旅游重点产业。外商在国家级旅游度假区内经批准可投资兴办中外合资的旅行社，并允许其在区外设立分支机构开展相关业务。经批准，外商可在国家旅游度假区、省级旅游经济开发区内投资建设别墅、度假村及配套服务项目。

I. Economic Situation

Fujian Province is located on the southeast coast of China, west to the Taiwan Straits, adjacent to Hong Kong and Macao and facing Taiwan. Having jurisdiction over eight cities, one prefecture and eighty-four counties, Fujian Province has an area of 121,400 square kilometres and a population of 32.99 million. With mountains and seas around, Fujian is abundant in tourist resources and has many places of historical interest and scenic spots. Wuyi Mountains

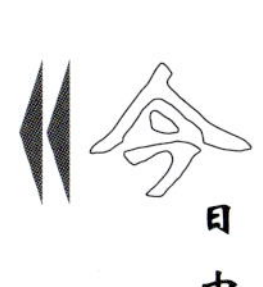

and Meizhou Island are classified as national scenic spots. Fujian Province is our country's key hometown of overseas Chinese, with more than 8 million Fujian Chinese nationals residing all over the world. As one of the first group of provinces taking the lead in carrying out the policy of reform and opening up, Fujian is an experimental zone in conducting overall reform. Regions opening to the outside world cover an area of 43,200 square kilometres, accounting for 35.6% of the total area of Fujian Province.

Over the past fifty years since the founding of the People's Republic of China, great achievements in the national economic and social development have received the world recognition. Over the past 20 years since reform and opening up, Fujian has stepped into a new stage of its overall development, during which a sustained and rapid development of economy has been achieved and the overall strength has been noticeably enhanced. In 1998, the gross domestic product of the province has reached RMB 333.018 billion, increasing by 11.9 times over that of 1978 and increasing by 13.6% annually on average in terms of comparable prices. Per-capita GDP was RMB 10,200, increasing by 8. 6 times compared with that of 1978, with an average annual increase of 12.0%. In 1998, the budgetary state revenue of the province was RMB 28.142 billion, increasing by 17.6 times over that of 1978, with an average annual increase of 15.7%. The province has opened wider to the outside world. Satisfactory achievements have been made in the export-oriented economy. A multilevel and omni-directional opening-up pattern has preliminarily taken form, which includes special economic zones, coastal opening cities, economic and technical development zones, Taiwan investment zones, duty-free zones, high-tech zones, experimental zones for overall reform. Since 1978, the actual funds from direct foreign investment totalled US$ 26.316 billion, including US$ 4.012 billion for 1998. The investment fields involve light industry, textile, clothing, electronics, machinery, chemical industry, metallurgy, building materials, agriculture, forestry, water conservancy, communications, power, real estate, finance and tourism service, etc. The export value totalled US$ 73.883 billion. In 1998, the export value was US$ 12.073 billion, increasing by 62.5 times as against that of 1978, with an average annual increase of 23.1% .

II. Investment Environment

Since the implementation of the reform and opening up policy, Fujian accelerated the construction steps of infrastructure, and readjusted the investment structure. Emphasis was laid on the construction of communications, post and telecommunications, power, and municipal administration. All these measures have obviously ameliorated the investment circumstances, and fostered the economic development of the province. Highways in Fujian radiate in all directions, with total mileage of 48 thousand kilometres. There are five national level highways within the boundaries of the province. Quanxia expressway has been completed and opened to traffic and Fuquan expressway shall be completed in 1999 as well. Fujian has railways of Yingxia, Waifu, Zhangquanxiao, and Hengnan, with a total mileage of 1068 kilometres. Fujian has airports of Fuzhou, Xiamen, Jinjiang, Wuyishan, with 119 airlines opened, leading to all China major cities, southeast Asia, Hong Kong and Macao. In terms of water transportation, the coastal port system has taken form, mainly including Fuzhou, Xiamen and Meizhouwan. 254 civil and international navigation lines have been opened, leading to 126 ports of Japan, Korea, Russia, Yugoslavia and some southeast Asian countries and regions.

The province has over 120 hotels open to foreign tourists, with over 30,000 beds, It has 143 star-rated hotels, including four five-star hotels. The hotels have the capacity of receiving foreign tourists of two million person-times.

Post and telecommunications of Fujian takes the lead in China. The capacity of telephone exchanges in the province surmounts 5.47 million lines. The capacity of long-distance automatic exchange boards amounts to 197,000 terminals. The mobile telecommunications system covers every city, county and developed coastal villages and towns. Rural and urban telephone subscribers amount to 3.475 million households. Mobile telephone subscribers amount to 1.422 million households. The popularity rate of telephones in urban and rural areas amounts to 16.56 sets every 100 people. The popularity rate of telephones and mobile telephones in urban areas amounts to 53.95 sets and 4.31 sets every 100 people respectively. The cooperation between Fujian and international financial institutions is becoming increasingly close. The province has 28 foreign and joint venture financial institutions, which have established agent and business intercourse relationship with over 4,400 foreign banks. Fujian urban infrastructure is becoming increasingly complete and perfect. Fujian has East China's biggest hydroelectric power plant Shuikou Hydroelectric Station as well as Fuzhou Huaneng, Xiamen Songyun and other big thermal power plants.

III. Development Perspects

The short-term objectives are, by the year 2000, that the overall national economic strength of Fujian shall take the lead in the whole country. Percapita GDP shall increase by eight times over that of 1980. "Better-off level" shall be realised completely. Fujian shall preliminarily establish and complete a socialist market economy, a foreign economic system agreeable with international practice, and form a perfect social developing system.

The long-term objective is, by the year 2010, that Fujian economic construction and the people's livelihood go up to a higher level. The GDP in 2010 shall quadruple that of 1996, which has increased by seven times over that of 1980. Fujian shall become one of the ten strongest provinces. The people's livelihood shall approach or reach the living standard of medium-income countries or regions. Relatively perfect and complete socialist market economic system and operating mechanism shall take shape. The overall quality of the national economy shall improve remarkably. Sustainable economic and social development shall be realised.

IV. Key Areas for Encouraging Foreign Investment

In order to further improve the level of the opening up and economic development, Fujian provincial government promulgated several stipulations on further encouraging foreign investment in Fujian Province, namely, foreign funds are encouraged to be invested in the following key fields. Foreign businessmen can enjoy preferential taxation policies, exemption from some charging items and enjoy favourable price of land. Foreign-funded enterprises may enjoy national treatment.

1. Foreign businessmen are encouraged to invest in petrochemical industry, machinery, electronics, building materials, forestry, aquatic product industry, textile industry and other pillar and key industries.

2. Foreign businessmen are encouraged to invest in agriculture, animal husbandry and other related items.

3. Foreign businessmen are encouraged to invest in ports, wharves, electric power and other infrastructure items.

4. Foreign businessmen are encouraged to invest in high-tech enterprises.

5. Foreign businessmen are encouraged to invest in building ordinary housing.

6. Foreign businessmen are encouraged to invest in Fujian tourist industry. Foreign businessmen may, on approval, invest to run joint-venture tourist agencies in na-

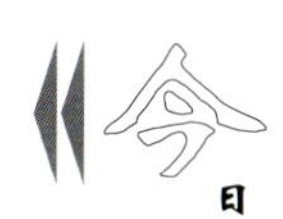

tional tourist and vacation zones. In addition, they are allowed to establish branches outside the zones to develop related business. On approval, foreign businessmen may invest to build villas, vacation villages and other related service items in national tourist and vocation zones as well as provincial tourist and economic development zones.

前进中的江西

Jiangxi: In Progress

一、经济发展情况

江西简称“赣”，位于长江中下游南岸。东邻浙江、福建，南连广东，西接湖南，北毗湖北、安徽。京九铁路和浙赣铁路纵横贯穿全境，交通便利，地理位置优越。素有“物华天宝，人杰地灵”之盛誉。现设6个省辖市、5个地区；辖71个县、15个县级市、13个市辖区，省会南昌市；全省总人口4191.2万人，人口密度为每平方公里251人，境内有43个少数民族，汉族是主要民族，占总人口的99%以上。

建国50年来，江西人民艰苦创业、创造了令人瞩目的业绩。特别是改革开放20年来，全省经济实力有了巨大的增长，教育、科技、文化、卫生、体育事业有了长足的进步，城乡人民的物质文化生活水平有了显著的提高。1994年全省提前6年实现了国民生产总值比1980年翻两番的战略目标。1998年全省国内生产总值达1852亿元，比1949年增长43.4倍；人均国内生产总值4440元，比1949年增长13.0倍，年平均递增5.5%。1950年全省财政收入只有1.17亿元，1998年达到145.70亿元，年平均递增10.6%；人均财政收入由1950年的8元增加到1998的349元，增长42.7倍。1998年，全省城镇居民可支配收入4251元，扣除物价因素，比1978年实际增长1.86倍；农民人均纯收入2048元，比1978年实际增长3.66倍；城乡居民储蓄存款已达1069.2亿元，比1978年末增加

南昌八一大桥
“August First” Bridge in Nanchang

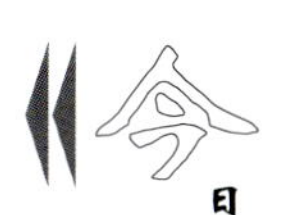

1065亿元，增长256倍。随着国家对外政策的调整，江西对外经济往来逐步扩大，特别是改革开放后，江西省外向型经济迅速发展。1981年发展了自营出口，开辟了九江港为外贸口岸，外贸进出口额快速增长，1998年全省外贸进出口总额达到18.80亿美元，其中出口额16.51亿美元，比1978年增长31.5倍；实际利用外资从无到有发展迅速，1998年全省实际利用外资7.09亿美元，比1985年增长68.4倍。

二、投资环境

建国50年来，江西投入了大量的财力加强基础设施建设，努力改善投资环境。尤其是改革开放以来，作为国民经济基础建设的交通运输、邮电通讯业得到迅猛发展。目前，江西省已初步形成一个铁路、公路、水运、航空等方式齐全，以省会南昌市为中心，以铁路、国道公路和赣江水路为干线的外通各省、内联各地、市、县、乡的四通八达的交通运输网。到1998年底，江西省公路通车里程已达36867公里，比1949年增长6.8倍，形成了以南昌为中心、二纵四横、六条国道为骨架，省道为干线，县、乡道路为支线，覆盖全省城乡，沟通毗邻六省的公路网，并已建成南昌至九江、南昌至樟树、温家圳至厚田高速公路共212公里，目前正在准备开工建设昌傅至赣州、温家圳至梨园高速公路；全省铁路营运里程达2197公里，比1949年增长2倍，特别是京九铁路和浙赣铁路复线的建成，有效地改善了江西省交通运输状况；自1957年开始，建立了第一个民用航空站—南昌航空站，以后又陆续成立了吉安、赣州、景德镇、九江等航空站。目前从南昌发往各大城市的航线已达23条，每周航班由1978年的不足10个班次发展到现在的100余班次，1999年南昌昌北机场（4D级）将正式建成通航。50年来，江西省先后建设了微波通讯工程、光缆通讯工程、DDN数据通讯工程、移动通讯网络工程等多项大型通讯工程，现已形成以程控交换、数字微波、光纤传输为主，设备、技术先进的电信网和以邮运自办、邮件计算机处理为主的现代邮政网。除了具有一定水平基础设施等硬环境外，江西还具备吸引外资、发展外向型经济的优越的软环境。为了加大引资的力度，制定和完善了一系列鼓励外商投资的政策、法规和章程。近几年，江西省坚持“积极、合理、有效”的利用外资的方针，制定了一系列保护港澳台投资者合法权益、鼓励来赣投资的优惠政策措施和规定，颁布了一些旨在促进对利用外资的管理、下放审批权限、简化审批程序、提高办事效率的法规。各地（市）县都制定了一系列适合本地区实际情况的鼓励外商投资的办法，为扩大招商引资创造了良好的条件。

三、发展前景

近期发展目标是：“九五”期间（1996-2000年），全面实现第二步战略目标，力争国民生产总值比1980年翻三番，初步建立社会主义市场经济体制，人民生活总体实现小康，解决现有贫困人口温饱问题，将一个经济繁荣、科技进步、文化昌盛、社会稳定、生活小康的江西带入21世纪，为迈向第三步战略目标奠定良好的基础。

远期发展目标是：到2010年，实现人均国民生产总值比2000年翻一番，使人民的小康生活更加宽裕，形成比较完善的社会主义市场经济体制，使经济管理体制和运行机制规范化、法律化；优化产业结构，加快城镇化步伐，基本实现工业化；实现资源的优化配置，显著提高国民经济的技术水平和整体素质，实现经济和社会可持续发展。

四、鼓励投资的重点领域

1.搞好灾后重建、移民建镇工作，建立一批与之配套的“退田还湖”、公路建设、兴修水利的建设项目，重点抓好一批移民建镇示范点，建成一批布局合理、环境优美的新型村镇。

2. 重点发展一批农业开发和农产品深加工项目，包括红壤开发、森林资源发展与保护项目开发以及以农产品为原料的食品工业项目，将潜在的资源优势转化为现实的经济优势，实现区域经济的协调发展。

3. 继续加强以交通运输为代表的基础设施建设，加快信息产业的开发力度，努力创造一个适应经济发展的投资环境。

4. 重点支持冶金、钢铁、有色金属、医药、纺织、建材、造纸、机械、电子等产业领域的一批国有企业的技术改造项目投资，引导企业加大更新改造投入力度，积极引进技术和先进设备，促进高新技术产业化，增强企业竞争力，加快以提高质量、增加技术含量、增加品种、节能降耗、防治污染为主的升级换代改造步伐。

5. 积极发展旅游业和生态环境工程建设，不断开发旅游资源，加强环境保护，努力创造一个促进经济可持续发展的优美、协调的自然环境。

I. Status of Economic Development

Jiangxi Province, known in short as "Gan", is located on the southern bank of the Yangtze River. It borders Zhejiang and Fujian provinces in the east, Guangdong Province in the south, Hunan Province in the west, and Hubei and Anhui provinces in the north. Jiangxi has convenient transport facilities and good geological status as the Beijing-Kowloon and Zhejiang-Jiangxi railways run through the province. In the history, it is famous for its fertility land and smart people. Now it has six cities, five prefectures, 71 counties, 15 county-level cities and 13 districts under its jurisdiction, and Nanchang is the capital of Jiangxi Province. It has a population of 41.912 million, averaging 251 people per square kilometers. There are 43 minority nationalities in the province, but the Han shares 99.5 percent of its total population.

Over the past 50 years since the founding of New China, the Jiangxi people have made noticeable achievements. Especially in the past 20 years since the reform and opening program was launched in 1978, Jiangxi has made considerable progress in its economic strength, education, science and technology, culture, public health and sports. The period also witnessed great improvement in people's living standards in cities and the countryside. In 1994, the GDP in the province amounted to 18.52 million yuan, 43.4 times over that of 1949; the per capita GDP hit 4440 yuan, an increase of 13 times over 1949, with annual average growth of 5.5 percent. In 1950 the provincial financial revenues were only 117 million yuan, while in 1998 the figure reached 14.570 billion yuan, with annual average growth rate of 10.6 percent. The per capita financial revenue has risen from eight yuan in 1950 to 349 yuan in 1998, increasing by 42.7 times. In 1998, the disposable income per person in cities and towns was 4,251 yuan allowing for price rises, an increase of 1.86 times over that of 1978. The net income for per farmer came to 2,048 yuan, 3.66 times higher than that of 1978. The amount of saving deposits in cities and the countryside in the province has reached 106.92 billion yuan, increasing 106.5 billion yuan, or 256 times higher than that of 1978. With the opening wider to the outside world, Jiangxi has gradually expanded its foreign trade and economic cooperations with foreign countries. Particularly since the opening and reform program, Jiangxi's foreign-oriented economy has developed rapidly. From 1981, the province began enjoying the right to manage exports and opened Jiujiang as foreign trade port. This has thus speeded up the development of its foreign trade. The total amount of its foreign trade in 1998 reached US$1.880

billion, among which, exports were valued at US$1.651 billion, or 31.5 times over 1978. The use of foreign capital developed rapidly. In 1998, the amount of foreign capital actually used reached US$709 million, 68.4 times over 1985.

II. Investment Environment

Over the past 50 years, particularly in the past 20 years, Jiangxi has allocated a large amount of money to strengthen the construction of infrastructure facilities to improve its investment environment. As a result, rapid progress has been made in construction of its traffic, transport, telecommunication facilities. At present, a transport network, including railways, highways, waterways and airlines, has taken form in the province, with Nanchang as the hub of its transportation. The transport network has directly connected with other parts of the country, as well as with foreign countries. By the end of 1998, the highway mileage in Jiangxi reached 36,867 kilometers, 6.8 times higher than that of 1949. Its well-developed highway network with Nanchang as center is formed by two national highways from north to south and four national highways from east to west, supported by provincial- and county-level highways, linking with all parts of the province. The province has completed Nanchang-Jiujiang, Nanchang-Zhangshu and Wenjiazhen-Houtian expressways, totaling 212 kilometers in length. In addition, two expressway projects, one from Changfu to Ganzhou, the other from Wenjiazhen to Liyuan, are under preparations. The railway milage in the province has reached 2,197 kilometers, 2 times over that of 1949. Particularly, the completion of the Beijing-Kowloon Railway and the Zhejiang-Jiangxi double-tracking railway has greatly improved the traffic situation in the province. From 1957, Jiangxi had its first civil aviation station--the Nanchang Aviation Station. Since then, it has established the Jiean, Ganzhou, Jingdezhen and Jiujia aviation stations. Now, it has 23 routes from Nanchang to major large cities throughout the country. The number of flight every week has increased from less than 10 in 1978 to more than 100. The Nanchang Changbei Airport, built according to 4D standards, is expected to be completed in 1999 and opened to the public.

Over the past 50 years, Jiangxi has completed many telecommunications projects, including those using microwave, optical fiber, DDN and mobile telecommunication technologies, thus forming an advanced telecommunication system. A modern post network handled by computers is also available. Apart from some modern infrastructure facilities, Jiangxi is also ready with excellent soft investment environment to attract foreign capital. To import more foreign capital, the Jiangxi government has worked out and improved a series of policies, laws and regulations encouraging foreign investment in Jiangxi. In recent years, Jiangxi, following the principle of "active, reasonable, effective use of foreign capital," has formulated a set of policies and regulations in protection of investment from Hong Kong, Macao and Taiwan. It also published some regulations favorable to rational use of foreign capital, simplification of examination and approval procedures. Various localities also worked out methods to attract foreign capital according to their actual conditions.

III. Investment Prospects

The short-term development targets are: During the Ninth Five-Year Plan period (1996-2000), Jiangxi will realize its second-step strategic goal, striving to octuple its 1980 GDP, thus initially establishing a socialist market economic system. People's living standards will be much improved up to a fairly well-off level. Jiangxi will enter the 21st century as a province with flourishing economy, progressive science and technology and stable society, thus laying a sound foundation for realization its third-step strategic goal.

The long-term targets are: by 2010, Jiangxi will double its 2000 GDP, and people's living standards will be much enhanced, forming a fairly complete socialist market economic system, and making its economic management system and operating mechanism standardized, legalized and industrialized. Efforts will be made to speed up the construction of cities and towns, basically realizing industrialization, optimizing allocation of resources, and enhancing the technological level and whole quality of the national economy, and realizing the sustained development of its economy and society.

IV. Key Fields for Investment

1. Doing a good job in rebuilding homeland after disasters, and building settlements for immigrants and other related projects, including the projects "returning fields to lakes", highway and water conservancy projects. Efforts should be made to build some demonstration settlements, with rational layout and beautiful scenery.

2. Priority should be given to development of agricultural projects, agricultural products processing projects, including development of red soil, development and protection of forest resources, and food industries using agricultural products. Efforts should be made to turn its potential resources advantages into economic advantages, and realize the co-ordinative development of its regional economy.

3. Efforts should be made to strengthen the construction infrastructure facilities, represented by traffic and transport facilities, accelerate the information industry, and strive to create an investment environment suitable for economic development.

4. Emphasis should be given to technical upgrading of state-owned enterprises in the fields of metallurgy, iron and steel, non-ferrous metal, machine, textile, building materials, paper making, machinery and electronics. We should guide these enterprises to put more efforts in technical transformation, import of advanced technologies and equipment so as to enhance their competitiveness. Enterprises should speed up their pace to produce quality products with hi-tech contents, and energy-saving and pollution-preventing functions.

5. We should actively develop tourism and protect biological environment. Continuous efforts should be made to develop tourist resources, strengthen environment protection, striving to create a well co-ordinated natural environment promoting the sustained economic development.

昌九工业走廊
The Changjiu Industrial Corridor

在现代化道路上奋进的山东

Shandong: Marching on the Road of Modernization

山东是中国东部沿海的一个重要省份，位于黄河下游，东临渤海、黄海，与朝鲜半岛、日本列岛隔海相望。特殊的地理位置，使山东省成为黄河经济带与环渤海经济区的交汇点、华北地区和华东地区的结合部，在全国经济格局中占有重要地位。山东总面积15.67万平方公里，约占全国总面积的1.6%。海岸线长3024.4公里，占全国大陆海岸线长的1/6。全省共有48个市(15个地级市，33个县级市)，2个地区，45个区，61个县，2309个乡镇。目前全省总人口8838.2万。

建国50年来，山东国民经济发展迅速，综合经济实力显著增强，特别是改革开放以来，全省经济一直持续、快速、健康发展，产业结构日趋合理，经济效益不断提高，国民经济主要指标走在全国前列，已成为名副其实的经济大省。1998年，全省实现国内生产总值7162.2亿元，比1952年增长42.6倍，年均增长8.6%，高于同期全国平均速度0.9个百分点；人均国内生产总值达8104元，是1952年的22.8倍，年均增长7.1%。

经过50年的发展，特别是改革开放20年的突飞猛进，山东国内生产总值占全国的比重由1952年的6.4%提高到9.0%。产业结构不断调整优化，一、二、三产业增加值占GDP的比重由1952年的65.8：18.1：16.1改变为17.2：48.2：34.6。1998年，全省实现社会消费品零售额2127.2亿元，比1949年增长340.4倍，年均增长12.6%。外贸规模迅速扩大，从1950年到1998年，山东外贸进出口总额由4149万美元增长到194.3亿美元，在全国居第四位，增长了467倍，年均递增13.7%。利用外资发展迅猛。改革开放以前，山东省利用外资的数量很少。改革开放以后，全省从社会主义初级阶段的实际出发，不断优化投资环境，吸收外资，以弥补省内经济发展的资金缺口，同时，山东省经济高速发展，市场前景广阔，对外国投资者具有巨大的吸引力，因此，全省利用外资规模不断扩大，水平日益提高。截止1998年底，全省累计批准外商投资企业20190家，从1979年到1998年，累计利用外资合同金额346.1亿美元，实际利用外资190.4亿美元，有效地弥补了国内建设资金的不足，促进了国内经济的发展。随着外商投资在全省的进一步发展，外资企业对国民经济的贡献也越来越大，其提供的税金也有显著增长，到1998年，外商投资企业累计交纳的税金及附加费达378亿元，所提供的税金已占地方财政收入的12.6%。利用外资的质量显著提高，到1998年已经有98个国家和地区的外商来山东投资，其中世界著名的跨国公司已近百家，世界排名前100名的跨国公司有26家已经来山东投资，过千万美元的利用外资项目近千个，过亿美元的项目近20个。利用外资对山东的国民经济和社会发展产生了重大而深远的影响，外商投资产业结构已构成全省经济结构的重要组成部分，到1998年，第一产业利用外资占1.6%，第二产业占73%，第三产业占25.4%，外资投向逐渐合理，形成了程控交换机、高清晰度电视、传真机、汽车发动机及零部件等高技术群体，促进了全省产业结构的调整优化，成为拉动经济增长的重要因素。目前山东利用外资在全国居第五位，农业利用外资在全国处于领先地位。到1998年，山东省第一产业增加值居全国第一位，二、三产业增加值、社会消费品零售额和地方财政收入均居全国第三，工业实现利税和利润总额均居第二。许许多多工业产品产量在全国居首位或前列。山东已被世界银行誉为“中国经济增长的引擎之一”。全省经济总量在1987年实现第一个翻番的基础上，1993年提前7年实现第二个翻番，1994年实现人均国内生产总值翻两番。山东是全国的农业大省，粮食产量居全国第二位，为全国最大的“菜园”和“果园”，而且是全国的“水产大省”。经过建国50年特别是改革开放20年的发展，山东形成了以能源、化工、机械、电子、纺织、建材、食品为支柱的产业群，一些新兴产业和高技术产业快速成长，轻重工业发展趋向协调，大中型企业和名牌拳头产品的支撑带动作用增强。经济的增长促进了社会各项事业的发展，反过来，社会各项事业也推动了经济的增长。科技事业硕果累累，建国50年来，全省共取得重要科技成果44919项，其中达到国际领先或先进水平的有4194项，属于国内先进水平的有23987项，有多项科技成果荣获国家科技进步奖和国家技术进步奖，1992年到1998年，获国家级科技奖励的项目数连续6年居全国首位。教育事业进一步发展，50年来，全省共培养大学毕业生70.61万人，为经济发展提供了宝贵的人才支持和智力支持。

威海港
Weihai Harbour

山东具有优越的投资环境。早在1983年7月就提出把发展对外贸易、扩大对外开放作为实现“提前翻番、富民兴鲁”奋斗目标的重要措施。山东的海、陆、空交通十分方便。公路以通车里程长、路面等级高闻名全国。中国的两大铁路干线京沪铁路和京九铁路均纵贯山东境内，胶济铁路和兖石铁路横跨东西。航空业迅速发展，现已建成包括济南、青岛两个国际机场在内的9处机场，开通了国际、国内航线106条。山东省沿海现有港口26处，港口密度居全国之首，并且所有的港口均对外开放，同100多个国家的300多个港口通航。山东省的邮电通讯基本实现了现代化。

山东鼓励投资的重点领域有：改造提高化工、冶金、建材、纺织、食品、造纸六大传统产业，以石油化工、机械电子、汽车和建筑业四大主导产业及以乙烯为基础的石化主导产品系列、以汽车为龙头的运输机械主导产品系列、以机电仪一体化设备为先导的机械制造主导产品系列、以计算机为中心的电子信息主导产品系列、以程控交换机为骨干的通讯设备主导产品系列、以新一代家电产品为重点的耐用消费品主导产品系列等六大主导产品系列等等。

山东作为沿海省份，各方面基础较好，在向现代化的历史进军中应当走在全国前列。山东省经济和社会发展总的目标是：实现由经济大省向经济强省的历史性跨越，确保本世纪末达到小康水平，到2010年基本实现现代化。到2000年的目标是：

1. 在不断提高经济素质和效益的前提下，实现国内生产总值比1980年翻三番，达到8000亿元，人均国内生产总值达到8920元。

2. 初步建立起社会主义市场经济体制，基本实现从计划经济体制向社会主义市场经济体制的转变。

3. 人民生活总体上达到小康水平，部分地区率先实现现代化。到2010年，国内生产总值比2000年再翻一番，经济结构进一步优化，整体素质明显提高，社会主义市场经济体制更加完善，人民的小康生活更加宽裕，社会更加文明，奠定实现社会主义现代化的坚实基础。

Shandong, an important coastal province in eastern China, is located on the lower reaches of the Yellow River. It is flanked by the Bohai and Yellow seas to the east, and faces the Korean and Japanese islands. This special geographical location enables the province to become a juncture of the Yellow River economic belt and the Bohai economic zone, as well as a bridge between northern and eastern China. It has an important status in the nation's economic pattern.

The province covers an area of 156,700 square km, with its coastline stretching 3,024.4 km, making up about 1.6 percent and one sixth of the country's total respectively. With a population of 88.382 million, Shandong is divided into 48 cities (including 15 prefectural cities and 33 county-level cities), two prefectures, 45 districts, 61 counties, and 2,309 towns.

In the past 50 years since the founding of the People's Republic of China, the province's economy has developed fast, and its comprehensive economic has notably strengthened. Especially since the practice of reform and opening in 1978, the economy has been developing in a rapid and sustainable way. The industrial structure has become more rational, economic returns constantly increased, and main national economic indices have taken the national lead.

In 1998, the province's GDP reached 716.22 billion yuan, increasing by 42.6 times from 1952 in comparable prices. The average annual growth was 8.6 percent, 0.9 percentage points higher than the national average. The per-capita GDP reached 8,104 yuan, 22.8 times higher than

1952, or an annual average growth of 7.1 percent.

The GDP has increased from 6.4 percent of the national total in 1952 to 9 percent now. The province's industrial structure has been continuously readjusted and optimized. The ratio of the primary, secondary and tertiary industries in GDP changed from 65.8:18.1:16.1 to 17.2:48.2:34.6.

In 1998, the province's retail sales of consumer goods hit 212.72 billion yuan, an increase of 340.4 times of 1949, or an annual average growth of 12.6 percent.

Foreign trade has expanded rapidly. From 1950 to 1998, the total foreign trade volume increased from US$41.49 million to US$19.43 billion, ranking fourth in China. The growth was 467 times higher, with annual average growth reaching 13.7 percent.

Foreign investment increased rapidly. Since 1978, the province, proceeding from the reality of the primary stage of socialism, has constantly optimized its investment environment so as to attract foreign funds and fill the capital gap in a developing economy. A fast-developing economy and vast prospects have attracted foreign investors, resulting in the foreign investment scale being enlarged by an increasingly high level.

By the end of 1998, the province had approved a total of 20,190 foreign-funded enterprises, involving US$34.61 billion of contractual foreign capital and US$19.04 billion in paid-in foreign funds.

With the further development of foreign investment, foreign-funded businesses have made more contributions to the national economy, and their tax payments have increased significantly. By 1998, foreign-funded enterprises have paid a total of 37.8 billion yuan of taxes and extra charges. Their tax payments account for 12.6 percent of local financial revenue.

Foreign investment quality has improved. Nearly 100 renowned transnational companies from 98 countries and regions have invested in Shandong, including 26 firms of the world's top 100. There are 1,000 foreign-funded projects with their capital exceeding US$10 million each, and 20 projects with funding of at least US$100 million each.

Foreign investment has had important and far-reaching effects on Shandong's economic and social development. The foreign-funded industrial structure has become an important part of the provincial economic structure.

By 1998, foreign investment used accounted for 1.6 percent, 73 percent and 25.4 percent respectively of the primary, secondary and tertiary industries. The foreign investment structure has become more rational. Foreign funds are mainly invested in program-controlled switchboards, high-definition television, fax machines, auto engines and parts and components. Readjustment and optimization of the province's industrial structure improved. Therefore, foreign investment has become an important factor to drive the province's economic growth.

Currently, Shandong ranked fifth in the nation in utilizing foreign funds, with its agricultural sector taking the lead in China. By 1998, the added value of primary industry led the country, the added value of secondary and tertiary industries, retail sales of social consumer goods and local financial revenue all ranked third, and total industrial profits and tax payment ranked second. Output of many products leads the country. As a result, Shandong was reputed as "one of engines promoting economic growth in China" by the World Bank.

Its GDP had doubled by 1987, and doubled again in 1993, seven years ahead of schedule. In 1994, its percapita GDP quadrupled.

Shandong is a big agricultural province in China, with its grain output ranking second. In addition to a largest "vegetable garden" and "fruit garden" in the country, it is also a big producer of aquatic products.

During the past 50 years, especially the past 20 years,

Shandong has created an industrial profile headed by the energy, chemicals, machinery, electronics, textile, building materials and foodstuff industries. Some new and high-tech industries have developed rapidly, with light and heavy industries tending towards coordinated development, and brand-name recognition and leading products of large and medium-sized enterprises have played a larger supporting role in the economy.

Economic growth has promoted development of social undertakings, and vice versa.

The province has achieved a total of 44,919 scientific and technological results. Of these, 4,194 have reached international advanced level, 23,987 domestic advanced level, and many have won prizes of state scientific and technological progress and state technical progress. The number of prize winners has stayed top in the nation for six consecutive years.

Education undertakings have developed further. During the past 50 years, the province has turned out 706,100 university graduates, providing vital personnel and intellectual support for economic development.

Shandong boasts an excellent investment environment. In July 1983, the provincial government decided to develop foreign trade and expand opening so as to materialize the target of doubling the GDP ahead of time and making the people rich and the province prosperous.

Transports by sea, land and air are very convenient. The province's highways are well-known in China for their long-mileage opening to traffic and high-grade road surface. The Beijing-Shanghai and Beijing-Kowloon, the country's two railway trunk lines, pass down the spine of Shandong, while the Jiaozhou-Jinan and the Yanzhou-Shijiazhuang railways traverse the province.

The aviation industry has developed fast. Now, nine airports, including the two in Jinan and Qingdao, have been built, and 106 international and domestic routes opened.

The province boasts 26 coastal ports, with port density taking the lead in the country. All these ports are open to the outside world, with links to 300 ports in 100 countries.

The posts and telecommunications sector has basically realized modernization.

Shandong has encouraged investment in the following fields: renovation and upgrading of such traditional industries as chemicals, metallurgy, building materials, textiles, foodstuffs and paper making; major industries like petrochemicals, machinery and electronics, automobile and construction; petrochemical products; transport machinery, including vehicles, machinery manufacture and mechatronics equipment; electronics information including computer, telecommunication equipment, and program-controlled switchboards; and durable consumption goods including a new generation of household electrical appliances.

As a coastal province, Shandong has sound foundations in all sectors, and determines to lead the country in its modernization drive. The general target of the provincial economic and social development is: to materialize an historical shift from a big economic province to a strong one, ensure a well-off living standard, and basically realize modernization by the year 2010.

Targets in 2000 are:

Firstly, to constantly improve economic performance, so as to octuple the GDP based on 1980 to 800 billion yuan, with per capita GDP reaching 8,920 yuan.

Secondly, initially set up a socialist market economic system, so as to basically shift from a planned economy to socialist market economic system.

And thirdly, enable people′s living standards to reach the well-off level, with some areas realizing modernization. By the year 2010, the GDP should double the figure of 2000, so as to further optimize the economic structure, improve the socialist market economic system, enable people to become wealthier and the society more civilized, and lay a solid foundation for realizing socialist modernization.

腾飞中的河南

Henan: A Rising Star

一、经济发展情况

河南省位于中国中部，黄河中下游，黄淮海平原的西南部，总面积约16.7万平方公里。1998年全省人口9315万。河南有得天独厚的地理和自然条件。处于温带与亚热带地区，兼有南北之长，气候温和，四季分明，雨量充沛，土地肥沃，动植物资源、矿产资源丰富，宜于工农业发展。

建国以来，河南的经济建设和社会发展取得辉煌成就。改变了贫穷落后的面貌，现代化进程不断加快。进入90年代以来，实施“开放带动”、“可持续发展”、“科教兴豫”的发展战略，开创了建国以来河南经济增长的最好时期，提前6年实现2000年国内生产总值比1980年翻两番的目标。1990-1998年，全省国内生产总值以年均11.3%的速度递增，1998年全省国内生产总值达4356亿元，经济总量在全国居第五位。粮、棉、油、烟产量分别达到4009.6万吨、72.8万吨、312.1万吨、31.1万吨，分别居全国第一、第二、第一和第三位，大牲畜头数居全国第一。以丰富的农副产品资源和矿产资源为依托，工业经济快速发展，形成了门类较为齐全的工业体系。1998年，工业增加值达1742亿元。具有现代工业特征的石化、电气机械、电子等新兴产业迅速崛起。一些主要工业产品产量跃居中国前列。如平板玻璃、原煤、卷烟、纱、发电量等分居全国第三、第二、第二、第四和第五位。

围绕培育大市场、搞活大流通，走贸易开路、金融活体、基础配套的发展思路，形成了以郑州为中心，门类齐全、城乡贯通、辐射中原、面向全国的市场体系。1998年，社会消费品零售总额1496.2亿元，居全国第六位。郑州商品交易所是中国最大的粮食批发市场和首家规范化的粮食期货市场，已与世界各大交易中心联网，被誉为“中国第一市”。郑州商品交易会是中国有影响的交易会之一。目前全省17个地市均拥有外贸自营

河南农业
Agriculture in Henan

出口权，拥有自营出口权企业100多家。年进出口额已达17亿美元。国际贸易伙伴由1978年的17个国家和地区扩大到140多个。河南已成为中国中西部改革开放的桥头堡和经济发展的龙头地区。

建国50年来，河南的教育、文化、科技、卫

生等社会事业快速发展，取得了一批达到国家和世界先进水平的科技成果，对国民经济发展起到了积极的推动作用。连续举办多届的洛阳牡丹花会、郑州国际少林武术节、温县国际太极拳年会等活动影响很大，成为河南扩大对外交流与合作的重要场所。

二、投资环境

河南是全国重要的枢纽地区之一，交通运输条件优越。京广、陇海、焦枝、京九等铁路干线纵横交错，新开通的亚欧大陆桥横穿全省。通过铁路出口的商品可以在郑州直接联检封关。洛阳—郑州—开封、新乡—安阳、郑州—许昌、许昌—漯河的高速公路已建成通车，许昌—平顶山，三门峡—洛阳，开封—商丘等高速公路正在积极建设之中。有四条国际集装箱运输线路通过郑州。目前河南的公路通车里程达57172公里，等级公路已延伸至偏远的乡镇。民用航空事业发展迅速。新建成的4E级的郑州新郑机场，年旅客吞吐能力达600万人，为河南省改革开放架起了便捷的空中桥梁。郑州、洛阳、南阳三个机场已开通了45条国内航线飞往国内40多个城市，另有多架次包机往返香港、澳门、曼谷和新加坡等地。郑州—莫斯科货运包机已开始试航。程控交换、光缆通信、数字通信成为河南通讯网的主体。1998年，全省城乡交换机总容量694.41万门，电话普及率达每百人6.54部。便利的交通通信设施使河南起着连南贯北、承东启西的重要作用。

目前，河南省同国外结交了20多对友好省(州、市)。建成投产的三资企业4254家，实际利用外资68.58亿美元。在日本、美国、德国、澳大利亚、泰国和香港等国家和地区设有40个经济贸易窗口。经国家批准，郑州被确定为享受沿海开放城市各项优惠政策的内陆开放城市。河南历史悠久，山川秀丽。洛阳、安阳、开封是闻名于世的历史文化名城。龙门石窟、少林寺、白马寺、石人山等闻名遐迩，是著名的旅游胜地。郑州、洛阳建立有国家级高新技术开发区，重点开发新材料技术及产品、电子信息技术及产品、生物工程技术及产品及其他领域的高新技术及产品。新乡、开封、漯河、商丘、鹤壁等大部分市也都建有各种形式的经济技术开发区。

三、发展前景

根据河南省“九五”计划（1996-2000年）和2010年远景规划:“九五”时期，国内生产总值力争在1980年的基础上翻三番，人均国内生产总值增长5倍，基本消除贫困现象，人民生活基本达到小康，初步建立社会主义市场经济体制，全面实现社会主义现代化建设第二步战略目标，为跨入21世纪、向第三步战略目标迈进奠定坚实的基础。

2001-2010年，实现国内生产总值和人均国内生产总值在2000年基础上再翻一番，按1995年价格计算，2010年，全省国内生产总值达到11100亿元，人口控制在1.04亿以内，人均国内生产总值10700元，人民生活达到比较宽裕的程度。形成比较完善的社会主义市场经济体制，实现经济管理体制和运行机制的规范化、法制化。产业结构趋于合理，国民经济整体素质和工业化、城市化水平明显堤高。社会主义精神文明建设和民主法制建设取得显著进展，实现经济和社会可持续发展。

四、当前河南省重点鼓励发展的领域

1. 农业、农副产品加工业、畜牧养殖业、林产品加工业;

2. 能源、交通、冶金、建材等基础设施和基础产业;

3. 高新技术产业、高效低耗产业;

4. 教育、科技、医疗等公益性事业;

5. 国家允许外商投资的第三产业。

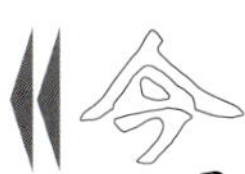

I. The Status of Economic Development

Henan Province is located in the central part of China, the middle and lower reaches of the Yellow River, and the southwest part of Huanghe-Huaihe-Haihe plain. It covers an area of 167,000 square kilometers, and has a total population of 93.15 million in 1998. Henan enjoys exceptional geographical conditions and natural resources. Located between the temperate zone and subtropics, Henan has advantages of both the South and the North. It has a mild climate, distinctive four seasons, abundant rainfall, rich soil, and plentiful natural resources in animals, plants and minerals. Hence, Henan is suitable for development of industry and agriculture.

Since 1949, Henan has achieved splendid success in economic construction and social development. It has changed its backward situation, and accelerated the procedure of modernization. Since 1990, Henan has implemented the strategies for development, including "opening up program", "sustained development" and "invigorating Henan through science and education". 1990s saw a best period in its economic development since New China was founded. Its GDP has quadrupled that of 1980, six years ahead of schedule.

Between 1990 and 1998, its GDP has increased annually at the rate of 11.3 percent, with its GDP hitting 43.56 billion yuan in 1998. Its aggregated economic strength ranked the fifth place in the country. The output of grain, cotton, edible oil and tobacco were 40.096 million tons, 0.728 million tons, 3.121 million tons and 0.311 million tons, and ranking the first, second, the first and third places respectively. The number of draught livestocks in Henan is on the top list of China. Relying on its rich resources of agriculture, sideline products and minerals, its industrial economy has developed rapidly and has formed a fairly complete industrial system. In 1998, its industrial added value amounted to 174.2 billion yuan. Its modern industries, including petrochemical, machinery and electronics, have emerged rapidly. The output of major industrial products jumped to the forefront in China. For example, the output of flat glass, coal, tobacco, cotton yarn, and electric power ranked the third, the second, the fourth and the fifth places respectively.

Guided by the thinking of fostering big markets, invigorating large-scale circulation, and taking the road of trade, Henan has established a market system radiating the Central Plain and facing the whole country. In 1998, the total amount of retail sales reached 149.62 billion yuan, ranking the sixth place. Zhengzhou Commodities Exchange is China's largest grain wholesale market and the first standardized grain futures market. It has been linked on the network with many large exchanges in the world, and is honored as the "First Market in China". It has become one of the most influential exchanges in China. At present, the province has more than 100 enterprises in 17 prefectures and cities enjoying the right to manage foreign trade business. The annual trade volume reached more than US$1.7 billion. It has established business relations with 140 countries and regions, instead of 17 in 1978. Henan has become the bridgehead for economic reform and development in mid-west provinces.

Since the founding of New China, Henan has made rapid progress in education, culture, technology and public health. Some of its scientific and technical results are up to the international advanced level, playing an active role to promotion of national economy. Popular events, such as Luoyang Peony Fair, Zhengzhou International Shaolin Martial Art Festival and Wenxian International Taiqi Boxing Annual Meeting, have become important places for foreign exchanges and cooperation.

II. Investment Environment

Henan is one of important hubs of traffic and transportation. The Beijing-Guangzhou, Lianyungang-Qinghai and Beijing-Kowloon railways, as well as the newly built Eurasian continental bridge, run through the province. The Luoyang-Zhengzhou-Kaifeng, Xinxiang-Anyang, Zhengzhou-Xuchang, and Xuchang-Luohe expressways are already opened to the public. In addition, the Xuchang-Pingdingshan, Shanmenxia-Luoyang and Kaifeng-Shangqiu expressways are under construction. There are four international container transportation routes passing through Zhengzhou. At present, mileage of highways in Henan totals 57,172 kilometers, linking with all parts of the province. Its civil aviation undertakings are developing rapidly. The Zhengzhou Xinzheng Airport, built at the standards of 4E, has the annual transport capacity of 6 million passengers. Three airports at Zhengzhou, Luoyang and Nanyang have opened 45 domestic routes to more than 40 cities, and offered chartered planes to Hong Kong, Macao, Bangkok and Singapore. The chartered plane for cargo transport from Zhengzhou to Moscow is on trial operation. Program-controlled switchboards, optical fibre and digital communications have become the mainstream of Henan's telecommunications network. In 1998, the total capacity of switchboards in the province reached 6.9441 million lines, and the rate of telephone popularization came to 6.54 sets per hundred people.

So far, Henan has established friendship ties with 20 provinces and cities of foreign countries. There are 4,254 foreign-funded enterprises in the province, involving actually used foreign capital of US$6.858 billion. It has opened economic and trade offices in Japan, the United State, Germany, Australia, Thailand and Hong Kong. Approved by the State, Zhengzhou has been designated as one of inland opening cities enjoying various preferential treatments as coastal cities have.

Henan province has beautiful mountains and rivers, with a long history. Luoyang, Anyang and Kaifeng have world-famous historic and cultural sites, including Longmen Grottoes, Shaolin Temple, the White Horse Temple and the Rock Men Mountain. In Zhengzhou and Luoyang, a number of state-level high-tech development zones have been established, with focus on development of new and high-tech products, electronical information technologies and biological industry. Local economic development zones are also available in Xinxiang, Kaifeng, Luohe, Shangqiu and Hebi.

III. Development Prospects

According to Henan's Ninth Five-Year Plan (1996-2000) and its long-term plan by 2010, its tasks for economic development are as following:

During the period between 1996 and 2000, its GDP will octuple that of 1980, and the per capita GDP will increase by five times. The Henan people will lead a fairly comfortable life. Henan will initially establish a socialist market economy system and realize the second-step strategic goal for construction of modernization.

Between 2001 and 2010, Henan province plans to double its GDP of 2000. Calculated based on 1995 prices, the GDP of Henan will reach 1110 billion yuan, with per capita GDP hitting 10,700 yuan. Its population will be controlled within 104 million, and the people will lead a well-off life. A fairly perfect socialist market economic system will be established. The economic management system and operating mechanism will be standardized and legalized. Efforts will also be made to raise the quality of national economy, as well as to enhance the level of industrialization and urbanization. Remarkable progress will be made in the socialist civilization and democratic legal system. A sustained development of economy and society will be realized.

IV. Key Fields for Investment

1. Agriculture, sideline products processing, livestock breeding, forest products processing;

2. Energy, traffic, metallurgy, building materials, infrastructure and basic industries;

3. High-tech industries, low energy-consumption industries;

4. Education, science and technology, and public health;

5. Foreign-funded service industries approved by the State.

湖北——朝着振兴崛起的目标奋进

Hubei: Witnessing Rapid Growth

一、经济发展情况

湖北位于中国的中部，长江中游的洞庭湖以北，总面积18.59万平方公里，1998年末人口5907.23万。湖北承东联西、南北交汇、得中独厚、维系四方，经济地理位置十分优越，有“九省通衢”之称的省会武汉区位优势尤为突出。举世瞩目的三峡工程就建在湖北境内。

湖北是中国中西部地区的工农业大省。拥有全部40个工业大门类，综合配套能力强，轻重工业均有一定的基础。湖北也是中国著名的“鱼米之乡”之一，农产丰富、品质优良。湖北教育与科技比较发达，有高等院校55所，仅非民营科研机构就超过1000个，各类专业科技人员4.6万人。

建国50年来特别是改革开放以来，湖北经济建设成效卓著。1995年提前5年完成现代化建设的第一步战略目标，国内生产总值比1980年翻了两番。1998年国内生产总值3704.21亿元，比1978年增长6.7倍，年平均增长10.7%；人均国内生产总值6289元，增长4.9倍，年平均增长9.3%；社会消费品零售总额1481.38亿元，比1978年增长23.8倍，年平均增长17.4%。在国民经济实力大大增强的同时，外向型经济发展也取得了可喜的成绩，与世界上140多个国家和地区有经贸往来。自建立外资统计的1986年开始到1998年，湖北累计利用外资90亿美元，其中外商直接投资累计达45.06亿美元。1998年末，湖北有外商投资企业6041家，企业经营状况良好。外贸出口大幅度增长。1979-1998年，湖北累计出口总额达236.50亿美元，年均增长15.4%。

二、投资环境

经过多年投资建设，湖北的基础设施更趋现代化，第三产业蓬勃发展，投资环境显著改善。

湖北水、电供应充足，并具有较完备的立体交通体系。中国三条重要的交通大动脉：京广、京九和焦枝—枝柳铁路纵贯全省、连通南北，襄渝—汉丹—武九铁路横亘东西。公路网四通八达，高速公路基本可由三峡坝址直通上海。有“黄金水道”之称的长江及其众多的支流水运通畅。武汉、黄石港直接对外籍船舶开放，江海联运十分便捷。1998年湖北已拥有7个民航机场，其中5个可起降波音737以上机型。武汉天河机场是国家干线民用机场，可满足目前世界最大型民用客机全载起降要求，并开通飞往香港、澳门、福冈等地的多条跨境航线。

湖北电信事业发展迅速。全省局内电话机容量超过600万门。1998年末电话普及率9.2部／百人。长途业务电路超过8万路；同时，湖北不断扩大的无线寻呼、移动通信网络为客户提供了更多、更有保障的通信服务。

湖北有口岸12处，海关7处，省级以上经济技术开发区27个，开放开发区1个。武汉、黄石、宜昌相继被国家批准为对外开放城市，享受同沿海开放城市相同的优惠政策。全省对外开放的县市已达90%以上。

1998年底，湖北已有9家外资金融代表机构，其中分行2家。省会武汉是华中地区的金融中心。中国人民银行武汉分行是中国中央银行9个跨省区市分行之一，管辖湖北、湖南、江西三省。法国还在武汉设立了总领事馆。

1998年，湖北共有旅游涉外饭店262家，客房28601间（套），床位8万多张，其中星级饭店126家。按国际五星级标准新建的武汉香格里拉大饭店于1999年建成开业。

三、发展前景

依据全国的发展大局和湖北的实际，湖北到2000年要达到的主要目标是：全面完成或超额完成现代化建设的第二步战略目标，实现由内陆地区工农业大省向经济强省的跨越，力争国内生产总值比1980年翻三番，人民生活达到小康水平，初步建立起社会主义市场经济体制，科技教育和精神文明建设取得明显进步。

湖北的远期发展目标是：到2010年，全省国内生产总值比2000年翻一番以上，年均增长10%，人均国内生产总值超过1万元，人民的小康生活得到更大改善，形成比较完善的社会主义市场经济体制，实现湖北振兴崛起。

四、鼓励投资的重点领域

1. 巩固加强农业：资源开发和创汇农副业，林业深加工项目，名特优畜产品、水产品的生产和加工项目。

2. 大力加强基础设施和基础工业建设：一是农林水利、交通通信、城市基础设施、城乡电网改造、粮食仓储设施、经济适用房等基础项目建设。二是壮大汽车、冶金、机电、化工、轻纺、建筑建材等六大支柱产业。重点是汽车及零部件、输变电设备、钢铁、水泥、新型建材、优质化肥、合成洗涤剂、制冷设备、纺织服装、维生素等10大主导系列工程建设。三是大力发展高新技术产业，重点是光纤通信、机电一体化、生物工程技术及现代医药、微电子、新材料和精细化工、高效节能与环保技术等领域。

3. 鼓励发展第三产业：加快发展符合国际规范，具有国际水准，能基本满足和适应第一、二产业发展和人民生活需要的第三产业体系，重点是金融、商贸、旅游、信息咨询、技术开发、工业设计、以旧城改造为主的房地产开发及城市道路、公共交通项目。

I. Economy

Hubei is located in the north of the Dongting Lake in the mid-Yangtze River Valley, with a total area of 185,900 square km and a population of 59.0723 million at the end of 1998. It enjoys a unique geographic position, and forms a communication hub connecting eastern and western, northern and southern China. The well-known Three Gorges Dam Project is within its boundaries.

Hubei, a big province of industry and agriculture in mid-west China, possesses 40 industries of both light and heavy with competent compatible capability. It is also a well-known land of fish and rice, its agricultural products being abundant and of good quality. There are 55 higher learning institutes and over 1,000 scientific research institutions (excluding non-governmental ones) in the province, with over 46,000 personnel of various disciplines.

The economic construction of Hubei Province has achieved marked results since the founding of the New China, especially since the reform and opening up. Hubei accomplished the first stage strategic goal in 1995, five years ahead of schedule, and its GDP quadrupled that in 1980. In 1998, its total GDP reached 370.421 billion yuan, increasing 6.7 times over 1978, with an average annual growth rate of 10.7 percent; per capita GDP valued at 6,289 yuan, up 4.9 times with an average annual growth rate of 9.3 percent; total retail sales reached 148.138 billion yuan, growing 23.8 times over 1978 with average annual growth of 17.4 percent.

The export-oriented economy has also recorded marked achievements. Hubei has established economic and trade relations with over 140 countries and regions. Between 1986 and 1998, the province introduced a total of $9 billion cumulatively, of which, direct foreign investment reached US$4.506 billion cumulatively. By the end of 1998, it had 6,041 foreign-invested enterprises, which are operating well. Exports have grown markedly, with total export volume reaching US$23.65 billion in the period 1979-1998, an average annual growth of 15.4 percent.

II. Investment Environment

Through years of construction, the infrastructure facilities in the province are becoming more modernized, and the tertiary industry has prospered, and the investment environment has markedly improved.

Hubei has a good supply of water and electricity, and a complete communications system. Three south-north traffic arteries, including Beijing-Guangzhou, Beijing-Kowloon railways run through the province. There are also railways, such as Xiangfan-Chongqing across the province from east to west. It also has a developed network of roads. There is a highway connecting the Three Gorges Dam with Shanghai. The Yangtze River, also referred to as the "golden waterway," and its numerous tributaries, provide smooth water transportation. The Wuhan and Huangshi harbors have opened to foreign ships. The river-sea joint transportation is convenient.

In 1998, Hubei already had seven airports, of which five could accommodate Boeing 737s and aircraft of the same level. The Wuhan Tianhe Airport is a key national civil airport able to accommodate the largest civil airplanes in the world, and it has opened international routes to Hong Kong, Macao and Japan's Fukuoka.

Hubei's telecommunications have developed rapidly, with a total capacity of over 6 million lines. By the end of 1998, telephones have been popularized at a rate of 9.2 phones per one hundred people. Long-distance lines exceed 80,000. At the same time, Hubei has expanded its radio paging and mobile telephone network.

Hubei has 12 ports, of which seven have customs facilities; and 27 economic and technological development zones at provincial level and above, and one open development zone. Wuhan, Huangshi and Yichang have been approved by the central authorities as open cities enjoying the preferential policies of coastal open cities. Now, over 90 percent cities and counties in the province have opened to the outside world.

By the end of 1998, nine foreign financial agencies have settled in Hubei, including two branch banks. Wuhan, the provincial capital, is the financial center of mid-China. The People's Bank of China Wuhan branch is one of the nine branches set up by the People's Bank of China across the country, with jurisdiction covering Hubei, Hunan and Jiangxi provinces. France also set up a general consulate in Wuhan.

By 1998, Hubei had established 262 foreign-oriented tourist hotels, with 28,601 rooms (including apartments) and over 80,000 beds, of which, 126 are star hotels. The Wuhan Shangari-la Hotel, built in accordance with international five-star standard, will go into operation in 1999.

III. Development Prospects

The goals set by Hubei Province by the year 2000 are: to fulfill or even overfulfil the second-stage strategic goal, realize the leap from an inland industrial and agricultural province to an economically powerful province and strive to octuple the GDP of 1980 with people's living standard reaching comparatively well-off level, initially set up the socialist market economic system, and make obvious progress in scientific and technological education and cultural and ethical construction.

The long-term targets are: by 2010, Hubei's GDP will double that of 2000 with an average annual growth rate of 10 percent; per capita GDP value will reach over 10,000 yuan annually; people's well-off living standard will be further improved; a relatively perfect socialist market economic system will be set up; and realizing that Hubei will rise as powerful province in China.

IV. Major Fields to Encourage Investment

1. The agriculture sector is oriented towards development of resources and side-lines for earning foreign currencies, timber processing items, brand and good quality products and local flavor and livestock products, production and processing of aquatic products.

2.The infrastructure facilities and basic industries include: firstly, projects of agriculture, forestry and water conservancy, transportation and telecommunication, urban infrastructure facilities, renovation of urban and rural electricity power grid, grain storage facilities, and economic comfortable houses. Secondly, expansion of pillar industries of automobile, metallurgical, machinery and electronics, chemical, light textile, and building materials with stresses laid on automobiles and parts, electricity transmission and power transformation equipment, iron and steel, concrete, new building materials, quality fertilizers, synthetic detergent, refrigeration equipment, textile clothes and vitamins. And thirdly, rapid development of new and hi-tech industries, which is oriented towards optical fiber communication, electromechanical integration, biological engineering technology and modern medicine, micro-electronics, new material, and fine chemical, high-efficiency power-saving and environmental protection technologies.

3. The tertiary industry: rapidly develop the tertiary industrial system that is in conformity with international standards, cater to the development of primary and second industries and people's life, stress will be laid on projects of finance, trade and commerce, tourism, information consultancy, industrial designing, real estate development with renovation of old-town at the core and urban roads and public transportation.

湖南——向更高目标奋进

Hunan: Aiming Higher Goals

湖南省位于世界第三大河——中国长江中游南部，总面积为21.18万平方公，划分为14个地州市，122个县区，省会长沙市。1998年末总人口6502万。

湖南资源丰富，物产丰饶，被誉为“鱼米之乡”、“有色金属之乡”、“非金属之乡”和“旅游胜地”。

湖南省拥有耕地面积321.87万公顷，拥有森林面积750.14万公顷，大小河流5341条，以湘、资、沅、澧四条水系较大，均流入洞庭湖，并与长江相通，河流可通航里程1.5万公里，内河航线贯通95%的县市和30%以上的乡镇。

矿产丰富，矿种齐全。世界已知的160多种矿产中，在湖南已发现134种，已探明储量的91

种，其中，煤炭储量为中国长江以南较多的省份之一。

湖南历史悠久，人才辈出。一代伟人毛泽东、国画大师齐白石、“杂交水稻之父”袁隆平等，都是湖南的杰出代表。湖南山川秀丽，古迹众多，旅游资源独特。省会长沙是一座有3000多年历史的名城，全省有省级重点文物保护单位154处，国家级重点文物保护单位12处。全省有10个集自然景观、人文景观和民族风情于一体的旅游景区，对外开放景点1360多处。中国五岳之一的衡山、江南三大名楼之一的岳阳楼（洞庭湖）、被列入《世界自然遗产名录》的武陵源（张家界、索溪峪、天子山）、被称为“天下第一漂”的猛洞河等风景名胜饮誉中外，为人瞩目。中华人民共和国的主要缔造者毛泽东的故乡——韶山，前往参观的中外游客络绎不绝。

90年代以来，湖南经济和社会发展进一步加快。1990-1998年，全省国内生产总值平均增长达10.97%。1998年，国内生产总值3211.4亿元，其中，第一产业828.31亿元，第二产业1294.17亿元，第三产业1088.92亿元。农业总产值1262.46亿元，全部独立核算国有及年产品销售收入500万元以上非国有工业企业工业总产值1289.43亿元。全省城镇居民人均可支配收入5434.3元，农民人均纯收入2064.85元。经过历年的努力，湖南的基础设施逐步完善，对外经济贸易与合作不断扩大，各项社会事业全面发展。

湖南农业在全国占有重要地位。主要农副产品如粮食、棉花、油料、苎麻、烤烟以及猪、牛、羊肉产量均为全国前10位，其中苎麻居全国第1位，猪、牛、羊居第2位，烤烟居第4位，粮食居第5位，稻谷产量多年为全国之冠，粮食单位面积产量比全国平均数高出1/4以上，接近世界先进水平。

湖南的工业基础较好，工业门类较齐全，已初步形成以机械、电子、仪器、能源、建材等工业为主体的产业结构体系。目前有工业企业28356个，其中，大中型企业724家，有一些大型企业已进入全国500家特大企业行列。

湖南交通便利，境内铁路总长达2620公里，公路总里程约6万公里。水运可通长江出海，岳阳城陵矶港口可停泊5000吨级货轮，长沙黄花机场、张家界机场开通了境内外30多条航线。

能源和通讯事业发展迅速。1998年全省发电量达345.7亿千瓦小时。全省长途、市内电话已实现数字程控化，农村电话也逐步向自动化、数字化过渡。

目前，湖南已与130多个国家和地区建立了经济贸易关系，并与美国、日本、法国、比利时、瑞士、加拿大、刚果、俄罗斯、乌兹别克斯坦、新加坡、保加利亚、乌克兰等国家缔结友好省、州、县、市关系24对。友好城市之间开展了经贸、科技、文化、艺术等多方面的交流，进行了富有成效的合作。

湖南教育、科技具有一定的实力，在城镇和部分比较发达的地区，基本实现了九年制义务教育。小学适龄儿童入学率达98.6%，中学教育实力较强，高中毕业升学统考成绩多年来一直稳居全国前列。

湖南综合科学技术实力列全国第6位。杂交水稻研究与应用居世界领先地位，铝箔轧机单辊驱动理论与应用、人类高分辨染色体技术、“试管婴儿”、银河-II亿次型计算机、地洼学说、齐次可列马尔可夫过程研究等均达国际先进水平。

1995年底，湖南省委、省政府提出了“呼应两东（广东、上海浦东），开放带动，生产者先导，兴工强农”的发展思路，并制定了《湖南省国民经济和社会发展“九五”计划和2010年远景目标纲要》。

“九五”期间，全省经济建设要强化农业基础，加速农业产业化进程；高质量、高效益地建设一批以路、电、水、通信为重点的基础设施；

大力发展冶金、机械电子、建材建筑、化学工业、仪器工业五大支柱产业。要加速科技进步、优先发展教育，积极发展第三产业，提高对外开放水平，加强环境、生态、资源保护，发展卫生、体育事业，加强社会主义精神文明建设，加强社会主义民主和法制建设等。

Hunan Province is located in the south of the middle reaches of the Yangtze River, the third biggest river of the world. It covers an area of 211,800 square kilometres and is administratively divided into 14 prefectures and cities, and 122 counties. The province has a population of 65.02 million. Changsha is the capital of the province.

Endowed with rich resoures and abundant produce, Hunan is famed for being a land of rice and fish, the home of nonferrous metals and nonmetallic minerals, and a paradise for tourists.

Hunan boasts 3.22 million hectares of cultivated land, and 7.50 million hectares of forests. Altogether 5,341 rivers and streams flow in Hunan's territory, among them the Xiang, the Zi, the Yuan and the Li rivers are the largest ones. Navigable mileage comes to 15,000 kilometres. Inland navigation lines extend to 95 percent of the counties and over 30 percent of the towns and townships.

With a fairly complete range of minerals, Hunan is rich in mineral resources. Of the 160-odd kinds of minerals already discovered in the world, 134 kinds have been found in Hunan, and the reserves of 91 have been ascertained. Hunan is one of the provinces in south China which have a comparatively large reserve of coal.

Myriads of celebrities have highlighted Hunan's age old history. Late Chairman Mao Zedong, one of the greatest men of the times, Qi Baishi, master of Chinese ink painting, and Yuan Longping, Father of Hybrid Rice, are distinguished representatives of native Hunanese.

Elegant landscape and numerous historic sites offer Hunan unique tourist resources. The capital city Changsha is a renowned 3,000 year old city. There are 154 sites of cultural remains in Hunan classified as provincial-level key protection units and 12 listed as national-level key protection units. Ten tourist scenic areas simultaneously presenting natural scenery, man-built sights and customs and life styles of the minority people are open to public, and 1,360 places of interest are open to foreigners. Mount Hengshan, one of China's five most famous mountains, Yueyang Tower, one of the three well-known ancient towers in the south of the Yangtze River. Wulingyuan Tourist Area (including Zhangjiajie, Suoxi Valley and Tianzi Mountain) which has been listed as one of the world natural heritages, and the Mengdong River known as No.1 Drifting all enjoy high reputation both at home and abroad and have become hot tourist spots. Streams of domestic and foreign visitors come to Shaoshan, the birthplace of Mao Zedong, the founder of the People's Republic of China.

Since the 1990s, the economic and social development in Hunan has been further accelerated. From 1990 to 1998, the province GDP has witnessed an average increase of 10.97%. In 1998, GDP was valued at 321.14 billion yuan, of which primary industry took up 82.831 billion yuan, secondary industry 129.417 billion yuan, and tertiary industry 108.892 billion yuan. The total output of agriculture was valued at 126.246 billion. The total industrial output value of non-state enterprises adopting independent accounting system and with annual sales income of 5 million yuan amounted to 128.943 million yuan. The average allocatable income of city and town citizens was 5,434.3 yuan per capita, and the net income of farmers was 2,064.85 yuan per capita. Through years of efforts, Hunan's infrastructural facilities have been gradually perfected, foreign economic cooperation and trade continuously expanded,

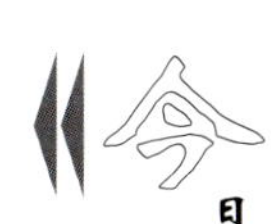

and all-round progress has been achieved in all social undertakings.

Hunan's agriculture takes up an important standing in China. The output of major farm products, like grain, cotton, oil bearing plants, ramie, tobacco, and pork, beef, and mutton, are all on the top ten lists in China. Specifically, Hunan is the country's largest grower of ramie, second largest supplier of pork, beef and mutton, fourth largest yielder of tobacco, and fifth largest grower of grain. Hunan's output of rice has been leading the whole country for years. The unit output of grain in Hunan surpasses the country's average by 1/4, and is close to the world advanced level.

Hunan's industry has a good foundation and covers complete industrial sectors. An industrial setup with machinery, electronics, food processing, energy, and construction material industries as the backbone has taken shape. Up to now, there are in the province 28,356 industrial enterprises, and 724 of them are large or medium sized ones. Some have even been listed among the country's top 500 extraordinarily large enterprises.

Hunan enjoys convenient transport. Railway mileage totals 2,620 kilometres, and highway mileage, about 60,000 kilometres. Water transportation allows ships to go via the Yangtze River to the sea.Chenglingji at Yueyang can harbor 5,000 tonnage ships. Over 30 domestic and international air routes are available at Changsha Huanghua Airport and Zhangjiajie Airport.

Energy and communications have witnessed a very fast development. The power generation in 1998 totaled 34.57 billion kmh. All long distance and city proper calls in the province are now controlled with digital programmes. Telephones in rural areas are gradually being upgraded with automation and digital technology.

So far, Hunan has established business relations with 140 countries and regions, and has set up sister relationship with 24 provinces, states, counties or cities in many countries such as the United States, Japan, France, Belgium, Switzerland, Canada, Congo, Russia, Uzbekistan, Singapore, Bulgaria and Ukraine. Exchanges in various respects including foreign economic relations and trade, science and technology, culture and art have been conducted between the sisters, and fruit-bearing cooperations have been carried out.

Hunan is considerably strong in education and science and technology. Nine-year compulsory education has been realized in nearly all cities, towns and the comparatively developed areas. As many as 98.6 percent of schoolage children are going to primary school. The province excels in middle school education. Scores of middle school graduates in college entrance examinations have been among the top ones in the whole country for years on end.

With regards to overall technical strength, Hunan ranks 6th in China. The province leads the world in hybrid rice research and application. The theory of one roll driving in aluminum foil rolling mill and its application, the high resolution technique of human chromosomes, the research in test-tube babies, the giant Galaxy computer II, the Geodepression theory, the research on Homogeneous Markov process are all up to the world advanced level.

At the end of 1995, Hunan Provincial Party Committee and Hunan Provincial Government developed the strategic thinking of making Hunan as open as Guangdong and Pudong, making opening up an impetus to development, making science and technology a first priority and making industry flourshing and agriculture highly developed; and formulated the Programme of Hunan Province for the 9th Five-Year Plan for Economic and Social Development and Long-term Goals for the Year 2010.

During the 9th Five-Year Plan period, focus of economic construction in Hunan will be set on the following aspects: To strengthen the agricultural foundation and accelerate the industrialization of agriculture; to construct

infrastructural facilities with high quality and high efficiency, laying stress on road, power, water conservancy, and telecommunications; to vigorously foster the five mainstay industries, i.e., metallurgical, mechanotronical, building material and construction, chemical, and food processing industries; to speed up the progress of science and technology; to give priority to education; to energetically develop tertiary industry; to improve the level of opening-up; to strengthen protection on environment, ecosystem, and natural resources; to further develop public health, physical culture and sports; to promote socialist ethical and cultural progress; to improve socialist democracy and the legal system, etc.

广东——阔步迈向新世纪

Guangdong: Marching Towards New Century

一、广东概况

广东是中国大陆最南端的省份之一，东连福建，西邻广西，北依湖南、江西，南临南海，毗邻港澳，是中国著名的侨乡之一。

全省土地面积17.79万平方公里，设21个地级市，21个省辖县级市，49个县（含3个自治县），1998年末全省总人口7115.65万人。广东由大陆和众多岛屿构成，境内山地、平原、丘陵交错，低山、丘陵广布。除粤北山区属中亚热带外，大部分地区属于亚热带季风气候，雨量充沛，海域广阔，海岸线绵长，河网纵横，水产资源丰富。

广东是中国近代民族工业的摇篮之一，也是中国近代史和现代史上许多重大历史事件的发生和策源地之一。1949年新中国成立以后，广东国民经济在曲折中取得长足的发展，尤其是1978年以后，改革开放给广东经济发展带来了生机活力，广东一跃成为全国经济发展最快的地区之一。1978年前，广东经济在全国几乎处于无足轻重的地位，主要经济指标增长速度处于全国平均线以下。然而，经过近20年的改革开放，广东实行特殊政策、灵活措施，对外开放，吸收外资，对内实行一系列改革，进一步调整生产关系，实现了经济发展的大跨越。广东GDP由1978年的185.85亿元增加到1998年的7937亿元，翻了三番多，年均递增14%。国民经济实力显著增强，国内生产总值、全社会固定资产投资、社会消费品零售总额、进出口总额、一般预算内财政收入（未含国税、关税等部分）、实际利用外资、邮电业务总量、城乡居民储蓄存款余额等指标多年均位居全国各省市之首，1998年分别占全国的10%、9.4%、11.1%、40.1%、6.5%、25.8%、17.2%和12.5%，远远高于广东人口占全国5.2%的比重。

二、投资环境

在经济快速发展的同时，广东还努力改善投资环境，集中财力和引进外资加强交通、邮电、通信、能源等基础建设，大力发展第三产业，各项服务设施日臻完善。1998年全省公路通车里程居国内首位，公路密度为52.12公里／公里^2，比1978年提高77.5%。等级公路比重占89.3%，比全国高5.6个百分点；高速公路里程已达810公里，居国内首位。航运及航空运输能力也有长足的发展，1998年全省拥有码头泊位2368个，其中万吨级深水泊位106个，沿海港口货物吞吐量12762万吨，为1978年的4.5倍。目前全省已有8个民航机场，国内航线90多条，国际航线13条，旅客运输量、吞吐量、飞行起降架次均居国内首位。全省电信能力有很大的提高，电话交换机总容量1998年比1952年增长426倍。电力生产已摆脱曾长期制约经济发展的瓶颈状态，全省发电设备装机容量已达2906.95万千瓦，比1978年增长10.5倍；发电量达1004.4亿千瓦时，比1978年增长9.9倍。

广东外向型经济格局基本形成。1998年末在广东登记注册的外商投资企业达5.77万家，约占全国的1/4；到广东投资的国家和地区已达80多个、跨国公司300多家；广东与世界上200多个国家和地区建立了经贸关系。粤港澳经贸合作关系进一步加强，1979-1998年，广东实际利用的港澳资金累计703.15亿美元，占全省实际利用外资总额的73.1%，广东对港澳的出口累计2892.79亿美元，占同期出口总额的83.4%。

金融服务体系逐步完善。境内的国内金融机构包括中央银行1家，政策性银行1家，国有商业银行4家，其他商业银行12家，保险公司4家，农村信用社1735家，城市信用社220家，以及各类齐全的其他金融机构。商业银行国际结算、汇兑、信贷、投资、租赁、担保、外汇买卖、代理等业务均得到良好的发展。至1998年底，全省共引进外资金融机构83家，其中营业性机构50家，代表处33家。

三、发展前景

广东正阔步迈向21世纪，展望未来，广东的发展前景将更加美好。1996-2010年经济开发的目标分为两个阶段：1996-2000年时期为第一阶段，2001-2010年为第二阶段。

第一阶段，总体上达到亚洲新兴工业化国家和地区1990年经济水平，一部分地区达到中等发达国家以上水平，其余地区达到小康水平。重点加强基础设施建设和人才培养，为产业升级作准备。全省国内生产总值年均递增11%。建立起社会主义市场经济体制的基本框架和与之相适应的运行机制。统一开放的市场体系初步形成。发展和完善商品市场，培育和规范要素市场。

第二阶段，总体上相当于世界中等发达国家和地区当年的经济水平，基本实现现代化。重点发展高附加值、低污染的技术密集型产业。到2010年，国内生产总值达16700亿元，2001-2010年年均递增10.5%。社会主义市场经济体制比较健全，运行顺畅。精神文明建设与物质文明建设互相适应，协调发展，基本实现共同富裕。

四、鼓励投资的重点领域

今后若干年内，广东重点鼓励发展电力、港口、公路、机场、通信等基础设施项目；长期依赖进口的原材料工业项目；汽车、电子、电器的零部件和精密模具制造、表面热处理等配套工业项目；电子信息、新材料、生物工程等新兴技术产业；农业技术工业；优良种苗引进和培育技术以及农产品加工项目；附加值高、以出口为主的各类加工工业项目。

属于广东重点鼓励发展的外商投资项目可享受下列优惠待遇：

1. 优先纳入省、市的固定资产投资计划和技术改造计划；

2. 建设生产所需资金和国家控制进口的物资予以优先安排；

3. 除享受国家规定的减免税外，继续给予一定时期免征或减征地方所得税；

4. 合作经营项目可加速折旧回收投资股本，折旧率一般为20%，高技术和风险性投资的项目

广东新建筑群
New Buildings in Guangdong

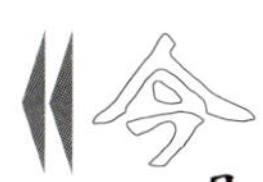

可增加至30%;

5.土地使用年限最高为50年，投资额大、回收期长的项目，可酌情延长;

6.依赖进口的原材料、零部件和新技术生产项目，其产品可优先替代进口;

7.投资于能源、交通等基础设施项目的，可实行综合补偿。

I. General Survey

Guangdong Provinces is located at the southern tip of the Chinese mainland. Guangdong borders on Fujian to the east, Hunan and Jiangxi to the north, Guangxi to the west, and the South China Sea to the south. Hong Kong and Macao are nestled in the southeastern coast of Guangdong. Many overseas Chinese families originated in this region.

The province, covering an area of 177,900 square kilometers, has 21 prefecture-level cities, 21 county-level cities, and 49 counties (including 3 autonomous counties) under its jurisdiction. In 1998, the province had a population of just over 71 million. Guangdong is made up of continental lands and numerous offshore islands. Its land form varies from mountains and plains to rolling hills. Although the mountains of northern Guangdong are part of an intermediate subtropical zone, most of the province is within the limits of a subtropical monsoon climate, which provides for plentiful rainfall. The lengthy coastline and Chinese territorial waters give the province a vast sea area. The continental portion of the province is crisscrossed by an extensive network of rivers teeming with aquatic products.

In addition to being a witness to many of the important historical events of Chinese civilization, Guangdong is a cradle of modern industry in China. Since the founding of New China in 1949, the economy of Guangdong has made considerable progress. This is especially true of the period since 1978. The reform and opening program has brought vitality to the development of Guangdong's economy. It has become an area enjoying the most rapid rate of development in China. Prior to 1978, Guangdong's economy was of little importance to China's overall economy, with a major economic index growth rate lower than the national average. However, after 20 years of reform and opening, Guangdong's economy has taken off by carrying out special policies and flexible measures to absorb foreign capital and further adjust the production structure. Guangdong's GDP increased from RMB 18.6 billion yuan in 1978 to RMB 793.7 billion yuan in 1998, an increase of eight times and an average annual growth rate of 14 percent. Growth in economic indices in the terms of total economic strength (10%), total output (9.4%), total fixed assets investment (11.1%), total retail commodities sales (40.1%), total imports and exports (6.5%), budgeted revenue excluding taxes and customs duties (25.8%), foreign capital utilized (17.2%), total volume of post and telecommunications (12.5%), and savings deposit balance between urban and rural residents (5.2%) rank first in all provinces and municipalities.

II. Investment Environment

While developing the economy at a faster rate, Guangdong is putting more efforts to improve the investment environment. It has concentrated financial resources and imported foreign capital to strengthen the construction of transportation, post and telecommunications, energy and other infrastructure facilities and to develop tertiary industries. These efforts have resulted in notable improvements in various service facilities. In 1998, the length of highways opened to traffic in the province took the lead in the country, with highway density reaching 52.12 kilometers of road for each square kilometer of territory. This reflects an increase of 77.5 percent over the total in 1978. Graded highways account for 89.3 percent, 5.6 percentage points higher than the national average. The total length of expressways reaches 810 kilometers, ranking the province first in the country. Considerable progress has also been made in sea and air transportation. In 1998, the province boasted 2,368 berths, of which 106 are deep-water berths capable of handling 10,000-dwt cargo vessels. The total cargo handling capacity of its coastal ports reached 127.62 million tonnes, 4.5 times the figure in 1978. The province has eight civil airports that operate more than 90 domestic air routes and 13 international routes. The volume of passenger transportation, cargo handling capacity, and the numbers of take-offs and landings rank first in the country. The province also witnessed rapid development in electricity production. The capacity of telephone switchboards in 1998 reflected an increase by 426 times the 1952 figure. Electricity production has shaken off the bottle-neck that had long restricted economic development. The total installed capacity in the province reached 29.07 million kilowatts, increasing by 10.5 times over the installed capacity realized in 1978. The generated energy came to 100.44 billion kilowatt hours, 9.9 times the figure in 1978.

An internationally-oriented economic pattern has taken shape in Guangdong. By the end of 1998, there were 57,700 foreign-funded enterprises registered in Guangdong, accounting for one-fourth of the nation's total. The financial backing for these enterprises comes from 80 countries and territories and involves more than 300 multinational corporations. Guangdong has established economic and trade ties with more than 200 countries and regions. Its economic and trade ties with Hong Kong and Macao have been further strengthened. Between 1979 and 1998, the accumulated foreign funds actually used in Guangdong reached US$70.3 billion, accounting for 73.1 percent of the province's total investments. Guangdong's exports to Hong Kong and Macao during the same period amounted to US$289.3 billion, accounting for 83.4 percent.

Financial services have been gradually improved. Guangdong now boasts all kinds of financial establishments, including a central bank, a policy-related bank, four state commercial banks, 12 commercial banks, four insurance companies, 1,735 rural credit cooperatives, and 220 urban credit cooperatives. Commercial banks have developed a variety of services, including international settlements, remittances, credit, investment, leasing, guarantees, foreign exchange and proxy transactions. By the end of 1998, the province had licensed the operation of 83 foreign financial institutions, of which, 50 are operating agents and 33 representative offices.

III. Prospects for Development

Guangdong's future is bright with prospects. Between 1996 and 2010, the province's economic development will be divided into two periods. The first period is from 1996 to 2000, and the second will be from 2001 and 2010.

The goals of the first period: The overall economic strength in Guangdong will reach the 1990 level of newly-industrialized Asian countries. Some areas are expected to reach the level of small developed countries, while the remainder will enjoy moderate development. The focus during this period will be on strengthening infrastructure facilities and training personnel in preparation for upgrading the industrial sector.

Total output will increase at an average rate of 11 percent. Guangdong will establish the basic framework for a socialist market economic system and its compatible operating mechanism. A unified and opening market system will be formed. Efforts will be made to develop and perfect commodity markets and to foster and standardize key elements within these markets.

The goals of second period: Its overall economic

广东中山纪念堂
Guangdong Zhongshan Memorial Hall

strengthen will reach the 1990 level of small developed countries, basically realizing modernization. Priority will be given to the development of technology-intensive industries with high added value and low pollutant output. By 2010, total output is expected to reach 1,670 billion yuan, rising at an annual average of 10.5 percent from 2001 to 2010. The socialist market economic system will operate in a sound and smooth way. Cultural, ethical, and material culture will be developed in a coordinated fashion so as to realize common prosperity.

IV. Key Fields for Investment

In the next few years, Guangdong will encourage the development of infrastructure facilities projects involving electricity, ports, railways, roads, airports, and telecommunications. Additional emphasis will be placed on projects to develop raw material industries that have long relied on imports, auxiliary industrial projects related to manufacturing spare parts for automobiles, electronics and electrical appliances, and precision molds, as well as conducting surface heat treatment. Newly emerging technological industries related to electronic information, new materials and biological engineering will be fostered. Agricultural technological industries, the importation of improved varieties of seeds and seedlings, cultivation technologies and farm product-processing projects will gain additional attention. And processing industries that involve high added value and focus on exports will be supported.

Foreign-invested projects belonging to key fields for investment will enjoy the following preferential treatment:

1. Priority listing in provincial and municipal fixed assets investment plans and technical transformation plans;

2. Priority will be given to funds needed for construction and production, and to State-controlled imported materials and goods;

3. In addition to State policies on tax reduction and exemption, foreign-invested projects will be allowed to continue enjoying local income tax exemptions or reductions during a certain period;

4. Cooperative projects are allowed to recover invested capital stock through speeding up depreciation. The general rate of depreciation is 20 percent, but the rate of depreciation in this case will be raised to 30 percent for high-tech and high-risk projects;

5. The maximum land-use time limit is 50 years. For projects with large amounts of investment and a long recovery period, the time limit can be extended appropriately;

6. Projects that produce with domestic raw materials and spare parts replacing imports, or projects using new technologies, are given the priority in replacing imports with their products;

7. Projects with investment in energy and traffic infrastructure facilities are given comprehensive compensation.

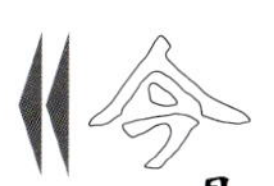

广西——中国西南地区重要出海通道

Guangxi: Important Passage to Sea in Southwest China

广西壮族自治区是一个沿海的省级行政区，位于中国的南端，是中国少数民族人口最多的自治区。面积23.67万平方公里，大陆海岸线长1595公里，1998年人口4675万。自东向西与广东、湖南、贵州、云南4省为邻，西南与越南交界，陆地边境线长1020公里。广西气候温和，北回归线横贯中部，日照充足，年平均气温16-22.7℃，雨量充沛，温暖的气候非常适于亚热带植物和农作物的生长。广西有丰富的矿产资源，是中国10个重点有色金属产区之一。探明的矿种近百种，其中，储量居中国首位的有14种（锰、锡矿储量均占全国总储量的1/3）；储量居中国第2-6位的有25种（锑矿储量占全国总保有储量的1/4）。北部湾海域面积12.92万平方公里，蕴藏着丰富的海洋资源，是中国四大渔场之一，鱼类资源初步探明近600种，比中国东海鱼类还多50多种，浅海滩涂栖有海洋生物149种。在南海大陆架北部湾盆地，石油和天然气储量也很可观。广西拥有十分丰富的旅游资源。其中最著名的桂林—漓江风景名胜区，以其独特的自然景观，享誉于世，自古

有“桂林山水甲天下”的美誉；位于北部湾海滨的北海银滩国家旅游度假区，沙滩洁净平缓，风轻浪细，阳光明媚，更是令人留连忘返。广西可供开发的景区、景点400多处，分布于8个地区、63个县；拥有3处(桂林漓江、桂平西山、宁明花山)国家级风景名胜区；7处国家级历史文物保护单位；11个国家级森林公园，1个国家级旅游度假区(北海银滩)。

一、经济发展与出海通道建设

新中国成立50年来，特别是改革开放以来，广西各族人民解放思想，开拓进取，紧紧抓住改革开放和建设西南出海通道的机遇，大力加强基础设施建设，增加农业投入，进行农业综合开发，加快工业化和城市化进程，积极引进外资，发展外向型经济，经济建设和各项社会事业取得了长足的发展。1998年，广西国内生产总值1903亿元，比1952年增长30倍，比1978年增长4.9倍，1979-1998年，全自治区国内生产总值年均增长9.3%，其中，第一产业年均增长6.5%，第二产业年均增长12.7%，第三产业年均增长9.3%。现已形成制糖、建材、机械、汽车和有色金属、电力、冶金、医药、林化、日化、轻工、纺织、橡胶、电子、食品等独具地方特色的工业体系。1998年广西的糖产量达340万吨，居全国首位。广西的亚热带农业已初具规模，形成区域性水稻、甘蔗、水产养殖、捕捞、牲畜饲养、水果种植农业带，农业的发展前景广阔。1998年，主要农产品产量水稻1424万吨、甘蔗3582万吨、水产品218万吨、猪牛羊肉268万吨、水果325万吨。1978-1998年年均分别增长2.3%、11.9%、15.5%、10.9%和16.3%。

广西以构筑“西南出海大通道”为主题的基础设施建设成果十分引人注目。目前，已初步形成海、空、陆、河立体交通运输网络和体系。基本竣工的桂林—柳州—南宁—北海高等级主干公路及密布全区四通八达的公路网，与黎湛、枝柳、南昆铁路干线及南防等6条地方铁路线与国内各地相连，构成独特的西南地区出海大通道。1997年，广西南宁到云南昆明的铁路全线通车，将中国西南地区和广西的沿海港口连接起来，中国西南内地省份和广西西部山区通过这条铁路把他们丰富的产品运往沿海口岸出口海外。

广西现有南宁、柳州、桂林、梧州、北海五个机场，拥有国内航线100多条，地区航线5条，国际航线4条，形成以南宁、桂林为中心，连结国内各大城市的航空网络，并已开通南宁至香港、河内、曼谷，北海至香港，桂林至香港、澳门、福冈、汉城的直达航线。桂林两江国际机场年旅客吞吐能力可达500万人次。

广西独具特色的沿海开放优势，已成为经济发展的重要动力。广西沿海港湾众多，可开发的大小港口21个，北海、防城、铁山、珍珠和钦州港可建成万吨级以上泊位深水码头。北海、防城和钦州港已建成万吨级以上泊位16个，吞吐能力已达1300万吨。大西南各省的货物从广西沿海港口可以直达港澳、东南亚、印支半岛、波斯湾和西欧各大港口。西江航道经过整治，从南宁以下可航行千吨级船队，是一条连接广东、港澳的黄金水道。

实行改革开放政策以来，广西对外经济贸易事业取得了较快的发展。目前已有20多家国际知名企业在广西开业经营，广西还与130多个国家和地区的5,000多家客户建立了贸易关系，同近220个外贸机构建立了经销代理业务关系。还在美国、日本、法国、德国、新加坡、巴拿马、冈比亚等国家及港澳地区设有62家贸易机构。1998年，广西有外资企业4565家，实际投入资金88613万美元。

经国家批准的广西沿海开放城市3个：北海市、防城港市、南宁市；沿海开放地区6个：梧州市、合浦县、防城港市防城区、钦州市钦南区、钦北区、玉林市；沿边开放市镇2个：凭祥市、东

兴市。对外开放的一类口岸16个，边境经济开发区2个：凭祥、东兴市边境经济合作区。广西边境有8个县(区、市)与越南接壤，现有边境口岸12个，其中凭祥、友谊关、东兴、水口是国家一类口岸，另外还有25个边境贸易点，每年边境进出口贸易额30多亿元。各边境口岸和边境贸易点都有公路相通，湘桂铁路与越南铁路连接，火车可直通河内。是中国发展与越南及东南亚国家的直接贸易、双边、多边或转口贸易以及出口加工的理想渠道。

二、发展战略与投资环境

中国西南地区是一个拥有两亿多人口的大市场，中国政府对中西部地区经济发展的倾斜战略，使广西的发展呈现出十分广阔的前景。广西"九五"时期至2010年的远景目标是：通过加大开发力度，促进国民经济和社会的持续、快速、健康发展。国内生产总值年均增幅10%以上，力争到本世纪末，实现国内生产总值达到全国中上水平。2010年国内生产总值比2000年翻一番，人均国内生产总值超过全国平均水平。

实现上述战略构想，需要国家及各省、市、自治区的支持和广西各族人民的共同努力，同时，也为海内外资金、技术、人才的投入提供了难得的机会。经自治区人民政府批准，当前利用外资的方向和重点领域：

农业方面重点是引进国外优良品种和先进技术，提高农业产业化水平和农产品科技含量的项目，调整优化农业结构，促进农业增长方式转变。鼓励利用外资发展良种（含粮食和经济作物、畜禽和水产、林木和花卉）产业化项目。

工业方面重点是通过结构调整和引进利用高新技术，改造提高制糖、食品、有色金属、汽车和机械制造、建材、冶金、化工、造纸等工业水平，开展节能降耗，开发新品种，促进产品升级换代，同时扩大海洋生物技术、制药、林化、电子、造船、铝材加工等市场开拓潜力大的行业，形成新优势。

第三产业方面要有步骤地推进旅游、服务贸易的对外开放。

基础设施方面重点是：水利、交通、通信、能源、城市基础设施、生态建设和环境保护项目。

高新技术产业方面重点是生物工程、海洋工程、信息工程以及新材料等项目。

外向型出口创汇方面重点是各类加工贸易和以富余的设备、原材料和国内技术向境外投资的项目。

Guangxi Autonomous Region, a coastal provincial administrative area with the greatest number of minorities, is situated in the south of China. It has a total area of 236,700 square kilometers and its coastline is 1,595 kilometers in length. In 1998, it had a population of 46,750,000. From the east to the west, it adjoins Guangdong, Hunan, Guizhou, and Yunnan. And it is bounded on the southwest by Vietnam. Its borderline is 1,020 kilometers.

Guangxi has a temperate climate and the Tropic of Cancer traverses the middle, so it is full of sunshine, the annual average temperature ranging from 16℃ to 22.7℃. And it has abundant rainfall. The temperate climate is good for the growth of the subtropical plants and crops.

Guangxi is rich in mineral resources and is one of the key areas of non-ferrous metal in China. In Guangxi, nearly one hundred kinds of minerals have been verified, among which fourteen kinds of mineral deposits rank the first place in China (the deposits of manganese and tin make up one-third of the total deposits in China), and twenty-five of them rank from the second to the sixth place in deposits (the antimony deposit accounts for one-fourth of the total deposit in China).

The sea area in Beibu Bay is 129,200 square kilometers, rich in ocean resources and it is one of the four big fisheries in China. The fishery resource is verified to be 600 species, 50 species more than that of the East China Sea, 149 kinds of marine organism dwell in shallow waters along coast. Petroleum and natural gas are also quite rich in the Beibu Bay basin on the continental shelf of the South China Sea.

Guangxi has very rich tourist resources, the most famous of which is the scenic spot between Guilin and Lijiang, which enjoys a worldwide reputation for its unique natural landscape, and it fames the world over from ancient times to present as "The mountains and waters of Guilin are the finest under heaven." The national tourist vocation area of the Beihai Silver Beach is situated along the coast of Beibu Bay. The beach here is clean, open and flat, the wind and waves gentle, the sunshine radiant and enchanting. In Guangxi 400 scenic areas and spots are available for exploitation, distributed over eight prefectures and sixty-three counties. It has three national scenic spots including Lijiang in Guilin, the Western Hill in Guiping and the Flower Hill in Ningming, seven national historic reservation units, eleven national forest parks and one national tourist vocation area (the Beihai Beach).

I. The Economic Development and the Construction of the Passage to Sea

50 years after New China was founded, especially after the reform and opening to the outside world, the people of different nationalities in Guangxi have emancipated their thinking and advanced in a pioneering spirit. They have seized the opportunity of the reform and openness and constructing of the southwest passage to sea, and they have been strengthening the construction of the projects for infrastructure facilities, increasing the income of agriculture, waging a comprehensive agriculture development, speeding up industrialization and urbanization, absorbing

foreign investment, developing the export-oriented economy. As a result, they have made rapid progress in economic development and in different social undertakings. In 1998, the gross domestic product of Guangxi was 190.3 billion yuan, 31 times that of 1952, and 5.9 times that of 1978. From 1979 to 1998, the gross domestic product of Guangxi increased by an annual average growth rate of 9.3%, among which the primary industry increases by an average of 6.5%, the second industry by 12.7% a year, and the tertiary industry by 9.3% . Now a unique local industrial system of sugar making, building materials, machinery, automobile, non-ferrous metal, electricity, metallurgy, medicine, silvichemistry, chemistry for daily use, light industry, textile, rubber, electronics, food and so on, has been formed. In 1998, the sugar output in Guangxi amounted to 3,400,000 tons, ranking the first place in China. The subtropical agriculture of Guangxi has begun to take shape, and an agricultural belt of the regional rice, sugar cane, aquaculture, fishery, livestock breeding, fruit growing, has also been formed, so the development prospect of agriculture here is broad. In 1998, the rice output, the main agricultural product, amounted to 14,240,000 tons, sugarcane to 35,820,000 tons, aquatic product to 2,180,000 tons, pork and mutton to 2,680,000 tons, fruit to 3,250,000 tons. Between 1978 and 1998, they increased by an average of 2.3%, 11.9%, 15.5%, 10.9%, and 16.3% respectively.

Guangxi has made noticeable achievements in constructing the projects for infrastructure facilities of the southwest passage to sea. At present, a three-dimensional communications and transportation network and system of sea, land and air, have been formed. And a unique southwest passage to sea is also formed after the completion of the advanced main highways between Guilin and Liuzhou, Nanning and Beihai, the road net reaching out all over the autonomous region, and the six local main lines between Litang and Zhanjiang, Nanning and Kunming, Nanning and Fangcheng Port, etc, linking up all parts of the country. In 1997, the whole highway between Nanning of Guangxi and Kunming of Yunnan, opened up to traffic, linking up the southwest areas of China and the coastal ports of Guangxi. Now the people in the southwest provinces of China and the west areas of Guangxi are transporting their abundant products to the coastal trade ports for export overseas through this highway.

Presently, Guangxi possesses five airports located in Nanning, Liuzhou, Guilin, Wuzhou and Beihai, and more than 100 domestic navigation lines, five regional ones and four international ones, consequently, a navigation network centering in Nanning and Guilin, linking up all big cities of China, is formed. Besides, direct navigation lines between Nanning and Hongkong, Hanoi, Bangkok, between Beihai and Hongkong, and between Guilin and Hongkong, Macao, Fu Kuo Ka, Seoul, have been opened. The passenger transport capacity of the Liangjiang International Airport in Guilin amounts to 5,000,000.

The unique coastal open superiority of Guangxi has become an important driving force for its economic development. Guangxi has numerous coastal docks and harbors, among which 21 ports of varying sizes are available for development. Beihai Port, Fangcheng Port, Tieshan Port, Pearl Harbor and Qinzhou Port can be built into deepwater berth wharves of ten thousand tons. Beihai, Fangcheng and Qinzhou have built 16 berths of ten thousand tons, the throughout of which amounts to 13,000,000 tons. Goods from all southwest provinces of China can be shipped directly to all big ports in Hongkong, Macao, Southeast Asia, Indo-Chinese Peninsula, the Persian Gulf and Western Europe. The channel of the West River having been dredged, fleets of ten thousand tons now can navigate from Nanning, and it is a gold waterway connecting Guangdong, Hongkong and Macao.

Since we put into effect the policy of the reform and

opening to the outside world, Guangxi has made rapid progress in foreign economic relations and trade. Now 20 world famous enterprises have opened and run business in Guangxi. Guangxi has established trade relations with 130 countries and regions and over 5,000 connections, and distributive and agency business relations with 220 foreign trade organizations. And it has also established 62 trade organizations in such countries as the United States, Japan, France, Germany, Singapore, Panama, Gambia, and regions in Hongkong and Macao. In 1998, Guangxi already had 4,565 foreign-invested enterprises, and the actual capital invested amounted to 886,130,000 US dollars.

Ratified by the state government, Guangxi has three coastal open cities: Beihai, Fangchengang, Nanning; six coastal open districts: Wuzhou city, Hepu county, Fangchen district of Fangchengang city, Qinnan and Qinbei districts of Qinzhou city, Yulin city; two border open cities: Pingxiang city, Dongxing city; sixteen first-rate open ports; two border economic development zones: Pingxiang, Dongxing.

Eight counties (districts and towns) in Guangxi lie on the border with Vietnam. There are now eight border ports, among which four of them including Pingxiang, the Friendship Pass, Dongxing, Shuikou are first-rate state ports. And there are twenty-five border trade areas. Every year the border import and export volume of trade amounts to over three billion yuan. There are highways leading to all border ports and trade areas. The Xianggui Railway links up Vietnam and trains run directly to Hanoi. It is the ideal medium through which we develop direct, bilateral, multilateral and entrepot trade and export processing with Vietnam and Southeast Asian countries.

II. Development Strategy and Investment Environment

The southwest area of China is a big market with a population of 200 million. The strategy of the state government, which favors the central and western areas, opens vast vistas for the development of Guangxi. The long-range objective of Guangxi from the period of the Ninth Five-Year Plan to the year 2010 is to accelerate the development of the national economy and society sustainedly, rapidly and healthily by enhancing development; the gross domestic product increases by over 10% a year so as to reach the above-average level. In 2010, the gross domestic product will be twice that of what it is now, and surpass the average country level.

To realize the above strategic blueprints, we need support from the state government, all provinces, cities and autonomous regions, and the joint efforts made by the people of all nationalities in Guangxi. Meanwhile, we have offered a rare chance for national and international capital, technology and talented personnel invested. Approved by the people's government of the Guangxi Autonomous Region, the present orientation and important fields of introducing foreign investment are as follows:

In agriculture, stress is laid on introducing good strains of seeds and advanced technology from abroad so as to raise the level of agricultural production, to increase projects of advanced science and technology, to readjust and optimize agricultural structure, to promote the transition of agriculture increase, and to encourage the introduction of foreign investment to develop projects of agricultural production of good strains of seeds, including grain and commercial crops, livestock, fowls and aquatic product, forest and flowers.

In industry, through readjusting structure and introducing high technology, stress is laid on increasing the industry level in sugar-making, food, nonferrous metal, auto and machinery manufacturing, building materials, metallurgy, chemical industry and paper-making, on promoting energy-saving and reduction of material consumption, on

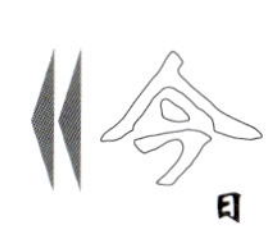

developing new variety of goods, on accelerating the upgrade and update of goods, on expanding the potentialities of market exploitation in such trades as marine organism, pharmacy, silvichemistry, electronics, shipbuilding, aluminium processing, etc.

In the tertiary industry, effective measures are adopted to promote opening wider to the outside world in tourism and service trade.

In infrastructural facilities, stress is laid on projects of water conservancy, transportation, communications, energy, city infrastructure, ecological construction and environmental protection.

In high technology industry, stress is laid on projects such as bioengineering, oceaneering, information engineering and new materials.

In the export-oriented industry of foreign exchange-earning, stress is laid on various processing trade and investment items in foreign countries with surplus equipment, raw materials and domestic technology.

海南——中国最大的经济特区

Hainan: The Largest Special Economic Zone in China

一、地理位置和经济发展

海南省简称琼，位于中国的最南端，北以琼州海峡与广东省划界，西临北部湾与越南民主共和国相对，东濒南海与台湾省相望，东南和南边在南海中跟菲律宾、文莱和马来西亚为邻。

1988年4月13日，经全国人民代表大会批准，设立海南省并建立海南经济特区。海南省的行政区域包括海南岛和西沙群岛、南沙群岛、中沙群岛的岛礁及其海域。海南省实行省直接管理市、县的行政管理体制，截止至1998年底，海南省共辖2个地级市，7个县级市，4个县，6个民族自治县，1个办事处（即西沙、南沙、中沙群岛办事处，县级），省会海口市。

1998年末，海南省有总人口733.31万，其中汉族人口605.50万人，占82.6%，少数民族人口127.96万人，占17.4%。海南省是中国主要侨乡之一，海外的华侨、华人近200万人，分布在世界50多个国家和地区。

海南岛是海南省陆地的主体，总面积（不包括卫星岛）3.39万平方公里，是中国仅次于台湾岛的第二大岛。

海南省地处热带、亚热带，属热带季风气候区域，是中国最具热带气候特色的地方。海南岛年日照时数约2500小时，年平均温度在23-25℃之间。西、南、中沙群岛属于热带海洋气候、夏长无冬，全年平均气温26.5℃。海南省是全国冬温最高的地区。海南岛平均降雨量为1500-2000毫米。海南省资源丰富，是中国热带作物基地，橡胶产量占中国60%以上，热带雨林中盛产珍贵木材、南药和鸟兽。海域盛产优质的海产品并蕴藏有丰富的石油和天然气。

海南建省办经济特区以来，海南的开发建设进入了新的发展时期，走上了一条富岛强省之路，从一个经济比较落后的边陲地区发展成为初步繁荣昌盛的经济特区。1998年全省国内生产总值达到438.92亿元，比1978年增长7.72倍，年均递增11.4%，全省人均国内生产总值由1979年的327元增加到1998年的6022元，增长6.78倍，年均递增10.8%。1998年全省地方财政收入36.49亿元（不包国税上缴部分），比1952年增长279.69倍，年均递增13.0%；全省人均地方财政收入由1952年的5元增加到1998年498元，增长98.6倍，年均递增10.5%。1999年初，国务院总理朱镕基在来琼视察时说："真正抓好了农业和旅游业，海南就可以富甲天下"。近10年来海南省的水果、冬季瓜菜、水产养殖等热带高效农业发展迅速，逐步向产业化、基地化和外向型方向发展。1998年全省农业增加值164亿元，比1978年增长4.43倍，平均年增长8.8%；旅游业迅速崛起，已成为海南省具有深远发展潜力和前景的优势产业。从1988年建省开始，海南省就把海岛旅游业作为全省的优势产业下大力气认真抓好，经过10年的建设，全省旅游基础设施不断完善，一大批新的景区、景点相继建成，已形成了热带海滨、黎苗风情、温泉康乐、热带植物、南中国海潜水、热带田园、美食、文化古迹、商务会议考察游等十个方面的系列旅游，服务质量明显提高。1998年全省接待旅游人数达855.97万人次，其中涉外宾馆接待旅游过夜人数达596.05万人次，比1987年增长6.94倍，年均递增20.7%；1998年旅游收入58.97亿元，其中国际旅游收入0.96亿美元，比1987年增长7.37倍，年均递增21.3%。对外开放迅速扩大，全方位开放格局已基本形成，1988至1998年全省累计实际利用外资87.38亿美元，其中外商直接投资62.21亿美元，对外借款24.97亿美元。来琼投资的国家和地区1998年达到20多个，大财团、大企业来琼投资的势头日益增大。随着对外开放和经济发展，极大促进了对外贸易发展。1998年全省出口总值达8.85亿美元，比1952年的42万美元增长2105.3倍，年均递增18.1%。

二、投资环境

1987年以来全省加强能源、运输、邮电业等基础设施建设，全省投资环境明显改善，已具备大规模开发建设的条件。

先后建设了大广坝等多个水库，确保了海南经济发展对水资源的需求。

电力建设超常规发展。至1998年底全省电力装机总容量达156.05万千瓦，跨入全国富电省份。

港口建设成效显著，万吨级泊位由1987年的3个增至1998年的10个，港口吞吐能力大大增强。

公路建设有新的突破，"三纵四横"的公路网络贯穿全岛，高速公路从无到有。环岛高速公路将在1999年底全线贯通，目前已经开通的高速公路有：环岛东线海口至三亚、西线海口至洋浦、三亚至九所高速公路。全省公路密度居全国先进行列。

航空事业得到超常规发展，按国际4E级建成了三亚凤凰国际机场、海口国际美兰机场，按股份制组建的海南省民用航空公司已成为中国民航中一支新生力量，经营管理水平居全国前列。建省前夕还是小机场的海口机场如今已跻身于全国前10名行列。海南省通往国内外的民用航空航线由1987年的5条增加到189条。

陆海铁路通道建设进展顺利，2001年将实现通车，届时海南铁路将跨过琼州海峡和全国铁路相连，海南省发展的空间将更加广阔。

海口经济开发区
Haikou Economic Development Zone

邮电通信业迅速发展，已形成包括数字微波、光纤通信、卫星通信、程控电话、移动电话、无线寻呼、分级交换等现代通信技术手段的完整的通信体系。电信网已经完成由人工网向自动网的过渡，基本实现了模拟技术向数字技术的转变。全省程控电话交换机总容量从1987年的1.67万门增加到1998年的66.79万门，移动电话从无到有发展到19.49万门。全省电话已全部实现程控化，1998年电话普及率为9.7部/百人，已处于全国先进行列。

三、发展前景

新中国成立50年来，海南走过了光辉的历

程。展望未来的发展前景，海南人民充满信心和希望。1988年，国务院对海南省提出了经济发展的战略目标要求，即“争取在三、五年内赶上全国平均经济水平。到本世纪末达到国内发达地区的水平”。海南省在1992年已经实现了第一步战略目标，全省人均国内生产总值赶上了全国的平均水平。海南省将继续实现第二步战略目标和第三步战略目标，基本实现现代化，即：到2000年人均国内生产总值比1990年翻两番，人均经济总量和整体经济素质达到国内发达地区水平，基本消除贫困现象，人民生活提前达到小康水平，建立起较为完善的社会主义市场经济体制；到2010年，实现国内生产总值比2000年翻两番，人均国内生产总值接近或达到中等发达国家和地区的水平，国民经济整体素质明显提高，人民的小康生活更加富裕，生活质量明显提高，社会主义市场经济体制进一步完善。届时，海南将成为基本实现现代化、经济发达、科技先进、人民富裕、政治民主、法制完备、社会文明的省份。

四、鼓励投资的重点领域

1. 高新技术工业。主要是高新科技、无污染或少污染工业，主要在海口市、琼山市、洋浦经济开发区和西部工业区，包括石油天然气加工；计算机、笔记本电脑、计算机软盘等电子信息产业；汽车、摩托车的生产、生物制药等。

2. 热带高效农业，包括农产品的增产增收技术；农产品的改良、改造技术；农产品的保鲜、加工、储藏技术；热带作物、热带水果、冬季瓜菜、南繁育种、海洋水产的生产、保鲜、加工、储藏技术等。

3. 海岛旅游业。包括旅游员工的培训、旅游景点的建设、旅游设施的配套等。目前主要引进一批档次高、管理先进的旅游项目。

4. 生态产业。包括绿色农业、无污染、无公害农业；建立无氟省，消灭白色污染；建立一批具有生态特色的旅游景点等。

5. 信息产业。以软件开发应用为主，并可开展各产业的信息应用，如把信息技术用于农业、旅游业等。

6. 生命产业。

(1)用生物技术开发现代农业。

(2)环保产业。主要有防治空气、水质污染和垃圾处理等绿色技术。

(3)医药产业。包括中草药开发、基因工程药物、医疗器械等。

I. Geographical Location and Economic Development

Hainan Province, also known as Qiong, is located at the southernmost tip of China. Qiongzhou Strait divides it from Guangdong Province in the north and Beibu Gulf from the Democratic Republic of Vietnam in the west. In the east, it looks towards Taiwan Province. While in the south and southeast, it is neighbored by Philippines, Brunei, and Malaysia in the South Sea.

On April 13, 1988, the establishment of Hainan Province and the Hainan Special Economic Zone was ratified by the National People's Congress. Regions under its jurisdiction include Hainan Island, Xisha, Nansha, and Zhongsha archipelagoes, together with the territorial waters around them. Its counties and municipalities are subject to the direct administration of the provincial government. By the end of 1998, there were altogether two regional-level and seven county-level cities, four counties, six autonomous counties, and one county-level office (which is in charge of Xisha, Nansha, and Zhongsha archipelagoes). The capital city is Haikou.

By the end of 1998, Hainan Province boasted a registered population of 7,333,100, among which 6,055,000 were Han, and 1,279,600 were national minorities. They comprised 82.6 percent and 17.4 percent of the total respectively. Hainan is also one of the major native places of many overseas Chinese, with about 2 million descendants living in more than 50 countries and regions across the world.

The main body of the province is Hainan Island, which covers an area of 33,900 square kilometers (excluding the small satellite islands). It is the second largest island in China.

Hainan lies in tropical and subtropical zones, and has the most characteristic tropical monsoon climate in China. It receives on average a total of 2,500 hours of sun per year. And its average annual temperature is 23-25 degrees centigrade. Xisha, Nansha, and Zhongsha archipelagoes have a tropical marine climate with an average annual temperature of 26.5 degrees centigrade. Therefore, its winter temperature is the highest in China. Its annual rainfall amounts to 1,500-2,000 millimeters. The province is also endowed with rich natural resources. Being one of the bases of tropical plants, Hainan yields more than 60 percent of the rubber output in China. Its tropical forests offer precious timber, herbal medicines, and rare birds and animals, while its vast territorial waters are endowed with fine aquatic resources, and abundant reserves of oil and natural gas.

The establishment of the Hainan Special Economic Zone heralds a new era for Hainan's rapid development. The province has, as a result, taken off economically, emerging as a fledging prosperous economic zone from a relatively undeveloped frontier region. In 1998, its gross domestic product (GDP) totaled 43.892 billion yuan, 7.72 times higher over that of 1978 after adjusting for inflation, with an average annual growth of 11.4 percent. Its per capita GDP rose from 327 yuan in 1979 to 6,022 yuan in 1998, an increase of 6.78 times after inflation, with an average annual growth of 10.8 percent. In 1998, Hainan realized provincial state revenues of 3.649 billion yuan (excluding those taxes turned over to the central government), 279.69 times higher over that of 1952, with an average annual increase of 13 percent. As a result, its per capita revenue rose from 5 yuan in 1952 to 498 yuan in 1998, an increase of 98.6 times, with an average annual growth of 10.5 percent.

At the beginning of 1999, Premier Zhu Rongji came to Hainan on an inspection tour. He asserted that Hainan's development depended on the good management of its agriculture and tourism. Over the past decade, Hainan's tropical, high-yield agricultural items, such as fruit, winter vegetables, and aquaculture, have witnessed rapid growth, becoming more and more industrialized and export-oriented. In 1998, the added value of agriculture of Hainan came to 16.4 billion yuan, 4.43 times higher over that of 1978, with an average annual increase of 8.8 percent.

Tourism is booming to become a pillar industry with great potential for development. Ever since its founding in 1988, Hainan Province has attached great importance to tourism. As a result, a decade's efforts have paid off handsomely. Tourist infrastructure has been improved, while a set of new scenic spots and scenic zones have been completed. So far, the province can offer ten specialized tour series, such as a tropical coastal tour, Li and Miao local customs, hot springs and body-building tour, tropical plants tour, diving in the South China Sea, country life in tropical fields, local delicacies tour, cultural relics tour, and business inspection tour. At the same time, the quality of service has also undergone remarkable improvements. In 1998, the number of tourists hosted by the province reached 8,559,700 visits, among which foreign tourists totaled 5,960,500 visits, 6.94 times higher over that of 1987, with an average annual increase of 20.7 percent. Tourism revenues in 1998 added up to 5.897 billion yuan, of which 96 million US dollars came from foreign tourists, 7.37 times higher over that of 1987, with an annual average increase of

21.3 percent.

At the same time, Hainan is quickening its pace of opening to the outside world, as its comprehensive, multi-layer framework of opening has basically taken shape. From 1988 to 1998, the total amount of foreign investment in the province reached 8.738 billion US dollars, of which 6.221 billion US dollars was direct foreign investment and 2.497 billion was foreign loans. The number of countries and regions investing surpassed 20 in 1998, and the momentum of investment by consortiums and large enterprises keeps rising. The deepening of the process of opening has consequently spurred the rapid growth of Hainan's foreign trade. In 1998, its export volume totaled 0.885 billion US dollars, an increase of 2,105.3 times over that of 1952, which was only 420,000 US dollars. It realized an average annual growth of 18.1 percent.

II. Investment Environment

Since 1987, Hainan has stepped up its efforts in infrastructure construction, including energy, transportation, and telecommunications. Therefore, its investment environment has been greatly improved, providing optimal conditions for large-scale development.

With respect to water resources, Hainan has completed the construction of many reservoirs, such as Daguangba, so as to meet the growing demands of water consumption.

Its electricity construction has developed very rapidly. By the end of 1998, its total installed capacity reached 1,560,500 kilowatts, becoming one of the provinces rich in electricity.

Harbor expansion and construction have also progressed remarkably. The number of berths with 10,000-ton handling capacities rose from three in 1987 to ten in 1998, thus greatly increasing the handling capacity of ports and harbors.

Highway construction has also witnessed quite a few breakthroughs. A highway network of three routes from north to south and four from west to east crisscrosses the whole island. In the past, Hainan did not have a single expressway, but now three expressways are already in operation. They are Haikou-Sanya Route, Haikou-Yangpu Route, and Sanya-Jiusuo Route. They, together with the remaining sections, will form a ring route circling the whole island. The remaining sections will be completed and in operation by the end of 1999. So Hainan's highway density is well ahead of other provinces in China.

The same is true with aviation. The Phoenix International Airport at Sanya and Meilan International Airport at Haikou were built according to the 4E international standards. Hainan Civil Airlines, established as a joint venture, has developed to become a new dynamic force in China's civil aviation industry and its management level is one of the most advanced in China. Haikou Airport, which was only a small facility before the founding of the province, is already ranked among the top ten in the country. The number of domestic and international civil airlines connecting Hainan rose from 5 in 1987 to 189.

Hainan's railway construction is proceeding smoothly. The railway will be completed and put into operation in 2001. Hainan Railway will span over the Qiongzhou Strait to connect the province with the railway network on the mainland, thus lending great potential for Hainan's development.

A complete network of telecommunications has already taken shape, including digital, optical fiber, satellite, program-controlled telephone system, mobile phones, wireless paging, and other means of communications. Its telecommunications network used to be staff-operated, but now it is automatically operated. Correspondingly, the applied technology has changed from analogue to digital communication. The total installed capacity of its switchboard for program-controlled telephone system increased from

16,700 sets to 667,900 sets in 1998. Mobile phones have increased to 194,900 sets from none. All the telephones in the province are linked up to a computerized system. By 1998, the number of telephones for every 100 residents reached 9.7 sets.

III. Prospects for Development

After the founding of the People's Republic of China, Hainan made remarkable achievements in development. So Hainan people have complete confidence and hope in their bright future. In 1988, the State Council put forward strategic goals regarding Hainan's economic development, that is, "it should try in three to five years to catch up with the average economic level of the country and to equal the advanced provinces by the end of the century." In 1992, Hainan realized the first step, and it will keep advancing to fulfill the second and third steps. By 2000, it plans to double its per capita GDP over that of 1990, and match the developed provinces in terms of overall economic power and strength. This should be accompanied by basic poverty eradication so people will live a better life, and the smooth functioning of the socialist market economy. By 2010, it plans to double its GDP over that of 2000, with per capita GDP approaching that of middle-level developed countries or regions. Its overall economic strength, quality of life, and the mechanisms of the socialist market economy will all be greatly improved. By then, Hainan will emerge as a modernized, democratic province with a developed economy, advanced technology, and a complete legal system. To sum up, its people will be able to enjoy better lives in an educated society.

IV. Key Fields for Investment

1. High and new technological industries with no or little pollution: including oil and natural gas processing, electronics and information technology, such as desktops, laptops, and computer software, and production of automobiles, motorcycles, and bio-medicine.

2. Tropical, high-yield agriculture: high-yield and high-profit agricultural technology, crop-improvement technology, technologies to preserve, process, and store farm produce, tropical plants, fruits, winter vegetable growing, and technologies to produce, preserve, process, and store aquatic products.

3. Island tourism: including training service staff, building up scenic spots, and providing tourist facilities. The main task at present is to import a set of high-level tourist projects or programs with advanced management.

4. Ecological industries: including non-polluting, green agriculture, eliminating white pollution, building up a set of scenic spots with ecological features, and developing into a fluorine-free province.

5. Information technology (IT): focusing on software development, and the application of IT in agriculture, tourism, and other fields.

6. Bio-industries:

(1) Using bio-technology to develop modern agriculture.

(2) Environmental protection industries, such as technologies to prevent air and water pollution and treat garbage.

(3) Medical industry, including developing traditional Chinese herbal medicine, genetically engineered medicine, and medical instruments.

三亚蜈支洲岛风光
Wuzhizhou Island Scene of Sanya

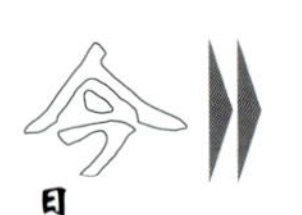

共和国最年轻的直辖市——重庆

Chongqing: The Youngest Municipality Directly Under the Central Government

一、经济发展情况

1997年3月14日全国人大八届五次会议决定设立重庆直辖市，辖原重庆市、万县市、涪陵市和黔江地区，共和国第四个直辖市诞生了。1998年底重庆市共辖13个区、23个县（自治区）和4个县级市，辐员面积8.24万平方公里，人口3060万，其中非农业人口614万。重庆已基本形成了大农业、大工业、大交通、大流通并存的格局，是中国西南地区和长江上游的经济中心城市，重要的交通枢纽和内河开放口岸。重庆是全国六大老工业基地之一，工业门类齐全，以重工业为主，轻工业也有较好基础。重庆是全国重要的机械工业基地、常规兵器生产基地、综合化工基地、医药化工基地和仪器仪表基地，重庆还是全国著名的优质水果、榨菜、桐油、烤烟产地，此外蚕茧、家禽、茶叶等农产品也有较高的市场占有率。重庆科技实力雄厚，全市有各类专业技术人员50余万人，其中高中级专业技术人员16万人。重庆拥有发达的高等教育体系，普通高等院校22所，在校学生达8.32万人。

建国以来，特别是中共的十一届三中全会以来，重庆坚持改革、不断开放，经济发展进入了高速增长期，社会经济面貌发生了翻天覆地的变化，50年来经济年均增长速度为5.6%，改革开放20年来平均每年增长9.1%，于1995年提前5年实现了经济增长翻两番的战略目标。1998年国内生产总值达1429亿元，人均国内生产总值从1949年的不足80元上升到1998年的4680元。社会消费品零售总额1998年达到553.70亿元，比1949年增长了120倍，年均增长10.3%，重庆的对外开放力度不断加大，从1983年第一家外商投资企业落户重庆以来，现已有2000余家外商企业在重庆扎根。累计实际利用外资47.2亿美元，世界级企业纷纷来渝，外资企业涉足行业从工业扩展到农业、交通、能源、商业和金融等行业。外贸出口大幅度增长，出口产品中机电产品比重不断上升，出口市场日趋多元化，1998年进出口总值10.34亿美元，其中出口总值5.14亿美元。

二、投资环境

重庆具有特殊的区位优势，拥有丰富的生物资源、矿产资源、水能资源和独具特色的三峡旅游资源，具有极大的开发潜力。举世瞩目的三峡工程建设和库区百万移民开发，三千万人的巨大需求市场，为重庆的投资者发展提供了广阔的市场空间。为改善投资环境，吸引外来资金和技术，重庆把直辖第一年定为“交通建设年”，集中财力进行交通、能源和市政建设，城市功能日臻完善。重庆已形成铁路、公路、水运、航空和管道运输相结合的综合运输体系。成渝、襄渝、川黔3条铁路干线与全国铁路网相连；21条干线公路、17条跨省公路构成四通八达的公路网络；重庆港是中国西部最大的内河港和西南地区唯一的对外口岸，吞吐能力超过1000万吨；江北国际机场现已

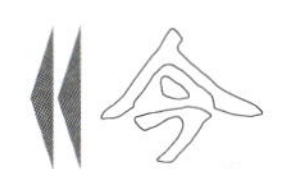

开通国内国际航线70多条，梁平机场也开通了国内航线。

重庆拥有完善发达的金融系统，中国人民银行总行在重庆设立直属营业部，中国银行重庆分行是国家一级口岸银行，业务联系遍及世界各地。加拿大丰业银行、汇丰银行在渝设分行。加拿大驻重庆领事馆已挂牌，日本大使馆在重庆设立了办事处。全市有涉外宾馆、酒店87家，共有客房5663间，床位11212张，其中星级饭店41家。重庆城市拥有出租车9418辆，重庆电讯事业发展迅速，全市电话装机总量330万门，主城区中电话普及率达32.6%，全市8.24万平方公里范围内实现了本地网覆盖，已建立卫星通讯地球站和实现程控交换。重庆水、电、天然气供应充足，为投资者提供了良好的投资环境。

三、发展前景

“九五”和2010年重庆国民经济和社会发展的目标是：以邓小平建设有中国特色社会主义理论和党的基本路线为指导，遵照江泽民总书记“努力把重庆建设成为长江上游的经济中心”的要求，紧紧把握解放思想，抓住机遇，“开发三峡，振兴重庆”，加快发展，富裕城乡的工作方针，实施科教兴渝和可持续发展战略，坚持以经济建设为中心，以改革开放统揽全局，积极推进经济体制和经济增长方式的根本转变；坚持富民为本，城乡一体共同繁荣；坚持物质文明建设和精神文明建设两手抓，依法治市，保持社会稳定，促进经济、社会协调发展。到2010年把重庆建设成为长江上游和西南地区的经济中心，形成长江上游新兴产业群，全市国内生产总值比1995年翻两番，综合经济实力力争达到全国省市中等偏上水平，人民生活富裕文明。

四、鼓励投资的重点领域

为鼓励外来投资，重庆市制定了比较完备的对外开放政策和地方性法规，建立了较为完善的招商引资工作制度，对外商投资审批和企业年检实现了“一站式”服务，特别是1998年11月4日市政府颁布了《关于进一步规范政务管理改善投资环境的决定》，简化了办事手续，提高了工作效率和服务水平，进一步优化了投资环境。根据重庆市经济结构调整的需要，鼓励外商投资的主要方向是：汽车工业、光电子工业、石化工业、冶金工业、通信设备制造业、仪器仪表制造业、精细化工业、化学纤维工业、电力、交通和通讯建设、农牧及食品加工和城市基础设施。

I. Economic Development

The establishment of Chongqing Municipality directly under the Central Government, which administers the former Chongqing municipality, Wanxian municipality, Fuling municipality and Qiangqing district, was decided at the Fifth Session of the Eighth National People's Congress on March 14,1997. Thus, the fourth municipality directly under the P.R.C.Central Government came into being.By the end of 1998, Chongqing Municipality had under it 13 districts, 23 counties (autonomous counties) and 4 municipalities at the county level. Chongqing covered 82,400 square kilometers, with a population of 30.6 million, of which the urban population numbered 5.95 million.The municipality has vigorous agriculture, and industry, convenient transportation and efficient communications. As an important hub of communications and an open port, Chongqing is the economic center of the southwest of China and of the upper reaches of the Yangtze River. Being one of the 6 national industrial bases, Chongqing has a wide variety of industries. Heavy industry is the key sector, while light industry is also on a sound basis. Chongqing is the country's major machinery industry base, and a defense industry, comprehensive chemical industry, pharmaceuticals and instruments and meters industry base. Chongqing is also famous for high-quality fruits, tuber mustard, tung oil and cured tobacco. Besides, such farm products as silk cocoons, poultry and tea have a fair market share. The scientific and technological strength of Chongqing is tremendous. There are more than 500,000 technicians of various specialties, of which those with high or medium ranks total 160,000. The higher education system in Chongqing is advanced, with 83,200 students enrolled in 22 institutions of higher education.

Since the foundation of the PR of China, and especially since the Third Plenary Session of the Eleventh CPC Central Committee, Chongqing has been carrying out the national reform and opening-up policy. The economic development has entered a high growth period. Earth-shaking changes have appeared in both social and economic aspects. The annual average economic growth has been 5.6 percent over the past 50 years. Since the advent of the reform and opening up, the growth has speeded up to 9.1 percent, and the target of quadrupling economic growth was realized in 1995, some five years earlier than planned. The GDP for 1998 accounted for 142.9 billion yuan, per capita GDP rose from less than 80 yuan in 1949 to 4,680 yuan in 1998. The retail sales revenue of consumer goods was 55.37 billion yuan, increasing 120 times over 1949, and the annual average growth was 10.3 percent. Chongqing is opening wider and wider to the outside world. More than 2,000 foreign-funded enterprises have been set up in Chongqing since 1983. A total of 4.72 billion US dollars in foreign

funds have been actually utilized. World-famous enterprises are coming to Chongqing in succession, involving industrial, agriculturial, transportation, energy, commerce, finance and other subjects. Exports have increased by a wide margin. Among exported articles, the proportion of equipment and machinery keeps rising. The total value of imports and exports in 1998 was 1.034 billion US dollars, of which total exports were valued at 0.514 billion US dollars.

II. Investment Environment

Chongqing has special regional advantages. With abundant resources of labor, minerals and energy, and the Three Gorges tourist attraction, the developing potentiality is great. The construction of the world famous Three Gorges Project, the relocation of one million people in the reservoir area and great demands for 30 million people provide great potential for investors. To improve the investment environment and absorb foreign funds and technology, the first year of the establishment of Chongqing Municipality directly under the Central Government was defined as the "Transportation Construction Year", and funds were concentrated on constructing transportation, energy and municipal facilities. As a result, Chongqing now has a comprehensive transportation system combining railways, highways, waterways and airways. Chengdu-Chongqing, Xiangyang-Chongqing and Sichuan-Guizhou railway lines connect with the national railway net; 21 main highways and 17 trans-provincial highways form a highway network extending in all directions; Chongqing Port is not only the biggest inland river port in western China but also the only port handling foreign ships in southwest China, with a handling capacity of over 10 million tons; Jiangbei International Airport has 70 domestic and international lines, and Liangping Airport has several domestic lines.

Chongqing's financial system is an advanced one. The Chongqing business department is directly under the Head Office of the People's Bank of China. Chongqing branch, of the Bank of China is a national bank in a first-grade port, whose business encompasses over the world. The Bank of Nova Scotia and Hongkong and Shanghai Banking Corp. have established branches in Chongqing. There are also a Canadian consulate and an office of the Japanese Embassy in Chongqing. There are 87 foreign hotels with 5,663 rooms and 11,212 beds, including 43 star-grade hotels. There are 9,418 taxis in Chongqing. Telecommunications services have developed rapidly. The volume of telephone exchanges totals 3.3 million lines and there are 32.6 telephones per 100 households in the city proper. Local telecommunications cover the whole of Chongqing. Satellite ground stations have been set up and long-distance telephone exchanges are in use. Plentiful supplies of water, electricity and natural gas provide an excellent investment environment.

III. Development Prospects

The guiding ideology for the Ninth Five-year Plan (1996-2000) and the plan for Chongqing's socio-economic development to the year 2010 is as follows: Guided by Deng Xiaoping Theory on building socialism with Chinese characteristics and the Party's basic line, in accordance with the call to "Make great efforts to build Chong-qing into the economic center of the upper reaches of the Yangtze River" by Secretary Jiang Zemin, we will firmly insist on emancipating our minds, seizing the opportunity, "developing the Three Gorges, to give vigor to Chongqing", pursuing economic development, and enriching both town and country. We will implement the strategies of developing Chongqing by relying on science and education, and sustainable development.We will concentrate our efforts on promoting the economy, take the whole situation into account in the course of reform and opening up, actively carry forward the fundamental change of the economic system and economic growth pattern, adhere to the principle of enriching the people, making both town and country flourish, working for material progress and meanwhile for cultural and ethical progress, and guarantee social stability under the rule of law to promote socio-economic coordinated growth. By 2010, Chongqing is to be the economic center of the upper reaches of the Yangtze River and of southwest China as a whole, promoting new and developing industries on the upper reaches of the Yangtze. The local GDP will be 4 times as much as that of 1995. The comprehensive economic strength will reach the medium-to-upper level compared to other provinces (municipalities).

IV. Major Fields in Which Investment Is Encouraged

To attract foreign investment, Chongqing has drawn up sound policies and local rules and laws for its opening up, and established a relatively complete system for attracting funds. The approval of foreign investment has been speeded up and there is an annual examination of enterprises. The municipal government issued the Decision On the Further Standardization of Administration and Improvement of the Investment Environment on Nov. 4,1998, simplified working procedures, raised work efficiency and service quality, and further improved the investment environment. According to the needs of economic structural readjustment, the major fields in which investment is encouraged are: automobile industry, fiber-optics, petrochemicals, metallurgy, telecommunications, instruments and metes, fine chemicals, chemical fibers, electric power, transportation and communications, agriculture, forestry, food processing and urban infrastructure.

重庆嘉陵摩托车
Chongqing Jialing Motorcycle

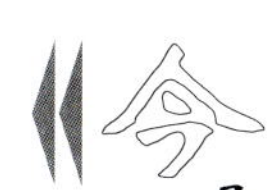

迈向21世纪的四川

Sichuan: Facing the 21st Century

一、经济发展情况

四川位于中国西南部的长江上游，与青海、甘肃、陕西、重庆、云南、贵州、西藏等交界，为西北、西南和华中三大地区的结合部，是中国内陆土地辽阔、市场巨大、资源丰富的大省，自古就以富饶的物产，秀美的山川被誉为“天府之国”。全省面积48.5万平方公里，1998年末常住总人口8493万。有53个少数民族，世居的少数民族有14个。全省工业门类齐全，在39个工业门类中，机械、电子、冶金、化工、建筑、建材、食品、丝绸、医药、皮革工业等在全国占有重要地位。四川是中国的科技、人才大省，在航空、航天、核能、光纤通信、生物工程、高分子化学等领域的研制能力居全国领先地位。目前在四川工作的中国科学院、中国工程院院士有35名，各类专业技术人员近120万人，高等院校43所。

建国50年，特别是改革开放20年以来，四川各方面发生了巨大变化，经济实力增强，大开放促进了大发展。1998年四川国内生产总值3580.3亿元，比1952年增长21.8倍，年均增长7.0%；比1978年增长4.9倍，年均增长9.3%；人均国内生产总值由1952年的69元、1978年的264元，增加到1998年的4319元；社会商品零售总额1298.6亿元，分别比1952年和1978年增长94.5倍、20.1倍，年均分别增长10.4%、16.5%。改革开放以来，四川省合同直接利用外资67.23亿美元，实际直接利用外资22.75亿美元，目前有“三资”企业近5000家。1979-1998年累计，四川进出口总额224.0亿美元，其中出口146.8亿美元，年均分别增长23.7%、25.1%。

二、投资环境

经济增长促进基础设施的快速发展，四川努力改善投资环境，交通、通信、城市、市政、第三产业等迅速发展。以成都为中心的交通、通信比较发达，全省铁路营运里程2974公里，有成（都）渝（重庆）、宝（鸡）成、成昆（明）、达（川）成主要干线，成都铁路口岸已开通直达上海、天津、青岛、连云港等地的国际集装箱列车。高速公路通车里程328公里，有成渝、成绵（阳）高速公路，即将建成通车和建设中的有成乐（山）、成雅（安）、成灌（都江堰）、成南（充）等高等级公路。成都航空港是全国第四大航空港，西南地区的空中枢纽，成都双流国际机场可通往国内外主要城市。成都是中国西南地区最大的物资集散地，商品市场十分活跃，购物十分方便。目前，在省会成都有星级宾馆58家，五星级酒店2家、四星级酒店3家、三星级宾馆16家。每两年分别举办中国四川国际电视节、中国成都国际熊猫节，诚邀世界各地宾朋相聚。目前四川县以上城市全部实现了电话交换程控化，17个城市进入国际电话自动网，可通达世界近200个国家和地区；成都国际邮件交换局已开通成都直达美国、日本等国家和地区的特快专递邮路；国际互联网成都中心站的开通，使四川驶向了“信息高速公路”。

三、发展前景

面向21世纪的四川，正以更加开放的姿态迎

成都新区
Chengdu New District

接明天。

到2010年，四川国民经济跨世纪的发展战略是：推进转变，优化结构，发挥优势，高效持续，加快发展。战略重点是：

1. 夯实四大基础。即夯实农业、交通、能源、科教基础。

2. 壮大六个支柱。即电子信息产业，机械冶金工业，建筑建材业，饮料食品业，化学医药工业，旅游业。

在大力发展支柱产业的同时，努力改造和提高轻纺工业，发展优势拳头产品，组建企业集团，提高市场占有率和经济效益。为抢占下世纪经济发展制高点，要积极培育以高新技术和高加工度为特征的先导产业，重点在生物工程、新材料、民用核技术、航空航天、高效节能和环保产业上下功夫。

3. 培育经济中心。即依托成都，构建成都平原经济圈，开发攀西、川南，扶持丘陵地区、盆周山区和民族地区，推动全省经济发展。

4. 坚持可持续发展。要正确处理人口、资源、环境同经济建设的关系，正确处理经济发展与社会进步的关系，始终把严格控制人口、节约资源、保护环境放在重要位置。

四、鼓励投资的重点领域

为让世界各地的客商，更好地投资中国西部这块热土。四川始终坚持“不求所有、但求所得、投其所好、对其负责”和“以诚相待，恪守信誉”的指导思想，共同开发，共谋发展，今后鼓励投资的重点领域和重点区域是：

重点领域：

1. 农业综合开发及其产业化；

2. 高新技术产业；

3. 国有企业嫁接改造；

4. 低耗能工业；

5. 建筑建材及装饰业；

6. 旅游业;
7. 环保产业。
重点区域:
1. 富饶的成都平原经济圈;
2. 得天独厚的攀西地区;
3. 国家级的成都高新技术产业开发区;
4. 国家级的绵阳高新技术产业开发区;
5. 国家级的成都海峡两岸科技产业开发区;
6. 省级成都经济技术开发区。

I. Economic Development

Sichuan, a province in southwest China, is situated on the upper reaches of the Yangtze River and shares boundaries with Qinghai, Gansu, Shaanxi, Chongqing, Yunnan, Guizhou and Tibet. It is at the junction of northwest China, southwest China and central China. It enjoys the name of natural Storehouse with its vast territory, huge market, abundant resources and products, and its beautiful mountains. It has an area of 485,000 sq.km and had a permanent resident population of 84,930,000 at the end of 1998. There are 54 minority nationalities, 14 of whom are residents who have lived here for generations. In fact, Sichuan is the largest region where the Yi ethnic group lives in compact communities and the only home of the Qiang nationality. It is also the second-largest area inhabited by Tibetan people.

Sichuan has a complete range of industry. Among its 39 industrial sectors, engineering, electronics, metallurgy, chemicals, construction materials, food, silk, medicine, and fur and leather play key roles in Chinese industry. Thus, it is not surprising that Sichuan leads in research and manufacturing in the fields of aerospace, nuclear energy, fiber-optical communications, biological engineering and polymer chemistry. There are 43 universities and colleges, and 35 academicians and 1,200,000 technicians in Sichuan.

Since the founding of the People's Republic of China in 1949, especially in the last twenty years of reform, great changes have taken place in Sichuan, and its remarkable economic achievements have in return promoted its development. In 1998, the GDP of Sichuan was RMB 358.03 billion, 21.8 times that of 1952, and with an average annual growth rate at 7 %, 4.9 times that of 1978, with an average annual increase at 9.3 %. The per capita GDP grew from RMB 69 in 1952 and RMB 264 in 1978 to RMB 4,319 in 1998. The total volume of retail sales is RMB 129.86 billion, 94.5 times that of 1952 and 20.1 times that of 1978, with average annual increases of 10.4 % and 16.5 %. Since the implementation of the reform and opening up policies, Sichuan's contractual value of foreign investment has amounted to US$6.723 billion, and its realised foreign investment is US$2.275 billion. Now there are about 5,000 joint ventures in Sichuan. From 1979 to 1998, the total export-import volume of Sichuan was worth US$22.4 billion, of which US$14.68 billion came from exports, with average growth rates of 23.7 % and 25.1 %.

II. Favourable Investment Environment

Economic growth has brought about a rapid development in Sichuan's infrastructure, which has resulted in the improvement of the investment environment, transportation, communications, urban construction and tertiary industry. Transportation and communications with Chengdu, the provincial capital, as the hub, are well developed. Sichuan's railways are 2,974 km long with the Chengdu, Baocheng, Chengkun and Dacheng main lines. Chengdu has international container train connections with Shanghai, Tianjin, Qingdao and Lianyungang. First-class highways connect Chengdu with Chongqing, Mianyang, Leshan, Ya'an, Dujiangyan and Nanchong. Chengdu, as a matter of fact, is also the air transportation hub of southwest China.

As an international airport, Chengdu vs Shuangliu Airport is the fourth-largest airport in China and is a major bridge between China and the rest of the world. Chengdu, as a goods-distribution centre of southwestern China, is a flourishing market. Chengdu has 58 hotels, including two five-star, three four-star, and 16 three-star hotels. In order to accommodate guests from all over the world, the Sichuan International Television Festival and the Chengdu International Panda Festival are held every other year. Sichuan's communications system is flourishing. At present, the city-level counties have program-controlled telephone exchange systems and 17 cities are connected via the automatic international telephone network to nearly 200 countries and regions. The Chengdu International Postal Exchange Bureau has opened express delivery services to the US, Japan and other countries and regions. The Chengdu Internet links Sichuan with the "information highway".

III. Development Perspective

Sichuan is facing the 21st century with a more open mind.

By 2010, Sichuan's cross-century development strategies are to promote & accelerate its development, to optimise its structure, to give a full play to its advantages, and to sustain high efficiency. The focus of these strategies will be:

1. Giving priority to four basics: Agriculture, transportation, energy, and science and education.

2. Expanding six pillar industries: Information technology, machinery and metallurgy, building materials, food and drinks, chemicals and pharmaceuticals, and tourism. In addition, Sichuan will make efforts to transform and improve its light and textile industry, develop its most competitive products, and establish its own enterprise groups, so as to increase its market shares and its economic efficiency. Moreover, Sichuan will stand in the forefront of economic development to explore high-tech and high-level processing industry such as biotechnology, new materials, nuclear technology, aerospace and aviation technology, energy saving and environmental protection.

3. Establishing economic centres: With Chengdu as its centre, the province will construct the Chengdu Plain economic zone, develop Fanxi and Chuan'nan, and support hilly regions and ethnic regions so as to promote its economic development.

4. Maintaining sustainable development. The province will co-ordinate the relations between economic development and population, and the environment, and resources, and between economic development and social advance, giving priority concern to birth control, resources saving and environmental protection.

IV. Key Areas for Encouraging Foreign Investment

In order to attract more investment from overseas, the Sichuan government will stick to the following principles in encouraging investment. They are "to benefit not to own, to serve & be responsible, and to be honest and abide by promises".

Key areas of investment:

1. Comprehensive agricultural development and its industrialisation;

2. High-tech industries;

3. Rationalization and transformation of state-run enterprises;

4. Energy-efficient industries;

5. Building materials and refurbishing;

6. Tourism;

7. Environmental protection.

Key regions of investment:

1. Chengdu Plain economic zone

2. Panxi region

3. Chengdu National High-tech Industry Exploration Zone

4. Mianyang High-tech Industry Zone

5. Taiwan and Chengdu Science and Technology Park

6. Chengdu Provincial Economic Technology Development Zone

奋起的贵州

Guizhou: On the Rise

贵州简称"黔"或"贵"，位于中国西南部，与湖南、云南、广西、四川和重庆等省、区、市相连，是一个山川秀丽、气候宜人、资源丰富、人民勤劳，发展潜力巨大的内陆省份。

贵州省国土面积17.61万平方公里，1998年底全省总人口3657.6万，辖贵阳、六盘水、遵义3个省辖市，黔东南、黔西南、黔南3个自治州，安顺、铜仁、毕节3个地区，86个县（市、区、特区）。

贵州是能源和矿产资源大省。水能蕴藏量1874.5万千瓦。列全国第6位，其中可开发量1683.3万千瓦，煤炭资源量2419亿吨，保有储量524亿吨，居全国第5位，保有储量相当于江南9省区的总和，居江南之首，煤层中还蕴藏着大量可开发利用的煤层气。水能与煤炭优势并存，为把贵州建成南方重要的能源基地奠定了坚实基础，为国家西电东送战略的实施提供了有力的支持。贵州已发现矿产110多种，其中76种探明了储量，有40种储量居全国前10位，21种列1至3位。贵州是中国富磷矿最多的省区，储量4.86亿吨；铝土矿质优量大，保有储量3.96亿吨，列全国第2位；重晶石甲冠中华，储量占全国的1/3；汞、锑、锰、硫铁矿和水泥原料等矿产优势明显；金矿储量居全国第12位，是中国新的黄金生产基地。

贵州是生物资源大省。全省平均海拔1000米，年平均气温15℃，无霜期约270天，年平均降雨量在1000-1300毫米，气候温和湿润，有利于动植物生长。全省有食用野生植物500多种，工业用野生植物600多种，绿化、美化及抗污染野生植物240多种，有药用植物3700多种。银杉、珙桐、秃杉、桫椤列为国家一级保护植物。有野生动物1000余种，其中黔金丝猴、黑叶猴、黑颈鹤、华南虎等14种列为国家一级保护动物。

贵州是旅游资源大省。奇特的自然风光、浓郁的民族风情，加上宜人的气候是海内外宾朋理想的旅游和避暑胜地。全省有黄果树瀑布、龙宫、红枫湖、织金洞、㵲阳河、赤水十丈洞瀑布群、马岭河峡谷、荔波樟江等8个国家级风景名胜区；有铜仁梵净山、茂兰喀斯特森林、赤水桫椤和威宁草海等4个国家级自然保护区以及众多的森林公园，数百处民族风情村寨和历史文物古迹。

经过50年的建设，特别是改革开放20年的快速发展，贵州经济社会面貌发生了深刻变化，基本形成了依托本省资源和技术优势的能源原材料工业体系，机械电子工业体系，轻工业体系，拥有航天、航空、电子三大基地以及电解铝、钢铁、铁合金、原料磨具、工业轴承、低压电器、仪器仪表、氮肥、磷矿石及磷肥、名烟名酒等一批在全国有影响的大中型企业或企业集团。1998年全省完成国内生产总值843亿元，比1997年增长8.6%，高于全国平均增长水平。由于坚持把农业放在国民经济的首位，强化农业基础，全省农村经济全面发展，农业连续6年丰收，1998年全省粮食产量达到1100万吨，初步实现了全省农村人口粮食自给的历史性跨越。在工业方面，坚持建立现代企业制度的改革方向，把国有企业改革作为各项工作的重中之重，1998年全省完成工业增

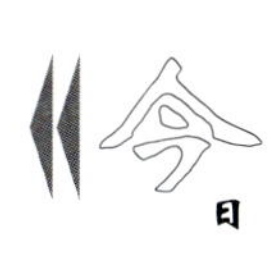

加值277亿元，比1997年增长10.5%。在经济发展的基础上，1998年全省财政收入完成122.84亿元，比1997年增长12.4%。固定资产投资增加，1998年全社会固定资产投资完成315亿元，比1997年增加22.6%，投资率达到37.4%，是改革开放20年来最高的年份。全省金融机构各项存贷款增加，1998年各项存款余额815.4亿元，各项贷款余额947.8亿元。城乡居民收入稳步增加，1998年全省城镇居民人均可支配收入4565元，农民人均纯收入1334元。

贵州是西南地区铁路交通枢纽。湘黔、贵昆、川黔、黔桂4条铁路干线在贵阳交汇，南昆铁路穿越贵州西南部。株（洲）六（盘水）铁路电气化复线、内（江）昆（明）铁路贵州段、水（城）柏（果）铁路已动工修建。贵阳南站是西南地区铁路运输最大编组站，日编解能力8000辆，已开通货运口岸，开办大型集装箱业务。贵州公路通车里程33604公里，其中等级公路14137公里。贵阳至黄果树、贵阳至遵义和贵阳东北绕城高等级公路已建成通车。贵阳至新寨、贵阳至毕节高等级公路正在加紧建设，全省高等级公路北上南下，东进西联的骨架初见端倪。贵阳龙铜堡4D级现代化机场已于1997年建成通航，年吞吐旅客400万人次，高峰期可满足每小时2000人次进出港。10多家航空公司开通贵阳至香港、北京、上海、广州、福州、杭州、南京、西安、武汉、成都、昆明、海口等30多个城市的航班。邮电通信发展迅速，全省开通了程控电话，主要城市开通了移动电话。基础设施日趋完善。

展望未来，贵州面临很好的发展机遇，也为外商提供了许多的投资创业机会。国家确定的增加投资，扩大内需的方针，决定了国家要进一步加大包括贵州省在内的中西部地区的开发和建设，沿海地区进一步发展也需要能源、原材料支撑，贵州将充分利用这种机遇、发挥资源优势和现有的物质技术基础，加快经济发展，1998年贵州省确定了全省跨世纪发展的奋斗目标和主要任务。今后贵州省将进一步加强基础设施建设，改善投资环境，认真执行《贵州省进一步放宽政策，改善投资环境的若干规定》，采取更加灵活的方式，以资源换资金，以存量换资金，放市场引资金，为外商投资贵州创造良好的环境和优越的条件。除国家明令禁止的项目外，对外来投资不搞行业限制，不受地域影响，不定投资比例。欢迎外商投资参与贵州各方面的建设，特别鼓励和欢迎外商投资贵州农业、能源、交通、原材料等基础产业和基础设施，投资开发旅游资源和其他资源，投资环境保护工程和生态环境建设工程，投资国有大中型企业的技术改造，投资高新技术产业开发等。

Guizhou is situated in southwest China and bounded by Hunan, Yunnan and Sichuan provinces, the Guangxi Zhuang Autonomous Region, and Chongqing Municipality directly under the Central Government.

The province has picturesque scenery, a pleasant climate, rich resources, industrious people and great potential for development.

Guizhou covers 176,100 square km. By the end of 1998, its total population had reached 36.58 million. It has jurisdiction over the three cities of Guiyang, Liupanshui and Zunyi directly under the provincial government, the three autonomous prefectures of Qiandongnan, Qianxinan and Qiannan, the three prefectures of Anshun, Tongren and Bijie, and 86 counties (county-level cities, districts and special regions).

Guizhou is rich in energy and mineral resources. Its hydropower reserves are 18.75 million kw, ranking sixth place in the country, of which 16.83 million kw are usable. Coal reserves are estimated at 241.9 billion tons, with the

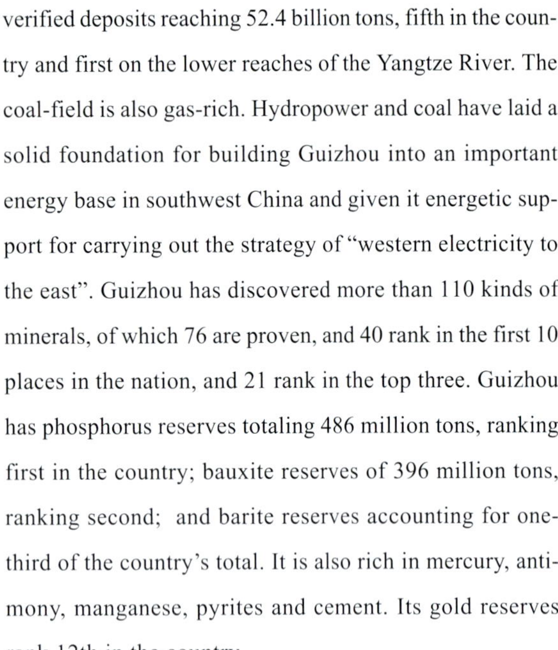

verified deposits reaching 52.4 billion tons, fifth in the country and first on the lower reaches of the Yangtze River. The coal-field is also gas-rich. Hydropower and coal have laid a solid foundation for building Guizhou into an important energy base in southwest China and given it energetic support for carrying out the strategy of "western electricity to the east". Guizhou has discovered more than 110 kinds of minerals, of which 76 are proven, and 40 rank in the first 10 places in the nation, and 21 rank in the top three. Guizhou has phosphorus reserves totaling 486 million tons, ranking first in the country; bauxite reserves of 396 million tons, ranking second; and barite reserves accounting for one-third of the country's total. It is also rich in mercury, antimony, manganese, pyrites and cement. Its gold reserves rank 12th in the country.

Rich in biological resources. Guizhou, lying around 1,000 meters above sea level, has an average annual temperature of 15 degrees centigrade. It has about 270 frost-free days, and the average annual rainfall is 1,000-1,300 mm. The temperate and humid climate are ideal for animals and plants to thrive in. The province has more than 500 species of edible wild plants, more than 600 species for cash crops, more than 240 species for afforestation, beautification and anti-pollution, and more than 3,700 species of medicinal plants. The China fir, dove tree, Taiwania flousiana and spinulose tree fern are listed as plants under state first-level protection. There are more than 1,000 species of wild animals, of which 14 are under state first-level protection, including golden monkeys, black leaf monkeys, black-necked cranes and South China tigers.

Rich in tourism resources. Unique natural landscapes, pronounced local colors, and a pleasant climate make Guizhou ideal for tourism. The province has eight state-level scenic spots, —Huangguoshu Waterfall, Dragon Palace, Hongfeng Lake, Zhijin Cave, Wuyang River, Shizhangdong Waterfalls in Chishui, Maling River Gorge and the Zhangjiang River in Libo. The province also has four state-level nature reserves: Tongren's Fanjing Mountain, Maolan's Karst Forest, Chishui's Spinulose Tree Ferns and Weining's Grassland, in addition to many forest parks, hundreds of ethnic villages, historical sites and cultural relics.

After 50 years of construction, especially since the implementation of reform and opening to the outside world in 1978, great changes have taken place in Guizhou's economy and society. Depending on its resources and technological advantages, the province has basically formed complete industrial sectors in energy, raw materials, electrical machinery and light industries. It also owns three large bases engaging in space, aviation and electronics, as well as a group of large and medium-sized enterprises or enterprise groups, producing electrolytic aluminum, iron and steel, ferroalloy, abrasives and abrasive tools, industrial bearings, low-pressure electrical appliances, instruments, nitrogenous fertilizer, phosphate minerals and phosphate fertilizer, cigarettes and liquor. In 1998, the province's GDP stood at 84.3 billion yuan, up 8.6 percent over the previous year and higher than the national average. Due to strengthening agriculture as the foundation of the economy, the province's primary sector has developed in an all-round way, reaping bumper harvests for six years running. In 1998, grain output reached 11 million tons, realizing the historic leap of the rural population achieving grain self-sufficiency. The province adheres to the reform orientation of establishing a modern enterprise system, and in all work stresses state-owned enterprise reform. In 1998, it achieved 27.7 billion yuan in industrial added value, up 10.5 percent over 1997. Revenue stood at 12.28 billion yuan, up 12.4 percent. Fixed-assets investment totaled 31.5 billion yuan, up 22.6 percent, with the investment rate reaching 37.4 percent, a record for the past 20 years. Loan deposits of financial institutions increased. In 1998, the

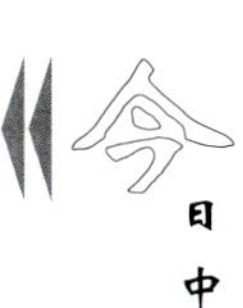

deposit balance stood at 81.54 billion yuan, and the loan balance at 94.78 billion yuan. Household income has steadily increased. The average per-capita income of urban residents stood at 4,565 yuan and farmers' real per-capita income was 1,334 yuan.

A hub of railway communications in southwest China. Guiyang stands where four railways meet, —the Zhuzhou-Guiyang, Guiyang-Kunming, Chongqing-Guiyang and Guiyang-Guilin lines. The Nanjing-Kunming Railway cuts through southwest Guizhou. The project to electrify the multiple-track Zhuzhou-Liupanshui Railway and projects to build the Guizhou section of the Neijiang-Kunming Railway and Shuicheng-Baiguo Railway are under construction. Guiyang South Railway Station is the largest marshalling yard in southwest China, with a daily marshalling capacity of 8,000 trains. It has opened cargo and container services. The road network totals 33,604 km, including 14,137 km of graded highways. The high-grade Guiyang-Huangguoshu, Guiyang-Zunyi highways, and the ring road in southeast Guiyang have been completed. The Guiyang-Xinzhai and Guiyang-Bijie high-grade highways are under construction. A framework of high-grade highways from north to south and from east to west has begun to take shape. The 4D-grade modern airport in Longdongbao, Guiyang, was completed in 1997, with the annual passenger volume reaching 4 million, handling 2,000 passengers an hour at peak times. More than 10 airlines have opened scheduled flights from Guiyang to more than 30 cities, including Hong Kong, Beijing, Shanghai, Guangzhou, Fuzhou, Hangzhou, Nanjing, Xi'an, Wuhan, Chengdu, Kunming and Haikou. Postal and telecommunications services enjoy rapid development. The province has opened computerized telephone services and the main cities have opened mobile telephone services. Infrastructure facilities are constantly improving.

Looking ahead, Guiyang faces a favorable development situation. Meanwhile, it provides many investment opportunities for foreign business people. The state policy of increasing investment and enlarging domestic demand means further enlargement in the development and construction of the provinces, central and western areas, including Guizhou. The further development of coastal areas also needs the support of inland energy and resources. Guizhou will fully use the opportunity and give full play to its advantages in resources and in its existing material and technological base to speed up its economic development.

In 1998, Guizhou successfully held its Eighth Provincial Party Congress, which defined the trans-century objectives and main tasks of the province. From now on, it will further strengthen its infrastructure facility construction, improve its investment environment, carefully carry out the Regulations of Guizhou on Further Introducing More Flexible Policies and Improving the Investment Environment, adopt more flexible measures to attract capital, and create a favorable investment environment and good conditions for foreign businesses.

Foreign investors are welcome to participate in the construction of Guizhou. The province especially encourages foreign businesses to invest in basic industries and infrastructure facilities related to agriculture, energy, transportation and raw materials, as well as in the development of tourism and other resources. Foreign investment is also guided to environmental protection and ecological environment construction projects, technological renovation of state-owned enterprises and high-tech industrial development.

云南——人与自然和谐相处的宝地

Yunnan: A Land Where People and Nature Develop in Harmony

一、经济发展的成就

云南是中国西南边陲一个多民族的山区省份，有着独特的自然风光，多彩的民族风情和丰富的自然资源，素有“植物王国”、“动物王国”和“有色金属王国”的美称。最近，通过中国，’99昆明世界园艺博览会，云南再次向世界展示了她神奇而灿烂的风采。

云南有16个地州市，共128个县（区市），总面积39.4万平方公里，人口4144万人，其中少数民族人口1486万人。

经过50年的经济建设，特别是1979年以来，云南人民坚定不移地推进改革，扩大开放，准确把握省情，探索出一条立足本省优势资源，发展特色经济之路，通过全省各族人民的努力奋斗，开创了建国以来经济发展的最好时期。到1998年国内生产总值达到1794亿元，同1952年相比，增长了28.7倍，年平均增长7.7%，人均国内生产总值达到4355元，比1978年增长4.8倍，年平均增长8.2%，社会消费品零售总额达500亿元，比1952年增长了102倍，全省财政收入也由1952年的1.87亿元增加到1998年的410亿元，实现了由中央净补贴到每年净上缴80多亿元的跨越。地方财政对国民经济的支撑能力大大增强。由于经济实力的增强和与世界各国的经济联系不断扩大，对外贸易和引进外资也得到快速增长。现在，云南同世界上100多个国家和地区建立了经贸关系，拥有进出口权的外贸、工贸公司、商贸公司、生产企业和科研单位已达128家。1998年全省进出口总额达20.35亿美元。到1998年，实际利用外资达2.98亿美元，1985-1998年累计签订对外承包工程、劳务合作合同359份，合同金额9.12亿美元。此外，近6年云南完成省际间各类联合协作项目6202项，引进省外到位资金78.49亿元。

二、加强基础设施建设，改善投资环境

改革开放以来，尤其是1991-1995年，为了改善云南的投资环境，坚持把基础设施建设放在经济社会发展的重要位置，集中财力进行重点建设，并取得了令人瞩目的成绩。全社会固定资产投资快速增长，1998年达到673亿元，年均增长19%，投资的重点是关系国计民生和经济发展后劲的建设项目。到1998年，全省共有水库5084座，公路通车里程7.7万公里，其中高等级公路1577公里，建成了以省会昆明为中心，幅射中心200公里范围的高等级公路网。完成了以省内6条干线公路为骨架，覆盖全省的公路网建设。除1949年之前建成的昆河铁路之外，又建成贵昆、成昆、南昆3条铁路通向省外，连结全国；省内新建了昆玉铁路、广大铁路，铁路营运里程达2310公里。新建和改扩建了9个机场，临沧机场正在抓紧建设。组建了云南航空公司，拥有大型客机21架，开辟了国际、国内航线98条。电力建设坚持水火并举，同步发展，发电装机容量达703万千瓦，成为全国能源供应最好的省份之一。通讯方面，全

省市内程控电话交换机容量已达到313万门，全部乡镇和98%的行政村通了电话，全省电话机普及率达到每百人有电话机6.1部。

1993年，在国务院的支持下，云南省与西南五省区六方联合在昆明举办了首届昆交会，到1998年已成功举办了六届，为世界了解云南，让云南走向世界创造了有利条件。

三、经济发展前景

到2010年云南经济和社会发展的目标是：到2000年，人均国内生产总值比1980年翻两番多，人民生活基本达到小康；到2010年，力争实现国内生产总值比2000年翻一番，农村居民生活全面达到小康，城镇居民生活在小康基础上更加富裕。改革的目标是：2000年前初步建立社会主义市场经济体制的框架；到2010年形成比较完善的市场经济体制。

四、云南省鼓励投资的重点领域

1. 基础设施建设

交通（公路、铁路、机场、桥梁）和能源的建设和管理。

2. 农业和生物资源开发

花卉、热带经济作物、天然香料、特种经济作物的种植、加工以及畜产品的开发等。

3. 旅游资源开发

旅游度假区和风景点的开发、建设以及配套的娱乐设施的建设。

4. 矿产资源开发

磷产品开发；黑色冶金工业及有色金属工业的开发；建材及非金属制品工业的开发。

5. 高新技术产业

一是现有高新技术的规模化和产业化；二是传统产业的高技术化；重点是机电、生物制药、食品、冶金、化工等行业。

6. 环保产业

主要是三废处理，城市卫生特种设备制造，生态环境整治，环境污染治理。

I. Achievements in Economic Development

Yunnan Province, located in mountainous southwestern China, is home to many of China's diverse national minorities. Featuring distinct scenic beauty, kaleidoscopic folk traditions, and rich natural resources, the province has gained renown as "The Realm of Plants," "The Kingdom of Wild Life" and "The Domain of Non-ferrous Metals." Its magic and wonder were revealed to the world during the '99 China International Horticulture Fair recently held in

云南石林
The Stone Forest in Yunnan

Kunming, the capital of Yunnan.

Comprising 16 cities and 128 towns, Yunnan covers an area of 394,000 square kilometers, with a population of 41.44 million, including 14.86 million people belonging to different national minorities.

After 50 years of economic progress, and especially since 1979, the Yunnan people have created their own style of building an innovative economy by unswervingly following the policy of reform and opening, based on local conditions. With the combined efforts of all its peoples, Yunnan is at present enjoying its best economic performance since the founding of the PRC. In 1998, its GDP reached 179.4 billion yuan, an increase of 28.7 times compared with 1952 and representing an annual growth rate of 7.7%. The per capita GDP reached 4,335 yuan, 4.8 times that of 1978, representing an annual growth rate of 8.2%. The total volume of retail sales reached 50 billion yuan, 102 times that of 1952. Fiscal revenue also grew from 187 million yuan in 1952 to 41 billion yuan in 1998. Yunnan turns over more than 8 billion yuan to the State every year, remarkable for a province to which the central government had to grant huge subsidies in the past. Its contribution to the national economy has been greatly promoted.

With strengthened economic capacity and expanded economic relations with other countries, Yunnan's foreign trade and foreign investment have also increased rapidly. It has established economic and trade relations with more than 100 countries and regions, and has granted import and export license rights to 128 companies, manufacturers or research institutes. In 1998, the total import and export value of the province was US$2.035 billion, and the foreign investment utilized amounted to US$298 million. From 1985 to 1998, altogether 359 foreign projects and labor service contracts were signed, with a total contract value of US$912 million. As well, in the past 6 years, a total of 6,206 interprovincial projects were accomplished, and investments totalling of 7.849 billion yuan were injected into the province.

II. A Strengthened Infrastructure Construction and an Improved Investment Environment

Ever since the introduction of the policy of reform and opening, particularly in the period 1991-1995, in order to improve Yunnan's investment environment, the provincial government has given priority to and concentrated financial resources on infrastructure construction for social and economic development. Remarkable achievements have been made so far in this regard. Investment in fixed assets involving projects giving priority to people's livelihood and national economic development has risen rapidly, with an annual growth rate of 19%, reaching 67.3 billion yuan in 1998. By that year, altogether 5,084 reservoirs had been constructed. Highways totaling 77,000 km cover the whole province with 6 trunk lines, including 1,577 km of high-quality highway with Kunming as the hub of a 200-km-wide network. In addition to the Kunhe Railway, built before 1949, three railway lines–the Guizhou-Kunming, Chengdu-Kunming and Kunming-Nanning lines–were built to connect Yunnan with other provinces, along with the newly constructed Kunyu and Guang-Da railways within the province. Thus, the total railway line length of the province reached 2,310 km. As for air transport, 9 airports have been constructed or expanded, and Lincang Airport is under construction. Yunnan Airlines has 21 planes, with 98 destinations. In the energy sector, the provincial government adheres to the harmonious development of thermopower and hydropower, making Yunnan one of the provinces with the best energy supply. In telecommunications, program-controlled switchboard capacity has risen to 3.13 million lines, with telephones available in all towns and 98% of all villages, averaging 6.1 telephones for every 100 people.

Supported by the State Council, the first Kunming Trade Fair was held in 1993, co-sponsored by Yunnan and 5 other provinces or autonomous regions in southwestern China. By 1998, altogether 6 fairs had been successfully held, helping the rest of the world get to know more about Kunming and helping Kunming open itself wider to the rest of the world.

III. Prospects for Growth

Yunnan's social and economic development target is to improve its people's living standards by quadrupling the 1980 per capita GNP by the year 2000, and further developing the people's livelihood by doubling the 2000 per capita GNP by the year 2010. The target of reform is to establish an initial framework for a socialist market economy before 2000 and to establish a mature market economic system by 2010.

IV. Priorities for Investment Decision-Making

1. Infrastructure Construction

Construction and management of transportation (highways, railways, airports and bridges) and energy.

2. Development of Agriculture and Bio-resources

The cultivation and processing of flowers, tropical cash crops, natural perfume and special economic crops, and the development of animal byproducts.

3. Development of Tourism Resources

The development and construction of tourism zones and scenic spots with facilities for recreation and entertainment.

4. Development of Mineral Resources

The development of phosphate products, ferrous metallurgy, non-ferrous metal industries, building materials and non-ferrous metal products manufacturing.

5. Hi-Tech Industry

To achieve large-scale industrialization of high technology and to enhance the hi-tech content of traditional industries, especially machinery, bio-pharmacy (bio-medicines), food, metallurgy and chemical industries.

6. Environmental Protection

The disposal of water, gas and solid wastes; the manufacture of special equipment for public health; ecological recovery and pollution control.

迈向 21 世纪的西藏

Tibet: Striding Forward into the New Millennium

一、经济发展情况

西藏是中国不可分割的一部分。勤劳、智慧的藏族人民是中华民族大家庭的重要成员。1965年9月1日，西藏自治区正式成立。全区现设拉萨市和昌都、山南、日喀则、那曲、阿里、林芝6个地区，有71个县、1个县级市和1个市辖区。首府设在拉萨市。全区面积120多万平方公里，约占全国总面积的1/8。西藏平均海拔在4000米以上。1998年底，全区总人口244万。其中藏族占总人口的95.4%，其它有汉族、门巴族、珞巴族、纳西族等。

1951年西藏和平解放以来，在以毛泽东、邓小平、江泽民为核心的中央三代领导集体的亲切关怀下，在全国各兄弟省、市、区的大力支援下，西藏的现代化建设取得了举世瞩目的成就，社会面貌发生了翻天覆地的变化。特别是1978年底中共十一届三中全会以来，西藏坚定不移地推进改革，扩大开放，开创了和平解放以来经济发展的最好时期，经济实力不断增强。1998年全区国内生产总值91.18亿元，比1978年增长4.4倍，年平均增长8.8%，其中第一、二、三产业增加值年平均分别增长5.1%、7.2%和14.8%；人均国内生产总值年平均增长6.9%。

改革开放20年间，是西藏自治区农牧业发展较快的时期，这一时期，自治区先后制定了一系列有利于农牧业和农牧区经济发展的重大政策和措施，实施科教兴农兴牧战略，使农牧区经济发展十分活跃，农副产品有效供给大幅度增加，进一步丰富了城乡居民的“米袋子”和“菜篮子”。粮食产量由1978年51万吨增加到1998年的85万吨，油菜籽由0.8万吨增加到3.4万吨，肉类产量由4.7万吨增加到12.9万吨，蔬菜和水果产量也有较大幅度的增长，1998年分别达到13.8吨和6300多吨。

和平解放以前，西藏基本没有现代工业。西藏的现代工业是从无到有、从小到大逐步壮大起来的。改革开放以来，自治区以市场为导向，以资源为依托，重点发展了采矿业、电力工业、建筑建材工业、以农畜产品加工为主的轻纺工业、民族手工业、食品工业和藏医药工业。尤其是在自治区成立30周年之际，由中央、各部委以及各省、市、区为西藏援建的62项工程中，有工业建设项目11个，这些工程的相继投产大大增强了西藏的工业生产能力。1998年，全区实现工业增加值9.02亿元，比1978年增长2.4倍。目前，一个以电力、采矿、建材、农畜产品加工和民族手工业为主的富有地方特色的工业体系基本形成。

固定资产投资规模扩大，基础设施建设成效显著。1978-1998年，全社会固定资产投资累计达261亿元，其中基本建设投资225多亿元。按照适度超前发展的方针，大力加强了关系经济社会发展全局的基础设施建设。这一时期，整治了青藏、川藏、新藏公路，扩建了贡嘎机场，改建邦达机场，修建羊湖抽水蓄能电站，拉萨电信枢纽大楼，拉萨分别至日喀则、林芝、江孜光缆等一批重点工程和“一江两河”（雅鲁藏布江、年楚河、拉萨河）农业综合开发等项目，使自治区投资环境和基本生产条件得到明显改善。特别是为庆祝自治区成立20周年和30周年，国家各部委和各省、市分别援建了43项和62项工程，投资分别达到4.81亿元和41.6亿元。这些项目的建设投产，为增强西藏经济发展后劲和改善人民生活发挥了重要作用。

改革开放20年来，是西藏城乡市场最为活跃，人民生活改善最为明显的时期。全区社会消费品零售总额由1978年的2.45亿元增加到1998年的34.99亿元，年平均增长14.2%。1998年，城镇居民人均可支配收入达到5438元，比1978年增长8.6倍；农牧民人均纯收入达到1158元，增长5.6倍，是西藏和平解放以来增长最快的时期。人们吃、穿、用、住、行等方面的消费水平有了很大提高，特别是高档耐用消费品的增加和居住条件的改善最为明显。城乡居民在物质生活提高的同时，文化生活也得到改善。

随着改革开放和经济的全面发展，对外经济贸易发展迅猛。1998年全区进出口贸易总额1.13亿美元，其中出口总额0.74亿美元，分别比1978年增长5.8倍和45倍。目前西藏有“三资”企业79家，企业经营良好。

二、投资环境

改革开放以来，尤其是1995年以后，自治区基础设施建设按照适度超前的发展方针，调整投资方向，大力加强关系经济社会发展全局的基础设施建设，通过多渠道筹集资金，加强了能源、交通、通信、市政等建设。大力发展第三产业，城镇设施日趋完善，投资环境明显改善。目前，全区基本建成了由公路、航空、管道等组成的交通运输网，公路通车里程已达 2.24 万公里；开通了北京、西安、成都、重庆、西宁等国内航线和加德满都国际航线。西藏电信事业发展迅速，目前全区 98% 的县以上行政建制所在地实现了卫星传输和电话程控化，并进入国内、国际长途自动交换网。到 1998 年底，全区金融机构有 581 家。全区有星级宾馆 14 家。

三、发展前景

近期目标：到 2000 年，在发展中理顺关系，调整结构，突出重点，稳定发展第一产业，有重点地发展第二产业，大力发展第三产业，适当超前发展基础设施建设，人均国内生产总值在 1980 年的基础上翻两番，基本完成脱贫任务，多数群众达到小康水平，国民经济和社会事业的整体水平有较大幅度提高，为下世纪初的更大发展奠定坚实基础。

远期发展目标：到 2010 年，在一、二、三产业稳定、协调发展，经济结构基本合理，经济增长方式显著改善的基础上，保持经济总量的快速增长，国内生产总值在 2000 年的基础上再翻一番，综合经济实力大大增强，人民生活逐步走向富裕。

四、鼓励投资的产业领域

1. 种植业、养殖业、林业用途的荒山、荒坡、荒滩开发；农田、菜地、果园、牧场的承租经营；农畜林产品加工；“高产、高效、优质”农业综合开发示范区；经济作物种植。

2. 工业用地开发：购买、租赁、承包经营全部或部分现有企业不动产；独资、合资、合作进行高新技术或一般工业产品生产加工。

3. 进行矿产资源勘探、开采、矿产品加工，中小型矿山租赁、承包。

4. 修建道路、桥梁、渡口等；经营汽车客货运输，开设修理厂、加油站等；合资、合作兴办民用航空运输企业（含直升机运输）及旅游包机、航空服务企业。

5. 利用水能、火力、地热、风能等资源进行各类电站建设。

6. 用于商、住、旅游的房地产开发和成片土地开发，物业经营，投资兴建或参与经营旅游饭店、餐馆、娱乐、健身、信息咨询、教育、卫生等领域的项目。

7. 鼓励客商利用中央赋予自治区的优惠政策和沿边地域优势，独资或联合建设边境贸易口岸设施，兴建出口生产基地或加工企业；试办合资商品零售业和合资外资企业（外贸企业嫁接外资）。

8. 兴办各类残疾人福利事业。

I. Economic Development

Tibet is an inseparable part of China. The industrious and intelligent Tibetan people are important members of the big family of the Chinese people. The Tibet Autonomous Region was established on September 1st, 1965. At present, the autonomous region has jurisdiction over Lhasa City, the prefectures of Changdu, Shannan, Rikaze, Naqu, Ali and Linahi, 71 counties, 1 county-grade city and 1 prefecture under the jurisdiction of the Lhasa municipal government. Lhasa is the capital of Tibet. The Autonomous Region has an area of over 1.2 million square kilometres, comprising approximately one-eighth of the country's total area. The average elevation of Tibet exceeds 4,000 meters. By the end of 1998, the total population of the autonomous region was 2.44 million, among whom the Tibetan ethnic group made up 95.4%. The other ethnic groups are Han, Hui, Monba, Lhoba, Naxi, etc.

Since the peaceful liberation of Tibet in 1951, with the kind attention of three leading collectives of the Central Government respectively headed by Mao Zedong, Deng Xiaoping and Jiang Zemin, and with the support of the other provinces, cities and prefectures of the country, Tibet has made remarkable achievements in the construction of modernisation. An earth-shaking change has taken place in the social setup. Especially since the Third Plenary Session of the Eleventh Central Committee of the Communist Party of China at the end of 1978, Tibet has unswervingly pushed ahead with reform and expanded its opening up, entering its best period for economic development since its peaceful liberation. In 1998, the GDP was RMB 9.118 billion, an increase of 4.4 times over 1978, with an average annual increase rate of 8.8%, of which the added value of the primary, secondary and tertiary industries had average annual increases of 5.1%, 7.2% and 14.8% respectively. The per capita GDP had an average annual increase of 6.9%.

In the 20 years since the adoption of the reform and opening-up policies, Tibet has experienced rapid development. The autonomous region has successively worked out a series of important policies and measures beneficial to farming and animal husbandry, through science and technology. The effective supply of farm produce and by-products has increased by a big margin, enriching the rice sacks and vegetable baskets of both urban and rural inhabitants. The grain yield increased from 510,000 tons in 1978 to 850,000 tons in 1998. The rapeseed yield increased from 8,000 tons to 34,000 tons. The meat output increased from 47,000 tons to129, 000 tons. The vegetable and fruit yields increased by a big margin to 13.8 tons and 6,300 tons, respectively, in 1998.

Prior to the peaceful liberation of Tibet in 1951, Tibet had no modern industries. The modern industries of Tibet grew out of nothing and expanded from small to large progressively. Since the adoption of the reform and opening-up policies, the autonomous region, oriented to markets and relying on its resources, has placed emphasis on the development of the mining industry, power industry, building materials industry, textile industry, local handicrafts industry, food industry and medicine industry. On the occasion of the 30th anniversary of the founding of the Tibet Autonomous Region, the central government, ministries and commissions, and various provinces, municipalities and prefectures assisted Tibet to construct 62 big projects, involving 11 industrial construction projects. These projects have gone into operation successively, greatly enhancing the industrial production capacity of Tibet. In 1998, the region realised industrial added value of RMB 902 million, an increase of 2.4 times over 1978. An industrial system full of distinctive local features has taken shape on the whole, mainly involving power, mining, building materials, processing of farming and livestock product and local handicrafts.

The investment scale in fixed assets was enlarged, and the effect of infrastructure construction was remarkable from 1978 to 1998. The accumulative investment in the social fixed assets amounted to RMB 26.1 billion, with infrastructure investment of RMB 22.5 billion. In accordance with the policy of developing moderately beyond the present stage, the Autonomous Region has made every effort to intensify its infrastructure construction, which has a bearing on the overall situation of social and economic development. During the same period, the Autonomous Region repaired the Qingzang Highway, Chuanzang Highway, and Xinzang Highway, extended Gongga Airport, rebuilt Bangda Airport, constructed Yanghu Hydroelectric

Station, Lhasa Telecommunications Building and laid electric cables from Lhasa to Rikaze, Linzhi and Jiangzi, and developed agriculture projects along the three Rivers (Yaluzangbu River, Nianchu River, and Lhasa River). These projects have improved the autonomous region's investment environment and basic production conditions. In order to celebrate the 20th and 30th anniversaries of the founding of the autonomous region, ministries and commissions under the State Council, and many provinces and cities helped to construct 43 and 62 projects, with investments of RMB 481 million and RMB 41.6 billion, respectively. The construction of these projects played an important role in the improvement of the Tibetan economy and the people's livelihood.

The last 20 years since the reform and opening-up started the period during which urban and rural markets of Tibet have been brisker than ever before and the people's livelihood has improved distinctly. The region's total volume of retail sales increased from RMB 245 million in 1978 to RMB 3.499 billion in 1998, with an average annual growth rate of 14.2%. In 1998, the per capita disposable income of urban dwellers amounted to 5,438 yuan, an increase of 8.6 times over 1978. The per capita net income of the peasants and herdsmen has reached 1,158 yuan, an increase of 5.8 times. People's consumption level in terms of food, clothing, dwelling and travelling has improved greatly, especially the obvious increase of high-grade durable consumer goods and the improvement of people's living conditions. The material lives of urban residents have improved as well as this cultural lives. With economic development during the reform and opening up, foreign trade has developed by leaps and bounds. In 1998, the region's total volume of imports and exports was US$ 113 million, with a total export value of US$ 47 million, an increase of 5.8 times and 45 times, respectively, compared with 1978. At present, Tibet has 79 joint-venture enterprises, which are all running well.

II. Investment Environment

Since the adoption of the reform and opening-up policies, and especially since 1995, in accordance with the policy of developing moderately beyond the present stage, the autonomous region has readjusted its investment orientation and made every effort to intensify its infrastructure construction which has a bearing on the overall situation of social and economic development. The region has intensified the construction of power, communications, telecommunications and municipal administration. It has devoted major efforts to developing tertiary industry. The urban infrastructure is becoming increasingly complete and the investment environment has been greatly improved. At present, the region has on the whole completed its communications and transportation network composed of highways, airlines and pipelines, with a highway mileage of 22,400 kilometres. Civil airlines routes to Beijing, Xi'an, Chengdu, Chongqing and Xining as well as an international route have been opened. Tibetan telecommunications have developed very quickly. At present, satellite transmission and program-controlled telephones have been achieved in 98% of the administrative location above the county-level. Three places have entered civil and international automatic exchange network. By the end of 1998, the region had 581 financial institutions and 14 star-grade hotels.

III. Development Prospects

The short-term objective is by the year 2000, to put all relations in order, readjust the structure, lay stress on the key points, develop primary industry steadily and secondary industry with focal points, devote major efforts to developing tertiary industry, promote infrastructure construction moderately beyond the current stage, quadruple the gross domestic product of 1980, accomplish the task of

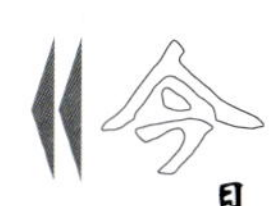

欢度旺果节
Tibetans in Celebration of the Wangguo Festival

basically shaking off poverty, enable the majority of the masses to enjoy fairly comfortable lives, and make the overall level of the national economy and social undertakings improve by a relatively big margin, which should lay a solid foundation for the next century's further development.

The long-term objective is, by the year 2010, on the basis of stable and coordinated growth in the primary, secondary and tertiary industries, to achieve a relatively rational economic structure and notable improvements in the mode of economic growth, to double the GDP of the year 2000, and to enhance overall economic strength and enable the people to become progressively well-off.

IV. Key Areas in Which Foreign Investment Is Encouraged

1. The exploitation of barren mountains, mountain slopes and flood plains for planting, aquaculture and forestry; leasing and management of farmland, vegetable plots, orchards and grazing land; processing of farming, animal husbandry and forestry products, exemplary zones for the overall development of high-yield, efficient and high-quality agriculture; planting of cash crops.

2. Exploiting lands for the use of industry; occupancy, purchase, lease, management under contract of all or partial real estate of the existing enterprises; conducting and processing of high-tech or ordinary industrial products by way of individual proprietorship, joint venture cooperation.

3. Undertaking exploration and development of mineral resources processing of mineral products, leasing under contract of small mines.

4. Constructing roads, bridges and ferries, etc.; managing passenger and freight transportation businesses; running garages and filling stations, etc.; initiating civil aviation transport enterprises (involving helicopter transport), chartered sightseeing airplanes and air service enterprises.

5. Undertaking the construction of all kinds of power stations by exploiting hydropower, thermal power, geothermal energy, wind energy and other sources.

6. Development and property management of real estate and vast stretches of land for commercial, dwelling and

tourism uses; investing in the construction or participating in the management of hotels, restaurants, entertainment centers, sports clubs, information consultation, education, sanitation and other fields.

7. Taking advantage of favourable policies offered to the autonomous region by the central government and the frontier trading ports; constructing production bases for export or processing enterprises; running pilot trading enterprises.

8. Initiating all kinds of welfare projects for the disabled.

迈向新世纪的陕西

Shaanxi: Striding Forward into the 21st Century

一、经济发展情况

陕西省地处中国内陆腹地，东起连云港，西至荷兰鹿特丹，跨亚欧的国际经济大通道“新亚欧大陆桥”横贯陕西中部。陕西地域狭长，北部是陕北高原，中部是关中平原，南部是秦巴山区。现辖7个省辖市，3个地区，107个县、市、区。全省总面积20.58万平方公里，人口3596万。省会西安人口675万，面积10108平方公里。陕西矿产资源蕴藏丰富，目前探明储量的有91种。储量居全国前10位的56种。矿产资源保有储量潜在总值8万多亿元，居全国第4位；平均每平方公里拥有资源潜值4千多万元，居全国第2位。

陕西是中西部农业比较发达的省份，农业产业化初具规模，已建成粮棉油、果品、奶山羊、商品瘦肉型猪、秦川牛、烤烟基地143个。陕西工业门类众多、基础雄厚，拥有相当规模和水平。机械、电子、能源、化工、医药、食品为全省的六大优势产业。飞机、高压输变电设备、工程机械、新型材料、家用电器、计算机、通信设备、医药化工等一批骨干产品在全国具有较强的竞争力。陕西是全国重要的教育基地，现有普通高校42所，在校本、专科学生15.1万人。科研力量雄厚，现有科研院所1066个，拥有各类专业技术人员81.5万。陕西是中华民族及华夏文化的重要发祥地，中国历史上先后有14个王朝在此建都，人文资源丰富，被誉为天然历史博物馆。秦始皇陵及被誉为世界第八大奇迹的秦兵马俑，被联合国科教文组织列入世界文化遗产清单。改革开放20年来，全省国际游客接待量年均递增20.2%，累计接待国际游客579万人次。

新中国成立50年来，陕西省的面貌发生了巨大的变化。特别是1978年底中共十一届三中全会以来，陕西省坚定不移地推动改革，扩大开放，开创了建国以来经济发展的最好时期。1998年国内生产总值达到1381.53亿元，比1978年增长5倍，年均增长9.4%；人均国内生产总值3834元，增长3.8倍，年均增长8.1%。国民经济综合实力大大增强。外向型经济发展取得了可喜的成绩。1998年全省新批准利用外资项目216个，实际利用外资6.78亿美元。从1983年陕西诞生第一家外资企业到1998年，累计批准利用外资项目3146个，实际利用外资额42.75亿美元。1998年利用外资额比1985年增长14.2倍，年均增长20.9%。外商投资的领域已涉及到农业、采掘业、加工业、公路交通、邮电通信及餐饮、娱乐、文化、教育、科研、信息咨询等各个行业。目前省内有外资企业2814家，企业经营状况良好。1998年全省进出口总额20.5亿美元，是1985年的20倍。出口产品遍及130个国家和地区，机电、轻纺、煤炭、技术出口占到出口总额的90%。

二、投资环境

改革开放20年来，尤其是进入90年代后，陕西多方位筹措资金，加强基础设施和基础产业建设，大力发展第三产业，使全省交通、能源、市政建设等均发生了巨大变化，餐饮服务业网点星罗棋布，旅游车队、购物中心、娱乐中心都有相当规模。陕西交通已形成以西安为中心，铁路、公路、民航相衔接的立体交通网络。现有13条铁路干支线，通车里程达2867公里。西安火车站及其12个编组站构成西北最大的铁路交通枢纽，陇海线、宝成线、襄渝线、宝中线分别连接西北、西南和华东。西安至安康、延安到神木的铁路正在加紧建设，西安至南京铁路、神木到黄骅和宝成复线亦即将动工。这些工程将会大大增强陕西与长江三角洲经济发达地区的经济交往。省境内等级公路累计通车里程42202公里，公路密度为每百平方公里20.53公里，"米"字型公路主骨架初具规模。高等级公路建设速度加快，已通车里程340公里，到2000年可达600公里。全省实现了乡乡通公路，行政村通路率达到94%。西安航空港咸阳机场是西北最大的空中交通枢纽，已开通国内航线107条、地区航线和国际航线6条，通航城市53个。咸阳机场扩建工程已列入国家重点基础设施项目，即将开工。全省电话网交换机总容量319.7万门，总用户181.9万户；移动电话和无线寻呼用户分别达到30.73万户和74.27万户；一、二级光缆总长度达2460公里，另有4条国家一级光缆干线全面加紧建设。国际长途电话可直拨235个国家和地区。陕西是西北地区的金融中

西安兵马俑
The Terra Cotta Warriors and Horses of Qin in Xi'an

心，到1998年底，全省共有金融机构1万多个。陕西现有旅游涉外宾馆饭店98家，客房1.7万间，其中五星级宾馆4家，四星级宾馆5家。

三、发展前景

基础设施建设方面，陕西计划三年内筹集1500亿元资金，建设96个涉及农林水利、交通、通信、城市基础设施、粮库、经济适用房等一批大的基础设施项目。到下世纪初，全省将形成两纵六横、贯通南北、直达沿海的铁路大通道和辐射四面八方的“米”字型公路骨架。

区域经济发展方面，集中力量建设西安经济中心，关中高新技术产业开发带、陕北能源重化工产业开发带，陕南水力、矿产、生物资源开发带。

培植六大新的经济增长点。从省情实际出发，瞄准下世纪的消费热点，调整产品结构，重点培育电子信息产业、旅游业、非公有制经济、住宅产业、环保产业、小城镇建设等六大新的经济增长点。重点建设家用电器、计算机及显示终端、通信产品、新型元器件、军转民电子产品等五个生产基地。在西安兴建具有相当规模的软业园区。精心开发秦陵石质铠甲坑、铜车马坑和汉阳陵从葬坑群，逐步形成世界一流的周、秦、汉、唐大型文化旅游区，实现旅游名省目标。使非公有制经济在增长速度、产业升级和经营规模上有一个大的突破，非公有制经济在国内生产总值中的比重由18%提高到30%以上。建立以经济适用房为主体的多层次住房供应体系。加快小城镇建设，使全省城市化水平2000年达到30%。

四、鼓励投资的重点领域

1. 基础设施项目。道路、桥梁、隧道、铁路、地铁、电厂、水利等大型基础设施建设。城市建设、城市供气、供热、供水、房地产开发、污水处理、环境保护等市政基础设施项目。

2. 资源性开发项目。煤炭、石油、天然气和金属、非金属矿产综合开发利用、深加工项目、原材料生产项目。

3. 农业项目。优质粮棉油菜果等新品种开发、保鲜、加工、新技术推广应用，畜禽鱼优良品种的引进、养殖和加工，高产优质高效农业项目开发。

4. 现有企业的技术改造。对国有企业进行嫁接改造，提高技术水平、生产规模和经济效益，扩大出口创汇。

5. 文物、旅游资源的开发建设。重点开发周、秦、汉、唐四个文化旅游区，兴建娱乐设施，更新旅游设备，开发旅游产品等。

6. 新兴产业开发区的建设。鼓励兴办集约化农业技术、电子信息技术、新材料技术、先进制造技术、能源及高效节能技术、生物技术等新兴产业。

I. Economic Development

Shaanxi Province is located in the hinterland of China, through the middle part of which runs the New Eurasian Bridg–an international economic thoroughfare, spanning Asia and Europe from Lianyungang in the east to Rotterdam in the west. Shaanxi is long and narrow in territory, with the Shanbei Plain in the north, Guanzhong Plain in the middle, and Qinba Mountains in the south. At present, Shaanxi has jurisdiction over seven municipalities, three prefectures, and 107 counties, cities and districts. The province has a total area of 205,800 square kilometres and a population of 35.96 million. The population of the provincial capital Xiían is 6.75 million and the area is 10,108 square kilometres. Shaanxi is rich in mineral resources. So far, 91 minerals have been discovered there with proved reserves,

56 of them in the first ten places in reserves in the country. The total potential value of the mineral resources is over RMB 800 billion, taking fourth place in the country; the average potential value of the mineral resources per square kilometre is over RMB 40 million, holding second place in the country. Shaanxi has developed agriculture and the industrialisation of agriculture has begun to take shape. The province has set up 143 bases for grain, cotton, oil, fruit, goats, lean-meat pigs, Qinchuan cows and flue-cured tobacco. A large variety of industrial departments in Shaanxi are of tremendous strength and considerable scale and levels. Machinery, electronics, power, chemicals, medicines and food staffs are the six pillar industries of the province. Airplanes, equipment for high-tension electricity transmission and transformation, engineering machinery, new materials, household appliances, computers, equipment for telecommunications, medicine, chemicals and other backbone products possess relatively strong competitive ability in the country. Shaanxi is an important educational base, with forty-two institutions of higher learning and 151,000 university and college undergraduates. With 1,066 scientific research institutions and 815,000 technical personnel, Shaanxi is of great importance for scientific research. Shaanxi is the birthplace of the Chinese people and China's ancient culture, and the capitals of 14 dynasties were set up here. The tomb of Emperor Qinshihuang and the Qin Dynasty's clay tomb figures of warriors and horses which are called "the eighth wonder of the world", are listed as part of the world cultural heritage by the United Nations Educational Scientific and Cultural Organisation. Since the start of reform and opening up, the province has received 5.79 million foreign tourist visits, an average annual increase of 20.2%.

In the 50 years since the founding of the People's Republic of China, an earth-shaking change has taken place in the appearance of Shaanxi Province. Especially since the Third Plenary Session of the Eleventh Central Committee of the Communist Party of China at the end of 1978, Shaanxi has unswervingly promoted its reform and opened wider to the outside world, pioneering its best period since 1949 for economic development. In 1998, the GDP of the province came to RMB 138.153 billion, an increase of 5 times compared with 1978, with an average annual increase of 9.4%; per capita GDP was RMB 3,834, an increase of 3.8 times over 1978, with an average annual increase of 8.1%. The overall economic strength was greatly enhanced. Gratifying achievements were made in the development of the export-oriented economy. In 1998, the province newly approved 216 foreign-funded projects, with utilised foreign investment of US$678 million. Since 1983, when the first foreign-funded enterprise in Shaanxi appeared, 3,146 foreign-funded projects have been approved, with practical utilised foreign investment of US$ 4.275 billion. Foreign investment utilised in 1998 increased by 14.2 times over 1985, with an average annual increase of 20.9%. The foreign investment was in agriculture, excavation, processing, communications, posts and telecommunications, food and drinks, entertainment, culture, education, scientific research, information consultation, and so on. At present, the province has 2,814 foreign-funded enterprises, all of which are operating well. The total volume of imports and exports of the province in 1998 was US$ 2.05 billion-worth, twenty times that of 1985. The products were exported to over 130 countries and regions. The export of mechanical and electrical products, textile products, coal and technology constitutes 90% of the total export volume.

II. Investment Environment

In the 20 years since the adoption of the reform and opening-up policies, and especially since the beginning of the 1990s, Shaanxi has raised funds through many channels and intensified the construction of infrastructure and basic industries, which brought great changes in communications, power and municipal construction. The province has made

"飞豹"机群
"Flying Panther" Fighters

great efforts to develop its tertiary industry. Commercial and catering networks are scattered all over the province. A three-dimensional communications network has taken shape, centering on Xi'an and linked by railways, highways and airlines. At present, the province has 13 arterial and feeder railways totalling 2,867 kilometres. The Xi'an railway station and its 12 marshaling stations compose the biggest hub of railway communications in the northwest. The Longhai, Baocheng, Xiangyu and Baozhong lines connect it with the Northwest, Southwest and East China, respectively. Railways lines from Xi'an to Ankang and from Yan'an to Shenmu are now under construction. The Xi'an to Nanjing and Shenmu to Huanghua and Baocheng double-track railway lines will be constructed soon. These projects will greatly promote the economic ties between Shaanxi and the developed regions of the Yangtze delta. The highways within the province total 42,202 kilometres. The density of highways is 20.53 kilometres for every 100 square kilometres. A radial highway framework has taken shape, and the construction of high-grade highways has been accelerated, with 340 kilometres of highways opened to traffic, which will be increased to 600 kilometres by 2000. Highways extend to every town in the province and 94% of administrative villages have highways passing through. The Xi'an air harbor and Xianyang airports are the biggest pivots of air communications in the northwest, with 107 civil air routes and local and international flights connect Xi'an with 53 cities. The extension project of Xianyang airport has been listed as a national key project of infrastructure construction. The total capacity of telephone switchboards of the province is 3.197 million sets, with telephone subscribers numbering 1.819 million households; The number of mobile phone and radio subscribers reaches 307,300 and 742,700 households respectively. The total length of the first-grade and second-grade optical cables amounts to 2,460 kilometres. Besides, another 4 national first-grade optical cables are under construction. One can dial to 235 countries and regions by international long-distance phone. Shaanxi is the financial centre of the northwest China with altogether over 10,000 financial setups all over the province. At present, Shaanxi has 98 foreign hotels with 17,000 guest rooms, among which there are 4 five-star hotels and 5 four-star hotels.

III. Developing Perspective

In the aspect of infrastructure construction, Shaanxi proposes to raise RMB 150 billion within 3 years to construct 96 infrastructure projects involving agriculture, forestry, water conservancy, communications, telecommunications, urban infrastructure, grain depots, economic houses and so on. By the beginning of the next century, a railway thoroughfare leading directly to the coast and composed of two north-south and six west-east railway lines and a radial highway framework will take shape.

In the aspect of regional economic development, the province will concentrate its efforts on the construction of "one centre and three development zones", i.e Xi'an economic centre, Guanzhong high-tech industry development zone, Shanbei power and heavy chemical industry development zone and Shannan hydraulic power, mineral and biological resources development zone.

The province will, proceeding from its practical situation and aiming at next century's hot consumption points, readjust its industrial structure and foster six new economic growth points, namely electronic information industry, tourism, non-public owned economy, housing construction, environmental protection, and construction of towns. The province will focus on the construction of five manufacturing bases of household appliances, computers, screen terminals, telecommunications products, new devices and electronic products. The province will construct a software spark in Xi'an, which shall be of considerable scale. In addition, Shaanxi will boost its tourism industry. The non-public ownership economy will see a big breakthrough in growth speed, industrial escalation and operating scale. The participation of the non-public ownership economy in the gross domestic product will increase from 18% to 30%. The province shall set up a multi-level housing-supply system laying stress on supplying economical houses. Shaanxi will accelerate the construction of towns, enabling the urbanization level of the province to reach 30 % by the year 2000.

IV. Key Areas in Which Foreign Investment Is Encouraged

1. Infrastructure projects. Foreign funds are encouraged in the construction of roads, bridges, tunnels, railways, subways, power plants, water conservancy and urban construction, gas supply, heating supply, water supply, real estate development, sewage disposal, and environmental protection.

2. Projects of resource exploitation, as well as exploitation, utilisation and processing projects and raw material production projects of coal, petroleum, natural gas, metals and non-metals.

3. Agricultural projects. The development, fresh-keeping, processing, spread and application of new technology of high-quality new strains of grain, cotton, oil, vegetables and fruits; introduction, breeding and processing of high-quality breeds of domestic animals, fowls and fish; development projects of high-yield, high-quality and efficient agriculture.

4. Technical innovation of existing enterprises. Foreign

funds are encouraged to be invested to graft and innovate state-owned enterprises, promoting their technical level, production scale and economic efficiency, and enlarging the export of their products.

5. The exploitation and construction of cultural relics and tourist resources. Stress will be put on developing four tourist zones of Zhou, Qin, Han and Tang Dynasty's culture, constructing entertainment facilities, renewing tourist facilities and developing tourism products.

6. The construction of development zones for new and expanding industries. Funds are encouraged to be invested to initiate information, new materials, advanced manufacturing technology, power, power-economising technology, and biological technology projects.

中国西部明珠——甘肃

Gansu: A Gem in West China

一、经济发展情况

甘肃省地处黄河上游，是中华民族和中国古文化的发祥地之一，闻名中外的古丝绸之路和新亚欧大陆桥横贯全境。全省土地面积45.4万平方公里，有汉、回、藏、蒙等45个民族，共2500万人，现设14个地、市、州，下辖87个县、市、区，省会兰州市是全省政治、经济、文化教育中心，现有人口280万人，也是中国西北第二大城市。甘肃拥有丰富的土地资源、矿产资源、水力资源、生物资源和文化旅游资源，开发潜力巨大。甘肃工业综合实力居全国第23位，已逐步形成了以电力、有色冶金、石油化工、机械电子、建材、轻纺等为主的较为完整的工业体系，并成为中国重要的能源、原材料工业基地。

建国50年来，甘肃经济得到迅速发展，国内生产总值由1952年的13.32亿元猛增到1998年的869.75亿元，年均递增7.22%，"八五"计划（1991-1995年）提前一年完成，并于1996年提前4年实现了翻两番的第二步战略目标；人均国内生产总值由1952年的125元猛增到1998年的3456元，年均递增5.2%；农业生产条件不断改善，生产能力大幅度提高，1998年农、林、牧、渔业总产值达335.8亿元，是1952年的6.38倍，年均递增4.44%；工业生产高速增长，1998年完成工业总产值1081.4亿元，按可比价格计算，是1952年的216倍，年均递增12.41%；消费品市场繁荣稳定，1998年实现社会消费品零售总额303.7亿元，是1949年的204倍，年均递增11.47%；对外开放成绩显著，1998年接待海外旅游者12.24万人次，旅游外汇收入达3018万美元，截止1998年底，全省共有外资企业840家，实际利用外资14.57亿美元，全省对外贸易出口实现40.33亿美元，年均增长24.67%。

二、投资环境

为了扩大对外开放，加快实施开放带动战略，甘肃省始终把改善投资环境作为重要环节来抓。全省的交通、通迅设施日趋完善，以兰州为中心的全省交通、通信网络已经形成，客观上已成为西北地区的交通通信枢纽，中川机场辟有通

兰州
Lanzhou

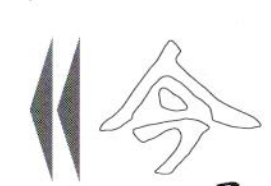

往全国主要城市的二十多条航线，312等四条国道穿境而过，陇海、兰新、包兰、兰青四大铁路干线交汇于此，形成了一个四通八达的立体交通网络。近几年，省内主要公路、铁路干线普遍得到了更新改造，开通了直飞香港的旅游包机，对敦煌机场进行了维修，中川机场跑道工程的改扩建已正式竣工投入使用，西兰乌、京呼银兰、西拉乌通信光缆和兰州电信枢纽工程已相继建成并投入使用，全省各地都可以直拨国内、国际电话；省内主要大中城市都普遍对基础设施进行了改造，城市交通、供电和供水状况有了较大改善；自建设兰州商贸中心以来，甘肃市场建设步伐大大加快，商品市场和生产资料市场体系初具规模，现已在工商管理部门登记注册的各类商品交易市场1819个，总成交额达318.57亿元；全省现有旅游涉外星级宾馆、饭店43个，国际国内旅行社79家。甘肃在改善软环境方面制定了一系列吸引外商投资的优惠政策，并在改进服务质量上狠下功夫，建立健全了外商投资企业投诉受理中心、法律咨询中心、争议调解中心以及外商投资企业协会，尽力为外商提供方便、快捷、满意的服务；以“兰交会”为载体，扩大对外宣传，加强与世界各国的外经贸往来，积极开展招商活动；先后开放了马鬃山口岸、中川机场航空口岸和兰州铁路货运口岸，成立了兰州海关和边防检查、商品检验、动植物检疫、卫生检疫机构，为甘肃的对外经贸活动提供便利；甘肃拥有较强的科研力量，截止1998年末，全省拥有科技活动单位671个，从事科技活动人员6.9万人，共取得科研成果986项。

三、甘肃的发展前景

近期发展目标：“九五”（1996-2000年）的后两年，经济发展略高于全国平均水平，人口增长略低于全国平均水平，到2000年实现人均国内生产总值比1980年翻两番；财政收入要与国内生产总值同步增长，努力建立稳固、平衡、有后劲的甘肃财政；形成能够参与国内外市场竞争的更大经济规模和实力，建成社会主义市场经济体制的基本框架，保持物价基本稳定；全省城乡居民收入显著提高，多数达到小康生活水平，为实现2010年远景目标打下坚实的基础。

远期发展目标：2010年实现国内生产总值比2000年翻一番，人口控制在2780万以内，全省范围内达到小康，向比较完善的社会主义市场经济体制过渡，社会主义精神文明和民主法制建设取得明显进展，社会生产力，综合经济实力，人民生活水平再上一个大台阶，为下世纪中叶实现第三步战略目标，基本实现现代化，开创新的局面。

四、甘肃鼓励投资的重点领域

对外开放是邓小平理论的重要组成部分，是一项长期不变的基本国策，也是甘肃省加快经济发展，推进实现现代化进程的重要途径。甘肃人民热忱欢迎海内外各界人士前来观光旅游，投资兴业，开展经济、科技、文化等方面的交流合作。今后甘肃省鼓励外商投资的重点领域是“二高一优”（高产、高效、优质）农业开发与农业产业化项目；布局合理的能源、交通及其他城市基础设施项目；短缺的原材料工业项目；引进先进技术，节能降耗，提高产品质量、增加花色品种，具有出口潜力的深度加工工业项目；能替代进口的机电产品项目和装备工业项目；资源开发与综合利用的项目；环保产品及环保装备制造项目；具有国际先进技术管理水平和典型示范作用的第三产业项目。

I. Economic Development

Gansu, located at the upper reaches of the Yellow

River, is one of the birthplaces of China's ancient culture and the Chinese nation. The world-renowned Old Silk Road and the new Eurasian Bridge travels the whole province.

Covering an area of 454,000 square km, Gansu is home to 45 nationalities including Han, Hui, Tibet and Mongolian, with a total population of 25 million. The province has jurisdiction over 14 prefectures, cities and autonomous prefectures, including 87 counties, cities and districts. Lanzhou, capital of the province, is the province's political, economic, cultural and educational center, with a population of 2.8 million. It is also the second largest city in northwest China.

Blessed with abundant land, mineral, hydrological, biological and cultural as well as tourist resources, the province has a huge potential to be developed. Its comprehensive economic strength now holds the 23rd position in the country, gradually forming a complete industrial system centered on the power, nonferrous metal, metallurgy, petrochemical, machinery and electronics, building materials, light and textile industries. Meanwhile, it has become an important industrial source of energy resources and raw materials in the country.

For five decades since the founding of the People's Republic of China, the province has made great headway in economic development. Its GDP soared to 86.975 billion yuan in 1998 from 1.332 billion yuan in 1952, which represents an annual average increase of 7.22 percent.

This figure shows that the province has accomplished the Eighth Five-Year Plan (1991-1995) one year ahead of schedule, and has also realized the strategic target of quadruple designated as the second step four years ahead of time in 1996. The per-capita GDP rapidly increased from 125 yuan in 1952 to 3,456 yuan in 1998, an annual average rise of 5.2 percent.

Besides, farming conditions have improved continuously, with its production capacity significantly increasing. In 1998, the total output value in agriculture, forestry, animal husbandry and fishery amounted to 33.58 billion yuan, 6.38 times more than 1952, representing an annual average rise of 4.44 percent.

The province has witnessed a rapid growth in industrial production. Its industrial output value was 108.14 billion yuan in 1998, 216 times more than 1952 or an annual average growth of 12.41 percent calculated according to the fixed price.

With a stable prosperity in the market of consumption goods, the total volume of retail sales in 1998 was 30.37 billion yuan, 204 times more than 1949, representing an annual increase of 11.47 percent.

A remarkable achievement has been made in the opening-up policy. The province received 122,400 tourists from home and abroad in 1998, earning foreign exchange income totaling US$30.18 million. By the end of 1998, the number of foreign-funded enterprises reached 840 throughout the province, with actual paid-in foreign capitals amounting to US$1.457 billion. The volume of exports in foreign trade for the province totaled US$4.033 billion, an annual average growth of 24.67 percent.

II. An Environment Suitable for Investment

In order to expand the scope of opening up and expedite the implementation of a strategy of pushing forward the social and economic development driven by reform, the province has always made the improvement of investment environment a priority. As a result, the infrastructure facilities of communications and telecommunications throughout the province have improved on a daily basis.

For example, the province's communications and telecommunications network centered in Lanzhou has now been formed, becoming a communications and telecommunications hub in northwestern areas. Zhongchuan Airport is open to more than 20 airlines leading to major cities of the

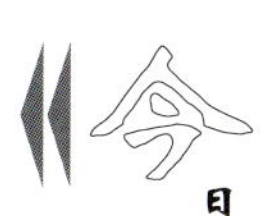

country, along with four national highways crossing the province. The four railway trunk lines—Lianyungang-Qinghai, Lanzhou-Xinjiang, Baotou-Lanzhou and Lanzhou-Qinghai— are converged here, forming a transport network extending in all directions.

In recent years, some major highways and railway lines across the province have been renovated, while at the same time chartered tourist planes flying directly to Hong Kong have been introduced. Moreover, Dunhuang Airport has taken a new look now since its facelift, the newly renovated runway of Zhongchuan Airport has been put into operation in the wake of its completion of the renovation.

Moreover, the province has witnessed some communication optical cable projects completed in some areas, along with the accomplishment of the Lanzhou telecommunications project. They have been put into use one after another. In addition, international and domestic direct dial telephones have been introduced in the province's various areas and technical renovations have been conducted in the infrastructure facilities in different major cities. As a result, the condition in the fields of urban communications and the power and water supply have been greatly improved.

Since the Lanzhou Commerce and Trade Center was set up, the local authority has redoubled its effort to accelerate the pace of market establishment, with the result that the commodities market and means of production are taking shape.

At present, the number of various markets to conduct commodities exchanges that registered in certain management departments of industry and commerce amounted to 1,819, with transaction volume amounting to 31.857 billion yuan. To date, there are 43 tourist star-rated hotels and restaurants funded by overseas capitals, as well as 79 international and domestic travel services.

The local provincial government has formulated a series of preferential policies in the areas of improving a soft environment aiming to attract overseas investment, in conjunction with more efforts to improve the quality of services.

Meanwhile, it has strengthened the management systems, including the establishment of foreign-funded enterprises' complaint center, the legal consultant center, the dispute mediating center, and the association of foreign-funded enterprises. These efforts have made it possible to provide overseas business people with convenient, quick and comfortable services.

Based on the Lanzhou Commodities Fair, the local authorities have enthusiastically expanded their influence to the outside world, seizing the opportunity to enhance the contacts with the world counterparts in business and trade areas and to actively conduct activities of introducing overseas business people.

In addition, the Mazongshan Port, along with the Aviation Port of the Zhongchuan Airport and the Lanzhou Railway Freight Transport Port were opened in the province. At the same time, the Lanzhou Customs, frontier inspection, commodities inspection, animals and plants quarantine agency, and hygiene quarantine have been established. This has provided a convenient environment for the local foreign trade activities.

Now, the province has a powerful scientific and technological force. By the end of 1998, it had 69,000 technicians in 671 scientific and technological institutions, with 986 scientific and technological achievements accomplished.

III. Development Prospects for Gansu

The short-term targets for development are: During the last two years for the Ninth Five-Year Plan (1996-2000), the level of economic development is somewhat higher than the country's average level, while the population growth lower than the nation's average level.

By 2000, the local average per-capita GDP will be quadruple that of 1980; financial revenue will increase accompanying the GDP growth simultaneously in an effort to establish a steady and balanced revenue system with potential.

More efforts will be dedicated to forming a strong economy with a larger scope in a bid to participate in the market competition at home and abroad, in conjunction with establishing a basic framework pertinent to the socialist market economy while basically maintaining the stability of the price.

In the meantime, the income for urban and rural residents throughout the province will be obviously promoted so as to improve people's standard of living, and pave the way for realizing the long-term target in 2010.

The long-term targets for development are: By 2010, the GDP will be double that of 2000, while the population will be controlled within the scope of 27.80 million. The people's living standard throughout the province is expected to significantly improve so as to accomplish the transition toward a more perfect socialist market economy.

Meanwhile, there will be remarkable achievements made in promoting cultural and ideological progress and building the democratic legal system. The social productive forces, comprehensive economic strength and the people's living standard will also be raised to a higher level which will create a new situation for realizing the third strategic target relating to basically fulfilling the modernization.

IV. Major Areas for Investment

The initiation of reform and opening-up policy, an important part of Deng Xiaoping Theory, is not only a long-term state policy that is unchangeable, but also an important way available for accelerating the local economic development while pushing forward the process of modernization.

Anyway, the local people warmly welcome people from all over the world to Gansu for sightseeing, investment, cooperation and exchange in the economic, scientific and technological and cultural fields.

Moreover, overseas investors are encouraged by the local government to invest in following main areas:

— Projects of high-yield, high-efficiency, top-quality agricultural development and industrialized projects featured by agriculture;

— Projects of energy and communications with rational structure and other infrastructure facilities in urban areas;

— Projects of raw materials industry in short supply;

— Projects of the deep-processing industry with export potential that require the introduction of advanced technology aiming to save energy, promote the quality of products as well as to increase the product's varieties;

— Projects of machinery and electronic products capable of displacing the imported products and projects of equipment industry;

— Projects of resource development and of comprehensive utilization;

— Projects of environmental protection products and equipment manufacturing for environmental protection;

— Projects of the tertiary industry with the international state-of-the-art management technology and with the typical demonstration role.

今日青海

Qinghai Today

一、经济与社会发展基本状况

青海省位于中国西北部，地处“世界屋脊”青藏高原的东北部，总面积72万多平方公里，平均海拔3000米以上。与甘肃、四川、西藏、新疆毗邻，是内地连接西藏、新疆的纽带。青海是中国四大牧区之一，拥有五亿亩草场。青海省内山脉纵横，湖泊众多。有祁连山、昆仑山、阿尔金山、巴颜喀拉山、唐古拉山等山脉。闻名世界的长江、黄河、澜沧江（即湄公河）均发源于青海，因此，青海又被称为“江河源头”。举世闻名的佛教胜地塔尔寺和青海湖也在省内。

青海地大物博，是中国的资源大省之一。水能总储量2000万千瓦以上。探明有储量的矿产105种，矿产保有储量在全国占前十位的矿种多达50种。其中锂矿、冶金用石英岩、芒硝、盐矿、钾盐、镁盐、石棉、锶矿等11种居全国首位。

青海省现设有1个省辖市、1个行政公署、6个民族自治州。州、地、市下设有46个县级行政单位。总人口502.80万，其中少数民族人口215.00万，占全省总人口的42.8%。在少数民族人口中，藏族占20.8%，回族占14.52%，土族占3.76%，撒拉族占1.73%，蒙古族占1.67%。

新中国成立50年来，青海的面貌发生了翻天覆地的变化，特别是改革开放20年来，国民经济和社会事业迅速发展。1998年，全省国内生产总值220.43亿元，比1949年增长40.9倍，年平均增长7.92%，人均国内生产总值4372元，年平均增长5.32%。工业生产飞速发展，1998年全省工业总产值已达122.00亿元（1990年不变价），比1949年增长367.65倍，平均每年增长12.82%。1998年，全省社会消费品零售额70.60亿元，是1949年的202.46倍，是1978年的8.21倍。1998年全省对外贸易进出口总额11405万美元，比1978年增长154.06倍。协议外商直接投资额7584万美，比上年增长43.5%，外商投资企业出口额342万美元，增长77.2%。1998年末全省自然科学与社会科学工作者队伍已达11万多人。现全省共有包括中国科学院青海盐湖研究所和西北高原生物研究所在内的各类科研机构53个，各类专业科技人员0.25万人。1978-1998年全省共取得1416项重要科技成果，获国家级奖励662项，省部级奖励670项，科技进步对经济增长的贡献率已由80年代的29.31%提高到41.56%。教育事业迅速发展，国民文化素质显著提高，基础教育和民族教育得到加强，职业教育、成人教育发展较快，高等教育有了新发展。全省适龄儿童入学率由1965年的73.07%提高到1998年的92.1%，1998年末，全省共有大中小学校3955所（不含农业中学和职高），在校学生70.33万人。其中大中专院校41所，在校学生2.17万人。卫生体育事业蓬勃发展，人民群众的健康水平显著提高。人均期望寿命由1982年的60.79岁提高到1990年的65.60岁。城乡居民收入逐年增加，生活水平明显提高。1998年，全省农牧民人均纯收入1426元，比1980年增长1.45倍，年平均增长5.10%；1998年城镇居民人均生活费收入3891.40元，比1985年增长37.45%，年均增长2.48%。坚持可持续发展战略，环境保护力度增大。1998年全省共有环境监测站15个，自然保护区4个，全年完成限期环境污染治理项目12项，完成环境污染治理项目投资额达2228.5万元。

二、投资环境

50年来，青海省一批水利、电力、交通、通信、石油、化工、机械、有色金属和原材料等基础产业与基础设施项目相继兴建投产，有力地推动了青海省经济建设的发展步伐。

“三北”防护林体系青海营林工程，湟中、互助、大通和贵南牧场三县一级商品粮基地建成投产。

已建成了黄河上游龙羊峡、李家峡两座装机容量分别为128万千瓦、200万千瓦的大型水电站;已形成东西贯通的330KV大电网和南北110KV电网覆盖全省的格局。青海的水电资源十分丰富，仅黄河上游青海段就可建大型水电站6座，中型水电站7座，总装机容量1100万千瓦，发展潜力巨大。

目前，青海省已形成以水电、石油天然气、盐化工、有色金属冶炼为支柱，包括机械、轻纺、食品加工、医药等行业在内的门类比较齐全的工业体系。“九五”期间全省的工业化进程进一步加快。

经过50年的建设，青海的铁路从无到有，1998年底，青海境内铁路营业里程1100公里。境内除兰青、青藏两条铁路干线外，还有海湖（海晏—热水）、宁大（西宁—大通）、柴达尔（哈尔盖—柴达尔）和茶卡（察汗诺—茶卡）4条支线，以及通往若干大型企业的59条专用线。青藏铁路一期扩建工程已完成，二期正在加紧前期准备工作。铁路运输的发展，对青海的经济振兴以及对祖国西部边陲的繁荣稳定，具有特殊意义。

青海地域辽阔，运输线长，特别是省内各地客货运输主要依靠公路运输来完成。50年来，先后修复、新建了青藏109线、青新315线、青康214线、宁张227线、柳格215线5条国道和临平、五河、宁果、民门等38条省道，基本上形成了以省会西宁为中心，以国道、省道为骨架，县乡道路为脉络的干支相连、脉络相通、辐射全省城乡的公路交通网。同时实现了西宁至六州一地的公路路面黑色化、州县公路等级化、县乡公路通车化的格局。兰宁高速公路正在加紧建设之中。

随着西宁曹家堡机场和格尔木机场的建成，现已开辟西宁至北京、上海、广州、西安、成都、乌鲁木齐、武汉、拉萨、沈阳等城市的多条航线。每周航班23班，通航里程达1.47万公里，1998年，青海民航局完成客运量6.93万人次，货物和邮件吞吐量达600余吨。

目前，青海设有邮电局（所）292处，实现了省会西宁通向国内外各大城市和地区及跨国长途电话全自动拨号，本省县以上城镇全部进入全国自动交换网。同时，无线通信业务发展迅猛。

青海共有旅游饭店、涉外宾馆14家。其中星级宾馆8家，拥有客房1685间，床位3533个。

三、发展前景

近期发展目标：初步建立起社会主义市场经济体制，形成覆盖全省、联结省外、信息灵敏、具有青海特色的商品市场体系和金融、信息、技术、房地产和劳动力等要素市场体系，基本建立起适应社会主义市场经济需要的地方经济调节体系和地方法规体系。

远期发展目标：形成比较健全和完善的社会主义市场经济体制和运行机制，社会经济生活基本走上规范化、法制化轨道。抓住机遇、加大投入，到2010年，依托优势资源，初步建成中国的水电基地、钾肥基地和西北的石油天然气，有色冶金和石棉建材的重要生产基地。基本实现粮食自给，积级发展第三产业。把江河源头建设成特殊生态环境保护区。人民群众小康生活更加富强，科技、教育等社会事业和精神文明建设提高

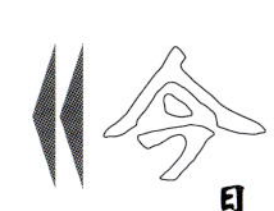

到一个新水平，综合经济实力和国民经济整体迈上一个新台阶。逐步建成文明富裕、繁荣进步的新青海。

四、鼓励投资的重点领域

1. 建立滚动开发机制，加快黄河上游水电资源开发。
2. 开发石油天然气资源，发展石化工业。
3. 加快开发柴达木盐湖资源，开展综合利用。
4. 大力开发有色金属和非金属矿产资源。
5. 建设畜牧业基地。
6. 加强农业基础建设，全面发展农村经济。
7. 建设高原独特的生态旅游业。

I. Economic and Social Development

Qinghai Province is in the northeastern part of the Qinghai Tibet Plateau, with a total area of more than 720,000 square km., and an elevation of more than 3,000 meters on average. It abuts Gansu, Sichuan, Tibet and Xinjiang. Qinghai is one of the four major pastoral areas in China, with 500 million *mu* (one *mu* = 1/15 hectare) of grasslands. The province has many mountains, lakes and rivers, such as the Qilian, Kunlun, Altun, Bayanhar and Tangula mountains, and the world-renowned Yangtze, Yellow and Lancang (or Mekong) rivers, which all originate in Qinghai. Hence, Qinghai is also known as the "source of rivers". The Tar Monastery, a famous Buddhist lamasery, and the Qinghai Lake are also located in Qinghai.

With vast territory and abundant resources, Qinghai has rich natural resources. Its hydropower potential comes to 20 million kw; and reserves of 105 kinds of minerals have been verified. Of them, deposits of 50 types rank in the top 10 nationally, and 11 hold first place, such as quartz, mirabilite, salt mine, sylvite, lithium, magnesium salt, asbestos and strontium.

Qinghai Province has jurisdiction over one city directly under the provincial government, one administrative office, and six ethnic autonomous prefectures. Under the autonomous prefectures, prefectures and cities are 46 counties. Qinghai has a total population of 5.028 million, including 2.15 million ethnic minority people, making up 42.8 percent of the province's total. Tibetan people make up 20.8 percent, Huis 14.52 percent, Tus 3.76 percent, Salars 1.73 percent and Mongolians 1.67 percent.

Tremendous changes have taken place in Qinghai in the past 50 years since the founding of New China. Especially in the past 20 years since the initiation of reform and opening to the outside world, its national economy and social undertakings have developed rapidly. In 1998, total GDP came to 22.043 billion yuan, or 41.9 times the 1949 figure calculated at constant prices, with an average annual growth of 7.92 percent. Per capita GDP was 4,372 yuan, or an average annual increase of 5.32 percent. Industrial production has developed at high speed. In 1998, total industrial output value of Qinghai Province reached 12.2 billion yuan (in 1990 prices), or 367.65 times the 1949 figure, with an average annual growth of 12.82 percent. In 1998, the retail sales volume of social consumer goods stood at 7.06 billion yuan, or 202.46 times the 1949 figure, and 8.21 times the 1978 figure. The import and export volume totaled US$114.05 million, or 154.06 times the 1978 figure. Agreed direct foreign investment reached US$75.84 million, or an increase of 43.5 percent over the previous year. The export volume of foreign-invested enterprises was US$3.42 million, or an increase of 77.2 percent.

At the end of 1998, Qinghai had more than 110,000 natural and social scientific personnel, 53 scientific research institutions including the Qinghai Salt Lake Research Institute of the Chinese Academy of Sciences, and the Northwest Plateau Biology Research Institute, involving a total of 2,500 scientific and technological personnel. Between 1978 and 1998, Qinghai made 1,416 important scientific and technological achievements, and won 662 national awards and 670 provincial awards. The contribution rate of scientific and technological progress to the economic growth increased from 29.31 percent to 41.56 percent. The province's educational cause has developed rapidly and the people's cultural quality has improved remarkably. Basic and ethnic education has been strengthened; vocational and adult education has developed rapidly; higher education has made new progress. In 1965, 73.07 percent of school-age children attended school. The figure rose to 92.1 percent in 1998. At the end of 1998, Qinghai had 3,955 institutions of higher learning, middle and primary schools (excluding agricultural middle schools and vocational schools), with a total of 703,300 students, including 41 universities, colleges and polytechnic schools, with 21,700 students. Its public health and sports causes have developed vigorously, and people's health has improved remarkably. The average life-span increased from 60.79 years in 1982 to 65.60 years in 1990. The income of urban and rural residents has increased year by year, and their livelihood has improved greatly. In 1998, the net income per farmer or herdsman of Qinghai Province came to 1,426 yuan, 2.45 times the 1980 figure, or an average annual growth of 5.10 percent. In 1998, average living expense income per urban resident reached 3,891.4 yuan, an increase of 37.45 percent over that of 1985, an average annual growth rate of 2.48 percent. Qinghai has adhered to the sustainable development strategy and strengthened environmental protection. In 1998 Qinghai Province had 15 environmental monitoring stations, and four nature reserves; completed 12 environmental pollution control projects; and invested 22.285 million yuan in improving the environment.

II. Investment Environment

In the past 50 years, a number of water conservancy, power, communications, telecommunications, oil, chemical, machinery, nonferrous metal, raw and processed materials and other basic industrial and infrastructure projects went into production one after another, thus powerfully promoting the economic development of Qinghai Province. The Qinghai Yinglin Project in the "Three Norths" Shelter-Forest System has been completed, and the three commodity grain bases in Huangzhong, Huzu and Datong counties and Guinan Pastureland have been completed and gone into production.

The Longyangxia and Lijiaxia large hydropower stations on the upper reaches of the Yellow River have been built up, with an installed capacity of 1.28 million kw and 2 million kw respectively. The large east-west 330-kv power network and the south-north 110-kv power network cover the whole province. Qinghai is rich in hydropower resources. On the upper reaches of the Yellow River in Qinghai Province, six large and seven medium sized hydropower stations can be constructed, with an installed capacity of 11 million kw.

At present, Qinghai has formed an industrial system with hydropower, petroleum gas, salt chemical, nonferrous metal and metallurgical industries as the mainstay, and including machinery, light textiles, food processing and medicine industries. During the Ninth Five-Year-Plan period, Qinghai's industrialization was accelerated.

Thanks to the construction in the past 50 years, Qinghai's railways have grown from nothing to reach 1,100 km at the end of 1998. Besides the two main railways—the Lanzhou-Qinghai and Qinghai-Tibet lines, there are the Haiying-Reshui, Xining-Datong, Harbai-Chaidar, and Chahannuo-Chaka railways, and 59 special railways leading to some large enterprises. The first-phase project of the expansion of the Qinghai-Tibet Highway has been com-

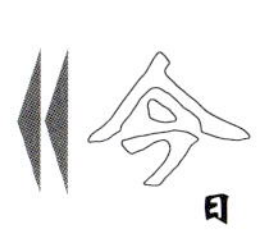

pleted; and the preparations for the second-phase project are in full swing. The development of railway transport is of special significance to Qinghai's economic development and to the prosperity and stability of the western border areas.

Qinghai has a vast expanse of land and a long transport line. Passenger and freight transport within the province mainly relies on highways. In the past 50 years, the province has renovated and constructed five national highways and 38 provincial highways, and a highway network with Xining, the provincial capital, as the center, and the national and provincial highways as the framework, has been formed, in addition to the highways radiating to all parts of the province. Meanwhile the highways from Xining to the prefectures and countries have been greatly improved, and each county and township is accessible by bus. The Lanzhou-Xining Expressway is under construction.

Along with the completion of Caojiabao Airport and Golmud Airport in Xining , flights from Xining to Beijing, Shanghai, Guangzhou, Xi'an, Chengdu, Urumqi, Wuhan, Lhasa, Shenyang and other cities have been opened. There are 23 regular flights every week, covering a total of 14,700 km. In 1998, Qinghai Civil Aviation Administration handled 69,300 passengers and more than 600 tons of freight and mail. At present, Qinghai has 292 post offices. In Xining, people can make phone calls to all domestic and foreign countries. All towns at or above the county level are connected with the national automatic exchange network. Meanwhile wireless communications services have developed rapidly.

Qinghai has 14 hotels catering for foreign tourists, including eight star-rated hotels, which have a total of 1,685 guest rooms and 3,533 beds.

III. Development Prospects

The short-term development objectives: Qinghai will, in a preliminary way, set up the socialist market economic system, and form a well-informed commodity market system. In addition, the province will establish the financial, information, technology, real estate, labor and other main factor markets, the local economic regulation system meeting the needs of the socialist market economy and the local legislation system.

The long-term objectives: Qinghai will form a comparatively perfect socialist market economic system and operation mechanisms, and the social and economic activities will basically get onto the standardized and legal tracks. The province will seize opportunities, and increase investment. By 2010, Qinghai will turn itself into the country's hydropower base, potash fertilizer base, as well as important production bases of oil/gas, nonferrous metallurgy and asbestos building materials in northweat China. Qinghai will be basically self-sufficient in grain, actively develop the tertiary industry, and turn the source of the rivers into a special ecological environment protection area. The people's lives will be better, and science, technology, education and other social causes and cultural and ideological progress will reach a higher level, and its comprehensive economic strength and the national economy as a whole will move to a new stage. A civilized, rich, prosperous and progressive Qinghai will be built up step by step.

IV. The Key Fields That Investments Are Encouraged

1. Establishing rolling development mechanisms and speeding up the development of the hydropower resources on the upper reaches of the Yellow River.

2. Exploiting oil natural gas resources and developing petrochemical industry.

3. Speeding up the exploitation and comprehensive utilization of the resources of the Salt Lake in the Qaidam Basin.

4. Making great efforts to exploit non-ferrous metal and non-metal mineral resources.

5. Setting up animal husbandry centers.

6. Strengthening the construction of the agricultural base and developing the rural economy in an all-round way.

7. Constructing unique plateau ecological tourism.

宁夏——中国西部的一块沃土

Ningxia: A Rich Land of the West China

宁夏回族自治区是全国五个省级建制的少数民族自治区之一。位于中国西北东部黄河上中游，周边与内蒙古自治区、甘肃省、陕西省接壤。土地面积5.18万平方公里。现辖3个地级市、1个行署、15个县、2个县级市。1998年末全区总人口536.57万，其中，回族人口182.97万，占总人口的34.1%，是全国最大的回族聚居区。

宁夏是全国重要的能资源基地之一。这里矿产资源丰富，人均自然资源潜在价值为全国平均值的163.5%，居第5位。已探明具有工业价值的有17种，以能源和非金属矿产为主。煤炭探明储量311.6亿吨，居全国第6位，预测储量2027亿吨，居全国第5位，平均每平方公里保有储量仅次于山西，煤炭品种齐全，品质优良。

丰富的煤炭资源和黄河水能资源的良好组合，使宁夏具有较好的能源优势。目前已形成了以煤炭、电力、石化、冶金等为龙头，以机械、纺织、食品、造纸、建材产业为支柱的门类比较齐全的工业体系。

一、经济发展情况

新中国成立前，宁夏经济和社会发展十分落后。1958年自治区成立后，特别是改革开放20年来，在国家和兄弟省区的大力支持下，经过回汉各族人民的共同努力，宁夏经济和社会面貌发生了根本性变化，综合实力显著增强，人民生活水平不断提高。1998年国内生产总值达到227.46亿元，比1952年增长50倍，比1978年增长4.5倍；人均国内生产总值由1957年的147元增加到4270元；地方财政收入由0.37亿元增加到17.72亿元，增长46.8倍。农业生产条件得到较大改善，粮食年产量连续几年稳定在25亿公斤，1998年达到29.5亿公斤。一些农产品人均占有量处于全国前列，粮食、牛奶人均占有量分别居全国第5位和第3位。乡镇企业迅速发展，已成为农村经济的重要支柱。工业从无到有、从小到大，初步形成了以煤炭、电力、机械、冶金、建材等为支柱，具有现代化水平和区域特色的产业体系，培育了一批在国内外市场有较强竞争力的优势骨干企业。主要产品产量大幅度增长，钽、铌、铍、金属镁、金属钠、双氰胺、石灰氮、电解铝、机床、轴承、轮胎等已在全国占有一席之地。改革开放成效显著。目前，宁夏已同60多个国家和地区建立了经济科技文化交流合作关系。1998年进出口总额达到3.13亿美元，比1978年增长10倍，出口商品达370多种。累计利用外资2.8亿美元，外商投资企业发展到400多家。与此同时，加强了与兄弟省区的经济技术交流与合作，经济外向型程度明显提高。与国际国内两个大市场的联系日趋紧密。人民生活水平显著提高，1998年城镇居民人均生活费收入和农民人均纯收入与1978年相比，分别增长9倍和13倍，城乡居民储蓄存款增长214倍。

二、投资环境

为了加速发展外向型经济，自治区努力改善投资环境，集中财力搞好全区的交通、通信、能源和市政建设，基础设施得到了显著改善。包兰、中宝铁路纵贯全境，宁夏已成为亚欧大陆桥的重要组成部分。由12条国道、省道组成的公路网，覆盖全区城乡。新建了银川河东机场，开通了银川至北京、上海、广州、西安、成都、重庆、昆明、杭州、乌鲁木齐等地的航线。邮电通信快速发展，实现了乡镇电话程控化，市话普及率达到全国平均水平。昔日落后封闭的状况从根本上得到了改变，宁夏与世界的距离已越来越“近”。宁夏不但大大改善了投资的硬环境，而且在投资的软环境方面制定了许多优惠政策。以此进一步扩大对外贸易和国际经济技术合作与交流，引进外资、引进技术、引进人才，促进经济与社会更快地向前发展。同时，简化工作程序，提高办事效率，为前来宁夏投资合作者提供便利条件和良好服务。

三、发展前景

世纪之交，宁夏各族人民焕发出前所未有的加快宁夏发展的积极性和创造性。自治区从宁夏实际出发，制定了跨世纪发展的宏伟蓝图：即以富民为本，以市场为导向，实施农业产业化、工业现代化、新技术应用全面推进，加快改革开放步伐，加快经济结构调整，加快非公有制经济发展，加快脱贫致富，加快社会进步，形成宁夏经济发展的新优势，实现经济社会协调发展，使全区各项事业三年上个新台阶，五年有个大发展。力争经济增长速度五年年均达到10%。到2002年，国内生产总值达到400亿元（现价），地方财政收入达到30亿元；到2010年，国内生产总值达到620亿元，地方财政收入达到67亿元。

四、鼓励投资的重点领域

宁夏是西部待开发的一块地方，土地、农副产品、煤炭、水利、电力和矿产资源丰富，开发潜力很大，随着时间的推移，必将成为西部经济开发的热点之一。今后宁夏鼓励和吸收外资的重点领域是：

1. 加大对农业的投资力度，用5–10年的时间，把宁夏引黄灌区建设成为国家级农业示范区。用3年左右的时间，初步形成以粮食加工、肉奶制品业、绒毛皮加工业、生物制药业、葡萄酿酒业、水果菜业为主的新的优势产业群，促进农业增值增效。力争用10–15年的时间，使灌溉水田面积由现在的3万公顷扩大到66万公顷，实现再造一个新灌区的目标。

2. 集中力量发展电力、化工、冶金、机械、建筑建材、医药和农副产品加工等支柱产业。在工业结构调整、行业整合、产业升级中，依托宁夏资源优势、人才优势和业已形成的技术优势，重点发展生物工程、新材料、光机电一体化、节能环保等高新技术产业。培育一批科技含量高、带动作用强、产品幅射广、经济效益好的高新技术企业，并成为宁夏经济新的增长点。

3. 宁夏是一个富饶美丽的地方，除了有丰富

宁夏银川镇海塔
Zhenhai Pagoda in Yinchuan, Ningxia

的土地、农副产品、水利、电力和矿产资源外，旅游资源也多姿多彩。东部有古人类活动的灵武水洞沟遗址，西部贺兰山脉有古老神奇的贺兰山岩画，南部是闻名遐尔的丝绸古道；在贺兰山下的西夏王陵，是大夏国兴衰的历史见证；新开发的旅游胜地—沙湖，是中国著名的王牌旅游景点之一；沙坡头风景区是世界治沙的典范，受到联合国表彰，吸引着众多中外旅客和考察者。对有利于发展旅游业的外商投资，自治区将给予政策上的更大优惠。

Ningxia Hui Autonomous Region is one of the provincial level minority autonomous regions in China. It is located in the middle reaches of the Yellow River in Northwest China, with Inner Mongolia, Gansu and Shaanxi as its neighbors. It covers a total area of 51,800 square kilometers and consists of three prefecture-level cities, one administrative office, 15 counties, and two county-level cities. Ningxia has a population of 5.37 million. Of them the Hui nationalities are 1.83 million, or 34.1 % of the total population. It is one of the biggest Hui nationality areas in China.

Ningxia is one of China's important energy bases. It is rich in ores and minerals and its per capita natural resources value is 163.5% of the national average level, ranking the fifth in the country. There are 17 varieties with commercial value with energy and non-metal minerals being the staple. The discovered reserves of coal is 13.5 billion tons, ranking the 6th in the country and its estimated reserves is 202.7 billion tons, ranking the 5th in China, while its per square meter reserves is only next to Shanxi.

With the rich coal and the Yellow River water resources, Ningxia has the energy advantage. It has a relatively well-established industrial structure with coal, power, petrochemical and metallurgical industries as the leading industries and machinery, textiles, food, paper, building materials as the pillar industries.

I. Economic Development

Ningxia is very backward before the People's Republic of China was founded. Since the autonomous region was established in 1958 and especially since China adopted the reform and opening up policy 20 years ago, Ningxia's economic and social situation has undergone remarkable changes with the support of the sister provinces and efforts by both the Hui and Han nationalities. Its economic strength has been much improved and so has the people's living standard. Its GDP for 1998 was 22.8 billion yuan, 51 times as much as for 1952, and 550% higher than 1978. Per capita GDP has been increased from 147 yuan in 1957 to 4,270 yuan at present, while its fiscal revenue from 37 million yuan to 1.77 billion yuan, up by 47 times.

With the improvement of its agriculture, its annual grain output was 2.5 billion kilograms in the past years and it reached 2.95 billion kilograms in 1998. For some agricultural products, its per capita consumption is the highest in the country, e.g. grains and milk.

In the past 20 years, Ningxia's industry has grown from nothing and now has a modern industrial structure with regional characteristics with coal, power, machinery, metallurgy, building materials as its pillars. A group of good companies and enterprises have shown competition in both the international and domestic markets. There is a great rise of output of its major products output such as tantalum, niobium, beryllium, metallic magnesium, metallic sodium, lime nitrogen, electrolytic aluminium, machine tools, bearings, tyre, etc.

Ningxia has established relations with over 60 countries and regions in economic, scientific and cultural cooperation. Its foreign trade volume reached US$ 313 million for 1998, up 10 times over 1978. Its export varieties num-

Sheepskin Produced by Ningxia

ber 370. Ningxia has attracted US$ 280 million of foreign investment by 400 foreign companies. It has also strengthened its economic cooperation with other provinces of the country. Now its economy is much outward looking, closer to both the domestic and international markets.

People's living standard has been much improved. The disposable income for urban and rural people has increased by 9 times and 13 times respectively since 1978, while their savings have increased by 214 times.

II. Investment Environment

In order to develop an export-oriented economy, the autonomous region government has been making efforts to improve investment environment in such areas as transportation, telecommunications, energy and infrastructure. Baotou-Lanzhou Railway and Zhong-Bao Railway cross the region and thus, Ningxia has become an important part of Europe-Asia continental bridge. 12 state and local high ways have composed a network across the region. The newly built Yinchuan Hedong Airport has opened up air traffic routes to Beijing, Shanghai, Guangzhou, Xi'an, Chengdu, Chongqing, Kunming, Hangzhou and Urumqi. Telecommunication industry has grown rapidly, with telephone popularization at the average level of the country.

Ningxia has improved not only the "hardware" for foreign investment, but also its "software" by introducing various preferential treatment policies concerning foreign investment.

All the above measures are adopted to improve Ningxia's foreign trade and international economic cooperation, attract foreign investment as well as technology and personnel so as to speed up the economic growth.

III. Development Perspective

At the turn of the century, all ethnic nationalities in Ningxia have shown more enthusiasm and creativity than ever before. The autonomous region has drawn up the development program for the new century in the light of its reality. With improving people's living stamdard and realizing market economy as its main goals, the autonomous region shall promote its agricultural industrialisation, industrial modernisation and the application of new technologies. Ningxia shall speed up the reform and open-up, the economic restructuring, the private economy growth, the poverty relief, and overall social development, form Ningxia's new advantages in economic growth, and realise a balanced social advancement so as to raise the various aspects of life in the whole region to a new level in three years and a big development in five years. It shall make efforts to reach 10% of an annual economic growth rate on the average in the next five years. By the year 2002, its GDP shall be 40 billion yuan (constant price) and fiscal revenue 3 billion yuan. And by the year 2010, its GDP shall reach 62 billion yuan and fiscal revenue 6.7 billion yuan.

IV. Key Areas for Encouraging Foreign Investment

Ningxia is a place in the western region waiting for development. With its rich natural resources, it has great potentials for development. It would become a favourable place for investment. Ningxia shall focus on the following areas in attracting foreign investment:

1. It shall increase the investment in agriculture and shall build the Yellow River area of Ningxia into an agricultural model area in 5-10 years and an industrial framework for such sectors as grain processing, milk and meat processing, wool and leather processing, biotechnology and pharmaceuticals, winery, fruit and vegetables in 3 years so as to raise the added value of the agriculture. It shall make efforts to increase the irrigated rice field from the existing 30,000 hectares to 660,000 hectares in 5-10 years.

2. Ningxia shall continue to develop power, petrochemicals, metallurgy, machinery, building materials, pharmaceuticals and agricultural by-products processing as its pillar industries. Its industrial restructuring and upgrading shall give full consideration to its advantages in natural resources, personnel and existing technology. Emphasis shall be given to the development of such new industries as biotechnology, new materials, the integration of optoelectronics and machinery, energy efficiency, and environment protection. It shall cultivate a number of enterprises which are of hi-tech, can play a leading role and have good economic returns.

3. Ningxia is a beautiful place and a fertile land. Apart from its rich natural resources, it has great tourist resources too. It boasts its historical site of Lingwu Water Cave in the east, the ancient Helanshan Mountain rock paintings in the west, the well known Silk Road in the south. The West Xia Dynasty Tomb against the Helanshan Mountain is a historical evidence of the rise and fall of the Great Xia Dynasty. Shapotou Scenic Site is a model of the world in dust and sand treatment, much appraised by the UN and having attracted many tourists both from home and abroad. Foreign investment in this sector shall also be treated favourably.

新疆——中国西部最大的待开发区

Xinjiang: The Largest Region to Be Developed in West China

一、经济发展情况

新疆维吾尔自治区通称新疆，简称“新”，古称“西域”，意即中国的“西部疆域”。新中国诞生后，于1955年10月1日成立了新疆维吾尔自治区。现辖5个自治州、8个地区、3个直辖市和86个县市，面积166万平方公里，是中国面积最大的省区。居住着维吾尔、汉、哈萨克、蒙古、回、柯尔克孜等47个民族，总人口1747万，其中少数民族1073万，占总人口的61%。新疆与蒙古、俄罗斯、哈萨克斯坦、吉尔吉斯斯坦、塔吉克斯坦、阿富汗、巴基斯坦、印度等8个国家接壤，边境线长达5400多公里，是中国陆地边境线最长的省区；新疆地处欧亚大陆腹地，是世界著名的古“丝绸之路”的重要组成部分和必经之地，是中国今后开放的前沿地区。自治区首府是乌鲁木齐市。新疆的地上地下资源都很丰富，是中国重要的资源型省区，其中石油和天然气储量约占中国总储量的1/4以上；新疆拥有发展农业、畜牧业、轻纺、食品工业和能源、建材、重工业等优越条件，是一个大有发展前途、有待大规模开发的地方。

建国50年来，新疆的经济建设取得了巨大成就，社会面貌发生了深刻变化，特别是中共十一届三中全会以来，国民经济快速增长，综合经济实力和人民生活水平都跃上一个新台阶，国内生产总值（GDP）从1978年的39亿元增加到1998年的1117亿元，比1978年增长6.5倍，年均增长10.6%；人均国内生产总值从1978年的313元增加到1998年的6229元，年均增长8.6%。农业总产值499亿元，比1978年增长4.1倍，年均增长8.5%；棉花产量140万吨，占中国棉花总产量的1/3强，从1994年起跃居全国首位。工业总产值758亿元，比1978年增长7.6倍，年均增长11.4%；主要产品产量有：原煤2927万吨，原油1628万吨，天然气23.8亿立方米，发电量157.8亿千瓦小时，钢108万吨，纱22.03万吨，糖47.59万吨等。随着改革开放的不断深入，对外贸易和利用外资快速增长，新疆已对外开放58个县（市）、6个经济技术开发区和15个对外口岸，1998年底，新疆已与世界80多个国家和地区建立了经贸合作关系。外贸进出口总额从1978年的2346万美元增加到1998年的15.3亿美元，年均增长19.9%；其中出口额8.1亿美元，进口额7.2亿美元。1980年以来，新疆累计签订利用外资协议合同金额33.5亿美元，实际利用外资24.1亿美元，外商直接投资3.2亿美元，年底实有三资企业597家。1998年，新疆接待海外旅游者20.66万人，旅游外汇收入4亿美元。

二、投资环境

新疆现已形成了以铁路、公路、民航和管道为主的交通运输网络。兰州—乌鲁木齐铁路、南疆铁路乌鲁木齐—库尔勒—阿克苏和北疆铁路乌鲁木齐—阿拉山口是新疆交通大动脉的主体；每

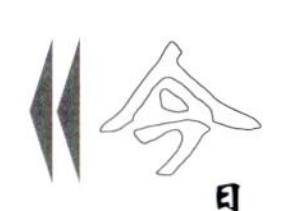

天都有乌鲁木齐开往北京、上海的特快列车以及乌鲁木齐至兰州、西安、郑州、成都的直达列车。公路运输在新疆占有特殊地位，1998年公路通车里程32762公里，以乌鲁木齐为中心，连接县镇、主要矿区和95%的乡村公路运输网已经形成；吐鲁番—乌鲁木齐—大黄山高等级公路也已开通运营。民航已拥有12个机场，开辟了40多条国内航线，其中有乌鲁木齐至北京、上海、广州、西安、昆明、南京、深圳、长沙、桂林、兰州和沈阳等国内大城市的航线，并开辟了4条国际航线，乌鲁木齐机场是中国六大国际机场之一，可以起降各种大型喷气飞机。新疆有1955公里输油管道，连接克拉玛依、独山子、乌鲁木齐、库尔勒等产油区。新疆拥有便捷的通讯系统，西安—兰州—乌鲁木齐光缆已铺通，长途自动交换机容量114200路，电话普及率达到9.5%，邮政特快专递、磁卡电话和移动通信等新兴业务成倍增长，光缆、微波和卫星地面站构成了新疆数字通信网的主体。近年来，第三产业已占国内生产总值（GDP）的1/3以上，餐饮业、证券业、信息咨询业、广告业、旅游业和房地产业快速发展，电子商务、国际互联网等现代信息业务不断涌现。金融、证券业快速发展，工商、农业、建设、中行等四大国有银行积极向商业银行过渡，此外，新疆还设有1家交通银行、4家保险公司、10多家证券公司和遍布城乡的数百家农村和城市信用社。目前，新疆还没有外资金融机构。城市基础设施建设和服务水平不断完善和提高。

新疆的教育、卫生、科技和文化事业与经济建设同步发展。1998年，新疆有17所高等学校，在校学生4.75万人，一些大学可培养研究生。现拥有各类卫生机构6615个，有病床7.11万张和卫

新疆天池
Tianchi Pond in Xinjiang

生技术人员9.76万。新疆重视科技事业发展，现拥有县以上自然科学研究机构127个，各类专业技术人员44万人，其中科学家和工程师2.7万人。文化事业欣欣向荣，拥有各类文化艺术表演团体89个，图书馆73个，出版各类报纸87种，广播电台6座电视台18座。

三、发展前景

新疆属于中国西部地区，开发新疆，使新疆成为中国21世纪经济建设的一个重要支点，是中国既定的战略方针。根据中共第十五次代表大会精神，新疆1999-2005年国民经济和社会发展总的战略设想是：继续深化改革，进一步扩大开放，不断增强综合经济实力，加快现代化进程，逐步建立社会主义市场经济体制；以科技进步为先导，以提高经济效益为中心，充分依托优势资源，加快资源优势向经济优势转变；保持国民经济持续、协调和稳定增长，1999-2005年，国内生产总值年均递增8-9%，逐步缩小同全国的经济发展差距，经济发展达到国内中等水平，为把新疆建设成为21世纪中国经济发展的一个重要支点奠定坚实的基础。

新疆将集中力量建设粮食、棉花、畜产品、糖料、石油及石油化工和有色金属6个国家商品生产基地，以农牧业、纺织和食品工业、石油和石油化工、有色金属工业、电力工业和建材工业为主导产业，以水利、交通通信等基础产业和基础设施为先导。

四、鼓励外商投资的重点领域

按照新疆1999-2005年国民经济和社会发展战略规划，国内生产总值年均增长8-9%，要实现这一目标，新疆要进一步扩大利用国际市场、资本、技术和资源，使对外贸易以快于经济增长的速度发展。按照平等、互利的原则，遵守国际惯例，采取更加灵活的措施，进一步开放区内市场，改善投资环境，改革经营管理体制，提高政府办事效率，完善法律法规体系，为外商投资创造便利条件。

新疆资源丰富，原料价格较低，能源供应充足，建厂选择余地大，土地和劳动力费用低廉。新疆热诚欢迎各国朋友、港澳和台湾同胞到新疆来投资。除吸收外商直接投资外，还可吸收和利用外国政府贷款和世界银行、国际货币基金组织等国际金融机构的低息和优惠商业贷款。合作的方式包括合资、合作和独资经营，开展补偿贸易，来料加工、来样加工、来件装配，租赁贸易等。今后10年，新疆全社会固定资产投资年均增长15%以上。为了增强对外商投资管理的透明度和预见性，新疆已经颁布了重点的投资建设和更新改造项目，这些项目涉及许多产业，新疆将积极引导外商重点投向农业、水利、能源、交通通信、石油化工、电力、原材料和其它基础产业和基础设施建设。鼓励投资的重点产业领域是：农牧业生产和加工业、交通运输和邮电通信业、电力工业、纺织和轻工业、冶金工业、有色金属工业、石油和石油化工、电子工业、建材及非金属矿物制品业、医药工业、新材料、生物工程、环保产业、电子信息产业、微电子以及包括金融证券业、批发零售业和旅游业在内的服务业。

I. General Situation of Economic Development

Xinjiang Uygur Autonomous Region, generally refered to as Xinjiang or Xin, was known in ancient times as Xiyu (China's Western regions). The territory became an Uygur autonomous region on October 1,1955, after the founding of the People's Republic of China. Consisting of 86 basic units, including counties and towns in 8 prefectures and 5 antonomous ones and 3 cities. Xinjiang, the largest of all Chinese provincial-level area, covers an area of 1.66 million square kilometers, inhabited by 47 ethnic groups, such as the Uygurs, Hans, Khazaks, Mongolians, Huis and Kirgizes. Of the total population of 17.47 million, 10.73 million or 61% belong to the ethnic minorities. It shares a more than 5,400 km common boundary with Mongolia, Russia, Kazakhstan, Kirghizia, Tadzhikistan, Afghanistan, Pakistan and India. It outstrips all the other administrative regions of China in the length of continental borderlines. Xinjiang lies in the hinterland of Eurasia. Following the ancient tradition of granting tree transits to the travellers along the Silk Road, it now opens its doors to all foreigners. The regional capital is Urumqi. Xinjiang is one of China's major administrative units remarkable for natural resources above the ground and under it. Oil and gas deposits in Xinjiang account for more than 1/4 of the national total. It is endowed with good material basis for the growth of agriculture, livestock raising, textile, food industry and the energy, building material manufacture and heavy industries. It is a region of promise and prospect.

Significant achievements in the past 50 years in economic and social development brought about tremendous changes to the region. Especially, since the 3rd Plenary Session of the 11th Central Committee of CPC, Xinjiang has undergone a rapid economic development in the past 20 years. Economy has registered rapid growth. People's living standard and comprehensive regional strength have been enhanced to a new level. The Gross Domestic Product (GDP) jumped from 3.9 billion yuan in 1978 to 111.7 billion yuan in 1998, an increase of 6.5 times over that of 1978 with an annual growth rate of 10.6%. The per capita GDP jumped from 313 yuan in 1978 to 6,229 yuan in 1998 with an annual growth rate of 8.6%. The production of agriculture, forestry, and animal husbandary amounted to 49.9 billion yuan, an increase of 4.1 times over that of 1978 with an annual increase of 8.5%. Xinjiang's cotton output added up to 1.4 million tons, about one-third of the national total and ranked first in China since 1994. Its gross industrial output amounted to 75.8 billion yuan, an increase of 7.6 times that of 1978 with an annual increase of 11.4%. Major products are as follows: 29.27 million tons of raw coal in 1998,16.28 million tons of crude oil, 2.38 billion cu.m of natural gas, 15.78 billion kwh of electric power, 1.08 million tons of steel, 220,300 tons of yarn, 475,900 tons of sugar. Xinjiang's total foreign trade volume as well as the total amount of foreign investment have been increasing markedly with the deepening of reform and opening to the outside world. Xinjiang has opened 58 counties and cities to foreign investment, six economic and technical development zones and 15 boundary ports. By the year of 1998, Xinjiang had established economic cooperation with more than 80 countries and regions. Its exports and imports increased from US$23.46 million in 1978 to US$1.53 billion in 1998, with an annual growth rate of 19.9%. Exports added up to US$0.81 billion, and imports US$0.72 billion. Since 1980, Xinjiang has signed foreign agreement, totalling US$3.35 billion and actually used US$2.41 billion. It attracted US$0.32 billion in direct foreign investment. By the end of the year, Xinjiang had 597 registered foreign-funded enterprises in the region. In 1998, Xinjiang received 206,600 overseas tourists, earning US$0.4 billion from tourism.

II. Investment Environment

Xinjiang has a modern communication-transport network consisting of railways, roads, airlines and pipelines, with the operation of the Lanzhou-Urumqi double-track Railway, the Southern Xinjiang railway Urumqi-Korla-Aksu and the Northern Xinjiang railway Urumqi-Alashankou as trunk lines. There are daily express train services from Urumqi to Beijing and Shanghai plus those connecting Urumqi with Lanzhou, Xi'an, Zhengzhou and Chengdu directly. Highway transportation plays an outstanding role in Xinjiang, and in 1998 the region was served by roads totalling 32,762 kilometers in length. The network, with Urumqi as its center, links up all of the towns, major mines and more than 95% of the villiges. The special expressway from Turpan to Urumqi and to Dahuangshan has been put into use. The civil aviation industry now has 12 airports, and more than 40 domestic flights are flying from Urumqi to such big cities as Beijing, Shanghai, Guangzhou, Xi'an, Kunming, Nanjing, Shenzhen, Changsha, Guilin, Lanzhou and Shenyang and there are 4 regular international flights. The Urumqi Airport is one of the sixth largest international airports in China, which has become an important point in the world's network of airlines with its modern equipment. More than 1,955 kilometers of petroleum and gas pipelines were built in Xinjiang to connect Karamay with such localities as Dushanzi, Korla and Urumqi. Xinjiang is having a convenient communications system. Xi'an-Lanzhou-Urumqi trans-province optical cables was going into operation, and the capacity of long distance automatic switching expand to 114,200 channels. Today, out of 100 Xinjiang residents there are 9.5 telephones. Emergency mail service (EMS), card phone and mobile telephone users are increasing at fast speed. With a cellular phone, a man in Xinjiang can call his friends in every city in China. The Xinjiang digital telecommunications network is being to take shape with its optical fiber cable, microwave telecommunications transmission and satellite ground stations being built. In recent years, service sector accounts for one-third of Xinjiang's GDP. Catering trade, as well as securities and bonds, information, advertising, tourism and real estate saw a rapid development. New services such as electronic paging, Internet Network emerged one after another. Finance and insurance are developing very quickly, and the People's Bank of China Xinjiang Branch serves as a central bank. Four state-owned banks including the Industrial and Commercial Bank, the Agriculture Bank, the Bank of China and the Construction Bank have been transformed into state-owned commercial banks. Xinjiang also has the Bank of Communications, four insurance companies, more than 10 securities bodies and hundreds of rural credit cooperatives and urban credit cooperatives. Xinjiang has no foreign financial institutions.

Fast growth was seen in Xinjiang's education, health, research and culture. By 1998, it had 17 institutes of higher education which had 47,500 students, and some colleges provided masterships. There are more than 6,615 medical and health institutions varying in size and form of service, equipped with 71,100 beds and operated by 97,600 medical workers. Xinjiang lays due emphasis on technology and science and there were 127 research and technological centers affiliated with the government institutions above the country level were operating in 1998, employing 440,000 persons, including at least 27,000 senior researchers. Cultural services are flourishing in the region, and there are 89 professional literary and art bodies, 73 libraries, 87 daily newspapers, six radio broadcasting stations and 18 television stations.

III. Prospect and Vision

It is China's firm decision to turn Xinjiang, her westernmost region, into an important place for further economic development in the 21st century. In the light of the decision made at the 15th National Congress of the CPC, Xinjiang set its own basic principles for its economic and social development in the period 1999-2005,which may be summarized as follows:

Xinjiang plans to further deepen reform, and opening to the outside world and will concentrate on acceleration of economic construction in order to improve the overall economic performance and comprehensive regional strength, while buildding up the system of a socialist market economy. Relying on Xinjiang's own achievements in technology and

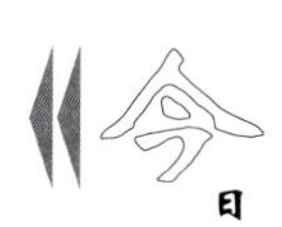

science as a guiding force and focusing on the endeavours for high economic benefits, the work will be done to develop the resources which Xinjiang enjoys safe superiority, and turnimg the superiority in resources into actual economic power. Thus Xinjiang's economy will develop in a persistent, well coordinated and steady way. The Gross Domestic Product will have an average annual increase of 8-9% between 1999-2005. The gap between Xinjiang and other parts of China in economic development will be narrowed, so that it will serve as an important factor in China's 21st century economic advance.

Xinjiang will build up six national important commodity production bases which include grain crops, cottons, sugar crops, animal husbandary, petroleum and petroleum chemical, and non-ferrous metals. Agriculture and livestock raising, textile and food industries, petroleum production and processing, non-ferrous metallurgical industries, power generating and building materials supply will form the mainstay of its economy, and building of water conservancy, communications and transport will be the guiding factors.

IV. Key Scope Where Foreign Investment Is Encouraged

Xinjiang has such superiorities as rich resources, cheaper raw materials, reliable energy supply and wide range for the choice. According to the Xinjiang's target to realize the strategic Program for National Economic and Social Development Between 1999-2005, the average annual rate of GDP growth will reach 8-9%. In order to meet this target, Xinjiang should make more and better use of the international market, capital, technology and resources to maintain an even faster growth rate of imports and exports. At the same time, in line with generally accepted international trade practices, Xinjiang will adopt more flexible measures to further open the domestic market, improve the investment environment, reform the system of business management, upgrade the efficiency of office work, and perfect the laws and ordinances to provide a better environment for the investment of foreign businessmen.

We cordially welcome foreign partners and those from Hongkong, Macao and Taiwan to come and invest in Xinjiang. Besides the direct investment by foreign businesses, we also absorb and utilize loans from foreign governments, low interest loans and commecial loans from such international financial organizations as the World Bank and International Monetary Fund. The mode of cooperation includes, running joint ventures, cooperative enterprises and solely foreign invested enterprises, doing compensation trade, processing with supplied material and processing according to specimens and samples provided, doing assembly of supplied parts and elements, and leasing .

Total investment in fixed assets of the region will increase by more than 15% during the next ten years. In order to increase the transparency of Xinjiang's foreign trade policy and enhance the confidence of foreign businessmen in terms of trade with Xinjiang, Xinjiang has announced major construction and technical renovation projects. The projects emphasize on raising the proportion of investment in agriculture and water conservancy, energy, communications, telecommunications, raw materials and other basic industries and infrastructure, electronics, petrochemicals and other backbone industries.

Industries that conform to one of the following cases shall be listed in the category of foreign-funded projects to be encouraged. They are agriculture, animal husbandry and related Industries, communications and transports, post and telecommunications, power industry, textiles and light Industry, ferrous metal industry, non-ferrous metal industry, petroleum and petrochemicals and chemicals industries, electronics industry, construction materials, non-metallic mineral products, pharmaceutical industry, emerging industry such as new materials, bio-engineering technology, environmental pollution control engineeing and control technologies, information and telecommunications systems networking technology, microelectronics technologies, service industry including finance, banks, retail sales and wholesales, and tourism.

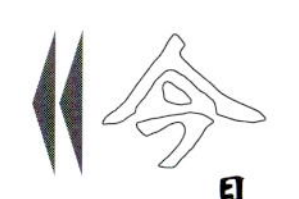

迈向新世纪的深圳

Shenzhen: Striding Forward into the 21st Century

一、经济发展情况

深圳市位于中华人民共和国广东省中南沿海地区，北与东莞市、惠州市接壤，南以深圳河为界与香港相邻，东隔大亚湾与惠东县的平海半岛相望，西临珠海口伶仃洋。深圳是中国唯一陆地与香港接壤的城市。1980年8月，深圳经济特区正式成立，1981年7月，深圳市升格为副省级，1988年10月，国务院批准深圳市计划单列。

深圳市面积2020平方公里，其中经济特区面积327.5平方公里。全市辖6个县级建制区，即特区内的罗湖、福田、南山、盐田区和特区外的宝安、龙岗区。深圳是一个移民城市，1998年总人口数395万，其中户籍人口114.6万，暂住人口280.4万。

深圳经济特区建立以来，始终坚持发展是硬道理，国民经济一直保持高速增长。1980-1994年的前15年成功地进行了“第一次创业”，创造了全国闻名的“深圳速度”，1995年开始“第二次创业”，在经济特区的政策优势开始弱化，经济规模和经济总量基数比较大的情况下，国民经济继续保持快速增长。1998年，全市国内生产总值1289亿元，居全国大中城市第6位，1979-1998年年均递增32.2%；工业总产值1848亿元，居第5位，年均递增49.6%；地方预算内财政收入165亿元，居第3位，年均递增43.5%；外贸进出口总额453亿美元，年均递增43.4%，出口总额264亿美元，占全国出口总额的1/7，从1993年起连续6年居全国大中城市之首。

在深圳经济发展格局中，工业始终发挥着基础和带动作用。90年代以后，深圳抓住时机大力发展高科技，高新技术产业迅速崛起。高新技术产品产值由1991年的22.86亿元增加到1998年的655亿元，年均递增61.5%，占工业总产值的比重由8.1%提高到35.4%，拥有自主知识产权的高新技术产品产值占高新技术产品总值的43%。计算机和通信产业的主要产品产量和技术水平在中国位居前列。高新技术产业已成为深圳的第一经济增长点和特色经济。经国务院批准，对外贸易经济合作部、科学技术部、信息产业部、中国科学院和深圳市人民政府每年秋季将在深圳市举办中国国际高新技术成果交易会，第一届交易会于1999年10月5日至10日举行。

二、投资环境

深圳在城市建设中始终保证城市基础设施适当超前发展，注重基础设施的建设，使城市功能日趋完善，城市环境不断优化。截止1998年，全市累计完成固定资产投资2400亿元，其中用于城市基础设施的投资占30%以上。建成了便利、高效的海陆空立体交通网络。深圳机场开通了4条国际航线、96条国内航线，机场旅客年吞吐量达515万人次，成为全国四大繁忙空港之一。深圳海岸线长230公里，分布着8个港区，拥有万吨级以上的泊位33个，其中盐田港是中国四大深水港

深圳夜景
Shenzhen at Night

之一和中国南部地区航运中心、转口贸易中心。城市道路四通八达，各类道路总长1200多公里，高速公路连接珠江三角洲主要城市。建成了国家第一条准高速铁路—广深准高速铁路。建成12个一类口岸、5个二类口岸，皇岗口岸成为中国最大的陆路交通口岸，形成了陆海空全方位开放的口岸体系，口岸管理逐步向国际惯例靠拢。全市供电、供水网络完善，发电装机容量327万千瓦，日供水能力338.7万吨，自来水普及率96.5%。1998年，深圳已与国外200多个城市、国内近2000个城镇开通了直拨电话，固定电话交换机容量167.48万门，移动电话交换机容量136万门，平均每百人拥有电话49部，其中固定电话31部，移动电话18部。深圳是华南地区重要的区域性金融中心，目前，深圳有金融机构92家，其中外资金融机构（不含办事处）26家。1998年末，全市金融机构各项存款余额2238.37亿元，各项贷款余额1550.37亿元，分居全国大中城市第4位和第5位。作为中国两个全国性证券市场之一，1998年，深交所上市公司数目413家，上市证券数目483只，市价总值8980.16亿元。深圳证券市场全年总成交金额11965亿元，深交所挂牌股票454只，其中A股400只，B股54只，总发行股本1065亿股，总流通股本361.21亿股。深圳旅游业从无到有，独具特色。成功开发了富有民族特色、“窗口”特色的文化旅游性质的锦绣中华、中国民俗文化村、世界之窗、野生动物园、欢乐谷、未来时代等。目前，深圳有星级宾馆86家，其中五星级宾馆6家，四星级4家。中国政府对到香港的外国人组团进入深圳经济特区旅游观光实行72小时免签证。深圳整体生态环境保护较好，城市绿化覆盖率44.0%，城市建设园林化，水、气、声质量处于较好水平，先后获得了“国家卫生城市”、“国家园林城市”、“国家环境保护模范城市”、“全国优秀旅游城市”等称号。深圳建有现代化的图书馆、书店、博物馆、科技馆、电视台、广播电台、新闻

中心、剧院、艺术中心、娱乐中心等文化设施。有全日制普通高校 2所，中小学364所，幼儿园488所。全市有医院77所，卫生技术人员1.5万人，医疗技术、设备比较先进。

三、发展前景

广东省第八次党代会要求深圳建设成为经济中心城市，在金融、科技、信息、商贸、交通、文化、旅游等方面成为区域中心，充分发挥在发展高新技术产业、带动广东城乡发展的龙头作用和经济特区的示范、辐射作用，带头实现现代化目标。

深圳已确定了迈向新世纪的发展战略：到2010年，深圳总人口控制在430万人以内，城区面积达到490平方公里，国内生产总值达到5000亿元，经济发达、文化繁荣、环境优美、法治完善，治安良好、管理先进、生活质量较高。以建设园林式、花园式城市，区域经济中心城市和现代化国际性城市为目标，坚持发展是硬道理，实现国民经济持续、快速、健康发展；大力推进高新技术、金融、物流三大支柱产业的发展，提高国民经济综合素质；建成较完善的社会主义市场经济体制和全方位开放的高水平外向型经济格局；坚持可持续发展战略，提高城市环境质量；依法治市，建设社会主义法治城市；坚持“两手抓，两手都要硬”，努力争取两个文明建设都走在全国前列，率先基本实现现代化。

四、鼓励投资的重点领域

1. 道路桥梁、港口码头、供电、环境项目、市政工程等基础设施建设；

2. 先进适用技术和高新技术产业，重点是计算机及软件、通信、微电子及基础元器件、机电一体化、视听、重点轻工、能源等七大主导产业；

3. 新材料、元器件等配套基础工业；

4. 能带动相关行业发展的大型骨干项目；

5. 以外销为主，增加出口创汇的项目；

6. 适应中国市场需求的替代进口产品项目；

7. 开发旅游资源，发展有民族特色、文化特色和地方特色的旅游项目。

此外，深圳在全面完善整体投资环境的同时，还建立了保税区、高新技术产业园区和大工业区等各具功能的特定投资区。这些区域比经济特区其他地区具有更加优越配套的投资环境和更为优惠的政策。

I. Economic Development Situation

Located in coastal area in Shandong Province, Shenzhen connects Dongguan and Huizhou cities to the north, facing Hong Kong across the Shenzhen River to the south, Pinghai Peninsular across the Daya Bay to the east, and Lingding Ocean of Zhuhai Port to the west.

Shenzhen is the only mainland city in China boarding on Hong Kong. In August 1980, the Shenzhen Special Economic Zone (SEZ) was officially set up. The city was promoted to a sub-provincial level in July 1981, and was approved by the State Council as a city with independent planning power in October 1988.

The city covers 2,020 square km, including 327.5 square km of SEZ. It has six county-level districts (Luohu, Futian, Nanshan and Yantian District in the SEZ, and Bao'an and Longgang District outside the zone) under its jurisdiction. Shenzhen is an emigration city with a total population of 3.95 million in 1998. In which, some 1.146 million are permanent residents, and 2.804 million are temporary living people.

Since the establishment of the SEZ, development has been emphasized. As a result, the city's national economy has been keeping a high-speed growing. During the first inaugurating period from 1980 to 1994, the city succeeded in creating the well-known "Shenzhen speed" in the country. In 1995, Shenzhen launched the second time of pioneering. The national economy continued to keep fast growing under the situation that the preferential policies began to weaken and the figure of total economic amount is large.

In 1998, the city's GDP topped 128.9 billion yuan, ranking sixth among the nation's large and medium-sized cities, or increased by 32.2 percent annually between 1979-98. The total industrial output value hit 184.8 billion yuan, ranking fifth, and the annual growth rate accounted for 49.6 percent. The local budgetary financial revenue reached 16.5 billion yuan, ranking third, rising by 43.5 percent annually. The total volume of import and export top US$45.3 billion, increasing by 43.4 percent annually. The total volume of export was US$26.4 billion, accounting for one seventh of the nation's total. Since 1993, the city has taken the lead of the nation's large and medium-sized cities for six consecutive years.

The city's industry has been playing a leading role in economic development. Since 1990s, the city highly developed high technology, resulting in fast booming of high-tech industry. Output value of high-tech products rose to 65.5 billion yuan in 1998 from 2.286 billion yuan in 1991, increasing by 61.5 percent annually, or accounting for 35.4 percent of the total industrial output value from 8.1 percent. Output value of high-tech products with self-owned intellectual property accounted for 43 percent of that of high-tech products.

Output of main products and technological level of computers and telecommunications lead the country. The high-tech industry has become the featured economy and the first indicator of economic growth in Shenzhen. Approved by the State Council, the China International New and High-Tech Achievements Trading Fair is slated to be held each autumn in Shenzhen, co-sponsored by the Ministry of Foreign Trade and Economic Cooperation, the Ministry of Science and Technology, the Ministry of Information Industry, the Chinese Academy of Sciences, and the Shenzhen municipal government. The first fair was held October 5-10 in 1999.

II. Investment Environment

Construction of infrastructure facilities in Shenzhen always takes the lead in its urban construction, so as to enable the city's function and environment to improve constantly. By 1998, the accumulated investment in fixed assets reached 240 billion yuan, with more than 30 percent of them going to urban infrastructure facilities.

An efficient and convenient sea, land and air transport network has been set up. Shenzhen airport opened up 4 international lines and 96 domestic lines, with passenger transport capacity reaching 5.15 million annually, becoming one of the four busiest airports in China. Along the 230-km-long Shenzhen coast spread eight harbors with 33 over 10,000-ton berths. Among them the Yantian Harbor, a shipping and entrepot trade center in south China, is one of the four deep-water harbors in the country. The city's road leading to all directions, with aggregated length of all roads reaching more than 1,200 km. Expressways connect main cities around the Pearl River Delta. China's first quasi-express railway from Guangzhou to Shenzhen was built, along with 12 first-class ports and five second-class ports. The Huanggang Port has become China's largest land port. All of which established an opened port system, with the port management gradually closing to international practice.

The city's power and water supply network is complete, with installed electricity generating capacity reaching 3.27 million kw, and water supply capacity hitting 3.387 million tons. Running water coverage rate amounts to 96.5 percent.

In 1998, Shenzhen has direct dial telephones connecting with more than 200 cities in the world and nearly 2,000 cities and towns in China. Telephone exchange capacity reached 1.67 million lines, and that of mobile telephones was 1.36 million lines. Per 100 persons boast 49 telephone sets, including 31 telephone sets and 18 mobile telephones.

Shenzhen is an important financial center in south China. It has 92 financial institutes at present, including 26 foreign-funded institutes (excluded representative offices). By the end of 1998, the aggregated savings deposits and total loans reached 223.837 billion yuan and 155.037 billion yuan respectively, ranking fourth and fifth. As one of the two stock markets, the Shenzhen Stock Exchange Market is home to 413 listed companies, listing 483 stocks. The total market value reached 898.016 billion yuan. Total transaction volume in the year was 1,196.5 billion yuan. Of the 454 listed shares, 400 are A shares, and the remainders are B shares. The total capital stock reached 106.5 billion shares, and capital stocks through circulation hit 36.121 billion shares.

Tourism of the city developed from scratch. The city successfully developed various tours with national characteristics. At present, the city is home to 86 star-grade hotels, including six five-star and four four-star hotels. The Chinese Government allowed foreign tourist groups visiting the SEZ via Hong Kong free of visa for 72 hours.

The cit's whole ecological environment are will protected, with 44 percent of the city covering with green plants. The urban construction is garden like, with quality of water, gas and sound keeping well. As a result, the city won many good titles at state level, such as a "hygienic city", a "garden city", a "model city of environmental protection", and an "outstanding tourist city".

It has such cultural facilities as libraries, book stores, museums, scientific and technological halls, television stations, broadcasting stations, theaters, art centers and entertainment centers.

There are two ordinary institutions of higher leaning, 364 primary and middle schools, and 488 kindergartens.

The city also has 77 hospitals, employing 15,000 doctors and nurses. The medical technology and equipment are fairly advanced.

III. Prospect

The Eighth Guangdong Provincial Party Congress requested the city to build into a economic center and a regional center of finance, science and technology, information, commerce, communications, culture and tourism. The aim is to fully play the role of leading and radiation in new and high-tech industrial development, and drive the urban and rural areas in Guangdong Province to realize the target of modernization.

The city's development strategy to stride forward into the new era is as follows:

By 2010, the population shall be controlled within 4.3 million, urban area expanded to 490 square km, and total value of GDP should reach 500 billion yuan. The city is to be more prosperous and thriving. The environment should be beautiful, legislation improved, social security good, administration advanced, and living standard high.

The city is striving to become a garden city, regional economic center and modern international city.

The city will adhere to the principle that development is of fundamental, so as to achieve the national economy's sustainable, fast and healthy development.

Efforts will be made to develop high-tech industry, fiance and material circulation, upgrade the comprehensive strength of national economy, and establish fairly complete socialist market economic system and a high-level export-oriented economy pattern that opened to all directions. Efforts will also be made to stick to sustainable development strategy, improve city environment quality, adminis-

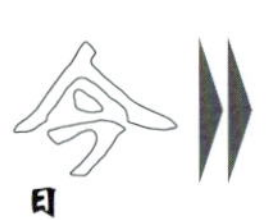

ter the city according to law, build up a socialist legislative city, stick to "do tow types of work at the same time", strive to take the lead in terms of material and spiritual civilization, and realize modernization.

IV. Key Fields Encouraged to Invest In

1. Such infrastructure facilities as roads and bridges, ports and docks, power supply, environmental projects, and municipal engineering.

2. Advanced and applicable technologies and new and high-tech products. The emphasis will put on such pillar industries as computer and soft ware, telecommunications and basic parts and components, integration of machinery and electronics, audio and video, key light industry and energy.

3. Basic industries such as new materials, and parts and components.

4. Large pillar projects that promote development of related trades.

5. Projects with the products marketing overseas to earn foreign exchange.

6. Projects met the needs of domestic market and able to take place of imported products.

7. Development of tourist resources, in an aim to open tourist items with national and local cultural features.

While improving the overall investment environment, Shenzhen set up special investment zones like free trade zones, new and high-tech industrial parks and large industrial areas. These areas enjoy more preferential policies and superior investment environment than other areas in the SEZ.

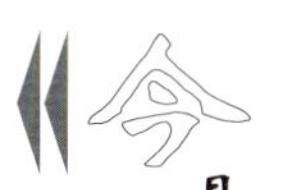

沧海桑田 珠海巨变

Great Changes of Zhuhai

美丽的南国明珠——珠海，座落在南海之滨、珠江口的西部，是一座著名的花园式海滨城市，为中国最早设立的经济特区之一，享有全国人大赋予的地方立法权。全市总面积7650平方公里，其中陆地面积1630平方公里，海域面积6020平方公里，总人口118万。

珠海市成立于1979年，1980年设立经济特区。20年来，珠海市经济持续快速增长，城市建设和基础设施不断完善，已建立起以工业为主，商贸、旅游、金融、房地产、信息、运输、农渔等各业协调发展的综合性外向型经济格局。珠海市是外商投资的热点地区之一。至1998年底全市累计批准利用外资合同7335项，合同利用外资119.89亿美元，实际利用外资65亿美元，已投产开业“三资企业”2511家，其工业总产值占全市工业总产值的70%，已有25家跨国公司落户珠海。经济发展总规模明显扩大。1998年，珠海GDP总量263.5亿元，社会商品零售总额100.3亿元，货运总量3354万吨，预算内财政收入18.7亿元，分别比1979年增长64.3倍、72.9倍、37.5倍和77.3倍。1979-1998年19年间GDP年平均增长24.6%。经济结构得到调整，产业结构日益优化。三大产业结构从1979年的38.5：30.6：30.9调整为4.8：52.3：42.9，工业已成为珠海经济的主导产业，形成了电子器材制造业、通信设备制造业、纺织制衣业、食品制造业、医药保健等30多个行业。新兴的信息产业增加值已占全市国内生产总值的15%左右，从业人员达5.5万人。

交通运输、邮电通信及能源等基础设施建设取得显著成绩，拓展了珠海发展空间，提升了珠海在区域经济中的地位。珠海港、珠海机场已建成投入运营，广珠铁路已经动工兴建。人民生活水平和生活质量得到明显改善。到1998年底城镇居民年人均可支配收入13622元，农渔民人均纯收入3775元，分别比1986年增长9.3倍和3.9倍。

一、投资环境

珠海市海、陆、空交通发达，交通运输十分方便。珠海港是中国南方主枢纽港之一，可实行河海联运，沟通广东中、西部至中国西南各省、区。港池可利用的海岸线长75公里，可建造1万吨级至25万吨级泊位100多个，年吞吐量可达1.5亿吨。目前，两个2万吨级码头、一个5万吨、一个8万吨级专用码头已经投入使用，另有一批5万吨级的专用码头将陆续竣工。此外，九洲、香洲、前山、万山、井岸、斗门等港口作业区，拥有500吨以上的码头泊位近100个。公路交通条件不断完善，公路运输事业迅猛发展。公路通车里程达700多公里，其中等级公路占86%。建起公路桥梁89座，总长9582米，在水网之乡实现了无渡口通车，汽车拥有量达6万辆。拥有各类型的客货运企业600多家，开通了省内外一百多个城市的客运班车；市区营运公汽线路30多条，出租小汽车2000多辆。

按现代化国际机场标准建设的珠海机场，占地400万平方米，机场跑道4000米，年旅客吞吐量可达1000万人次，已开通国内航线30多条，每周130多个航班。广珠铁路于1997年10月23日动工建设，全长142公里，总投资34亿元，按国铁1级标准建设，预留电气化条件和澳门运道，计划2000年建成，年货运量可达950万吨，客运量可达1.6亿人次。

邮电通信发展迅速。城乡电话交换机总容量为42万门，用户24万户，移动电话交换机总容量为21万门，用户16.5万户。电话、移动电话普及率居全国前列。长途交换机容量为1.7万路端，可直拔世界各地及国内1800多个城市。开办了特快专递、数字数据专线、分组交换、电子数据交换、无线传呼、移动通讯、图文传真等数十种邮电业务，对外通信快捷方便。

供水设施。珠海市拥有丰富的淡水资源，枯水期淡水流量达1000m²/秒。已建成香洲水厂、拱北水厂、西区水厂等一批供水设施，日供水能力达150万吨，除能满足全市生活和生产用水需要外，还保证向澳门供水。

供电服务。珠海市主要依靠广东省大电网供电，同时已建成前山柴油机发电厂、洪湾燃机发电厂和洪湾柴油机发电厂等一批电力生产设施；全市发电装机容量已达65万千瓦，372万千瓦的珠海电厂正在建设中，年底将有一台机组投产，可以充分保障全市生活、生产用电需要。

金融服务。珠海市金融业发展良好，网点众多，目前全市已达600多个。除国有商业银行外，还有南通、渣打、东亚、大西洋等多家外资银行。

珠海在狠抓经济发展的同时，十分重视对环境和资源的保护，先后被国家和有关部门评为“园林城市”、“国家卫生城市”、“国家环境保护模范城市”、“全国优秀旅游城市”。获得联合国人居中心授予的“国际改善居住环境最佳范例奖”。

二、发展前景

珠海的今天令人振奋，珠海的明天更富魅力。

近期发展目标是：到2005年，珠海将更好地利用和发挥经济特区作为改革“试验场”和对外开放“窗口”的重要作用，在经济体制改革、对外开放理念、市场配置资源、生态环境管理等方面努力创新，增强竞争实力，加快发展步伐、进一步完善投资环境特别是“软环境”，扩大利用外资的规模、质量和水平，扩大对外贸易；巩固提升第一产业，发展、优化第二产业，多领域、大力度推进第三产业，依靠科技进步，优化经济结构，以高新技术产业为先导，促进产业升级，增大经济总量，实现经济全面发展的目标，提高城乡人民生活水平。

远期发展目标是：到2010年，珠海市将形成大城市的经济规模和综合经济实力，人民生活迈入富裕水平，市场经济运行机制与运行方式实现与国际接轨，在省内率先实现现代化和国际化，建成现代化花园式海滨城市，发展成外向型经济的重要基地和珠江三角洲西部的大城市。

Zhuhai, a bright pearl in the beautiful south China, is located in the western part of the mouth of the Pearl River into the South China Sea. A well-known garden-like city, it is one of China's first special economic development zones and enjoys the regional legislative power granted by the

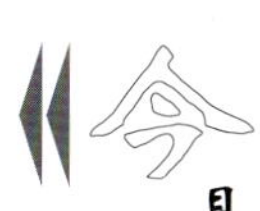

National People's Congress. Zhuhai occupies an area of 7,650 square kilometers, of which 1,630 square kilometers are continental area and the rest 6,020 square kilometers are oceanic area. The city has a population of 1.18 million.

Zhuhai city was founded in 1979 and established its special economic development zone in 1980. In the past two decades, its economic construction has increased steadily and its urban construction and infrastructure facilities have been constantly improved. Up to now, the cith has established a comprehensive foreign-oriented economic structure with industry as the main body, trade, tourism, finance, real estate, information, transportation, agriculture and fishing developed coordinately. Zhuhai has become one of the hotspots of foreign investment. By the end of 1998, the city had approved 7,335 projects for using foreign investment. Of the US$11.989 billion contractual foreign investment, US$6.5 billion had been actually used. A total of 2,511 joint ventures, foreign-funded and wholly foreign-owned enterprises have gone into operation and their industrial output value accounted for 70 percent of the city's total. In addition, 25 transnational corporations have settled down in the city. The overall economic development scale has expanded remarkably. In 1998, the GDP amounted to 26.35 billion yuan, social commodity retail sales totaled 10.03 billion yuan, the total volume of goods transportation reached 33.54 million tons and the budget revenue was 1.87 billion, an increase of 64.3 times, 72.9 times, 37.5 times and 77.3 times that of 1979 respectively. In the 19 years from 1979 to 1998, the GDP increased at an average annual rate of 24.6 percent. The economic structure has been readjusted and the industrial structure has optiimized. The proportion of the three industries has readjusted from 38.5:30.6:30.9 in 1979 to 4.8:52.3:42.9. Industry has become the main body of Zhuhai local economy. Now it has more than 30 trades including the manufacturing of electronic equipment, manufacturing of telecommunication facilities, textile and garment industry, food industry and medicine and health products. The added value from the newly developed information industry has accounted for 15 percent of the GDP and a total of 55,000 employees are working in this field.

Zhuhai has achieved remarkable progress in the construction of infrastructure facilities such as communications and transportation, post and telecommunications and energy. All these has increased room for the city's development and increased the position of Zhuhai in regional economic construction. The Zhuhai Harbor and the Zhuhai Airport have put into use. The construction of Guangzhou-Zhuhai Railway has started and the people's life and the quality of the life have greatly improved. By the end of 1998, the per-capita annual income in urban areas reached 13,622 yuan while that of farmers and fishermen being 3,775 yuan, an increase of 9.3 times and 3.9 times that of 1986 respectively.

I. Investment Environment

Zhuhai has good land, water and air transportation facilities. Zhuhai Harbor is one of the main hub harbors in south China and connects with inland rivers. The harbor connects central and western parts of Guangdong Province with various provinces and autonomous regions in southwest China. The harbor area boasts a coastline of 75 kilometers which is long enough for building more than 100 berths for 10,000-250,000 ton ships. The harbor has a yearly loading and unloading capacity of 150 million tons. Now it has two 20,000-ton-class berths, one 50,000-ton-class berth and one 80,000-ton-class special berth in use. A group of 50,000-ton-class berths will be put into operation soon. In addition, the Jiuzhou, Xiangzhou, Qianshan, Wanshan, Jingan and Doumen harbor operation districts have nearly 100 berths for 500-ton ships or larger ones. The road transportation conditions have improved continuously and the road transportation industry has developed rapidly. More than 700 kilometers of roads are in use and 86 percent of them are standard. The city has built 89 highway bridges with a total length of 9,582 meters. Zhuhai has 60,000 motor vehicles and has more than 600 passenger and goods transportation enterprises. It has opened passenger coach routes to more than 100 cities inside or outside the province. The city has opened 30 public bus routes in urban area and has more than 2,000 taxis.

The Zhuhai Airport built according to the standards for international modern airports occupies an area of 4 million square meters. The runway is 4,000 meters long. The yearly handling capacity of passengers is 10 million persons/times. The airport has opened more than 30 airlines to various parts of the country and there are 130 flights each week. The construction of the Guangzhou-Zhuhai Railway started on October 23, 1997. The 142-kilometer-long railway needs an investment of 3.4 billion yuan. It is built according to the national standards for the first-class railways and leaves rooms for being electrified and being connected with that in Macao in the future. The railway is expected to be completed in 2000. Then the annual goods transportation volume will be 9.5 million tons and the passenger transportation volume 160 million persons/time.

The city registers a rapid development in its post and telecommunications industry. It has a telephone capacity of 420,000 lines in urban area and 240,000 users. Also it has a mobile telephone capacity of 210,000 lines and 165,000 users. Zhuhai is among the leaders in the country in the popularization of telephone and mobile phone calls. The city has 17,000 terminals for long-distance phone calls and connects with more than 1,800 cities at home and abroad. It has also developed dozens of services including express mail, digital and data special lines, group exchanges, electronic data exchange, wireless page, mobile telecommunications and fax. It is very convenient to contact with outside world through telecommunications facilities.

Water supply. Zhuhai is rich in fresh-water resources. In dry season, the fresh-water flow is 1,000 square meters per second. A group of water supply facilities have been built incuding he Xiangzhou Water Work, Gongbei Water Work and West District Water Work. The daily water supply capacity is 1.5 million tons. These water works not only meet the needs in daily life and production but also supply water to Macao.

Electricity supply. Zhuhai relies on Guangdong grid for power supply. But it has built a group of power production facilities including the Qianshan diesel oil power plant, Hongwan oil power plant and Hongwan diesel oil power plant. In total it has an installed generation capacity of 650,000 kilowatts. The Zhuhai Power Plant with an installed generation capacity of 3.72 million kilowatts is under construction. By the end of 1999 the first generating unit will go into operation which will meet the needs of the life and prodution.

Monetary facilities. The monetary industry in Zhuhai has developed smoothly. At presnt, the city has more than 600 financial centers. In addition to the state-owned commercial banks, there are some foreign-invested banks opened by Nantong, Chartered, East Asia and Pacific banks.

While focusing its efforts on economic development, Zhuhai has attached great importance to the production of environment and resources. For its effort, it was once appreciated by the central government or the related departments as the "garden-like city", "a national pace-setter in sanitation", "an exemplary city in environment protection", and "an advanced tourist city of the country". Also it won the UN award for its efforts in improving living environment.

II. Development Prospects

Zhuhai of today is inspiring and Zhuhai of tomorrow

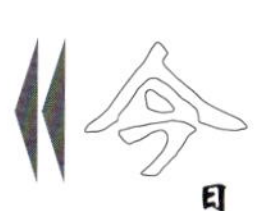

is more imposing.

The short-range development targets: by 2005, Zhuhai will play the important role of the special economic zone as an experimental center and a window to the outside world and made its efforts to make breakthroughs in the reform of economic structure, the concept of opening up, allocation of market resources and the management of ecological environment in order to increase its competitiveness, further improve the investment environment and expand the scale, quality and standards of the use of foreign investment. Also the city will strengthen the first industry, develop and optimize the secondary industry and promote the tertiary industry. By relying on the progress in science and technology, optimizing economic structure, putting on the top the production of high and new technology, upgrading industries, increase economic strength, thus realizing the overall development of the city and increasing the standard of the people's life.

The long-range development targets: by 2010, Zhuhai will have an economic of scale and comprehensive economic strength for big cities. The people's life will be rich and comfortable. The market economic operational mechanism and operation methods will be close to the international ones. It will be first in the province to realize modernization and internationalization. It will be built into a modern garden-like coastal city, an important foreign-oriented economic base and a big city in the western part of the Pearl River Delta.

向现代化国际港口城市迈进的汕头

Shantou: Marching to a Modern International Port

一、经济发展概况

汕头市位于广东省东南部，地处潮汕平原南缘，倚山临海，是中国对外开放的港口城市，全国五大经济特区之一和著名侨乡。现辖5区1县，代管2个县级市，总面积2064.4平方公里，总人口417.95万，其中市区人口111.32万。汕头是粤东地区的中心城市。外向型经济较为突出，以轻工业为主的汕头工业，有超声电子工业，纺织服装工业，化学工业，机械工业，食品工业，医药工业六大门类。工业产品大部分外销，感光、超声、电子、陶瓷、抽纱、纺织服装、医药、工艺品都是传统工业出口产品。

改革开放20年来，汕头市抓住机遇、深化改革、扩大开放，开创了建国以来经济发展的最好时期。1995年，全市人均国内生产总值比1980年提前实现第三个翻番。1998年全市国内生产总值423.18亿元，人均国内生产总值10184元，其中特区人均国内生产总值20380元。1998年全市国内生产总值比1978年增长17.23倍，年均递增15.6%；地方财政收入32.74亿元，增长27.47倍，年均递增18.2%；社会消费品零售总额178.10亿元，增长39.94倍，年均递增20.4%。国民经济实力大大增强。1992年汕头进入“全国投资硬环境40优城市”和“中国城市综合实力50强”之列。1994年汕头经济特区成为全国首批55个人均国内生产总值超万元的城市之一。1997年，汕头市再次进入“中国城市综合实力50强”，列第41位。外向型经济发展取得可喜成绩。1979-1998年汕头签订利用外资项目共13184个，合同利用外资金额89.88亿美元，实际利用外资64.41亿美元，外资投向由加工业逐步扩展到电力、交通、通讯等基础产业，以及商业、旅游、房地产行业。目前汕头有“三资”企业2553家。全市外贸出口大幅度增长。1979年以来，累计出口总额为236.96亿美元，年均增长16.8%。

二、投资环境

为了加速外向型经济发展，汕头努力改善投资环境，集中财力和吸引外资大力推进基础设施建设，城市环境日臻完善。1979-1998年全市累计全社会固定资产投资860.75亿元，其中基础设施建设投资236.85亿元。初步构成了海陆空综合配套的立体交通网络。广梅汕铁路与京广线、京九线相连接；深汕高速公路和324、206国道使汕头四通八达；汕头港成为全国19个枢纽港之一，与世界上47个国家和地区的210个港口有货运往来，拥有万吨级泊位9个，港口年综合通过能力2112万吨；汕头机场与国际国内44个城市通航。全市发电能力140.5万千瓦，电力自给有余。汕头市区日供水能力77万吨，生活、生产用水充足。全市电话交换机总容量110万门，电话69.64万部，移动电话23.90万户，国际长途电话可直拨国际246个城市和国内2100个城市，建立了亚欧和中美国际海底光缆汕头登陆站。全市共有金融机构

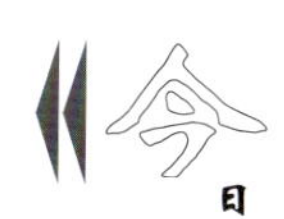

网点1259个，其中外资银行5家，有五星级酒店2家，四星级3家，涉外宾馆、酒店35家。汕头市区有公共交通汽车241辆、线路16条，出租车3243辆。

三、发展前景

近期发展目标是：在本世纪内，仍将贯彻速度与效益并重，素质提高与总量扩张并举的原则，扬长避短，优化产业结构，重点是尽快构筑能适应现代化国际港口城市的现代化工业基础，加快农业现代化步伐，发展提高第三产业。

远期发展目标：全面推进第三产业高度发展，优化提高第一、二产业，到2010年形成先进技术型工业、交通运输业、商贸业、金融保险业、信息通信业、旅游服务业、现代化农业产业等七大支柱产业。

四、鼓励投资的重点领域

在符合国家、省产业政策的前提下，鼓励符合下列原则要求的投资行为：具有较高经济效益和市场前景的新产品（新技术）开发，促进生态环境良性循环的资源开发与利用，符合规模经济要求且不增加城市市政、人口、环保压力的产业综合开发；有利于加快全市产业结构优化和升级换代、强化本市在粤东及闽西南、赣东南经济区域的中心城市地位的资本、技术较密集的二、三产业。

1. 第一产业：农林牧渔业、农用及相关工业、水利建设。

2. 第二产业：石化工业、电子信息及超声设备制造业、机械工业、冶金加工业、轻工纺织业、食品工业、医药工业、能源工业、建筑业与建材工业。

3. 第三产业：交通运输、邮电信息产业、仓储业、城镇基础设施、科研和产业服务、信息咨询业、贸易业、金融保险业、旅游业、房地产业、社会服务业、文化教育与卫生、社会福利和社会保障。

I. Economic Development Overview

Located in the southeast part of Guangdong province, on the Chaoshan Plain, the open port of Shantou, with mountains at its back and the sea before it, is one of the five special economic zones (SEZs) in China and the ancestral home of many overseas Chinese. With five districts and three towns under its jurisdiction, and covering an area of 2,064.4 square km, Shantou has a population of 4.1795 million, of whom 1.1132 million people live within the city itself. As an important city in Guangdong, Shantou lays special emphasis on its export-oriented economy. The principal industries include ultrasonic electronics, textiles, chemicals, machinery, food staffs and pharmaceuticals, the product of most of which are for export. Photosensitive materials, electronic products, chinaware, garments, medicines and handicrafts are also among Shantou's traditional exports.

Twenty years after the policy of reform and opening were introduced, Shantou's government took the opportunity to extend the reform and open wider to the outside world, thus creating its best economic situation since the founding of the PRC. In 1995, the per capita GDP of the city was 6 times that of 1980, and its share of the national GDP also increased greatly. In 1998, the city's GDP reached 42.318 billion yuan, an increase of 17.23 times compared with 1978 and with an annual growth rate of 15.6%. The per capita GDP in that year had reached 10,184 yuan, and the per capita GDP within the SEZ amounted to 20,380 yuan. Local revenues reached 3.274 billion yuan, up 27.47 times, or 18.2% annually. Retail sales reached 17.810 billion yuan, up 39.94 times, or 20.4% annually. In 1992, Shantou was listed among the "top 40 cities with an optimal investment environment" and among the "top 50 cities with strong comprehensive power." In 1994, it became one of 55 cities with a per capita GDP over 10,000 yuan. In 1997, Shantou was again listed as one of the "top 50 cities with strong comprehensive power," ranking 41st. Its export-oriented economy has achieved an admirable level of development. From 1979 to 1998, altogether 13,184 international contracts were signed, involving US$8.988 billion in foreign investment, of which US$6.441 billion has been utilized. Sectors accepting foreign investment have also expanded from processing to electricity, communications, telecommunications, commerce, tourism and real estate. At present, there are 2,553 enterprises with foreign funds in Shantou. Export volume has been increasing rapidly since 1979, totaling 23.696 billion yuan, with an annual growth rate of 16.8%.

II. Investment Environment

In order to spur the development of its export-oriented economy, Shantou's municipal government has expended great efforts in improving its investment environment by concentrating resources and absorbing foreign investment for the construction of infrastructure. From 1979 to 1998, accumulated investments in fixed assets totaled 86.075 billion yuan, of which 23.685 billion yuan went to infrastructural facilities. A three-dimensional transportation network combining land, air and marine transport has started to take shape. The Beijing-Guangzhou Railway and the Beijing-Kowloon Railway have linked up with the Guangzhou-Meishan-Shantou Railway. The Shenzhen-Shantou Superhighway and National Highways No. 324 and No. 206 make the city accessible from all directions. Shantou Port, with 9 ten-thousand-ton berths and a transportation capacity of 21.12 million tons, has become one of 19 key ports in the country and does business with 210 ports in 47 countries around the world. Air routes connecting Shantou with 44 cities in China and other countries have also been established. The power-generating capacity of the city is 1,405 MW, and its water-supply capability is 770,000 tons per day, sufficient for daily and industrial needs. With switchboard capacity topping 1.1 million lines, the number of telephones has reached 696,400 units, alongside 239,000 mobile phone users. Through its IDD service, people in Shantou can easily connect with 2,100 cities in China and 246 cities in other countries. Landing stations of Asia-European and Sino-American international optical cables have been built. There are 1,259 branches of financial institutions, including 5 foreign-funded banks, 2 five-star hotels, 3 four-star hotels, and 35 foreign-related hotels, as well as 16 bus routes with 241 buses, and 3,243 taxis.

III. Prospects for Development

Shantou's short-term development targets are: to optimize its industrial structure within this century, making the best use of its advantages by following the principle of laying equal emphasis on speed and results, as well as quality and quantity; to establish an industrial base that befits a modern international port city; to quicken the pace of modernization of agriculture; and to promote the development of tertiary industry.

The city's long-term development targets are: to complete the development of tertiary industry; optimize the structure of the primary and secondary sectors; and to strengthen the 7 industrial pillars of the city: hi-technology, transportation, trade and commerce, finance and insurance, information and telecommunications, tourism and services and modern agriculture.

IV. Key Sectors Given Investment Priority

In accordance with the national and provincial industrial policies, investments in the following sectors are encouraged: new high-yield technological products providing high economic benefits and market share; the utilization of resources which favor the maintenance of the ecological balance; the comprehensive development of industries according to an economically sustainable scale that will not exert undue pressure on the administration, population and environment of the city; and secondary and tertiary industries utilizing intensive capital and technology which are conducive to optimizing and upgrading the industrial structure of the city, strengthening Shantou's status as the economic center of the region comprising southern Guangdong, southwestern Fujian and southeastern Jiangxi.

1. Primary industries: agriculture, forestry, animal husbandry, fisheries, agriculture-related industry and irrigation.

2. Secondary industries: petro-chemicals, electronics, information, manufacturing of supersonic equipment, machinery, metallurgy, textiles, food, pharmacy, energy, building and building materials.

3. Tertiary industries: transportation, telecommunications, warehousing, infrastructural construction, R&D and related services, consultancy, trade, finance and insurance, tourism, real estate, social services, culture and education, health and social security.

厦门——朝着国际港口风景城市迈进

Xiamen: Heading Toward an International Port and Tourist City

一、社会经济发展情况

厦门是中国对外开放的五个经济特区之一。是中国东南沿海传统的对外通商口岸，也是一座美丽的海滨旅游城市，港区自然岸线达64.5公里，拥有可停泊5-10万吨巨轮的天然良港；厦门是中国著名的侨乡和台胞祖籍地，旅居海外的华侨和港澳同胞达40万。全市总面积1565平方公里，户籍人口126.6万人。

建国50年来，厦门市发生了巨大变化，特别是改革开放、创建经济特区的20年，厦门市社会经济的发展更是日新月异、引人注目。1998年，全市实现国内生产总值418.06亿元，比1978年增长29.3倍，平均年递增18.6%；人均国内生产总值31727元，比1978年增长19.9倍，平均年递增

鼓浪屿
Gulangyu Scenery

16.4%；财政收入56.66亿元，比1978年增长35.67倍，平均年递增19.7%。

在国民经济实力大大增强的同时，城市建设和管理水平有了显著的提高，近几年，厦门市先后被授予“国家卫生城市”、“国家园林城市”、“国家环境保护模范城市”和“中国优秀旅游城市”等称号。市民的社会公德水准和文明素质有很大提高，1996-1998年连续三年荣获“全国双拥模范城市”称号，还先后被评为“全国共建社会主义精神文明口岸”和“全省精神文明建设先进城市”。

二、投资环境

为了提高对外开放水平，厦门市把基础设施建设作为优化投资环境，开发城市功能的重中之重纳入经济社会发展计划之中，从而带动了城市建设由适度性构造向功能性开发、直至适度超前发展转变。1981-1998年，全市基础设施建设投资累计达238.3亿元，相当前31年累计投资额的37.2倍。首先建成了东渡码头第一期工程4个万吨级泊位、厦门国际机场、引进万门程控电话和960路微波通信工程，以及供水、供电、道路等工程的建设；其后又陆续进行厦门大桥、海沧大桥、3号泊位、博坦油码头、嵩屿电厂一期、特区供水工程等一系列基础设施建设。厦门市已形成比较发达的海、陆、空交通网络和现代化通信网络，城市运载能力不断提高。目前全市已有大小码头81个，开辟了日本、新加坡、韩国、地中海及美国西海岸等远洋集装箱航线，1998年海港货物吞吐量1639万吨，集装箱吞吐量达65万标箱。已开辟国内外航线62条，其中国际、地区航线有新加坡、槟城、吉隆坡、马尼拉、雅加达、大阪、香港和澳门的航班。信息港建设也有了较大发展，邮电光缆传输网络已延伸到全市农村，有线电视光缆骨架已形成，建成了电力调度自动化系统、厦大公共教育互联网、商情国际互联网。金桥工程开通了国家经济信息网络。金卡工程全市实现了银行卡跨行使用。同时其他生活服务设施配套，投资环境日臻完善。

三、发展前景

厦门市“九五”计划和2010年远景发展目标纲要中提出：到2000年，全市国内生产总值达到480亿元（1990年不变价），在经济体制和运行机制上，率先建立社会主义市场经济体制，在市场机制的主要环节上按国际惯例运作；在经济体制和运行机制上，率先建立社会主义市场经济体制，在市场机制的主要环节上按国际惯例运作；在经济综合实力上，完成工业化进程，主要综合指标达到世界中等收入国家和地区90年代初的中上水平，人均国内生产总值达到3.6万元，在城市功能布局上，初步建成现代化国际性港口风景城市框架，成为中国重要的招商口岸和海峡两岸交流与合作的桥梁，成为与国际金融市场密切联系的区域性金融中心，成为具有国际航运功能的直达港，成为国内航线发达的区域性航空枢纽和沟通海内外的重要信息港，成为国际性海滨旅游城市；在精神文明建设上，成为环境优美、科教发达、法制健全、政风廉明、社会治安良好、文化生活丰富、社会道德高尚的城市；到2010年，基本实现现代化，国内生产总值达到2000亿元（1990年不变价），比2000年翻两番，建成社会主义现代化国际性港口风景城市。

四、鼓励投资的重点领域

厦门市鼓励投资的重点领域：

一是新兴产业，包括微电子技术；新材料技术、生物工程技术；新能源及节能技术；同位素辐射及激光技术；海洋开发、综合治理及利用；环境污染处理技术等。

二是先进技术型工业，除了要优先发展电子、机械、石化和电力四大支柱行业外，还要积极发展高新技术产业和产品出口型企业。

三是农业方面，主要有水利设施建设；优质高产新品种（苗种）引进、开发、培育、推广；大型畜禽生产加工基地；名优特水产品养殖；远洋渔业；农、畜、水产品储藏、保鲜加工新技术；花卉基地建设。

还鼓励投资城市基础设施建设、基础产业、高新技术产业、市场信息设施、市场服务业等。

厦门市对上述投资规模大、回收周期长、风险性大的项目，将扩大与其相关的经营范围，并给予更优惠的待遇。

I. Social and Economic Development

Xiamen is one of the five special economic areas in China. It is traditionally an open port in Southeast China and a beautiful seaside tourist city. The port can accommodate 50,000 to 100,000 dwt vessels. Xiamen is the ancestral home of some 400,000 overseas Chinese and Taiwan people. The city covers an area of 1,565 square kilometres and has a population of 1.266 million.

In the past 50 years since the People's Republic of China was founded, Xiamen has undergone great changes; and especially in the past 20 years, Xiamen's social and economic development has made remarkable progress. In 1998, its GDP was RMB 41.81 billion, 29.3 times that of 1978, and an annual increase of 18.6 % on the average. The per capita GDP was RMB 31,727.21, 19.9 times that of 1978,and an annual increase of 16.4 % on the average. The city's fiscal revenue was RMB 5.67 billion, 35.67 times that of 1978, and an annual increase of 19.7 %.

With economic growth, the city's construction and administration have been much improved. It has been cited as a National Clean City, National Forest City, National Model for Environmental Protection and the Best Chinese Tourist City. Its residents' social moral values and quality have also been greatly improved. The city was chosen as a model city for its spiritual civilization and good relationship between the residents and army there for three years from 1996 to 1998.

II. Investment Environment

Xiamen has put infrastructure construction as its priority for economic and social development, in order to optimise its investment environment as well as to develop urban construction. The city invested RMB 23.83 billion in infrastructure construction from 1981 to1998, 37.2 times the amount for the previous 30 years. Big projects include 4 berths for 10,000 dwt vessels in the Dongdu Port Phase I project, Xiamen International Airport, import of telephone exchanges with over 10,000 lines and a 960-gate micro-telecommunications project, Xiamen Bridge, Haicang Bridge, No. 3 Berth, Botai Petroleum Port and Songyu Power Plant Phase 1, as well as other water, energy and road projects.

Now Xiamen has well developed sea, land and air transport, and a modern telecom network. It has 81 harbours and a freight turnover of 16.39 million tonnes, and handled 650,000 containers in 1998. It operates container-shipping lines to Japan, Singapore, the Republic of Korea, the Mediterranean countries and the American west coast. It has opened 62 shipping lines altogether, both domestic and international. The international lines attend to such cities as Singapore, Penang, Kuala Lumper, Manila, Jakarta, Osaka, Hong Kong, and Macao.

The information industry has developed well in the past few years. The telecom network has spread to the rural outskirts of the city. Cable TV, an automation system for power distribution, Xiamen's public education website and International economic information website are in place. The "Golden Bridge" project has opened the state economic in-

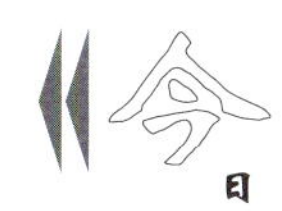

formation network, while the "Golden Card" project has realised the interbank recognition of credit cards.

III. Development Perspective

Xiamen's Ninth Five-Year Plan and 2010 Development Program to the year 2010 indicate that by the year 2000, the city's GDP will have reached 48 billion yuan (based on 1990 constant prices). It will also establish a socialist market economy operating according to international practice. The city aims to complete its industrialisation process and reach early 1990s the level of the world's well-off countries in terms of its comprehensive economic strength. Per capita GDP is to reach RMB 36,000. The city will build up a modern international tourist city framework, become an important port for foreign investment and a bridge for exchange and cooperation across the Taiwan Straits. It will also endeavour to become a regional financial centre with close relations to the international financial market, an international port, a regional air-traffic hub in China and an information harbour with both domestic and international connections. Xiamen will also establish itself as a city with a beautiful environment, developed education, sound legal system, honest government, good social security, rich cultural life and sound social ethics. By the year 2010, the city shall realise basic modernisation. Its GDP will reach RMB 200 billion, based on 1990 constant prices and triple that of Year 2000.

IV. Key Areas for Encouraging Foreign Investment

The key areas in which encouraged for foreign investment include:

1. New industries such as microelectronics, new materials technology, biotechnology, new energy and efficiency technology, isotope radiation and laser technology, the development and comprehensive use of marine resources, environmental pollution technology, etc.

2. Advanced technology industries. Apart from the priority areas of electronics, machinery, petrochemicals and power, the city will develop hi-tech and new industries and export-oriented companies.

3. In the area of agriculture, stress will be put on water conservancy projects, the import, cultivation and promotion of high-quality and high-yield new seed varieties, large animal husbandry farming and processing bases, specialised aquatic products farming, overseas fisheries, the storage and processing of agricultural, livestock and aquatic products, and the construction of horticultural bases.

Foreign investment is encouraged in urban infrastructure construction, hi-tech industries, market information provision and some services. Xiamen will give favourable treatment to projects with big investment, long-term investment returns and high risk, including allowing them broader business scopes.

迈向新世纪的大连

Dalian: Marching Toward the New Century

一、经济发展情况

大连是中国14个沿海开放城市之一，是中国东北地区重要的港口、工业、贸易、科技、旅游城市和对外开放"窗口"，是国家计划单列市，享有省级管理权限。现辖6个区、3个县级市和1个海岛县，土地面积12574平方公里，总人口543.2万人。建国50年来，大连市社会经济面貌发生了巨大的变化。特别是中共十一届三中全会以后，大连市各族人民在邓小平建设有中国特色社会主义理论的指导下，深化改革，扩大开放，推动国民经济快速发展，社会事业全面进步，综合实力显著增强，取得了令世人瞩目的辉煌成就。与改革开放初期的1978年相比，1998年全市实现GDP935亿元，增长6.8倍；地方预算内财政收入64.4亿元，增长2.2倍；农业总产值185.7亿元，增长3倍；工业总产值1769亿元，增长15倍；固定资产投资总额263.5亿元，增长91倍；社会消费品零售额410.7亿元，增长38倍。全方位、多层次、宽领域的对外开放格局已基本形成。1985-1998年间，全市累计批准利用外资项目9622项，合同外资金额179.8亿美元，实际使用外资金额91.7亿美元，完成外贸自营出口总值196.4亿美元。截至1994年，大连市已提前6年实现GDP比1980年翻两番的战略目标，从而为下个世纪初叶国民经济再度腾飞奠定了坚实可靠的物质基础。1999年，恰逢大连建市100周年。3月18日，江泽民总书记为之欣然题词："百年风雨洗礼，北方明珠生辉"。这既是对大连市社会经济发展历程的高度概括，也是对大连市改革开放成果的充分肯定。

二、投资环境

改革开放以来，大连市全面实施"外向牵动"战略，集中财力努力搞好城市基础设施建设，投资环境日臻完善。1992年，经中国城市评价中心评价公布，大连市名列全国投资环境40优城市之一。在大连市境内，现已建成了中国沿海地区最大的经济技术开发区以及东北地区唯一的保税区、国家旅游度假区和国家级高新技术产业园区。大连市地理位置得天独厚，海陆空交通运输发达，形成了集铁路、公路、民航及输油管道等多种运输方式为一体的立体交通网络。沿海良港众多，其中大连港以水深港阔、终年不淤不冻而驰名中外。境内盛产苹果，水产资源丰富，名胜古迹与自然景观遍及城乡各地，是著名的渔果之乡和独具特色的海滨消夏型风景旅游城市。工业基础雄厚，行业门类齐全，在40个工业大门类中已拥有36个。第三产业发展迅速，在GDP中的构成比重已达44.3%。科技、教育事业综合实力较强，拥有市属以上科研机构53所，高等院校13所，各类专业技术人员25万。截至1998年末，全市拥有电话交换机总容量140.8万门，各县（市）区都开通了国内国际直拨程控电话；旅游涉外饭店150多家，其中星级饭店55家；国内国际航线66条，航线总里程10.3万公里；外资金融机构26家，其中外资银行分行10家；累计批准外商投资企业7549家，其中3600家已投产（营业）。

三、发展远景

面临世纪更替、千年之交的今天，大连市已经确立了迈向21世纪的宏伟目标，“北方明珠”将放射出更加璀璨的光辉。

近期发展目标：至2000年，全面实施外向牵动、口岸经济、科教兴市和区域共同发展四大战略，以提高国民经济整体素质和经济效益为中心，以发展农业、搞好国有大中型企业、提高对外开放质量为重点，积极调整产业结构，实现城市功能和面貌的重大转变，加快农村城市化和城市现代化进程，全面提高市民素质和人民生活水平，基本建立起社会主义市场经济体制。

远期发展目标：至2010年，把大连基本建成现代化国际性城市，成为东北亚地区的商贸、金融、旅游、信息中心城市之一；综合经济实力、人民生活质量、城市建设水平再上一个大台阶，社会主义精神文明建设再上一个新水平；形成健全和完善的社会主义市场经济体制和运行机制；国民经济发展基本与国际经济融为一体；经济结构高级化，GDP中三次产业的比重为6∶44∶50；基本实现人口、资源、环境、经济、社会的可持续发展和富强、民主、文明的社会主义现代化。

四、鼓励投资的重点领域

大连市作为中国东北地区和环渤海地区经济基础发展最具活力、对外开放程度最高的城市之一，现已成为海内外客商理想的投资热点。今后，大连市鼓励和引导外商投资的重点领域是：

1. 基础设施领域。以发电和供热为目的的电厂建设、以改善城市交通条件为目的的港口建

大连海港之夜
Dalian Port at Night

设。

2. 工业加工领域。以提高附加值、增加出口创汇为主要内容的电子、自动化仪表、轻工机械、数控机床等行业的加工装配项目，以及精细化工、服装纺织、冶金、建材、食品等行业的开发与加工项目。

3. 其他投资领域。以旅游度假区的旅游开发建设以及相关项目；以安居工程为主的房地产开发建设项目；以信息、金融为主的服务业项目；以高技术和实用技术为主的高新技术项目；以品种改良和保鲜为主的农业开发项目；以劳动密集型为主的工业开发小区项目；以转口贸易、仓储加工为主的保税区内的项目。

I. Economic Development

Dalian is one of the 14 Chinese coastal open cities and an important port and center of industry, trade, science and technology and tourism. It is also a "window" opening to the outside world in the northeast region of China. Dalian has the same administration rights as a province. It has 6 districts, 3 counties and 1 island county under its jurisdiction, covering an area of 12,574 square km and with a population of 5.432 million. In the 50 years since the founding of the People's Republic of China, there have been tremendous changes in Dalian. Remarkable and brilliant performance has been achieved particularly since the Third Plenary Session of the 11th Central Committee of the Communist Party of China, which, held in 1978, decided to launch a reform and opening-up drive in China. Compared with 1978, the city realized a GDP of 93.5 billion yuan in 1998, an increase of 6.8 times. The local revenue was 6.44 billion yuan, an increase of 2.2 times. Total agricultural output was 18.57 billion yuan, an increase of 3 times. Total industrial output was 176.9 billion yuan, an increase of 15 times. Investment in fixed assets was 26.35 billion yuan, an increase of 91 times. Consumer goods retailed at 41.07 billion yuan, an increase of 38 times.

From 1985 to 1998, the city approved the use of foreign funds for 9,622 items. The contracted foreign funds came to US$17.98 billion and the sum actually used was US$9.17 billion yuan. The total export value was US$19.64 billion yuan. By 1994, Dalian had realized the strategic objective of doubling its 1980 GDP six years ahead of schedule, and thereby laying a solid and reliable material foundation for its economic take off in the next century. The year 1999 marked the 100th anniversary of Dalian. On March 18, President Jiang Zemin wrote an inscription in honor of the occasion: "Severely tested by wind and rain for one hundred years, the bright pearl of the north will shine more splendidly".

II. Investment Environment

Since the introduction of reform and opening policies, Dalian has implemented the strategy of drawing on foreign capital and amassed financial resources to make a good job of the city infrastructure construction. The investment environment has greatly improved. In 1992, Dalian was declared one of the country's 40 cities with excellent investment environment. The city has set up the biggest economic and technological development zone of any Chinese coastal region, and the only bonded zone, national tourism zone and national hi-tech industrial zone in the northeast region.

Dalian is richly endowed by nature; ocean, land and air transportation is well developed. The Dalian Port is well-known for its deep water, spacious berths and freedom from silt and ice. Dalian abounds in apples, aquatic resources, famous historic and cultural sites and natural scenery. It is known as a "land of fish and fruit" and a coastal

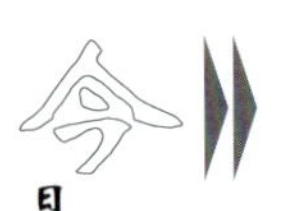

summer resort. The local industrial foundation is solid, with 36 categories of industry. The service sector has also developed rapidly, accounting for 44.3 percent of the GDP. The city boasts 53 research institutes, 13 higher-learning institutes and 250,000 professionals and technicians.

At the end of 1998, there were telephone exchanges 1.408 million. Every county had opened international direct-dialing telephone service. There are more than 150 hotels catering to foreign tourists, of which 55 are star-rated. Domestic and international air routes total 66, covering a total of 103,000 km. Foreign financial agencies number 26, among which 10 are branches of foreign banks. Some 7,549 foreign-funded enterprises have been approved of which 3,600 have gone into operation.

III. Long-Range Development Perspective

Facing the new millennium, Dalian has set an ambitious goal for stepping into the 21st century.

The short-term development objectives: by the year 2000, the four strategies of drawing on foreign capital, developing port economy, rejuvenating the local economy through science and education and achieving common development regionally will be carried out in a comprehensive way to improve the overall quality of the national

大连新区
DaLian New District

economy. Priority will be given to the development of agriculture and large and medium-sized state enterprises and to the improvement of the quality of opening up. Greater efforts will be made to readjust industrial structure, achieve a significant shift in the functions and outlook of the city, accelerate the process of urbanization of the countryside and modernization of the city, improve people's quality and living standard, and establish a socialist market economic system.

Long-term objectives: by the year 2010, Dalian will have become a modern international metropolis, one of the trade, financial, tourism and information centers in the northeast Asia. Its overall economic strength, people's living standard, the level of urban construction as well as social ideological and ethical progress will reach a higher scale. The socialist market economic system and its operational mechanism will be greatly improved. The local economic development will be integrated with the world economy. The economic structure will be upgraded, with the ratio of primary, secondary and tertiary industry in the GDP being 6:44:50. The sustainable development in terms of population, resources, environment, economy and society as well as socialist modernization shall be generally achieved.

IV. Key Areas for Encouraging Investment

Dalian, as one of the cities in northeast region and the rim of Bohai Sea with most vigorous economy and opening to the outside world at the highest degree, has become an attraction to both domestic and foreign business people. In coming years, foreign investment are encouraged in following areas:

1. Infrastructure including the construction of power plants for electricity generation and heat supply and port construction to improve urban communication facilities.

2. Industrial processing including processing and assembly projects related to electronic, automatic apparatus, machinery and numerical control machine industries as well as projects related to precision chemical industry, garment and textile processing, metallurgy, building materials and food processing.

3. Other fields include: development of tourism resorts and related projects, development of real estate centering on economic and functional buildings, service projects centering on information and finance, hi-tech projects, agricultural development projects; labor-intensive industrial development projects, and transit trade and warehousing projects within bonded zone items.

秦皇岛——渤海之滨的明珠

Qinhuangdao: The Pearl on the Shore of the Bohai Sea

秦皇岛市是河北省省辖市，位于河北省东北部，南濒渤海，北依燕山，东邻辽宁，西近京津；联结华北、东北两大经济区，处在环渤海经济区的中间地带，是华北、东北、西北地区重要的出海口；海岸线全长126公里。现辖海港、山海关、北戴河三个城市区和抚宁、昌黎、卢龙、青龙四个县，陆域总面积7812平方公里。人口263万，其中市区人口67.3万。

新中国成立后，秦皇岛市经过50年努力，特别是近20年来的改革开放与发展，经济实力显著增强，社会事业全面进步，人民生活明显改善。1998年，全市实现国内生产总值249.5亿元，比改革开放初期的1978年增长8.6倍，比建国初期的1952年增长40倍，提前6年实现了“翻两番”

秦皇岛经济开发区
The Qinhuangdao Economic Development Zone

的目标；人均国内生产总值由1952年的133元、1978年的392元，提高到1998年的9508元；1998年全市财政收入19.09亿元，是1978年的19倍，人均财力连续6年全省排列第一；城市居民人均可支配收入达6156元，农民人均纯收入2980元，均比1980年翻了4番，全市7个县区中有6个县区实现了小康；人均绿地面积6.5平方米，高于园林城市标准。

截止1998年底，有42个国家和地区在秦投资办企业，全市累计批准外资项目988个，合同外资27.05亿美元，实际进入外资13.4亿美元。世界排名500强的企业如日本的三菱、丸红和德国的曼内斯曼德马格、韩国的现代以及LG国际公司纷纷落户秦皇岛；戴卡轮毂、渤海铝业等十多家企业年产值在亿元以上，首钢板材、中阿化肥进入全国最大500家三资企业行列。

秦皇岛市是中国优秀旅游城市。北戴河海滨气候宜人，是中外闻名的旅游避暑胜地；古万里长城从山海关老龙头入海，并有保存完好的城防建筑群；祖山风景区素有“北国黄山”之称。凭借得天独厚的自然、人文资源优势，以旅游为发展龙头，形成了以海、关、山旅游为主，集观光、餐饮、住宿、娱乐、购物于一体的旅游经济体系。目前全市有各具特色的旅游景区22个，景点300多个，近年来每年接待国内外游客都在600万人次左右。

秦皇岛市具有良好的投资环境。近年来重点加强港、路、航、讯、水、电、气等基础设施的建设。秦皇岛港建港已有百年历史，现有泊位49个，年货物吞吐量8000多万吨，年设计通过能力1.24亿吨，是目前世界上最大的能源输出港，也是中国晋煤外运、北煤南运的一个重要枢纽港，与世界100多个国家和地区和港口保持着经常性的贸易往来；京秦、京哈、大秦三条铁路干线和102、205两条国道贯通全境，京秦准高速列车已开通，境内公路通车里程达2446公里；秦皇岛机场已开通至国内十几个大中城市的航线，每周航班最多达34个；秦皇岛新开河港开通了至大连、烟台、旅顺的海上航线；全市连续三年开展“绿化美化年”活动，城市绿化美化工作逐年上新台阶，城市道路达708条，人均道路面积居全省首位；在省内首先建成以市区为中心，城乡一体化的本地电话网，程控电话装机容量达43.7万门；电、水、气供应充足。秦皇岛市是全国投资硬环境“40优”城市，社会治安综合治理先进城市，并跻身于“全国卫生城市”和全国城市容貌综合整治“24优”行列。

时间的脚步即将跨入21世纪，机遇与挑战并存，任务艰巨而光荣。1996-2000年期间乃至2010年，秦皇岛市经济和社会发展将大力推进经济体制和经济增长方式的转变，优化产业、产品内部结构，继续加强基础设施建设和加工投资力度，大力发展新兴电子、汽车配件、环保设备、精细化工等新兴产业和新技术产业项目的投资；坚定不移地实施科教兴秦、开放带动、以港兴市三大主体战略，加快建设外向型、高科技、富有产业特色的现代化工业港口城市和花园式旅游城市；到2000年，国内生产总值比1980年翻三番半以上，2010年，人均国内生产总值达3000美元以上，实现经济和社会发展的第二次跨越。

Qinhuangdao is a city under the jurisdiction of the Hebei provincial government. It is situated in the northeast of Hebei Province with the Bohai Sea in the south, the Yan Mountains in the north, Liaoning in the east, and Beijing and Tianjin in the west. Qinhuangdao, situated between the North China economic area and Northeast China economic area, is located in the middle of the Bohai Rim economic zone, which is an important outlet for North China, Northeast China, and Northwest China. Its coastline is about 126

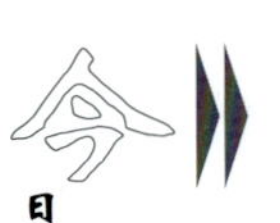

km long. Qinhuangdao includes three city areas: Haigang, Shanhai Pass, and Beidaihe, and four counties: Wuning, Changli, Lulong, and Qinglong. Its total area is 7,812 sq km and its population is 2.63 million, among whom 673,000 live in the cities.

In the 50 years since the founding of the People's Republic of China, and especially in the past 20 year of reform and development, Qinhuangdao has undergone great changes, with its economic strength and the people's living standard much improved. In 1998, the city's GDP was RMB 24.95 billion, 9.6 times that of 1978 and 40 times that of 1952. Its per capita GDP rose from RMB 133 in 1952 and RMB 392 in1978 to RMB 9,508 in 1998. The city's fiscal revenue was RMB 1.909 billion in 1998, 19 times that of 1978. Its urban residents' per capita disposable income has been at the top of the whole province for six consecutive years–RMB 6,156 for urban residents and RMB 2,980 for rural residents, five times the figures for 1980. Six out of the seven counties and districts have reached the well-off level; the per capita possession of green land area is 6.5 sq. meters-- beyond the garden city standard.

By the end of 1998, the Qinhuangdao government had approved 988 foreign investment projects from 42 countries and regions, with a total contractual investment of US$ 2.705 billion and actual foreign investment of US$1.34 billion. Some of the world's top 500 companies such as Mitsubishi, Mannesman, Hyundai, and LG have set up plants in Qinhuangdao. The turnover a dozen of companies is 100 million yuan each, and some are among the national top 500 joint ventures.

Qinhuangdao is a famous tourist city in China. Beidaihe, owing to its favourable climate, has a reputation as a tourism and summer resort. The ancient Great Wall at Laolongtou on the Shanhai Pass extends to the sea, with its walls well preserved. The Zusan Mountain scenic spot is well-known as the "Yellow Mountain of North China". With its advantages of unique natural and human resources, Qinhuangdao develops tourism as its leading economic sectors, integrating sightseeing, accommodation, amusement, and shopping. There are more than 300 scenic spots in 22 special tourist areas in Qinhuangdao, which receive about 6 million domestic and foreign tourists annually now.

Qinhuangdao has a good investment environment. In recent years, the city government has attached great importance to infrastructure construction covering the harbour, highways, aviation, communications, water supply, electricity, and heating. Qinhuangdao Harbour has a history of 100 years, with 49 berths. Its annual freight turnover is over 80 million tonnes, while its designed capacity is 124 million tonnes. It is the largest-energy export harbour in the world and a major harbour for the transportation of coal in China. It has regular business relations with more than 100 counties and regions across the world. The three railway lines of Beijing-Qinhuangdao, Beijing-Harbin and Dalian-Qinhuangdao and the No. 102 and 205 state highways run through the whole city. The Beijing-Qinhuangdao express railway is now in operation. There is a 2,446 km highway network covering the whole city. Qinhuangdao airport is connected with a dozon large and medium-sized domestic cities, with 34 flights each week.Qinhuangdao's Xinkaihe Port has opened sea routes to Dalian, Yantai and Lushun.The city government has launched an "Afforestation and Beautification Year" movement for three years running. There are 708 roads in Qinhuangdao and the per capita possession of road area is the first in the province. A telecom network has integrated the urban and rural areas and its digital exchanges have 437,000 lines. There are sufficient supplies of electricity, water and gas. Qinhuangdao is a "40 Superiorities" city in terms of foreign investment environment and has good public security. It has been cited as a "National Clean City" and one of the "24 Superiorities" cities in terms of its appearance.

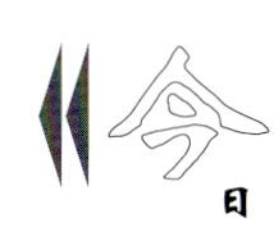

Opportunities and challenges coexist, and our task is both difficult and glorious in the coming 21st century. From 1996 to 2000 or to 2010, Qinhuangdao will make great efforts to promote the transformation of its economic system and growth models, optimise the industrial and product structure, and continue the investment and construction of infrastructure. It will increase investment in such new industries and technological projects as electronics, automobile parts, environmental protection equipment and fine chemicals. The city will stick to the three strategies of developing Qinhuangdao through science and education, opening up, and taking advantage of its port facilities. It will speed up the construction of an export-oriented, hi-tech modern industrial port and a garden-like tourist city. By 2000, its GDP will be triple that of 1980, and by 2010, its per capita GDPwill reach US$ 3000 so as to realise the second stage of economic and social development.

北戴河海滨
Beidaihe Seashore in qinhuangdao

青岛——山东对外开放的龙头

Qingdao: Flagship in Shandong Province in Opening to the Outside

一、历史的回眸

青岛市位于山东半岛南端，东、南濒临黄海，西、北连接内陆。是中国东部沿海重要的经济中心和港口城市，是国家历史文化名城和风景旅游胜地。新中国成立50年来，特别是改革、开放以来，青岛市国民经济和各项社会事业都取得了前所未有的成就，社会生产力迅猛发展，综合经济实力显著增强，成为中国北方对外开放的重要门户，被国家确定为沿海开放城市、国家计划单列城市和副省级城市。

青岛市现辖七区五市，总面积10654平方公里，人口699.57万。其中，市区1102平方公里，人口229.58万。1998年全市国内生产总值888.4亿元，比1978年增长8.4倍，年平均增长11.9%，人均国内生产总值增长6.3倍，年平均增长10.5%，社会消费品零售额242亿元，比1978年增长23倍，年平均增长17.3%。外向型经济取得进一步发展，到1998年末利用外资项目5832个，协议外资金额94.2亿美元，实际利用外资45.5亿美元。目前，青岛市已有外商投资企业3890家，1998年三资企业出口额达26.6亿美元，占全市出口额69.4%。

二、山东对外开放的龙头

近年来，青岛作为山东省确定的对外开放龙头，始终在为进一步提高对外开放水平，改善投资环境，完善城市设施，提高综合经济实力而不懈努力。

青岛农业基础条件较好，资源丰富，石墨、黄金、大理石、重晶石的储量和开采量居全国重要地位。海区港湾众多，岸线曲折，滩涂广阔，水质肥沃，具有广泛的开发利用潜力。青岛工业基础雄厚，门类齐全。啤酒、家用电器等产品享誉海内外。拥有海尔、海信、澳柯玛、双星、青岛啤酒5个全国驰名商标，在全国居前列。青岛是中国、山东省重要的商品流通中心。

青岛是中国重要的沿海开放城市，现已有30多个国家和地区的1245家商社、公司和金融机构在青岛市内设有常设办事机构。青岛与8个外国城市结为友好城市，与5个外国城市结为友好合作关系城市，还有8个外国城市分别与青岛的县级市结为友好城市和合作关系城市。青岛市政府还聘请了日、韩、德等国13名外国经济界人士为经济顾问。

青岛港是中国重要的外贸港口，历史悠久，现为中国五大海港之一。流亭国际机场可起降波音767等大型客机，已开通国内航线35条，国际航线5条和香港、澳门两条地区航线。

青岛依山临海，风景优美，冬暖夏凉，气候宜人，是中国对外开放的重点旅游城市和八个国际会议城市之一。全市共有涉外酒店76家，客房总数10432间。其中，五星级2处，四星级3处，三星级9处，二星级9处。

青岛的海洋科研力量雄厚，有各类海洋科研机构17个，还有全国唯一的综合性海洋大学——

青岛海洋大学。青岛云集了中国50%以上的海洋科学家，是中国海洋科研学术交流的中心。

三、让黄海明珠更加璀璨

根据《青岛市国民经济和社会发展第九个五年计划和2010年远景目标纲要》的设想，到2000年，全市国内生产总值达到1150亿元，人均国内生产总值15800元。2001年至2010年，国内生产总值年均增长10%，人均国内生产总值比2000年再翻一番以上。以尽早实现建设社会主义现代化国际城市目标，使青岛—镶嵌在黄海之滨的明珠更加璀璨。

为此，市政府提出要加大体制改革、产业升级、全面开放、城乡一体、可持续发展和社会全面进步等方面的力度，在今后5年基本实现经济体制、增长方式、产业结构三个转变，加快与国际经济接轨，使全市的综合经济实力、对外开放水平和城市整体素质实现阶段性跨越，增创口岸、产业、名牌、人才、资金等方面的新优势，把青岛建设成区域性的经济中心、贸易中心、金融中心和国际航空中心，初步建成现代化国际城市。

四、跨世纪的选择

面对新世纪的到来，围绕建设社会主义现代化国际城市的目标，青岛市将重点鼓励国内外资金的投入。坚持高技术优先、扩大需求、增加出口优先和可持续发展的原则，推动青岛市的产业结构达到新的层次和水平。

鼓励外商投资的产业重点是青岛对外开放的跨世纪选择：

——近期重点支持利用外资开发和发展电子信息、生物工程、海洋工程、新材料、环境保护等新兴产业，努力形成新的产业主导；鼓励利用外资进行农业开发和农产品深加工；鼓励外资以多种方式和模式对交通能源和城市基础设施投资建设。

——鼓励利用外资扩大新型家电、新型饮料、石油化工、船舶制造、汽车和车辆制造、电力设备等支柱产业的规模和能力；同时，鼓励利用外资和新型实用技术改造提高纺织服装、轻工、食品、橡胶、机械加工的传统产业，提高其技术水平。

——鼓励外资对文化、教育、卫生、旅游、信息咨询等服务贸易领域的投资建设。

I. History Review

Qingdao City is situated at the southern end of the Shandong Peninsula, with the Yellow Sea to the southeast and the hinterland to the northwest. It is one of the economic centres and port cities on China's east coast as well as a historical, cultural and tourist site. In the past fifty years since the P. R.of China was founded, and especially since China adopted the reform and open policies, Qingdao's economy and its other aspects of society have made outstanding achievements. It has become the most important open port in North China and been approved as an open coastal city, and given sub-provincial status by the central government.

The city of Qingdao consists of 7 districts, covering an area of 10,654 square kilometers and with a population of 7 million. Its urban area is 1,102 square kilometers with a population of 2.3 million. The city's GDP in 1998 was RMB 88.84 billion, 9.4 times that of 1978, and an increase of 11.9% annually on the average. The per capita GDP has increased by 630 %, in the past 20 years, an increase of 10.5 % annually on the average. Its aggregate retail sales reached RMB 24.2 billion, 24 times as much as in 1978, and an annual increase of 17.3 % on the average. Further progress has been made in foreign trade and economic cooperation. By 1998, there were 5,832 foreign-invested projects and their contractual value was US$9.42 billion, while the realised foreign investment was US$4.55 billion. At present there are 3,890 foreign-invested enterprises, and their exports in 1998 accounted for US$ 2.66 billion, 69.4% of the city's total exports.

II. The Leader of Shandong's Opening up to the Outside World

As the leader of Shandong Province's opening up to the outside world, Qingdao has been making efforts to further open up, to improve the investment environment and urban infrastructure, and to raise its comprehensive economic strength.

Qingdao has a good agricultural base, with rich natural resources. Its graphite, gold, marble, and barite reserves and extraction volumes are all the biggest in the country. It has fine harbours and the coastline has wide beaches and a good water quality, with great potential for development. Qingdao has a strong industrial foundation. Its beer and home appliances enjoy good reputations on the world market. It boasts the five well-known brands of Haier, Hisense, Aokema, Double Star and Qingdao Beer. It is a commodity distribution centre for both Shandong Province and China, as a whole.

Qingdao is one of China's most important coastal cities open up to the outside world. Now 1,245 companies and financial institutions from over 30 countries and regions have set up offices in the city. It has sister relations with 8 foreign counterparts and cooperative relations with 5 other foreign cities. Furthermore, 8 other foreign cities and its county cities are twins. The city government has invited 13 economic experts from Japan, Korea, Germany, etc. as its advisers.

Qingdao is an important trading port in China with a long history. It is one of the five largest ports in China.

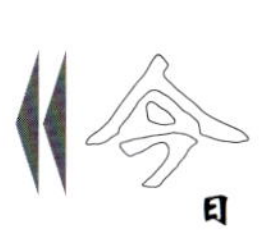

Liuting International Airport can accommodate Boeing 767 planes. It has opened 35 domestic air routes, 5 international routes and one route cach to Hong Kong and Macao.

Qingdao is a scenic city with beautiful weather, facing the sea and against the hills. It is one of the key tourist cities and one of the 8 international conference centres in China. The city has 76 hotels with 10,432 rooms. Of them, there are 2 five-star ones, 3 four-star ones, and 9 three-star ones.

Qingdao city is famous for marine research, with 17 scientific research institutions in this sector. It also boasts the only marine university in this country—Qingdao Marine University. It is also home to 50% of the Chinese marine scientists and is the centre of China's marine research and academic exchanges centre in this sphere.

III. Bright Future for the Pearl of the Yellow Sea

According to Qingdao's Ninth Five Year Plan and 2010 Long Term Development Program, the city's GDP will reach RMB 115 billion, with per capita GDP at RMB 15,800 by 2000 and this will be increased by 10 % annually on the average until 2010 when per capita GDP will double that of 2000, so that the city will realise the target of becoming a modern international city with socialist characteristics.

The municipal government has been making efforts in structural reform, industrial upgrading, further opening up, parallel development in both urban and rural areas, sustainable growth and overall development. In the next five years, it will complete the three transitions economic system, growth model and industrial structure and speed up its connections with the world economy. It will raise its comprehensive economic strength, the level of opening up to the outside and its overall quality. Qingdao will endeavour to take further advantages of its port, industries, well-known brands, human resources and capital to establish itself as the regional economic centre, trade centre, financial centre and international airport.

IV. Cross-Century Focus

With the new century, Qingdao will encourage investment both from at home and abroad. It will prioritise the development of hi-tech, expand social demand, increase exports and adopt sustainable growth so as to further improve its industrial structure.

Encouragement of foreign investment is another focus in Qingdao's opening up in the new century. It will give key support to the development of such new industries as electronics, information, biotechnology, marine engineering, new materials and environmental protection. Foreign companies are also encouraged to invest in agricultural development and further processing, and in infrastructure, energy and urban infrastructure construction in various forms.

Foreign investment is also encouraged to expand the scope and capacities of such pillar industries as new domestic appliances, beverages, petrochemicals, shipbuilding, automobile manufacturing and power equipment, as well as improving the technological levels of textiles and garments, light industrial products, food, rubber, and machinery .

Qingdao also encourages foreign investment in such sectors as culture, education, health care, tourism and consultancy.

烟台——日益崛起的现代化国际性港口城市

Yantai: A Rising Modern International Port

一、经济发展情况

烟台位于山东半岛东部，濒临黄河、渤海，与辽东半岛及日本、韩国、朝鲜隔海相望，是山东省及环渤海经济圈内的重要城市。现辖四区七市一县，总面积13745.95平方公里，人口643.35万。其中市区人口156.77万。烟台自然资源丰富，矿藏众多，是中国海产、水果的主要产地之一，农业比较发达，工业形成了以机械、电子、食品、饮料、冶金、纺织等行业为支柱、门类齐全的体系，各类企业3.3万家。烟台依山傍海，冬暖夏凉，气候宜人，有“人间仙镜”蓬莱阁等多处旅游景点，是旅游避暑的胜地。是中国首批14个沿海开放城市之一。

建国50年来，烟台市的各方面发生了翻天覆地的变化，特别是1978年底，中共十一届三中全会以来，烟台市坚定不移地推进改革，扩大开放，开创了建国以来经济发展的最好时期，国民经济实力大大增强。1998年国内生产总值740亿元，比1978年增长9.5倍，年均增长12.5%，于1997年提前三年实现国内生产总值比1980年翻三番；人均国内生产总值增长8.2倍，年均增长11.7%；社会消费品零售总额212亿元，比1978年增长26.8倍，年均增长18%。外向型经济发展取得了可喜的成绩。自1984年成为首批沿海开放城市以来，截止到1998年，全市合同利用外资65.8亿美元，实际利用外资38亿美元。目前烟台已建成三资企

业2461家，外资投向遍及工业、农业、商业、房地产、能源等四十多个行业，企业经营良好。1997、1998两年，分别代表国家成功举办了第二届APEC国际贸易博览会和第二届APEC中小企业技术交流暨展览会，扩大了烟台的国际影响。

二、投资环境

为了加速发展外向型经济，烟台市努力改善投资环境：实行了社会服务承诺制，推行了“办事效率监督卡”，设立了外商投资服务中心，建起了一个窗口对外、一条龙服务的工作体制；集中财力和引进外资搞好全市的交通、能源、市政建设，大力发展第三产业，城市设施日臻完善，是“全国投资硬环境40优”城市之一。烟台交通通信四通八达，全市公路通车里程5407公里，沟通所有乡镇和村庄；境内蓝烟铁路横贯东西，火车直达北京、上海、西安、佳木斯、济南等8个城市，蓝烟铁路复线和德（州）龙（口）烟（台）铁路已开始建设，烟台——大连的铁路轮渡已被列入国家1999年预开工项目，随着这些项目的建成，烟台将成为环渤海地区的重要交通枢纽：全市现有港口9处，年吞吐量近3000万吨，烟台、龙口、莱州和蓬莱港为国家一类开放口岸，其中烟台港是中国北方重要的对外贸易枢纽港，与国内外的100多个港口直接通航，年吞吐量达到1400万吨，客运可直达天津、大连、釜山、群山。年旅客运送量300万人次；烟台空港为国家一类开放口岸，目前已开通北京、上海、广州、香港、澳门、汉城、大阪等国内外航线23条，旺季每周航班120个；全市电话全部实现程控化，装机容量达到130.7万门，普及率达到14.3%，其中市话普及率达到38.4%，此外还开通了GSM全球通移动电话；全市发电总装机容量150万千瓦，市区自来水供应充足，主要居民区实现了集中供热，气化率达到98.7%，正在规划建设的渤海天然气项目最终达产后，每日可向境内供气150万立方，其中生活用气80万方。全市有涉外宾馆、酒店100多座，其中三星级以上酒店18座；金融服务网点2140家，多家银行均可办理国际业务，其中中国银行烟台分行与171个国家和地区的4000多家银行建立了代理关系。烟台市教育基础良好，科技力量雄厚，被评为“全国科教兴市先进城市”和“全国技术创新示范城市”。1998年，烟台又获得“国家环境保护模范城市”和“中国优秀旅游城市”称号，标志着烟台整个投资环境又迈上了一个新台阶。

三、发展前景

近期发展目标是：到2000年，国内生产总值按可比价格计算比1980年翻四番，人均水平居全国、全省前列；人民生活全面实现小康，并向富裕阶段迈进；加快建立现代企业制度，基本建立起社会主义市场经济体制格局。到2002年，全市人均国内生产总值达到2万元，地方财政收入在1997年的基础上力争翻一番，农民人均纯收入突破5000元，城镇居民人均可支配收入突破1万元。

远期发展目标是：立足烟台特有的区位优势，面向21世纪，顺应世界特别是亚太地区经济发展的大趋势，着力提高国民经济的整体素质，在21世纪的前20年里，基本建成现代化国际性港口城市。

四、鼓励投资的重点领域

为加快发展，烟台将大力改善投资环境，以成为海内外客商理想的投资热土。今后烟台鼓励和吸引外商投资的重点领域是：

1. 可持续优质、高效农业和农产品加工业。

2. 六大系列加工工业：以轿车及其零部件为龙头的主导产品系列，以机电一体化为先导的机械主导产品系列，以计算机及软件、通信设备、新型电子元器件为主导的电子产品系列，以化纤及深加工为主体的纺织主导产品系列，以名优产品为重点的食品、医药主导产品系列，以合成革及其深加工为重点的聚氨酯主导产品系列。

3. 新型能源和原材料的开发利用。

4. 金融保险、旅游、信息咨询和社会中介服务等新兴第三产业。

5. 采用新技术、新工艺、新设备、新型建设材料的建筑业，以及进行“安居工程”和经济适用商品住宅建设的房地产业。

6. 水利、交通运输、邮电通信和城市基础设施建设。

I. Economic Situation

Yantai is situated in the east of the Shandong Peninsula, with the Yellow Sea and Bohai Sea around it. It faces Japan, South Korea and the North Korea, and it is an important city in Shandong Province and the Bohai Sea Economic Zone. There are four districts, seven cities and one county under it, with a total of 13,745.95 sq km land area and a population of 6.43 million, among whom 1.5677 million are urban residents. With rich natural resources, Yantai is one of the major production areas in China for minerals, sea products and fruits. It has developed agriculture, and its leading industries are machinery, electronics, food staffs, beverages, metallurgical industry, and textiles. It has 33,000 enterprises. Yantai enjoys a mild climate, a warm winter and a cool summer. Penglai, and many other tourist spots are summer resorts. Yantai was one of the first 14 open coastal cities in China.

In the past 50 years since the founding of the People's Republic of China, and especially since the Third Plenary Session of the Eleventh CPC Central Committee at the end of 1978, great changes have taken place in Yantai. Yantai pushes on the reform and open-door policy and has created a fine economic development period. With its economy strengthened, Yantai's GDP reached 740 billion yuan in 1998, 0.5 times that of 1978, and an average annual increase of 12.5%, which was 3 times more than that of 1980 and three years in advance, 8.2 times the per capita average GDP, and a 11.7 % of annual increase. The total retail sales of consumer goods were 21.2 billion yuan, 27.8 times the sales of 1978, an 18 % annual increase on the average. The export-oriented economy made remarkable achievements. By 1998, the contractual value of foreign investment in Yantai had reached US$6.58 billion, and US$3.8 billion actual foreign investment had been realised. Now 2,461 joint ventures have been established in Yantai, and foreign investment has boasted more than 40 well-managed enterprises in industry, agriculture, commerce, real estate, energy, etc. In 1997 and 1998, Yantai represented the central government in successfully organising the 2nd APEC International Trade Exhibition and the 2nd APEC Technology Exchange Exhibition of Medium and Small-Sized Enterprises, which promoted Yantai's international status.

II. Investment Environment

In order to accelerate the development of export-oriented companies, Yantai's government has made efforts to improve the investment environment, such as by establishing a responsibility system for social services, management efficiency supervising feedback card and a service centre for foreign investment so as to guarantee a complete service mechanism. Therefore, Yantai has gained the honour of being one of the best 40 investment cities in China. Yantai's transportation, energy, urban construction and tertiary industries have been increasingly improved due to its rational use of foreign investment. For example, transportation extends in all directions, with 5,407 km of highways. It is connected by rail directly with eight cities, including Beijing, Shanghai, Xi'an, Jiamusi and Jinan.A Lanyan sub-line and Dezhou-

Longkou-Yantai line have been built, and the train ferry from Yantai to Dalian has been listed as a 1999 national project. With all these projects completed, Yantai will become an important transportation hub to the Bohai Rim. Now there are 9 ports which can handle 30 million tons of freight annually. The harbours at Yantai, Longkou, Laizhou and Penglai are national first-class open harbours, and Yantai harbour is north China's key foreign trade hub open to direct navigation with more than 100 foreign and domestic beaths with an annual volume of freight of 1,400 tonnes and 3 million of passengers transported every year to Tianjin, Dalian, Fushan and Qunshan. Yantai Airport has become a national first-class airport, and has 23 airlines direct routes to Beijing, Shanghai, Guangzhou, Hong Kong, Macao, Seoul, Osaka, etc. The average weekly flights reach 120 in the busy seasons of the year. The city is served by a digital telephone system with a capacity of 1.307 million telephones lines. The telephone popularisation rate is 14.3%, and 38.4 % in the urban areas. Besides, a GSM mobile phones service is also operating. The whole city has a power-generating capacity of 150 megawatts, has sufficient running water and central heating in major residential areas and the gas supply reaches 98.7% of households. Upon the completion of the Bohai Sea natural gas project, 1.5 million cubic meters of gas will be provided to the city daily, of which 800,000 cubic meters will be for civil use. There are more than 100 hotels, among which 18 are three-star hotels or above. The 2,140 banks or financial service bodies can do international business. The Yantai Branch of the Bank of China has established agency relations with more than 4,000 banks in 171 countries and regions worldwide. Yantai has a solid foundation for education and has a strong faculty of technology. Yantai has earned the titles of "National Advanced City for Strengthening the Country through Science and Education" and "National Model City for Technology Innovation". In 1998, Yantai earned the title of "National Model City for Environmental Protection" and "The Best Tourist City in China".

III. Development Perspective

Yantai's short-term development goals: By 2000, its GDP will increase by 4 times, based on 1980 fixed price and the average per capita income will be among the top in both the country and the province so as to raise the living standard of the people from being well-off to being wealthy in the long run. It will accelerate the establishment of a modern enterprise system so as to set up a socialist market economy structure. By 2002, the per capita GDP will reach RMB 20,000, and the local financial revenue shall increase by 100% on the basis of 1997. The farmers' per capita net income is to reach RMB 5,000, and that of urban residents RMB 10,000 on the average.

Yantai's long-term development goal is to follow the international and especially the Asia-Pacific economic development trend and to take advantage of its favourable location to welcome the 21st century. By 2020, Yantai will be an international modern harbour city .

IV. Key Areas for Encouraging Foreign Investment

In order to speed up its development, Yantai will make every effort to improve its investment environment and make policies to attract more foreign funding. The key areas in which foreign investment are encouraged:

1. Sustainable, efficient and excellent agriculture and agricultural product processing industries.

2. Six processing industries: vehicles and parts; mechanical and electrical products; computers and software, communication facilities, new types of electronic devices; chemical fibre and major textile products, food stuffs and medicines, and synthetic leather and polyurethane products.

3. New energy and raw material development and utilisation.

4. Tertiary industry such as finance and insurance, tourism, information consultancy and intermediary services.

5. Construction industry with new technology, new facilities, and new building materials, and low-price apartments.

6. Irrigation works, transportation, communication, and urban infrastructure construction.

不断前进的南通

Nantong: Making Constant Progress

一、经济发展

沐浴着改革开放的春风，南通的国民经济得到了较快的发展。80年代初以市区人均工业产值超万元、人均国民收入超千元被列为全国46个重点城市之一，1989年跨入全国25个国内生产总值逾百亿元的城市行列，1992年被列为全国“综合实力50强”城市之一，1995年在全国84个人均国内生产总值超万元的地级以上城市中居第31位。1998年，全市实现国内生产总值624亿元，按可比价计算(下同)，比上年增长10.5%；财政收入40.3亿元，增长10.5%，综合经济实力进一步增强。

第一产业。近年来，南通市坚持把农业放在国民经济发展的首位，全面贯彻党在农村的基本政策，不断深化农村改革，大力改善农业生产条件，积极实施科教兴农和贸工农一体化战略，农业综合生产能力稳步提高。1998年战胜晚春大雪、连续阴雨、特大洪水、持续高温等历史罕见自然灾害的频繁袭击，全市第一产业实现增加值124.6亿元，增长2.5%；完成农林牧渔业总产值235.6亿元，增长2.4%。南通农业有五个显著特点：一是综合生产能力高。“八五”(1991-1995)以来，在粮食播种面积有所下降，其他作物播种面积基本稳定的情况下，粮棉油总产稳中有升，单产水平逐年提高。1998年，粮食总产326.40万吨，超额完成年度计划。“五肉”、禽蛋、水产品总量、家禽饲养量和上市量均保持较高水平。二是土地产出率高。全市耕地复种指数达194.4%，形成了一年三熟、两年五熟、三年七熟等多熟制。三是农产品商品率高。南通是全国35个综合商品生产基地之一，所辖6县(市)中，有5个县(市)被列为全国粮棉生产大县，农产品综合商品率大大高于全省平均水平。四是农业科技水平高。农业科技进步贡献率为51.7%。良种覆盖率在95%以上。五是创汇率高。农副产品及其加工品出口占全市一般贸易出口总额的60%以上。

第二产业。南通工业起步较早，发展较快，门类齐全。早在清朝末年，著名实业家张謇就在南通兴办纺织工业，使南通成为中国民族工业的发祥地之一。经过一个多世纪的发展，现已初步形成轻纺、机械、电子、化工、医药、建材、船舶、冶金、电力相配套的现代化工业体系。纺织工业实力较强，纺、织、染整、服装配套成龙，是全国12个纺织品出口基地和10个服装出口基地之一。在全国42个重点服装生产城市中，南通服装工业各项主要经济技术指标连续6年名列前茅，成为全国十大服装生产出口基地之一。轻工产品有86大类、5000多个品种，薄荷脑、柠檬酸、工艺鞋帽、扎染制品、丝绸绣衣、蓝印花布、红木雕刻等名特产品饮誉海内外。机械工业现有产品550个系列、1500多个品种，出口比例居全国之冠。化学工业以精细化工为主，是全国15个精细化工生产基地之一，拥有一批骨干企业和拳头产品，在国内同行业中享有一定知名度。电子基础产品具有相当优势，江苏华容集团是国内最大的元器件生产基地。船舶工业形成一定规模，建成了国内最大的远洋船舶修理基地、设施一流的大型造船基地、大型拆船基地以及渔船修造企业群。1998年，全市完成工业总产值1024亿元，比

南通经济开发区
The Nantong Economic Development Zone

上年增长4.3%。其中国有及年销售500万元以上企业产值539亿元，产销率为95.78%，盈亏相抵后的利润总额为9.9亿元。乡镇企业在经济总量进一步扩张的同时，运行质量进一步提高。建筑业实力雄厚。全市现有建筑施工企业430家，其中国家一级资质企业17家，二级企业60家，从业人员30万以上。建筑队伍遍布全国各地，其中上海、新疆、山东、北京、南京、大庆等地均在万人以上。对外建筑劳务输出达32个国家和地区。1998年，全市建筑业完成总产值250亿元，施工面积3800万平方米，竣工面积1800万平方米，年全员劳动生产率达到每人8.3万元，工程质量合格率为100%，优良品率为42%，有5项工程新获中国建筑业最高奖“鲁班奖”。历年累计获“鲁班奖”18项，高居全国地级市之首。

第三产业。把第三产业作为全市经济发展的重要生长点和繁荣经济的战略产业，实施重点突破。1996年，产业格局实现了“二一三”向“二三一”的历史性转变。1998年，第三产业实现增加值208亿元，增长13%，占全市GDP的比重达到33.6%，比上年提高1.4个百分点。市场建设成效显著。全市现有各类商品交易市场664个，形成了叠石桥绣品城、永兴商城、华东轻纺城等一批辐射广、影响大的专业批发市场，年成交额亿元以上的市场达61个。南通王府井、伊丽名店百货相继开业，给全市商界注入了新的活力。全市流通业初步形成了商场与市场并举，综合经营与专业经营互补，高中低档次齐全，城市商业中心与新村、乡村商业网点配套的格局。1998年全市社会消费品零售总额213亿元，增长4%。金融保险业运行平稳。年末，金融系统各项存款余额620.28亿元，比年初增加87.51亿元；贷款余额368.89亿元，比年初增加30.48亿元。邮政、电信顺利分营，业务总量保持较快增长。专卖店、连锁店、超市、商业银行、证券公司、旅游度假区、物业管理、信息服务网络、会计师和律师事务所、社会办学等新的产业形式和服务方式发展较快。

二、基础设施

南通区位优势得天独厚，基础设施比较完备，投资环境优越。1992年被评为“全国投资环境40优城市”。交通已初步形成以水路为特色、水陆空相配套的立体大交通网络。南通港是全国十大港口之一，长江第二大港口，共有万吨级码头26座，与世界上64个国家和地区178个港口通航。1998年，南通港口货物吞吐量2017万吨，创历史最高记录；集装箱运输量13.03万标箱，在长江港口中跃居首位。宁通一级公路、204国道、328国道穿境而过，市内公路纵横交错，通沙、通常、海太三座汽渡通大江南北。新长铁路南通段已开工建设。苏通长江大桥项目已由省计经委上报国家审批。南通兴东机场和联航如皋机场有至北京、广州、深圳、厦门、大连、武汉、成都等空中航

线。邮电通信快速发展，在江苏省率先实现长话、市话、农话数字化交换。1998年末，全市电话交换机总容量达112万门，移动通讯交换机总容量达35万门。城市电话用户达27.9万户，增长15.4%；农村电话用户达42万户，增长44.8%；移动电话用户达11.6万户，增长51%。城市建设规模空前，面貌大为改观。近年来，市区以打通老城道路卡口、建设外环快速通道和新城区中轴线为重点，先后开工建设了外环东路、外环北路、工农路、204国道市区段、疏港公路、南大街等一批骨干路桥工程，拉开了新的城市框架。围绕创建全国卫生城市，强化城市综合管理，市区环境卫生状况明显改观。各县（市）高度重视城乡建设管理工作，加大了旧城改造、新区开发、村镇建设和创建工作的力度，环境面貌焕然一新。海门市、启东市为全国卫生城市，通州市、如皋市为省级卫生城市。

I. Economic Development

Bathed by the spring wind of reform and opening to the outside world, Nantong's economy has developed rapidly. In the early 1980s, the per capita industrial output value in the urban area exceeded 10,000 yuan, and the per capita national income was over 1,000 yuan. Hence it was listed as one of the 46 key cities of China. In 1989, it was among the 25 domestic cities whose GDP was more than 10 billion yuan. In 1992, it was listed as one of the nation's 50 top cities in terms of "comprehensive strength." In 1995, it ranked 31st among 84 cities at or above prefectural levels with GDP per capita exceeding 10,000 yuan. In 1998, its GDP reached 62.4 billion yuan, or an increase of 10.5 percent as compared with that of the previous year at constant prices; its financial income stood at 4.03 billion yuan, or a growth of 10.5 percent.

Primary Industry. In recent years, Nantong has given first priority to the development of the national economy, implemented the Party's basic rural policies in an all-round way, constantly deepened rural reform, greatly improved the conditions for agricultural production, and actively implemented the strategy of developing agriculture through science and education, and integrating trade, industry and agriculture. Consequently, its comprehensive agricultural production ability has been constantly improved. In 1998, it conquered natural disasters rarely seen in history, such as heavy snow in late spring, continuous rain, serious floods and constant high temperatures. The total output value of primary industry increased by 12.46 billion yuan (2.5 percent) to 23.56 billion yuan. The agriculture of Nantong has five remarkable characteristics:

1. High comprehensive production capacity. Since the Eighth Five-Year Plan, the area sown to grain crops has been reduced, while that sown to other crops has been basically stable. The total output of grain, cotton and oil-bearing crops has risen slightly, and per-unit area yield has grown yearly. In 1998, the total grain output came to 3.264 million tons, over-fulfilling the annual plan. The total output of the five kinds of meat, eggs and aquatic products was high,as was the amount of domestic fowls raised and sold on the market.

2. High land output rate. The multiple crop index of Nantong is as high as 194.4 percent, with three crops a year, five crops within two years and seven crops within three years.

3. High commodity rate of agricultural products. Nantong is one of the 35 national comprehensive commodity production bases. Of the six counties (cities) under its jurisdiction, five have been listed as national major grain and cotton production counties.

Its comprehensive commodity rate of agricultural products is much higher than the province's average level.

4. High agricultural scientific and technological level. The contribution rate of scientific and technological progress to agriculture is 51.7 percent; and the coverage rate of improved varieties is over 95 percent.

5.High foreign exchange-generating rate. The export volume of agricultural, and side-line products and processed products make up more than 60 percent of the city's total export volume.

Secondary Industry. Nantong's industry started fairly early, and has developed rapidly. At the end of the Qing Dynasty (1644-1911), Zhang Jian, a leading industrialist, founded the textile industry in Nantong, thus making the city one of the birthplaces of this industry in China. Thanks to development over the past century or so, Nantong has formed a modern industrial system, including light industrial and textile products, and the machinery, electronics, chemicals, medicines, construction materials, shipbuilding, metallurgical and power industries. Its textile industry is fairly outstanding, consisting of spinning, weaving, dyeing and garment-making sectors. Nantong is one of the 12 export bases of textile products and one of the 10 clothing export bases in China. Among the 42 national key clothing production cities, Nantong has led for six successive years in terms of various major economic and technological indices, thus becoming one of the 10 major clothing production centers in China. Nantong produces more than 5,000 varieties of light industrial products, which fall into 86 categories. Its peppermint, citric acid, shoes and hats, silk clothing, blue printed cloth, padauk carvings and other famous local products are well known both at home and abroad. Its machinery industry produces more than 1,500 varieties of products, which fall into 550 series, and ranks first in export volume in the country. Nantong is one of the 15 fine chemical industrial production bases in China, with a number of backbone enterprises. Its fine chemicals industry enjoys a high reputation among enterprises of the same trade in China. Its basic electronics products occupy a dominant position, and the local Jiangsu Huarong Group is the largest producer of components and parts in China. Its shipping industry includes the largest ocean-going vessel repair base in China, a well-equipped shipbuilding base, a large ship-demolition base and fishing boat repair and building enterprises. In 1998, the city's total industrial output value came to 102.4 billion yuan, or an increase of 4.3 percent over the previous year, of which the output value of state-owned enterprises and enterprises with annual sales volume exceeding five million yuan was 53.9 billion yuan, with a production and marketing rate of 95.78 percent, and profits totaling 990 million yuan. While further expanding their total economic volume, township enterprises have further improved their operational quality. The construction industry is particularly strong. Nantong has 430 construction enterprises, including 17 first-class qualification enterprises, and 60 second-class qualification enterprises, employing more than 300,000 people. Its construction workers are spread all over the country, with at least 10,000 each in Shanghai, Xinjiang, Shandong, Beijing, Nanjing and Daqing. In addition, it has sent construction workers to 32 countries and regions. In 1998, the total output value of its construction industry registered 25 billion yuan, and the construction area came to 38 million square meters, of which 18 million square meters were completed. The annual per capita labor and production rate of all staff and workers reached 83,000 yuan and the quality of all projects reached the required standard. Among them, 42 percent were rated as excellent projects and five won the "Lu Ban Award", the highest award in China's construction industry. Nantong has won 18 Lu Ban awards, ranking first among prefectural-level cities in China.

Tertiary Industry. Nantong takes tertiary industry as an important growth point for its economic development and a strategic industry for economic prosperity. In 1996, historical changes took place in the industrial setup. In 1998, the output volume of the tertiary sector increased by 20.8 billion yuan (13 percent), making up 33.6 percent of Nantong's GDP (growth of 1.4 percentage points). Remarkable progress has been made in the construction of markets. Nantong has 664 various kinds of commodity trade markets, including a group of specialized wholesale markets, such as Dieshiqiao Embroidered Products City, Yongxing Commercial City and East China Light and Textile City. Of them, 61 markets have an annual business volume exceeding 100 million yuan each. Nantong Wangfujing and Yili Famous Department Store have gone into operation, injecting new vitality into the commercial sector. A new setup has been formed featuring the simultaneous development of shopping centers and markets, the mutual complement of comprehensive and specialized operation, complete grades, and urban commercial centers supported by new village and rural commercial networks. In 1998, the total retail sales volume of Nantong's social consumer goods came to 21.3 billion yuan, or an increase of 4 percent. The financial and insurance undertakings are operating steadily. At the end of 1998, the remaining sum of various kinds of deposits was 62.028 billion yuan, or an increase of 8.751 billion yuan over that at the beginning of the year; the remaining sum of loans was 36.889 billion yuan, or a growth of 3.048 billion yuan over that at the start of the year. Postal services and telecommunications were smoothly separated, with the business volume growing rapidly. Some new industrial forms and service means have developed at high speed, such as specialized shops, chain stores, supermarkets, commercial banks, securities companies, tourist and holiday resorts, property management, information service networks, accountancy and law offices,and community schools.

II. Infrastructure Facilities

With exceptional locational advantages, Nantong has perfect infrastructure facilities and an excellent investment environment. In 1992 Nantong was named as one of the "40 cities with excellent environments in China." A three-dimensional communications network with water routes, highways and airlines has been formed. The Nantong Port is one of the 10 major ports in China, and the second largest port on the Yangtze River. With 26 ,10,000-dwt wharves, the port has links with 178 ports in 64 countries and regions. In 1998, the port handled 20.17 million tons of freight, the highest figure ever, along with 130,300 standard containers, ranking first among all the ports along the Yangtze River. Nantong is on the Nanjing-Nantong first-class highway, and No. 204 and No.328 national roads, and has a crisscross network of roads and three steam ferries. The construction of the Sutong Yangtze River Bridge has been submitted to the state for examination and approval by the planning and economic commissions of Jiangsu Province. Flights from Nantong to Beijing, Guangzhou, Shenzhen, Xiamen, Dalian, Wuhan and Chengdu are available. Nantong led Jiangsu Province in adopting digital exchanges for long-distance, city and rural telephone services. At the end of 1998, the total telephone exchange capacity of Nantong reached 1.12 million circuits, and its mobile telephone exchange capacity 350,000 circuits. In urban areas, there were

27,900 telephone users, or an increase of 15.4 percent; in rural areas, 420,000 users, or a growth of 44.8 percent; mobile telephone users rose 51 percent to 116,000. The urban construction scale is unprecedented, and great changes have taken place in the face of Nantong. In recent years, Nantong has constructed a number of key roads and bridges.

The Outer-Ring Road, North Outer-Ring Road, Industry and Agriculture Road, the city section of the No.204 National Road, Shugang Road, South Street, etc., thus forming the framework of the new city.

The environment and sanitation in Nantong have been remarkably improved. All counties (cities) have attached great importance to the management of urban and rural construction, and have strengthened the transformation of the old city, the development of new areas, and the construction of villages and towns. As a result, Nantong has taken on an entirely new look. Haimen and Qidong cities are national sanitary cities, and Tongzhou and Rugao cities, provincial ones.

连云港——黄海之滨的明珠

Lianyungang: A Pearl on the Shore of the Yellow Sea

一、经济发展状况

江苏省的连云港市，地处中国沿海中部的黄海之滨，位于横贯中国大陆东西的陇海铁路东端，新亚欧大陆桥的东桥头堡，是中国最早实行改革开放的沿海城市之一。全市共辖四县四区，总面积7444平方公里，人口443.53万。连云港山海奇观，景色壮丽，名胜古迹浑然一体，享有："东海第一胜境"的美誉。自然资源丰富，平原、山丘、水面、滩涂具备。东临大海，盛产鱼、虾、盐；中耸云台山，盛产茶、磷矿及水晶石；西南北三面平川环抱，盛产稻麦、花生、棉花。

建国50年来，特别是近20年以来，连云港市以改革、开发、发展为主线，创造了惊人的业绩。1998年国内生产总值264.67亿元，是1978年的25.34倍，年均增长10.9%；人均国内生产总值增长18.72倍，可比价年均增长9.2%；社会消费品零售总额84.47亿元，是1978年的22.72倍，年均增长16.9%。国民经济实力大大增强。外向型经济发展取得了丰硕的成果。1984-1998年，连云港签订利用外资项目近2000个，合同利用外资17.66亿美元，实际利用外资7.27亿美元，外资投向遍及农业、工业、建筑业、交通运输业、饮食娱乐和房地产等产业。目前连云港有三资企业上千家，运营状况良好。外贸出口大幅度增长，1988年以来，累计出口总额14.93亿美元，年均增长5.77%。

二、投资环境

为了加速发展外向型经济，连云港市努力改善投资环境，集中财力和引进外资搞好全市的交通、能源、市政建设。大力发展第三产业，城市建设日臻完善。连云港河海相通，港路相接，水陆空相连。海上可通往世界各国，陆上经新亚欧大陆桥直达西亚和欧洲各国。连云港位于中国海洋和铁路联运的T型结构交汇点处，是内地11个省区对外贸易最便捷的出海口，年设计吞吐能力已达2265万吨，是全国500家最大服务企业之一。公路网密集，宁连一级公路和连徐、同三高速公路使连云港便捷地通向全国的东西南北；内河可与江淮及京杭大运河相通；航空开通了全国主要城市的航线，组成一个四通八达的水陆空立体交通网。目前连云港已与世界各大洲的85个国家和地区有贸易往来。连云港市吃、住、行便利，拥有二十多家星级、涉外宾馆和酒店，出租小汽车众多，服务热情周到。电信事业发展迅速，1998年底，全市拥有市话机36.85万部，国际电话可直拨195个国家和地区的500多个城市。同时，无线电话传呼机、移动电话、磁卡电话齐全。全市供水、供电充足。

三、发展前景

远期发展目标是：人民的小康生活更加宽裕，全市初步实现现代化，初步建成区域性国际贸易中心、环境优美的旅游中心、现代化的交通枢纽和国际性海港城市，基本确立在亚欧大陆桥经济带的龙头地位。

近期奋斗目标是：到本世纪末，人均国内生产总值翻一番，人民生活实现小康，初步建立适应社会主义市场经济要求的经济体制，为实现现代化打下坚实的基础。

四、鼓励投资的重点领域

1. 优化本市产业结构，逐步建立一批能迅速转化为生产力的高新技术产业。工业重点发展化学、机械、纺织、皮塑、轻工业、工艺、建材、医药、冶金等行业；农业重点发展优良品种的引进、农副产品深加工、养殖业、蔬菜水果的加工、储藏、保鲜技术，开发创汇农业新项目。

2. 围绕建设现代化海港枢纽城市的目标，加大配套基础设施建设力度。重点扩大港口建设，新建散装水泥装卸码头、危险品装卸码头、集装箱转运站，扩建机场，修建高速公路，改造内河运输码头，对站埠、管道、大桥、电厂、供水、供气、城市道路、旧城改造、污水处理及其他环保设施、水库治理、闸坝、泵站的建设和改造。

3. 充分开发本市旅游资源，使现代化旅游和传统旅游协调发展，合理发展涉外房地产业，建立与贸易、旅游相配套的文化娱乐、旅馆和餐饮业。

对于围绕资源开发、基础设施建设、产业结构调整、现有企业嫁接改造和农业产业化的项目，连云港将给予政策上更大的优惠。

I. Economic Development

Lianyungang, one of the pilot coastal cities for the implementation of the reform and opening policies, is located on the shore of the Yellow Sea. It is at the eastern terminus of the Lianyungang-Qinghai Railway, which connects eastern and western China, and is the eastern bridgehead of the new Eurasian Continental Bridge. It administers four districts and four counties, with a total area of 7,444 square km and a population of over 4.4 million.

The city boasts beautiful scenery, with mountains, the sea and well-known historical sites, and is praised as "the first landfall along the East China Sea." It has rich natural resources, and its geography varies from plains and hills to shoreline and shallows. The Yellow Sea provides fish, shrimp and salt. The Yuntai Mountains produce tea and provide phosphorus ore and rock crystals. The plains in the north, south and west are fertile ground for the cultivation of wheat, rice, peanuts, and cotton.

Since the founding of the New China 50 years ago, and especially in the 20 years of reform and opening, Lianyungang has created magnificent records. In 1998, the city's GDP value stood at 26.467 billion yuan, 25.34 times the figure in 1978, with an average annual growth rate of 10.9 percent at a constant price level. The per capita GDP value increased 19.72 times, with a growth rate of 9.2 percent. Total value of retail sales was 8.447 billion yuan, 22.72 times the figure in 1978, with an annual growth rate of 16.9 percent. The local economy has been greatly strengthened. One result has been massive development of the export-oriented economy. Between 1984 and 1998,

Lianyungang signed nearly 2,000 contracts involving foreign investment, with contracted capital of US$1.766 billion and actual investment of US$727 million. Foreign investment was primarily directed towards agriculture, industry, construction, transportation, catering, recreation and real estate. There are approximately 1,000 joint ventures, cooperative enterprises and solely foreign-funded ventures in the city. Exports have increased markedly. The total export value from 1988 to 1998 was US$1.493 billion, with an annual growth rate of 5.77 percent.

II. Investment Environment

To accelerate the development of the export-oriented economy, the Lianyungang municipal government has made efforts to improve the investment environment, with the emphasis on transportation, energy and urban construction, through financial allocations and the introduction of foreign investment. The government has also stressed the development of tertiary industry and urban construction. Lianyungang links sea and land, it reaches various countries by sea and is connected with Central Asia and Europe through the new Eurasian Continental Bridge. The harbor, located in the T-shaped hub of sea and railway transportation, is close to 11 provinces and regions. The annual cargo handling capacity of the harbor amounts to 22.65 million tons, forming one of the top 500 service enterprises in the country.

The city also has a network of radiating highways. Its first-grade Ningbo-Lianyungang Highway and Lianyungang-Xuzhou Expressway connect it to all parts of the country. The river that flows through the city links it with the Huaihe and Yangtze rivers and the Beijing-Hangzhou Canal. The city has opened air routes to major cities in the country. Lianyungang has established trade relations with 85 countries and regions around the world. It also provides convenient accommodation, with over 20 star-rated hotels and numerous taxis offering cordial services.

The city's telecommunications network has developed rapidly. By the end of 1998, there were 368,500 telephone lines and international direct dialing services linked Lianyungang with over 500 cities in 195 countries and regions. It also has full facilities for personal pagers, cellular telephones, and magnetic card telephones.

III. Prospects for Development

The long-term target is to improve living standards, initially realize modernization and turn Lianyungang into a regional center for international trade, tourism, communication and ocean cargo handling, so as to establish the city as the dragon-head of the economic belt along the Eurasian Land Bridge.

The short-term target is to double per-capita GDP by the end of this year, to basically realize improvements in living standards, and to set up an economic system in conformity with the socialist market economy so as to lay the foundation for the realization of modernization.

IV. Major Fields in which Investment Is Encouraged

1. To streamline local industrial structure and gradually establish a group of new and hi-tech industries that can be quickly turned into production. Major industries include chemicals, machinery, textiles and leather, plastic, light industries, handicrafts, building materials, medicines and metallurgy. The development of agriculture will emphasize the introduction of hybrid seeds, the processing of agricultural and side-line products, aquatic products, the processing of vegetables and fruits, storage technologies, and new foreign-currency earning projects.

2. Redoubling efforts for the construction of complementing basic facilities to reach the goal of building a modernized hub harbor. Stress will be laid on expanded con-

struction of the harbor, the building of a concrete quay and a hazardous materials dock, establishing a transfer station for containers, expanding the construction of the airport, building expressways, renovation of the canal dock, building and renovating stations and docks, pipelines, bridges, power plants, water and gas supply lines, urban roads, the old city, drainage treatment and other environmental facilities, a reservoir, floodgates and pumping stations.

3. To fully tap tourism resources in the city, to coordinate the development of modern tourism with that of traditional tourism, and to rationally develop foreign-related real estate, establish cultural and recreational facilities and hotels, and the food and beverage industries related to trade and tourism.

Lianyungang will provide additional preferential policies to encourage the development of resources, basic infrastructure construction, industrial adjustments, the reform and renovation of existing enterprises, and projects involving agricultural industrialization.

宁波——东方大港初具规模

Ningbo: A Large Prospering Port in the East

宁波简称“甬”，是中国沿海四大深水中转港与重要贸易口岸，宁波位于东海之滨，中国大陆海岸线中段，长江三角洲东南翼，全市总面积9365平方公里，总人口535万。宁波地理位置优越，是著名的历史文化名城，更是具有7000年文明史的“河姆渡文化”的发祥地。宁波自古以来就是重要的通商口岸，包括北仓港、宁波港、镇海港在内的宁波港集内河港、河口港、海峡港于一体，港口综合吞吐能力居中国大陆港口第二位。宁波作为著名的侨乡，“宁波帮”名扬海外，目前有30多万宁波籍人士旅居在世界60多个国家和地区，是宁波经济建设和对外开放的又一大优势。

一、经济和社会发展

新中国成立以来，特别是1979年6月，国务院正式批准宁波港对外开放以后，宁波立足深水大港，适时制定和实施了“以港兴市、以市促港”的发展战略，利用得天独厚的港口优势，综合经济实力不断迈上新台阶。改革开放以后的20年时间里，宁波市的国内生产总值年均递增15.5%，1998年国内生产总值达973.4亿元，比1949年增长121倍，综合经济实力1997年在219个城市中居第27位，成为进步最快的城市之一；1998年的财政收入达87.6亿元，较之1949年的0.3亿元，50年扩大了291倍。

目前，宁波经济结构合理，特色产业形成实力，块状经济初具规模，乡镇企业异军突起。宁波拥有杉杉、雅戈尔、一休、罗蒙、帅康、方太、玉立等一大批明星企业，在国内同行中的竞争力迅速上升。一些乡镇和村的块状经济已初具规模。乡镇企业的异军突起，使宁波县域经济不断发展壮大，所辖6县（市）中有5个县（市）跻身“全国百强县”行列，蓬勃发展的乡镇企业成为宁波经济的一大特色。

同时，宁波的城市建设和管理水平不断提高。宁波市中心城市环境优美，道路通畅，阳光广场、中山广场等休闲场所风格各异，成为甬城的一道亮丽风景线。近年来，宁波市先后被授予“全国首届优秀旅游城市”、“历史文化名城”、“全国双拥模范城”等。

二、投资环境

根据“宁波经济主体要转向外向型开放型经济”和“以港兴市、以市促港”的发展战略，宁波不断加强基础建设，开发城市功能，优化投资环境。从1988年起，宁波共投入近百亿元人民币用于城市基础设施建设，还吸收10多亿美元外资投向基础设施，使城市交通、通讯供水、环保等条件明显改善。以宁波港为中心的交通集疏运网络基本形成，居大陆港口第二位。在已建成的万吨级以上泊位中包括中国目前最大的20万吨级兼靠30万吨级船舶的码头、25万吨级原油码头、5万吨级散装液体化工专用码头，管理服务日臻完善。宁波港已与84个国家和地区的518个港口开通了航线，并已开通至美国东、西部，欧洲，日本神户、横滨，澳大利亚，新西兰，韩国，香港的定期集装箱班轮；宁波栎社机场已开通了国内外航线26条；萧甬铁路年通过能力提高到1200万吨。此外，邮电通信事业快速发展。1996年全网实现交换程控化、传输数字化，同期还相继开通了移动和数据通信网。邮政也形成了以宁波为中心的快速邮运网，引进自动化信函分拣系统，开通了邮政金融计算机网。信息港建设初见成效，Internet 宁波节点站、Chinanet宁波节点接入平台以及教育网、科技网、经济信息网、经贸网等资源网络相继建成开通。在能源、原材料的供应上，北仑电厂、镇海电厂、镇海炼化等重点工程的相继建成投产，确保了能源、原材料供应。随着投资环境的不断改善，很多国际知名企业如美国埃索、印尼金光、协和石化等纷纷落户宁波。

三、发展前景

宁波市2010年远景发展目标纲要中提出：到2000年国内生产总值按1995年价格计算，达到1300亿元，人均23600元，城乡居民收入年均增长5%以上；要提高宁波在全国中心城市综合实力评估中的地位，争取县（市）都进入全国百强县，并力争位次有所提高；宁波港初步建设成为中国大陆沿海重要的国际深水中转枢纽港和大型远洋集装箱转运基地，港口货物吞吐能力达到1亿吨以上，集装箱吞吐能力达到100万标箱，以港口为中心的集疏运网络和揽货系统初步形成；更好地发挥宁波口岸作为长江三角洲地区第二大口岸的功能作用，口岸进出口额争取突破200亿美元，年均递增30%以上；争取到本世纪末形成5家年销售收入超100亿元、10家超亿元的大型企业集团；建成和建设一批事关宁波长远发展的重大基础设施、基础工业项目，供水、交通、供电、邮电通信基本适应经济发展和人民生活需要，重化工业基地初具规模。到2010年，全市国民经济和社会发展主要指标达到目前中等发达国家水平，人均国内生产总值比2000年翻一番以上，把宁波基本建设成为经济实力雄厚、对外开放度高、科学文化发达、人民生活富裕、社会风气良好、城市环境优美的社会主义现代化国际港口城市。

宁波城市风貌
The Scene of Ningbo

四、鼓励投资的重点领域

为实现宁波的发展目标，结合实际情况，宁波鼓励投资能够优化工业结构、提升产业的领域。

一是大力发展临港工业，以港口为依托，确立临港型工业在工业体系中的重要地位，加快发展炼油、电力、钢铁、化工、造纸、修造船等产业。

二是积极发展高新技术产业，在现有的行业中选择电子信息、机电一体、新材料、精细化工、新能源及节能技术等高新技术产业重点培育，实现产业化。

三是大力推动农业产业化，鼓励全社会办水利的投资体制。引进开发、培育农业新品种，发展出口创汇农业；发展专门基地种植；推广科技农业，立足资源，面向市场建立现代化综合农业产业体系；发展加工农业和远洋渔业。

四是结合城市建设和产业结构调整，鼓励基础设施建设投资、高新技术产业及市场服务业的投资。

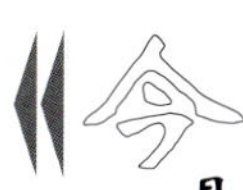

Ningbo, also known as Yong, is one of the four largest deep transit ports in China. In 1987, Ningbo became a city specially designated in the state plan. It is located on the southeastern tip of the Yangtze Delta along the coast of the East China Sea, which is in the middle of China's coastline . Covering an area of 9,365 square kilometers, it has a population of 5.35 million. As the birthplace of the 7,000-year-old Hemudu culture, Ningbo is a famous cultural and historical city in China. Ever since ancient times, Ningbo has been an important trade port, including the sections of Beilun, Ningbo, and Zhenhai. It simultaneously serves the functions of inland, delta, and oceanic water transport. Compared with other ports on the Chinese mainland, its comprehensive handling capacity ranks second. Ningbo is also the ancested home of many overseas Chinese, with more than 300,000 descendants currently living in over 60 countries and regions across the world. This is another big advantage of Ningbo for its economic development and opening to the outside world.

I. Social and Economic Development

In June 1979, the State Council placed Ningbo among the first set of ports opened to the outside world. Seizing this opportunity, Ningbo soon laid down its strategy of "first developing the city through the port, then advancing the port through the city." Based on its status as a large and deep port, Ningbo has fully tapped its transportation advantages, while its overall economic strength keeps rising to new levels. Two decades after the introduction of the reform and opening policies, Ningbo's GDP (gross domestic product) realized an average annual growth of 15.5 percent. In 1998, its GDP came to 97.34 billion yuan, an increase of 121 times over that of 1949, after adjusting for inflation. In 1997 its overall economic strength ranked 27th among 219 cities in China, becoming one of the most rapidly developing cities. In 1998 it realized a regional state revenue of 8.76 billion yuan, with an increase of 291 times over that of 1949, in the past 50 years, from 30 million yuan in 1949.

At present, Ningbo enjoys a rational economic structure, powerful characteristic industries, an emerging specialized sub-regional economy and fast-growing township enterprises. Ningbo boasts quite a few star enterprises, such as garment factories like Shanshan and Yagor, and manufacturers of household appliances like Shuaikang and Fangtai. Their competitive strength keeps rising ahead of other similar enterprises in the domestic market. Specialized sub-regional economies in towns and villages have already taken shape. Among the six counties under its jurisdiction, five have been numbered among the "One Hundred Most Powerful Counties in China." Ningbo's prospering township enterprises are a salient feature of its economy.

At the same time, Ningbo's urban construction and management level have also progressed greatly. The city center has a beautiful environment and easy access to transportation. Its recreation sites like Sunshine Square and Zhongshan Square all possess styles of their own, becoming new places of interest in the city. In recent years, Ningbo has been conferred honorary titles such as "Outstanding Tourist City," "Key Historical and Cultural City," and "National-level Model City in the Dual Support Movement" (a movement calling on civilians to support the army and give preferential treatment to families of soldiers and martyrs).

II. Investment environment

Ningbo's development strategy is to switch its economy to an open and export-orientated one, and to develop the city through the port and advance the port through the city. Based on that strategy, Ningbo has strengthened its infrastructure construction, exploited its urban functions, and improved its investment environment. Since 1988,

Ningbo has invested almost 10 billion yuan in infrastructure construction, together with more than 1 billion US dollars in foreign investment. As a result, its transportation, communications, water supply, and environmental protection capacities have been greatly improved. A transportation network with Ningbo as the center has taken shape. In 1998, the handling capacity of the Ningbo port came to 87.06 million tons, its containers handling capacity reached 352,000 standardized containers, ranking second among ports on the Chinese mainland. Among China's completed berths with 10,000 dwt handling capacity, Ningbo alone boasts China's largest iron ore wharf with a 200,000-dwt handling capacity (it can also serve 300,000 dwt ships). It also has a wharf for crude oil and one for liquid chemicals in bulk with a handling capacity of 250,000 tons and 50,000 tons respectively. Its corresponding services and management level have improved considerably. At present, Ningbo is connected with 518 ports in 84 countries and regions. It has also opened regular container shiplines to terminals in Europe, Australia, New Zealand, South Korea, Hong Kong, Japan's Kobe and Yokohama, and along the eastern and western coasts of the United States. As for air transportation, Ningbo's Lishe Airport is linked by 26 airlines with both domestic and international destinations. And the Xiaoyong Railway has a handling capacity of 12 million tons per year.

With respect to telecommunications, Ningbo has also witnessed rapid growth. In 1996, the city achieved its goal of digital transmission and a regional program-controlled telephone system. Subsequently, it has opened networks of mobile and data communications. Concerning postal services, Ningbo has imported an automatic letter-sorting system and started a computer network for postal banking. A network of EMS (express mail service) with Ningbo as the center has already been set up. Construction of information technology has also begun to result in handsome gains. Internet Ningbo site, Ningbo cutover flatform to Chinanet, Cernet, Cstnet, Ceinet and Chinatrade have been set up. With respect to energy and raw materials, a set of key projects, such as the Beilun Power Plant, Zhenhai Power Plant and Zhenhai Petrochemical Works, have been completed and put into operation, ensuring a steady supply of energy and raw materials. As Ningbo's investment environment has improved, many famous international corporations such as Esso have flocked to the city.

III. Prospects for Development

Ningbo's Ninth Five-Year Plan for Economic and Social Development and Outline of the Long-Term Target for the Year 2010 have proposed a GDP target of 130 billion yuan RMB (calculated at 1995 prices), 23,600 yuan per capita, with an average annual increase of over 5 percent in per capita income by the year 2000. Ningbo should enhance its ranking in the evaluation of the comprehensive economic strength of key cities in China. All its counties should join the "One Hundred Most Powerful Counties in China." Ningbo also plans to build itself into a key international deep-port transit hub and a large oceanic-container transit terminal with a handling capacity of more than 0.1 billion tons and 1 million standardized containers. A goods collecting system and a collection, distribution and transportation network with the port as the center will develop. The city will better tap its potential and function as the second-largest harbor in the Yangtze Delta so as to attain an import and export volume of over 20 billion US dollars, with the average annual increase exceeding 30 percent.

By the end of the 20th century, Ningbo plans to establish 5 industrial groups with annual sales incomes exceeding 10 billion yuan RMB cach and 10 smaller groups with the corresponding figure surpassing 0.1 billion. It will construct a set of key infrastructure and basic industrial projects for the benefit of long-term development. Its wa-

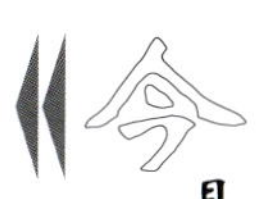

ter supply, transportation, electricity supply, postal service and telecommunications will be able to meet the demands of economic development and the local people's lives. It will also become an emerging base for the heavy and chemical industries.

By 2010, Ningbo plans to double or more than double its per capita GDP over that of 2000, and to raise its main regional state economic and social development indicators to the current levels of middle-level developed countries. By that time, Ningbo will have emerged as a modern international port, with great economic power, and high levels of science and culture, where people can enjoy a better life in a progressive society.

IV. Key Fields for Investment

According to Ningbo's existing reality and development strategy, the city encourages investment in fields which can rationalize its industrial structure and enhance the technological level of its industries. They are:

1. Emphasizing port industries so as to make them the main pillar of the city's industrial matrix. Port industries include oil refining, electricity, iron and steel, chemicals, paper-making, ship-building and repair, and so on.

2. Developing new- and high-tech industries. Its priority is to nurture high-tech industries like electronics, information technology, new materials, fine chemicals, new energy, energy-saving technology and electrical machinery.

3. Mechanizing agriculture and encouraging a system in which all social sectors invest in water conservancy projects. It is imperative to import, develop and cultivate new strains of crops for the development of an export-oriented agriculture. Ningbo should also step up efforts to popularize agricultural technology and grow specialized crops in bases so as to establish a modernized, comprehensive agricultural system which meets market demands. Food processing and oceanic fishing are also important.

4. In combination with urban construction and adjustment of its industrial structure, Ningbo should encourage and direct investments towards infrastructure facilities, new- and high-tech industries, and other sectors which serve market needs.

温州——东海之滨的明珠

Wenzhou: A Pearl on Coast of the East China Sea

温州市位于中国黄金海岸线中段，受长江、珠江三角洲经济带双重辐射，与沪穗经济联系十分密切。温州是全国首批沿海开放城市、农村改革试验区和城市综合配套改革试点城市之一。全市土地面积11784平方公里，市区建成区面积76平方公里；人口718万，辖3区2市6县。

温州以气候温和而得名，年平均气温16.1-18.2摄氏度，降水量1500-1900毫米，无霜期260-300天。温州地理位置优越，辖区有8个县（市、区）临海，大陆海岸线355公里，拥有大小港湾80多个，海岛436个。港口资源得天独厚，可建5000吨到10万吨级码头泊位100个。市区以东100余公里的大陆架蕴藏着丰富的油气资源，已有5.4平方公里的海域由中外知名石油公司勘探开发。全市水资源总量为141亿立方米，理论可开发蕴藏量为82万千瓦。矿产以非金属矿为主，明矾矿储量占全国80%，有“世界矾都”之称。温州山奇水秀，旅游资源丰富，有国家级风景区2个、自然保护区2个，省级风景区7个，景区面积占土地面积1/5强。雁荡山、楠溪江、南麂岛、乌岩岭等均是闻名的旅游胜地和自然保护区。温州环境条件较好，市区空气污染指数为一至二级，在全国46个重点城市中处于比较清洁的城市。全市主要水系为一类或二类标准，森林覆盖率为56.1%。

经过50年的建设，温州发生了巨大变化。1998年与1949年比较，全市农业总产值增长11.5倍，粮食总产量增长1.8倍，工业总产值增长1793倍，社会消费品零售额增长679倍，固定资产投资增长3万多倍，财政收入比1952年增长160倍。教育、文化、科技、社会、保障等各项社会事业也取得了飞速的发展。

温州人素以“敢为天下先”而著称，改革开放以来，温州人民凭着自己的勤劳智慧，率先进行市场取向改革，成为经济发展最快、最活跃和综合实力较强的地区之一。1978年至1998年，全市经济平均每年递增15.9%，大大高于全国、全省平均发展水平。全市国内生产总值由13.31亿元增加到677.19亿元，财政收入由1.35亿元增加到46亿元，分别翻了4和5番。人民生活总体水平实现小康，1998年城市居民人均可支配收入8942元，农村居民人均纯收入3833元，城市经济实力跃升为全国第47位。工业生产已形成了机械、化工、轻纺、食品、服装、制革、塑料、建材、电子、电器、冶金、造船、电力等工业生产体系，主导性产品主要有服装、鞋类、低压电器、打火机、灯具、眼镜、机械阀门、医疗仪器等，是全国著名的“服装城”、“鞋城”、“低压电器城”。

经过20年的改革与发展，温州形成了“小商品、大市场”的格局，“小资本、大辐射”的优势和“小区域、大发展”的态势，走出了一条颇具特色的经济发展路子。民营经济成为国民经济的主体，市场机制成为经济发展的内在动力，社会投入成为城市建设资金的主渠道，小城镇的崛起

成为经济增长的主要支撑。在改革领域中，温州率全国之先，创出了许许多多个全国第一，在全国以至世界享有很高的知名度。温州是全国股份合作制经济的发祥地，商贸业和私营个体经济发达。在工业和贸易业中，民营比重占到八成。1998年，全市私营个体工商户达20.5万户，从业人员35.5万人；有各类市场533个，年成交额407.23亿元。商品经济异常活跃，在全国各地经商办企业达100多万人，同时也有百余万人口流入务工和从事服务活动。

温州作为沿海开放城市，投资环境有许多优势。温州是著名的侨乡，在世界各地的华侨有30多万人，聚集着信息、科技、文化、资金等方面的优势。全市有6个县（市、区）被列为对外开放地区，有1个国家级经济技术开发区和3个省级经济技术开发区，60个建制镇为对外开放重点工业卫星镇，形成了多层次的对外开发布局。基础设施日臻完善。水、电、路、港、通讯等基础设施成为政府和全社会投资的重点，90年代投入城市建设资金达280多亿元。温州交通初步形成了港口、铁路、航空、公路相配套的立体交通网络。温州机场已开通国内和境外航线56条，温州火车站是全省第二大站，温州港辟有国际航线。温州目前在建和筹建的交通投资项目主要有：温（州）福（州）铁路、甬（宁波）台（州）温（州）铁路和高速公路、金（华）温（州）高速公路、温州七里港区一期等项目。仅高速公路温州段总投资100多亿元，已完成投资额30%。港口项目投资4.6亿元，新建1–2.5万吨级码头3座，1000–5000吨级码头4座，使港口吞吐能力达到2000万吨，温州交通正向着全国区域性枢纽中心迈进。温州也是通信设施最完善的城市之一。1998年全市电话装机容量达到142.6万门，移动电话装机容量达到120.1万门，全市每百人拥有电话24.3部，

温州大桥
Wenzhou Bridge

市区达到74部，全年邮电业务量29.7亿元，居全省之首。水电紧缺的“瓶颈”制约已根本解决。温州电网年最高负荷80万千瓦，1998年全市用电量55.7亿千瓦时，比1990年增长2.7倍，年均递增17.7%。市区自来水日综合生产能力已达到61万吨。目前在建的重点水电建设项目总投资103亿元，电力装机总容量333万千瓦，水利枢纽工程总库容18亿立方米。为提高抗御自然灾害能力，按50年一遇标准建设浙东标准海塘，温州段总长度226公里，总投资10.9亿元。

温州涉外机构齐全，港口、航空港、开发区均设有海关、商检、保险、外运、金融、税务、法律等机构。外国投资事务办公室、外商“三胞”投资咨询中心和外商投资企业协会，为海外投资者提供高效、优质服务。国家级开发区温州经济技术开发区建设颇具规模，一批“三资”企业相继在温州落户。对外开放以来，全市累计签订外资协议项目1460个，协议项目金额13.5亿美元，已开业投产的“三资”企业264家。对外贸易以每年50%速度递增，目前温州已与世界上120多个国家和地区建立贸易关系。出口商品达26类500多个品种，1998年外贸进出口总额8.6亿美元。

温州城市发展方向是建设现代化工业、商贸、港口、旅游的生态型城市。到2010年率先基本实现现代化，到2020年经济达到中等发达国家水平。近阶段围绕建设现代化新温州发展目标，把现代化导向作为跨世纪的发展战略，并将提高产业现代化、城市现代化和城乡一体化、人的现代化作为今后发展的三个战略重点，全面实施产业升级计划、基础设施优化计划、文化升位计划和跨世纪人才发展计划。力争今后五年，国内生产总值年均递增12%以上，到2002年，全市GDP达到1100亿元，人均GDP接近2000美元，第三产业比重达到40%。中、远期目标，2002年到2020年，GDP年均递增低方案8%，高方案10%，到2020年，GDP分别达到5000亿元和8000亿元，人均GDP分别达到57000元和100000元。

温州未来的发展为国内外投资者提供了广宽的投资场所和新的机遇，尤其是近阶段大规模的基础设施建设为投资者开辟了新的投资渠道。今后几年，温州市引资项目的重点主要是基础设施建设项目，包括港口、铁路、高速公路、水利、电力等；高新技术产业，包括机械电子工业、精细化工、新型材料、轻纺工业、石油开发等；开发性农业及滩涂围垦；旅游业等。

Located in the middle of the golden coastline of China, and flanked by the Yangtze River delta and Pearl River delta, Wenzhou is the economic, political, cultural and transportation centre of south Zhejiang Province. It was also one of the first coastal open cities, one of the first experimental area for rural reforms, and one of the first experimental cities for a whole range of urban comprehensive reforms. Wenzhou occupies an area of 11,784km^2, including 76km^2 of urban districts. It has a population of 7,180,000, 3 districts, 2 cities and 6 counties.

Wenzhou derives its name from its temperate climate. The annual average temperature is 16.1-18.2℃, the annual rainfall amounts to 1500-1900mm, and there are 260-300 frost-free days. With great advantages in its geographic location, Wenzhou has 355km of coastline, with 8 counties (cities and districts) facing the sea, where there are 80 gulfs and 436 islands, and about 100 berths for 5,000- dwt to 100,000- dwt ships can be constructed.

Stretching over 100km to the east of the urban district, the off-shore continental shelf of the East China Sea is rich in resources of oil and natural gas, which are being explored and developed by both the domestic and foreign oil companies.

Wenzhou is also rich in resource of water, amounting

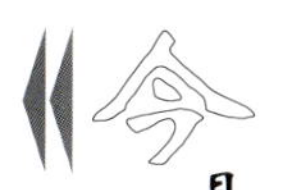

to 820,000kw. Having 80% of the reserve of aluminite in the country, Wenzhou is reputed to be the capital of aluminite in the world.

With fantastic mountains and graceful waters, Wenzhou has rich tourism resource, including 2 state-designated scenic resorts, 2 state-designated nature protection areas and 7 province-designated scenic resorts. Yandang Mount, the Naxi River, Nanji Islands and Wuyanling Ridge all boast their distinctive features and flavour of magnificence or elegance.

Now, after 50 years of construction, Wenzhou has made great progress both economically and socially. From 1949 to 1998, its economic strength increased many times. For example, the gross output of agriculture: expanded 11.5 times, the output of grain crop:1.8 times, the gross output of industry: 1,793 times, the total retail sales of consumer goods:679 times, and the total investment in fixed assets:30,000 times. The education, culture, science, technology, social welfare have also improved greatly.

The Wenzhou people have long been distinguished for their courage of "daring to be pioneers in the world". Since the start of the reform and opening up, they have taken the lead in carrying out the market-oriented reform. Wenzhou is one of the cities which have the fastest growing, most flexible, and strongst economies.

In the last 20 years, the annual average economic growth of Wenzhou was 15.9%, much higher than those of the state and Zhejiang Province. In 1998, the Gross Domestic Product reached 67.7 billion yuan, 4 times 1978s, and the financial revenue reached 4.6 billion yuan, 5 times 1978s.

The people's general livelihood has reached the better-off level on the whole. In 1998, the per capita disposable income of urban residents came to 8,942 yuan, and the per capita net income of rural residents came to 3,833 yuan.

The economic strength of Wenzhou has leapt to 47th among the cities at the prefecture level in the country. Wenzhou has now established an industrial production system of machinery, chemicals, textiles, foodstuffs, clothing, leather, plastics, building materials, electronic goods, metallurgy, shipbuilding, electronic power, shoes, cigarette lighters, lamps, glasses, valves, and medical instruments, and is called as the "City of Clothing", and "City of Shoes", "City of Low- voltage Electronic Appliances".

With 20 years experience of reform and opening up, Wenzhou has formed the setup of "Big Market with Small Commodities", the superiority of "Great Radiation from Small Funds", and the situation of "Great Development in Small Regions". Wenzhou has blazed a path of economic development with unique features. The private economy has become the mainstay of the local economy, the market mechanism has become the intrinsic motive force of economic development, and social investment has become the main source of funds for urban construction. In the field of reform, Wenzhou has created the Shareholding Cooperative Economy. In 1998, there were 205,000 self-employed and private bussiness, employing 355,000 people. There are 533 markets of all kinds, with a total turnover 40.72 billion yuan.

About one million native of Wenzhou are running industrial and commercial establishments in all parts of the country, and meanwhile, about one millioun outsiders are employed in Wenzhou.

As a coastal open city, Wenzhou has a superior investment environment. Wenzhou is a famous ancestral home of overseas Chinese, as over 300,000 overseas Chinese are from Wenzhou, and they have the advantages of information, science, technology, culture and funds. There are 6 counties (cities and districts) ranked as open regions, 1 state-level Economic and Technological Development Zones, 3 province-level economic and technological development zones, and 60 towns appointed as major industrial open satellite towns. Wenzhou has formed a multi-level setup of opening up to the outside world.

Wenzhou has achieved great improvement in the construction of infrastructural facilities, such as water, electric power, communication, and telecommunications. In the 1990s, 28 billion yuan was invested in urban construction. Now a 3-dimensional communication network with a whole range of port, highway, airway and railways has come into being. There are 56 domestic and international airlines and international shipping lines, and the railway station ranks second in Zhejiang Province.

At present, there are lots of projects of communication construction, such as the Wenzhou-Fuzhou Railway, Ningbo-Taizhou-Wenzhou Railway, Ningbo-Taizhou Wenzhou expressway, Jinhua-Wenzhou expressway, and Qiligang harbor. Wenzhou is coming to be a regional center of communication in the country.

Wenzhou is one of the cities with the best improved telecommunications. In 1998, the number of telephones reached 1.426 million and the number of mobile telephones reached 1,201,000. The total business revenue of postal and telecommunication services reached 2.97 billion yuan, ranking first in Zhejiang Province.

All foreign related institutions, including customhouse, commodity inspection, finance, insurance, sea transportation, tax, and law are in place. And the Foreign Investment Affairs Office, the Investment Consultancy and Service Center for Foreign Businessmen and Hongkong, Macao, Taiwan and Overseas Compatriots and the Foreign-funded Enterprises Association offer efficient and excellent services to overseas visitors.

The state-designed Wenzhou Economic and Technological Development Zone has been built on a considerable scale, and a number of joint ventures, cooperative enterprises and sole foreign-funded enterprises have settled in Wenzhou one after another.

Since the opening up, 1,460 projects have been signed, with an agreed investment of 1.35 billion US dollars, and 264 joint ventures, cooperative enterprises and sole foreign-funded enterprises have started operations.

Wenzhou has established trade relations with more than 120 countries and regions worldwide, with the export commodities amounting to over 500 varieties in 26 categories and the total imports and exports to 860 million US dollars in 1998. Wenzhou is carrying out in an all-round

雁荡山
Yandang Mountain

way a modernization guiding strategy with the basic realization of modernization ahead of time as the target, the reform and opening up as the motive power, and the advance of science and technology as the main means, so as to guide the national economy and social development to the fulfillment of the modernization of enterprises, city and people. To this end, it has worked out the 4 implementation plans of "upgrading of enterprises", "optimization of infrastructural facilities", "promoption of culture" and "development of transcentury talented people". In the next five years, the Gross Domestic Product is expected to keep increasing by over 12% on annual average. By the year 2002, the city's Per Capita Gross Domestic Product will approach 2,000 US dollars, the proportion of tertiary industry will reach 40%, and the contribution rate of scientific and technological advance to economic growth will reach over 50%.

The development prospects for Wenzhou offer both domestic and foreign investment chances. In the next few years, the emphasis of investment will be on the construction of infrastructural facilities, including harbors, railways, expressways, electric power, high-tech industry, agriculture and tourism.

福州——迈向21世纪

Fuzhou: Striding Forward into the 21st Century

福州，又名“榕城”、别名“三山”，是福建省省会，位于中国东南沿海，濒临东海，全市海岸线长1137公里，占全省海岸线的1/3。1984年被列为全国第二批国家历史名城和全国对外开放的十四个沿海港口城市之一。

全市辖五区、二市、六县。土地面积1.2万平方公里，市区面积1043平方公里，建城区面积80平方公里；总人口579.8万，市区143.7万人。

福州是中国重点侨乡，旅居海外的福州籍华人侨胞有250万人。福州也是台胞的主要祖籍地，与台湾仅一水之隔，最近处仅68海里。

目前，全市有各种科研机构100多所，高等院校23所，普通中学、职业中学和中等专业学校360所，有各种专业技术人员10多万人。全市工业门类齐全，有电子、机械、化工、纺织、轻工、食品、塑胶、制鞋、冶金、工艺美术等产业。福州是中国最早实现长途电话自动化的城市，有程控电话容量123万门、移动电话68万户、无线电传呼容量150万台。程控电话可与世界150多个国家和地区直接通话；国际特邮业务遍及100多个国家和地区。福州还拥有装机容量均为140万千瓦的华能火电站和水口水电站；新建成的长乐国际机场首期客运能力达650万人次，货运能力达20万吨，可起降B747-400和MD-11大型客货机，现辟有国内外航线35条，每周210个航班。福州铁路、公路运输比较发达，已建福泉高速公路。福州海运有悠久的历史，古代就是海上丝绸之路的要道。全市已投入使用的码头泊位有57个，其中，万吨级以上的深水泊位12个。马尾港距台湾基隆港仅148海里，距离香港488海里；通往国内各大港口和30多个国家和地区。福沽、罗

源湾可兴建1-20万吨级深水码头泊位100多个，发展前景十分广阔。

1998年，全市国内生产总值863.92亿元，比上年增长17.64%，比1978年增长23倍，年平均

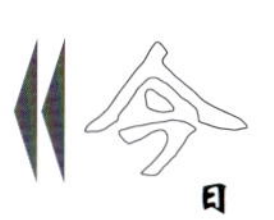

增长17.3%，人均国内生产总值增长17倍；工农业总产值1282.97亿元，比上年增长21.1%，比1978年增长29.7倍，年平均增长18.7%；社会消费品零售总额277.02亿元，比上年增长18.2%，比1978年增长38.9倍，年平均增长20.2%。“八五”、“九五”期间，福州近台、近港澳、近东南亚的区位优势得到充分发挥，外经、外贸工作不断取得新成果。1998年全市完成进出口总值达58.08亿美元，比上年增长1.8%，其中，进口总值18.96亿美元，下降9.5%；出口总值39.12亿美元，增长2.5%。1979-1998年，全市累计批准外商投资项目5755项，协议金额146.93亿美元，实际利用外资61.36亿美元，其中，台资项目1312项，协议台资27.09亿美元。1998年共接待境外旅游人数22.41万人，其中，外国游客7.08万人次，港澳同胞4.93万人次，台胞9.07万人次。

近年来，福州市扎实推进投资环境建设取得成效。

一是建章立制，规范税费征收。

二是减少环节，下放审批权限。

三是突出重点，积极营造宽松的投资环境。

福州2000年发展目标是实现国民生产总值和人均GNP比1980年翻4番之多，基本实现经济和社会的协调发展。

2000年主要控制目标：计划2000年，全市国民生产总值770亿元（1990年不变价，下同），“九五”期间（1996-2000年）年均增长17.8%；人均国民生产总值1.3万元，年均增长15.7%；第一、第二、第三产业结构之比为10∶40∶50；农业总产值114亿元，年均增长8.4%；工业总产值1542亿元，年均增长25.8%；财政收入85亿元，年均增长17.6%；全社会固定资产投资年均增长18.5%；自营出口总值32亿美元，年均增长15%。2000年末市中心城区面积达到125平方公里，人口145万。

福州市2010年发展目标：全市国民生产总值和人均国民生产总值在2000年水平基础上再翻两番。全市国民生产总值超过2400亿元。2001-2010年10年年平均增长12%，人均国民生产总值超过3.6万元；10年年平均增长11%。支柱产业得到确立、主导产业已经形成，整体产业结构和产业水平得到很大优化和提升、基本实现了“两个转变”，初步实现经济与国际市场的接轨。城市交通实现现代化，对外交通实现陆海空立体化便捷联系；基本确立两岸交流中心的多种功能。全市形成以中心城市为核心的多极次、紧密协作、功能强劲的区域经济中心，实现经济、社会与资源、环境协调发展，城市人民生活水平大幅提高，经济发展水平和人民生活多项指标接近或达到亚洲中等发达国家或地区的水平。

福州市2020年战略目标。全市国民生产总值达5700亿元，10年年平均增长9%，人均国民生产总值超过7.8万元，经济社会发展水平和人民生活水平达到中等发达国家和地区水平，把福州建成为海峡两岸闽江口繁荣带。经济全面实现市场化、高效化、国际化、建成高效率、多功能的两岸交流中心，成为商贸金融中心、交通通信中心、产业管理中心，经济总体实力和影响力跃入全国一流城市水平。

福州市鼓励投资的重点领域：

一是基础设施。继“八五”期间，全市投入140亿元资金进行基础设施建设，“九五”的头两年，即1996、1997年又投入119亿元资金。近期，鼓励外商投入福州基础设施的主要项目有：平潭海峡大桥，总投资7000万美元；福沽江阴钢铁厂配套专用码头，总投资6000万美元；闽侯县大目溪水电站，总投资8000万美元等。

二是基础工业。其中重点培育电子、机械、轻纺、化工四大支柱产业，加快发展电子信息、精细化工、电气机械、汽车及动力、化纤、运动鞋、塑胶、水产加工、食品加工等行业。

三是农业科技。农业作物良种选育、粮油作

物栽培技术、果蔬技术、林木技术、畜牧技术、淡水养殖技术、农业工程技术、海洋科技等。

四是旅游业。吸引外资形成以福州旅游口岸为中心，以历史文化名城为依托，以海、江、山三大特色为主线的旅游的黄金通道。

Fuzhou, also known as "Rongcheng" or "Sanshan", is the capital of Fujian Province. Lying on the southeastern coast and facing the East China Sea, it has a coastline of 1,137 kilometers, a third of the provincial total. In 1984, it was among the second group of national historical and cultural cities listed by the state, and one of the 14 coastal port cities opened to the outside world.

Fuzhou has jurisdiction over five districts, two cities and six counties. It covers an area of 12,000 square kilometers, including 1,043 square kilometers of urban area and 80 square kilometers of the city proper. It has a total population of 5.798 million, including 1.437 million urban residents.

Fuzhou is an important ancestral home of overseas Chinese. There are some 2.5 million Fujian natives living overseas. Fuzhou is also the hometown of many Taiwan compatriots, as it faces Taiwan Province across the Taiwan Straits, and is only separated from it at its closest point by 68 nautical miles.

The year 1998 was the 2000th anniversary of the founding of Fuzhou. The city's major symbols are "three mountains, two towers, three lanes and seven alleys". The biggest water system of the province, the Minjiang River, runs through the city proper into the sea.

Since the implementation of the reform and opening-up policies, Fuzhou has given full play to its advantages of mountains, and the sea, and its status as a special zone, the capital city, and made great efforts to construct an economic, trading and tourist harbour city at the advanced international level.

At present, Fuzhou has more than 100 scientific research institutions, 33 institutions of higher learning, and 360 middle, vocational and polytechnic schools, in addition to more than 100,000 technical personnel in various fields. The city boasts a wide variety of industries, such as electronics, machinery, chemicals, textiles, food, plastics cement, shoes, metallurgy and arts and crafts industries. It led the country in automating long-distance telephone services. Its program-controlled telephones total 1.23 million circuits; there are 680,000 mobile telephone users, while its pager capacity is 1.5 million. Through program-controlled telephones, people in Fuzhou can directly reach more than 150 countries and regions. Its international express mail service covers more than 100 countries and regions.

Fuzhou also boasts the Huaneng Thermal Power Plant and the Shuikou Hydropower Station, with an installed capacity of more than 1.4 million kw. The newly-completed Changle International Airport has a capacity of 6.5 million passengers, and 200,000 tons of freight a year, and can handle B747-400 and MD-11 aircraft. It now has 35 domestic and international air lines operating 210 scheduled flights a week. Fuzhou's railways and highways are comparatively advanced. The Fuzhou-Quanzhou Expressway has been completed. The city's ocean shipping has a long history. In ancient times, Fuzhou was an important stage on the Maritime Silk Road. Now, it has 57 berths, including 12 deep-water ones, which can handle ships of more than 10,000 dwt.

Mawei Port is only 148 nautical miles from Keelung Port in Taiwan and 488 nautical miles from Hong Kong, It has links with all major ports in China and more than 30 countries and regions. More than 100 deep-water berths ranging up to 200,000 dwt can be built in Fugu and Luoyuan Bay, promising bright development prospects.

In 1998, the GDP of Fuzhou stood at 86.392 billion

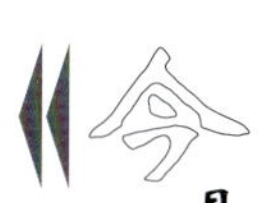

yuan, an increase of 17.64 percent over the previous year, or 24 times the 1978 figure, with an average annual growth rate of 17.3 percent.

The GDP per capita has increased by 18 times in past 20 years. The total industrial and agricultural output value reached 128.297 billion yuan in 1998, an increase of 21.1 percent over the previous year, or 30.7 times the 1978 figure, with an average annual growth rate of 18.7 percent. The retail sales volume of social consumer goods totaled 27.702 billion yuan, an increase of 18.2 percent over the previous year or 39.9 times the 1978 figure, with an average annual growth rate of 20.2 percent. During the Eighth Five-Year Plan and the Ninth Five-Year Plan periods, Fuzhou's locational advantage close to Taiwan, Hong Kong, Macao and Southeast Asia was brought into full play, and its foreign economic and trade operations have constantly made progress. In 1998, the city's total import and export volume reached US$5.808 billion , a 1.8 percent increase over the previous year; its import volume came to US$1.896 billion, or a decrease of 9.5 percent; and its total export volume to US$3.912 billion, a 2.5 percent increase. Between 1979 and 1998, Fuzhou approved 5,755 foreign-invested projects, with an agreed capital of US$14.693 billion, of which US$6.136 billion were actually used. Among them, Taiwan-funded projects numbered 1,312, involving a total of US$2.709 billion in agreed capital.

In 1998, Fuzhou received 224,100 tourists from overseas, including 70,800 foreign tourists, 49,300 Hong Kong and Macao compatriots and 90,700 Taiwan compatriots.

In recent years, Fuzhou has made progress in its construction of the investment environment.

First, establishing rules and regulations and standardizing taxation.

Second, reducing links and transferring examination and approval authorities.

Third, putting stress on key points and actively creating a relaxed investment environment.

The development objectives of Fuzhou in 2000 are that the GNP will be 16 times the 1980 figure, and coordinated economic and social development will be basically realized.

By 2000, Fuzhou's total GDP will be 17 billion yuan (calculated according to 1990 constant prices); the average annual growth rate during the Ninth Five-Year Plan (1996-2000) will be 17.8 percent; per capita GNP will be 13,000 yuan, with an average annual growth rate of 15.7 percent; ratio among the primary, secondary and tertiary industries will be 10:40:50; total agricultural output value, 11.4 billion yuan, with an average annual growth rate of 8.4 percent; total industrial output value, 154.2 billion yuan, with an average annual growth rate of 25.8 percent; financial income, 8.5 billion yuan, with an average annual growth rate of 17.6 percent; average annual growth rate of the investment in fixed assets of the whole society will be 18.5 percent; and total export volume 3.2 billion US dollars, with an average annual growth rate of 15 percent. In 2000, the central area of the city will cover 125 square kilometers, and have a total population of 1.45 million.

By 2010 Fuzhou's GNP will quadruple the 2000 figure, exceeding 240 billion yuan. The average annual growth rate between 2001 and 2010 will be 12 percent; per capita GNP will exceed 36,000 yuan, with an average annual growth rate of 11 percent during the 10 years. Pillar industries will be set up; the industrial structure as a whole and the industrial level will be greatly improved; the "two changes" will be basically realized; and Fuzhou will initially bring its economy into line with the international economy. Urban communications will be modernized, and the city will have adequate transport facilities by water, land and air. The Exchange Center for Both Sides of the Taiwan Straits will have multiple functions. A regional economic center with the central city as the core will be formed, featuring multipolarity, close cooperation and multiple functions; coordinated development between the economy and society, and natural resources and the environment will be realized; the urban people's livelihood will be greatly improved; and the economic development level and various targets for the people's livelihood will be close to or reach the level of the medium-advanced countries and regions in Asia.

According to Fuzhou's strategic objectives, by 2020 the city's GNP will be 570 billion yuan. The average annual growth rate in the 10 years from 2010 to 2020 will be 9 percent; per capita GNP will exceed 78,000 yuan; the economic and social development and people's livelihood will reach the level of the medium-advanced countries and regions, so that Fuzhou will become a prosperous city at the outlet of the Minjiang River. Its economy will be marketized, highly efficient and internationalized. Fuzhou will be a highly-efficient exchange center between both sides of the Taiwan Straits, a commercial, trade and financial center, a communications and telecommunications center, and an industrial management center. Its overall actual strength and influence will reach the level of the first-class cities in China.

The key fields in which Fuzhou encourages investment are as follows:

First, infrastructure facilities. During the Eighth Five-Year Plan period, Fuzhou invested 14 billion yuan in the construction of infrastructure facilities; in the first two years of the Ninth Five-Year Plan period (1996 and 1997), the city invested another 11.9 billion yuan. Fuzhou encourages foreign business people to invest in the following infrastructure facilities: The Pingtan Strait Bridge, with a total investment of US$70 million; a special wharf for the Jiangyin Iron and Steel Mill, involving an investment of US$60 million; and the Damuqi Hydropower Station in Minhou County, with a total investment of US$80 million.

Second, basic industries. Fuzhou will focus on the development of its four pillar industries—electronics, machinery, light industrial goods and textiles, and chemicals, and speed up the development of electronic information, fine chemicals, electrical machinery, automobiles and motive power, chemical fibers, sports shoes, plastics cement , and the processing of aquatic products and foodstuffs.

Third, agricultural sciences and technologies, involving seed selection and cultivation, cultivation technologies for grain and oil-bearing crops, technologies for growing fruit, and vegetables, forests and timber, animal husbandry, freshwater breeding, agricultural engineering technology, and ocean science and technology.

Fourth, tourism. Fuzhou will absorb foreign capital to form a "golden tourist thoroughfare" with Fuzhou as the core, consisting of famous historical and cultural cities and featuring by the three main local mountains.

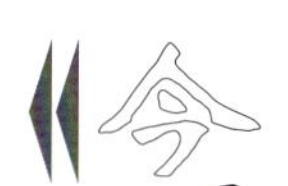

广州——朝着现代化国际大都会奋进

Guangzhou: Becoming an International Metropolis

广州是广东省省会，广东省政治、经济、科技、教育和文化的中心。广州市是中国南方对外的重要门户，是沿海开放城市和副省级市。现辖八区四市（县级），总面积7434.4平方公里，人口674.14万，其中市区人口399.30万，市区日平均流动人口约170万。广州是华南地区工业中心。工业门类比较齐全，规模较大，综合配套能力强。在40个工业大门类中，除受资源条件限制的黑色金属采选业和其他矿采选业两个行业外，共拥有38个行业。目前，广州工业产品的销售在省内、省外、国外的比例约为62%、16%和22%。广州已成为名副其实的工业生产基地。由于实施科教兴市战略，广州市科技实力有了较大提高，科技事业有了较大的发展，科技进步因素对经济增长和社会发展的作用日趋明显。1998年各类研究机构有566个，各类专业技术人员41.55万，高等院校27所。广州是全国著名的华侨之乡，华侨居全国各大城市之首。

一、经济发展情况

建国50年来，广州市的方方面面发生了翻天覆地的变化。特别是党的十一届三中全会以来，广州市坚定不移地推进改革，扩大开放，开创了建国以来经济发展的最好时期，取得了显著的成就。改革开放以来，广州经济以年均14%的速度持续快速发展，“八五”时期（1991-1995年），增长速度高达20.18%，高于全国和全省，成为中国乃至亚太地区主要的经济增长点，积累了雄厚的经济实力。1998年国内生产总值1841.61亿元，比1978年增长13.4倍，年平均增长14.3%；人均国内生产总值2.75万元，按当年平均汇率折算为3319美元，超过现代化的国际标准（3000美元）；社会消费品零售总额904.57亿元，比1978年增长50.3倍，年平均增长21.8%。国民经济实力大大增强。外向型经济发展取得了可喜的成绩。1979年至1998年累计，广州实际利用外资169.91亿美元。1998年与1979年比较，增长300倍以上，年均增长35.2%。利用外资比率（实际利用外资占全社会固定资产投资总额的比例）由2%提高到33.2%。来穗投资国家（地区）增至46个，外商投资企业达8470家。外资投向遍及工业、农业、市政建设、建筑、能源、交通、旅游服务等行业。外贸系统出口大幅度增长，全年出口总值80.18亿美元，比1978年增长58.7倍，年平均增长22.7%，大大超过前29年年平均增长8%的速度。

二、投资环境和投资重点

为了加速发展外向型经济，广州市努力改善投资环境，集中财力和引进外资搞好全市的交通、能源、市政建设。大力发展第三产业，城市设施日臻完善。广州海、陆、空运都十分方便，铁路南有广九线，西有广三线，北有京广线，东有广梅汕铁路与京九线连接；公路网四通八达；广州港已与世界183个国家和地区的港口有业务来往，成为华南地区最大的物资集散地；广州白云机场旅客吞吐量1241.12万人次，成为国内最繁忙的三大航空港之一。广州新白云国际机场计划于2002年建成，未来的新机场将成为中国南方最大的航空枢纽。广州是中国对外贸易的重要口岸。自1957年起，每年两届中国出口商品交易会都在广州举行。广州是华南地区的金融中心。目前，广州市营业金融机构网点达2813家，外资金融和保险机构在广州设立的代表处和营业性机构63个。全市有五星级酒店5家，主要宾馆（酒店）315家，共有客房6.46万间。广州市内交通车不断增加，1998年汽（电）车增加到5163部，出租车增加到15142部。地铁一号线1998年底全线建成开通。广州电信事业发展迅速，1998年末移动电话达100.84万户，居全国各大城市之首，市内电话达到了164.73万户，市话普及率达每百人67部，市民每户平均拥有电话达1.1部（包括副机）。广州已初步建成规模宏大、技术先进、功能齐全的公用信息网络。1998年，广州城市自来水日供水能力351万吨，年供电168.15亿千瓦时，按人口计算的气化率1998年达到91.89%。

今后广州鼓励外商投资的重点领域和项目是：

鼓励外商投入广州东南部大型国际综合开发区。这个区总面积达219平方公里，区域中有广州经济技术开发区、广州保税区、天河高新技术产业开发区、南沙经济技术开发区、莲花山对外加工区、新塘加工区和云埔工业区等。该地区将形成较高层次的二、三产业群。并使之成为广州现代化大都会高层次的对外开放区。

鼓励外资加快广州市基础工业和城市基础设施的建设，投资新电厂、钢厂、乙烯工程、聚丙稀工程、广州客运站（东站）、高速公路、地下铁路、轻轨列车、港口码头、广州新国际机场等。

鼓励外资大力发展技术先进型企业。拟发展电子与信息、新材料生物技术、机电一体化、新能源、高效节能与环保、精细化工和轻纺高新技术等七大领域产业，以及汽车、摩托车、电梯等重点产品。

鼓励外资加快广州第三产业的发展。欢迎外商从事与引进先进配套及高档次的房地产开发和市民安居工程建设，鼓励外商参与旧城区、新城区的房地产开发。拟利用外资发展信息咨询、金融、旅游服务等行业。积极尝试商业领域的利用外资。

鼓励外资加快老企业的技术改造。近5年内广州要使2/3以上老企业得到技术改造，鼓励外商对老企业进行改造，并可与老企业合作易地改造后，原厂房旧址进行房地产的综合开发结合起来。

鼓励利用外资建设出口商品生产基地。今后的三、五年间广州各外贸公司拟利用外资建立一批以出口商品为主导的生产企业。包括轻工、工艺、纺织、食品、化工、机械、土产、畜产、医药保健品等行业，扩大广州市出口规模。

鼓励外资发展农业综合开发项目和城市环境保护项目。引进优良品种、栽培技术，提高广州农业生产技术水平，建立创汇农业、高效农业生产基地。引进外资建设环保项目，提高城市环境质量。

鼓励外资银行在广州设立机构，把广州建成国际性、区域性金融中心。

三、广州发展前景

迈向21世纪的广州，确立了建设现代化中心城市的发展目标，制定了跨世纪的发展蓝图。到2000年，广州国内生产总值比1980年翻三番半，人均国内生产总值比1980年翻三番，“九五”期间（1996-2000年）年平均增长分别为13%和10%，朝着基本实现现代化的目标迈出更大的步伐。

Guangzhou, capital of Guangdong Province, is the south China region's political, economic, industrial, scientific and technological, educational and cultural center. As an important gateway of southern China to the outside world, a coastal open city and a sub-provincial municipality, Guangzhou has jurisdiction over eight districts and four cities (county-level), with an area of 7,434.4 square kilometers and a population of 6.7414 million, including 3.993 million in the urban area. On average, 1.7 million people pass through the city proper each day. Guangzhou has a wide variety of industries and a strong comprehensive supporting ability. Its 40 industrial categories involve 38 trades, except ferrous metals mining and other mineral resources mining industries whose presence is restricted by inadequate resources. Its industrial products are sold all over the country and the world. The proportion of Guangzhou-made products sold in Guangdong, other regions in China and abroad are 62 percent, 16 percent and 22 percent, respectively. Guangzhou has become a true industrial production base. Thanks to the implementation of the strategy of developing the city by science and education, its scientific and technological sectors have made greater progress, and their role in economic growth and social development has become prominent. In 1998, Guangzhou had 566 research institutions, involving 415,500 technical personnel, and 27 institutions of higher learning. Guangzhou is the leading ancestral home of overseas Chinese in China.

I. Economic Development

Since the founding of New China in 1949, tremendous changes have taken place in Guangzhou. Especially since the Third Plenary Session of the 11th Party Central Committee, Guangzhou has unswer-vingly promoted reform and opening to the outside world, thus creating the best period for its economic development and achieving great successes. Since the initiation of reform and opening to the outside world, the average annual economic growth rate of Guangzhou has been 14 percent. During the Eighth Five-Year Plan period (1991-1995), its average annual economic growth rate reached 20.18 percent, higher than the national and provincial levels. Hence Guang-zhou has become a major economic growth area in China and of the Asian-Pacific region as well, and has accumulated great economic strength. In 1998, its GDP reached 184.161 billion yuan, or 14.4 times that of 1978, with an average annual gowth rate of 14.3 percent. The GDP per capita stood at 27,500 yuan, which could be converted into US$ 3,319 according to the average exchange rate in 1998, exceeding the international standard for modernization (US$ 3,000). The total retail sales volume of social consumer goods came to 90.457 billion yuan, or 51.3 times the 1978 figure, with an average annual growth rate of 21.8 percent. Consequently its economic strength has greatly improved, and its export-oriented economic development has made encouraging achievements. Between 1979 and 1998, Guangzhou used US$ 16.991 billion in foreign capital, the 1998 figure being 301 times greater than that of 1979, with an average annual growth rate of 35.2 percent. The proportion of the foreign capital actually utilized to the total investment in fixed assets of the whole society increased from 2 to 33.2 percent. A total of 46 countries (regions) have invested in Guangzhou, and there are 8,470 foreign-invested enterprises, involving industry, agriculture, municipal works, construction, energy, communications, tourism services, etc. The export volume has increased by a large margin, reaching US$ 8.018 billion, or 59.7 times the 1978's figure, with an average annual growth rate of 22.7 percent, greatly exceeding the average annual growth rate of 8 percent.

II. Investment Environment and Key Investment Projects

In order to speed up the development of its export-oriented economy, Guangzhou has spared no effort to improve the investment environment and concentrated domestic and foreign funds on the construction of communications, energy and municipal works. The city has greatly developed its tertiary industry, and its urban facilities are improving with each passing day. Guangzhou has transport facilities by sea, land and air. It has many rail links with other parts of the country, such as the Guangzhou-Kowloon, Guangzhou-Sanshui, Beijing-Guangzhou, and Guangzhou-Meizhou -Shantou lines. Its highways radiate in all directions. Guangzhou Port has business contacts with 183 countries and regions, thus making it the largest goods and materials collection and distribution center in the country. Guangzhou's White Cloud Airport is one of the three busiest airports in China, handling 12.4112 million passengers annually. The New Guangzhou White Cloud International Airport, to be completed in 2002, will be the largest aviation hub in south China. Guangzhou is an important foreign trade port of China. Starting in 1957, the China Export Commodities Fair is held twice a year. Guangzhou is also a financial hub of southern China. Now the city has 2,813 financial business institutions and 63 representative offices and business agencies of foreign financial institutions and insurance companies. The city has five five-star hotels and 315 other major hotels with 64,600 guest-rooms. Public transport has continuously improved. In 1998, there were 5,163 buses and trolley buses, and 15,142 taxis. The No.1 Subway Line opened to traffic in 1998. Guangzhou's telecommunications have developed rapidly. At the end of 1998 there were 1,008,400 mobile telephone users, ranking first among large Chinese cities. There were 1.6473 million telephone users, with a penetration rate of 67 telephones per 100 people, each family owning an average of 1.1. Guangzhou has initially formed a

羊城春色
The Spring Scenery in Guangzhou

public information network featuring a large scale, advanced technology and complete functions. In 1998, it had a capability of supplying 3.51 million tons of running water a day; its annual electricity supply reached 16.815 billion kw; and 91.89 percent of the people in the city used gas.

Guangzhou encourages foreign investors to invest in the following key fields and projects:

The large-scale international development area in the southeastern part of the city. With an area of 219 square kilometers, this development area includes the Guangzhou Economic and Technological Development Zone, Guangzhou Free Trade Zone, Tianhe High-tech Industrial Development Zone, Nansha Economic and Technological Development Zone, Lianhuashan Foreign-oriented Processing Zone, Xintang Processing Zone and Yunpu Industrial Zone. This development area is also home to a group of high-level secondary and tertiary enterprises.

Construction of the city's basic industries and urban infrastructure facilities, power plants, steel mills, ethylene projects, polypropylene projects, the Guangzhou Passenger Terminal (East Station), expressways, subways, light railways, ports and wharves, the Guangzhou New International Airport, etc.

Technologically advanced enterprises, which involve seven major industries, namely electronics and information, new materials biological engineering, electromechanical integration, new energy sources, high-efficiency and energy-saving projects and environmental protection projects, and fine chemical and light industries, in addition to the production of key products, such as automobiles, motorcycles and elevators.

Development of tertiary industry. Foreign business people are welcome to introduce advanced supporting technologies, and engage in real estate development and the construction of the Living-in-Peace Project for urban citizens. They are also encouraged to participate in the real estate development of both old and new city areas. The city also plans to develop information consultancy, finance, tourism services, etc., with foreign capital, and make use of foreign capital to develop its commerce on a trial basis.

Speeding up the technological transformation of old enterprises. It is planned that in the coming five years more than two-thirds of the old city areas in Guangzhou will undergo technological transformation. Foreign business people are encouraged to help transform old enterprises. If an old enterprise is moved after transformation, foreign investors may develop real estate on the original site in cooperation with the original occupant.

Constructing export commodity production bases with foreign capital is encouraged. In the coming three to five years, foreign trade companies in Guangzhou will make use of foreign capital to set up a group of production enterprises with export commodities as the mainstay, involving light industrial goods, handicrafts, textiles, foodstuffs, chemicals, machinery, livestock products, medicines and health-care products, so as to expand the local export trade.

Foreign investors are encouraged to invest in comprehensive agricultural development projects and urban environmental protection projects. Guangzhou plans to import fine varieties of crops and cultivation technologies, improve the agricultural production technology level, set up the agricultural production bases that can generate foreign earnings, and high-efficiency agricultural production bases, establish environmental protection projects with foreign capital, and improve the urban environmental quality.

Foreign-funded banks are encouraged to set up agencies in Guangzhou so as to turn the city into an international and regional financial center.

III. Guangzhou's Development Prospects

While greeting the 21st century, Guangzhou has set up development objectives for turning itself into a modernized central city, and has worked out a cross-century development blueprint. In 2000, Guangzhou's GDP will be 12 times the 1980 figure; and the GDP per capita, eight times the 1980 figure. During the Ninth Five-Year Plan period, the average annual growth rate of its GDP will be 13 percent, and that of the GDP per capita, 10 percent.

湛江——美丽丰饶的南方港城

Zhanjiang: A Beautiful and Richly Endowed Port City in South China

一、经济发展情况

广东省湛江市，在1899年法国租借后称为“广州湾”，1945年起定名为“湛江市”。湛江是个美丽的海滨城市，也是中国首批对外开放的14个沿海港口城市之一。下辖二县、三市、四区，有一个国家级经济技术开发区和五个省级经济开发试验区。全市总面积12471平方公里，其中市区1460平方公里。总人口636万人，其中市区130万人，为全国一类市。

建国50年来，湛江市各方面发生了巨大的变化，特别是1978年实行改革开放政策以来，湛江市开创了建国以来经济发展的最好时期，国民经济实力明显增强。1998年国内生产总值359亿元，比1978年增长7倍，年平均增长11%，人均国内生产总值5686元，比1978年增长4.2倍，年平均增长8.6%。农业总产值172亿元，比1978年增长4.2倍，年平均增长8.6%。农业生产向产业化推进，形成了糖蔗、远洋捕捞、海水养殖、优质肉牛、外运蔬菜、优质水果，短轮伐期商品林、剑麻等一批有相当规模的生产基地。工业总产值395亿元，比1978年增长24.8倍，年平均增长17.4%。工业有石油天然气开采、制糖业、石油加工业、汽车制造、电力生产、机械仪表、建筑材料、医药、食品等。现拥有年销售收入500万元以上工业企业445家。其中大中型企业111家。目前正筹建全国最大的50万吨木浆厂。社会消费品零售总额158亿元，比1978年增长28.8倍，年平均增长18.5%。对外开放逐年扩大。1979年首次利用外资7万美元，于1998年累计实际利用外资12.17亿美元。1998年外贸出口总额4.14亿美元，比1978年增长16.1倍，年平均增长15.2%。全市已同60多个国家和地区建立了贸易关系。综合科技实力增强，现有各级各类科研机构48个，专业技术人员近10万人。普通高校3所，中等专业学校17所，成人高校3所。各级各类学校在校生164.4万人。各类卫生机构525个，其中医院162间，床位11849张，医生7264人。

二、投资环境

湛江位于中国大陆的南端，地处广东、广西、海南三省区的交汇处，背靠中国华南和西南腹地，面对东南亚国家，是中国西南各省通往国外的主要出海口，亦是中国大陆通往东南亚、非洲、亚洲和大洋洲海上航程最短的重要口岸，湛江在北部湾、东南亚和亚洲太平洋经济圈中具有重要的战略地位。

湛江资源丰富，最重要的是三大资源：

一是港口资源。全市拥有交通运输港口22个，泊位170个，年吞吐量能力3164万吨，初步形成了以湛江港为主，环雷州半岛中小港口为辅的相互配套的港口群。湛江港是全国八大枢纽港之一。现拥有泊位33个，其中万吨级以上泊位25个，最大泊位为5万吨级。年吞吐量达1800多万吨。目前湛江港已与世界100多个国家和地区通航。在全国率先开办了铁路——港口集装箱联合运输业务。湛江港发展前景广阔，港内岸线长达241公里，其中深水岸线97公里。港内的东海岛蔚律港有水深26至40米，可建30万吨级以上货轮、50万吨级以上油轮码头泊位的海岸线6.5公里。现正积极筹建可通航10万吨货轮的航道。

二是海洋资源。湛江是海洋大市，5县（市）4区均面临海洋，海岸线长达1556公里，占广东省海岸线长的46%，人均拥有海岸线系数超过全国人均海岸线系数10倍，与海洋大国日本相当。沿海岛屿30多个，港湾101处。有10米等深线浅海滩涂49万公顷，为陆上耕地面积的1.4倍，滩涂面积10万公顷，占全国的5%，占全省的48%。有可供常年进行捕捞生产的北部湾和粤西两个近海渔场，面积达15万平方公里。湛江市海岸带具热带性、多样性和旺盛性三大特点，有经济鱼类520余种，虾类28种、贝类547种。水产品总量连续多年居全省之首，其中海养珍珠产量占全国的2/3。海盐产量占全省的一半。湛江周围海域蕴藏着丰富的油气资源现已从勘探进入大规模开发的阶段，为香港输送油气的中国石油南海西部公司总部设在湛江。湛江风光旖旎，景色秀丽，阳光和防护林带、国家级红树林保护区为特色的滨海旅游资源十分丰富。目前已建有东海岛和吉兆湾两个省级旅游度假区。

三是热带亚热带资源。湛江处于热带、亚热带过渡地区，年平均气温23℃，年平均雨量1417-1870毫米，年平均日照时数1817-2106小时，年均积累温度8309-8519℃，光热资源充足，地理环境和气候条件独特，可大量开发许多其他地区不能种植的热带、亚热带作物。目前，湛江是全国重要的糖蔗产区，拥有全国最大的桉树、剑麻生产基地，盛产并外运多种蔬菜和优质水果。

湛江的基础设施日趋完善，湛江在省内是仅

湛江高速公路
Zhanjiang Expressway

次于广州的海陆空交通齐全的港口城市。被评为"投资硬环境40优城市"之一。有黎塘至湛江、广州至湛江两条铁路，与国家铁路干线连接通往全国各地。黎塘至湛江铁路复线正在建设，广州至湛江的粤海大通道已动工，湛江至茂名、洛阳到湛江的铁路正筹建之中。公路纵横成网，四通八达，广州至湛江高速公路正在分段建设。湛江机场现有航线20条，每周上百个航班，通往全国各地大城市。还有坡头南油直升机场。通讯方面已具备各种现代化通讯手段。湛江市城区面积60.8平方公里，以椹川、海滨、人民三条大道为主干的市区道路四通八达。城市气化率达90%以上。绿化覆盖率35.4%，1991年被评为全省第一个全国绿化达标市。全市旅行社16家，其中国际社4家；星级宾馆23家，其中四星级1家，三星级9家。供电、供水、供气情况良好，各种生活服务设施配套完善。

I. Economic Development

Zhanjiang had been called "Guangzhou Bay" since 1899 when it became a French concession. It was formally named Zhanjiang in 1945. Zhanjiang is a beautiful coastal city, as well as one of the first 14 coastal ports opened to the outside world. It has two counties, three cities, and four districts under its jurisdiction. There is a state-level economic and technological development zone and five provincial-level economic development experimental zones.

With a total area of 12,471 square km, the city proper covers 1,460 square km. Zhanjiang has a total population of 6.36 million, of which 1.30 million are living in urban districts. Zhanjiang is listed as a first-class city.

Tremendous changes have taken place in the city since New China was founded in 1949. But it has witnessed its best development period in the past 20 years since the reform and opening drive was launched in 1978. Its economic strength has been greatly enhanced. Its GDP in 1998 reached 35.9 billion yuan, eight times higher than 1978, with annual average growth of 11 percent. Per-capita GDP was 5,686 yuan, an increase of 4.2 times over 1978, with annual average growth of 8.6 percent. Agricultural output value came to 17.2 billion yuan, 5.2 times higher than in 1978, with annual average growth of 8.6 percent. Agricultural production has been gradually industrialized, forming a batch of production bases for sugar cane, oceangoing fishing, sea aquaculture, quality beef, vegetable transportation, quality fruit, and commercial forests, and sisal hemp.

The industrial output value stood at 39.5 billion yuan, an increase of 24.8 times, with an annual average growth of 17.4 percent. Its industry features petroleum and natural gas exploitation, sugar, petrochemicals, automobile manufacturing, power, machinery, apparatus and meters, building materials, medicine and food. There are 445 industrial enterprises with annual sales income of 5 million yuan each. Among them, 111 are large and medium-sized enterprises. At present, a 500,000-ton wood pulp mill, the largest of its kind, is under preparation. The retail sales of commodities reached 15.8 billion yuan, 29.8 times over 1978, with an annual average growth of 18.5 percent. Along with the opening wider to the outside world year by year, its accumulated funds actually used in 1998 came to US$1.217 billion compared with US$70,000 in 1979. In 1998, its foreign trade volume stood at US$414 million, 17.1 times higher than in 1978, with an annual average growth rate of 15.2 percent. The city has established trade ties with more than 60 countries and regions worldwide. Its comprehensive scientific and technological level has improved greatly. Zhanjiang now boasts 48 scientific research institutions of various kinds at different levels, employing 100,000 specialized technicians. There are three institutes of higher learning, 17 secondary technical schools and three adult colleges. The total student population is 1.644 million. The number of hospitals and public health establishments has reached 525, of which 162 are hospitals, with 11,849 beds and 7,264 doctors.

II. Investment Environment

Zhanjiang is located on the southern tip of China's mainland, where Guangdong, Guangxi and Hainan provinces meet. Lying against south China and the southwest hinterland, Zhanjiang also faces the countries of Southeast Asia. It is a major sea outlet for various southwestern provinces, as well as an important port leading to Southeast Asia, Africa, Asia, and Oceania. It occupies an important strategic position in the economic spheres of Beibu Bay, Southeast Asia and the Asia-Pacific region.

Zhanjiang is richly endowed with natural resources, especially the following three :

1. Port resources. It has 22 transportation ports, with 170 berths and an annual handling capacity of 31.64 million tons, initially forming a port complex with Zhanjiang as the center supported by the Huanlei Peninsula and other medium-sized and small ports. Zhanjiang is listed as one of the eight major hub ports in China, and operates 33 berths. Among them 25 are deepwater berths accommodating 10,000-dwt vessels, and even one handling 50,000-dwt. Its total handling capacity reaches more than 18 million tons. At present, Zhanjiang has shipping services to more than 100 countries and regions. It was the first in the country to provide a through container service by train and ship. Zhanjiang Port has bright prospects for development. Its coast line stretches 241 km, of which 97 km are deepwater. Its Weilu Port near Donghai Island is 26-40 meters deep, making it possible to build berths for 100,000-ton-class freighters and 500,000-ton-class oil tankers along a 6.5-km coast line. Now, a sea-lane for 10,000-ton-class freighters is under preparation.

2. Marine resources. Zhanjiang is a city with five counties and four districts facing the sea, and their coast line stretches 1,556 km, accounting for 46 percent of the total of Guangdong Province. Its per-capita coastline coefficient is 10 times higher than the 100,000 hectares of the nation's average level, and is equal to that of Japan. Along the coast, there are more than 30 islands and 101 havens, as well as 490,000 hectares of shallows 10 meters deep or more, equivalent to 1.4 times of its cultivated land. The tidal-flat area covers 100,000 hectares, accounting for 5 percent of the country's total, and 48 percent of the provincial total. Zhanjiang has a well-developed inshore fishing industry. Its Beibu Bay and Yuexi fishing farms, covering a combined area of 150,000 square km, have good conditions for aquatic breeding and fishing all year round. Zhanjiang produces 520 species of economic fish, 28 species of shrimps and prawns and 547 species of shells. Its aquatic products, featuring tropical species, a wide variety and large numbers, have ranked first in the province for many years running. Among them, the output of pearls accounts for two-thirds of the national total. Its salt production is half of the province's total output. There are rich oil-gas deposits in the offshore area near Zhanjiang , and exploration has turned into large-scale drilling. The Western Company of the South China Sea Oil Corp. is headquartered in Zhanjiang, supplying oil and gas to Hong Kong.

Zhanjiang has beautiful scenery, featuring beaches, sunshine, shelterbelts, and state-level mangrove forests, constituting rich tourist resources. So far, two provincial-level tourist and holiday resorts on Donghai Island and in Jizhao Bay have opened to the public.

3. Zhanjiang has rich tropical and sub-tropical resources, having an annual average temperature of 23 degrees centigrade, and annual average rainfall of 1,417-1,870mm. Its annual average sunshine reaches 1,817-2,106 hours. With its

unique geographical and climatic conditions, Zhanjiang can cultivate tropical and sub-tropical plants not suitable for growing in other places in China. It is one of major sugar cane producing areas in China. In addition, it also has eucalyptus and sisal hemp production bases, and abounds in vegetables and quality fruits which are shipped to other parts of China .

Zhanjiang has greatly improved its infrastructure facilities. It is a port city, next only to Guangdong, in sea-land-air transportation facilities. It has been cited as one of the "40 cities with excellent investment environments". The Litang-Zhanjiang and Guangzhou-Zhanjiang railways link the city with the nation's railway trunk network. The construction of double-tracking from Litang to Zhanjiang is underway. The thoroughfare from Guangzhou to Zhanjiang's Yuehai is under construction. Two railway projects from Zhanjiang to Maomin and from Luoyang to Zhanjiang respectively, are under preparation. Zhanjiang also has a highway network radiating in all directions. The Guangzhou-Zhanjiang expressway is under construction. The Zhanjiang Airport is now used by 20 airlines offering more than a hundred scheduled flights a week to all big cities throughout the country. There is also a helicopter airport at Podounanyou, Zhanjiang. Now, various modern telecommunications facilities are available in Zhanjiang. The city district covers an area of 60.8 square km, with Shenchuan, Haibin, Renmin avenues crisscrossing it. The rate of household gas use in the city has reached more than 90 percent and the rate of afforestation 35.4 percent. In 1991, Zhanjiang was cited as the first city in the province up to the state-set standards of afforestation. The city now has 16 travel agencies, four at international level, and 23 star-graded hotels, including 1 four-star and 9 three-star hotels. The city has a good supply of electricity, water and gas, as well as various services.

北海——北部湾畔的明珠

Beihai: A Pearl on Beibu Bay

一、经济发展情况

北海市位于中国广西壮族自治区南陲，北部湾东北岸，三面临海，是全国少数民族地区唯一列入国家首批对外开放的14个沿海港口城市之一，经过20年的改革开放与发展，初步建成为北部湾沿岸功能较为齐全的现代化港口旅游城市。现辖合浦县、海城区、银海区和铁山港区，总面积3337平方公里，其中市区面积957平方公里，总人口137.8万，其中市区人口49.7万。

北海的区位优势独特，背靠中国大西南，面向东南亚，邻近广东、海南、港澳和越南，处于“一城系四南”的枢纽位置之上。既是中国西南地区以及华南、华中部分地区便捷的出海口，也是中国大陆距离东南亚、西亚、非洲及欧洲最近的出海口，在西南经济区、亚太经济区的发展格局中，具有重要的战略地位。

北海市地理位置优越，自然资源丰富，风景秀丽，气候宜人。丰富的自然资源，以港口、淡水、土地、旅游、海洋水产、矿产、石油及天然气、亚热带农业尤为突出。全市海岸线长500公里，优良天然港湾众多，可建1-10万吨级泊位200多个，10-20万吨级泊位20个；市区土地70%属平原台地，地质承荷力强，适合成片开发和大型工业项目建设，淡水资源丰富，现探明储量118.8亿立方米，年可利用量43亿立方米；北海濒临的北部湾是中国重要的海上石油和天然气产地，又是中国四大著名渔场之一，北海近海盛产珍珠，是著名的“南珠”之乡。

北海拥有十分丰富的旅游资源，是新兴的重点旅游城市，1998年被评为首批“中国优秀旅游城市”，旅游资源以海滩、海岛、红树林最为突出，集“海、滩、岛、湖、山、林”于一体，自然风光和人文景观兼备，主要有北海银滩、星岛湖、涠洲岛、红树林、大士阁、东坡亭、珍珠城遗址等自然景观和风景名胜。北海至越南——“海上桂林”下龙湾海上国际旅游航线已开通。北海银滩的海水浴，海上运动、沙滩运动，以及大型雕塑、音乐喷泉、旅游娱乐等，构成了北海旅游度假的主要特色。逐步形成以银滩为中心，涠洲岛、星岛湖为两翼的旅游格局。

北海还是广西主要的侨乡，侨居海外及港澳的侨胞有3.8万人，归桥1.74万人。

建国50年来，特别是1978年以来，北海市进一步解放思想，不断深化改革，扩大开放，抓住机遇，加快发展，经济建设和各项社会事业都取得了显著的成就。1998年全市国内生产总值102.6亿元，比1950年增长89.6倍，年平均增长9.8%；北海工业发展迅速，1998年全市工业总产值86.9亿元，比1950年增长834倍，年平均增长15%；工业产品结构有效调整，逐步建立了一个传统工业与新兴工业并举，外向型经济初具规模，门类较为齐全的工业体系。农业和农村经济全面发展，北海特色的主要农业优势初现，发展前景十分广阔，粮食、水产品产量连续创历史最好水平，主要农产品产量成倍增加，1998年全市粮食产量达41.5万吨，水产品产量78万吨，甘蔗产量165.3万吨。

二、投资环境及跨世纪发展战略思路

大西南出海通道建设步伐加快，北海市基础设施超前发展，投资环境不断改善，北海已形成水陆空四通八达的立体交通网络，机场、港口、码头、铁路、公路等基础设施完备。北海港与世界98个国家和地区的218个港口有贸易往来；钦（州）北（海）铁路已建成通车，北海至南宁和成都已开通客货列车；北海机场开通了至北京、上海、广州、深圳、香港、成都、昆明等20多个城市航线，每周航班82次；南宁至北海高速公路全线近期内将建成通车，北海至玉林、北海至山口的高速公路正抓紧建设；邮电通信业快速发展，已建成了本地电话网、寻呼网、分组数据交换网、高速数据通信网、移动电话交换网、数字移动电话网、会议电视网和长途交换网，实现了城乡电话一体化和线路传输光缆化。供电供水方便充足。

北海市精神文明建设和物质文明建设同步发展，荣获自治区级“文明城市”、“双拥模范城”、“卫生城市”和“园林城市”等称号。

北海市到本世纪末和2010年的总体发展战略和发展目标是：以工业为主导，港口为中心、贸工农和旅游、金融并举，综合发展。在经济体制和运行机制上，朝着经济形式多元化、产业结构合理化、经济运行市场化、基础设施现代化的社会主义市场经济方向发展，综合实力上，力争成为广西名列前茅的经济强市。在城市功能上，力争成为西南和中南部分地区发展国际贸易的窗口、连接国内外市场的重要桥梁；力争成为海、陆、空全面发展，联结东南亚和大西南两个扇面的交通枢纽；力争成为富有时代气息和滨海特色的花园式城市和旅游度假胜地。在精神文明建设上，力争成为善于吸收人类社会文明成果，促进社会全面进步的先进地区和卫生城、双拥模范城、文明城。力争成为广西区率先全面达到小康水平，并向富裕水平过渡的较发达地区，把北海建设成为初步现代化的港口城市。

以十大农业基地为重点，大力发展农村社会生产力。充分发挥高产、高效及优质农业所具有的海洋资源优势、土地成片优势、区位交通优势和城市品牌优势，围绕规模农业、高新技术农业和观光农业的发展，积极推进具有鲜明特色的十大农业基地建设，如珍珠基地、名贵鱼类养殖基地、优良品种与种苗繁育基地、名特优水果基地、无公害大棚蔬菜基地、畜禽出口创汇基地、纯精田示范基地、花卉基地、观赏性动物养殖基地。以此带动北海农业生产结构的调整，增强农产品的市场竞争力。

以重点扶持十大高新技术企业为突破口，优化产业结构。高新技术产业是北海市经济发展方向和新的经济增长点。以电子信息、生物制药、海洋生物、新材料、节能技术五大领域为重点，从21家新技术企业中优选10家作为政府重点扶持对象，促进它向规模化、产业化方向发展。尽快形成一个在全广西乃至全国具有领先水平、有竞争力的高科技产业群、进而带动相关产业的发展。

以十大基础设施项目建设为重点，进一步完善大西南出海通道功能。北海市抓住国家加大基础设施投资的有利时机，以三港（海港、陆港、空港）建设为龙头，集中力量搞好交通设施、市政设施、城市建设方面的十大项目，带动基础设施建设。

I. Economic Development

Beihai city is located in the south of the Guangxi Zhuang Autonomous Region, surrounded by sea on three sides. It is the only minority ethnic region among the first 14 cities opened to the outside world listed by the State.

During the past 20 years of development and practice

of reform and opening, it has taken the initial steps to become a modern tourist port city with fairly complete amenities along Beibu Bay.

Covering 3,337 sq.km and including 957 sq km of urban area, the city now has Hepu County and Haicheng, Yinhai and Tieshangang districts under its jurisdiction, with a total population of 1.378 million, including 497,000 urban people.

With southwest China behind and southeast Asia in front, the city, neighboring Guangdong, the South Sea, Hong Kong, Macao and Vietnam, enjoys an advantageous position. It is an outlet for the southwest, north, and part of central China, and the nearest opening to the sea of Southeast and West Asia, Africa and Europe. Therefore, the city occupies an important strategic position in the economic circle of southwest China and the Asia-Pacific region.

With beautiful scenery and a pleasant climate, the city has abundant natural resources, featuring ports, fresh water, land, tourist attractions, marine products, minerals, oil and natural gas, and semi-tropical agriculture.

The coastline is 500 km long, dotted with many natural ports, where it is possible to build more than 200 berths able to accommodate 10,000-100,000 dwt vessels, and 20 berths with the ability of accommodating 100,000-200,000 dwt vessels.

Some 7 percent of the land is plain terrace which is able to bear heavy loads. Most of the area is suitable for development and for the construction of large industrial projects.

Fresh water resources are ample, with proven water resources reaching 11.88 billion cubic meters. The annual water consumption amount is 4.3 billion cubic meters.

Beibu Bay facing Beihai is an important production base of oil and natural gas, and is one of the four main fisheries bases in China. The inshore waters are rich in pearls.

It is a booming tourism city, rich in attractions. In 1998, the city was rated as "China's outstanding tourism city". The tourist attractions feature natural scenery and cultural relics, integrated with the sea, beaches, islands, lakes, mountains and forests. There are many such natural scenic spots and cultural sites as the Beihai silver Beach, Xingdao Lake, Weizhou Island, mangrove swamps, Dashi Pavilion, Dongpo Pavilion and Pearl City. An international tourist route on the sea from Beihai to Vietnam has opened. The Beihai holiday resort features sea bathing, water sports and beaches, as well as large statues, musical fountains and many forms of entertainment. A tourist pattern has basically formed with Silver Beach as the center and two islands as wings.

Beihai is also a major ancestral home of overseas Chinese in Guangxi, with 38,000 compatriots living abroad, and in Hong Kong and Macao. There are 17,400 returned overseas Chinese there.

During the past 50 years, and especially since 1978, the city, emancipated the mind further, has constantly developed the reforms, expanded the opening up, and seized opportunities to accelerate its development, making remarkable achievements.

In 1998, the city's GDP reached 10.26 billion yuan, a rise of 89.6 times over 1950, and an annual increase of 9.8 percent. Industry witnessed rapid development. The total industrial output value hit 8.69 billion yuan, 834 times higher than in 1950, representing an annual increase of 15 percent. The structure of industrial products was effectively readjusted. A complete industrial system has been formed, with an export-oriented economy taking shape and traditional and booming industries developing together.

Agriculture and the rural economy have also enjoyed overall development. Main agricultural advantages with the city's characteristics began to emerge, showing great potential. The outputs of grain and aquatic products recorded the best level for several successive years. Primary farm production has increased by many times. In 1998, grain out-

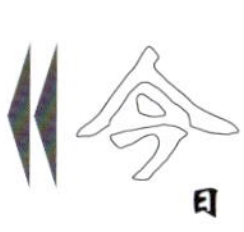

put reached 415,000 tons, the output of aquatic products hit 780,000 tons, and that of sugarcane hit 1.653 million tons.

II. Investment Environment and Trans-Century Development Strategy

Construction of access to the sea has been accelerated. The city's infrastructure facilities have developed ahead of time and the investment environment has improved continuously. Beihai City has formed complete transportation infrastructure facilities, with an airport, ports, docks, railways and highways. Beihai Port trades with 98 countries and regions. The Qinzhou-Beihai Railway has been put into operation. Passenger and cargo trains are now running along the Beihai-Nanning-Chengdu Railway. Beihai Airport has connections with more than 20 cities, including Beijing, Shanghai, Guangzhou, Shenzhen, Hong Kong, Chengdu and Kun-ming. There are 82 regular flights each week. The Nanning-Beihai Expressway will be completed and ready for traffic soon, and the Beihai-Shankou Expressway is under construction.

The postal and telecommunications sector has developed rapidly. So far, the city has set up networks of local telephone, paging, group-divided data exchange, high-speed data communication, mobile telephone exchange, digital mobile telephone, conference telephone, and long-distance exchange, using optical cable transmission. There were ample supplies of water and power.

The city's material progress and cultural and ideological progress have developed together. It has won the titles of "Progressive City", "Model City ", "Hygienic City" and "Garden City" at the autonomous region level.

Beihai's general development strategy and targets for 2010 envisage comprehensive development in terms of industry, ports, trade, agriculture, tourism and finance, with the emphasis placed on the former.

The economic system and operation mechanisms will develop toward a socialist market economy, featuring multi-layer economy, rational industrial structure and modern infrastructure facilities. The aim is to enable the city to have the economic strength to lead Guangxi.

The city will strive to become a window to develop international trade in southwest and central China, which will link markets at home and abroad; develop sea, land and air facilities to become the main traffic link between Southeast Asia and southwest China; and become a garden city with seaside features and a tourism resort.

Concerning cultural and ideological progress, the city will endeavor to be an advanced, clean city, culturally progressive and a model city, so as to improve overall social progress; and take the lead in Guangxi to reach a high standard of living, and become a first-rate modernized port city.

Efforts will be made to develop the social productive forces in rural areas focusing on the construction of 10 agricultural bases for pearls and fish breeding, fine varieties of seeds, high-quality production, sugar cane, flowers, and domestic animal breeding.

Construction of 10 agricultural bases will be actively promoted. The aim is to spur the readjustment of the agricultural structure and strengthen the market competitive power of farm produce.

Efforts will also be made to support 10 high-tech enterprises, so as to optimize the industrial structure. High-tech industry is the economic development orientation and a new economic growth indicator of the city. With priorities in the fields of electronic information, biological pharmacy, marine biology, new materials and energy conservation, the city government chose 10 enterprises out of 21 to support. The aim is to help the city develop toward industrialization, and to form a high-tech industrial group with competitive power which will lead Guangxi or even the country, so as to encourage related industries.

The focus will also be placed on the construction of 10 infrastructure facility projects, in an effort to further perfect the function of the southwest's access to the sea. Seizing the opportunity of the country to expand investment in construction of infrastructure facilities, the city will, headed by the construction of seaports, docks and airports, make extra efforts to improve transportation facilities, urban facilities and buildings.

中国科技工业园

CHINA'S SCIENCE AND TECHNOLOGY INDUSTRIAL PARKS

中国科技工业园

CHINA'S SCIENCE AND TECHNOLOGY INDUSTRIAL PARKS

中国的科技工业园区

High-Tech Industrial Parks in China

中国的高新技术产业开发区（科技工业园区）是1978年改革开放以后，涌现的新生事物。是在中国火炬计划的推动下，在中国政府和各地方领导的支持和关怀下成长起来的，主要目的就是要在各高新区的范围内给予一定的优惠政策，创造一个局部优化的环境，促进高新技术成果的商品化、产业化和国际化。几年来，高新技术产业开发区建设与发展灿烂夺目，已成为各地经济增长快、投资回报率高、创新能力强、具有极大发展前景的高新技术产业的发展基地和新的经济增长点。

中国国家主席江泽民指出："本世纪在科技产业化方面最重要的创举是兴办科技工业园区。这种产业发展与科技活动的结合，解决了科技与经济脱离的难题，使人类的发现或发明能够畅通地转移到产业领域，实现其经济和社会效益"。1998年，全国53个国家级高新区已开发土地273平方公里，高新区内企业达1.6万家，创造了180万个就业岗位，实现技工贸总收入4839.6亿元、人均技工贸总收入达27.8万元，工业销售额4333.6亿元，税收477亿元，出口85.3亿美元。1991-1998年上述指标的平均增长率为75%。技工贸总收入亿元以上的高新技术企业达到678家（不包括区级高新技术企业），有2060项国家863攻关、成果推广计划项目在高新区实现了产业化，产生了众多的名牌产品和杰出的企业家群体。

联想公司靠20万元起家，1988年的营业额仅有1.3亿元，高新区的沃土为他们的成长提供了坚实基础和良好的发展环境，1998年在激烈的计算机市场竞争中，联想公司依靠自主知识产权和可靠的质量及良好的售后服务实现了176亿元的营业收入，名列中国电子百强企业第1名。

方正公司依靠自己强大的技术实力开发的激光照排系统，使中国的印刷业告别了铅与火，跨入光与电的时代，1988年该公司的销售额仅有4000万元，1998年则达到74.4亿元。

华为公司、远大公司、长虹公司、海尔集团等一批国内外知名的企业已在各高新技术产业开发区迅速崛起，他们正用其高质量的产品给社会和家庭带来进步和欢乐。

为扶植创新和科技型小企业的发展，各高新技术产业开发区在中国政府的支持下，借鉴国外建设企业孵化器的发展经验，结合中国国情建立了100余家高新技术创业服务中心，这些创业服务中心完全是社会公益型科技服务机构，依靠国家制定的有关政策和各级政府提供的必要条件，为入住企业提供全方位的服务，从孵化高新技术企业入手，培育新的经济增长点，促进高新技术成果的商品化。

据对77家高新技术创业服务中心的统计，1998年拥有孵化场地88万平方米，在孵企业4138家，其中当年新孵企业1244家，累计毕业企业1316家，其中当年毕业企业554家，这些创业服务中心已转化科技成果7000多项，创造就业机会15万个，已有多家企业年销售额达亿元以上，开发的项目包括新材料、生物技术、电子信息、光机电一体化、新能源和环保技术等。创业服务中心已成为各高新技术产业开发区强化创新，推进科技成果商品化的有效手段。

为适应海外学人回国创业的需要，全国各地依托创业服务中心建立了20多家海外学人回国创业园以及良好的软、硬件服务，为海外学人搭起了施展才华的舞台。

为使各界人士对中国的高新技术产业有一个全面的了解，这里选择了几十家国家级高新技术产业开发区，选择了若干孵化器（即创业服务中心）；还选择了若干省级高新技术产业开发区以及国家科委批准的民营科技实验区，加以具体介绍。

综上所述，高新技术产业开发区是现在中国最具活力的地方，这块热土为广大中华儿女和外国朋友大展宏图提供了必要的基础，成为培养高新技术企业家的摇篮。高新技术企业发展的勃勃生机和日新月异的形象也为所在城市带来了希望。高新技术产业开发区内企业自主开发、产业发展的创新实践，已初步走出了一条具有中国特色的发展高新技术产业的道路。

China's high-tech industrial development parks are new things arising in the process of its opening to the outside world. Thanks to the support and concerns of the central and local governments, the high-tech industrial parks have developed along with the implementation of the Torch Program of China. The establishment of high-tech industrial parks is to promote commercialization, industrialization and internationalization of high-tech achievements. In recent years, the construction and development of the high-tech industrial parks, with the characteristics of fast economic growth, high repayment rate of investment, strong capability of blazing new trails and vast range of prospects for development, have drawn great attention of the world, and developed as new growth points in different regions.

Chinese President Jiang Zemin said that the establishment of high-tech industrial parks is the most important pioneering work in the industrialization of science and technology. The development of the industry, in conbination with scientific activities, has solved the problem of divorcing science and technology from eccnomy. In 1998, there were 53 high-tech industrial parks of state level in China with a total area of 273 square kilometers. There were 16,000 enterprises settled in the parks providing 1.8 million posts for employment; total income of technical and industrial trade was 483.96 billion yuan while per capita income of technical and industrial trade was 278,000 yuan; industrial sales was 433.36 billion yuan; tax revenue was 47.7 billion yuan and volume of export reached US$ 8.53 billion. The average growth rate of the indicators mentioned was 75% from 1991 to 1998. There were 678 enterprises with an income of technical and industrial trade of 100 million yuan (not including the high-tech enterprises outside the parks). There were 2,060 projects under the 863 Program, and achievement-spreading program became industrialized in the high-tech parks, thus giving birth to a large number of famous-brand products and a group of outstanding entrepreneurs.

Legend Company has built itself up by starting with 200,000 yuan. It had only 130 million yuan of volume of business in 1988. The rich land provides it with a sound basis of growth and a favorable environment of development. In 1998, the turnover of Legend Company reached 17.6 billion yuan, ranking first among 100 top electronic enterprises in China.

Founder Company, depending on its strong technical capability, developed laser phototypesetting software, thus entering the times of electronic typesetting. In 1988, the gross sales volume of the company was only 40 million yuan, but in 1998, it reached 7.44 billion yuan.

Some national and world famous companies, such as

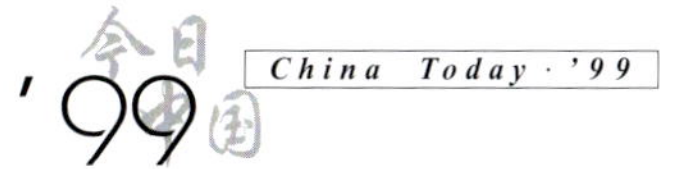

Huawei Company, Yuanda Company, Changhong Company and Haier Group, etc. emerged quickly in the high-tech industrial parks. They brought progress and happiness to the society and households with high-quality products.

To foster small high-tech enterprises, over 100 pioneering service centers were established in the high-tech industrial parks under the support of the Chinese government. These pioneering service centers, a type of scientific and technical service center of public welfare, provide services to all enterprises in the parks in the light of related policies and favorable conditions put forward by local governments. They started their work from incubating new high-tech enterprises to fostering new economic growth points, thus promoting commercialization of new high-tech achievements.

Statistics from 77 pioneering service centers showed that the area used for incubating enterprises totaled 880,000 square meters, with 4,138 enterprises under incubation in 1998, of which, 1,244 enterprises were incubated within the year. The enterprises which were incubated successfully totaled 1,316, of which, 554 enterprises were successfully incubated in 1998. These pioneering service centers have transferred over 7,000 scientific and technical achievements into productive force and created 150,000 jobs. There are several enterprises each with sales volume of over 100 million yuan. The projects for development involve new materials, biological techniques, telecommunication, optical and electrical integration, new energy and environmental protection, etc. The establishment of the pioneering service center has become effective means for commercialization of scientific and technical achievements.

To meet the needs of returned scholars for running business, over 20 pioneering parks have been established. These parks offer good services, making overseas scholars have an arena to show their abilities.

To let people of various circles have an overall understanding of the high-tech industries of China, we have made a detailed introduction to dozens of State-level high-tech industrial development parks, several incubators (the pioneering service centers), provincial high-tech industrial parks and non-governmental high-tech parks approved by the Ministry of Science and Technology.

In short, the high-tech industrial development parks, are the most active places in China where the Chinese people and foreign friends are provided with necessary bases to achieve their great plans. The enterprises, with full vitality and improved image, also have brought hopes to the cities in which they are located. These high-tech industrial parks have opened a way for development of high-tech industries with Chinese characteristics.

北京市新技术产业开发试验区

Beijing Experimental Zone for the Development of New Technology Industry

北京市新技术产业开发试验区（以下简称北京试验区）是1988年5月经国务院批准建立的中国第一个国家级高新技术产业开发区。北京市新技术产业开发试验区管理委员会是其业务领导机关，代表市政府对试验区实行统一领导和管理，经市政府授权，具有市级经济管理权限。

北京试验区覆盖了北京市科技、智力、人才和信息资源最密集的100平方公里区域，包括海淀试验区、丰台科技园区、昌平科技园区、电子城科技园区和亦庄科技园区。海淀试验区位于海淀区，以被誉为“科学城”的中关村地区为核心，其中建有1.8平方公里的上地信息产业基地和4平方公里的永丰中试基地；丰台科技园区位于南郊的丰台区，昌平科技园区位于北郊的昌平县，作为高科技产业基地，两园区面积各占地5平方公里；亦庄科技园区位于北京东南郊京津塘高速公路起点，面积7平方公里；电子城科技园区位于首都东北郊酒仙桥，面积10.5平方公里，五园区共同构成环京高新技术产业带。

北京试验区的核心区域——中关村地区，是中国科技智力资源最密集的地区，拥有一流的科技人才和科研成果，具有发展高新技术产业的良好基础和条件，国家科技部已把中关村地区建设正式列为国家科技创新示范工程。北京试验区将在市委市政府的领导下，积极配合国家有关部门，努力改善中关村地区的投资环境和创业环境，力争用10年左右的时间，把中关村地区建成：国家科技创新示范基地、科技成果转化和科技产业的孵化基地、高素质创新人才的培育基地、推动科教兴国战略、实现两个转变的改革试验区和世界一流的科技工业园区，为全国高新技术产业的发展发挥示范作用。

作为中国第一个国家级高新技术产业开发区，在过去的10年里，试验区经济发展始终保持30%以上的增长速度。1998年，实现技工贸总收入513.86亿元，国内生产总值157亿元，工业总产值（不变价）332.5亿元，出口创汇3.34亿美元，上缴税费17.98亿元，分别比上年同期增长35.7%、20.9%、42.4%、10.4%和40.4%，对北京市工业增长贡献率达50%以上，成为北京市经济发展的重要增长源。涌现出了一大批拥有自主知识产权的新技术企业，目前试验区拥有新技术企业6057家，技工贸总收入超过10亿元以上的企业有7家，过亿元的企业达60家，纳税500万元以上的高新技术企业达52家。

北京试验区十分重视发展国际经济技术合作，积极参与国际经贸活动，充分利用国际各类资本发展高科技产业。到1998年底，试验区拥有三资企业1000多家，约占企业总量的17.3%；外商投资企业累计投资总额达16.4亿美元。

1997年北京试验区已被批准作为中国政府首批对亚太经合组织（APEC）成员开放合作的科技工业园区之一。同时，北京试验区作为国际科技园区协会（IASP）的正式会员单位，于1995年

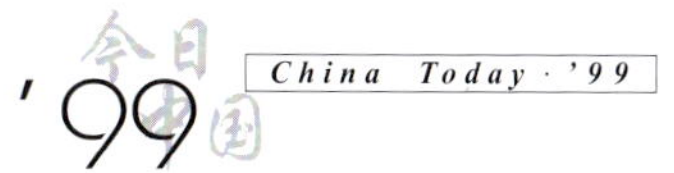

在北京成功举办了“科技工业与研究园第四届世界大会”，1997年又被推举为该协会亚太分会理事单位，与国际高科技组织保持着密切联系。

国家为促进试验区内的高新技术企业发展给予了优惠政策：外商投资的高新技术企业减按15%税率征收所得税，企业出口产品的产值达到当年总产值40%以上的，减按10%税率征收所得税；自开办之日起，3年内免征所得税，第4至第6年可按前项规定的税率，减半征收所得税等。

北京市政府制定出台了《北京市进一步促进高新技术产业发展的若干政策》（简称33条），重点支持具有良好产业基础和发展前景的高新技术及其产业。

北京试验区愿意同世界各国企业和机构在平等互利的原则下，开展多领域、多样化的广泛合作，共同发展高新技术产业。

Established in May 1988, with the approval of the State Council, the Beijing Experimental Zone for the Development of New Technology Industries (hereinafter referred to as BEZ) is the first State level high-tech industrial development zone in China. On behalf of Beijing Municipal Government, the administration commission of BEZ, authorized by the government, has the municipal level rights of economic management and leadership on the zone.

BEZ covers an area of 100 km^2 with the most intensified science & technology, intelligence, and talents as well as information, and includes five areas, i.e., Haidian Experimental Zone (HEZ), Fengtai S&T Park, Changping S&T Park, and Electronic Town S&T Park, as well as Yizhuang S&T Park. HEZ, located in Haidian District, takes Zhongguancun known as "Science Town" as its center. It has the 1.8 square km Shangdi Information Industry Base, the 4-square-km Yongfeng Intermediate Trial Site. Fengtai Park is situated in Fengtai District, the southern suburbs of Beijing, and Changping Park lies in Changping county, in the northern suburban of Beijing, each having an area of 5 square km as high-tech industry sites respectively. Yizhuang Park is at the starting point of Beijing-Tianjin-Tanggu Expressway in the southeast of Beijing, with an area of 7 square km. Situated in Jiuxianqiao, northeast of Beijing, Electronic Town Park has an area of 10.5 square km. All the five parks constitute a high-tech industrial belt surrounding Beijing.

For its highly intensified intelligence resource in China, Zhongguancun is the kernel part of BEZ as a leading place for the development of nationwide new-and high-tech industrial zones, with first-class S&T talents and achievements as well as great potentials. Its intelligence sources can be compared with the "Silicon Valley" in the United States. Under the leadership of the municipal government, BEZ will try its best to reach the following targets in the next 10 years by improving its investment and innovation environment, namely, the demonstration site for S&T innovation, transformation site for S&T achievements and incubating base for S&T industries, training site for high-quality innovation talents, pushing forward the strategy of "developing the country with science & education," and reforming the polit zone. BEZ will play a demonstration role in the development of nationwide new-and high-tech industries.

In the past ten years, the BEZ's growth rate has been over 30 percent annually. In 1998, its total revenue of technology, industry and trade amounted to 51.386 billion yuan, its Gross Domestic Production (GDP) reached 15.7 billion yuan; its industrial output value (unchangeable price), 33.25 billion yuan, and export volume of US$ 334 million; taxes, 1.798 billion yuan, or an increase of 35.7 percent, 20.9 percent, 42.4 percent, 10.4 percent and 40.4 percent over those of the previous year respectively. Moreover, their contributions to Beijing's industrial growth was over 50 percent. Hence, an important increment source of Beijing's economy. In addition, a large number of new-tech enterprises have appeared with intellectual property rights on their own. At present, there are 6,057 new-tech enterprises in BEZ, of which, 7 enterprises have a total income of over 1 billion yuan each year, 60 enterprises have more than 100 million yuan each year, and 52 enterprises pay taxes of over 5 million yuan each year. Furthermore, a large number of new and high-tech enterprises have been set up conforming to the market economy. They have laid a foundation for the development of new and high-tech industries.

BEZ pays much attention to international cooperation in economy and technology, and takes an active part in a variety of economic and trade activities, so as to develop high-tech industries by means of international capital. By the end of 1998, BEZ had over 1,000 foreign-invested companies, making up 17.3 percent of the total; and the total investment amounted to US$1,640 million.

With approval of the Chinese government in 1997, BEZ was one of the first group of high-tech parks open to the members of APEC. BEZ was elected as a council member of Asian-Pacific area Branch of International Association of Science Parks (IASP) in 1997. BEZ has close relationships with the international high-tech organizations.

Approved by the State Council, the preferential policies are implemented to encourage the development of the new and high-tech industrial enterprises in BEZ, i.e. for foreign-invested new and high-tech industrial enterprises, the income tax will be levied at a reduced rate of 15 percent. Furthermore, the enterprises, whose export volume exceeds 40 percent of the total output in the same year, will be levied their income taxes at a reduced rate of 10 percent. Newly established enterprises shall exempt from income tax in the first three profit-making year; and shall enjoy a 50 percent reduction of their income tax in the 4th to 6th profit-making year.

The Beijing Municipal Government issued "The Policies on Further Promoting the Development of new and high-tech Industries" (i.e. 33 Articles for short), so as to support new and high-tech industrial enterprises with an excellence industrial base and a prosperous future.

BEZ would like to cooperate broadly with enterprises and organizations from the whole world on the principles of equality and mutual benefits in various forms, to promote the development of new and high-tech industries.

北京市新技术产业开发试验区管委会大楼
The Building of the Administration Commission of BEZ

武汉东湖新技术开发区

Wuhan East Lake High-Tech Industrial Development Zone

武汉东湖新技术开发区（简称东湖高新区）位于中国武汉市东南部，是中国国务院批准的首批国家级高新区之一。武汉作为中国特大中心城市，地处中国腹地的中心，素有“九省通衢”之称。在中国经济发展战略布局中，起着承东启西、荟萃南北的重要作用，是中国经济中心和科教中心。

武汉东湖高新区是中国智力最密集的地区之一，是华中人才、技术、高新技术产业的源头，享有“华中硅谷”的美誉。区内聚集了包括武汉大学、华中理工大学等著名院校在内的23所高等院校，有中科院武汉分院、武汉邮电科学研究院等56个国家级科研设计单位，10个国家级重点开放实验室，4个国家工程技术中心，20家国有大中型企业，700多家高新技术企业，汇集了10万多名专业技术人员，平均每平方公里科技人员达到5000人，年获科技成果1000多项。在通信、生物工程及新医药、激光技术、电子信息、先进制造技术、新材料等领域有雄厚技术实力和人才优势。

武汉东湖高新区依托区内人才、技术、科研条件、高等教育、工业基础的资源优势，改善投资环境，优化区域性政策条件和服务体系，突出发展有区域性优势的特色高新技术产业，确立了以通信产业为重点，以生物工程及新医药、电子信息、先进制造技术、新材料、激光技术等为基础的六大高新技术产业。1998年实现科工贸总收入130亿元，其中通信产业38亿元，约占30%，是中国光通信产业基地；生物工程及新医药产业24.6亿元，约占20%；激光技术领域已有10多家企业从事开发、生产与经营。

目前，武汉东湖高新区已有32家高新技术企业年科工贸总收入过亿元。区内企业与国际交流十分活跃，一批高新技术企业纷纷在境外设立分公司或分支机构。一批国际知名大公司纷至沓来，世界经济500强工业企业中有美国施乐、西屋电气、荷兰菲利浦、日本NEC、住友、三井物产株式会社、瑞典爱立信、瑞士ABB、英国英之杰和香港汇丰银行等11家到区内投资兴业，高新技术产业化、国际化特征日益明显。

根据武汉科技新城总体规划，科技工业园将按国际标准建设成30平方公里高新技术产业化基地，实行统一管理，目前已开发土地10平方公里，实现“六通一平”，60余家中外企业在新区安家落户。

Wuhan East Lake High Technology Industry Development Zone (EDZ), located in Wuhan, is one of first group of high-tech parks approved by the State Council.

Lying in the center of China, Wuhan has long been known as the “thoroughfare of nine provinces”. It is right in the middle of the nation’s main water and land communication artery. As one of the important centers of economy, scientific research and education in China, Wuhan is an important link between the east and the west and joins the north with the south in the strategic layout of China's economic development.

The EDZ was one of the national high-tech industrial development zones approved by the State Council.

Being one of China's most intelligence-concentrated area, EDZ is the source of talents, technologies, and high-tech industries in Central China. Thus it enjoys high reputation of "Silicon Valley in Central China". In the zone, there are 23 universities, such as the well-known Wuhan University, Central China Science and Engineering University, etc., and 56 national scientific research and design institutes, namely Wuhan Branch of the Chinese Academy of Science (CAS) and Wuhan Research Institute of Telecommunications.

There are also 10 national key open-up laboratories, 4 national engineering technology centers, 20 large- and medium-sized State-owned enterprises, and over 700 high-tech enterprises.

With over 100,000 specialized technical personnel working in the zone (5,000 scientific and technical personnel/km), over 1,000 items of scientific and technical research achievements are made a year on average. The fact shows EDZ has the advantages of sound technical strength and well-known talents in the fields of telecommunications, bioengineering, laser technique, electronic information, and new materials.

By relying on its advantages of talents, technology, scientific research conditions, higher education, abundant resourses for the industrial base, improved environment, favorable policies and food service systems, it has decided that six pillar industries will be developed, with telecommunications industry as the mainstay, and bioengineering, electronic information, advanced manufacturing technique, new materials, and laser technique as the base. Through five years' construction and development, the layout of the six pillar industries has generally been formed.

In 1998, EDZ achieved a revenue of 13 billion yuan in the fields of science and industry, among which 3.8 billion yuan came from the telecommunication industry, accounting for 30%, forming a national optical communication industry base. Among the revenue of 13 billion yuan, 2.46 billion yuan came from bioengineering, accounting for 20%. In the field of laser technique, over 10 enterprises are engaged in development, production and management.

At present, there are 700-odd high- and new-tech industrial enterprises in the zone, with 32 achieving 100 million yuan of revenue a year each. Some enterprises are very active in international exchange, and a group of high- and new-tech enterprises have established branch offices and organs abroad. A number of well-known international big companies have invested or set up representative offices in EDZ, such as NEC, Mitsui from Japan, Siemens from Germany, Xerox and Westing House Ele. Cor. from USA, ABB and CIBA from Switzerland, etc. By now, EDZ has attached 350 foreign-invested enterprises, showing its more and more obvious characteristics of the industrialization and internationalization of high- and new-tech industry.

A new area of 30 km^2 has been developed into an industry park to provide a good investment environment for foreign investors. With centralized management, the park will be built into a new industry base according to international standards. At present, a piece of 4-square km land has been developed and 60 domestic and foreign-invested enterprises have been established in the park.

南京高新技术产业开发区

Nanjing New & High-Tech Industrial Development Zone

南京高新技术产业开发区（以下简称高新区）1988年5月由江苏省人民政府与南京市人民政府共同创建，1991年3月被国务院批准为国家级高新技术产业开发区。

南京高新区地处长江大桥脚下，是五条国道、省道的枢纽，毗邻珍珠泉国家级旅游渡假区和老山国家森林公园，环境优美，景色秀丽，周围有南京大学、东南大学等7所高等院校，科技及人才资源雄厚。

高新区由产业区、金融贸易区、教学科研区等组成，总面积为16.5平方公里。此外，在南京市繁华地段开辟了8公里长的“科技一条街”。

高新区产业区已完成首期开发3.2平方公里，建成40万平方米工业厂房和配套的基础设施。区内道路四通八达，上、下水管网齐全。已建成的3万门程控电信分局可为客商提供国内外电信服务；日供水能力达15万吨的浦口水厂为高新区供水；11万伏双回路变电站可保证区内用电；供热、供气系统实行集中供应，方便了区内企业。此外，包括餐饮、住宿、交通、办公、娱乐、学校、医疗、进出口、保税仓库、储运等多项服务内容的综合保障体系已基本配套。

为加快高新区的建设，南京市政府授予高新区市一级经济管理权限。市工商、税务、财政、公安、电信等部门在区内设立了分局，供电、供水、银行、保险、海关、会计、审计、法律、邮政、消防等单位在区内设立了分支机构，形成了完善的支撑服务体系。

高新区建立了精干、高效的管理机构。高新区管理委员会作为南京市政府的派出机构对高新区行使管理服务职能。

为扶持高新区的发展，国家公布了一系列的优惠政策，在高新区内兴办企业可享受税收、进出口、人员出入境等多方面的优惠。

优惠的投资环境，吸引了美国、日本、英国、德国、荷兰、香港等国家和地区的客商在高新区投资，其中有世界上知名的美国联信 (Allied Signal)、荷兰阿克苏 (Akzo Nobel)、德国西门子 (Siemens)、美国可口可乐 (Swire CocaCola)、荷兰特恩驰 (Twentsche) 等跨国公司已在高新区内创办了合资企业。

依托南京强大的科技优势和雄厚的工业基础，高新区的电子信息、生物工程与医药、航空航天及新材料等高新技术企业已初具规模。以国内大企业、大学、科研单位为支撑的一批高新技术企业在区内已形成一定规模，民办科技企业也得到蓬勃发展。

高新区现有企业1000余家，其中高新技术企业157家，占南京市高新技术企业总数的76%，成为南京地区高新技术最密集的地区，并成为南京重点发展的两大高新技术产业即电子信息、生物医药工程的重要产业基地。1998年全区技工贸总收入165亿元，实现利税17亿元，税收4.2亿元。经济总量在全国53个国家级高新区中位居前五名，并荣获国家科技部授予的"火炬计划先进管理奖"。

根据规划，南京高新区将建成园林式的高科技园区和高尚的生活社区，形成外向型的高新技术开发试验基地和产业基地。

Nanjing New & High-Tech Industrial Development Zone (the following is shortened as NHZ) was jointly established in May, 1988 by the Jiangsu Provincial Government and the Nanjing Municipal People's Government. It was approved as a "National Hi-Tech Zone" by the State Council in March, 1991.

The NHZ is situated at the foot of the Nanjing Yangtze River Bridge. As a pivot of 5 State and provincial-grade highways, it is adjacent to a State-class tourist & holiday resort-Pearl Spring Park, and a state-class forest park-Laoshan Scenery Zone, well known for a nice environment and beautiful scenery. Surrounded by Nanjing University, Southeast University and other five universities and colleges, it has the advantage of science and technology.

NHZ consists of an industrial area, a financial and trade area, and an educational and scientific research area, with a total area of 16.5 square kilometers. NHZ has also set up a "scientific market street" in downtown Nanjing, which is 8 kilometers long .

At present, NHZ has completed the first-phase development of 3.2 square kilometers, with such infrastructure facilities as water supply, power supply, heating, and communications, and such public living facilities as hotels, service centers, bus service, office buildings, hospitals, entertainment, import and export, bonded warehouse and other service system.

In order to speed up the construction of NHZ, the Nanjing Municipal Government grants the NHZ first-class management authorities. For convenience of the investors in NHZ, the departments concerned such as administration bureau for industry and commerce, tax bureau, finance bureau, public security bureau, telecommunication bureau, power supply, water supply, insurance company, banks, accounting, audition, post office and lawyer office, have established their branches or offices in NHZ.

NHZ has established an effective and capable administrative organization. As an agent of Nanjing Municipality, the NHZ Administrative Committee exercises the management and service functions.

In order to support the development of NHZ, the State formulated a series of preferential policy. The enterprises in NHZ can enjoy preferential treatment in tax, import and export, and entry and exit formalities.

Its good investment environment has attracted a lot of investors from USA, Japan, UK, Germany, Netherlands and Hong Kong. Some of the investors are well-known transnational corporations, such as Allied Signal and Swire Coca Cola from USA, Akzo Nobel and Twentsche from Netherlands, and Siemens from Germany, etc. They have invested and established joint-ventures in NHZ.

Relying on its advantages of science and technology and sound industrial foundation, the NHZ has developed electronics & information, biomedical engineering, mechanical-electronic integration, new materials, and space and aviation industries. A group of high-tech enterprises invested by the universities, large research institutes and large enterprises in NHZ have formed a certain superiority in its scale. The private enterprises have developed vigorously in NHZ.

In NHZ, there are 1,000 enterprises, and 157 of them are new and high-tech enterprises, making up 76 percent of the total new and high-tech enterprises in Nanjing. Hence the NHZ is the area with the most intensive new and high-tech enterprises in Nanjing. It has become an important production base of the two large industries—electronics &

information and biomedical engineering industries. In 1998, the NHZ had accomplished such economic indicators as the total income of 16. 5 billion yuan from technology, industry and trade, the pre-tax profit of 1.7 billion yuan and revenue of 420 million yuan. The economic strength of NHZ ranks the fifth among the 53 national high-tech zones in China; and NHZ won the prize of "Advance Management for Torch Plan" awarded by the Ministry of Science and Technology.

In accordance with the planning, Nanjing New & High Technology Industry Development Zone will be built into a garden-like high-tech zone and high level living quarters, and become an expor-oriented experimental and industrial base for new and high technology.

高新区管理委员会大楼
The Building of the Administration Commission of NHZ

沈阳国家高新技术产业开发区

Shenyang High-Tech Industrial Development Zone

沈阳高新区创建于1988年5月，是被国务院首批批准的国家高新技术产业开发区和综合改革试验区。高新区总体规划面积34.2平方公里，总体发展格局为“一城、两区、四园”，即：中国电脑软件城、浑南产业区、南塔产业区、沈阳海峡两岸科技工业园、大学科学园、留学人员创业园、环保科技工业园。

沈阳高新区实行封闭式管理，行使市级管理权限，统一领导和管理区内的经济和社会发展工作。

经过11年开发建设，高新区已成为沈阳发展高新技术产业的重要基地，东北地区最大的电子信息技术和产品的集散地。高新区已创办高新技术企业1200户，外商投资企业522户，开发高新技术2300项，其中列入国家“863计划”7项，列入国家火炬计划39项。初步形成了以电子信息、生物工程、新材料、机电一体化、能源与环保等五大高新技术领域为主体的产业发展框架。高新区年工业总产值已达120亿元，技工贸总收入150亿元。

南塔产业区已有32个项目进区生产，初步形成了以三普、昌普和科金公司为代表的新材料生产基地；以机器人工程中心、北商技术和东宇电器公司为代表的自动化产品的生产基地。

浑南产业区，一期工程2.7平方公里土地已开发完毕1998年又新开发土地1.1平方公里，总开发面积达到3.8平方公里，现有50个项目进区建设和生产。东软集团开发生产的全身CT扫瞄机、彩色多普勒填补了国内空白；他们自行开发的分布式多媒体、应用系统与平台、嵌入式软件环境与系统等工程软件从这里走向世界。LG公司生产的大屏幕彩电和电视机、万普公司生产的万普牌电脑，具有广阔的市场前景。协合公司生产的愈肤灵、接骨素、BM828等系列生物药品，在国内处于领先地位。

21世纪大厦
21st Century Mansion

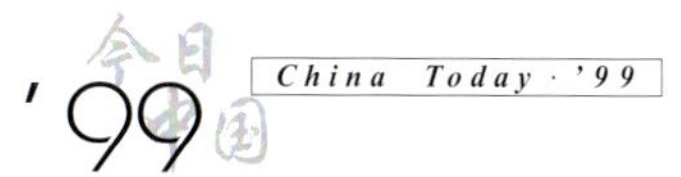

座落在三好街和西文萃路的中国电脑软件城，云集了世界多家著名电子信息企业的名牌产品，是国内仅次于中关村的电子信息产品集散地。

电脑软件城已投入经营的6座功能齐全的科技商厦和630多家科技门点，年贸易额达41亿元。正在建设中的裕宁大厦、长白大厦、泰阳电脑市场、诚大电脑市场、创业中心大厦等将使科技商城经营面积由现在的30万平方米增加到70万平方米，年贸易额将大幅度增长。

随着对外开放工作的不断深入和拓展，沈阳高新区已成为辽沈地区对外交流与合作的重要窗口。已与日本、芬兰、美国、德国、加拿大等一流科学园建立友好关系。美国微软、IBM、康柏、太阳、日本东芝、比利时贝尔、加拿大北方电讯、韩国乐金电子和三宝集团等18个国家和地区的知名跨国公司相继进区投资经营，外商投资总额已达14.89亿美元，使区内高新技术企业与巨人同行。

沈阳高新区持续、快速发展，为沈阳经济发展注入了新鲜血液。展望21世纪，高新区将义不容辞地承担起沈阳跨世纪的历史重任。高新区将瞄准世界一流园区，围绕产业和市场"两个升级"，全力实施"八大工程"，将一个高科技、国际化、现代化、高度文明、充满生机和活力的新区，带入21世纪。

Shenyang National High-tech Industrial Development Zone was established in May, 1988. It is one of the earliest national new- and high-tech industrial development zones approved by the State Council. The zone is planned to cover an area of 34.2 square km, which consists of China Computer Town, Hunnan Industry Park, Nanta Industry Park, Shenyang Science and Technology Industry Park for Both Sides of the Taiwan Strait, University Science Parks, Returned Scholars' Creation Park, Environmental Protection Science and Technology Industry Park.

The zone is authorized to practise an internal management at municipal level in the aspects of economic and social development of the zone.

Through eleven years of construction and development, the zone has become an important base of new- and high-tech industry of Shenyang and the largest distributing center for electronic information products in Northeast China. The zone has established 1,200 new and high-tech enterprises and 522 foreign-invested enterprises, and developed 2,300 new and high-tech projects (including 7 projects of the "National 863 Plan" and 39 projects of the "National Torch Plan"). The zone has set up an industry framework majored by electronic information, electromechanical integration, bioengineering, new material, new energy, and environmental protection. The annual industrial output value of the zone totals 12 billion yuan; and the income of technology, industry and trade, 15 billion yuan.

There are 32 enterprises in Nanta Industry Park. This park has become a new material production base (represented by Suppo, Changpu and Kejin Co.) and a base of automation products (represented by Robot Engineering Center, Beishang Technology Co. and Dongyu Electrical Co.).

An area of 3.8 square km of Hunnan Industry Park (with a total planned area of 10 square km) had been developed by the end of 1998. Now there are 50 projects in the Hunnan Industry Park. Neusoft has designed and produced the CT scanner and color Doppler for the first time in China. Neusoft is marketing its products to all over the world, such as distributed multimedia, application system and platform, embedded software environment and system. The large TV by LG Electronic (Shenyang) Co., Ltd. and monitor by Wanpum Co. have a broad marketing prospect. The biological medicine of Xiehe Co. is on the leading place in China.

China Computer Town is the second largest electronic information products distributing center in China, only next to Zhongguancun. Here you can find almost every world-famous computer product. There are six well-functioned markets of computer products and 630 companies with technological background. The annual turnover of the town comes to 4.1 billion yuan. Once the construction of Yuning Building, Changbai Building, Taiyang Computer Market, Chengda Computer Market and Incubating Center is finished, the operating area will increase from 300,000 m^2 to 700,000 m^2, and the turnover will grow greatly.

With the deepening of opening to the outside world, Shenyang High-tech Industrial Development Zone has become a showcase of international cooperation and exchange. The zone has established sisterhood with science parks of Japan, Finland, U.S.A., Germany, Canada and so on. Famous transnational corporations such as Microsoft, IBM, Compaq, Sunmicro, Toshiba, Bell, Nortel, LG and Trigem have established partnership with the companies in the zone. The total foreign investment in the zone has reached US$1.489 billion.

The continuous and rapid development of the zone makes Shenyang full of vitality. Looking forward to the 21st century, we're trying to build a high-tech, internationalized, vital and world famous development zone.

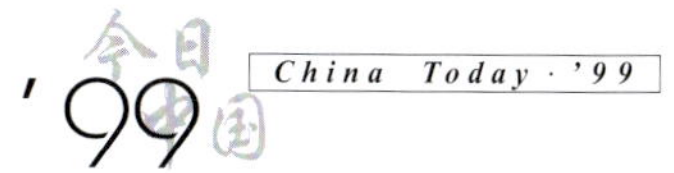

天津新技术产业园区

Tianjin New Technology Industrial Park

天津新技术产业园区于1988年3月经市人民政府批准建立，1991年3月经国务院批准为国家高新技术产业开发区，总面积21.85平方公里，由华苑产业区、政策区和辐射区三部分组成。政策区位于本市智力密集区，是园区的基础和起步区，已建有包括创业中心在内的科研基地、科贸街、南开工业园和天津大学科学园。经过几年的发展，政策区已成为天津市高新技术成果、信息产业、技术交易的最大集散地。辐射区，已建有武清开发区、北辰科技工业园和塘沽海洋科技工业园。随着战略的发展，用布点连线的方法，将建成一条京津塘高科技走廊。

天津新技术产业园区依托于国际大都市，充分利用天津集港口、工业、金融、人才、交通等方面的整体优势，努力营造国际化投资环境。今后将重点建设好华苑产业区。华苑产业区是天津园区的发展重点，位于市区西南部，可开发面积10平方公里，外环线以内2平方公里基础设施建设基本就绪；外环线以外8平方公里起步区开发建设已全面展开。产业区有良好的区域优势，其发展的主要支撑条件是：华苑产业区规划面积10平方公里，形成了土地资源优势，为高科技产业发展提供了广阔的天地，特别是产业区地处天津市西南部，处于长年主导风向的上风口，外环线绿化带起着天然净化作用，大气条件优越，该地区无工业污染，空气洁净，排污设施齐全；北边以复康路为界的西青区候台风景区相连，是正在兴建集商贸、居住、娱乐为一体的风景区。优美的环境为华苑吸引投资，发展高科技产业提供了条件。

同时，华苑产业区依托天津市近百家科研机构、9所大学及创业中心、天津图书馆、中德培训中心、中日培训中心等科技服务设施，有4000多名高级人才、9096名中级人才、博士111名、硕士706名、大学本科学历10017名，为发展高科技产业提供了人才保证。华苑周围的张窝和汪庄两个大型发电厂及第一煤气制造厂是产业区内高科技产业发展的能源保障。

华苑距市中心百货大楼、劝业场、华联商厦、服装街、食品街、旅馆街、喜来登、利顺德大酒店等均在10公里以内，购物旅游极为方便。全市最大的第一中心医院及市总医院、环湖医院等都很近，周边幼儿园．中小学分布密集，为华苑产业区发展提供了良好的外部服务条件。

华苑产业区还与本市安居工程的起步区“华苑安居工程”相连，这是拥有安居小区、全国示范小康住宅区和高级别墅区的全国最大的现代化居住区。这里地理环境优越、基础设施齐备、公建完善、绿化布局合理。

此外，天津园区在市委、市政府的支持下，华苑产业区全面行政管理的基础已经形成，将大大增加华苑产业区招商引资以及高新技术企业招纳人才的吸引力。

华苑产业区的发展重点：一是建设好绿色能源、生物制药和电子信息工程技术三大产业基地，并发展配套产业。目前已初具规模。二是建设好华苑软件园和国际创业中心。华苑软件园是经国家科技部评审和认定，由市科委和天津园区共建的“国家火炬计划软件产业基地”，进入该基地的软件企业可在税收、土地出让、房租等多方面享受各种优惠。国际创业中心是为高新技术企业的诞生与成长提供帮助的公益性服务机构，今年底在孵企业达到100家，其中三成以上产品达到国内领先或世界先进水平。一半以上企业为软件开发企业，为软件园的建设奠定了基础。三是搞好与美国纽约州中小企业环保产业的展示交流活动，已于今年6月份开展。

天津新技术园区
A Corner of TNTIP

Tianjin New Technology Industrial Park (TNTIP) was originally built with the approval of the Tianjin Municipal People's Government in March, 1988, and authorized to become a state high-tech industry development area by State Council in March, 1991. With an area of 21.85 square kilometers, it is composed of three parts. Located in intelligence-intensive district in city, Policy Area is the primary part of TNTIP. Here we have built four scientific and technological parts. They're the scientific research base including the incubator center, the scientific and technological trading street, the Nankai Industrial Park and the Tianjin University Scientific and Technological Park. After several years' development, this area has become the biggest collecting and distributing center of high-technological achievments, information industry, and technological trade. Radiating areas have three parts: Wuqing Development Area, Beichen Scientific and Technological Industry Park and Tanggu Marine Scientific and Technological Industry Park. All of them are developing progressively. Both sides of the industrial belts along Beijing-Tianjin-Tanggu Highway will become the access of the High-Tech in North China in the future.

As a metropolitan city, Tianjin is the largest open coastal city in North China. It has many advantages: trading port, industries, finance, personnel, communication and so on. Huayuan Industry Development Area (HIDA) is the most important part in TNTIP. Located in the southwest in the urban district, HIDA covers a space of 10 square kilometers. So far, within 2 square kilometers of the Outer Ring Road, its fundamental facilities have been accomplished. And for the other area whose total area is 8 square kilometers out of the Outer Ring Road, all preparations have begun. HIDA has plenty of advantages to investors. The main condition for development in HIDA is that TNTIP is rich in land resources, and HIDA covers a space of 10 square kilometers. It's advantageous to the development of hi-tech industry. Especially, located in the southwest of Tianjin, HIDA is in the windward area. The air in the area is fresh due to the purification by a tree belt of the Outer Ring Road. We have fresh air, and completed waste water pipes without industry pollution here. Houjiatai Scenic Resort in Xiqing district neighboring on its north is a site where there are markets, houses and amusement parks. All of them make it possible

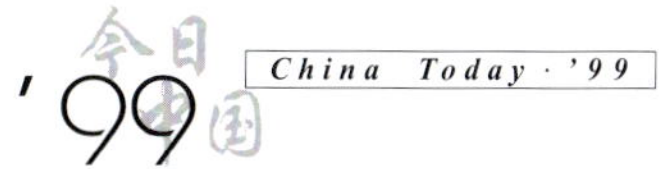

to develop hi-tech and absorb the investment in HIDA.

Meanwhile, HIDA is adjacent to almost 100 science and technology research institutions, nine universities and colleges, Tianjin Library, China-Germany training center, and China-Japan training center. They provide rich personnel resources. There are 111 people with doctor's degree, 706 people with master's degree, more than 13,000 people with mid-rank and senior professional titles, and 10,017 people with higher education. Close to Zhangwo and Wangzhuang power plants and the first gasworks, HIDA has enough energy to develop hi-tech industries.

The distance to Tianjin Department Store, Quanye Bazaar, Hua Lian Department Store, the Food Street, the Clothing Street, the Hotel Street, Tianjin Astor Hotel, Tianjin Sheraton Hotel is within ten kilometers, so it's convenient for shopping and travelling. It's near to hospitals, such as First Center Hospital—the biggest hospital in Tianjin, Huanhu Hospitals, etc. The nursery schools, elementary schools and high schools locate closely. All of these provide perfect exterior service conditions for the development of industries.

Modern and large-scale Huayuan Housing Project is in its south. There are different styles of apartment buildings and comfortable residential houses. This area is the biggest residential quarter in the state. Here we have favorable geographical location, completed infrastructure facilities and a beautiful natural environment.

Besides, with the support of Tianjin Municipal Party Committee and Tianjin Municipality, HIDA has founded the administrative base. This will greatly increase the attraction of HIDA to the hi-tech enterprises, domestic and overseas investors and excellent personnel.

In HIDA, it will firstly establish three industrial bases, —new energy resources technology, electronics information technology and biomedical engineering. We'll also develop assembly industries. Our focal point of the work in the future is to develop Tianjin Huayuan Software Park (THSP) and Tianjin International Business Incubator (TIBI) secondly. THSP is the first batch of the software industrial bases for Torch Program of the State approved by the State Science and Technology Ministry, and established by Tianjin Committee of Science and Technology and Tianjin Hi-ghtech Industry Park. Those enterprises entering the Park will enjoy preferential treatment on financial credits and bank loan. TIBI, also called as "incubation machine", begins to provide service. About 100 enterprises will come into the TIBI at the end of this year, one third of them manufacture advantageous products. Half of them are software enterprises, which are the base to develop the TIBI. The environmental business trade show of New York State Small Business Development Center (NYS/SBDC) was held in June,1999.

天津新技术园区
Tianjin New Technology Industrial Park

西安高新技术产业开发区

Xi'an High-Tech Industrial Development Zone

西安是一座闻名世界的文化古都，有着三千多年的辉煌历史，13个王朝在此建都，她丰富的历史人文景观每年都会吸引国内外数百万游客前来品味这悠悠的古韵与令人留连忘返的中国古代文明。1998年6月，美国总统克林顿就是从此开始他的中国之行。

走出古城墙，你会发现西安是一个充满活力的现代都市。作为亚欧大陆桥沿线最大的城市，她有着雄厚的科技工业基础。510所大中型科研院所，49所大专院校和强大的现代工业，为西安发展高科技产业奠定了坚实的基础。

1991年正式成立的西安高新技术产业开发区，经过8年发展，已成为西安现代化的一个标志。面积为29.15平方公里的科技工业园区之内，聚集了2500多家科技型企业，1998年全区实现技工贸总收入141.6亿元。不仅吸引德国、日本、美国、新加坡等350家世界性跨国公司到西安投资，还培育出一批具有市场竞争力的民族高科技企业，在国内外颇有知名度的大唐程控交换机，庆安集团的空调压缩机，联合汽车电子汽车发动机电子喷射系统等都出自这里，咸阳彩虹、西飞国际、大唐电信、长岭、黄河、金花、达尔曼等一批上市公司总部落户西安高新开发区。

地处内陆的西安高新开发区注重创造良好的软硬投资环境，吸引国内外科技人员到西安创业，西安高新区建立起政策到位、服务高效的管理体系，深得企业界认可。经过高水平规划建设，这里不仅建成了适合科技产业发展的产业环境，还形成了舒适高雅的生活休闲娱乐环境。一流的中学、小学、幼儿园、公园、俱乐部成为吸引投资者来这里安居乐业的重要因素。另一方面，西安高新区着重依靠西安的科技优势，为科技成果转化创造条件，培育出一批颇具特色的科技小巨人企业。除政府的服务功能外，西安高新区还陆续成立了以下服务机构：为小型科技企业发展提供全面孵化服务的高新区创业服务中心，为企业融资进行担保并进行风险投资的科技风险投资公司，为企业人才流动服务的人才交流中心，为企业发展提供全面中介服务的生产力促进中心等，这些机构构成了促进企业科技成果转化的良好的外部环境。

8年来，高新区累计引进28个国家的外商投资企业的投资5.18亿美元，吸引国内投资100多亿元。园区内产业发展生机勃勃，形成了以电子信息、光机电一体、高效节能、生物制药、新材料为主的支柱产业，作为全国五个对亚太经合组织开放的科技工业园区，西安高新区对国际开放与合作也进入了一个新境界。西安高新开发区管委会主任张龙虎对西安高新区的发展充满信心，他说：到2000年，西安高新区的各项工作将上一个新台阶，技工贸总收入将达到250亿元。

Xi'an is a world-famous ancient city with a splendid history of 3000 years, which was once the capital of 13 federal dynasties. Every year, millions of tourists from home and abroad come to visit Xi'an, one of cradles of

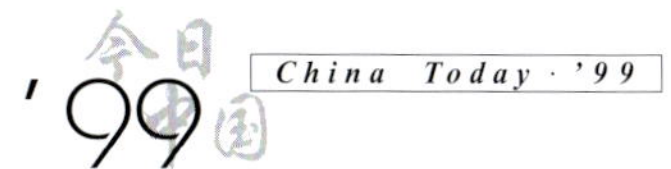

Chinese civilization with abundant historical relics. In June 1998, Mr.Bill Clinton, the President of the United State, chose Xi'an as the first stop of his China Trip.

Walking out of the ancient city wall, you will find that Xi'an is a modern metropolis full of vitality. As the biggest city along the Euro-Asian Land Bridge, it has 501 large- and medium-sized research Institutes, 49 universities and colleges and powerful modern industry, which lay steady foundation for the development of high-tech industry in Xi'an.

Xi'an High-tech Industry Development Zone (XHIDZ), formally established in 1991, has become a symbol of Xi'an's modernization after 8 years' development. In its Science & Technology Industrial Park with an area of 29 square kilometers are 2,500 scientific and technological enterprises, 350 of which are invested by large international corporations from America, Germany, Japan, Singapore, etc.; and many of which are national high-tech enterprises with strong competiveness. There are many well-known high-tech products, such as super digital exchangers produced by Datang telecommunication, air-conditioning compressors produced by Qing'an Group, electronic petrol ejection system for the engines of cars produced by United Automobile Electronic System Companies. The headquarters of a group of listed companies, such as Xianyang Rainbow, Datang Telecom, Changling, Huanghe, Jinhua, Diamond, are also located in the Zone . In 1998, the total revenue of technology, industry and trade reached 14.16 billion yuan (RMB).

As an inland development zone, XHIDZ has paid great attention to creating a superior investment environment in order to attract technical professionals from home and abroad to work and invest in Xi'an. With complete policy and efficient service, the management system of XHIDZ is highly appreciated by the companies in the Zone. With reasonable construction planning, the Zone is not only suitable for the development of high-tech industry, but also has a comfortable, elegant environment of life and entertainment. There are first-class primary schools, middle schools, kindergartens and an international club, which attract the investors to invest and set their home in the Zone. On the other hand, relying on its superiority of science and technology, XHIDZ has created optimum conditions for converting R&D results into production in order to establish distinctive small-sized "Giant" companies with high capital return rate. Beside providing the service as a local government, XHIDZ has also set up such service organizations as the international incubator, venture fund companies, talent exchange center, high-tech productivity promotion center in order to promote the process of converting R&D results into production.

By 1999, the total investment of foreign-funded enterprises with foreign investors from 28 countries reaches 518 million USD, while the investment of national companies is 10 billion yuan (RMB). The Zone has established such dominant industries as electronic information, opto-electric-machinery integration, biomedical engineering, energy-saving technology and new materials. Mr. Zhang Longhu, the director of the Administrative Committee of XHIDZ, is so confident for the development of the Zone that he says: "Until the year of 2000, the Zone will make greater progress, and the total revenue of technology, industry and trade will hit 25 billion yuan (RMB)."

成都高新技术产业开发区

Chengdu High-Tech Industrial Development Zone

自1988年创立以来，成都高新区以“发展高科技，实现产业化”为宗旨，以产业发展、招商引资、基础设施建设和体制改革为重点，经济和社会各项事业都取得了长足发展，成为成都市、四川省乃至中国中西部地区最具活力的开放型经济的先导区。1993年，成都高新区被国家科委授予“先进高新技术产业开发区”称号，同时被列为国家重点开发区；1994年被评为“四川省先进开发区”；1998年荣获国家科技部“火炬先进管理奖”。

10余年来，成都高新区在加大基础设施建设力度、创造良好硬环境的基础上，千方百计创设一流的投资软环境。一方面全力营造仿真国际环境：首先，健全延伸了自己首创的“一站式”服务内涵，使高效、务实、全新的运行机制在投资者中有口皆碑，独具匠心的“税务工商银行服务大厅”更是成为全国税务系统和高科技领域优质服务的一面旗帜；同时，围绕用活用好各种优惠政策，在企业从立项、用地选址、土地价格到人才引进等，全方位不断推出更加灵活、开放、务实的操作措施，为企业进区发展奠定了良好基础；此外，强化了法制、教育、文化、卫生等配套设施建设，努力创建高科技企业和产业发展的“温床”。另一方面，着眼企业长远利益，强化和优化对已进区企业的后续服务：一是择优扶持重点企业。对科技含量高、发展潜力大、投资风险大的项目和以自我创新为主、拥有自己知识产权的高新技术企业，在政策、资金方面给予重点扶持，积极促进支柱产业形成和发展。二是促进科技成果转化，积极培育新的经济增长点。着力扶持和培育中小高科技企业，增强了高科技企业发展后劲，促成了一大批科研成果在区内转化和发展。

今日的成都高新区，已由当初的阡陌田畴变成了一座有数千家企业落户的现代化科技新区。目前该区已累计认定高新技术企业248家，高新技术产业实现产值占全区工业总产值的比例已超过50%；三大优势产业产值占全区工业总产值的82%。经过成都高新区的精心培育，以几十万元在此起家的中科院成都地奥制药公司，已经成为国内外有较大知名度的高科技企业；成都国腾通信有限公司，在短短一年多的时间里，实现了科研成果产业化，销售收入也实现了从零到亿的突破。成都高新区已愈来愈牵动着国内外知名公司的目光，成为中西部地区最具吸引力的投资热土：到目前为止，德国西门子、日本住友、富士重工、法国阿尔卡特、沙特ALJ等已纷纷来此落户；美国GE、深圳华为、清华大学等一批著名企业和学府已进行投资申报或实质性洽谈；美国摩托罗拉、日本NEC等一批大集团也正对成都高新区进行意向性考察和洽谈。

创造新业绩，迎接新世纪。成都高新区将抓住世纪发展的机遇，朝着建设“体制新区，经济强区”的目标，不断优化投资环境，努力培育和发展高新技术产业，把自己建设成为推进知识经济和高新技术产业的高地。

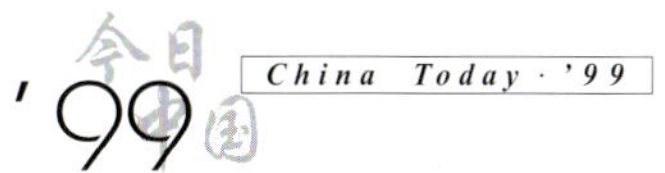

Since its establishment in 1988, Chengdu Hi-tech Development Zone (hereinafter reffered to as the "zone") has focused on "developing hi-tech and realizing industrialization" and stressed on industry development, investment and capital invitation as well as infrastructure construction and institutional reform. Consequently it has emerged as an outstanding zone with the most active open economy in central and western China. In 1993, the zone was honored an "Advanced National Hi-tech Zone" by the State Science and Technology Commission, and was listed asthe national major hi-tech development zone. Furthermore it was rated as the "Advanced Development Zone of Sichuan Province" in 1994 and awarded the "Advanced Management Unit of Torch Program" by Ministry of Science and technology in 1998.

For 10 years, Chengdu High-tech Zone has endeavored to present a first-class soft investment based by enforcing infrastructure construction and achieving a well-matched hard environment. In terms of conducting a kind of internationalized environment, "one-station" service was initiated and has been improved with propounded and extended service connotation. Accordingly it has won universal praise for high efficiency, a practical style and brand-new operating mechanisms, whereas the "Taxation, Industry and Commerce & Bank Service Hall" of a distinctive style has even upheld a banner of quality service in the field of nationwide taxation and hi-tech. Moreover, on purpose to lay a foundation for further development of the enterprises within the zone and making flexible and the best use of various preferential policies, the zone has adopted elastic and substantial open measures throughout project ratification, land utilization and price preference to employment. In addition, it has striven to fulfil the accessory policies such as legality, education, civilization and hygiene and to found a hotbed of development for hi-tech enterprises and industry. On the other hand, it has carried on a policy of strengthening and optimizing the follow-up services: to preferentially foster key enterprises, promote the transformation of scientific achievement and cultivate new origin for economic growth. Namely it has stressed on propelling the production and promotion of the pillar industries by favoring key enterprises which emphasize self-innovation, with privileges on policies and funds, whose projects are backed by high technology, with bright prosperity, of great capital venture as well as of self-owned intellectual property. By means of fostering and nurturing, the strength for future progress of the small and medium- sized hi-tech enterprises has been enforced, and a large-scale transformation and promotion of scientific achievements have been accomplished.

Today Chengdu Hi-tech Zone has become a new district of modern technology far from the original farmland. At present it obtains 248 hi-tech enterprises organized by relevant authorities in total. The total output value of the hi-tech industry is over 50 percent of that of the whole zone, the total output value of the three pillar industries even up to 82 percent. Under the comprehensive cultivation of the zone, Chengdu Di'ao Pharmaceutical Company, which set up with a capital of several hundred thousand yuan, has become a hi-tech enterprise well known both at home and abroad. Chengdu Guoteng Communication Co., Ltd. successfully made a breakthrough at its sales income up to 10 billion out of a blank and accomplished the industrialization of scientific achievements. Hence the zone has attracted a number of noted companies worldwide and become the most brilliant land for investment in central and western China. Accordingly international groups like Siemens, Alkatl, Fuji Heavy Industries have set up factories in the zone. In addition, a group of well-known enterprises and universities headed by GE, Shenzheng Huawei and Qinghua University have applied for investment or staged business talks. Meanwhile investigations and business talks have been taking place between the zone and some groups like Motorola and NEC.

Striving for further achievement and greeting the new century. To construct "a district with new mechanisms and a strong economy," the zone is to seize the opportunity for century development, adhere to promoting and developing hi-tech industry, and build an upland featuring a knowledge economy and hi-tech industry.

威海火炬高新技术产业开发区

Weihai Torch High-Tech Industrial Development Zone

威海火炬高新技术产业开发区是1991年3月6日经国务院批准成立的国家级高新技术产业开发区，由国家科委、山东省政府和威海市政府共同创办的，也是全国四个火炬高新技术产业开发区之一。

开发区位于威海市区西北部的风景游览区和文教科研区，总面积39.2平方公里。开发区三面环海，有绵延10多公里的松林带环绕，三大天然海水浴场沙质柔细，水清滩缓。整个开发区依山傍海，空气清新，风光绮丽，环境优美。是国内外专家公认的发展高新技术产业的理想之地。

威海高区是一个新建区，开发前是一片荒滩、沼泽。经过8年的开发建设，一个初具规模的高科技产业城已经形成。累计完成固定资产投资45亿元，完成基础设施工作量6.2亿元，7平方公里区域的“七通一平”工程基本完成。批准进区高新技术项目350项，投资总额47亿元；外资项目580项，合同外资额3.7亿美元，实际利用外资2.3亿美元，合同外资到位率达到69.7%。成为威海市高新科技项目最为集中、外向度最高的区域。

为扶持高新技术产业的发展，威海高新技术开发区制定了《关于促进高新技术产业发展的若干规定》，从税收、土地出让价格、基础设施费用等方面给高新技术项目以优惠，并设立了高新技术发展基金，用以扶持高新技术产品的开发和高

威海火炬大厦
Torch Mansion in Weihai

威海火炬高技术产业开发区一角
A Corner of WHDZ

新技术企业的发展。在项目引进上，严把项目审批关，坚持技术含量低的项目不引进，能耗高的项目不引进，有污染的项目不引进。同时，加强与大院大所、科研机构和科技实体的联合与协作，先后引进了国家有关部委厅局的17家科研院所和19所高等院校的科研机构进区建立中试或产业基地，累计研制开发新技术、新产品200多种，实施火炬、星火、科研计划项目100多项，申请专利80多项。目前，被认定的高新技术企业45家，高新技术产品70多种。程控式交换机、小型胶印机、热敏打印头、图像传感器、镇脑宁胶囊、促肝细胞生长素等100多个高新技术项目已经投试产，40多个项目正在建设中。区内已经和正在形成以通讯设备、计算机及应用产品、数字传输检测设备、电子元器件为龙头的电子信息产业；以办公自动化设备、电子医疗器械为龙头的机电一体化产业；以抗癌生物制药，医用高分子制品、基因生物技术产品为龙头的医药生物工程产业；以电控透光幕、热敏材料制品、碳素渔具系列产品为龙头的新材料产业；以高效电子节能灯为龙头的新能源产业等五大高新技术产业群体，构成了高新技术产业的发展框架。高新技术企业及产品形成的产值、利税均占区内工业总量的80%以上。

The founding of the Weihai Torch Hi-Tech Industrial Development Zone (hereinafter reffered to as the "WHDZ") was approved by the State Council on March 6, 1991 as a State-level hi-tech industrial development zone. It was jointly sponsored by the State Science and Technology Commission, the people's government of Shandong Province and Weihai city. It is also one of the four torch hi-tech industrial development zones in China.

WHDZ is located at the scenic and cultural area, northwestern part of Weihai, with a total area of 39.2 square km. The zone is surrounded by the sea at three sides and ringed by a lush and verdant pine tree belt extending over 10 km all along the zigzag coastline. The three natural bathing beaches feature fine and soft sand, azure sea water and gently-bevelled sands.

Embraced by mountains and sea, the whole zone enjoys fresh air, gorgeous scenery and a graceful environment

and therefore generally recognized as an ideal place for developing new- and high-tech industries.

Now standing exquisitely, the zone was once a vast expanse of desolate beach and marsh. After 8 years' development and construction, a hi-tech industrial town has taken shape. The investments in fixed assets total 4,500 million yuan, in which infrastructure input accounts for 620 million yuan. So far, an area of 7 square km has been completed with power, water, gas, steam, drainage, communications, road and levelled ground. High and new projects amount to 350, with a total investment of 4,700 million yuan; foreign-funded projects 580, with a total contractual foreign investment of US$ 370 million and the actual investment of rate of 69.7 percent, so WHDZ boasts the most hi-tech intensified and foreign-oriented zone in Weihai.

In order to foster the development of hi-tech industries, WHDZ has worked out "Stipulations on Promoting the Development of the New- and High-Tech Industries", rendering the qualified projects a package of preferential policies in taxation, land transferring price and infrastructure fee and so on. A hi-tech development fund has also been instituted to promote the R&D of the hi-tech products and the development of hi-tech enterprises. The zone persists in strictly examining and approving the want-to-enter projects by stringent rules against those with low-tech contents, high energy consumption and pollution. In the meantime, WHDZ strengthens integration and coordination with institutes of high learning and scientific entities by introducing 17 research institutes and 19 research organs affiliated to universities and colleges, which have now yielded 200 items of new technologies and products, implemented 100-plus torch, sparkle and research plan projects and won over 80 patents. So far, 45 enterprises have been appraised as new- and high-tech enterprises and over 70 diversities of products as high and new products. Over 100 high and new technologies, including program-controlled exchange, offset press, TPH, image sensor, Zhennaoning capsule and liver cell auxinmone, have been put into production or trial production, and 40-some projects are under construction. The five hi-tech industries, which are being formed or have been formed, including electronic information industry spearheaded by communications equipments, computer and applied products, digital transmission & measurement sets, electronic components; machinery & electricity-integrated tech industry spearheaded by office automatic equipments and electronic medical appliances; pharmaceutical and bioengineering industry spearheaded by anticancer biomedicine, medical polymer products and genetic bio-tech products; new material industry spearheaded by electronic controlled transparency screen, thermal sensitive materials and carbonic fiber fishing tackles; new energy industry spearheaded by high efficiency & energy-saving lamps, constitute the development framework of high and new industries. New- and high-tech enterprises and products make up 80 percent of the total output value and profits and tax of the zone.

中山火炬高新技术产业开发区

Zhongshan Torch High-Tech Industrial Development Zone

位于广东省中山市东部的中山火炬开发区1998年荣获国家科技部授予的火炬先进高新技术产业开发区管理奖。开发区的两个文明建设已跨入全国53个国家级开发区的先进行列。

经过8年的艰苦创业，开发区不仅具有毗邻港澳的区位优势、完善的设施优势、优惠的政策优势，而且具备了外向带动优势、科技创新优势和管理体制优势。初步形成“一区两园”格局，占地15.1平方公里的火炬工业园和13.4平方公里的健康医药园蓬勃发展。国家“863”计划项目和46项国家和省级火炬计划项目顺利实施；41家高新技术企业迅速壮大；初步形成电子信息、新材料、新能源、生活医药技术等六大产业群；日本东芝集团、台湾宏碁电脑公司等30多个跨国公司、大财团先后进区投资设厂，并与全国20多家重点院校挂钩设点、创办科研机构，共组建和成立了国家新型储能材料工程开发中心、中国包装科学技术研究所及通信技术、生物工程、真空技术等九家科研机构。1998年工业产值达103.38亿元，利税4.5亿元，科技对经济增长的贡献率达49%。开发区已由初创阶段进入高新技术产业化和国际化的重要发展阶段。

面对知识经济的挑战，开发区人决心实施“外向带动，科技兴区，可持续发展”的发展战略，抢抓机遇，振奋精神，再攀高峰，以实施工业产值200亿元、利税10亿元的新成绩跨进21世纪，进而把中山火炬开发区办成“高新技术产业的先行区、新经济体制的试验区、现代化城市建设的示范区”。

中山火炬开发区一角
A Corner of the Zhongshan Torch High-Tech Industrial Development Zone

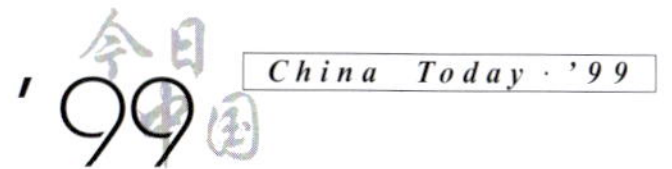

Located at the east of Zhongshan City, Guangdong Province, Zhongshan Torch Hi-tech Industrial Development Zone was named as the "Torch Advanced Hi-tech Industrial Development Zone Administrative Prize" by the Ministry of Science and Technology in 1998. The construction of spirit civilization and material civilization in the zone is in the front rank among 53 state-level development zones.

After eight years' efforts, the zone has not only the advantages of closing to Hong Kong and Macao, the improved infrastructure facilities and preferential policies, but also the superiority in extroversion promotion innovations, scientific and technological and an administration system. "One zone with two parks" has taken shape in the zone. The Torch Industrial Park with an area of 15.1 square kilometers and the Health Technology Park with an area of 13.4 square kilometers are developing rapidly. In the zone, the State "863" Plan Program and 46 state-level and provincial-level Torch Programs have been carried out smoothly; 41 hi-tech enterprises are growing consistently; and six industrial groups are taking shape, such as electronic information industry, new material industry, new energy industry and pharmaceutical technology etc. Toshiba Group Corporation from Japan, Acer Computer Corporation from Taiwan and other 30 international companies and big financial groups have established factories in the zone in recent years. Nine research and development institutes, such as State New Storage Material Engineering Development Center, China Package Science and Technology Research Institute, and institutes for communication technology, biogenic engineering and vacuum technology, have been set up. In 1998, the industrial output value reached 10.338 billion yuan, profit and tax 0.45 billion yuan. The ontribution of science and technology to the economic development came to 49 percent. Started from the initial stage, the zone now has entered an important stage of industrialization and internationalization of the high and new technology.

Facing to the challenge of the knowledge economy, and under the guidance of the spirit of the Party's 15th National Congress, the people in the zone are determined to carry out the developing strategy of "flourishing the zone with science and technology and consistent development". The people will seize the chance, make great efforts and climb to the higher peak. The industrial output value of 20 billion yuan, profit and tax of 1 billion yuan will be realized at the turn of the 21st century. Zhongshan Torch Hi-tech Industrial Development Zone will be built into be "a pioneer zone of high and new technology industry, an experimental zone with a new economic system, and an example for modernized urban construction".

长春高新技术产业开发区

Changchun New and High-Tech Industrial Development Zone

长春高新技术产业开发区是于1991年3月经国务院正式批准的首批27个国家级高新技术产业开发区之一。经过7年的艰苦创业，高新区建设取得了令人瞩目的丰硕成果。到1998年底，区内注册企业已经达到1400户，认定的高新技术企业达到930户，年产值逾亿元的企业达到24户，超千万元的企业达到120户。区内企业实施高新技术项目1369项，已实现商品化的808项，实现工业化生产的236项。全区技工贸总收入由1991年的1.6 亿元猛增到1998年的130亿元，利税由2300万元大幅度提高到21亿元，分别增长81倍和84倍。综合经济指标在全国53家开发区中名列前茅。1993年，高新区曾被国家科委授予“先进高新技术产业开发区”称号；1998年，在纪念火炬计划实施10周年全国高新技术产业开发区评比中又荣获“优秀管理奖”。

长春高新区位于全国著名的高智力密集区长春市区南部的自然延伸部分，总面积49平方公里，其中政策区27平方公里，科技新城规划22平方公里。区内有18所全日制高等院校，39个国家、省直属科研机构和11个国家重点开放实验室，有28位学部委员、科学院士、工程院士集中在开发区内，科技人员占人口总数的16.6%，具有丰富的智力资源和雄厚的科研创新能力。这里交通发达，高新区与长春至大连高速公路相连接，距长春火车站仅2.5公里，距长春飞机场仅10公里，可任您来去自如。这里通信便捷，全市国际直拨程控电话装机容量已达100万门以上，可任信息遨游四方。这里生活舒适、环境优雅，市区内三星级以上饭店达20多家，可使您宾至如归。这里供水、排水、电力、供气、热力、通信等基础设施完善。金融、工商、税务、保险、会计师事务所、律师事务所、人才交流服务中心、信息中心等支撑服务体系健全。开发区企业在财政、税收、进出口、信贷等方面享有国务院及地方政府赋予的一系列特殊优惠政策。1994年8月，经吉林省人大常委会批准，《长春高新技术产业开发区管理条例》正式颁布实施，使省、市政府对高新区的扶持有了可靠的法律保障。1998年12月，长春市政府下达了对开发区实行封闭管理和对外商投资企业实行全面保护的文件，使开发区的投资环境进一步改善。

高新区的良好投资环境和巨大发展潜力不仅吸引了一汽集团、四川长虹等国内较大的企业集团，而且更引来一批批海外客商。截止1998年底，已有香港、美国、日本、韩国、台湾、德国、新加坡、泰国、澳大利亚、加拿大等21个国家和地区的客商来开发区投资兴办了240多家三资企业，其中包括美国的通用、福特，日本的伊藤忠商事、丸红，德国的奔驰、西门子，马来西亚的金狮集团等著名跨国公司和厂家，一批企业已获得了丰厚的投资回报。

现在，开发区的高新技术产业格局已经基本形成，生物工程、汽车工程、新材料、光机电一

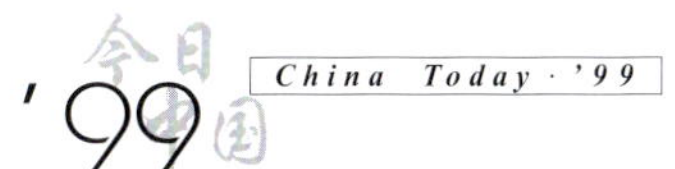

体化、电子信息五大主导产业产值已占区内总产值的80%以上。在带动全市乃至全省经济发展方面，正在发挥着越来越重要的作用。

目前，长春高新区正在全力以赴进行第二次创业，到2005年，将在已具规模的生物制药园、汽车工业园、计算机软件园基础上，再创办及完善教育产业园等功能区，形成各具特色的十大园区。五大支柱产业将进一步壮大。全区技工贸总收入要达到800亿元，比1998年翻两番；利税达到160亿元，比1998年翻三番。同时还将兴建现代化的广场、四星级宾馆、国际电讯大厦和别墅区等一批高档服务设施。到那时，被誉为“东北硅谷”的长春高新技术产业开发区将以现代化、多功能、高度文明的崭新姿态屹立在广袤的黑土地上。

Changchun New-and High-tech Industrial Development Zone is one of the first 27 national new- and high- tech industrial development zones approved by the State Council. Thanks to the efforts in the past 7 years, the Development Zone has made great achievement. At the end of 1998, there were 1,400 enterprises registered in the Zone and 930 were recognized as new- and hig- tech enterprises. There are 24 and 120 enterprises whose output value exceeded 100 million yuan and 10 million yuan respectively. A total of 1,369 new- and high-tech projects were carried out by the enterprises in the Zone, and 808 items were commercialized and 236 industrialized. The total income of technology, industry and trade increased from 160 million yuan in 1991 to 13 billion yuan in 1998. The revenue from the profit and tax were raised largely from 23 million yuan to 2.1 billion yuan, or an increace of 81 times and 84 times, respectively.

It leads the 53 development zones all over the country in the comprehensive economic index. In 1993, the New- and High-tech Zone was conferred the title “Advanced New and High Technology Development Zone” and won the “Excellent Management Award” in the nationwide new- and high-tech industrial competition aiming at commemorating the 10-year implementation of the Torch Plan.

Changchun New-and High-tech Industrial Development

Zone is situated in the naturally extending part in the south of the city, a nationwide famous high intelligence-intensive area. The total area is 49 km^2, of which 27 km^2 are the policy region and 22 km^2 the science and technology new city.

There are 18 full-time universities and colleges, 39 scientific research institutes directly under the state and the province, 11 major public laboratories, and 28 academicians of the Academy of science and the technology of Engineering Academy in the Development Zone. Scientific personnel hold 16.6 percent of its population. The Development Zone has abundant intelligent resources and a strong ability for scientific research. It has transport facilities. The New-and High-tech Zone is adjacent to the Changchun-Dalian Highway, 2.5 km from the Changchun Railway Station, only 10 km away from Changchun Airport. You can go anywhere freely. Communication is very comfortable and swift. The total capacity of its international direct-dial program-controlled telephone is over one million circuits. The information will spread all over the world. You can enjoy comfortable life and a fine environment with 20 hotels opened to foreigners. The infrastructure facilities such as water, power, and coal gas supply, heating and communication have been perfected. It has a perfect supporting service system, such as finance, industry and commerce, taxation, insurance, certified public accountant, certified public lawyer, qualified personnel exchange center and information center. The enterprises in the Development Zone enjoy special preferential policies in banking, taxation imposing, import, export, and credit. In 1994, "Administration Regulations of the Changchun New- and High-tech Industrial Development Zone", approved by Jilin province People's Congress Standing Committee, promulgated and came into effect in August 1994. In December 1998, Changchun City issued the documents on carrying out close management and protecting the foreign-funded enterprises in the zone, thus greatly improving the investment environment.

With a good investment climate and great developing potentials, the Development Zone attracts not only domestic large-scale enterprises groups, such as the 1st Automobile Group and Sichuan Chang Hong, but also lots of foreign merchants. Up to the end of 1998, the merchants from more than 21 countries and regions, such as Hong Kong, U.S.A. Japan, South Korea, Taiwan, Germany, Singapore, Thailand, Australia, Canada etc. had invested and established foreign-funded enterprises, including well-known transnational corporations of GSM, Ford from America, Itoucyuu Co., Marubeni Co. from Japan, Benz, Siemens from Germany, Goldlion Group from Malasia. A lot of them have gained generous profits from their investment.

And now, the pattern of new- and high-tech industry in the Development Zone has been basically formed. The output valuee of five main pillar industries, bioengineering, automobile engineering, new materials, engineering, optics-mechanism-electricity integral systematization, makes up more than 80 percent of the total output value of the whole Zone. It has been playing key role in promoting economic development of the city and the province.

At present, Changchun New- and High-tech Industrial Development Zone is sparing no effort to do pioneering for the second time. On the present basis of biopharmaceutic district, automobile industry district and computer software district, the Zone will create and perfect education industry district in 2005, forming ten districts with its own distinguishing features. The five main pillar industries will develop further. The total revenue from technology, industry and trading will be 80 billion yuan, quadupling the 1998 figure. The profit and tax will be 16 billion yuan, eight times of the 1998 figure. Meanwhile, several high- level service facilities, such as a modern square, four-star hotels, an

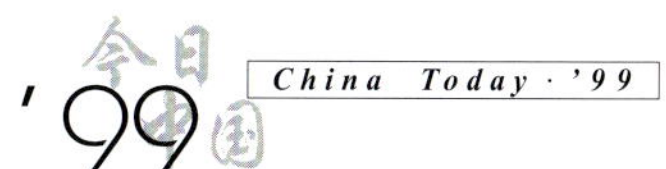

international telecommunication building and villas will be built up. Famed as "Notheast Silicon Valley", Changchun New- and High-tech Industrial Development Zone will stand on the vast blackland with modernization, multifunction, high civilization and new shape.

长春高新区〝科技新城区〞一角
A Corner of Changchun New and High-Tech Industrial Development Zone

哈尔滨高新技术产业开发区

Harbin High-Tech Industrial Development Zone

哈尔滨高新技术产业开发区1988年9月创建。1991年3月成为全国首批、黑龙江省第一家国家级高新技术产业开发区。建区10年来，哈高新区遵循特色办区、创新强区的方针，大力弘扬“拼搏创新、高效敬业、举贤荐能、远望争先”的开发区精神，艰苦创业，两个文明建设连年大丰收。截至1998年末，全区累计实现技工贸总收入348亿元，完成工业总产值316亿元，创利税44亿元，其中1998年实现技工贸总收入101亿元，实现工业总产值95亿元。1998年全区工业总产值占哈尔滨市工业总产值的份额达14.7%。哈高新区以具有特色、成绩显著而跨入国家先进高新区行列，并荣获国家科技部颁发的火炬先进高新区管理奖。

哈高新区始终坚持以高新技术项目为灵魂，以高新技术企业为依托，以高新技术产业为核心，突出了高科技特色。目前，累计发展高新技术企业946家，共开发高新技术项目1300项；其中国际先进水平的98项。国内先进水平的1090项；累计实施火炬计划项目128项，其中国家级34项，地方级94项；全区实施火炬计划项目占全市的70%。

哈高新区按照“抓大育小”的方针，实施了高新技术产业化工程、技术创新工程等，培育了一批骨干企业，构建了集团带重点、重点带一般的产业发展格局。1998年全区技工贸总收入或工业总产值超千万元企业已达60家，其中超亿元企业18家。已初步形成以光机电一体化、电子信息、生物工程、新能源与高效节能、新材料五大产业为支柱的高新技术产业群。

哈高新区先后创办了哈工业大学、哈工程大学、哈理工大学和哈农业大学四个大学科技园区，推进了产、学、研一体化的进程，还创办了学府信息产业园，构建了“以区带园、一区多园”发展格局。同时，积极探索用高新技术改造传统产业新路，吸引国有大中型企业入区创办高新技术企业已达117家，并采用“一厂一角”、“腾笼换鸟”、“嫁接移植”、“引进吸收”等方式，在65家企业试点，取得显著效果。

哈高新区积极优化投资环境，正逐步建立特区型管理体制，基本健全了支撑服务体系，初步建成了占地1平方公里的具有高科技特色的现代文明小区。积极发展外向型经济，加大招商引资力度，目前，已有18个国家和地区的145家外商投资企业入区发展，总投资额4.6亿美元，注册资金2.5亿美元，外资到位额1亿美元。资金到位率达73%，开业率为71%。

知识经济即将叩响新世纪的大门，“创知识经济之业”的号角已经吹响。哈尔滨高新区人决心高擎火炬，向特区型国际化科技园区的目标迈进，为省、市经济发展做出新的更大贡献。

Harbin High- and New-tech Industrial Development Zone began its construction in Sept. 1988, and became the state-level high-tech zone in March, 1991. Through ten years' development, always following the zone's spirit of "striving after creation, high efficiency, recommending and electing the best and trying to be the best", it has made significant progress. Up to end of 1998, the grand total revenue from technology, industry and trade was 34.8 billion yuan, total industry output value 31.4 billion yuan, and profit and tax 4.4 billion yuan. In 1998, revenue from technology, industry and trade was 10.1 billion yuan, total industry output value 9.5 billion yuan. The zone's total industry output value made up 14.7% of that of Harbin. The zone has become one of advanced high-tech zones in China, and was awarded the High-tech Management Prize of Torch Program by the Ministry of Science and Technology.

Harbin High-tech Zone always sticks to high-tech projects. To date, the zone has 946 high-tech enterprises, which have developed 1,300 projects, including 98 internationally advanced projects, and 1,090 domestically advanced projects. The grand total of 128 of Torch Program projects have been conducted, including 84 state-level and 94 province-level projects. The Torch Program projects implemented in the zone account for 70% in Harbin.

Harbin High-tech Zone has implemented high-tech industrialization projects and creation projects, and fostered a batch of enterprises. In 1998, there were in the zone 60 enterprises, each with the total industry output value or revenue from technology, industry and trade of over 10 million yuan, including 18 enterprises whose total industrial output value exceeds 100 million yuan each. The zone has initially formed five pillar industries of electronic information, integration of optics, mechanics and electric, bioengineering, new energy, and energy-conservation and new materials.

Harbin High-tech Zone has founded successively four university technology parks: Harbin Institute of Technology, Harbin Engineering University, Harbin University of Science and Technology and Harbin Agriculture University, thus promoting the integration of production, study and research. The zone has created information industry park of universities, and formed the pattern of "a zone with parks, one zone and many parks". Meanwhile, many big and medium-sized enterprises have been attracted to set up 117 high-tech enterprises in the zone. Significant results have been achieved in 65 experimental enterprises of them.

Harbin High-tech Zone is improving its investment environment constantly and following the management system of special zones, which has amplified the enterprise service system. A modern opening economy has been promoted, 18 countries and regions have established 152 foreign-funded enterprises in the zone with a total investment of 460 million USD and registered capital of 250 million USD.

Knowledge economy is knocking at the gate of the new century. People of Harbin High-tech Zone are confident of striving forward to be an international science park.

长沙高新技术产业开发区

Changsha High-Tech Industrial Development Zone

长沙高新技术产业开发区创建于1988年10月，1991年3月经国务院批准为首批国家级高新区，总规划面积18.6平方公里。由岳麓山高科技园、星沙工业高科技园、马坡岭农业高科技园、远大高科技园和政策区组成。截止1998年底，长沙高新区累计完成高新技术工业总产值266.3亿元，技工贸总收入282.3亿元，实现利税44.3亿元，上缴国家税金15.4亿元，出口创汇1.85亿美元。1997年在全国53个国家级高新区主要经济指标排名中，长沙高新区总产值居第18位，上缴税金居第8位，人均利税居第7位。目前，全区共有高新技术企业568家，其中三资企业158家；开发高新技术项目812项，其中156项列入国家、省（部）重点计划。支柱产业逐步形成，在全区高新技术产品产值中，电子信息、光机电一体化、生物医药、新材料及精细化工等四大支柱产业分别占29.5%、26.7%、11.6%和10.5%。1998年，高新区完成产值106亿元，技工贸收入119亿元，实现利税17.1亿元，出口创汇7233万美元，分别比上年增长51.4%、52.6%、42.5%、55.5%。高新技术总产值占全市国有工业企业及销售收入500万元以上非国有工业企业产值的比例达到27%，成为地方经济增长最具活力的区域。

长沙高新区具有明显的科技、人才、政策、基础设施、地理位置优势，有着良好的投资环境。四个科技园以319国道为轴，形成高新技术产业开发带。319、107国道在此交汇，紧联黄花国际机场、湘江水运码头，水、陆、空交通十分便利；水、电、路等基础设施完善，与长沙市区形成一体；区内医院、学校、写字楼、住宅小区等一应俱全。长沙高新区管委会作为长沙市人民政府的派出机构，享有市一级经济管理权限和与之相适应的行政权限，对所辖园区的产业发展实行统一有效管理。进区企业按“自筹资金、自愿组合、自主经营、自负盈亏、自我约束、自我发展”的“六自”方针运作，除享受国家给予高新区的各项优惠政策外，还享受省、市政府给予的特殊优惠待遇。财政、工商、税务、国土、规划、建设等部门在园区均设立了分支机构，实行“一站式办公”。区内INTERNET服务中心、创业服务中心、投资咨询服务中心、对外科技交流中心、人才交流培训中心以及审计、律师、金融、保险、物业管理等支撑服务机构健全，为企业和投资者提供全方位优质服务。

在新的世纪到来之际，长沙高新区将牢牢抓住良好的发展机遇，继续坚持“科技兴区、产业强区、依法管区”的方针，以产业发展为中心，以招商引资为重点，以优化环境为突破口，进一步抓好各高科技园基础设施建设，搞好产业和企业发展的协调服务，按“封闭式管理，开放式动作”的原则，为高新技术产业的发展营造更有利的环境，推动长沙高新技术产业健康、快速、持续发展，为长沙市的经济增长再作贡献，为科技兴市战略的全面实施再铸辉煌。

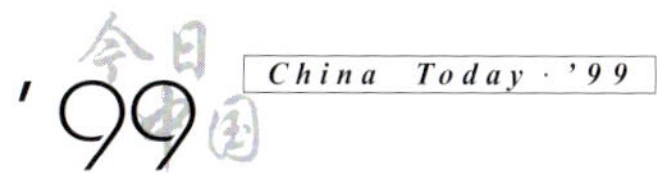

Changsha High-tech Industrial Development Zone (CHIDZ) was founded in October 1988. In March 1991, with approval of the State Council, it became one of the first state-level development zones. The total planned area of the zone is 18.6 km², consisting of four high-tech parks (Yuelu Hill High-Tech Park, Xing Sha High-Tech Industrial Park, Mapoling High-tech Agricultural Park and Broad High-tech Park) and Policy Zone. There are 568 high- tech enterprises in the zone, and 158 are foreign funded. CHIDZ has developed 812 high-tech projects. 156 projects have been listed in the state, and provincial (ministry) development plans. Pillar industries have been formed up (see Fig.3). CHIDZ takes up 27% in the total output value of the state-owned and private enterprises (sales income above 5 million yuan) in the city. It has become the most vigorous area in local economic development.

The advantageous technological, talent, policy, infrastructure and geological conditions make CHIDZ well known for its fine environment .The four high-tech parks, with No.319 National highway as the axle, shaped up a high-tech industrial development belt. No.319 and No.107 national highways cross here, connecting the nearby Huanghua International Airport with Xiangjiang water transport wharf, which provide transport convenience for investors. Infrastructure facilities (water, power, road) have been perfected and integrated within the city networks. Hospitals, schools, office buildings and residential quarters are available in CHIDZ. As an agency of Changsha City People's Government, CHIDZ Administrative Committee is authorized of a municipal-level competence to manage economic affairs, and some appropriate administrative rights. CHIDZ Administrative Committee guides the industrial development with unified and efficient management. Running the zone enterprises is based on the "self-responsibility" (capital, combination, operation, profit & loss, restrain, development) principal. Besides the state preferential policies, province and city also offer favorable treatment. Functional departments of finance, industry and commerce administration, tax, land, planning and construction have set up their agencies in CHIDZ, offering a "one-stop" office system. CHIDZ has perfect supportive facilities, such as the Internet Service Center, Enterprise Service Center, Investment Consulting Center, Foreign Technology Exchange Center, Talents Exchange Center and auditing, law, finance, insurance, real estate management, which will provide investors with excellent services.

Fig1 **Economic Data**

Item	Grand Total (by the end of 1998)	Total (1998)	Growth Rate (compare 1997)
Output Value	26630	10600	51.4%
TIT* Income	28230	11900	52.6%
Profit & Tax	4430	1710	42.5%
State Tax	1540		
FE*	185(US$)	72.33(US$)	55.5%

TIT: Technical, Industrial & Trade FE: Foreign Exchange Earned Throuth Export

Fig2 **CHIDZ Among 53 National Zones (1997 Major Economic Quota)**

Item	Ranking
Total Output Value	18th
State Tax	7th
Per Capita Profit & Tax	8th

Fig3 **Proportion of 4 Key Industries in CHIDZ Total Output Value**

Industry	Percentage
Electronic information	29.5%
OEM Integration	26.7%
Biology & Medicine	11.6%
New Material & Fine Chemiary	10.5%

OME:Optical-Mechanical-Electronic

长沙高新区岳麓山高科技园
Yuelushan High-Tech Park of CHIDZ

福州市科技园区

Fuzhou Science & Technology District

福州市科技园区创办于1988年，1991年经国务院批准为国家级高新技术产业开发区，规划面积5.5平方公里，下设马尾、洪山、仓山三个科技园。作为53家国家高新技术产业开发区之一，福州市科技园区肩负着“科教兴国”、发展福州地方民族高科技产业、抢占科技战略制高点的重任。经过10年努力。在高新技术基础设施建设、“产、学、研”相结合、培育支柱产业、增加经济总量等方面取得一定成就。培育出：实达、新大陆、创识、中银BOC、中华映管、建榕、福龙、梅生、亚仿、福光、福晶、瑞迪、瑞达、力之源、金得利、瑞闽等一大批民族高科技企业。目前在福州市科技园区从业的2万多人中，大中专以上学历占10417人，其中：博士生36人、硕士生389人、留学回国人员30人、大学本科生4197人。在具有专业技术职称资格的7238人中，高级职称的为483人、中级职称的为2045人，占专业技术人员总数的34.95%。至1998年底，园区累计兴办科技型企业246家，认定高新技术企业79家，5家企业列入国家重点高新技术企业，7家企业被国家科技部批准为国家软件产业基地重点骨干企业；形成高新技术产品产值超10亿元的企业2家，超亿元的企业13家，超5000万元的企业27家；25个高新技术项目列入国家级火炬计划项目，56个高新技术项目列入省火炬计划；实现高新技术产品产值240亿元，出口总值6.4亿美元。1998年科技园区掀起“向百亿冲刺”创优竞赛活动，在新一轮创业热潮中重点实施了上规模、上台阶的高新技术项目，高新技术产品产值突破100亿元，比上一年60亿元增长66.6%。

福州软件园
Fuzhou Software Park

福州市科技园区“一区三园”分布如下：

1. 马尾科技园面积1.4平方公里。马尾科技园依托马尾区五位一体的综合优势，以外向型经济为主体，以国际经贸为导向，发展成为以出口创汇为重点的外向型科技工业区，重点建设了“百亿电子城”、“光大科学园”以及“国家863计划智能计算机成果转化基地”。

2. 洪山科技园面积3.6平方公里。洪山科技园依托福州大学、中科院福建物质结构研究所等大专院校科研院所的智力优势。集孵化、中试与产业化为一体，发展以电子信息、生物工程为重点的新型科技工业区和民营高新技术产业群体的基地。重点建设了“实达科技城”、“福建留学生创业园”和“福州软件园”以及以高校为主力的集科研、成果转化、中试和成果交易、“产、学、研”相结合的“福大新大陆科学园”。

3. 仓山科技园面积0.5平方公里。仓山科技园依托仓山教育文化区内大专院校、科研院所密集以及高速公路、港口等优势，重点发展现代通信器材、新材料等产业。

面临知识经济的挑战，为加大发展高新技术产业的力度，福州市科技园区规划构筑福州市高新技术产业群体：马尾科技园、洪山科技园、仓山科技园、福清电子工业基地、闽侯双福科技工业园、闽侯上街生物科学园、闽侯荆溪农业科学园、长乐“闽台科技园”以及罗源湾“海洋科学园”，在现有5.5平方公里国家级高新技术产业开发区的带动下，扩大政策辐射面积，以产业政策带动产业群的形成和发展，实行“一区多园、一区多制”的管理体制，合理配置资金、人才、技术等要素，推进福州市高新技术产业经济总量和经济质量的持续发展。

Fuzhou Science & Technology District (Fuzhou S&T District) was established in 1988, and was approved as a national high-tech industry development district by the State Council in 1991. It was laid out to be a district with 5.5 sq km, including three science & technology zones (Mawei, Hongshan, and Cangshan S&T zones). Being a member among 52 national hi-tech industry development districts, Fuzhou S&T District undertakes the task of "constructing our country by science and education," aiming at developing local national high-tech industries and seizing technical top points. Its ten years' efforts led to great achievement in the following items: high-tech infrastructure construction, combination of "Produce, Study, Research," fostering core industries, and increasing the total economical amount. A number of national high-tech enterprises have developed well in the district, such as Start Group, New Continent Group, Chase Group, BOC Group, Chunghua Picture Tubes Co., Ltd, Fujian Jianrong Telecommunication Cable Co., Ltd, Fuzhou Fulong Biological Product Co., Ltd, Fuzhou Meisheng Medical Equipment Co., Ltd, Asia Simulation & Control System Engineering Co., Ltd, Fujian Fortune Sharp Optics Instrument Co., Ltd, Fujian Castech Crystals, Inc., Rady. Electronic Co., Ltd, Reida (H.K.) Co., Ltd, Fujian Power Origin Co., Ltd, Fujian Jindeli Co., Ltd, Fujian Reimin Co., Ltd. Now, there are over 20,000 employees in the whole district, of whom 10,417 have received academic education, including 36 doctors, 389 masters, 4,197 bachelors, and 30 personnel who once studied abroad. There are 7,238 technicians with professional technical titles in the district, among whom 483 have senior titles and 2,045 have secondary titles, making up 34.95% of the professional technical staff. By the end of 1998, 246 enterprises have been established there, among which 79 are assessed as hi-tech enterprises, and 5 are ranked as national key hi-tech enterprises. Besides, 7 are ratified as key skeleton enterprises in national software base. There are 2 enterprises with gross hi-tech product value over 1 billion yuan, and 13 enterprises over 100 billion yuan, 27 enterprises over 5 billion yuan; 25 hi-tech items are included in the national Torch Program, and 56 hi-tech items are listed in the provincial Torch Plan. In 1998, the S&T District held a competition "sprinting for gross product value over 10 billion yuan", and focused on implementing the important hi-tech items, which led to gross high-tech product value over 10 billion yuan, or an increase of 66.6% over 6 billion yuan of 1997.

Fuzhou Science & Technology District is constituted by three zones:

1.Mawei S&T Zone occupies an area of 1.4 sq km. Relying on the integrated advantage "Five in One", it is an export-oriented science and technology industrial zone. Its important projects include "Electronic Town," "Forever Bright Science Ground" and " Intellectualized Computer

Achievement Exchange Base in National 863 Plan."

2. Hongshan S&T Zone occupies an area of 3.6 sq km. Depending on the intelligence advantages of Fuzhou University and Fujian Substance Structure Institute under Chinese Academy of Sciences, it combines "research, trial and manufacturing," and is planned to be a new s&t industrial estate and nongovernmental hi-tech industry base oriented at developing electronic information and bioengineering. Its main projects include "Start S&T Complex", "Career Ground for Students Who Once Studied Abroad" "Fuzhou Software Ground ," and " Fuzhou University & New Continent Science Ground " which combines "production, study, research" with the intelligence support of colleges.

3. Cangshan S&T Zone occupies an area of 0.5 sq km. Relying on the advantages of a number of colleges and research institutes in the zone and some highways and ports, it emphasizes on developing industries like modern communications equipment and the new material industry.

Challenged by the information economy, Fuzhou S&T District program to construct Fuzhou hi-tech & new industry colony, including Mawei S&T Zone, Hongshan S&T Zone, Cangshan S&T Zone, Fuqing Electronic Industry Base, Minghou Shuangfu S&T Industrial Estate, Minghou Shangjie Bioscience Estate, Minghou Jingxi Agri-science Estate, and " Fujian & Taiwan S&T Estate " in Changle and " Oceanography Estate" in Luoyuan Bay, in order to speed up new hi-tech industry's development. Besides, supported by the national hi-tech & new industry development zone with an area of 5.5 sq km, it will enlarge the policy-radiated area, and utilizes industrial policies to accelerate the formation industry groups. Furthermore, it will implement the management system— "Numerous Zones in One District, Numerous System in One District", and make best use of capital, manpower, and technology, so as to have Fuzhou's hi-tech & new industry's gross product value and quality develop continuously.

福州市科技园区
Fuzhou Science & Technology District

广州高新技术产业开发区

Guangzhou High-Tech Industrial Development Zone

广州高新技术产业开发区是1991年3月经国务院批准成立的首批国家级高新区之一，地处广州市东部。为加速广州高新技术产业的发展，1997年广州市政府对高新区管理体制进行了调整，形成由广州科学城、天河科技园、黄花岗科技园和民营科技园组成的"一区多园"的新格局。1998年下半年，经市委、市政府研究决定，报请国家科技部同意，广州经济技术开发区与广州高新区合署办公。

广州高新区地处广州中心城市组团与东南部组团的交汇处，知识密集、人才荟萃，区内有华工、暨大、华农等高等院校12所，有中科院广州分院、广东农科院等科研机构44个，国家级重点实验室3个，各类科研人员2万多人，为高新技术企业的发展提供了良好的技术人才依托。

广州经济技术开发区与广州高新区合署办公是区域经济资源共享、优势互补、联动发展模式的创新。广州经济技术开发区具有建区早、基础设施好、经济实力强、体制健全、动作高效、开发建设和招商引资经验丰富等特点。广州高新区体制新、地理优、产业发展前景广阔、开发建设空间大。两区合署办公可以有效地利用两个开发区的有利条件加快广州科学城的开发建设速度。

广州高新区经过8年多的开发和建设，具备了较好的软硬投资环境。其中，科学城位于广州旅游景点世界大观和航天奇观东北侧，规划面积24平方公里，起步区4平方公里，基础设施建设正在进行中，1999年6月开始可提供第一批用地；天河科技园位于广州市天河区，开发面积1.37平方公里，建筑峻工面积71.33万平方米；黄花岗科技园位于广州市环市东路区庄立交桥北侧，占地1.5平方公里，建筑峻工面积1.62万平方米；民营科技园位于广州市白云区太和镇，规划面积0.8平方公里，首期开发0.23平方公里，1999年底前完成。

截止1998年年底，全区共有科技企业1275家，其中，被认定的高新技术企业225家，"三资"企业179家。1998年实现技工贸总收入92.1亿元，完成工业产值44.4亿元，其中，高新技术产品产值32亿元，出口创汇7794万美元，全年实现利税8.35亿元。全区累计实施火炬计划项目103项，占广州市火炬计划项目的71.5%，其中，国家级火炬计划项目39项，市级火炬计划项目64项，通过火炬计划项目的实施，培养出一批高新技术骨干企业，形成了以电子信息、生物制药、机电一体化为主的支柱产业。

Guangzhou Hi-tech Industrial Development Zone is one of the first state-level hi-tech industrial development zones which were approved by the State Council in March 1991. GHIDZ is located in the east of Guangzhou. In order to accelerate the development of high technologies, Guangzhou Municipal Government adjusted the management system in 1997. A new form "One zone with multiple parks" has taken shape. They are Guangzhou Science City, Tianhe Scientific Park, Huanghuagang Scientific Park and Individuals Scientific Park. In Aug., 1998, in accordance with the decision of Guangzhou Municipal Committee of CPC and Guangzhou Municipal Government and with the approval of Ministry of Science and Technology, Guangzhou Economic and Technological Development District and Guangzhou Hi-tech Industrial Development Zone were incorporated into one administrative setup.

Guangzhou Hi-tech Industrial Development Zone lies in the border of downtown Guangzhou and southeastern part of Guangzhou with intensive knowledge, a galaxy of talent. There are 12 universities, such as South China University of Science and Engineering, Jinan University, South China Agricultural University, and 44 scientific research institutions, such as China Scientific Academy, Guangzhou Branch, Guangdong Agricultural Scientific Academy, etc. There are also 3 state-level laboratories and more than 20,000 scientific research personnel. All these provide technical talents for the development of hi-tech enterprises.

The incorporation of GETDD and GHIDZ is a new way to enjoy economic resources, advantages and joint development. GETDD has the following features: earlier establishment, good infrastructures, strong economic strength, a sound system, high efficiency and rich experiences of construction and introducing foreign capital. GHIDZ is a new zone with a new system, advantageous geographical location, broad industrial development prospect and big construction space. The incorporation of the two zones can utilize the favourable conditions of both parties efficiently to accelerate the development and construction of Guangzhou Science City.

After 8 years of construction and development, GHIDZ has a good investment environment including infrastructure facilities and services. Science City is located in the northeast of World Grand Sight and Space Wonder, which are the tourist sights of Guangzhou. Its planned area is 24 square kilometers, the first phase is 4 square kilometers, the infrastructure is under construction now, and the first piece of land will be available in June 1999. Tianhe Scientific Park is located in Tianhe District of Guangzhou; the development area is 1.37 square kilometers, and the finished building is 713.3 thousand square meters. Huanghuagang Scientific Park is located in the north of Quzhuang Flyover across Huanshi Road. It covers 1.5 square kilometers. The finished building is 16.2 thousand square meters. Individuals Scientific Park is located in Taihe Town of Baiyun District of Guangzhou, the planned area is 0.8 square kilometer, the first development area will be 0.23 square kilometer, and it will be finished in 1999.

By the end of 1998, there were 1,275 technical enterprises in GHIDZ, among which 225 were ratified high-tech enterprises and 179 were joint ventures.

In 1998, the total industrial, technological and trade income was 9.21 billion yuan (RMB), the industrial output hit 4.44 billion yuan, among which 3.2 billion yuan was the value of high-tech products. The export volume reached 77.94 million US Dollars. The total profits tax was 835 million yuan.

The Torch Plan projects total 103, which took up 71.5% of those from Guangzhou, among the total Torch Plan projects, 39 are state-level ones, and the other 64 are city level projects. Through the implementation of Torch Plan projects, a group of high-tech enterprises have been fostered, and electronic information, biological pharmacy and mechanical and electrical integration have become the pillar industries of GHIDZ.

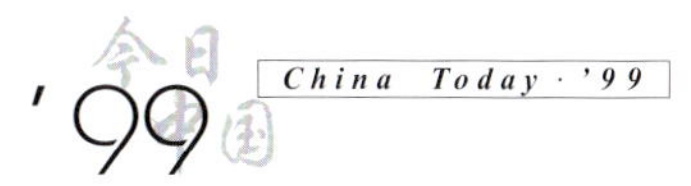

合肥国家高新技术产业开发区

Hefei State New and High Technology Industrial Development Zone

在中国中部的安徽省合肥市，迅速崛起了一座荟萃现代文明的科技新城，人们称之为“安徽硅谷”。这里路网纵横，四通八达；建筑物鳞次栉比，错落有致；绿化带绿树成群，花团锦簇；公园里，小桥流水，碧草如茵……，这就是蜚声中外的合肥国家高新技术产业开发区、中国亚太经合组织科技工业园区。

合肥是全国重要的科教基地，国家首批园林城市，环境优美。

合肥高新区位于合肥西郊风景区，和老城区连成一体，西临景色秀丽的大蜀山和郁郁葱葱的森林公园，北濒碧波荡漾的董铺水库，合肥地区70%的大专院校和科研院所星罗棋布在高新区周围。

高新区1990年10月隆重奠基，1991年3月经国务院批准首批进入国家级高新技术产业开发区行列，1997年9月被国务院批准为向亚太经合组织（APEC）成员特别开放的科技工业园区。

合肥高新区总体规划面积40平方公里，由科技工业园、农业科技园、创业服务中心和政策区组成。目前已在5平方公里范围内全面实现了道路、供水、排水、供电、煤气、热力、通信、有线电视和土地平整等“九通一平”，兴建了130多万平方米的工业厂房、公建服务配套设施和住宅。规划建设高标准，基础设施高效能，生态环境高质量，社区管理高水平。被省市政府授予“花园式开发区”、“文明单位”等称号。

合肥高新区是全国开发区行政管理体制和机构改革的试点单位，建立了全新的与国际惯例接轨的现代行政管理体制和运行机制，为投资者提供全过程高效优质服务，依法保障投资者的合法权益。

美国、德国、瑞士、意大利、日本、韩国和香港、台湾等几十个国家和地区的客商在高新区投资，兴办了130多个外商投资企业，总投资达6亿多美元。截止1999年2月底，高新区进区企业已达518家，项目581个，总投资达8亿多美元。

一批技术水平高，投资规模大，市场前景好的项目在高新区迅速成长。世界上第一台VCD就诞生在合肥高新区；中日合资的合肥三洋荣事达电器有限公司，投资3400万美元，生产人工智能模糊控制全自动洗衣机和微波炉，现已成为全国最大的模糊控制洗衣机生产基地；荣事达集团与美国美泰克公司共同投资1.8亿美元，生产系列化智能家电产品；中美日合资的达西浦国际实业（安徽）有限公司，总投资1.1亿美元，将形成120万台飞歌牌节能型空调器生产和出口基地等等。

高新区是实施火炬计划项目的重要基地。区内现有国家级和省级火炬计划项目56项，其中第一个国产基因工程a、b干扰素新药“安达芬”；生物药业“兆科降纤酶”；新材料“KG型印染助剂”；交通事故预防研究“汽车事故预防系统”等还是国家重点火炬计划项目。

In Hefei, Auhui Province, in central China, there is a new science and technology city Anhui Silicon, where there is a well-developed road network, rows and rows of buildings, green trees and blossom flowers. The well-known Hefei State New- and High-tech Industrial Development Zone (NHZ), and China APEC Science and Technology Industrial Park are located here.

Hefei is an important science & education base, and one of garden-like cities of China with a pleasant environment.

Located in the scenic west suburb of Hefei, Hefei NHZ connects with the old city, adjacent to the pleasant Dashu Hill and green forest park in the east and the blue rippling Dongpu Reservoir in the south, with 70% universities and colleges in Hefei spotted around.

Founded in October 1990, Hefei NHZ was approved as a national new- and high-tech indutrial development zone in March 1991, and a science and technology park specially open to APEC members approved by the State Council.

With a planned area of 40 km^2, Hefei NHZ comprises of the science and technology park, the agriculture technology park, the incubator, and the policy area. Within 5 km^2, infrastructure facilities, such as road, water supply, drainage, power supply, gas, heat, communication, cable TV and prepared land, are well done. Factory buildings of more than 1.3 million m^2 supporting facilities and living apartments have been constructed. Planning and construction are of high standards, infrastructure facilities, of high efficiency, and ecology environment and community management of high quality. Hefei NHZ was awarded as a civilized one by the municipal government.

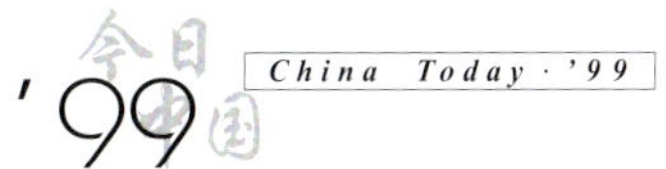

Hefei NHZ is a polit unit for the administration system and structural reform. A brand new modern administration and operation system has been established, providing all procedure, high efficiency and quality services and protecting investors' legal rights.

Investors from America, Germany, Swiss, Italy, Japan, Korea, Hong Kong, Taiwan etc. have established more than 130 foreign-invested enterprises in the zone, involving more than 600 million USD. By the end of February 1999, Hefei NHZ boasted 518 enterprises and 581 projects with a total investment of over US$800 million.

A bunch of prospect programs with high technology and large investments have been growing rapidly in Hefei NHZ. The first VCD player in the world was invented here. Hefei Sanyo Rongshida Electric Appliance Co. jointly invested by China and Japan, with an investment of 34 million USD, has become the largest producing base of fuzzy-logic controlled washing machines. Rongshida Group and the U.S. Maytag Co. have jointly invested 180 million USD in AI household electric appliances. W.C.P. International Industrial Co., a China-America-Japan joint venture, is going to become a production and export base for energy-saving air conditioners with a capability of producing 1.2 million sets annually.

Hefei NHZ is an important base to carry out the China Torch Program. At present, Hefei NHZ is host to 56 Torch Program Projects at the state or province level, among which the first China made gene engineering interferon a-2b, *Anterfon*®, biomedicine *Zhaoke*® Defibrase, new material KG type assist agent for printing and dyeing, and traffic accident prevention system of Traffic Accident Prevention Institute are the key projects.

合肥高新区环境优雅，企业与公园融为一体
The Fine Environment of NHZ

重庆高新技术产业开发区

Chongqing High- and New-Tech Industrial Development Zone

重庆高新区位于重庆西大门，周边几条城市主干道连接市内几个中心区，距重庆江北机场36公里，距重庆火车站8公里，距重庆港和集装箱码头10-13公里。

重庆高新技术产业开发区一角
A Corner of Chongqing NHZ

重庆高新区始终把营造良好的投资环境，特别是投资软环境作为头等大事来抓。在管理机构建设上，坚持“小政府、大社会”的原则，力求少而精，人员严格控制在50人以内；实行“一幢楼办公，一个窗口对外，一站式服务”，到高新区新办企业，一般只需一个星期即可办完所有手续。目前，高新区正着力营造法制、政策、体制、人才、金融、市场、舆论、社区等八大环境，把高新区的政策优势转移到功能优势、体制优势、机构优势和环境优势上来，形成高新区的综合竞争优势。

1991年以来，高新区经济指标连续几年实现

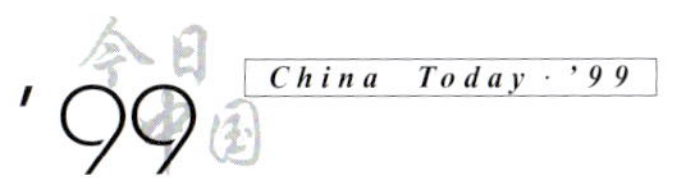

翻番增长。1998年，高新区各项经济指标继续高速增长，实现技工贸总收入111亿元，比1997年增长82.3%，工业总产值85亿元，增长58.0%，利税11.7亿元，增长80.0%，出口总额增长16.7%，已成为全市新的经济增长点。

重庆高新区以发展高新技术产业为中心，通过优惠出租标准厂房、提供信贷担保、提供产业发展基金、提供专家公寓等产业扶持措施，培育了一批以水润滑复合橡胶轴承、杜氏高压邮封、金属条码、血液透析仪、超声聚焦刀等为代表的拥有自主知识产权的高新技术产品；初步形成了信息产业、汽车摩托车配套新型产品产业、生物生化制药及医疗器械产业、新材料、节能和环保产业等四大产业群，已成为重庆高新技术产业基地。

目前，高新区已有“三资”企业300家，总投资9.75亿美元，协议外资4.18亿美元，实际利用外资3亿美元，分别占重庆市的11.78%、13.0%、12.23%和15.56%，成为重庆对外开放的重要窗口。1998年新办内资企业844家，比1997年增长10.0%；新办“三资”企业38家；协议引进外资7000万美元；实际利用资金4500万美元，绝对值列重庆市首位。

迄今为止，已有日本、美国、意大利、法国、德国、芬兰、俄罗斯、瑞典、加拿大、香港、台湾等24个国家和地区前来投资办厂；引进了日本五十铃、日本川崎、芬兰诺基亚、法国液化空气、泰国正大、中国联通、北大方正、中国联想、清华紫光等一批国内外知名企业。

面对新世纪的到来，为迎接知识经济的挑战，重庆高新区将继续以培育发展高新技术产业群、进一步扩大招商引资、加快产业基地建设为主要任务，力争到2001年实现技工贸总收入200亿元，2010年实现技工贸总收入600亿元。

Chongqing High- and New-tech Industrial Development Zone is situated at the west gateway of Chongqing. Its several peripheral municipal arteries connect a few central areas. It is 36 km from Chongqing Jiangbei Airport, 8 km from Chongqing Railway Station and 10-13 km from Chongqing Port and Container Dock.

Chongqing High- and New-tech Industrial Development Zone regards it as the most important task to build up a good investment environment, especially a soft investment environment. As far as the establishment of management institution is concerned, it upholds the principle of "Small Government, Big Society," seeks fewer but better by restricting the number of personnel within 50 persons, implements "one building for office work, one window open to the outside, one stop service." All formalities of opening a new enterprise in the zone can be completed within one week. At present, it pursues the construction of 8 major environments of legality, policy, system, talent, finance, market, public opinion, community, etc., transfers the policy advantage of the zone to the superiority in function, system, institution and environment, so as to enhances the zone's overall competitiveness.

Since 1991, its economic targets have been doubled for years running. In 1998, all of its economic targets rose continuously. The total income of its technology, industry and trade was 11.1 billion yuan, 82.3% higher than that of 1997; its total industrial output value, 8.5 billion yuan, 58.0% higher; its profit and tax, 1.17 billion yuan, 80.0% higher, total export volume increased by 16.7%. It has become a new factor contributing to the economic growth.

Chongqing High- and New-tech Development Zone focuses on the sector of new and high technology. Through preferential renting of factory buildings, provision of credit guarantee, industrialization development funds and expert apartment and other supporting measures, it has developed a range of new and high technology products with intellectual property rights, featuring water lubricating compound rubber bearing, DUC high pressure oil seal, metal bar code, blood dialysis instrument, ultrasonic focus cutter, etc. It has initially formed the 4 major sectors of information, new assorted products of vehicles and motorcycles, biochemical pharmaceuticals and medical equipment, and new materials, energy-saving and environmental protection products. It has become a new- and high-tech sector in Chongqing.

At present, it has 300 foriegn-invested enterprises, with a total investment of US$975 million, negotiated foreign funds of US$418 million, and actually utilized foreign funds of US$300 million, making up 11.78%, 13.0%, 12.23% and 15.56% of those of Chongqing, respectively. It has become an important window to the outside world. In 1998, 844 new domestic enterprises were established, 10.0% higher than that of 1997; 38 new foriegn-funded enterprises were founded; negotiated foreign funds came to US$70 million; actually utilized foreign funds, US$45 million; and the absolute value topped the list in Chongqing.

Up till now, investors from 24 countries and regions, such as Japan, USA, Italy, France, Germany, Finland, Russia, Sweden, Canada, Hong Kong and Taiwan, have come to the zone to make investment and build up factories; a series of worldwide and nationwide famous enterprises have been introduced to the zone, such as Isuzu and Yazaki from Japan, Nokia from Finland, Air Liquid from France, Zhengda from Thailand, China Union, Beida Founder, China Legend, Qinghua Zhiguang, and so on.

Confronted with the forthcoming new century and the challenge of knowledge economy, Chongqing High- and New-tech Development Zone will concentrate on developing continuously high- and new-tech industrial complex, furthering foreign investments and speeding up the construction of industrialization base. It endeavors to realize a total of 20 billion yuan income of technology, industry and trade by the year 2001, and 60 billion yuan by 2010.

杭州国家高新技术产业开发区

Hangzhou New and High-Tech Industrial Development Zone

在有“天堂”赞誉的中国浙江省省会杭州市美丽的西子湖畔，一座欣欣向荣的科技工业城正在兴起。被科技界人士称为“天堂硅谷”的杭州国家高新技术产业开发区，以其优越的地理位置、强大的科技依托、良好的工业基础和优越的政策环境而蜚声中外。

杭州高新技术产业开发区（简称杭州高新区）系1991年3月国务院批准的第一批国家级高新技术产业开发区之一。由主区块、之江区块等组成。1998年，全区实现工业总产值95.9亿元，技工贸总收入96.3亿元，利税总额9.7亿元，已成为省、市重要的经济增长点。

主区块位于杭州市区西北部，紧邻西湖，环境整洁。在这片原文教、电子仪表工业等为主的区域内，大专院校、科研院所密集，科技实力雄厚，基础设施齐全，毗邻机场、火车站、沪杭甬高速公路，交通便捷。

之江区块位于钱塘江南岸、萧绍平原，与六和塔等风景区隔岸相望，通过钱江一桥、二桥、三桥与北岸市区相连，是发展高新技术产业的理想之地。中国最大的通信产业基地“东方通信城”、国家火炬计划软件产业基地—杭州高新软件园、浙江省留学人员创业园区杭州高新区基地、国际跨国公司科学园、浙江大学辰光科技股份有限公司科研生产基地等项目已落户该区。杭州高新区正以高起点的规划、高质量的开发以及优惠的政策措施，全力推进之江科技工业园建设。一座21世纪杭州高科技新城正崭露头角。

杭州高新区致力于发展信息微电子、生物医药、新材料、光机电一体化、计算机及应用等技术领域。区内现有企业530余家，其中外商投资企业119家，218家被认定为高新技术企业745项高新技术产品及项目进入商品化生产或推广应用阶段。一批产品和项目已居国内外领先水平，一批科技型小巨人和规模企业正迅速崛起。

杭州高新区管委会是杭州市人民政府的派出机构，行使市政府授予的经济和社会管理职权，具有较高的办事效率。入区企业均可享受高新区相应的优惠政策。“天堂硅谷”正以崭新的面貌迎接国内外客商前来投资。

之江科技工业园街心花园
Street Garden of the Zhijiang Science and Technology Industrial Park

Hangzhou, the capital city of Zhejiang Province, has always enjoyed the name of the "Paradise on earth." Now, by the beautiful West Lake, a science and technology center–Hangzhou New- and High-tech Development Zone is prosperously emerging. Acclaimed as the "Silicon Valley in Heaven," it enjoys a high prestige within and outside of China due to its favorable geographic location, strong scientific and technological supports, solid industrial foundation, and preferential policy environment.

The Hangzhou New and High Technological Development Zone is one of the first of its kind ratified by the State Council in March 1993. It is comprised of the main section and the Zhijiang section. In 1998, its industrial output value totaled 9.59 billion yuan, with technological, industrial, and trade earnings of 9.63 billion yuan, contributing capital taxes of 0.97 billion yuan, thus becoming an important focal point of regional and provincial economic development.

Situated in the northwestern part of the city proper, the main section of the development zone has easy access to a variety of facilities. First, its natural environment is clean and good. Second, this area, once the center of higher education and electronic industry, enjoys a full range of infrastructure and strong scientific and technological supports with its many colleges and research institutes. Third, it also offers convenient transportation with easy access to the airport, railway station, and Shanghai-Hangzhou-Ningbo Expressway.

The other part, the Zhijiang section, lies on the southern bank of the Qiantang River in the Xiaoshao Plain. Facing the Liuhe Pagoda Scenic Area, it is connected with the northern district by the First, Second, and Third bridges over the Qiantang River. An ideal place for developing new- and high-tech industries, it has attracted a variety of high-tech projects, including: the Eastern Communications Center, the largest base of China's telecommunications industry; the Hangzhou high-tech and new software zone, the software industry base of the state Torch Program; the Hangzhou subzone of the pioneering zone of Zhejiang returned students from abroad; the scientific zone of international conglomerates; and the research and production base of Chenguang Science and Technology Company Ltd. under Zhejiang University. Relying on high-quality planning, and development and preferential policies, the development zone is tapping all its energy and resources to promote the development of the Zhijiang industrial zone into a new, fledging high-tech center in the 21st century.

The Hangzhou New- and High-tech Zone is committed to developing such high-tech industries as information technology, micro-electronics, bio-medicines, new materials, computer technology and its application, and integration of optical, machinery, and electrical technology. There are all together 530 enterprises in the zone, of which 119 are funded by foreign investment, and 218 are recognized as new- and high-tech enterprises. Seven hundred and forty-five items of high-tech products and programs are either in the process of commercial production or of promotion or application. Some products and programs have already been ranked at the forefront of domestic or international markets. Some large-scale scientific and technological enterprises are growing rapidly .

The Hangzhou New- and High-tech Zone is administered by a committee, an agency carrying out the social and economic administrative duties authorized by the People's Government of the Hangzhou Municipality. Its work efficiency is high. Any enterprise coming into the zone can enjoy the preferential policies of new- and high-tech zones. The "Silicon Valley in Heaven" is preparing to welcome both domestic and international investors with a new look.

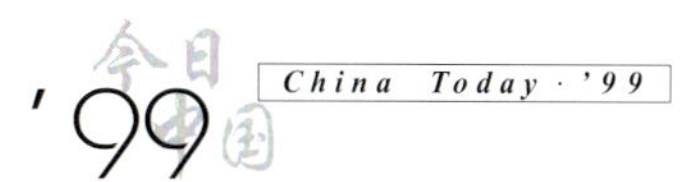

桂林高新技术产业开发区

Guilin High and New Tech Industrial Development Zone

桂林高新技术产业开发区创建于1988年5月，1991年3月经国务院批准为首批国家级高新技术产业开发区，是中国五个少数民族自治区建立的第一个国家级高新技术产业开发区。桂林高新区位于桂林市区漓江东畔，区划面积83平方公里。

桂林是享誉中外的风景游览城市和历史文化名城，千峰环立，一水抱城、山青水秀、洞厅石美。桂林是广西区的中心城市，广西对外开放的重要窗口之一，城市生态环境优美洁净，基础设施日臻完善。桂林高新区聚集了一批国家级科研院所、大专院校，具有雄厚的技术优势。高素质的人才资源和信息优势，为发展高新技术产业奠定了良好的基础。桂林高新区建立以来，在中央、自治区和桂林市领导的关怀和支持下，以“发展高科技、实现立业化”为宗旨，“务实为本，开拓争先”，大胆探索改革发展之路，全区经济、社会和新区建设取得了长足发展。

桂林高新区作为桂林市综合体制改革的试验区，对外开放的窗口，高新技术产业化的基地、经济发展的重要新增点，正发挥着愈来愈重要的作用，在全市经济社会发展中的地位和作用日益明显。桂林高新区与桂林市七星区政区合一，按照“小机构、大服务”原则设置精简高效的管理机构，全面行使市一级经济管理权限和相关行政管理权限，并按国际惯例设立相关的中介服务体系；高新区新建区已具备成片开发的“五通一平”土地，一批高新技术项目已建成投产，新建一批现代化办公设施、标准厂房和配套生活服务设施。目前，高新区为投资者提供了良好的环境条件和发展空间。

至1998年底止，桂林高新区累计实施高新技术项目164项，其中国家火炬计划项目等国家级项目38项，自治区火炬计划项目等自治区级项目111项；拥有各类企业近900家，其中，经认定的高新技术企业112家，三资企业175家，基本形成了电子与信息、机电一体化和办公自动化、新材料、生物医药工程、环保等五大支柱产业。招商引资势头良好，英国皮乐金顿公司、日本NEC公司、芬兰诺基亚公司、美国英格索兰公司等著名跨国公司相继进入高新区。1998年，高新区实际利用外资数占全市实际利用外资数的20.6%。高新区经济总量占全市的比重自1994年的7%提高到1998年的22%。

桂林高新区的发展目标是，建成全国最具特色的高新开发区之一，着力突出五大特色：环保特色、高科技工业与高科技农业结合的特色、高新技术产业与旅游结合的特色、高新技术产业与商贸结合的特色、现代化新城区特色；建设光纤传输、特种轮胎、生物医药和环保产业研究开发生产基地；规划建设环保、食品、综合产业园及软件园。

桂林高新区将继续坚持“统一管理、全市共建、外引内联、政策灵活、管理创新”的20字发展方针，为建设一个工业先进、农业现代、生产发达、商贸繁荣、市政完善、环境优美、生活优质的现代文明新城区而努力奋斗。

The Guilin High- and New-tech Industrial Development Zone (GIDZ) was set up in May 1998 , and was ratified by the State Council in March 1991 as one of the first batch national high- & new-tech industrial development zones. It is also the first one of the kind among five minority autonomous regions in our country. The GIDZ is situated on the easten bank of the Lijiang River, Guilin City proper, with an area of 83 sq km.

Guilin is a famous city at home and aboard for its beautiful scenery and historic cultural relics, where thousands of peaks stand uprightly and with a river winds its way through the city. Guilin is a hub of the northern part of Guangxi, an important window opening to the outside world in Guangxi. The urban ecological environment is fine, clear and elegant, and the infrastructures facilities have been getting better day after day. In the GIDZ, there are a group of national-level scientific and technological research institutes and colleges, with a strong technological superiority, high-quality talent resources and information advantages. All these factors have laid a good foundation for the development of the GIDZ. Since its establishment, under the concern and support of the leaders of the central government, the Government of the Autonomous Region and Guilin Municipality, the GIDZ has taken "developing high technology, and realizing industrialization" as its proinciple. It has achieved great progress both in the economy and social construction.

The GIDZ is regarded as an experimental base for the reform of the Guilin comprehensive system, a window towards the outside world, a base for high- & new-tech industrialization and an important growth bud of economic development. It is playing more and more important role in the whole city's social and economic development. The GIDZ and the Guilin Qixing District are united as one in administration. According to the principle of "small organ and broad service," it has set up a managerial organ with conciseness and high efficiency, fully exercising municipal level economic management power and relevant administrative power. At the same time the relevant medium service agencies have been set up according to the international practice. The GIDZ has developed a piece of land featuring "five facilities and flat land" (power & water supplies, water drainage, telecommunications, roads and even land) and has put a batch of high -& new-tech projects into operation. A batch of modern official installation facilities, standard workshops and living services installations for coordination have been built recently. At present, the GIDZ has prepared a fine environmental conditions and a vast space for the development by investors. Up to the end of 1998, the GIDZ has implemented 164 new- & high-tech projects in total, of which 38 projects are included in the Torch Plan as national projects, and 111 projects, in the Torch Plan of the Autonomous Region. There are 112 enterprises, and 175 foriegn-funded enterprises, thus basically forming five cornerstone industries: electronic & information, mechanical-electronic entity and official automation, new materials, bio-medicinal engineering and environmental protection, etc. The trend of soliciting business and luring foreign investment is fine. A lot of famous international corporations, such as Pilking ton (United Kingdom), NEC (Japan), Nokia Corporation (Finland), Ingersoll-Rand (USA) etc., have entered the GIDZ one after another. In 1998, the foreign fund used by the GIDZ accounted 20.6% of that of the whole city. The total economic output of the GIDZ in the whole city increased from 7% in 1994 to 22% in 1998. The target of the GIDZ in development is to build up a High &

New IDZ with most outstanding features, such as environmental protection, high-tech industry combined with high-tech agriculture, high- & new-tech industry combined with tourism, high- & new- tech industry combined with commerce and trade, and modern new urban district. It will build up the bases for studying, developing and producing fiber transmission, special tier, biomedicine and environmental protection products, and plan a comprehensive industrial park for environmental protection and foods, and a software industrial park. The GIDZ will persist in holding the development policy: "unifying administration, mobilizing the whole city for construction, luring foreign investments and cooperating with domestic enterprises, and adopting flexible policies and innovative management," so as to build up a new modern urban district with the advanced industry, modern agriculture, developed education, prosperous commerce and trade, sound public installations, elegant environment and a good-quality life.

郑州高新技术产业开发区

Zhengzhou High-Tech Industrial Development Zone

郑州高新区始建于1988年10月31日，1991年3月6日被国务院批准为国家高新技术产业开发区。位于郑州市西北隅，距市中心13公里，距市区边缘2公里。依托郑州市良好条件，地处中原，交通便利，是京广、陇海铁路干线交汇处，又是107、310两条国道交汇点，是亚欧大陆桥上的重要交通枢纽，距郑州国际机场仅35公里，科研机构密集，物质及劳力资源丰富，工业基础较雄厚。高新区总体规划面积18.6平方公里，现已开发6平方公里，4平方公里内布满项目。截止1998年，共批准成立企业697家，总投资64.3亿元，形成了电子信息技术、生物制药技术、新材料、节能环保等四大支柱产业。经济实力持续高速增长，1998年技工贸总收入达到82亿元，到2010年，将达到500亿元。初步建成了以高新技术产业为主导，基础设施配套、支撑服务体系完善，经济繁荣的现代化新社区。国家科技部领导高度赞扬郑州高新区产业形象与建设形象并举，形象、功能、效益全面发展，是中国中西部地区独具特色的有代表性的高新区。

郑州高新区致力于加强投资环境建设，成为中外客商投资兴业的理想场所。

硬件设施配套 目前基础设施建设累计投入5亿元，6平方公里内实现了道路、供电、电信、给排水、供热“五通一平”。道路总长35公里，已建成110KV变电站，供电能力2 × 3.15万KVA，已建成万门程控电话分局，最终容量4万门；建立专供水源，供水能力达50000吨／天；集中供热站设计规划8 × 35吨，目前供热能力40蒸吨／小时。

支撑服务体系完善 设立了公安、工商、税务、金融、保险、邮政、电信、供电、供水、供热、市政、商业、文化、教育、律师、会计、公证、医疗卫生、创业服务、房产交易、人才交流等服务行业和部门。

政府服务优质高效 按照市场经济的要求，遵循国际惯例，建立了新型的管理体制。按照“精简、效能、务实”的原则，建立机构，配备人员；实行一幢楼办公、一站式审批、一枚公章生效。为项目提供从审批到入区的全程优质、高效服务，对企业实行依法管理。

投资政策优惠 到高新区投资的高新技术项目和外商投资项目除享受国家规定的有关优惠政策外，还可享受高新区制定的地价、税收等方面的更加优惠的政策。

真诚欢迎中外客商到郑州高新区投资兴业，共创美好明天！

Zhengzhou High- and New-tech Industrial Development Zone (hereinafter referred to as the “Zone”) was established on Oct. 31, 1988, and ratified as a state development zone on Mar. 6, 1991. The Zone, situated in the sub-

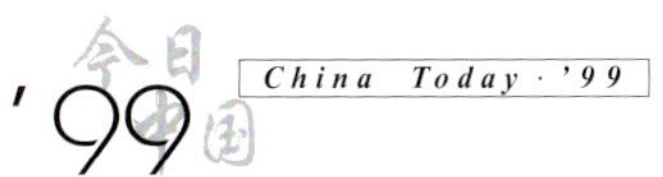

urban area of the city, is only 13 kilometers from the city proper, and 2 kilometers from the edge of the city. The two main railways, Beijing-Guangzhou and Lianyungang-Lanzhou railways, meet in Zhengzhou. It is also at the juncture of No.107 and No.310 National Highways. The Zone is 35 kilometers away from the Zhengzhou International Airport. The city has many research institutes, and is adequate in material and labor force resources. The Zone covers a total area of 18.6 square kilometers, of which 6 km^2 are ready for construction, and 5 km^2 are fully occupied by various enterprises. By the end of 1998, 697 enterprises had been approved to be set up in the Zone, and the total investment reached 6.43 billion yuan. In 1998, the total technology, industry and trade income reached 8.2 billion yuan. It is expected that, by 2010, the value will have reached 50 billion yuan. The Zone has initially become a new modern city area with complete basic facilities and supporting service systems under the high-tech industries. The leaders of the Ministry of Science and Technology highly praised the Zone's industrial and construction images saying that the Zone is a representative one with its own characteristics.

Hardware Facilities: Uuntil now, the Zone has invested 500 million yuan in the basic facilities. Within 6 square kilometers, there are roads, electricity power, telecommunications, water supply and drainage, and steam networks. The total road length reaches 35 kilometers. The Zone has been equipped with a 110 KV transformer station, a telephone bureau with a 10,000 telephone-controlled circuits, a water supply station with the capacity of providing 50,000 tons a day, and a concentrated steam station with a capacity of supplying 40 steam tons an hour.

Supporting Service System: There is a police station, the Industrial and Commercial Administration Bureau, Taxation Bureau, finance department, insurance department, post office, communication bureau, power supply station, water supply station, steam supply station, education department, CPA service, law office notary public, hospitals, and department stores in the Zone.

Government Service: The Zone is administrated only by the Administrative Committee. The administration of the zone is according to law.

Preferential Policies: For high-tech enterprise and foreign-invested enterprises, the Zone offers its own preferential policies on land use fees and taxation besides those policies set by the Central Government.

We sincerely welcome domestic and foreign investors to make investments in the Zone to create a bright futrue!

兰州高新技术产业开发区
兰州经济技术开发区

Lanzhou High-Tech Industrial Development Zone and Lanzhou Economic and Technological Development Zone

兰州高新技术产业开发区是国务院批准的全国首批27家国家高新技术产业开发区之一，其政策区面积为4.7平方公里，新建区面积为7.56平方公里。

兰州经济技术开发区由甘肃省人民政府按照国务院的精神，于1993年初批准成立的，其规划控制面积9.42平方公里。按照市委文件，兰州高新技术产开发区管理委员会与兰州经济技术开发区管理委员会合署办公，一个机构，两块牌子。

开发区经过几年建设，已经形成了以“精细化工、生物技术与新医药、节能环保、信息产业”为支柱产业，以高新技术企业为主体，集国营、集体、民营、“三资”等各种经济成份并存的产业格局。截止1998年底，进区企业达501家，其中高新技术企业253家，外商投资企业60家。

目前，开发区已基本具备了供水、排水、供热、电力、通信、道路的“六通一平”条件；三纵二横的城市主干道路已联成网络；银滩黄河大桥、110KV变电所和20万门程控电话的电信枢纽工程正在建设；金融、商业、文体中心等服务设施逐步配套，具备了良好的投资环境，正在成为集科、工、贸于一体，具有产、学、研功能的产业基地。与此同时，开发区按照市场经济要求和国际惯例，实行全新的管理体制，制订投资优惠政策，简化办事程序，大大便利了来区投资的客商；对外公布和严格执行的各类法规，有效地保障投资者的合法权益。

开发区作为深化改革的实验区，对外开放的窗口，科技与经济结合的示范区，带动和改造传

高新区管理委员会综合办公大楼
The Building of the Administration Committee of Lanzhou New- & High-Tech Industrial Development Zone

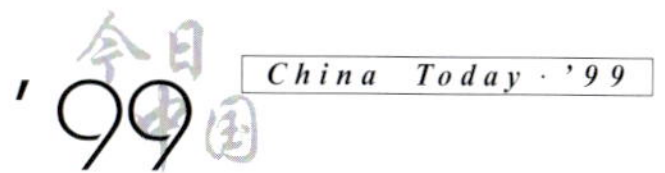

统产业发展的辐射源，新的经济增长点，正以软硬兼优的环境向投资者展示着广阔的发展前景。经过努力，力争在2005年建设成为以高新技术产业为依托，以工业为主体，集金融、商贸、生活、文化娱乐为一体的现代文明新城区。

兰州电信第二枢纽中心
Lanzhou Second Telecommunication Hub

The Lanzhou New- & High-tech Industrial Development Zone was one of the 27 national-class new- & High-tech industrial development zones firstly approved by the State Council. It embraces a 4.7-square-kilometer developed area, and a 7.56-square-kilometer newly built area.

The founding of the Lanzhou Economic and Technological Development Zone was approved by Gansu Provincial Government in light of the instructions by the State Council in 1993. It covers an area of 9.42 square kilometer. According to the documents of the Lanzhou Municipal Committee of the Chinese Communist Party, the administrative committees of the two zones are combined into an organ with two names.

After several years'efforts, the projects in Zones involve refined chemical industry, bioengineering, pharmaceutical science, medical engineering, energy-saving and environment protection, and information industry which are the pillar industries, with new- & high-tech enterprises as the mainstay and including state-owned, collective,and private enterprises and sino-foreign joint ventures. By the end of 1998, 501 enterprises, including 253 new- & high-tech corporations and 60 foreign-invested enterprises, had been established in the Zone.

At present, the Zones have completed ground leveling, water supply, water draining, heat supply, communication and road traffic, plus three horizontal highways and two vertical highways. The Yintan Bridge over the Yellow River, 110 KV transformer station, and the telecommunication hub with 200,000 program-controlled telephones are under construction. The service facilities, such as the bank, supermarket, museum, cultural and sports centre, and so on are being completed step by step. A good investment environment is taking shape and science, technology, industry and trade are integrated into one to form an industrial base. Meanwhile, according to the market economy and international rules, the administrative committee of the Zones adopts preferential policies and simple procedures to provide convenience to investors. The legal right of investors can be effectively guaranteed in accordance with regulations and rules. The zones are pilot areas for further reform, a window to outside world, an illustrative area to combine science and technology with the economy, a radiation source to push forward the traditional industries, and a new increment point to the economic development. It shows investors a bright future for development with a good soft and hard environment. In 2005, the Zones will become a new town with all functions and service facilities with the industry as the mainstay.

石家庄高新技术产业开发区

Shijiazhuang High and New Technology Industrial Development Zone

石家庄高新技术产业开发区（简称石家庄高新区）是1991年3月经国务院批准设立的全国首批国家高新技术产业开发区之一。经过几年建设，开发区注册企业已达864家，建设项目投资总额80亿元。其中，外资企业111家，实际利用外资2.58亿美元，涉及美国、英国、意大利、日本、加拿大、瑞典、马来西亚、波兰、韩国等十多个国家及香港特别行政区和澳门、台湾地区。1996年开发区完成工业总产值30亿元。在已建成的企业中，电子信息、生物医药、新材料产业的产值占70%以上。总体目标是到2000年全区工业总产值超过100亿元。

石家庄高新区总规划面积18平方公里，分东部区和西部区。

西部区位于石家庄市西南部城区，为建成区。目前，已投产的大部分企业集中于此，西部区具有十分雄厚的科技开发能力，有各类高等院校8所，有代表中国通信和微电子技术领域最高水平的两个国家级研究所以及导航设备检测中心，半导体行业技术发展中心等20多个国家和部级科研发展机构，有国家级试验室100多个，有上万名高、中级科研人员和近千项科研成果。

东部区位于石家庄东部，规划面积9.8公里，规划人口20万，是一个以工业为主，集商贸、科研、文教、生活、居住和文化娱乐为一体的现代化新城区。东部区交通便利，地势平坦，基础设施完善，具有广阔的发展前景。区内有四条主干道与石家庄市区连接，北侧有中国西部宁夏银川至本省（河北省）黄骅港的307国道通过，北京至深圳的高速公路直通区内，石家庄至山东德州的铁路在开发区北侧与307国道并行，经高速公路北行30公里即可到达石家庄国际机场。基础设施建设投入资金3.4亿元。在5.8平方公里的起步区内已实现道路畅通；区内两座11千伏安变电站双向供电，可以满足进区企业的用电需要；开发区热电厂已投入运行，对区内企业实行集中供热；区内2000门程控电话已投入使用，华北第二信讯枢纽正在建设，建成后可提供10万门程控电

石家庄高新区中美合资棉种有限公司
The Chinese-American Cotton Seed Co., Ltd. Within the Zone

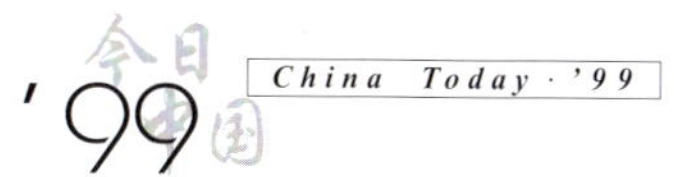

话，以大大增强开发区通讯能力；现有供水设施已形成日供水4万吨的能力，10万吨水厂正在建设之中；排水、排污管道已全部铺设完成，部分住宅楼和别墅已开始建设。目前，该区企业已达80多家，其中，投资28亿元生产电视机彩色玻壳的宝石电子玻璃有限公司和投资3000万美元年产3千克VC的维生药业（石家庄）有限公司都已投入生产，均取得了明显的经济效益。

石家庄高新区机构健全，办事程序简便，投资额3000万美元以下的项目可以直接批准设立。并设有土地、规划建设、工商、税务、物价、保险等机构和警察署、法院、检察院等法律机关，对来区投资的外商既可提供全程服务，又可提供良好的法律、安全保证。

Shijiazhuang High- and New-Tech Industrial Development Zone was established in March of 1991, and is one of the first batch of national development zones approved by the State Council.

After several years of construction, 864 enterprises have been registered in the zone with a total investment of 8 billion yuan RMB. Among these enterprises, 111 are foreign-funded with a total investment of 258 million US dollars. The foreign investment comes from over 10 countries and regions. The industrial output of the zone in 1996 was 3 billion yuan.

The output of the enterprises engaged in telecommunication, biotech medicine and new material takes over 70% of the whole. The total industrial output will be 10 billion yuan RMB by the end of the year 2000.

The zone covers an area of 18 square kilometers and is composed of two parts: East Park and West Park in the east area and southwest area of Shijiazhuang City.

The West Park is a developed area where most enterprises are productive. There are eight universities and two research institutes which represent the national level in the telecommunication and microelectronics staffed by over 10 thousand researchers.

The East Park covers an area of 9.8 square kilometers with a planned population of 200,000. It will be turned into a modern urban district with industry as its leading factor and other service facilities.

The East Park has good prospects with convenient transportation, smooth terrain and perfect infrastructure.

A total of 340 million yuan RMB have been invested in construction of the infrastructure of the East Park. Now in 5.8 square kilometers of initiative building area, a convenient road net, sufficient power supply, high quality centralized heat service have been built. A PABX with 2,000 ports has been installed. The second communication pivot in North China is being built here. The communication capacity will be increased remarkably. The daily capacity of water supply is 40,000 tons and a 100,000-ton water plant has been projected. Some apartments buildings and villas are being constructed.

Baoshi Electronic-Glass Company with a total investment of 2.8 billion yuan RMB for manufacturing color TV picture tubes and Weisheng Pharmaceutical Ltd. with a total investment of 30 million US dollars for manufacturing annually 3,000 tons of Vitamin C have been put into production and have got satisfactory economic benefits.

The administrative departments in the development zone are complete and efficient. Any project with total investment below 30 million US dollars can be approved in the office building of the committee of the zone. Our excellent service can meet any requirements from investors concerning land acquisition, project plan and construction, administration of industry and commerce, taxation, price control, insurance, public security, dispute treatment, etc.

济南高新技术产业开发区

Jinan High-Tech Industrial Development Zone

济南高新技术产业开发区位于济南市市区的东部，是1991年3月经国务院批准建立的国家级开发区。

济南高新技术产业开发区地理环境优越，她东距济南国际机场15公里；北临济南—青岛高速公路；南依景色秀丽的浆水泉风景区和龙洞风景区；西接繁华市区。分为建成区和集中新建区两部分。建成区为高等院校、科研院所和大中型企业的集中地；集中新建区由1.76平方公里的科技城和7.5平方公里的东部新区组成。科技城已基本形成以电子信息、生物工程、机电一体化、新材料为主体产业，融生产、生活、娱乐为一体的现代化新建区。现集中开发的东部新区已完成3平方公里起步区的基础设施一期工程建设，规划了齐鲁软件产业园区、大学产业园区、电子产业园区、轻骑集团产业园区、化纤产业园区、小鸭集团产业园区、综合加工工业园区等园区，是大型科工贸项目建设的理想投资之地。

“发展高科技，实现产业化”是高新技术产业开发区的根本任务。济南高新技术产业开发区内工业基础雄厚，有大中型骨干企业60余家，已培养认定高新技术企业230多家，认定高新技术产品近350种，实施火炬计划项目200多项，高新技术产业各项经济指标在全国同类开发区中位于前列。

济南高新技术产业开发区日益受到越来越多的中外客商的青睐。建区以来，已有美国、日本、加拿大、瑞士、意大利、新加坡等20多个国家和香港、台湾地区的客商前来洽谈投资。济南高新技术产业开发区已与世界上30余家知名企业财团建立了合作关系。目前，开发区已拥有三资企业130多家，外商投资企业正成为济南高新技术产业开发区经济群体中最活跃的一部分。

“有朋自远方来，不亦乐乎”，济南高新技术产业开发区热诚欢迎海内外各界朋友来开发区开拓伟业，携手共创一个更加美好的未来。

轻骑铃木摩托车有限公司生产车间
A Workshop of SUZUKI Motocycle Co., Ltd.

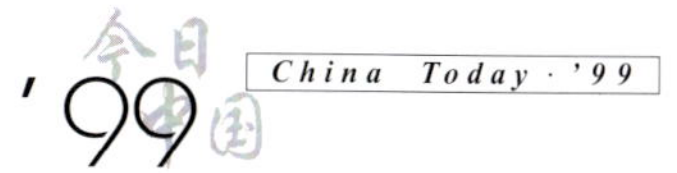

Located to the east of Jinan City proper, Jinan High-Tech Industrial Development Zone is a state-level development zone founded in March 1991 with approval of the State Council.

Jinan High-Tech Industrial Development Zone has geological and environmental advantages. About 15 kilometers to its east is Jinan Internationa Airport; Jinan-Qingdao Expressway passes by to the north; to its south are the Jiangshui Spring Scenic Area and the Dragon Cave Scenic Area; and to its west is the booming business district of the city. The development zone is around the East Outer Ring Road and consists of two sections: to the west of the Ring Road is the completed section and to the east is the section under construction. The former includes institutions of higher learning, scientific research institutes and large and medium-sized enterprises; and the latter is composed of the 1.76 square-kilometer Science and Technology City and the 7.5 square-kilometer Eastern New Subzone. At present, the Science and Technology City has been built into a modern facility for high-tech industries including electronic information, biological engineering, integrated machinery and electric equipment and new materials, as well as residential and recreational centers. In the Eastern New Subzone, the first-phase of the infrastructure construction covering an area of three square kilometers has been completed. The subzone is divided into sections respectively for the Qilu Software, university industrial development, electronics, the Qingqi Group, chemical fiber, the Xiaya Group and comprehensive industrial processing, an ideal place for large-scale technological, industrial and trade projects.

The fundamental task of all the high-tech development zones is to "develop high-tech and realize industrialization". Jinan High-Technology Industrial Development Zone has a solid foundation for industrial development and now there are over 60 large and medium-sized key enterprises in the development zone. In addition, 230 high-tech enterprises and 350 kinds of high-tech products have been identified, and more than 200 Torch Program projects have been carried out in the development zone. The development comes on the top in national high-tech industrial economic index of the development zones of the same kind.

An increasing number of both domestic and foreign businessmen have cast bright prospects on the Jinan High-Technology Industrial Development Zone. Since its founding, business people from over 20 countries and regions, including the United States, Japan, Canada, Switzerland, Italy, Singapore, Hong Kong and Taiwan have visited the development zone for business talks. At present it has established cooperative relations with more than 30 world famous companies and banks. There are now more than 130 joint ventures, cooperative enterprises and exclusively foreign invested enterprises established in the development zone, and these foreign-invested enterprises have become the most active part in economic development of the development zone.

"What a pleasure to have friends coming from afar!"

Jinan High-Tech Industrial Development Zone warmly welcomes Chinese and foreign friends to invest and engage in cooperation in the development zone, and create a more splendid future together with us.

深圳市高新技术产业园区

Shenzhen High-Tech Industrial Park

深圳市高新技术产业园区（以下简称高新区）成立于1996年9月。她位于深圳经济特区西部，北起广深高速公路，南到滨海大道，西临麒麟路，东至沙河路，总面积11.5平方公里（已开发土地面积7平方公里）。据统计，1998年高新区主要经济指标继续保持快速增长，工业总产值239.22亿元，与高新区成立之初的1996年相比，增长139%；高新技术产品产值213.12亿元，增长238%：出口创汇6.71亿美元；实现利税7.6亿元。1998年产值超过1亿元的企业18家，深圳高新区同年荣获国家科技部“火炬先进管理奖”。

高新区定位于“大规模、高效益的高新技术产业区、企业运行机制试验区、科技成果转化区、经济技术合作区和高层人才培养教育区”。发展模式是依靠园区优良的投资环境和资金优势，引进技术和人才，扩大自主知识产权比例，带动传统产业向高新技术产业转化，使深圳特区经济再度腾飞。

政策法规 早在1990年，市政府就确定了“以科技为进步动力，大力发展高新技术产业和第三产业”的2000年战略方针，随后颁布了《关于进一步扶持高新技术产业发展的若干规定》、《深圳市高新技术企业（项目）认定标准》、《深圳市高新技术产业园区发展规划》和《深圳市高新技术产业园区管理规定》等。

管理体制 高新区实行开放式管理，即在国家有关法律、法规之下，不改变政府各部门现有职权管辖范围；不中断各种审批链条，仅在高新企业能否入区方面赋予高新办权限，充分发挥政府各部门的积极性、协调性。高新区根据目前状况，实行了决策层（高新区领导小组）、管理层（高新办）、经营服务层（服务中心）三级管理体制。

产业结构 高新区重点发展电子信息、生物工程、新材料和光机电一体化等四大产业。电子信息产业主要有中国长城计算机、华为公司、中兴通讯、联想集团、北大方正，日本的爱普生、奥林巴斯，与IBM合作的海量存储和万国软件，加拿大的哈里斯通信等。生物工程产业主要有科兴公司、康泰制药、通海生物和海王制药等。新材料产业主要有方大意德新材料公司、长园应用化学公司、天鼎精细化工公司、永和科技公司和深圳大学反光材料厂等。光机电一体化产业主要有奥沃公司、思创太阳能公司等。

研发单位 深圳大学、深圳清华研究院、深圳中国工程院院士咨询活动中心、中国科技开发院、深圳中国生化中心、深圳生物工程产业基地等。

Shenzhen High-tech Industrial Park (hereinafter referred to as “High-Tech Park”) was established in September, 1996. It is located in north Shenzhen. Its range is from Guangshen High-Speed Road in the north, reaches to the Binhai Road in the south, borders on the Qilin Road in the west, and reaches to the Shahe Road in the east, covering 11.5 square kilometers (exploited land covering 7 square kilometers). According to the statistical data, the main eco-

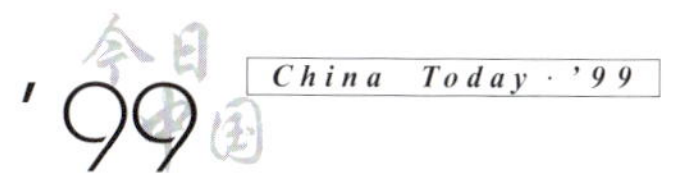

深圳市高新技术产业开发区一角
A Corner of Shenzhen NHE

nomic index increased rapidly in 1998, the gross industrial output value was 23.922 billion yuan, compared with the initial stage of the High-tech Park in 1996, increased by 139%; the output value of high-tech industrial products reached 21.312 billion yuan, increased by 238%, export income was US$ 617 million, the profit tax was 760 million yuan. In 1998, there were 18 enterprises whose industrial output value exceeded 100 million yuan. In the same year, Shenzhen High-Tech Park won the prize of "Torch Seniority Management" from the Ministry of Science and Technology.

The objective of High-Tech Park is to build an industrial park which has a large scale and high efficiency; an experiment park of the enterprise mechanism; a technology achievement transfer park, an economic technical cooperation park and an advanced talent cultivated park. Its development mode is depending on the good investment environment and fund superiority, introducing the technology and talent, enlarging the independence knowledge property right's proportion; spurring the traditional industry transferring to the high-tech industry, which makes the economy of Shenzhen prance and leap again.

Policies and Regulation In 1990, the municipal government definitive the strategy guidance for 2000 is "depending on the science and technology as the motive power for the progress, with efforts developing the high-tech industry and tertiary industry." After that it published "Regulation on Supporting the Development of High-Tech Industry", "Concluding Standard of the Shenzhen High-Tech Industrial Enterprise (item)", "Development Plan of Shenzhen High-Tech Industrial Park" and "Management Regulation on Shenzhen High-Tech Industrial Park" etc.

Management System High-Tech Park practices open management style, according to the related laws and regulations, it doesn't change the existent authority administer scope of all the government departments, nor it break off all the examination and approval chain, gives the Leading Group Office of High-tech Industrial Park the decision-making power on the establishment of enterprises in the park,bring into full play the role of the positive nature and coordination nature of all the government departments. According to the present situation, the High-tech Park carries out the policy-making stratum (by the leadership of the Park), the management stratum (by the High-tech Office) and management service stratum (by the Service Centre).

Industrial Structure The High-Tech Park emphasizes on developing the electronic information, bio-engineering , new material , and optical – mechanical – electrical industries , etc. The electronic information industry mainly includes the Great Wall Computer Company of China, the Japanese enterprises, such as Huawei Company, Zhongxing Telecom, Regent Company, Founder Company, Epson, Olympus, Savers and Wanguo Software Company which are cooperated with IBM. The bio-engineering industry mainly includes Kexing Bioproducts Company, Kangtai Biological Company, Tonghai Biology and Neptunus Bioengineering, etc. The new material industry includes Fang-Da Co., ChangYuan Applied Chemical Co., TianTing Chemical Co., Yonghe Tech. Co. and Reflect Light Material Factory of Shenzhen University. The optical-mechanical-electrical production industry includes Our Co. and Strength Co., etc.

Study and Research Institutes Shenzhen University, Shenzhen Qinghua University Research Institute, Shenzhen Cae Consultant Center, the Science and Technology Development Institute of China, Shenzhen State Biochemical Engineering Center, Shenzhen Biochemical Industrial Base, etc.

厦门火炬高新技术产业开发区

Xiamen High-Tech Industrial Development Zone

厦门火炬高技术产业开发区是53个国家高新区之一，也是国家科技部与地方政府共同创办的全国四个火炬高新区之一，1990年12月创办，规划面积2.67平方公里，目前已开发0.81平方公里。至1998年年底，累计境外客商协议投资额2.5亿美元，1998年开发区实现工业产值40亿元，出口创汇3亿美元，分别比上年增长23%、10%。开发区内道路畅通，环境优雅，政策优惠，服务周到，各种配套设施逐步完善，高新区已初具规模。

厦门高新区的主要特点是：

一是区内企业产品的技术档次较高，一个以电子信息产业和机电一体化为支柱的高新技术产业群体基本形成。高新区现有企业74家，电子信息产业和机电一体化产业的工业产值占高新区工业总产值95%。其中电子信息产业有远销海外的混合集成电路，有国际先进水平的红外光敏器件和光耦合器件，有全国市场占有率第一的各种家电微型控制器，有世界知名的德尔电脑；机电一体化的产品有国际先进水平的ABB中压开关柜，有全国最大的微型碳化钨钻头生产厂家。截止1998年底，开发区已认定的高新技术企业有34家，这34家高新技术企业实现工业产值34.5亿元，出口创汇2.8亿美元，分别占全开发区86%和93%。

二是外资企业的比例较大，一个以外资企业为主的外向型经济框架已基本形成。厦门火炬高新区充分利用厦门的区位优势、环境优势、政策优势，8年来先后引进外资企业共42家，占高新区企业总数57%，外资企业的工业产值占全部工业产值93%。这些外资企业主要有ABB电气开关公司、日本富士电气化学株式会社、日本松下音响公司、美国柏恩氏公司、美国戴尔电脑公司等。目前，这些外资企业都取得较好的经济效益。例如ABB中压开关去年人均技工贸总收入达107万，利税3000多万，是ABB总部在中国创办22家分公司中效益最好的企业。实践证明，厦门有较好的投资环境。因此外资投资规模扩大化是厦门高新区外资企业的一个显著特点。例如日本富士电气公司由原来投资的900万美元扩资到4300万美元。

为了加快厦门高新技术产业的发展，市政府已批准厦门火炬高新区实施“一区三园”，即厦门火炬高新区、海沧高科技园、集美高科技园、五通高科技园，规划总面积达8.17平方公里。预计到2000年，厦门火炬高新区技工贸总收入将达100亿人民币，出口创汇4.5亿美元。

Xiamen Hi-Tech Industrial Development Zone is one of 53 national hi-tech zones. It's also one of four zones which are sponsored by the Ministry of Science & Technology and local government. Founded in December 1990, it has 2.67 km^2 of total planning area. Now, high-tech zone has developed the area of 0.81 km^2. By the end of 1998, it attracted US$ 0.25 billion. It realized gross output value of 4 billion yuan . The value of exports amounted to US$0.3 billion. They rose respectively by 23% and 10%. There are open roads,elegant environment, favorable policies, thoughtful services and necessary facilities for living and working in the zone. Our high-tech zone is beginning to take shape.

厦门 ABB 开关有限公司
Xiamen ABB Switch Co., Ltd.

Our zone has the following main characteristics:

First, the technology of products is higher and hi-tech industries which depend on electronics & information industry and mechantronics industry have basically formed. Among 74 companies, the industrial output of the two industries makes up 95 percent of the total output value. The electronics & information industry includes integrated circuits which find a good market overseas, infrared photosensitive devices and photo-coupled devices with advanced international standard, all kinds of mini-controlled devices of electrical household appliances which rank first in domestic market, world-known DELL computers. The mechantronics products include ABB metal-clad metal-enclosed switchgear, the largest company in our country which produces mini-calcium wolfram bit. By the end of 1998, there were 34 companies awarded the title of "high-tech company". Their output value accounted for 3.45 billion yuan and the value of the exports totalled US$0.28 billion, respectively making up 86 percent and 93 percent of the zone's total.

Second, the proportion of foreign enterprises is high and the framework for export-oriented economy has basi-

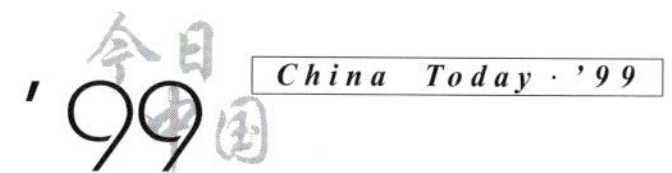

cally formed. Xiamen Torch High-tech Industrial Development Zone makes full use of region advantage, environment advantage and policy advantage of Xiamen. It has attracted 42 foreign enterprises in the eight years, making up 57% of the total. The industrial output value of foreign enterprises amounts for 93% of the total. Those foreign enterprises include ABB Xiamen Switchgear Co.Ltd., Xiamen FDK Corporation, Matsushita Audio Xiamen Co. Ltd., Bourns (Xiamen) Ltd., DELL Computer Co. Ltd., etc. All of these foreign enterprises gain very good economic benefit, such as ABB Switchgear Co. Last year, its income per person was 1.07 million yuan and profit & tax was 30 million yuan. It obtains the best benefit among 22 enterprises in China founded by ABB headquarters. Practices prove Xiamen has a better investment environment. So foreign capitals is an outstanding characteristic. Take FDK Corporation for example. It expanded investment from US$9 million to US$43 million.

In order to speed up the development of Xiamen high-tech industry, municipal authorities have approved Xiamen Torch High-Tech Industrial Development Zone to develop "one zone with three parks". They are Xiamen torch high-tech zone, Haicang high-tech park, Jimei high-tech park, Wutong high-tech park. The total planning area is 8.17 km^2. The income of Xiamen Torch High-Tech Zone will reach 10 billion yuan while the value of exports will be US$0.45 billion.

海南国际科技工业园

Hainan International Scientific and Industrial Park

自1991年创立以来，海南国际科技工业园立足于高新技术商品化、产业化、国际化的目标，以推动海南经济特区高新技术发展和产业化为己任，积极致力于促进海南省产业技术的升级和社会经济的发展。担负园区开发并对园内企业的发展和产业的形成进行导向、协调、帮助任务的海南国际科技工业园股份有限公司也发展壮大成为拥有24500万股本，业务领域涉及高新技术项目开发、房地产经营、贸易、旅游、教育等各方面的大型股份制规范化企业。

海南国际科技工业园位于海口市西部，距市中心9公里，园区南3公里处紧接海口火车站；东距美兰国际机场30公里；东北6公里处是琼洲海峡轮渡码头；北3公里处有海南第一大港口秀英港。园区北临海榆西线公路，南接环岛高速公路及两条城市主要交通干线，整个园区为规划中的

花园式厂房
Garden-Style Factory

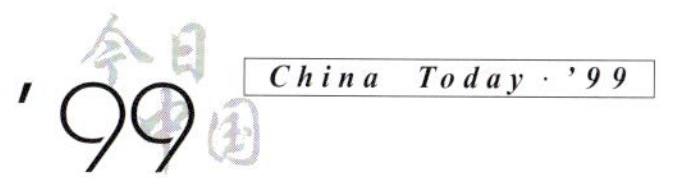

城市快速干道和绿化带所环绕。园区优越的地理位置、自然环境和交通条件为投资者提供了良好的外部投资环境。

根据国务院批准的总体规划，园区总开发面积为4.67平方公里，规划强调科研、教育与企业的联合机制，使园区成为海南经济特区科研、开发、生产、经营等多个环节协调发展的高新技术产业基地，成为向全省扩散高新技术的辐射源和与国际高新技术交往的窗口。

园区拥有一整套从生产、生活到服务的完备设施，可为投资者提供较为完善的综合配套服务体系。

海南国际科技工业园为海内外所有高新技术产业投资者开放，园内实行多种所有制并举，谁投资，谁所有，谁受益；自筹资金，自我决策，自主经营，自负盈亏，自愿组合。对企业入园实行土地出租、转让、折价入股、厂房出售、租赁等多种投资形式和独资经营、合资经营、租赁、承包经营等多种合作形式。

海南国际科技工业园股份有限公司为入园企业提供"一条龙"服务，从项目招商、评估筛选、入园审批、项目计划、基建报建、房产办证到物业管理、安全保卫等各方面实行专人专项负责，简明高效管理。

依据海南省经济发展需要、科技成果优势以及本省自然资源优势三个方面的因素，海南国际科技工业园将下列产业列为园区的重点发展产业：

●电子、信息技术

●生物制药技术

●新材料技术

●新能源和高效节能技术

●热带高效农业

入园高新技术企业除可享受中央、国务院给予海南经济特区和高新技术开发区的一系列优惠政策待遇外，海南省政府为促进园区的超常规发展，在税收、产品进出口、资金、土地转让、外汇留成及管理人员出入境等方面给予了更为优惠、更为特殊的政策，主要有：

1. 园区高新技术企业，从开始获利年度起，两年内免征企业所得税，第3-5年减半征收。其中，经省人民政府确认为技术先进的企业，第6-8年减半征收所得税。

2. 园区高新技术企业生产的产品，在省内销售的，免征增值税。信息企业产品在省外销售的，自投产年度起3年内，由财政以列收列支的方式，返还地方留成部分的60%，4-6年返还40%。

3. 信息企业和园区教学、科研单位为生产经营、技术产品开发、研究、教学、试验所需进口的自用设备，凡符合国家有关规定的，免征进口关税和进口环节增值税。信息企业生产的出口产品，除国家另有规定外，免征出口关税。

4. 园区信息企业和高新技术信息项目新建、新购置生产经营场所，免收报建费；生产经营用地，只收征地费，免收土地使用权出让金。

海南国际科技工业园近期发展战略首先是利用身处大特区的优势，努力创造更加科学的管理方式及更为优良的服务体系，在各方面树立自己的特色。集中优势力量，重点引进高科技基础产业、新兴电子信息产业、生物制药、高效节能和环保、热带高效农业项目，作为园区稳定发展的基础。积极扩大国内国际合作，参与国内国际资本市场的运作，以低成本、快速度的形式扩张园区实力，促进园区发展规模质的飞跃，充分发挥国际科技园在海南省高技术产业的龙头带动作用。

Since its founding in 1991, Hainan International Scientific and Industrial Park (HISIP), based on the goal of new hi-tech commercialization, industrialization and internationalization, has taken development and industrialization of new high-tech into consideration as its own responsibility.

Hainan International Science and Industry Park Co. Ltd. is responsible for the development of the park and offers guides, coordination and help to the enterprises in development and industrialization. It has developed into a large-scale regular enterprise of stock system that has 245 million shares. Its business deals with new high-tech development, real estate operation, trade, tourism and education.

HISIP is located in the west of Haikou City, 9 km away from the downtown, 3 km away from the Haikou Railway Station to its south. To its east, Meilan International Airport, one of the ten biggest airports in China, is 30 km away, to the northwest, Ferry Pier of Qiongzhou straits is 6 km away, 3 kilometres to the north is Xiuying Harbor, the biggest in Hainan with 10,000 berths. In the north Park borders, Haiyu West Highway, one of three main highways, and in the south of it is close to the around-the-island Expressway. The whole park is surrounded by main roads and green area. The excellent position of the park, natural environment and transportation facilities provide a good investment environment for the foreign investors.

According to the overall plan approved by the State Council, the development area of the park is 4.67 km^2. The plan stressed on construction of a unified system for scientific research, education and enterprises to make the park into a new high-tech industrial base with scientific research, development, production and operation coordinately developed. The park will become a new high-tech source radiating over the whole province and a window for international new high-tech exchange.

The park has been well equipped for production, life and service, and offers complete and comprehensive services for investors.

Hainan International Scientific and Industrial Park (HISIP) is opened to all investors from home and abroad to establish new high-tech industry. The park carries out the system of various ownerships simultaneously. The people who invest are owners and will get the profit, are responsible for raising capital, making decision, operating, and loss and profit. There are many types of investments for the enterprises which want to enter into the park, such as land-leasing, transferring, changing into stocks according to the price, the workshop can be purchased and rented. The operation can be sole operation, joint venture, leasing and contract.

HISIP Co. Ltd. can offer a series of services for the enterprises which want to enter into the park, in project invitation, evaluation selection, approval for entering the park, project plan, infrastructure submission, building certificates and real estate management, and public security. They are personnel in charge of each project, the management is simple but high efficient.

According to the demands of the economic development of Hainan Province, the advantage of scientific achievements and natural resources of Hainan Province, Hainan International Science and Industry Park has listed the following industries on development with importance.

(1) Electronic, information technology;

(2) Biological pharmaceutical technology;

(3) New material technology;

(4) New energy and high-efficient energy saving technology; and

(5) Tropical high-efficient agriculture.

The new high-tech enterprises of the park can not only enjoy a series of preferential policies issued by the Central Committee and the State Council for Hainan Special Economic Zone and new and high-tech development areas, but also the more preferential and special policies of Hainan Province for encouraging hyper-normal development of the park in tax, product import and export, finance, land-leasing,

foreign exchange retaining and managarial personnel in and out of the area. The main policies are as follows:

1. New- and high-tech enterprises in the park should be exempted from income taxes of the enterprises for two years from the year of profit making and at a 50% rate from the third year to the fifth year. Those enterprises which are confirmed by the People's Government of Hainan Province as technically advanced enterprises will be levied income taxes at a reduced rate of 50% from the sixth year to the eighth year.

2. The products made by the new high-tech enterprises in the park should be exempted from added-value taxes, if they are sold on the island. The products of the information enterprises that are sold outside the province can be returned 60% of the added value taxes retained by the local government within three years from first year of their production, and 40% from the fourth year to the sixth year, with the method of financial payment and collection.

3. Information enterprises and education and scientihic research institutes within the park, can be exempted from import customs duty and added value tax of the self use equipment imported for production operation, development of technical products, research, education and experiment in accordance with the related state regulations. The exported products made by the information enterprises shall be exempted from export customs duty, except of those specified by the state.

4. The information enterprises and new high-tech information projects in the park shall be exempted from construction submission charge for their new projects, newly purchased production and operation grounds. The land of production and operation will only pay for purchase without payment for land-use right.

The recent development strategy of HISIP is, at first, to use the advantages of the large size of the special zone, to do its best to create better scientific management model and more superior service system to set up its own characters in all aspects. It will concentrate its advanced force to introduce high-tech basic industry, newly built electronic information industry, biological pharmacy, high-efficient energy- saving and environment protection, tropical high-efficient agricultural projects, as the base for stable development of the park. It will actively develop domestic and international cooperation, take part in the operation of domestic and international capital market, to expand the strength of the park with lower costs and a rapid speed, to promote the development of the park in scale, to fully play its leading role in high-tech industry of Hainan Province.

配套服务设施
Comprehensive Service Facilities

苏州高新技术创业服务中心

Suzhou New & High-Tech Innovation Service Center

一、宗旨

苏州高新技术创业服务中心、苏州国际企业孵化器、中国苏州留学人员创业园是由苏州新区管委会全额财政投资的公益型科技服务机构，作为苏州新区实施科技兴区战略的重要工程，通过提供国际化的孵化服务，创造出一个局部优化、适合技术创新的环境和条件，使国内外中小科技型企业能够依托国际资源迅速发展。

二、目前现状

苏州创业服务中心1993年创立。1996年10月成为国家科委确认的全国首批三家“国际企业孵化器”试点单位之一。1998年2月苏州新区管委会与国家教委留学服务中心、国家科委火炬办等单位联合组建了“中国苏州留学人员创业园”。

1997年11月被原国家科委评为“国家高新技术创业服务中心”；1998年8月，被国家科技部授予“火炬先进创业服务中心管理奖”。

目前有孵化面积38公里。进驻企业累计超过200家（其中有40多家留学人员企业）。毕业企业历年累计数达36家。进驻企业销售收入1998年达3.11亿元。进驻企业开发的项目历年累计超过450项，其中包括国家及省级火炬项目、重点攻关、重点推广项目等。

三、良好的软、硬条件为企业全过程服务和孵化功能发挥提供了有力保证

创业园提供适合科技型企业国际化发展要求的硬件条件：智能化大楼，配备有设备优良的会议室、CAD中心、多功能学术报告厅、计算机中心、信息中心等公用服务设施，引进了会计师事务所、律师事务所、国际货运代理、报关代理、企业策划等社会中介服务机构，基本形成了与国际通行做法相似的企业运行环境和氛围。创业园还有完善的生活配套服务，如宿舍、健身房、洗衣房、活动室等生活设施。

创业园为进驻企业提供全过程服务。工商注册、银行开户、税务登记、人才支撑服务、信息服务、技术服务、知识服务、项目服务、资金引导等全方位服务，优惠的税收政策等完善的软环境，为企业发展提供了有力保证。科技支撑服务：良好的科技、人力资源合作关系，初步形成产、学、研一体化的组织体系，产前、产中、产后全过程跟踪管理的服务体系，跨地区、跨学科、跨行业的协作体系等。人才支撑服务：苏州新区健全的人力资源市场，博士后工作站，留学人员服务站，各种人才培训中心等机构，形成了系列化的人才支持体系。信息服务：所有孵化单元内每10个平方米就有一个网络信息接口，进驻企业共享着INTRANET/INTERNET信息资源。技术服务：行业协会、专家网络体系为企业提供产品开发及相应的技术指导和技术服务。知识服务：定期举办技术、法律、财务、市场和企业管理等方面的讲座、培训和座谈会，创造良好的知识氛围、技术氛围和创新氛围。项目服务：帮助企业进行高新技术企业和高新技术产品申报，向进驻企业介绍和推荐合作项目，帮助进驻企业申报各类科技项目。资金服务：努力为企业解决发展资

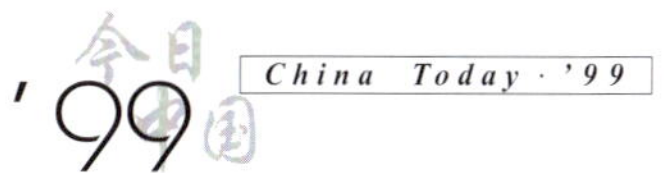

金不足的“瓶颈”问题。苏州新区经济发展集团总公司建有5000万元的风险投资资金，创业中心又与有关单位联合组建了“苏州高新技术投资担保公司”。此外，创业园努力加强银企交流，引入金融资本。优惠税收政策：苏州新区管委会制订了在所得税、增值税、营业税方面一系列优惠政策，鼓励科技型企业进驻。

I. Objective

As an implementation project of the development strategy of Suzhou New District (SND) to invigorate the district through science and technology, Suzhou New & High-Tech Innovation Service Center (also known as Suzhou International Business Incubator and China Suzhou Pioneering Park for Overseas Chinese Scholars) has developed with the financial investment wholly from SND Administrative Committee. It aims to create a favorable climate for technology innovation in which tenant enterprises could gain the benefit or access to international resources.

II. Progress Today

Suzhou New & High-tech Innovation Service Center (SISC) was set up in 1993. In October 1996, it was approved by the State Science & Technology Commission (SSTC) to be one of the first three pilot international business incubators in China. Based on SISC, six sponsors including SND Administrative Committee, Chinese Service Center for Scholarly Exchange, and the Torch Program Office jointly set up China Suzhou Pioneering Park for Overseas Chinese Scholars (CSPP).

SISC was approved by SSTC as a national innovation service center in November 1997. The Ministry of Science and Technology granted it the prize of "Outstanding Management of Innovation Service Center" in August 1998.

Up till now, SISC has developed incubation sites of 38,000 sq.m. Tenant enterprises have increased to 200 (including 40 enterprises run by overseas or returned Chinese scholars), among which 40 enterprises have graduated from SISC. The total sales income of the tenant enterprises amounted to 311 million yuan in 1998. These enterprises have developed 450 projects, some of which have been listed among national-level or provincial-level Torch projects, key problem-tackling projects and key generalization projects.

III. Excellent Hardware and Software Facilties

Tenant enterprises of SISC are accessible to facilities, including:

—intelligent building;

— well-equipped conference room;

— CAD center;

—lecture hall ;

— computer center;

— information center;

— intermediary agencies like Accountant Office, Law Firm, International Forwarding Agency, Customs Declaration Agency; and

— (on CSPP) dormitories, laundry, gym, and recreation room.

Tenant enterprises could also benefit from all-round services. In addition to incorporation service, SISC focuses on the following areas:

Support for Technology Development:

— rich reserve of technology and talent resources;

— close links among industries, universities and research institutes;

— following-up management in the process of industrialization; and

— trans-area, trans-field and trans-subject cooperation.

Talent Resource:

— fully-developed human resource market in SND;

— post-doctoral station;

— service station for returned Chinese scholars; and

— variety of training programs.

Information:

— access to INTRANET and INTERNET through communication connection in every 10 sq.m.

Technology Service and Consultation:

— guilds and specialists network .

Training:

— regular lectures and training programs on new technologies, legal knowledge, financial affairs, market exploitation and business management.

Project :

—assistance in applying for certificates of new & high-tech enterprises and products;

— introduction and recommendation of projects with cooperation perspective; and

— assistance in applying for financial support of different technology development programs.

Capital Investment :

— 50 million yuan venture capital investment of SND Economic Development Group Corporation;

— Suzhou New & High-Tech Investment Guarantor Corporation set up by SISC and its partners.

Preferential Policies :

— taxation incentives focusing on income tax, VAT, and business tax.

苏州新区全景
A Full View of Suzhou New District

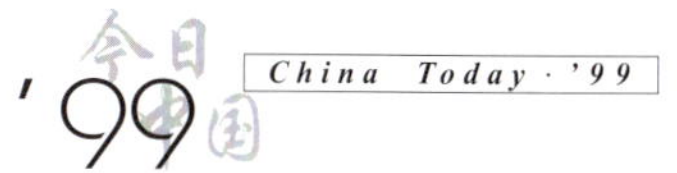

无 锡 新 区

Wuxi New District

无锡新区是在无锡国家高新区（启动于1992年11月，1993年5月经国务院批准正式授牌，规划面积5.45平方公里）和无锡新加坡工业园（1993年12月由无锡市开发区发展总公司和新加坡科技工业有限公司合资共同开发，规划面积为10平方公里）的基础上，于1995年3月经局部区划调整组建而成的，总面积约83平方公里，人口近10万。

无锡新区南濒太湖，沪宁高速公路、312国道、京沪铁路、京杭大运河穿境而过，距上海只有1个多小时的车程，到长江港口（江阴港、张家港）均只有40公里，具有得天独厚的区位优势。

6年多来，无锡新区累计投入资金20多亿元用于基础设施建设，形成了近6平方公里范围内较高质量“八通一平”的开发区域，一区一园的绿化、洁化、亮化、美化工程基本完成。为进区企业提供支撑服务的银行、保险、保税仓库、国际学校、国际医疗诊所、外商俱乐部等设施相继建成。与此同时，无锡新区强化对进区企业的服务，建立了“三个一”服务体系，即全面落实赋予新区管委会市级经济管理权限，由管委会“一个窗口”对外服务；由市、区23个职能部门进驻新区服务中心，为外商提供“一站式”服务；所有对园区企业的行政事业性收费，均由管委会规费征收管理所“一个头”收取，收费项目只有19项，杜绝了乱收费现象。投资环境的改善，使无锡新加坡工业园从1996年至今，连续三年被英国《企业测位》杂志评为亚太地区科技工业园投资环境综合评分第一名，并被国务院特区办定为直接联系点。无锡高新区也被评为中国投资环境优秀开发区50强，荣获1998年度全国火炬计划开发区优秀管理奖。

迄今为止，无锡新区已累计批准外商投资企业240多家，总投资22亿美元，实际到位外资11亿美元，投资额超过1000万美元的大项目达54个（其中超3000万美元的项目24个），列入全球500强的跨国公司已有22家共26个项目落户园区，包括美国柯达，日本夏普、日立、东芝、松下，德国西门子、拜耳，瑞典阿斯特拉，台湾统一集团等，形成了电子信息、精密机械、精细化工、生物医药和新型包装材料等五大高新技术支柱产业。1998年，实现工业总产值200亿元，国内生产总值40亿元，自营出口超过11.44亿美元，财政收入4.65亿元。

现在，为适应跨世纪发展的新形势，无锡新区不断完善“九五”发展规划，提出了建设一流的绿色城、生态城、高新技术产业城的战略构想和跨世纪奋斗目标，即不仅要把无锡新区建成拥有国际先进水平的、国内一流的高科技工业城，更要建设成拥有蓝天碧水的绿色城、生态城，率先基本实现现代化。目前，一座基础设施完善、配套功能齐全、中外客商青睐、高新技术企业云集的现代化高科技工业城，正在无锡市东南郊碧水蓝天之间、绿色生态镶嵌的优美环境中崛起。到2000年，无锡新区将建成城市化框架面积10平方公里，人口12-15万；实现工业总产值450亿元，其中高新技术产业产值占80%以上，国内生产总值80亿元，出口创汇20亿美元，财政收入8亿元。

无锡新区将以崭新的姿态迈入 21 世纪。

In November 1992, Wuxi High-Tech Industrial Development Zone (with a planning area of 5.45 km^2) was set up and was approved by the State Council in May 1993. Meanwhile, Wuxi Singapore Industrial Park (with a planning area of 10 km^2) was jointly established by Wuxi Development Zone Economic Development Company and Singapore Technologies Company in October 1993. Based on these two development zones, Wuxi New District was founded with a total area of 83 km^2 and a population of 100,000 in March 1995.

Wuxi New District enjoys a unique transport network. With Lake Taihu to its south, Wuxi city has Shanghai-Nanjing Expressway, No. 312 State Highway, Beijing-Shanghai Railway and the Grand Canal crossing it. It only takes more than one hour riding from the city to Shanghai and there are merely 40 km from the city to Jiangyin Harbor and Zhang Jiagang Harbor, along the Yangtze River.

In the past six years, a total of 2 billion yuan have been invested in infrastructure facilities and biult a 6 km^2 ideal area with leveled land, roads, sufficient water supply, power supply, gas supply, steam supply, telecommunication, drainage and sewage. Excellent greenery, lighting and cleaning have been realized here. Those supporting services of banks, insurance, bonded warehouse, international school, international clinic, foreign investors' club and so on have been established. At the same time, the "three first" service system has been completed. A unique authoritative "one-window-service" representing the New District Administrative Commission is open to the outside for service; "one-stop-service" promotes the settlement of problems encountered in the enterprise operation. Officials from 23 related bureaus of the city are appointed to work together in this stop in order to save time for investors; "one-place-charging" is in charge of all fee collection in the New District. It is responsible for the fee checking and collection so as to get rid of illegal and unreasonable fees charging. Now, according to the state law, there are only 19 items of fees are charged. The improvement of investment climate, Wuxi-Singapore Industrial Park has been voted as the most excellent industrial park in Asia-Pacific region by British magazine *Corporation Locatio* consecutively for three years. Last year, Wuxi National High-Tech Industrial Development Zone was evaluated among the 50 top development zones with the best environment in China and was granted the "Excellent Administrative Prize of China's Development Zone in Torch Plan".

Up to now, with a total investment of US$ 2.2 billion and actually utilized foreign capital of US$ 1.1 billion, there have been 240 foreign-invested enterprises settled down in Wuxi New District, among which 54 projects were invested with US$10 million (24 ones over US$30 million) and 26 projects were invested by 22 trans-nation copanies listed in *Fortune 500*, such as Kodak, Sharp, Hitachi, Toshiba, National, Siemens, Bayer, Astra and Tongyi, etc. Five main pillar industries of electronic information, precision machinery, fine chemical, bio-medicine and new packing materials have been formed in WND. In 1998, total industrial output value of 20 billion yuan, GDP of 4 billion yuan, self-export volume of US$1.144 million and fiscal income of 465 million yuan were realized.

According to the development trend of the new century, Wuxi New District has announced its great target to set up a modern green, ecological and high-tech industrial city. It means that, the New District will be an industrial city with international high technology, blue sky and clean water. Now the promising industrial city is erecting in the south-east suburb of Wuxi City. By the end of 2000, there will be an area of 10 km^2 with a population of 120,000-150,000.

Total industrial output value will reach 4.5 billion yuan, GDP 8 billion yuan and export volume US$2 billion and fiscal revenue 800 million yuan in Wuxi New District.

Wuxi New District is striding to the 21st century.

无锡新区管理委员会办公大楼
The building of the Wuxi New District Administration Commission

常州新区

Changzhou New District

在常州国家级高新技术产业开发区基础上发展起来的常州新区，经过6年来的开发建设，一个以机械制造、电子信息、生物医药、化工产业等四大高新技术产业为主体的高新技术企业群已在此崛起。著名的有意大利雷迪斯集团投资7500万美元的工程塑料项目、美国华生制药（亚洲）有限公司投资的医药制剂项目、日本小松制作所投资的装载机项目等，都已相继在新区内投产。目前区内已云集了200多家外商企业，其中总投资1000万美元以上的项目已达40个。

常州新区得以迅速崛起，有多方面的因素。在区位和交通条件上，常州新区就有着得天独厚的优势。常州新区的前身是1992年经国务院批准成立的国家级常州高新技术产业开发区，现在辖区扩大到5个乡镇和1个街道，总面积约116平方公里。常州新区南接铁路沪宁线，北濒长江边，沪宁高速公路、312国道、101省道穿区而过。常州民航机场又近在咫尺，形成了铁路、公路、航空、水运齐全的立体交通优势，这在苏南各个开发区是仅有的，在全国也是少有的。沪宁高速公路在新区设有大型出入口，从新区到南京仅需60分钟，到上海仅需90分钟。新区的江边工业区已经启动，长江常州港第一个万吨级通用码头已建成，并已开通了国际远洋运输。距新区仅20公里

常州新区一角
A Corner of the Changzhou New District

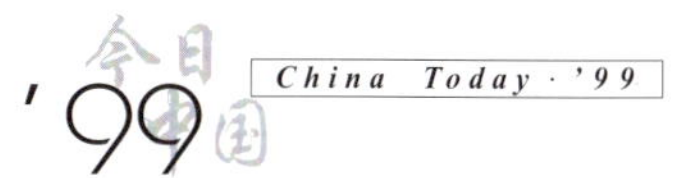

的常州民航机场，已开通国内37条航线，可到达北京、广州、深圳、厦门、大连、武汉、天津等20多个大中城市。

常州新区的基础设施也已配套完善，已累计投资27亿元，完成了15平方公里的基础设施开发，其中新建道路80公里，实现了20平方公里道路大环通。新建了11万伏变电所、日供5万吨的自来水厂、2万门程控电话交换局、5.3万千瓦的调峰电厂和5万吨级污水处理厂，建造了供热供气的热电工程，从而在高新区实现了通路、通电、通水、通气、通讯、供热、排污、场地平整“七通一平”。

常州新区尤为注重软环境建设，新区管委会按照国际惯例建立精简、高效的管理体制，海关、商检、工商、环保等行政机构都集中在一幢楼办公，提供一条龙服务，一个窗口收费，涉及外企的行政事业性收费由原来的36种压缩到8种，竭力使投资者获得最大的投资回报。

随着常州行政中心北移，一批服务中介机构以及文化、教育、卫生、体育、旅游设施等都将进入辖区，有效地加快新区功能性开发，使新区成为常州市政治、经济、科技、文化中心。

展望新世纪，常州新区必将建设成为科教发达、经济繁荣、环境优美的可持续发展的现代化新城区，成为长江三角洲上的一颗耀眼的明珠。

Changzhou New District, developed from the Changzhou New and High-Tech Industrial Development Zone, has formed a new and high-tech industrial base on four pillar industries of machinery, electronics & information, biological pharmaceuticals and chemical industry within the past six years of development. By now, a number of world famous companies have settled in the New District. For instance, the plastics project with the imvestment of US$ 75 million from Radici Group from Italy, the medical preparation project by Watson (Asia) Pharmaceuticals Co. Ltd. from the USA, and the loading machines project by Komatus from Japan have already been put into operation one by one. Totally there are more than 200 foreign enterprises in the district, among which there are 40 projects each with an investment of over US$ 10 million each.

The rapid development of the Changzhou New District is due to a series of advantages. First, it has an advantage in its location and convenient transportation network. Developing from the state-level high-tech industrial zone approved by the State Council in 1992, Changzhou New District has expanded to five towns and one neighbourhood under its jurisdiction with a total area of 116 square kilometres. The New District boasts an easy access to railways, highways, airlines and water routes. In the south of the district is the Shanghai-Nanjing Railway and in the north is the Yangtze River. The Shanghai-Nanjing Expressway, No.312 State Highway and No.101 Provincial Highway run across the New District. Changzhou Airport is only 20 km away from the district. Such a convenient transportation network is unique both in South Jiangsu Province and in the country.

The entrance and exit of the Shanghai-Nanjing Expressway in Changzhou is right in the New District. It is just 60 minutes' drive from Changzhou New District to Nanjing, and 90 minutes to Shanghai. A Port Industrial Zone is initiated nearby the Yangtze River. The first 10,000-ton dock has been accomplished in the Changzhou Port and the ocean-going shipping routes have been put into use. The Changzhou Civil Airport is only 20 km from the New District and by now there have been 37 airlines connecting Changzhou City with over 20 large and medium-sized cities such as Beijing, Guangzhou, Shenzhen, Xiamen, Dalian, Wuhan, Tianjing and so on.

The completed and perfected infrastructure of Changzhou New District is another advantage. More than 2.7 billion yuan has been accumulated for the development of the infrastructure in a 15-sq km area. There are 80 km of new roads forming a ring road covering 20 sq km. The new district has buit a 110,000-volt transformer station, a water plant with a capacity of 50,000 tons/day, a telecommunication switch bureau with a capacity of 20,000 program-controlled lines, a peaking power plant of 53,000 kw, a waste water treatment plant with a capacity of 50,000 tons/day, and a thermal power plant to provide heat and steam. In a word, the New District has completed the constrution of infrastructure facilities including roads, power and water supply, gas and steam supply, telecommunication, sewage treatment and land leveling.

Changzhou New District has always attached great attention to the construction of the software of the investment climate. According to the international practice, the New District Administrative Committee has set up a high efficient administration system. All relevant administrative departments, such as the Customs, Commodity Inspection Bureau, Industry & Commerce Bureau, and Environment Protection Bureau, provide package services within one building. In order to guarantee investors to have the highest profit return rate, the New District has reduced the administrative fees from 36 to 8 items.

With the moving of its adminstrative center of Changzhou to north, a great number of service organizations and some public facilities of culture, education, sanitation, sports and tourism will be moved into the New District to enhance its functional development. Undoubtedly, the New District will be developed into a new political, economical, scientific and cultural center of Changzhou City.

Looking ahead the 21st century, Changzhou New District will become a modernized and sustainable development city proper area with advanced science and education, prosperous economy and beautiful environment. The New District has become a pearl shining in the Yangtze River Delta.

常州新区科技创业服务中心
The Science and Technology Incubation Base of the Changzhou New District

淄博高新技术产业开发区

Zibo New & High-Tech Industrial Development Zone

淄博开发区辖区面积77.2平方公里，其中国家级高新区批准规划面积7.04平方公里，自1992年被批准为国家级高新技术产业开发区以来，淄博高新区产业规模迅速扩大，经济运行质量不断提高，呈现出良好的发展势头。截至目前，累计完成基建总投资51亿元，其中基础设施建设投资26亿元。建筑开工面积138.3万平方米，竣工面积112.5万平方米。各类进区企业1100余家，其中三资企业123家，高新技术企业35家。开发高新技术产品52项。累计合同利用外资3.2亿美元。形成了柳泉路科技街、北部科工贸综合区和东部医药化工区"一街两区"的格局。1998年，淄博高新区实现国内生产总值21亿元，技工贸总收入47.4亿元，工业总产值46.5亿元，各项经济指标均比1992年翻了几番。

淄博高新区拥有便利的交通条件，距离济南国际机场60公里，济青高速公路、胶济铁路、淄东铁路、205、309国道在区内交汇。同时，区内具备了完善的基础设施。交通网络发达。起步区"七通一平"全部实现。通信、信息、污水处理、保税仓库、集装箱中转站、标准厂房等设施配套齐全。经过几年的发展，淄博高新区已经成为一座环境优美、设施齐全的现代化新型城区，为区内经济和一流质量的提高奠定了良好的基础。

淄博高新区投资软环境建设取得了长足进展，逐步形成了一套灵活高效的管理体制和运行机制。高新区管委会突出以开发建设为中心，以为企业服务为宗旨，以精简、统一、高效为特色，对区内经济的高效运转和企业的快速发展起到了有力的推动作用。在政策建设方面，相继制定了一系列旨在鼓励投资、推动科技创新和产业化的优惠政策。民营科技工业园的创办、高新技术产业发展基金的建立、高新技术成果奖励办法的出台、"无费区"试点的推行，进一步增强了高新区的吸引力、凝聚力。在功能配套方面，创业中心孵化面积不断扩大，孵化功能不断提高；商品、生产资料等市场体系逐渐健全，金融、审计、会计、律师等中介组织体系初步形成。在强化服务方面，逐步向国际惯例靠拢，简化办事程序，加强与外部协调，减轻企业负荷，为企业创造了宽松的外部环境。

几年来，淄博高新区已经初步形成了以医药化工、新型材料、电子信息三大产业为主导的高新技术产业群体，按照产业发展的总体规划，淄博高新区将在"一街两区"布局的基础上，形成中心区、科工贸综合区、医药化工区、加工贸易区、商住区、游乐区6个功能区。并围绕三大主导产业重点培植新药物、精细化工、合成纤维、新型建材、医疗器械、光电材料、信息产品及开发、包装材料、高技术加工、加工出口10大产品基地，为区域经济的腾飞做出更大贡献。

The total area of Zibo development zone is 77.2 square kilometers, of which, the planned area of state-level new-and-high-tech industrial development zone is 7.04 square kilometers. Forming the pattern of "One street, Two zones", namely Eastern Medical and Chemical Industrial Zone, the Northern Industrial & Trade Comprehensive Zone and Scientific & Technological Street on Liuquan road. By the end of 1992, Zibo new-and-high-tech industrial development zone was approved by the State Council to be a state-level development zone. Its industrial scale has expanded rapidly, economic operation quality increased continuously, which present a good developing tendency. Till now, It has invested 5.1 billion yuan, of which investment for infrastructure is 2.6 billion yuan. There are 1.383 million square meters of buildings are under construction and 1.125 million square meters of which has finished. There are more than 1,100 enterprises in the zone, of which 123 are foreign-invested enterprises, 35 are high- and new-tech enterprises with 52 high-tech products and the total contractural foreign investment reached US$320 million. In 1998, the development zone's gross domestic product was 2.1 billion yuan, the total income of technology, industry and trade was 4.74 billion yuan and the total industrial output value was 4.65 billion yuan.

Zibo new- and high-tech industrial development zone has convenient transportation conditions. It is 60 kilometers away from Jinan International Airport, while Jinan-Qingdao Expressway, Jiaodong-Jinan Railway, Zibo-donga Railway, No.205 Highway, No.309 State Highway cross each other in the zone. At the same time, the zone's infrastructure with its full functions has been constructed, including water, electricity, steam, heat, road, telecommunication, sewage treatment systems and leveled land. Bonded storehouse, international container transfers station and standard factory building, etc. have completely sets of facilities. Through several years development and construction, Zibo new- and high-tech development zone has become a new-type modernized city with excellent environment, complete sets of equipment and laid a good foundation for the increase of economic and life quality of the zone.

Zibo new-and-high-tech development zone has made a good progress in the soft environment construction. Forming sets of flexible & high efficient management system and operation system. In the aspect of policy construction, it has drawn up a series of preferential policy in succession aimed for encouraging investment, promoting science and technology innovation and industrialization. The foundation of private science & technology industrial park, the establishment of new- and high-tech industrial development fund, the enactment of new & high-tech achievement awarding measures and the practice of free of charge have further strengthened the attraction and cohesion of the zone. In the aspect of supporting function, the incubation area of pioneering service center has expanded constantly, the incubation function increased continuously. Marketing system as commodity and means of production, etc., has strengthened gradually. The intermediary organization systems such as finance, audit, accounting, lawyer, etc., have formed in first step. In the aspect of service, the administrative committee of Zibo new- and high-tech development zone has concentrated on development and construction, narrowed gaps with international market, simplified work procedure, enhanced coordination with outside, lightened the burden of enterprises, and created better environment for them.

Over the past six years, Zibo development zone has been formed a new- and high-tech industrial group with three key industries: medical & chemical industry, new materials and electronics & information. According to the overall plan of industrial development, Zibo development zone will form six function areas of central area, science, technology & trade comprehensive area, medicine & chemical industry area, trade processing area, business & housing comprehensive area and entertainment area. Based on three key industries ten prodution bases will be developed of new medicine, fine chemical industry, synthetic fiber, new type building ma-

terial, medical equipment, photoelectric material, information products & development, packing material, high technology process and process export. This will make a great contribution to the rapid development of local economy.

淄博高新技术产业开发区科技一条街
A Science and Technoloty Street of the Zibo New & High-Tech Industrial Development Zone

昆明国家高新技术产业开发区

Kunming New- & High-Tech Industrial Development Zone

昆明国家高新技术产业开发区（简称"昆明高新区"）是1992年经国务院批准建立的全国53家国家级高新技术产业开发区之一，总规划面积11.5平方公里，由新区、金鼎科技园和云南民办科技园等部分组成。

昆明作为云南省政治、经济、文化中心和交通、通信的枢纽，发展高新技术产业有着良好的投资环境和广阔的发展前景。昆明高新区具有良好的区位优势，地处昆明市的西区，在国家及省、市领导的关怀指导下，充分发挥中心城市的技术优势、人才优势、资源优势、信息优势，以"发展高科技、实现产业化"为目标，为带动和促进地方社会经济的可持续发展作出了贡献。

昆明高新区作为发展高新技术产业的基地，是以大开放促进大发展的示范区，探索知识经济的先行者，促进云南产业升级的技术辐射源，昆明市和云南省重要的新的经济增长点和经济、科技、行政管理体制改革创新的试验区，对推动高新技术产业化发展起着示范、辐射和带动作用。作为昆明市政府的派出机构，昆明高新区管委会本着面向市场经济、衔接国际规范的原则，在政府机构设置、职能转变和运行机制等方面进行了

昆明国家高新技术产业开发区管理委员会大楼
The Building of the Kunming High & New Technology Industrial Development Zone Administrative Commission

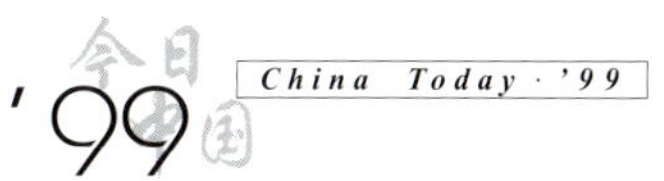

大胆创新和实践。按照“小机构、大服务”的管理模式，实现了“一幢楼办公、一个窗口对外、一条龙服务、一个图章管到底”，为发展高新技术产业创造良好的投资环境。

经过几年的开发建设，昆明高新区目前已拥有进区企业400家，其中经国家和省、市认定的高新技术企业150家，外资企业46家，投资和正在试制阶段的项目有国家火炬计划项目16项、“18生物工程”11项。昆明高新区已初步形成以生物工程及生物医药工程、光机电一体化工程、电子信息技术、新材料技术等高新技术领域为主的新兴产业；已在区内实施的有“小儿麻痹疫苗”、“甲肝疫苗”、“云大20植物生长调节剂”、“数字用户环路通信系统”、“辐照电缆”等一批市场前景好、技术含量高的高新技术项目。一座集多学科技术于一体的现代化科技新城已见雏形。

昆明高新区将努力把自己建设成为全省、全市改革开放的试验区、示范区；新的经济增长点、高新技术产业基地、现代科技新城区。以崭新的风貌，为科技兴滇，为迎接知识经济的挑战，做出应有的贡献。

Kunming State High and New Technology Industrial Development Zone (abbreviation: Kunming High & New Tech Zone) is one of 53 State Council granted high technology industrial development zones in 1992. It covers 11.5 sq.km in total as planned, consisting of New District, Jinding Science & Technology Garden, and Yunnan Nongovernmental Science & Technology Garden and so on.

As a center of politics, economics and culture, as well as the intersection of transportation and communication, Kunming proves to be an excellent place for investment and command a bright future in high and new technological industrial development. Kunming High & New Tech, Zone has a good location in the western area of the city. Under the close guidance of leaders from all levels, national, provincial and municipal, it has taken its full advantages in techniques, human resources, material resources, and information. Guided by "highly scientific and technological development and their industrialization", Kunming High Tech Zone has made great contributions to the regional social and economic sustainable development.

As the base to develop high and new technology industry, Kunming High Technology Zone will serve as a model for wide opening and rapid development, and as a pioneer in exploring knowledge economy, to promote Yunnan industry and upgrade technological dissemination. It will also serve as a new economic increase point and new experimental zone for economics, science and technology, administration and management system reform so as to play a leading role in modeling, disseminating and guiding others to promote high new technological industry development. As an outreach organization from Kunming Municipal Government, the administration committee of Kunming High & New Technology Zone, following the principles of the market economy and consistency with international rules, has taken bold measures in originality and practice in building government structure, functionary transformation and operational mechanism and so on. Based on the administrative principle of "small organization and large service", a model of "one office building, one window for outsiders, a series of services and one seal stamp administers all" has been realized. In this way, an excellent investment environment has been created for new and high technology industry development.

After these years' development and construction, up to now Kunming High and New Technology Zone has had 400 enterprises, among which 150 are accredited by the state, the province and the municipality. Forty-six are foreign ventures and 16 projects are under the State Torch Program which are invested in their experimental phase. There are 11 "Eighteen Bio-engineering" projects. Kunming High and New Technology Zone has now initially formed a new industry based on bio-engineering and bio-medical engineering, fiber-machinery-electronic synthesizing engineering, electronic information technology, new material technology and so on. Some projects being implemented in the region are poliomyelitis vaccine, Hepatitis A vaccine, Yunda-20 plant growth conditioner, digital circuit communication system for consumers and irradiation cable. All of these projects have a good future with high technological components. A new modern science and technology city in which many fields of studies are integrated is taking shape.

Under the guidance of the 15th Plenary Session of the Communist Party of China, we will do our best to turn the zone into an experimental model, open to the whole city and the whole province. It will become a new city for new economic increase, a base for high and new technology industry, and a new area for modern science and technology. With a brand new face, we are making our necessary contributions to develop Yunnan with knowledge of science and technology and to welcome challenges from knowledge economy.

贵阳高新技术产业开发区

Guiyang New & High-Tech Industrial Development District

贵阳高新技术产业开发区(简称贵阳高新区)是1992年经国务院批准设立的国家新技术产业开发区，也是贵州省唯一的国家级开发区。

贵阳是贵州省政治、经济、文化中心，气候宜人，全年平均气温16℃-22℃，年降水800毫米，冬无严寒、夏无酷暑，有“第二春城”之美誉。境内有储量丰富的煤、磷、铝等矿产和有“中国田纳西”之称的水力、磷化工、磨料磨具、机械制造、仪器仪表等支柱产业。在全区职工人数中，中级技术职称占9.5%，高级技术职称占3.5%，可为投资者进区办企业提供素质较高的各类技术人才。

贵阳高新技术产业开发区地处贵阳市东北面，距市中心区仅6.5公里，距龙洞堡国际机场25公里，距火车站12公里，规划面积11.32平方公里，可供开发面积5.3平方公里。

贵阳高新区从建立以来，投入基础设施建设资金近20亿元，完成道路、电力开闭所、自来水厂、给排水管网工程、煤气管网工程、标准厂房、行政大楼、通信等基础配套设施。建成全省唯一的高新技术企业“孵化器”和支撑服务体系。

贵阳高新区以高技术成果的商品化、产业化、国际化为宗旨，以军工企业为依托，积极扶持民办科技企业的发展，逐步形成了汽车零部件、表面贴装技术（片式电子元器件及贴装设备)、液压技术、新材料、制药、精密光学仪器为支撑的产业格局，为企业按照社会化大生产的要求，实现企业间的协作、配套提供了有力保障，截止1998年10月，进入高新区企业超过410家，其中，高新技术企业94家。

贵阳高新区在享有国务院批准的国家级开发区各项优惠政策的基础上，又配套采取了一系列的优惠措施，采取多种形式，吸引投资者进入高新区。工商、税务、土地等部门已在高新区建立分局；会计事务、审计事务、律师事务等中介机构也建立办事机构，为进区企业提供全方位服务。

根据国家产业政策，结合贵阳新技术产业开发区支柱产业现状，鼓励投资者在基础设施、汽车零部件、电子元器件、新材料及光、机一体化等领域进行投资。

贵阳高新技术产业开发区完备无缺的基础设施、优势明显的支柱产业、高素质但价格低廉的劳动力资源、优惠的政策以及全方位的支撑服务体系，必将是投资者的“乐园”。

Guiyang New & High-Tech Industrial Development District (abbreviation Guiyang New and High-tech District) is a new national industrial and technical development district which was approved by the State Council. It is also the sole state-level development district in Guizhou Province.

Guiyang is the center of politics, economy, culture in

Guizhou.The city enjoys agreeable climate, the annual average temperature being 16℃ –22℃, the annual average precipitation being 800 mm. Winter is not severely cold while summer is not sweltering hot. It has enjoyed a reputation of "the Second Spring City". It boasts abundant resources, such as coal, phosphorus, aluminum, and it has a reputation of "Chinese Tennessee" for the hydro electricity. The city has established a set of basic industry, such as aluminum production, phosphorus chemical industry, grinding materials and tools, mechanical production, instruments and meters. The intermediate professional personnel make up 9.5% of the district's total staff members; the senior professional persnonnel make up 3.5%. We can supply different kinds of qualified technical personnel for enterprises in the district.

Guiyang New and High-Tech Industrial Development District is situated in northeast of Guiyang city. The district is only 6.5 km from the city proper, 25 km from Longdongbao International Airport and 12 km from the railway station. The district covers 11.32 sq km, 5.3 sq km of which can be developed.

Since its founding, Guiyang New and High-Tech District has input 2 billion yuan for infrastructure construction. It has finished many infrastructure facilitities such as roads, power substitutions, water works, water-supply and drainage projects, coal-gas project, standard workshops, administration buildings, and communication.

It has established an "incubation center" for development of new and high technology enterprises.

Guiyang New and High-Tech District has the aim of commercialization, industrialization, internationalization of high technical products. Based on military enterprises, we support to develop non-state owned high-tech enterprises. We have gradually established an industrial network focusing on automobile accessories, surface sticking technology (electronic parts and sticking instrument), liquid pressure technology, new materials, pharmacy, precise optics. We advocate cooperation among all enterprises. There were more than 410 enterprises in the district by the end of October 1998, of which, 94 were high-tech enterprises.

The district has not only provided preferential policies as other national development zones do but also adopted a set of special preferential treatment to attract investors. Package service is offered by industry and commerce, tax and land departments in the district. Medium-sized organizations dealing with accountant affairs, audit affairs, lawyer affairs have been also set up in the district.

According to state industrialization policies, and proceeding from present situation of Guiyang, the district encourages investment in infrastructure facilities construction, automobile accessories, electronic parts, new materials and optics-machines.

Guiyang New and High-Tech Industrial Development District is an ideal place for investment as the district has good infrastructure facilities, advantageous basic industry, cheap laborer resources, preferential policies, and perfect services.

贵阳高新区
Guiyang New & High-Tech District

南昌高新技术产业开发区

Nanchang High-Tech Industrial Development Zone

南昌高新技术产业开发区创建于1991年，1992年11月被国务院批准为国家级高新开发区。高新区座落南昌市城东高教科研密集区，距市中心3公里，交通便捷，风景秀丽，地势平坦，投资环境优良。高新区总面积为19.5平方公里，其中集中新建区6.8平方公里。产业区已实现道路、供水、排水、电力及通信“五通一平”，区内公建配套设施齐全，建有工业标准厂房、电信分局、变电站及科技人员公寓和设施优良的学校，是功能齐全的现代化新城区。

高新区管委会是市政府派出机构，行使项目审批、土地征用、规划建设、人事劳资、办理出国审批手续等市级管理权限，对高新区实行统一领导、统一管理，高新区建立了精干高效的管理机构和完善的社会支撑服务体系，实行“一站式”公开服务，七个工作日内可为企业落户办完所有手续。产业开发方面，拥有进区企业355家，其中高新技术企业163家，外资企业62家。截止1998年底，高新区研制开发各类高新技术项目200余项，组织实施35项国家和省级火炬项目及重点新产品试制项目，先后有30多项产品在国际、国内获奖。全区技工贸总收入由1991年初创时的3000万元增长到1998年的38.2亿元，出口创汇由50万美元增长到1078万美元。在进区企业中，产值上千万元的有27家，其中上亿元的7家。江西省规模最大、水平最高的微电子信息技术企业，最大的民营科技企业，注入现资最多、技术最先进的新型金属建材企业，外商投资规模最大的企业均集中高新区，并逐步形成了电子信息、机电一体化、生物工程及现代化工、新材料、现代农业及食品工业五大支柱产业的分布格局。

高新区环境优美、设施完善、政策优惠、服务高效，已成为中外企业家竞相投资的首选之区。

Nanchang High-Tech Industrial Development Zone was founded in 1991, and approved by the State Council as a national new & high-tech industry development zone in November 1992. It is situated in the concentrated higher education and scientific research area in east part of the city. Here the investment environment is good since it is only three km away from downtown, with convenient transportation facilities, flat land and beautiful scenery. The zone covers an area of about 19.5 sq km, including the area of about 6.8 sq km^2 for concentrated development. In the industrial starting district of the zone, the infrastructure facilities such as roads, water and power supply, and drainage systems and telecommunication have been completed. Here, the public installations including the standard factory buildings, telecommunication bureaus, transformer substations, spacious apartment buildings and well-equipped schools have been accomplished. So it is a modern new urban area with comprehensive services.

The administrative committee of the zone is an agency of the Nanchang Municipal Government, which has the centralized and unitary administrative power over the zone. It enjoys the municipality-level administrative power such as examining and approving applications for projects, land requisition, planning and approving the construction, personnel and labor matters, and examining and approving the foreign affairs. By now, the administrative departments and supporting service system have been established which provide open, efficient and high quality services for enterprises. All the procedures and formalities for enterprises entering the zone can be finished in seven days.

At present, there are 355 enterprises in the zone, including 163 new & high-tech enterprises and 62 foreign invested enterprises. By the end of 1998, more than 200 new & high-tech projects had been developed, including 35 projects listed as national or provincial Torch Program ones, and 30 projects awarded international or national prizes. In the year of 1998, the total income of technology, industry and trade reached 3.82 billion yuan foreign exchange earnings US$10.78 million in1998, against 30 million yuan and US$ 0.5 million in 1991 respectively. In the zone, 27 enterprises's output value has reached 10 million yuan, of which , 7 enterprises's output value has reached 100 million yuan. The biggest and the most advanced micro-electronic information venture, the largest foreign invested enterprise and the largest private enterprise, the most advanced metal enterprise with the largest investment of the province are all in the zone. Now, the zone is gradually forming an industrial structure of mainly depending on the industries of electronic information industry, integration of mechanics and electronics industry, genetic engineering & modern chemical industry, new material industry and modern agriculture & food engineering industry.

The beautiful environment, complete infrastructure facilities, preferential policies for investment, and the high-quality services of the zone has made it the first choice for investors from home and abroad.

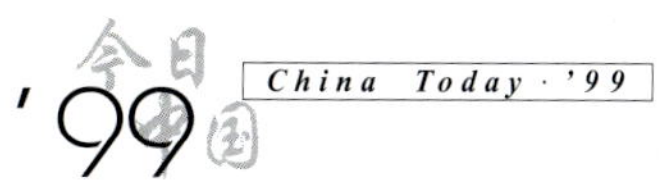

南宁高新技术产业开发区

Nanning New & High-Tech Industrial Development Zone

南宁高新技术产业开发区（简称南宁高新区）是1992年经国务院批准设立的国家高新技术产业开发区，她位于智力密集的南宁市西部，规划面积18平方公里，其中新建区8.5平方公里，功能规划为“一园四区”即：科技工业园、中心区、农业生物工程示范区、保税仓储区、相思湖别墅区。

基础设施配套齐全。高新区累计完成基础设施投资15亿元，现已有一批建成的写字楼、标准厂房和住宅楼投入使用，交通、通信方便，供排水、供电、供气等基础设施齐全。

管理体制精简高效。高新区管委会是南宁市人民政府的派出机构，在高新区范围内行使市一级规划、土地、建设、工商、税务、财政、劳动人事、项目审批、外事审批等经济管理权限和部分行政管理权限。此外，高新区还设有一系列社会化服务机构，可为入区企业提供一条龙全方位服务。1995年8月，自治区人大常委会审议通过的《南宁高新技术产业开发区管理条例》，为高新区的建设和管理提供了法律保障。

产业发展初具规模。至1998年底，高新区累计开发新产品170多项，实施国家级火炬计划项目14项，高新区企业已达510多家，初步形成了以生物工程及制药、电子信息、新材料、机电一体化等为主导的高新技术产业体系。

南宁高新区真诚地希望国内外各界朋友到此大展宏图。作为回报，她将致力提供优质高效的服务和实行优惠让利的政策。

Nanning New & High-Tech Industrial Development Zone (NNHIDZ), a national new & high-tech industrial development zone approved by the State Council in 1992, is situated in the intellect-intensive area in west Nanning. The High-Tech Zone possesses a planning area of 18 square km, functioning as "one park and four districts", which including the Science and Technology Park, Central District, Agricultural Bio-engineering Demonstration District, Bonded District, Xiangsi Lake Villas District.

Infrastructures facilities are perfect. The zone has put aside 1.5 billion yuan into the construction of infrastructure facilities, and has brought numbers of office buildings, standard workshops and dwelling buildings into use. Transportation and communication facilities are convenient and supply of water, power and LPG are complete.

Administrative system is efficient and pithy. Under the direct leadership of Nanning People's Government, the Administrative Committee of Nanning New & High-Tech Industrial Development Zone exercises municipality-level economic and administrative authorities in planning, land administration, construction, industrial and commercial administration, taxation, personnel, project examination and foreign affairs examination. Moreover, NNHIDZ provides an overall and perfect services through her social service network.

The Rules of Administration for Nanning New & High-Tech Industrial Development Zone, which is adopted by the Standing Committee of Guangxi People's Congress in August 1995, is a guarantee for the construction and management of the zone.

Industries are beginning to take shape. By 1998, NNHIDZ had developed over 170 new products and 14 projects of national Torch Program. Presently, there are 510 enterprises in the zone, which have formed a new & high-tech industrial system headed by bio-engineering and pharmacy, electronic information, new materials, machinery and electronics integration, etc.

We heartily welcome friends of various circles at home and abroad to invest in Nanning High-Tech Zone. We'll devote ourselves to providing a satisfactory service and preferential policies.

南宁高新区中心区一角
A Corner of the NNHIDZ

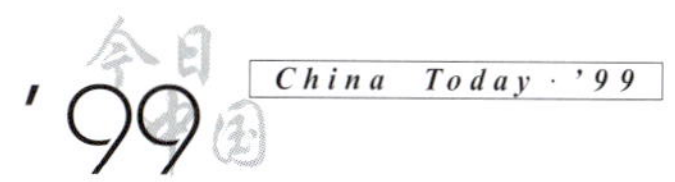

乌鲁木齐高新技术产业开发区

Urumqi High-Tech Industrial Development Zone

乌鲁木齐高新技术产业开发区成立于1992年8月25日，同年11月9日被国务院批准为国家高新技术产业开发区。这是新疆第一家，也是目前新疆唯一的一家国家级高新技术产业开发区。

乌鲁木齐高新技术产业开发区位于乌鲁木齐建成区内，总体规划面积9.8平方公里，首期开发2.4平方公里。这里，铁路、民航近在咫尺，交通、通信等十分便捷。临近地域智力密集，大中型企业遍布，周边地区城市基础设施条件较好，是建设高科技工业园区的理想场所。

建区6年来，高新区在首期开发的2.4平方公里土地上，已基本建成了“三区两街”，即“钻石城第一招商区”、“产业区”、“卫星广场第二招商区”和“贵州路科技一条街”、“钻石城科技一条街”。累计投入基础设施建设资金2.8亿元，完成基建项目投资6.4亿元。基本完成了1.6平方公里的“七通一平”。总开工面积已达64.91万平方米，竣工面积36.9万平方米，区内新修道路10.9万平方米，绿化面积6万平方米。硬环境建设日趋完善，为投资者提供了水、电、热、交通、通信、邮电、商住、办公等诸方面的基本保障。建成区内，楼房林立，绿树成行，道路开阔纵横，具有现代化风貌。高新区还不断优化软环境，先后出台了税收返还等一系列颇具吸引力的优惠政策，为投资者提供“一站式”高效服务，对进区的高新技术项目，采用“特事特办”的原则，不断完善支撑服务体系，为企业提供全方位服务等。优良的投资环境吸引了一批批有识之士来此发展置业。截止1998年底，高新技术企业143家，三资企业45家。累计实施高新技术项目300项，已实现商品化的134项，其中，列入国家和省级“火炬计划”项目43项。累计实现技工贸总收入48.76亿元，年平均递增46.4%；累计完成工业产值11.09亿元，年平均递增55.9%；累计实现税收2.45亿元；年平均递增62.7%；累计实现进出口额6893万美元，年平均递增106.5%。

乌鲁木齐高新技术产业开发区以其快速的发展势头和强有力的后劲，已成为乌鲁木齐乃至新疆重要的经济增长点。

Urumqi High-Tech Industrial Development Zone was set up on August 25, 1992, and in the same year on November 9, it was approved by the State Council, and granted as a state ranking high & new technological and industrial zone.

Urumqi High-Tech Industrial Development Zone is located in Urumqi City. The total programmed area is 9.8 square kilometers and the first-phase construction area covers 2.4 square kilometers. With the railway and the airport nearby, the transportation and communication are very convenient. With condensed intelligence of more then 20 universities and institutes and medium-sized industries around it, and the favourable basic construction conditions, the zone is an ideal location for building up the high-tech industrial garden. During the 6-year development, the first opening up area has been 2.4 square kilometers, three districts and two streets have been completed, i.e, the first merchandise enlist district of "Diamond City", "Industrial District", the 2nd merchandise enlist district of the satellite square, Guizhou Road Science and Technology Street, and the Diamond City Science and Technology Streeet. A total of 280 million yuan and 640 million yuan have been put aside for the construction of infrastructure facilities and projects respectively. The area of 1.6 square kilometers' basic construction has nearly been finished. The total construction area is 649.1 square meters, of which construction of 369,000 square meters has been completed.

Within the zone, 109,000 square meters of roads have been built, and 60,000 square meters of area have been afforested. The hard environment of construction is getting perfect which ensures the investors of water supply, electricity, heating, transportation, communication, postal service, accommodation, and office service, etc., demonstrating a new look of modernization. On the other hand, for the improvement of soft environment, early or later, a series of attractive preferential policies, such as tax return, has been announced. Following the one-spot, efficient service rule, every high-tech project which has been enlisted in the zone, will be dealt with according to the principle of "Dealing with as a special case, with specific methods", we constantly improve our supporting service system, offers overall services to the enterprises. Favorable conditions of investment attract flock of men of insight coming to do their business here. By the end of 1998, there were 599 legal-person enterprises registered in the zone, among which 134 were high-tech enterprises, 45 foreign-funded enterprises. Totally 300 high-tech projects had developed, of which 134 items had been turned into production, 43 items were enlisted into State and provincial "Torch Program". Totally, in 1998, the zone made the income of 4.876 billion yuan with an average increase of 46.4 percent a year and achieved tax revenue of 1.109 billion yuan with an average increase of 55.9 percent a year. Import and export trade reached US$ 68.93 million with an average increase of 106.5 percent a year.

With a rapid development trend and strong strength, Urumqi High-Tech Industrial Development Zone has become an important economic increasing spot in the city and even in Xinjiang .

乌鲁木齐高新区火炬大厦
The Torch Mansion of Urumqi High-tech Industrial Development Zone

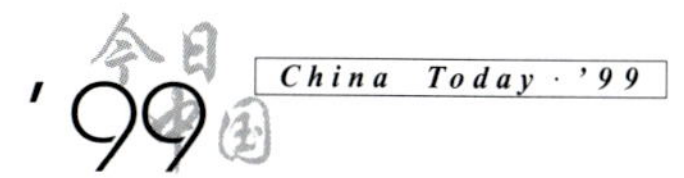

包头稀土高新技术产业开发区

Baotou Rare Earth High-Tech Industrial Development Zone

包头稀土高新技术产业开发区于1992年11月经国务院批准成为国家级高新技术产业开发区，是全国53个国家级高新技术产业开发区中唯一冠以稀土专业名称的高新技术产业开发区。

开发区区域规划面积为10.4平方公里，其中新建区规划面积为5.4平方公里。区内基础设施完善，已实现“六通一平”。开发区的交通条件十分便利，距火车站仅11公里，区内形成四通八达的公路交通网络与市内相通，民航机场距开发区仅28公里。通信线路和市邮电中心联网，能够很好地保证进区客商的通信要求。位于市中心的23000多平方米的开发区科技创业中心大楼是自治区唯一的、也是全国最大的科技孵化中心之一，现已成为内蒙古地区高新技术产业培育和转化的基地，其设备先进的国际会议厅已多次成功地举行了国际国内的各种大型会议。包头市是中国西北地区重要的交通枢钮，为开发区与国内外客商的联系提供了有利的条件。

开发区采取“封闭式管理、开放式运行”的特区管理模式，本着“小政府、大社会”、“小机构、大服务”以及精简、统一、高效的原则，构筑了与社会主义市场经济相适应的开发区管理体制和运行机制，建立了“产业引导，政策扶持，跟踪服务”的新型政企关系。开发区管委会作为市政府的派出机构，在开发区范围内行使行政、经济、社会管理职能，对开发区实行统一规划、统一领导。管委会内设办公室、综合经济发展局、财政局、土也规划建设局、人事劳动局等职能机构；有关部门在开发区设立工商分局、国家税务分局、地方税务分局、公安分局等派驻机构；同时开发区内建立起包括金融、邮电、法律事务、审计事务和会计事务等的支撑服务体系。开发区除执行国家高新技术产业开发区的优惠政策外，内蒙古自治区和包头市根据民族区域自治法和少数民族边疆地区的具体情况，制定了一系列比沿海和内地其它地区更加优惠的政策。

开发区产业发展坚持“一业为主，五业并举”的方针，即在以稀土高新技术产业为主导的同时，大力发展新材料、机电一体化、电子信息、化工、纺织等高新技术，同时吸收效益好、无污染的各类高新技术项目进区建设。1998年，开发区实现工业总产值22.3亿元，技工贸总收入23.5亿元，出口创汇3301万美元，利税2.4亿元。目前，开发区新建区已有企业253家，有美国、法国、德国、英国、日本等国及香港、台湾地区合资、独资创办的企业30家，有高新技术企业51家。全新的思维，全新的机制，优越的投资环境，使包头稀土高新技术产业开发区已经成为国内外投资者的理想发展园地。开发区热忱欢迎和期待着国内外各界朋友前来投资发展。

Baotou Rare Earth High-Tech Industrial Development Zone (hereinafter BRDZ) was approved to be a national high-tech industrial development zone by the State Council in November 1992. It is also the only rare earth development zone of the total 53 national high-tech development zones in China.

BRDZ has the planned construction area of 10.4 square kilometers including 5.4 square kilometers new construction area. The infrastructure facilities here are perfect and water supply, water drainage, electricity, gas, and heating systems and roads are all available in the zone. The transport here is very convenient. It is only 11 kilometers away from the railway station and 28 kilometers away from the airport. The telecommunication lines are linked with the city post & telecommunication network, which can well ensure the requirements of telecommunication for the clients of BRDZ. The 23,000-square meter science & technology promoting center of BRDZ is located in the city center and is the only one in Inner Mongolia and also one of the biggest of its kind in China. Now it has become a base for high technology cultivation and transformation in Inner Mongolia and many important international and national meetings have been held successfully in its advanced modern international conference hall. Baotou is a very important transport hub in northwest China and provides very beneficial conditions for BRDZ to keep contact with foreign and domestic clients.

BRDZ is implementing the management policies of special administration region of "closed management and opening operation", "simplest" but "high efficient", "united"principles and has established a new management system and operation structure, built up a new relationship between administration units and enterprises by carrying out the policies of "industry oriented, policies aiding and service in time", the high efficient working method, perfect services, super soft and hard investment environment and adequate opening policies have been realized in BRDZ. As a subsidiary organization of Baotou municipal government, the management committee of BRDZ has implemented its functions of administration, economic and social management. There are administration office, comprehensive economic development bureau, finance bureau, land planning and construction bureau, personnel bureau under the management committee. The related departments have also established the subsidiary departments such as industry and commerce bureau, national tax affairs bureau, local tax affairs bureau and police station. Furthermore, some service units have also been set up here such as finance, post & telecommunication, statute affairs, audit affairs and accountant affairs. Besides implementing the preferential polices of national high-tech industrial development zone, BRDZ has also taken into consideration the local situations of autonomous and inland area and established a set of more favorable policies than the other inland and coastal areas.

BRDZ insists on the policy of "keeping one leading industry as mainstay and developing the other four simultaneously". In another words, BRDZ has made its efforts on developing rare earth high-tech industry as the leading industry and motivated the development of the new materials, integration of machinery and electrical applicances, electrical information, chemical engineering and textile industries. Up to now, BRDZ has a total of 300 enterprises and 51 high-tech enterprise and 30 joint ventures and solely foreign-owned companies with funds from the United States, France, Germany, Britain, Japan and the regions of Hong Kong and Taiwan.

The new concepts, the new operational system and superior investment environment have made BRDZ an ideal developing place for foreign and domestic investors. We warmly welcome both domestic and foreign visitors and clients to BRDZ and we are also looking forward to your guidance and making your investment in BRDZ. We sincerely wish that you would work with BRDZ people together to create a splendid future in next century.

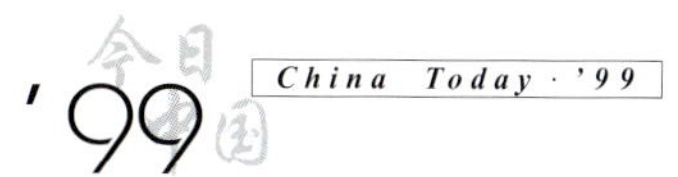

襄樊高新技术产业开发区

Xiangfan High and New Technology Industrial Development Zone

襄樊高新技术产业开发区是1992年11月经国务院批准的国家级高新技术产业开发区，中西部经济的结合部和辐射源，是“内陆特区”。

“水陆空”立体交通网优势明显。高新区位于襄樊市区北部，南靠市区中心，西接老工业园，东临东风汽车公司襄樊基地，北距刘集飞机场6公里。一条汉江黄金水道，二座飞机场通往全国大中城市，焦柳、汉丹、襄渝三条铁路在此交叉，316、207国道贯穿全城。

基础设施完善配套。高新区控制面积46平方公里，政策区面积7.5平方公里，目前已投入9亿多元，在2.7平方公里建成区内全面实现了道路、供水、供电、供热、有线电视、土地平整等“五通一平”，工业厂房、生活住宅、商业、服务业、文化、教育、娱乐等设施配套完善。

智力资源丰富。襄樊是国家级历史文化名城，三国时期政治家、军事家诸葛亮、唐代大诗人孟浩然等历史名人均留下足迹。而今，这里又聚集了众多中外高科技人才，共创现代文明。40家高新技术企业设立了25个科研开发机构，拥有科研人员1726人，其中3个科研院所被教育部指定为博士生教育、培养基地，是鄂西北技术和智

襄樊高新技术产业开发区全景
Panorama of the Xianfan High and New Technology Industrial Development Zone

力最密集地区。

招商引资势头良好。进入高新区的外商投资企业已达30多家，投资总额超过20亿元。投资开发区的客商主要来自美国、日本、新加坡、南非等20多个国家和中国的香港、台湾地区。其中，南非钻石、香港雄辉等公司已经进区，美国康宁、通用等大公司开始关注高新区，已组团考察洽谈项目，有30多个项目已达成进区意向。

创新能力不断增强。目前高新区已建成创业孵化基地8000平方米，在孵中小科技企业60多家，以创业中心为核心的创新体系正在建立，创新能力不断增强。几年来，高新区通过技术市场开发科技项目200多项，80多项转化为高新技术产品，40多个科研成果被国家、省、市列为火炬计划、攻关计划等。高新技术产业占工业经济的80%以上。以华光器材厂的光学玻璃、特种玻璃，江汉航空救生装备工业公司的航空救生产品，湖北东力公司的重、中型汽车冲焊车桥，湖北通力高新公司的高压合成绝缘子，襄阳轴承集团的汽车系列轴承为代表的产品已形成五大全国规模的产品开发和制造基地。

高新技术企业迅速崛起。高新区全面实施高科技强区、项目兴区、人才旺区、市场活区战略，重点打好"国牌"、军工牌和高新技术牌。几年来，共发展科技型企业645家，其中高新技术企业40家，民营科技企业近百家，初步形成了航空航天、汽车配套、机电一体化、新材料等四大企业群体，成为区域经济的重要增长源。6年来，累计实现国内生产总值38.7亿元，工业总产值103.4亿元，高新技术企业产值95.3亿元，实现利税10.6亿元。国务院发展研究中心、国家科技部组成专家组考察襄樊高新开发区后评价：技术含量高，开发后劲大，产业有特色，发展势头强。

襄樊高新区热忱欢迎国内外志士仁人来襄樊高新区考察、投资、兴办实业、共图发展。

Xiangfan High and New Technology Industrial Development Zone, established in November 1992 and one of the state level new and high technology industry development zones with the approval of the State Council, is located in the bordering part between China's central and western sections and is a radiant source to the both sections and an "inland special zone".

Obvious advantage in "water, land and air" three-dimensional traffic network. The zone is situated in the northern part of urban district of Xiangfan City and to its south is the downtown district, to its west is old industrial park, to its east is Xiangfan Base of Dongfeng Automibile Corporation, and the zone is 6 kilometers away from Liuji Airport to its north. The Hanjiang River, a golden traffic line, two airports, three railways (Jiaozuo-Liuzhou, Hankou-Danjiang and Xiangfan-Chongqing), No.316 and No.207 State Highways go through the city and connect it with all the large and medium-sized cities of China.

The infrastructure is well equipped. Controlled area of the zone is 46 square kilometers and that enjoying preferential policies is 7.5 square kilometers. More than 900 million yuan RMB has been invested in the zone. The infrastructure, including roads, water supply, power supply and steam supply, cable television and land leveling, has been finished and necessary factory buildings, residential quarters, shopping areas, services, and cultural, educational and recreational centers have been built in the constructed area of 2.7 square kilometers.

Rich intellectual resources. Xiangfan, one of famous historical and cultural cities at state level, Zhuge Liang, a statesman and strategist in the period of the Three Kingdoms, and Meng Haoran, a great poet of the Tang Dynasty, left their brilliant footmarks in it. And now many highly qualified scientists and technicians have gathered in the zone to create modern civilization. Some 40 high and new technology enterprises in the zone have set up, 25 scientific

research institutes have 1,726 scientific research personnel, three of these institutes have been appointed by the Ministry of Education as education bases for training the students who study for the doctorate. The zone is the highest intelligence-intensive area in northwest Hubei Province.

Good trend of introducing foreign investment. More than 30 foreign enterprises, with a total investment of over 2 billion yuan RMB, from more than 20 countries, such as the United States, Japan, Singapore, South Africa and China's Hong Kong and Taiwan regions. South Africa Chenshia (PTY) Ltd. (Hubei) and Hong Kong Hung Hung Fai (Int'l) Enterprise Development Co. etc., have invested in the zone. Some large firms, such as Corning Co. Ltd. (USA) and General Motors Corporation (USA) have begun to pay close attention to the zone and have organized groups to discuss business and have reached agreements on over 30 projects which are intended to enter the zone.

Creative ability increases with each passing day. The zone has built an enterprise incubation base of 8,000 square meters and it has incubated over 60 small- and medium-sized technology-intensive enterprises. The creative system with creation center at the core has been building up and the creative power increased day by day. In the past few years, more than 200 scientific and technological projects have been developed through technical markets in the zone, 80 and more of them have been turned into high-tech products. Over 40 scientific research achievements have been listed in Torch Program or in Key Problem Tackling Program at the state level, provincial level or city level. High-tech industries make up 80 percent of total industrial economy in the zone. The zone has formed five nationwide scale products development bases represented by the optical glass and special glass of Huaguang Equipment Factory, aviation life-support products of Jianghan Aviation Life-Support Industries Co., medium and heavy-duty punched and welded automobile axles of Hubei Dongli Co., high-voltage compound insulators of High-Tech Co. under Hubei Tongly Corporation and automobile bearings series of Xiangyan Bearing Group Corporation.

High-tech enterprises are emerging rapidly on the horizon. The zone has implemented in an all-round way the strategy of vitalizing it by relying on high science and technology, projects, qualified personnel and on the market, and made full use of its state, military and high-tech brands. In the zone 645 technology-intensive enterprises, including 40 high-tech ones, and about 100 private enterprises have been developed, four enterprise groups of aviation and spaceflight, automobile parts and components, integration of mechanical and electrical equipment and new materials that are the important growth sources of the regional economy have formed. In the last six years, it has accumulatively achieved 3.87 billion yuan of the GDP, 10.34 billion yuan of industrial output value, including 9.53 billion yuan from high-tech enterprises, and 1.06 billion yuan of profits and tax payments. The specialist group consisting of the persons from the Development and Research Center of the State Council and the Ministry of Science and Technology gave its evaluation after it made investigation on the zone: High technological content, strong strength for future development, industrial characteristics and good development trend.

Xiangfan New and High Technology Industry Development Zone warmly welcomes the domestic and overseas friends to visit, invest and do business in the zone.

株洲国家高新技术产业开发区

Zhuzhou High-Tech Industrial Development Zone

株洲高新技术产业开发区于1992年12月经国务院批准为国家级高新区。辖区面积35平方公里，政策区8.8平方公里，起步区3.78平方公里。经过7年建设，株洲高新区已初步建成一座布局科学合理、基础设施成龙配套、产业进区发展迅速、社会事业管理有序的文明新城区，正成为株洲市新的经济增长点。

基础设施完善配套。株洲高新区已累计投资达27.53亿元，在7.2平方公里范围实现五通一平，七纵六横城市主次干道网络状连通，道路总长达45公里，完成各类建筑151万平方米，绿化面积85万平方米，绿化率达40%。日供水能力30万吨，区内建有110千伏变电站，装机容量5万千瓦，供热能力150吨／小时的热电厂正抓紧筹建，程控电话装机容量6.4万门，可满足各类现代化通讯需要；管道煤气送至各功能小区。

支撑服务体系齐全。为方便进区企业办事，促进产业发展。株洲高新区建有商检、海关、进出口公司等涉外服务机构及财政、工商、公安、税务、房产、银行、保险、创业服务中心、人才交流中心、劳务市场、律师事务所、会计师事务所、公证处等支撑服务体系。4万平方米的标准厂房设施齐全、可租可售；全国城市住宅试点小区——滨江村——功能配套；占地15公顷的炎帝广场和高365米的广播电视塔气势恢宏；有3所三星级涉外宾馆、一个大型会议中心、大型文化宫；各类学校、幼儿园、医院、购物中心和农贸市场一应俱全。

管理体制精简高效。高新区管委会作为株洲市政府的派出机构，设有高效、精简、务实的职能部门。运用新的管理体制全权行使对高新区的统一领导和管理，在项目进区、立项、审批、国土、规划、建工、环保等方面享有市级行政和经济管理权限。以“小政府、大服务、有权威”的方式为企业提供优质、高效的服务和一站式办公，创造了一个经济发展的宽松环境。

享有特殊优惠政策。株洲高新区除享有国家级高新区的优惠政策外，还享有地方政策规定的优惠政策。为进一步优化投资环境，切实解决投资者各种税外费负担，增加投资者的信心，株洲高新区在全国53个国家级高新区中率先对科技园区的工业企业和高新区的高新技术企业实行只收税不收行政事业性收费的“无费区”政策。

产业进区发展迅速。株洲高新区坚持大项目、高起点、新领域的产业发展方向，走产业兴区之路。目前已形成了一区三园（工业、农业、民营科技园）产业发展格局，拥有各类企业700家，其中工业企业107家，高新技术企业58家，外商投资企业29家，初步形成新材料、机光电一体化、能源和环保等骨干产业。1998年实现工业总产值19.5亿元，其中高新技术企业总产值18.2亿元，技工贸总收入26.5亿元，出口创汇1080.9万美元，财政收入1.25亿元。高新区区域经济实力不断增强，并将继续向更高、更快、更好的方向发展。

Zhuzhou High-Hech Industrial Development Zone was

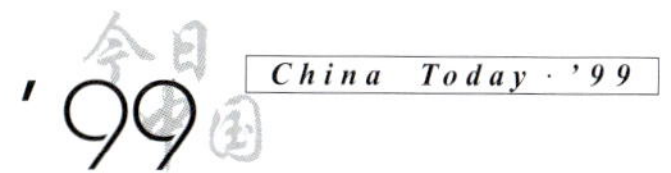

established in December 1992. The State Council recognized it as a state-level development zone in China. The development zone covers a total area of 35 square km, including the policy area of 8.8 square km, and the starting area of 3.78 square km. After 7 years of preparation, the development zone has been built into a new town with rational distribution, sound infrastructure facilities, fast-developing industries and orderly administration. It is becoming a new economic development place of Zhuzhou City.

Sound infrastructure facilities: Zhuzhou High-Tech Industrial Development Zone has invested 2.753 billion yuan on infrastructure facilities. Within an area of 7.2 square km, water supply, drainage, gas, electric power, road and land leveling can meet the requirements. As a crisscross network of highways, Zhuzhou has 7 north-south highways and 6 west-east highways, the total length of which is 45 km. The development zone has finished various construction projects with 1.51 million sq. m, of the floor space, 850,000 square meters of gardens make over 40 percent of vegetation cover. It can supply 300,000 tons of water daily. A power system with a substation of 110 kilovolts, and a thermal power plant with installed capacity of 50,000 kw and heat supply of 150 ton/hour are under intensive construction. A program-controlled digital telephone exchange system with a capacity of 640,000 terminals can meet the needs of modern communication. The gas plant provides piped gas to the development zone.

Complete service system: In order to promote industrial development, Zhuzhou High-Tech Industrial Development Zone has a supporting system including customs, commodity inspection, foreign exchange administration, industrial and commercial administration, state revenue, local taxation, land management, municipal planning, environmental protection, real estate companies, commercial banks, insurance companies, a service center for starting an undertaking, a service center for expertise exchange, a labor market and agencies for laws, accounting, auditing and notarizations. Standard plant buildings with 40,000 square meters floor space can meet different needs for rent or sale. The development zone has Binjiang No.1 Village, as one of the nationally experimental districts, the Square of the King of Yan covering 15 hectares of land area, a 365-meter-tall TV broadcasting tower, three "three-star" hotels, one convention center, one great cultural palace, elementary and secondary schools, kindergartens, hospitals, shopping malls and open-air markets that form convenient and comfortable surroundings.

Efficient and simple administration system: As the administration governmental agency authorized by Zhuzhou municipal government, the Administration Commission of Zhuzhou High-Tech Industrial Development Zone administrates the development zone with a new administration system, and is granted the administrative authority at the metropolitan rank in approval of a project application, state-owned land management, planning, construction, environment. It provides excellent, efficient service and one-stop office by the mode of "little government, great service and authoritative", which creates loose environment for economic development.

Special preferential policy: Besides preferential policy granted to state-level high-tech industry development zone, Zhuzhou High-Tech Industrial Development Zone enjoys preferential policy granted by the local government. To further improve the investment environment and to enhance investors' confidence, the development zone puts into effect the policy of "charge-free zone" for industrial enterprises in the science and technology park and high-tech enterprises in the development zone.

Quick industrial growth: The development zone insists on the guideline of big project, high starting point and new field. At present, the development zone consists of three parks: industrial, agricultural and entrepreneur parks.

It owns 700 enterprises including 107 industrial enterprises, 58 high-tech enterprises and 29 foreign-invested enterprises. New material, optical-mechanics-electronics integration, energy and environment have begun to become key industries. In 1998, industrial output value reached 1.95 billion yuan, among which high-tech enterprises output value accounted for 1.82 billion yuan, total income of technology, industry and trade totaled 2.65 billion yuan, foreign exchange earnings reached US$10.8 million and fiscal revenue totalled 125 million yuan. The economic strength of the development zone has increased, and continued to develop at a higher speed.

洛阳高新技术产业开发区

Luoyang High-Tech Industrial Development Zone

洛阳高新技术产业开发区于1992年11月被国务院批准为国家级高新技术产业开发区，目前开发面积已达3.5平方公里，拥有完备的路网、供排水网和供电网络，程控电话装机容量达2万门，并已建成功能完善、服务配套的商业、办公、居住、教学、旅游、餐饮、娱乐等各项设施。一个园林化的科技工业新城区初步形成。

洛阳高新区由周山电子工业区、三山科技工业园、科技工业园二期工程、外商投资小区、政策区等五部分组成。截止目前，已有483家各类企业进区落户，其中高新技术企业125家，外商投资企业114家，产值超亿元的企业6家，生产高新技术产品199项，初步形成了以镀膜玻璃、陶瓷棍棒、轿车缓冲制位块、高档玻璃纤维、新型耐火材料为主体的新材料产业；LED电子图文显示屏、以光纤连接器、交换机二次电源、无线电负荷控制系统为主体的电子信息产业；以茶叶包装机、测功机、并条机自匀装置、水下切粒设备等为主体的光机电一体化产业；以工具酶、病历试剂盒、醋蛋滋养素等为主体的生物工程产业。形成了洛阳高新区四大支柱产业框架，显示出巨大的发展前景。

洛阳高新区已成为中西部吸引投资最富成效的地区之一，被中国投资环境评估权威部门评选为“中国投资环境优秀开发区50强”。目前已有来自世界上20多个国家和地区的100多家企业进区发展。洛阳高新区自建区以来，各项经济指标持续高速增长，1992年至1998年累计实现技工贸总收入153亿元，技工贸总产值136亿元，利税总额12亿元，出口创汇3.14亿美元，其中1998年四项主要经济指标分别达到45.11亿元、42.04亿元、3.47亿元和5098万美元，四项指标年均增长速度均在60%以上，成为洛阳市一个新的颇具活力的经济增长点。

为鼓励高新技术企业的建设和发展，开发区制定了《洛阳高新技术产业开发区优惠政策》、《洛阳高新技术产业开发区企业管理条例》、《洛阳高新技术产业开发区劳动人事管理规定》、《洛阳高新技术开发区土地管理办法》、《洛阳高新技术产业开发区项目审批程序》等10余项政策法规，形成了开发区比较完备的政策法规体系。

Luoyang National New & High-Tech Industrial Development Zone was established in November 1992 with approal of the State Council. By now, 3.5 square kilometers of land have been developed with complete road, water supply and drainage, electrical power, telecommunication service with the capacities of 20,000 program-controlled telephone lines, as well as its perfect commercial, office, residential, teaching, tourism, food and entertainment service facilities. A new industrial garden is taking its shape.

The development zone is composed of Zhoushan Electronic Industry Park, Sanshan Science and Technology Industry Park, the 2nd Sanshan Science and Technology Industry park, Foreign-Funded District and Policy District. Up to now, 483 enterprises of various categories have invested here, among which, 125 are new and high technology enterprises with 199 new & high technology products, 114 are foreign-funded enterprises, 6 have over 100 million yuan output value. A framework has been formed as the key industries with new material, which mainly including coating glass, ceramic rolling, high-level glass fiber, and new refractory material, electronics which mainly including LED electronics display screen, optical-fibre cable coupling, and wireless electric load control system, optical-electric-mechanical integration, which mainly including tea-packing machine, eddy current dynamometer, automatic evening and adjusting system, and underwater strand granulator, and bioengineering , which mainly including tool ferment, medical record box and nutritional uineganed-egg oral liquid. All of them indicate a bright future for development.

The development zone has become one of the most fruitful areas to draw foreign capitals in central and western China, and was listed among the top 50 outstanding development zones with nice investment environment by the state authoritative investment environment evaluation department. Up to now, more than 100 enterprises from 20 countries and regions in the world have made their investment here. Since its setup, the development zone has recorded an average economic increase of over 60 percent. The total income of technology, industry and trade from 1992 to 1998 was 15.3 billion yuan. The total output value reached 13.6 billion yuan. The profit and tax was 1.2 billion yuan. The export value totaled US$314 million. The four mainly economic records in 1998 were 4.511 billion yuan, 4.204 billion yuan, 347 million yuan and US$ 50.98 million in turn. The development zone has become a new point of economic growth with great vigor in Luoyang.

洛阳高新区掠影
Luoyang New & High-Tech District

宝鸡高新技术产业开发区

Baoji Development Zone for High-Tech Industries

宝鸡高新技术产业开发区位于宝鸡市工业区。宝鸡市是陕西省第二大工业城市，总面积1.8万平方公里，人口360万。宝鸡属温带大陆性气候，年平均气温13℃，平均降水量710毫米。宝鸡交通便利，陇海铁路、宝成铁路、宝中铁路在此交汇，加上亚欧大陆桥的全线开通，使宝鸡东西贯通，南北纵深与各大铁路网相连，腹地广阔，出口顺畅。宝鸡工业基础雄厚，以机械、电子、食品、有色金属四大行业最具实力。宝鸡技术人才密集，科技力量比较雄厚。全市拥有大中专院校24所，各类专业研究所（院）30多个，厂办技术研究所60多个，民办科研组织百余所，各类专业技术人员10多万名。

宝鸡高新技术产业开发区1992年12月经国务院批准成立，总规划面积5.77平方公里，分东西两个各具特色的小区。西区1.49平方公里，位于市中心商业区和电子工业区之间，是科研单位、军工企业、技术人才最密集的地方，重点发展电子信息、机电一体化、新型食品、生物工程等高新技术产业。东区4.28平方公里，重点发展稀贵金属新材料等产业。

西区新建区"七通一平"基础配套设施完备。工业厂房、供热中心、110KV变电站、写字楼、商品住宅楼、创业中心孵化楼、宾馆等生产、生活配套设施齐全。海关、商检、卫生检疫、药检疫以及工商、税务、邮电、公安、金融等支撑服务机构，均在区内设有独立分支机构。科技创业园、民营科技园、军工科技园的建设格局已经形成，火炬科技电子一条街已初具规模。

宝鸡高新区管委会以招商引资为龙头，不断优化高新区的软、硬环境建设，各方面工作都取得了显著的成效。截止1998年底，全区注册的各类工商企业340多家，其中从事工业、科技开发、科技服务的企业139家，高新技术企业66家。民营企业106家，高新技术企业产值占全区产值的80%左右。1998年实现技工贸总收入达到23亿元，工业总产值26.1亿元。全区企业职工人数1.6万余人，其中技术人员5200余人。基本形成了以通信、计算机软硬件产品为主的电子信息产业；以数控机床、纺织电子新产品、高压真空开关及开关柜为主的机电一体化产业；以稀贵金属钛材及其深加工产品为主的新型材料产业；以及正在兴起的以研制生产rtPA为主的生物制药产业。

宝鸡高新区作为陕西省关中高新技术产业开发带的西部龙头和宝鸡市对外开放的窗口，得到国家科委、省市政府的大力支持，授予高新区管委会市一级经济管理权限，实行"封闭式管理、开放式运行"，为投资者提供优质、快捷的服务和优越、舒适的环境。

Baoji High-Tech Industrial Development Zone is situated in the industrial area of Baoji, the second large industrial city in Shaanxi Province in China. The city occupies a total area of 18,000 square kilometers with 3.6 million population. The weather here belongs to the continental climate of moderate with average annual temperature 13℃ and average rainfall 710 mm. Being located at a crosspoint of Longhai, Baoji-Chengdu and Baozhong railways and in addition to the whole way transportation from Asia through to Europe by the continental bridge, Baoji City thoroughly links with the east and the west and broadly stretches to the south and to the north, connecting with each large national railway network for convenient traffic in vast inland for smooth export. The industries in Baoji possess strong bases of four professions as machinery, electronics, food and nonferrous metal. And the city has a plenty of technical personnel and strong forces of science and technology. There are 24 universities and polytechnic schools and more than 30 all kinds of special institutes and more than 100 scientific researching organizations run by the local people as well as over 100,000 technical personnel.

Baoji High-Tech Industrial Development Zone was established by the approval of State Council in December 1992. The total planned area is 5.77 square kilometers, which is divided into the east and west parts of special characteristics. The west part with an area of 1.49 square kilometers locates between the city's shopping center and the electronic industrial district concentrating scientific researching units, military enterprises and technical personnel mainly developing new and high-tech industries as electronic information, combination of machinery with electronics, new type food and biological engineering. The east part with an area of 4.28 square kilometers mainly develops new materials as rare and precious metal.

The newly-built district in the west part has a complete and perfect matching base with industrial workshops, heating center, office buildings, commodity lodgings, hatching building and hotels, etc. for production and living. The independent branch organizations of customs, commodity inspection, hygiene quarantine, medicine quarantine and industry & commerce, tax, post office, public security, finance, etc. for supporting service. The construction of science and technology garden and the garden run by the local people and the garden for military industry have been finished. The street for developing science and technical electronics in Torch Road is now in the scale.

The Management Committee of Baoji development zone deals with inviting merchants and attracting funds as their leading tasks and continually optimizes the soft and hard environmental construction in the zone. So prominent achievements have been made in all aspects. By the end of 1998 more than 340 industrial and commercial enterprises have been registered including 139 enterprises for industry, technology development and service and 66 high-tech enterprises and 106 local people-run enterprises. The total output value of high-tech enterprises has made up about 80% of that of the whole zone and the total income of technology, industry and trade has reached 2.3 billion yuan and the total industrial output value 2.61 billion yuan. The number of employers is about 16,000 including about 5,200 technical personnel. The electronic information enterprises have been basically established as for their main products for communication and soft and hard ware for computers; the enterprises work in combination of machinery with electronics as NC machines, electronic products for textile, high-voltage vacuum switch and switching cabinet; the new-type material enterprises for rare and precious metal, i.e. titanium production and further processing work have been formed; the biological medicine enterprise for rtPA is now developing.

Being greatly supported by the Ministry of Science & Technology and Provincial and Municipal Governments, the Baoji High-Tech Industrial Development Zone as the west leading zone and open window for foreign countries along

Guanzhong S.D.Z. has been granted the municipal-level management right to adopt the policy of "Closed management and open operation" and providing optimum and quick service for investors and superiority, comfortable environment.

绵阳国家高新技术产业开发区

Mianyang High and New Technological Industrial Development Zone

1992 年由国务院批准建立的绵阳国家高新技术产业开发区，南接成都平原，北依中国电子科学城—绵阳，是“三国”旅游热线的黄金站点和成都北去九寨沟的必经之地。境内有以中国工程物理研究院和中国空气动力研究中心为代表的科研院所 43 家，各类科技人员 16 万人，其中享受政府津贴有突出贡献的专家近 800 名，两院院士 15 名；有宝成铁路复线、成绵高速公路穿境而过，航空港亦将在年内投入营运；铁路口岸、海关、商检的工作正逐步实现与国际接轨；程控电话、通信光缆遍布全区。

绵阳国家高新区坚持“小政府、大社会，小机构、大服务”的管理体制和“一站式”工作原则，以境内的军工技术为强力支撑，大力发展电子关键零部件配套产业，培养良好的制造和工艺配套环境，形成了以电子技术为龙头，以精细化工、新材料、光机电一体化、生物工程为重点的产业框架，吸引了长虹、泰国正大、日本精化株式会社等一批国内外知名企业及大量中小型企业进区发展。为加强高新技术的商品转化工作，绵阳高新区管委会采取低员工工资、低商品房价格、低成本工业厂房、控制地价、财税扶持和培育一大批技术工人队伍等一系列措施，降低中小型科技企业的营运成本，促进这些企业快速成长，使一批军工企业和科研院所的技术成果得到有效转化。截止 1998 年底，进区工业性企业 384 家，高新技术企业 45 家，建成投产的工业项目 279 个，累计完成固定资产投资 48.6 亿元，技工贸总收入、工业总产值 5 年平均增长速度 138.7%，1997 年这两项指标分别以 139.9 亿元和 129.9 亿元，排名 53 个国家高新区的第三和第六。

绵阳高新区正确处理环境与发展的关系，极力营造现代城市体系，实现了基础设施的“九通一平”，已建成 6.1 平方公里的高科技园区。配套完备的现代城区里，火炬大厦与 80 亩绿地相依相映，庄严典雅，雄踞一方，显现出绵阳高新区的开放和大气；现代、气派的长虹总部及横贯启动区的“十里绿化长廊”，张扬着高新区人的发展思想；而外国语学校、康复中心、医疗中心、商贸中心、科技游乐园、21 世纪花园无疑给这里的人们提供了良好的生活环境。

作为民族产业的代表——长虹公司所在地，绵阳高新区正致力于把这块土地建成长虹公司 21 世纪初进入世界工业 500 强的重要制造和技术开发基地；建成中国工程物理研究院等一大批军工企事业单位军民两用技术创新基地；建成中国西部电子信息产业制造基地；建成四川省跨世纪经济发展的重要经济增长点；建成西南地区一座亮丽的现代科技工业城。

Mianyang State High and New Technological Industrial Development Zone, which was established in 1992

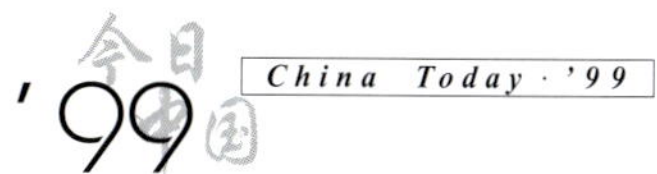

with approval of the State Council, with the Chengdu Plain to the South and with the China Electronics Science City of Mianyang, to the North, is a golden service station for touring "the Three Kingdoms" and the only way to the Nine-Stockade-Village Ravine from Chengdu by taking the northward way. There are 47 scientific research institutes here, represented by the Mechanics Physics Research Institute of China and the Aeromechanics Research Center. Among the 160,000 scientific and technological workers from various fields, there are 800 experts who have enjoyed the governmental subsidies for their outstanding achievements, and there are 15 academicians. The double tracks of the railway between Baoji and Chengdu, and the expressway between Chengdu and Mianyang cross this area. The new airport will have been put into use within this year. The affairs concerning the railway stations, the Customs, and the commodity inspections gradually conform to the international standards. Program-controlled telephones and cables are installed everywhere all over the region.

Mianyang High and New Technological Development Zone upholds the administration system of "the small government, the large society; the small setup, the perfect service" and adheres to the working rule of "one station" It makes good use of military industrial technology, devoting its major efforts to developing the industry which produces complete sets of the key electronic units, and fostering a good situation for manufacturing and technological complete sets. The industrial frame, headed by electronic technique and centered on refined chemical industry, new materials, the combination of machine and photoelectricity, and biological engineering, draws a number of famous national and international small and medium-sized enterprises such as Changhong, Zhengda of Thailand, and the Refined Chemical Industry Company of Japan. In order to strengthen the transformation of high and new technological commodities, the administration committee of the zone adopts a series of measures such as lower wages, lower prices of commodity houses, lower costs of factory buildings, controlling land prices, favorable financial taxes, and the training of a great number of technical workers. Consequently, the production costs and the expenses of the small and medium-sized technological enterprises have been developing very rapidly, realizing the effective transformation of a batch of achievements in scientific research of some enterprises and research institutes. By the end of 1998, there had been 384 industrial enterprises and 45 high and new technological enterprises here; there had been 279 industrial items put into production; The investment in fixed assets reached 4.86 billion yuan, the average yearly increase rate of the total income of technology, industry and trade, and the total industrial output value increased by 138.7 percent in the last five years, which amounted to 13.99 billion yuan and 12.99 billion yuan separately in 1997, ranking the third and the sixth separately among the 53 national high and new technological zones.

Mianyang High and New Technological Zone has correctly handled the relationship between the environment and the development, made great efforts to construct a modern city system, built infrastructure facilities and the land levelling and constructed the high scientific and technological fields of 6.1 square kilometers. Within the well-equipped modern town, the Torch Building, standing there solemnly and elegantly, forms a delightful contrast with the green fields of 80 *mu*, showing the lofty quality and the openness of Mianyang National High and New Technological Zone. The Changhong headquarters, with its modern architectural style, and "the ten-*li* Green Corridor" traversing the zone, are making public the people's developing thought. Moreover, the Foreign Languages School, the Health Rehabitation Center, the Medical Center, the Shopping and Trading Center, the Amusement Park of Science and Technology, the 21st-Century Garden, etc., will undoubtedly provide the local inhabitants with good living conditions.

Mianyang High and New Technological Zone has been working for changing itself into an important manufacturing and technique developing base for Changhong Company to become one of the 500 world's top powerful industrial enterprises in the next century; changing itself into a base for the Academy of Mechanic Physics of China and numbers of other military industrial enterprises and civil institutions to practise new technology; changing itself into a manufacturing base of electronic information industry in Southwest China; changing itself into an important place of Sichuan's economic growth in the next century; changing itself into a splendid modern scientific and technological industrial city in Southwest China.

绵阳高新区管理中心—火炬大厦
The Torch Mansion of Mianyang High and New Technological Industrial Development Zone

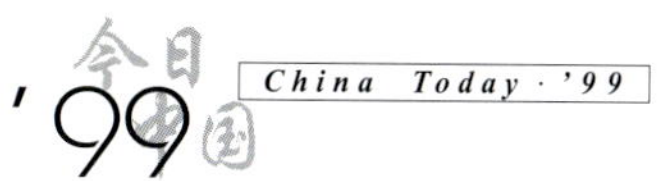

保定国家高新技术产业开发区

Baoding New and High-Tech Industrial Development Zone

保定位于河北中部，地处北京、天津、石家庄三大城市构成的金三角中心地带，素有“京畿重地”、“首都南大门”之称。保定具有2300多年的历史，是中国的历史文化名城、对外开放城市和中国综合实力50强之一，具有雄厚的工农业基础和优越的科技人才优势。保定国家高新区的建设与发展，已经成为保定新的经济增长点。

保定国家高新区是1992年11月9日经国务院批准的国家级高新技术产业开发区。1996年9月经国家科委批准，调整为“一区三园”格局，即：中心科技园、华北工业园、八达工业园三个园区。高新区管委会行使市级管理权限，全区实行“开放式运行，封闭式管理”。

建区6年多来，保定国家高新区不断解放思想、更新观念，注重发挥保定地理位置优越、工农业基础雄厚、文化底蕴深厚、技术创新能力强等诸多优势，坚持“大手笔、快运作、跳跃式”的发展原则，努力完善区内软硬环境，为高新技术企业和国内外投资者创造了优越的发展环境、保持了快速发展的势头。截止到1998年底，在高新区注册企业839家，拥有三家上市公司，累计完成工业总产值80.4亿元，实现利税11.6亿元。

保定国家高新区始终以促进高新技术商品化、产业化、国际化为目标，大力营造高新技术产业发展环境，投巨资兴建了近10万平米的标准厂房，出台了引进高级人才条例，为高新技术成果产业化创造了必要条件。截止目前，保定国家高新区共认定高新技术企业93户，认定高新技术产品106项，培育国家“863计划”项目一项，实施国家火炬计划项目14项，省火炬计划项目12项，转化科技成果80余项。形成新材料、电子信息、机电一体化、生物工程、食品工业等产业体系，已经成为保定产业结构调整和经济快速发展的样板，成为新的经济增长点。

保定国家高新区交通、通信、生产生活等基础设施日臻完善，建立起了海关、商检等外经贸服务体系。功能布局科学合理，整体形象富有现代气息，成为保定市招商引资的重要基地和开放窗口，截止到1998年底，共有美、英、德、日、法、菲律宾、台湾和香港等十几个国家和地区在这里投资，著名的生力啤酒集团、台湾威京集团等公司在此得到很好的发展。到目前，保定国家高新区三资企业已达118家，实际利用外资3.4亿美元，对外开放和外经贸事业发展迅速。

保定国家高新区面对新世纪的召唤，正以更加豪迈的热情，谱写着新的壮丽篇章。

Baoding is located in Hebei Province in the golden triangle zone composed by Beijing, Tianjin and Shijiazhuang.

Well-known as the “South Gate” of the “satellite city” of Beijing, Baoding benefits from a 2,300-yeae-long history and culture . It is also an opening city to the outside world.

Baoding is one of the "50 comprehensively powerful cities in China", has a foundation of industry, agriculture and technician talents. The construction and development of Baoding New and High-Tech Industrial Development Zone have played an important role in our local economy.

Our zone was approved by the State Council on November 9, 1992 as a national-level high-tech development area. In September 1996, the zone with its Central Science and Technology Park was enlarged by two other parks, the North China Industrial Park in the east subdistrict and the Bada Industrial Park in the West. The Administration Committee of the zone is authorized to exercise municipal administration with performing an executive management and offering overall services to the outside world.

For more than six years of construction, the Baoding high-tech zone has continuously adopted new concepts and ideas, and attached more importance to taking advantage of its strategic geographical location, its solid foundation in industry and agriculture, long historical heritage and its ability of technology innovations.

Pertinent analysis of situations, quick actions and constant improvements, that is our motive to develop the soft and hard environment inside and outside the zone, continuously creating an appropriated environment for high-tech enterprises and investors at home and abroad to lead them to a bright future. As a result, we maintain and strengthen our development orientation.

By the end of the year 1998, there were 839 enterprises registered in the zone and three companies listed in stocking exchange. The total industrial output value amounted to 8.04 billion yuan, profit and tax reached 1.16 billion yuan.

The Baoding high-tech zone continues to focus on promotion, commercialization, industrialization and internationalization of high technology, paying more and more attention to create a suitable environment for developing high-tech industries. Thus, large efforts in investments (100,000 square meters of new standard factories) and regulations about scientists', technicians' qualifications were deserved.

Until now, the Committee of Science and Technology of Hebei Province has approved 93 high-tech enterprises and 106 high-tech products. One of those firms is listed in the national "863" program, which carries out high-tech research and development.

The Baoding National High-Tech Zone has greatly improved its public infrastructures for transportation, communication, production and residents, establishing a foreign commercial service system including customs house, commercial inspection.

Within a rational distribution of industry and an integral imagination in a rich and modern atmosphere, it has become an important base of introduction for foreign investments as well as an opening window to the outside world. By the end of year 1998, more than ten countries and regions including the United States, Great Britain, Germany, Japan, France, the Philippines, Taiwan and Hong Kong have invested here. We can quote the San Miguel Brewery Group and the Taiwan Core Pacific Group, which have chosen our zone to set up their company and develop their business.

Until now, 118 foreign-funded enterprises and joint ventures have been set up in the Baoding New and High-Tech Industrial Development Zone. The foreign investment used, is equivalent to US$340 million . The fast growing economy of Baoding is due to the opening towards its international environment and foreign economic trade.

Our zone is very confident and enthusiastic to pass through the 21st century and write a new magnificent page of history.

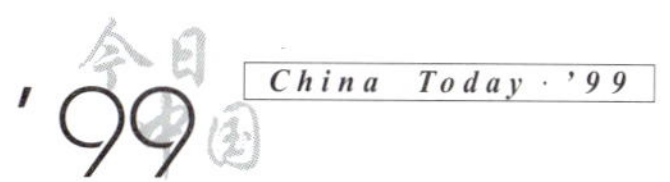

鞍山国家高新技术产业开发区

Anshan High & New Technology Industrial Development Zone

鞍山国家高新技术产业开发区位于辽宁省鞍山市市区东部，三面环山、一面傍水，距中心3.5公里，交通便捷畅达。

鞍山高新区1992年经国务院批准，规划面积7.9平方公里，是一个以高新技术产业为主体，包括科研、教育、生活服务、文化娱乐、行政管理等区域化、多功能化、现代化的综合性新城区。鞍山高新区是鞍山近期工作重点和下个世纪经济发展的核心、是深化改革的试验区、对外开放的窗口、经济发展的新的增长点、高新技术产业基地、现代化城市建设示范区。

1. 鞍山高新区作为国家级高新技术产业开发区是全面实施国家“火炬计划”的开发区之一，直接接受国家的扶持与促进。鞍山高新区享有国家规定的最为优惠的各项政策，是正在崛起和十分活跃的经济带。在高科技产业发展政策、资金和工作指导等方面，鞍山高新区还会直接得到国家、省、市政府科技主管部门支持。

2. 鞍山高新区是鞍山经济的增长点，得到市委、市政府的高度重视和热切关注，处于鞍山经济发展极为重要的战略地位。为了加速鞍山高新区的建设与发展，市政府先后投入了大量资金，采取了重大举措，给予了决定性的支持，形成以高新区为主体，实施城市建设向东拓展、人才资金向东流动、高新技术企业向东集结、政治文化中心向东转移的东部发展战略。

3. 鞍山高新区招商引资思路明朗开阔。招商引资的着眼点是，面向世界，面向未来，面向发展，与国家经济接轨。基本原则是：“你发财、我发展、互惠互利、风险同担，利益共享”。鞍山高新区在提供和实施税收、用地、用工等各项优惠政策方面完整切实。

现代文明新城区：鞍山
Anshan: The New City Anshan with Modern Civilization

4. 鞍山高新区自身功能完备，能够对中外投资商提供全方位高质量的服务。按照行使市级经济管理权限和区级行政管理权限并实行封闭式管理的规定，鞍山高新区形成了"小政府、大社会"的精干、高效的行政管理格局和门类齐全的支撑服务体系，为中外投资商在投资前后提供"一揽子"和"一条龙"的服务，为投资商赢得工作效率和经济效益创造条件。

5. 鞍山高新区高科技项目资源丰富，对外联系渠道坚实，高新技术产业化进程具有明显发展势头。鞍山高新区在电子信息、新材料、生物工程、静电环保、机电一体化等领域的高科技产业开发现已具备一定规模。"鞍山钢铁学院科技园"、"大康民营科技园"已经开始启动。鞍山高新区与中国科学院及其140余家科研院所形成了密切关系，高新技术项目的储备达到了相当规模；与欧美、亚太等国家的企业界建立了广泛联系；还在北京、上海、厦门建立了招商联络处。目前，加拿大中国东北投资贸易促进会正在鞍山高新区兴办加拿大工业园，首批入区、总投资近500万美元的八个外商独资企业已开工建设。

6. 鞍山高新区总体规划起点高，基础设施条件基本完备。由清华大学编绘的总体规划设计，被国家建设部和科技部确定为东北地区高新技术产业开发区的样板，为鞍山高新区全面开发建设奠定了坚实基础。目前，鞍山高新区起步区道路骨架基本形成；给排水系统基本完备；通信联络畅通无阻；有线电视网络现已开工；工业用地电容量已达到用户要求；管道煤气、集中供热工程1999年全部完工。特别对利用外资的高新技术大项目（科技园区）的大配套，政府予以优先支持，保证同步实施和投产需要。

7. 鞍山高新区已经开工建设的"绿色家园"小区是香港沿海房地产（集团）公司与鞍山高新区联合开发建设、由国家建设部和科技部立项的2000年小康住宅示范工程，体现了人居环境新思想，是融建筑与自然相结合，集商业服务、会所、广场、学校、绿化等社区配套于一体的综合开发的高智能化的绿色住宅小区，并实施当代高集成度的物业管理。"绿色家园"是鞍山新城区建设的重要标志，是中外投资商及其公务人员生活的最佳选择。小区的建设与竣工，必将对高新技术产业发展带来巨大拉动，给中外投资商在鞍山高新区工作提供优越的生活环境。

Anshan High & New Technology Industrial Development Zone (Anshan Hi-Tech Zone) is situated in the east districts of Anshan City, Liaoning Province, facing the river with its one site and lying against the mountains with its other three sides. It is 3.5 kilometers away from the center of the city of Anshan, 13 kilometers away from the Mt. Qian, the national level Scenic Spot. And the communication of the zone is convenient and unimpeded.

Anshan High-Tech Zone was approved by the State Council in 1992 with planned area of 7.9 square kilometers. With the industries of high and new technologies as its main body, it is a regionalized, multifunctional, modernized, comprehensive new urban district, including the fields of scientific research, education, living service, culture, entertainment and administration. Anshan High-Tech Zone is a recent important working point of Anshan City and the core of economic development of Anshan City, an experiment area of deepening reform, a window of opening to the outside world, a new increasing point of economic development, a basis of high and new industry and a demonstration area of modern city construction.

1. As a national level high and new technology industrial development zone, Anshan High-Tech Zone is one of the 52 development zones that completely implement national "Torch Program". It directly accepts the support and aid

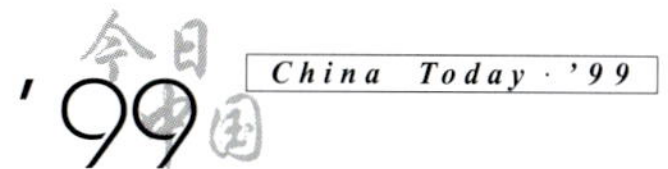

from the central government. Anshan High-Tech Zone enjoys the most preferential policies stipulated by the state and is a very active economic zone on the rise. In the aspect of the development policy of high and new technology industry, fund, the work guidance, etc., Anshan High-Tech Zone and high scientific and technology enterprises in the zone will get the forceful support from the science and technology jurisdiction departments of the state, province and city.

2. Anshan High-Tech Zone is a new point of economic growth in a very important strategic position for economic development of Anshan, to which the Anshan Municipal Party Committee and the Anshan Municipal Government are attaching great importance and paying close attention with warmth. In order to accelerate the reconstruction and development of Anshan High-Tech Zone, the Anshan Municipal Government has successively invested a large amount of capital in Anshan High-Tech Zone, taken a number of major actions and given decisive support to it. It has formed an eastward development strategy that taking Anshan High-Tech Zone as the main body, executed an eastward construction, eastward flow of talented persons and funds, eastward gathering of high and new technology enterprises and eastward transfer of political and cultural center.

3. The strategic thinking of Anshan High-Tech Zone is clear and broad for inviting businessmen, while all preferential policies are complete and practical. Facing to the world, the future and development and to be on the track of international economy, Anshan High-Tech Zone has invited businessmen and introduced capital on the principle of "coming and making money while we are developing, on the principles of reciprocity and mutual benefit, sharing risk and benefit in common." Various preferential policies like tax revenue, land use, workers, recruitment, etc., Anshan High-Tech Zone has provided are complete and practical.

4. With perfect functions , Anshan High-Tech Zone, can provide the Chinese and foreign businesses with all dimensional and high quality services. It has exercised the economic administrative power of competence at the municipal level and the administrative power of competence at the district level, implementing a closed-type administrative regulation. It has formed an administrative frame and a work structure of "small government and big society", which is small in scale but highly efficient and a support system of service with complete departments. On this basis, Anshan High-Tech Zone will provide the Chinese and foreign investors with perfect and overall services and create conditions for the investors to obtain high work efficiency and economic benefit.

5. Anshan High-Tech Zone abounds rich resources of high sciences and technologies and connects with the outside world via firm and solid channels , an obvious momentum for development in the process of industrialization of high and new technologies. Now, a basic framework has established in the fields of industries of high sciences and technologies such as electronic information, new materials, bioengineering, electrostatic environmental protection, merging the mechanical and electric equipment into an organic whole. Furthermore, Anshan High-Tech Zone has established close relations with the Chinese Academy of Sciences and 140 scientific research institutions under it , thereby the projects of high and new technologies being in considerable reserve. Anshan High-Tech Zone has set up extensive relations with many businesses from countries in Europe, America and Asian-Pacific region. The zone has also established the liaison offices for inviting businessmen in Beijing, Shanghai and Xiamen. Now, Canada-China Northeast Investment Promotion Association is establishing a Canadian Industrial Park in Anshan High-Tech Zone. The first eight foreign companies with a total investment of US$50 million have settled in the park in the zone.

6. The zone's overall plan starts on a high level and the

conditions for the construction of infrastructure facilities are all consummate. The design made by Qinghua University for Anshan High-Tech Zone plan has been appreciated by the Ministry of Construction and the Ministry of Science and Technology as an example of the development zones of high and new technologies in Northeast China, thus laying a firm and solid foundation for all-round development and construction of Anshan High-Tech Zone. Up to now, the skeleton of roads is basically completed in the "takeoff" area of Anshan High-Tech Zone, the system of water supply and drainage is almost finished, the telecommunication is in good position for use with the installation of 3,000 sets of telecommunication equipment and the completion of the buildings for 10,000 sets of communication, the wire net of television sets is under construction, the industrial electric capacity meets the requirements of users, the gas pipelines and the centralized heating system will be completed in the next year. The government will give support in priority to the big set of supporting facilities of the major projects of high and new technologies with foreign capital (the park of sciences and technologies), thus ensuring the requirements synchronously for both enforcing the projects and the commissioning thereof.

7. In Anshan High-Tech Zone the "Green Homeland" is a subzone, which is the best choice for the Chinese and foreign investors as well as the government employees to make residence. The "Green Homeland" is an important symbolic mark of new urban construction of Anshan, which is jointly developed by the Anshan zone and Hong Kong Coastal Real Estate (Group) Co. The project has registered with the Ministry of Construction and the Ministry of Science and Technology as a demonstrative project of dwelling houses for comfortable families in 2000, embodying a new concept for the environment where the human beings are living, combining the buildings with nature, merging the commercial service, the gathering places, the square, the schools, the plants into one body as necessary parts of a social community, and a comprehensive development of the green small residential zone with high intellectual facilities. The "Green Homeland" is an important symbol of Anshan new urban area construction and an ideal life selection of Chinese and foreign investors and other persons. The construction of this small zone will bring about huge impetus to the development of Anshan High-Tech Zone and provide an excellent living environment to the Chinese and foreign investors working in Anshan High-Tech Zone.

佛山国家高新技术产业开发区

Foshan High-Tech Industrial Development Zone

佛山高新技术产业开发区是1992年12月经国务院批准建立的国家级高新技术产业开发区。

全区面积10平方公里，由城南、城西高新技术产业开发园和小黄圃高新技术产业开发岛组成，并已建立了佛山高新区政策区。依照规划，区内支柱产业和产业发展重点为电子与信息技术、电器、仪器仪表及医疗器械等光机电一体化技术，医药及生物技术，塑料及精细化工技术等。建区以后，佛山市政府成立了高新技术产业开发区领导小组，由市长任组长，下设高新技术产业开发区管理委员会。目前开发区已征用土地7.55平方公里，开发土地6.46平方公里，区内已竣工各类建筑78万平方米，全区批准进区的有与美国、日本、瑞典、加拿大、意大利、台湾、香港等国家和地区合资、合作或内资企业40多家，已投产或试产的企业有30多家，其中一些项目的技术处于国内外先进水平，如：电磁四通换向阀、复合包装材料、电脑显示器、DMS-100程控交换机、特种医疗导管和生物工程有机复合肥等。生产的各种高新技术产品除供应国内市场外，还出口美

区内高新技术企业先进的生产线
An Advanced Assembly Line of the High-tech Enterprise in the Zone

国、日本、香港等世界各地。1995年和1996年，在全国53个国家高新技术产业开发区各项指标排序中，佛山高新区人均产值名列第三位，并有两家企业被列入“全国百强高新技术企业”。1997年，全区实现技工贸总收入35.9亿元，工业总产值36.4亿元，利税3.5亿元，初步显示出高新技术产业的强大生命力，成为佛山市经济新增长点。

为了加快高新区的建设，市政府先后投入资金20多亿元完成了佛山新港码头、佛陈大桥、季华邮电大楼和湾华变电站等大型配套设施的建设，从而解决了高新区的交通运输和通信等关键问题。目前，开发区的运输、商业、海关、金融、资讯、生产、住宅等各种服务设施配套齐全，同时，进区的高新技术企业享受国家和省、市给予税收、金融、信贷、进出口、用地、人才引进和人员出入境等方面的优惠政策，形成了优越的软硬投资环境。佛山高新区还设立了留学人员创业园，为海外学子回国创业，报效祖国创造条件。

佛山高新区水、电供应充足；通讯条件良好；交通便捷，通过新港码头（在开发区内），可以经东北、东南及西南三条河流，分别通往广州、香港、澳门、江门等珠江三角洲各地，甚至还可抵达广西梧州、柳州、南宁等地。通过区内公路（六车道）同样可通往全国各地，佛山机场及佛山火车站也是佛山与全国各地联系的重要途径。

佛山国家高新技术产业开发区环境优美、社会治安良好，适于发展经济，企业投资回报率较高，是各种投资和办企业的好去处。热诚欢迎国内外客商和各界人士前来进行各种形式的经济技术合作，共同发展，共创辉煌。

Foshan High-Tech Industrial Development Zone was established in December 1992 with approval of the State Council.

The total area of the zone is 10 square km, consisting of Southern High-Tech District, Western High-Tech District and Shunde Xiao Huangpu High-Tech Island, and the Policy Zone of Foshan High-Tech Industries Development Zone. According to the plan, the following industries have been chosen as the priority industries to be developed in Foshan High-Tech Industrial Development Zone such as electronics and information technology, optics-machinery-electronics integration and electric appliance technology, medicine, medical care apparatus and biological engineering technology, pollution-free fine chemistry and modem plastics technology and so on. The Supervising Group was established by Foshan government while the development zone was set-up. The mayor of Foshan is the leader of the group. The Administration Committee of Foshan High-Tech Industrial Development Zone is in charge of daily administration. So far, 7. 55 square km of land had been taken over and 6.46 square km had been developed. About 0. 78 million m^2 of various buildings had been completed. The companies from the United States, Japan, Sweden, Canada, Italy, Taiwan, Hong Kong, and other areas have set up over 40 joint ventures in the zone. Of which, many technologies of projects are up to the advanced international levels such as 4-way reversing valve, complex packaging box, scan color monitor, DMS-100 program control switch equipment, special catheter, bioengineering organic complex fertilizer and so on. The high-tech products made in the development zone are sold not only in domestic market but also exported to the Unite States, Japan, Hong Kong and other places in the world. In 1995 and 1996, Foshan High-Tech Industrial Development Zone was ranked third in output value per person among 53 national high-tech development zones of China. Two enterprises were listed as two of the 100 top high-tech enterprises of China. In 1997, the gross revenue of the development zone was

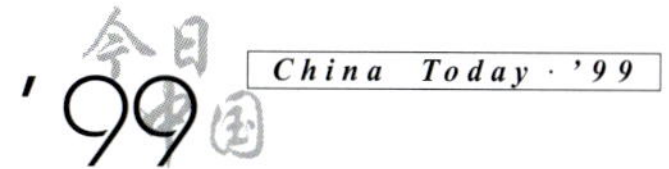

3.59 billion yuan. The industrial output value was 3.64 billion yuan. The profits and taxes were 350 million yuan. Great importance had been attached and wide support had been given to the development zone by the state, Guangdong Province and Foshan Municipality. The government had invested 2 billion yuan for constructing big infrastructure facilities such as Foshan New Port, Fochen Bridge, Jihua Telecommunication Building and Wanhua electricity substation, etc. So far, various service facilities had been built, such as transportation, water and electricity, commerce, finance, customs, communications, production, residential buildings and so on. Meanwhile, high-tech enterprises in the development zone can enjoy all the preferential policies given by the state, Guangdong Province and Foshan Municipality concerning taxation, finance, credit, import and export, land use, personnel introduction, entry and exit, etc. All of these made the development zone to form an excellent investment environment. A Creating Enterprises' Garden of Chinese who come back from their study abroad was set up in the development zone. It provids conditions for them to create their enterprises and to do something for the construction of their motherland after they come back from abroad.

The development zone has plenty water and power supply. The telecommunication is developed. The communication is convenient. Through the Foshan New Port in the development zone the goods can be shipped to Guangzhou, Hong Kong, Macao, Jiangmen and other places in the Pearl River Delta through three rivers in northeast, southeast and west. The goods can even be shipped to Wuzhou, Liuzhou and Nanning of Guangxi Zhuang Autonomous Region. Through the highways it connects with everywhere of China. Foshan Airport and Foshan Railway Station are the important channels of connecting Foshan with other places through China.

Foshan National High-Tech Industrial Development Zone with a fine environment and a sound social security is suitable for developing economy. The ratio of return on investment of enterprises in the development zone is much higher so that it is good place for investing and establishing enterprises. It sincerely welcomes the friends from all circles, both domestic and abroad, to come for extensive economic and technical cooperation, to make joint efforts for further development and achieving glory.

山西省高新技术创业中心

Shanxi High-Tech Service Center

1992年，在山西省科委科技体制改革总体框架的构筑过程中，山西省高新技术创业中心应运而生。它是以促进科技成果转化、培育高新技术小企业成长为目的的公益性科技服务机构，是太原高新技术产业开发区支撑服务体系的重要组成部分。

经过几年的努力，创业中心已经具备了一定的企业孵化基础条件，建成了4400平方米的企业孵化大楼，形成了集办公、开发、生产经营及商务、展览、会议、娱乐为一体的多功能孵化基地，为小型高技术企业提供了较为优越的创业环境。特别是省科委于1995年在创业中心建立企业孵化基金以来，创业中心的孵化功能得到进一步强化，科技风险投资在企业孵化工作中的强大作用日益显现。目前已形成孵化基金规模1300万元。经过几年的探索，创业中心在全国同行中率先提出了风险投资型企业孵化器的概念，制定了一整套科技风险投资工作规范，初步建立了适应社会主义市场经济体制、符合山西省实际情况的风险投资管理方式和运行机制，一个以科技风险投资为特色的企业孵化器雏形已见端倪。

在短短的几年时间里，创业中心共孵化高新技术企业34家、科技成果转化项目40余项。目前在孵企业就业人员800余人，保守估计1999年在孵企业技工贸总收入可达1亿元，利税2000万元。其中，雏龙电子、大恒通用电气、特美食品等三家孵化企业的产品年销售额均可达到千万元以上；中绿环保公司的烟气自动记录仪作为大气排放监测手段已被列入1998国家标准，并列入全国重点推广环保项目；瑞丰管件公司开发的PE电熔管件以全国同行业之首的名誉引起塑料管道行业的重视，并在农田灌溉和城镇供水工程中开始大面积推广应用。这些孵化项目的成功，不仅为山西省产业结构调整和经济发展培育了新兴产业和新的经济增长点，而且在促进科技成果转化、调动科技人员积极性、树立科技显示度项目、提高社会科技意识以及增加社会就业等方面都显示出了创业中心的企业孵化工作所产生的巨大社会效益。

Shanxi High-Tech Service Center was founded in 1992, under the leadership of the Science & Technology Commission of Shanxi Province. It is a public science & technology service institute aiming at accelerating the transfer of science & technology achievements, promoting the development of high technology and developing small business. It is also an important component of the serving system offered by Taiyuan High-Tech Development Zone.

After years of hard work, the center has developed a superior infrastructure environment for the launching of small high-tech projects with building areas of 4,400 square meters for business incubating, integrating administration, research, development, production, commercial meetings, exhibitions and amusenent. Now, its incubating function has been enforced, and science & technology investment officiancy is remarkable. Until now, the incubating fund

reached 13 million yuan. During years of efforts, center has initially set up a management mechanism saitable to a socialist market system and the practical conditions of Shanxi Province. A marker based upon science & technolog investment has emerged.

In a few years, the center has incubated 34 advanced small businesses and transferred 40 scientific research achievements. The incubated companies employ 800 staff members; the estimated total income of 1999 is about 100 million yuan and the profit and tax payment is 20 million yuan. The annual sales income of some incubated companies payment is such as Chulong Electronics, Daheng General Electrical, Temei Food etc., can reach more than 10 million yuan each. The auto fume recorder developed by Zhonglu Environment Protection Company has been regarded as the criteria of the produsts of the kind in China and has been introduced to all over the country. The PE electric melted pipes of Ruifeng Pipe Company ranks the first of the industry and has shown great attractiveness. The pipes have been widely used in agriculture irrigating projects and city water supplying projects. With the success of incubated items, the center are making more and more contributions not only to cultivating new industries and new economic growing point in the economic structural adjustment and the economic development of Shanxi Province, but also to accelerating the transfer of scientific & technological research achievements, and promoting enthusiasm of researchers.

山西省高新技术创业中心孵化大楼
The Business Incubator Building of Shanxi High-Tech Service Center

甘肃省高科技创业服务中心

Gansu High-Tech Pioneering Service Center

甘肃省高科技创业服务中心成立于1992年1月，是隶属于甘肃省科委领导下的全民性质的服务机构。中心位于兰州高新技术产业开发区科技街。现有员工14人，其中大专以上学历的员工占职工总人数的80%以上。中心下设办公室、政策项目部、企业管理部、物业管理部，可为企业提供政策咨询、项目孵化以及场地、物业管理等多项服务。

近年来，中心根据自身发展的需要，提出“以壮大自身经济实力为主导，挖潜、创收为手段，管理孵化为目的”的工作思路，不断优化中心的软、硬孵化条件，拓展服务功能。在省科委的支持下，1997年将原办公大楼进行了整体改造，使中心具有了3000多平方米的孵化基地，从此结束了甘肃省高科技创业服务中心无孵化场地的状况。在建成孵化基地后，中心先后落实和完善了《甘肃省高科技创业服务中心管理暂行规定》、《甘肃省高科技创业服务中心及其孵化企业税收优惠政策》。根据甘肃省产业政策和兰州高新区产业基础，确定了以电子信息、生物医药、机电一体化、计算机软件开发为主的孵化领域及项目。从1993年开始接纳孵化企业22户，毕业3户，孵化企业高新技术总收入累计达2133.8万元。

Gansu High-Tech pioneering Service Center,founded in January 1992, is under the leadership of Gansu Science and Technology Committee. It's located at Science-Technology Street of Lanzhou New and High-Technology Development Zone. There are 14 staff members in the center. More than 80 percent of its personnel have college education background. The center has an office, a policy related item department, enterprise management department and a property managent department.

Recently, according to the needs of its development, the center has the work idea: strengthening its economical power, tapping the potentials and increasing income, and promoting the incubation of high-tech enterprises. Under the guidance and help of Gansu Science and Technology Commission, its old office building was renovated and decorated in 1997. Now there is a 3,000-square-meter incubation base in the center. Following this, the center has implemented and improved the Tentative Management Regulations of Gansu High-Tech Pioneering Service Center and Preferential Treatinent on Taxation of Gansu High-Tech Pioneering Service Center.

Based on the Gansu industrial policy, Lanzhou high-new development zone fouses on development of electronic information, biological and medical science, electro-machinery, and computer software. Some 22 pioneering enterprises have been operated since 1993. Three of them have been successfully incubated. Total accumulative income of high-new technology of these enterprises amounted to 21.338 million yuan.

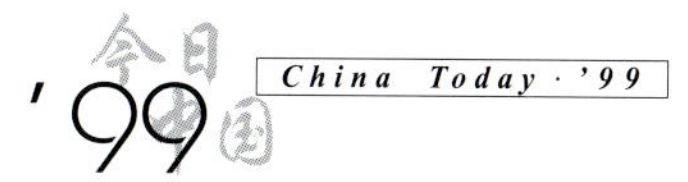

杨凌示范区创业服务中心

Yangling Agricultural Business Incubator

杨凌农业高新技术产业示范区创业服务中心于1998年3月正式成立，是中国第一家农业科技企业孵化器，是示范区管委会直属的具有独立法人资格的社会公益性科技服务事业单位，亦是杨凌示范区海外学子创业园的组织服务机构。

创业中心依托中国杨凌农科城，突出农业高新技术产业特色，创造良好的环境和条件，培育具有市场竞争力的高新技术企业和科技型企业家。

创业中心建在示范区产业区内，拥有一定孵化场地和示范基地，可提供不同规格水、电、暖、气配套的办公、生产用房和中试基地，设有共用的会议室、接待室、展示厅和文讯室等。现有孵化场地2000多平方米，建筑面积20000多平方米的创业大厦正在施工建设中，可望在2000年投入使用。

创业中心在管理上采用企业化管理模式。内设综合业务部、项目发展部、咨询培训部、服务管理部，为进驻企业提供全方位服务。入孵企业除享受示范区优惠政策外，还享受创业中心在资金、房租等方面的扶持发展政策和企业工商注册登记、项目申报、高新技术企业认定、人员培训、财务管理、政策法律咨询及INTERNET国际互联网络、电子商务、文讯等综合服务。

创业中心以农业科技型小企业为主要孵化对象，优先孵化与支持良种繁育、旱作农业、节水灌溉、生物工程、农副产品深加工及其它符合示范区产业发展规划的科技企业。成立一年多来，已进驻孵化企业24家，其创办者大都是杨凌各科教单位拥有一定技术成果的科技人员，其中博士5人，硕士3人，研究员7人，开发的产品紧密结合生产实际，市场潜力大，具有广阔的发展前景。

创业中心是高新技术企业孵化器，是科技创业者摇篮，是示范区技术创新体系的重要组成部分。创业中心将以优惠的条件、优良的环境、优质的服务支持科技人员创办高新技术企业。热忱欢迎国内外有识之士来杨凌创业中心一展宏图。

Yangling Agricultural Business Incubator (YABI) of Yangling Agricultural High-Tech Demonstration Zone was established in March 1998. YABI, first of its kind in China, is a non-profit and an independent operating institution. It is also the service organization for the business incubating garden of Yangling Agricultural High-Tech Demonstration Zone opened up for oversea Chinese scholars.

YABI depends on Yangling Agricultural Science Town to spotlight the distinctive features of agricultural high-tech industries in order to create favorable conditions for agricultural business, develop highly competitive agricultural high-tech business and train the entrepreneurs who have good mastery of agricultural science and technology.

YABI is located in the Zone and has certain business incubating facilities and demonstration bases. It can provide different-sized offices, workshops and mid-experiment bases equipped with water, electricity, heating and stream systems. It has public meeting-rooms, reception rooms, exhibition halls, document room as well as correspondence rooms. Its business incubating facilities have an area of 2,000m^2. The 20,000 sq m incubating building is under construction. It is expected to be put into use in 2000.

YABI has three branches, they are Comprehensive Affairs Section, Project Development Section and Advisory & Training Section. These sections provide all-round services for enterprises established within YABI. The being incubated enterprises will enjoy preferential policies. In addition, they can also enjoy privileges on fund, rent and services and so on.

YABI is mainly oriented to incubate small business of agriculture and give priority to the crop breeding, seed reproduction, dry-land farming, water-saving irrigation, bioengineering, farm-product processing and other respects in accordance with the policy of the demonstration zone. YABI was founded over a year ago.A total of 24 companies have registered in it. Most of the managers of these companies are scientists from research institutions or universities, of whom there are five with Doctorate degree, three with Master's degree and seven research workers. The developed products have a great market potential and bright future.

YABI is a high-tech business incubator, an important part of the zone's technology innovatory system. It will create favorable conditions, providing preferential policies and better services to support scientists who want to establish business in YABI.

People both at home and abroad are warmly welcome to Yangling.

正在建设中的创业大厦
Inncovation Mansion is under construction

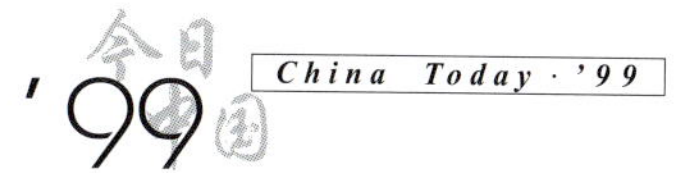

湘潭高新技术产业开发区

Xiangtan High Technology Industrial Development Zone

湘潭高新技术产业开发区地处长沙、株洲、湘潭“金三角”的重要位置。湘潭公路一大桥、二大桥、铁路大桥和正在兴建的三大桥临区飞架，四面贯通，107、320国道和京珠高速公路在此交汇；湘黔、京广铁路从这里穿越；傍区有湘潭千吨级码头，船舶可通江达海；长沙黄花国际机场距区仅60公里，经长潭高速公路40分钟可达；装机容量180万千瓦的湘潭新电厂一期工程2 × 30万千瓦机组已并网发电，二期工程正在抓紧进行施工，区内有22万伏和11万伏变电站各一个；区内有日供水能力25万吨水厂一个，日供水能力40万吨的新水厂正在筹建；煤气管道已接通进区；集中供热系统也正在抓紧进行筹建；市内18万门程控电话可直拨世界各地，光纤通信、移动传呼、图文传输等各项国际业务均已开通；海关已在区内定址兴建。

湘潭高新区坚持以发展高新技术产业和利用高新技术嫁接、改造传统产业相结合，开发区建设与湘潭新城建设相结合，以发展高新技术产业为主攻目标，积极招商引资，大力加强基础设施建设，不断改善和优化环境。

湘潭高新区正按照“拓展框架、主攻产业、招商筹资、建设新城”的思路，开拓奋进，力争早日建成湘潭发展高新技术产业的基地，对外开放招商引资的窗口，改革创新的样板，经济发展的龙头和现代文明的新城！

Xiangtan High Technology Industrial Development Zone is situated in the juncture of Changsha, Zhuzhou and Xiangtan, Zhuzhou, well-known as a “Golden Triangle”. Three expressways–No.107, No. 320 State Highways and Beijing-Zhuhai-Highway are intersected and the First, and Second Highway Bridges and the Railway bridge are in this zone, and the Hunan-Guizhou, and Beijing-Guangzhou railways are passing through this zone. At the side of this zone there is a 1,000-ton dock ships can go to rivers and seas. The Huanghua International Airport seated in Changsha City is only 60 kilometers or a 40-minute drive from the zone. The newly built Xiangtan power plant has an installed generating capacity of 1.8 million kw and its two 300,00 kilowatt generation units have put into use. There are two transformer stations with a capacity of 220,000 and 110, 000 volts respectively. Also this zone can supply 250,000 tons of water a day. A new water work with a daily supply capacity of 400,000 tons is under construction. The gas pipes have been laid into the zone. The concentrated-heating system has also been put in hand. The 1.8 million lines of program-controlled telephone system will connect the zone with the rest of the world. The optic-fiber communication, movable-calling and fax services for international businesses have been opened. The customs building has been built up already.

Xiangtan high-new development zone aims to develop new and high technical industry, to combine with that utilizing high-new technology with grafting, to reform the traditional industry and to combine the zone construction with that of Xiangtan new city .With the development of new-high technical industry as a main goal, the zone has made great efforts to attract cooperators and capital for the constructions of infrastructure facilities in order to better the environment conditions.

Now the high-new technology development zone is going forward in accordance with the principle of "developing the industries, and attracting partners and capital for the construction of a new city". We will build up a development base of high-new technology industry and a window of soliciting partners and drawing into capital so as to build it into a reforming sample, an economical development pace-setter and a modern city.

济宁高新技术产业开发区

Jining High and New Tech Industrial Development Zone

1992年，和着邓小平南巡讲话的东风，济宁高新技术产业开发区应运而生。她地处327国道两侧，总体规划面积13.2平方公里，位于济宁、兖州、曲阜、邹城经济发展的金三角地带，是济宁构建大城市格局的关键部位，是实施国家科委建设齐鲁高新技术产业带的重要组成部分。沿京沪高速铁路、新石铁路、京九铁路、104国道、105国道、327国道、京福、日荷高速公路，乘北京、上海、广州、香港至济宁的航班可便捷抵达，水运有京杭大运河和沿海近港日照、青岛、连云港可利用。

建区以来，济宁高新区从实际出发，重点选择光机电一体化、新材料、生物工程和电子信息等四大产业为主导产业，多措并举，全力促进高新技术产业发展。从1998年起，围绕产业规划而设立的外资工业园、大学工业园、农业高科技园等陆续启动。小松山推、英克莱集团、黄淮集团、冠宇集团、菱花集团、如意集团等国内外享有盛誉的高新技术企业集团相继在此崛起，美国、澳大利亚、日本、南非、韩国、香港等国家和地区的大财团、大商社、大企业陆续看好这方热土，竞相来此投资办厂或设立分公司。

济宁高新区还努力构建精简效能、运转有序、小政府大社会的管理体制和现代化、科学化、法制化、国际化的运行机制，以高效一流的工作，一流到位的服务让中外客商满意，并简化办事程序，实现了“一个窗口对外，一个公章管到底”。

济宁高新区愿与国内外投资者携手并进，共创未来。

In 1992, under the atmosphere of the speech of Deng Xiaoping, the Jining High and New Tech Industry Development Zone came into being. She is located along the two sides of the No.327 State Highway. This zone, with a planned area of 13.2 square kilometers, is situated in the golden delta formed by the robust economic development districts of Jining, Yanzhou, Qufu, and Zoucheng. It is the key area for the agglomeration of the macro Jining city, and an important constituent part for the organized construction of Qilu High-Tech strip currently in implementation with the approval of the State Science and Technology Commission. Convenient transportation by the Beijing-Shanghai express Railway, the Xinxiang-Shijiusuo Railway and the Beijing-Kowloon Railway or by the No.104,105 and 327 state highways, the Beijing-Fuzhou expressway, the Rizhao-Heze expressway, or by the airlines from Beijing, Shanghai, Guangzhou, Hong kong can bring travelers directly to the development zone. The Beijing-Hangzhou Grand Canal and the nearby harbors of Rizhao,Qingdao, and Lianyungang provide easily accessible water transportation approach for the zone.

After its initiations, the zone, on basis of the practical reality, chose the light /machinery/electricity integrated industry, the new material industry, the biology industry and electrical information industry as the four leading fields of development. Diversified measures have been taken to stimulate and promote the full-speed development of the high technological industries. Since 1998, foreign-invested industrial park, university industrial park and high-tech agricultural park have been built in accordance with the industry development plan. The Komasu-Shantui, the Incu Group, the Huanghuai Group, the Guanyu Group, the Linghua Group, the Ruyi Group, etc., of high technologies and enjoying great honor at home and abroad have been established here one after another. Business consortia, big merchandise businesses, big enterprises from countries and regions such as the United States, Australia, Japan, South Africa, Korea, and Hong Kong gave favorable views for this square of hot-land, and came to make their investments and set up factories or affiliates.

The Jining Development Zone is setting up a mechanism that is concise and efficient, orderly operated, scientific, legalized and international to obtain the first-rate high efficient work for providing the national and international investors and customers with the very satisfactory services they need. Also the governmental affairs are simplified to realize the goal of "one service window, one effective seal" policies.

The bright pearl of the Holy Land, Jining high-tech zone is expecting that the investors from home and abroad will seize the opportunity and create the bright future together with us.

济宁高新技术产业开发区一角
A Corner of Jining High and New-Tech Industrial Development Zone

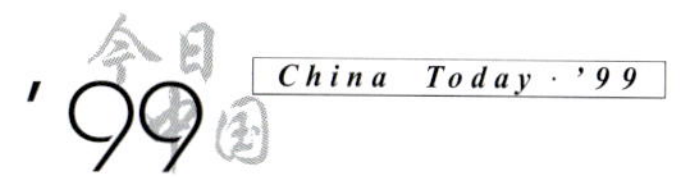

烟台高新技术产业开发区

Yantai High-Tech Industrial Development Zone

烟台高新技术产业开发区是1992年12月份成立的，规划面积75平方公里，封闭管理区25平方公里。1998年4月，国务院批准烟台高新区为APEC科技工业园区；1998年12月14日，中国国家科技部正式下发文件批准在烟台高新区设立中俄高新技术产业化合作示范基地。1998年实现技工贸总收入19.3亿元，财政收入和国内生产总值达到4510万元和15.8亿元，累计实际利用外资4050.73万美元，出口创汇13966.46万美元。

烟台高新区成立以来，按照“发展高科技，实现产业化”的建区宗旨，围绕烟台市委、市政府确定的“高新技术产业密集区、科技教育新兴区、国际商贸旅游中心区和改革开放示范区”的发展目标，不断加大基础设施建设投资，几年来已累计投入资金7亿多元，使产业集中区形成了良好的基础条件，公路、供电和通信网络已全部形成，产业支撑功能基本完善，旅游、金融、商贸、科教、文化、娱乐等设施建设都日趋完善。借助沿海开放区的政策、环境优势和已有的基础条件，把发展定位在开放带动上，已新批准成立外资企业95家，项目总投资12849.5万美元。在高新区内开辟了留学人员创业基地；联合区内国防科技交流中心、高技术产业公司、烟台大学和思可达高新技术产业基地，共同创办高创中心，对40多项高新技术成果进行了孵化。聘请丹麦、日本、俄罗斯以及国内专家进区搞技术攻关、短期合作开发达10余项。几年的建设成果增强了烟台高新区的吸引力和项目承载力，各类企业发展到760多家，其中高新技术企业从建区初期的两家发展到26家；机电信息、海洋生物制药、新材料、精细化工等正逐步成为支柱产业。

Yantai High-Tech Industrial Development Zone was set up in December 1992. Its mapped out area is 75 square kilometers, within which 25 square kilometers are used as a closed administrative quarter. In April 1998, with the approval of the State Council, it became the APEC Yantai Scientific and Technological Industrial Park. On December 14 of the same year, the Ministry of Science and Technology officially approved the establishment in the industrial park of a Model Base for Sino-Russian High-Tech Industrial Joint Venture. In 1998, the total income of Yantai High-Tech Industrial Development Zone in the scopes of technology, industry and trade amounted to 1.93 billion yuan RMB. Its financial income and gross domestic production reached the amount of 45.1 million yuan RMB and 1.58 billion yuan RMB respectively. The actual utilization of foreign capital added up to US$40.5 million and its foreign exchange earning through export was US$139.665 million .

Since its establishment, Yantai High-Tech Industrial Development Zone has been built with the aim of "developing high technology and realizing industrialization". Its goal set by the Municipal Party Committee and City Government is to build this zone into an area with dense high-tech industries, an new area for science and technology education, an international trade and tourist center and a demonstrative base for the reform and opening policies. In order to achieve this goal, the investment in infrastructure projects has been constantly enforced and the total investment in the past few years has amounted to 700 million yuan. Up to now, the dense industrial area within the zone has very good infrastructure conditions. Roads, electricity and communication networks have been built. These facilities are practically enough to support the industrial activities. Other facilities for tourism, finance, trade, education and entertainment are also improved day by day. With the help of the preferential policies, favorable environment and the existing infrastructure conditions of coastal areas, 95 foreign enterprises have recently been approved to set up. The total investment of these enterprises will amount to US$ 128.495 million. A base for returned Chinese students and scholars to start an undertaking has also been established in the zone. The Yantai High-Tech Incubation Center, which was jointly set up by the Defense Science and Technology Exchange Center, the High-Tech Industrial Company, Yantai University and Sikeda High-Tech Industrial Base, has incubated more than 40 high-tech scientific research achievements. The High-Tech Industrial Development Zone has hired domestic experts and foreign experts from Denmark, Japan and Russia to cooperate in tackling difficult technological problems. Ten technological programs have been carried out after a short period of cooperation. Following the development of these few years, the High-Tech Industrial Development Zone has greatly improved its ability in attracting and supporting industrial enterprises. When the high-tech zone was first established, there were only two high-tech industrial enterprises, but now the number of high-tech enterprises has reached 26. The total number of industrial enterprises in the zone has reached 760. Mechanical and electrical industry, communications industry, halobios medicine industry, new materials industry and fine chemical industry are gradually becoming its principal industries.

新乡高新技术产业开发区

Xinxiang High and New Technology Development Zone

新乡高新技术产业开发区（以下简称高新区）始建于1992年8月，1994年3月被河南省政府批准为省级高新区。

新乡高新区地处河南省北部，毗邻新乡市市区，规划面积18平方公里。交通便利，京深高速公路沿边而过，京广、太石铁路在此交汇，新荷铁路由新乡直达石臼港。

新乡在河南经济发展中的地位十分重要，是河南省的电子、纺织、医药、建材等工业的主要基地。

新乡高新区经过7年的创业，取得了令人瞩目的成绩，基础设施建设已具规模，在3平方公里的范围内实现了"六通一平"，竣工建筑面积70多万平方米，一个环境优美、功能齐全、设施配套、发展强劲的高新技术产业基地已经崛起。

良好的投资环境，吸引了包括美国、加拿大、德国、日本、新加坡、台湾等国家和地区在内的众多投资者。目前，进区工业企业达138家，其中，三资企业30多家，年产值超亿元的高新技术企业11家，一批高新技术项目被认定为火炬计划项目，初步形成了以全密封免维护高比能蓄电池为龙头的新能源产业，以聚四氟乙稀微孔薄膜层压面料、ZA新型锌基合金为龙头的新材料产业，以人血白蛋白、丙种球蛋白为龙头的生物工程等三大高新技术支柱产业。1998年区内实现技工贸总收入25.1亿元，工业企业销售产值23.55亿元，利税总额4.2亿元，新乡高新区已经成为新乡市乃至河南省发展高新技术产业的基地和新的经济增长点。

Xinxiang High and New Technology Development Zone (hereafter referred to as High-Tech Zone) founded in August 1992, was confirmed and approved as a provincial standard high-new zone by the Government of Henan Province.

Xinxiang High-Tech Zone is located in the north of Henan Province, close to the Xinxiang City, with a total planned area of 18 square kilometers. The transportation here is connvenient with Beijing-Shenzhen Highway passing by, Beijing-Guangzhou and Taiyuan-Shijiazhuang railways running through it. Furthermore Xinhe Railway directly joins Xinxiang City to Shijiu Harbor.

Xinxiang plays a very important role in the economic development of Henan Province as a main base of electrical, textile, curatorial and construction industries in Henan Province.

Xinxiang High-Tech Zone has made outstanding achievements through seven years of hard work. The construction of infrastructure facilities has reached a primary scale. In the area of three square kilometers, water, power, gas, communication, stream and telecommunication facilities have been built and the land has been leveled. The completed construction area has reached over 700,000 square kilometers. A high-new technology industrial development zone has been growing up with beautiful surroundings, multiple functions, complete facilities.

The favorable investment environment has attracted many foreign investors from the United States, Canada, Germany, Japan, Singapore, Taiwan, etc., to invest and set up enterprises of various kinds. Up to now, there are already 138 industrial enterprises in the zone, among which over 30 enterprises are joint ventures, 11 enterprises are high-tech corporations which have an annual output value of more than 100 million yuan RMB. Some high-tech projects were regarded as Torch-Program projects, basically formed three kinds of high and new technology industries. The first is new energy resource industry whose main body is totally-enclosed maintenance-free storage battery; the second is new material industry whose main body is PTFE micro-porous film laminated fabric; the third is bioengineering industry whose main body is human albumin (IVIG, IMIG).

The total income of the Xinxiang High-Tech Zone has reached 2.51 billion yuan in 1998. The industrial sales value reached 2.355 billion yuan, the total profit and tax totalled 420 million yuan. Xinxiang High-New Zone has become an important base for developing high and new technology industry, a new economic growth point of Xinxiang City and Henan Province.

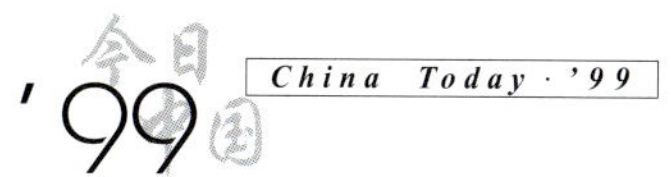

长治高新技术产业开发区

Changzhi High-Tech Development Zone

长治高新技术产业开发区是1992年经山西省人民政府批准成立的省级开发区。长治市地处山西省东南部，现辖13个县、市、区，人口300万，是山西省第三大城市。

高新区成立以来，注重于基础设施的建设和产业发展，目前区内道路、通信、水、电、气等市政设施已成龙配套，并已形成以生物工程、新材料产业为支柱，以机电一体化、电子信息、精细化工、新型建材、医疗器械、保健食品、高效农业为重点的产业发展框架。全区共有各类企业300余家，在建项目十余项。随着中国经济发展"北上西移"战略的逐步实施，必将会给长治高新区的发展带来更加有利的外部条件和新的发展机遇。

为了推动高新区的快速发展，长治高新区管委会在抓好硬件建设的同时，也十分注重软环境的建设。工商、税务、土地、保险、治安、房管等支撑服务体系实行一体化服务，并制定了《财政扶持企业发展的暂行规定》、《招商引资奖励办法》等优惠政策，对企业上缴的各项税收，通过财政予以适当比例的返还，形成了良好的投资环境，可为海内外客商投资兴业提供优质的服务、可靠的保证。

世纪之交的长治高新区将全方位、大跨度、多渠道地走向全国，走向世界。热诚欢迎海内外朋友到长治来考察访问、投资兴业、扩大友好往来和经贸合作，促进共同发展、共同繁荣!

Changzhi High-Tech Development Zone is a provincial-level development zone approved by Shanxi People's Government and was established in 1992. Changzhi is located in the southeast of Shanxi Province, and has 13 counties under its jurisdiction. It has 3 million population and it's the third largest city of Shanxi Province.

Since Changzhi High-Tech Development Zone has gone into operation, the zone's committee has paid more attention to the development of infrastructure facilities and industries. Now the water, power, roads, telecommunications and gas are in good supply. The pillar industries of the zone are biological projects and new material industry. Its framework is machinery and electronics industry, electro-information technology, fine chemicals, new building material, health food and high efficient agriculture. There are altogether 300 enterprises of various sectors. Some 10 projects are under construction. Along with the shift of China's economic development to "northward and westward", it would be a precious opportunity for Changzhi development zone's further development.

For the high-speed development of the hi-tech zone, the administrative committee is not only paying its attention to the construction of the infrastructure facilities but also the construction of investment environment. The integration services of the agencies such as industry and commerce, taxation, land, insurance, public security and housing, added with the publication of a series of favorable policies such as "Temporary Provisions Concerning Financial

Assisting Enterprises" and "Attracting Foreign Investment Rewarding Policy", which return a proportion of tax to enterprises through the agency of finance have made the development zone an ideal investment area, and have ensured the foreign investors the high-quality services and reliable credit.

In the new century, Changzhi High-Tech Development Zone will be nationalized and internationalized in fast steps and with multi-channels.

You will be warmly welcomed to come to Changzhi and make an investigation and investment, so that we can begin our cooperation and seek for common development and prosperity.

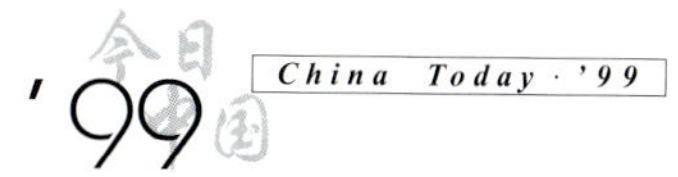

黑龙江省南岗民营科技企业示范区

Nangang Nongovernmental High-Tech Enterprises Demonstration Zone of Heilongjiang Province

黑龙江省南岗民营科技企业示范区于1995年6月经省政府批准，由省科委、哈尔滨市科委和南岗区政府三家共建，同年8月正式启动，1996年7月晋升为国家级示范区。示范区启动3年来，按照国家科技部和省、市提出的“推进当地民营科技企业向产业化、规模化、国际化方向发展和在改革发展上起到示范作用的技术密集型产业区”要求，充分发挥南岗区科技力量雄厚和城市基础设施齐全的优势，通过政策引导、强化服务、优化环境、向区域传统产业辐射高新技术，向“三大”单位（大学、大所、大企业）辐射新机制，为区域经济和科技事业发展注入了生机和活力，有力地促进了科技经济的双向结合，拉动了区域经济的快速发展。

示范区建立以来，以盘活区域内存量资产为途径，逐步形成了以大学、大所、大厂为点，以大直街、学府路为轴心的科技一条线，以区直和街乡工业小区为基础的科技园，辐射全区的民营科技企业群体，走出了一条具有南岗特色的少投入、高产出、快发展的路子。截止1998年底，民营科技企业发展到900户，注册资金10亿元，累计实现产值29亿元利税3.2亿元。产值超千万元的民营科技企业已达40户，并形成了光宇电源厂产值上亿元的大型民营科技企业，对本省市民营科技企业的发展起到了辐射带动作用。3年来示范区共吸引科技人员5580名，其中具有中高级职称的约占70%，吸纳各类科技成果580项，实施填补国内、省内空白的项目248项，有7项被列为国家级重点成果推广计划。

南岗区为扶持民营科技企业的发展，在全区范围内创造了各部门协调一致为示范区提供宽松环境的良好氛围。建立了融资、资产重组等七大服务体系，并由示范区办公室、科委协调工商、税务、公安、审计、卫生、环保、技术监督、银行、市容、文化、劳动、财政等部门集中联合办公，为企业提供一站式办照服务。仅1998年，新办民营科技企业354户。今年，南岗区政府以推进科技成果产业化为重点，建立了经济发展服务中心，集中全区为经济发展服务的职能部门，加大了服务工作力度，规范了服务行为。南岗区经济发展服务中心设有招商引资、办照一站式、科技服务等7个工作部和“博士俱乐部”、“企业家活动中心”，建立了科技成果市场化体系和加快科技型企业发展的催化体系以及壮大规模企业的培育体系，为民营科技企业向产业化、规模化发展创造良好的外部环境。

With the approval of the government of Heilongjiang Province, Nangang nongovernmental High-Tech Enterprises Demonstration Zone of Heilongjiang Province was jointly founded by the provincial scientific and technological commission, Habrin city scientific and technological commission and the Nangang District Government in June of 1995. It was formally operated in August of the same year and promoted as a state level demonstration zone in July of 1996. In the three years after its founding, the zone has always followed the principle of "promoting the development of local nongovernmental high-tech enterprises and making it industrialized and internationalized"set by the Ministry of Science and Technology and governments of the province and the city. It has fully displayed the advantages of strong scientific and technological strength and complete urban infrastructure facilities. Through policy guidance, strengthening services and optimizing the environment, the demonstration zone has radiated its high-tech functions to traditional regional industries and introduced new mechanisms to universities, research institutes and enterprises, bringing a vitality and vigor to the development of regional economy and strongly promoting a combination of technology and economy.

Since its founding, the demonstration zone has speeded up the circulation of the existing assets in the region. A scientific and technological belt has been formed, with universities, large-scale research institutes and factories as the mainstream and with Dazhi Avenue and Fuefu Road as axis. By the end of 1998, it had a total of 900 nongovernmental high-tech enterprises, with total registered capital of one billion yuan and accumulated output value of 2.9 billion yuan and profit and taxes of 320 billion yuan. The nongovernmental high-tech enterprises each with output value of more than 10 million yuan numbered 40. Guangyu Power Source Works has realized output value of more than 100 million yuan. They played a radiating and driving role in the development of nongovernmental high-tech enterprises in the city and even in the province. In three years, the demonstration zone has attracted a total of 5,580 technical personnel. Among them, some 70% have medium- or high-level technical titles. Some 580 scientific results have been introduced to the zone, filling the gap in 248 items in China and the province. Of which, 7 are listed in the national popularization program.

In order to support the development of nongovernmental high-tech enterprises, Nangang District has created a good investment environment. Seven service systems, including financing and assets reorganization have been established. Package service has been offered by local industrial and commercial department, taxation department, public security department, auditing department, health departments, environment protection departments, technical surveillance, banks, municipal environment, culture, labor and finance bureau or departments.

In 1998, 354 new nongovernmental high-tech enterprises have settled in the zone. Nangang District has set up a department in charge of foreign investment. A market of scientific results has been established as an effort to quicken the development of high-tech enterprises.

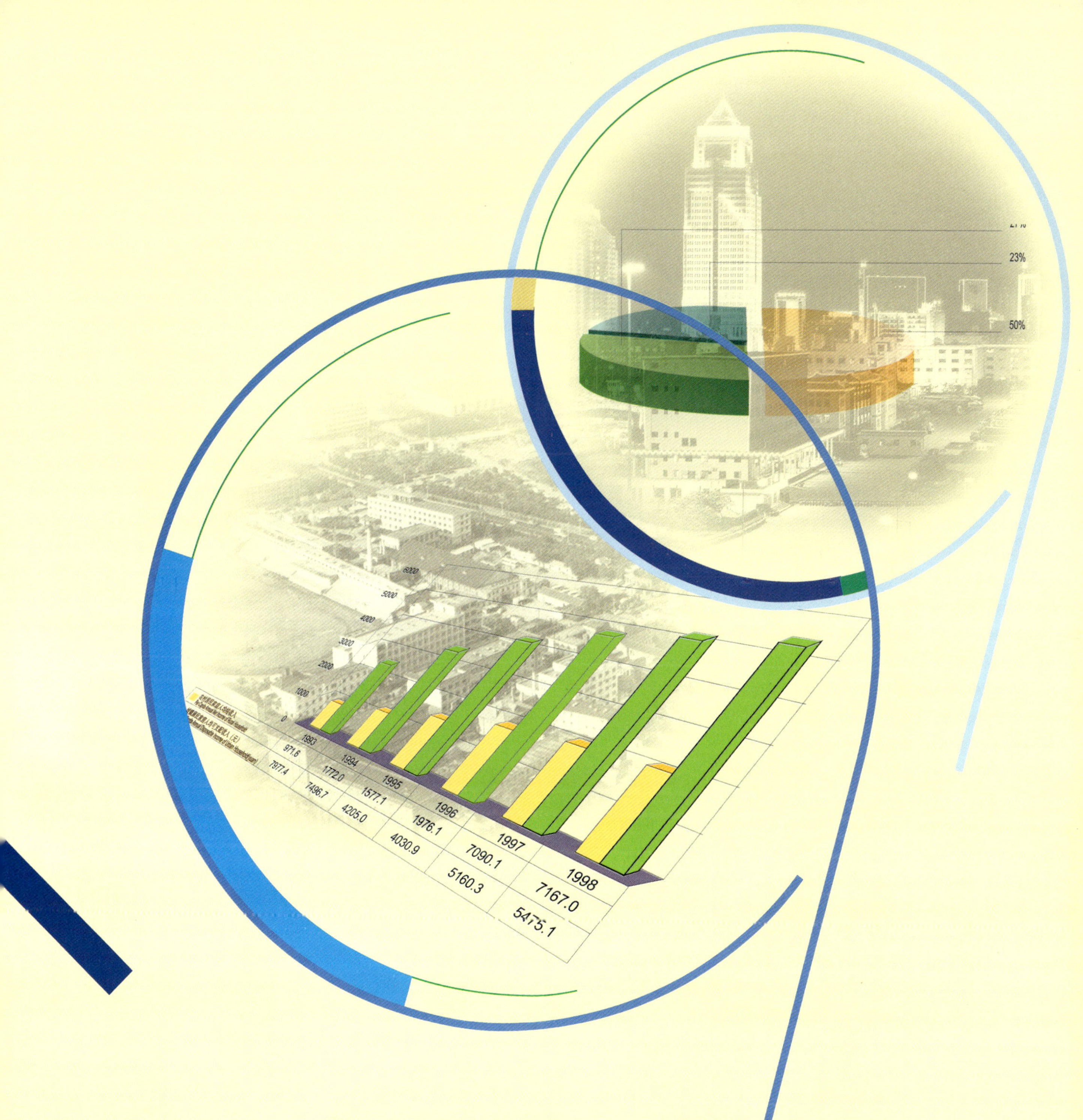

资　料　篇

DATABASE

资 料 篇

DATABASE

1998年国内生产总值构成
Composition of Gross Domestic Product in 1998

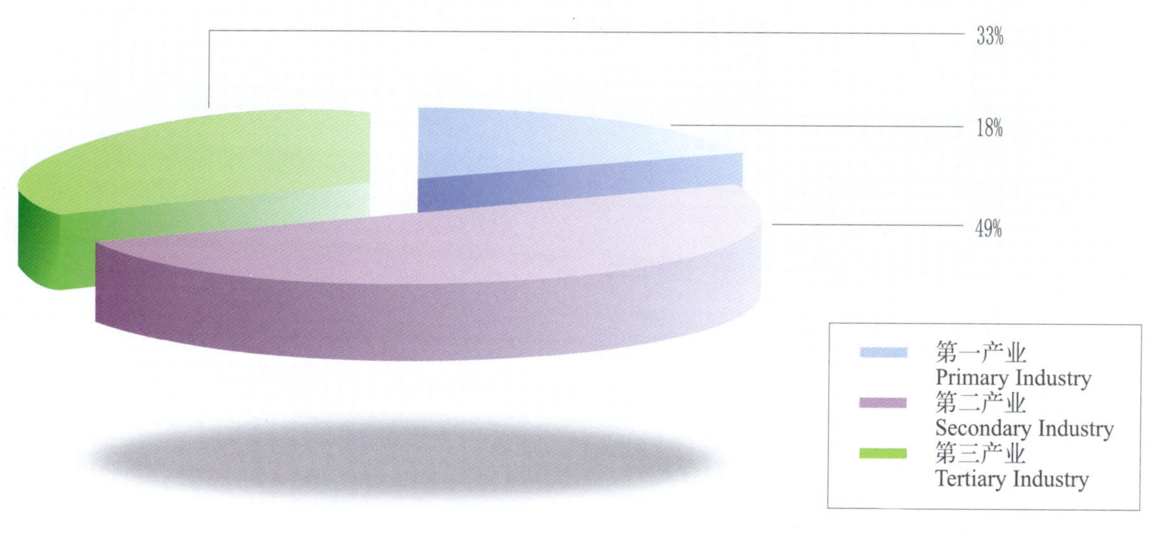

1998年从业人员产业构成
Composition of Employed Persons in 1998

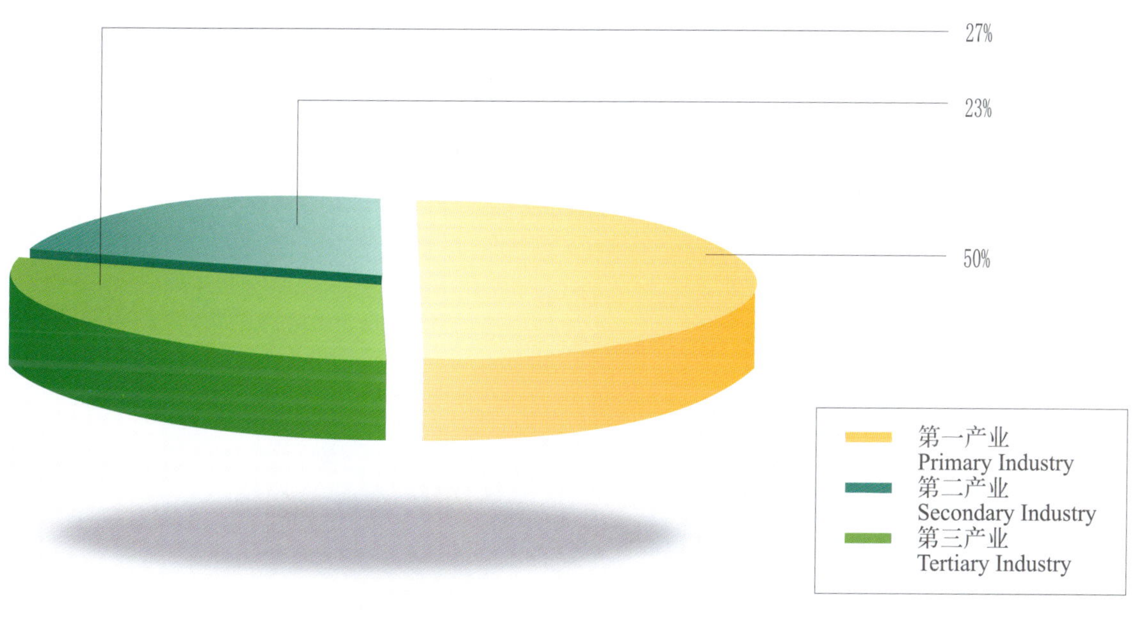

国家财政收支总额

Total Government Revenue and Expenditures

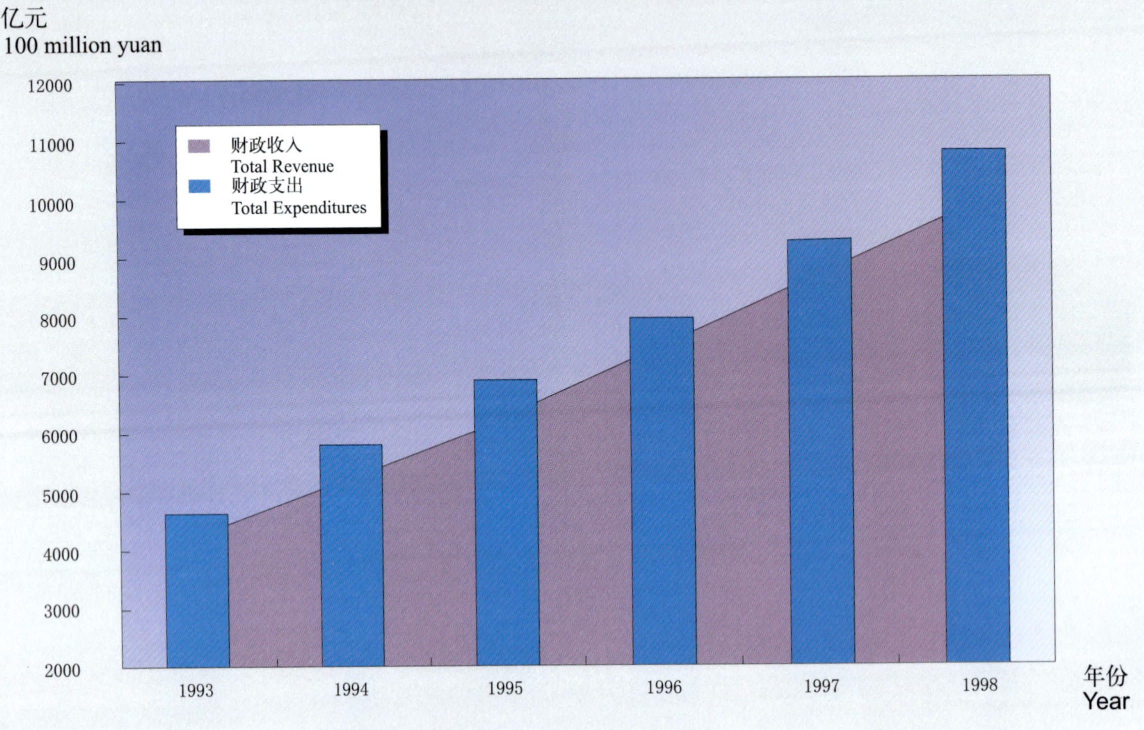

建筑业增加值与总产值

Value Added and Total Output Value of Construction

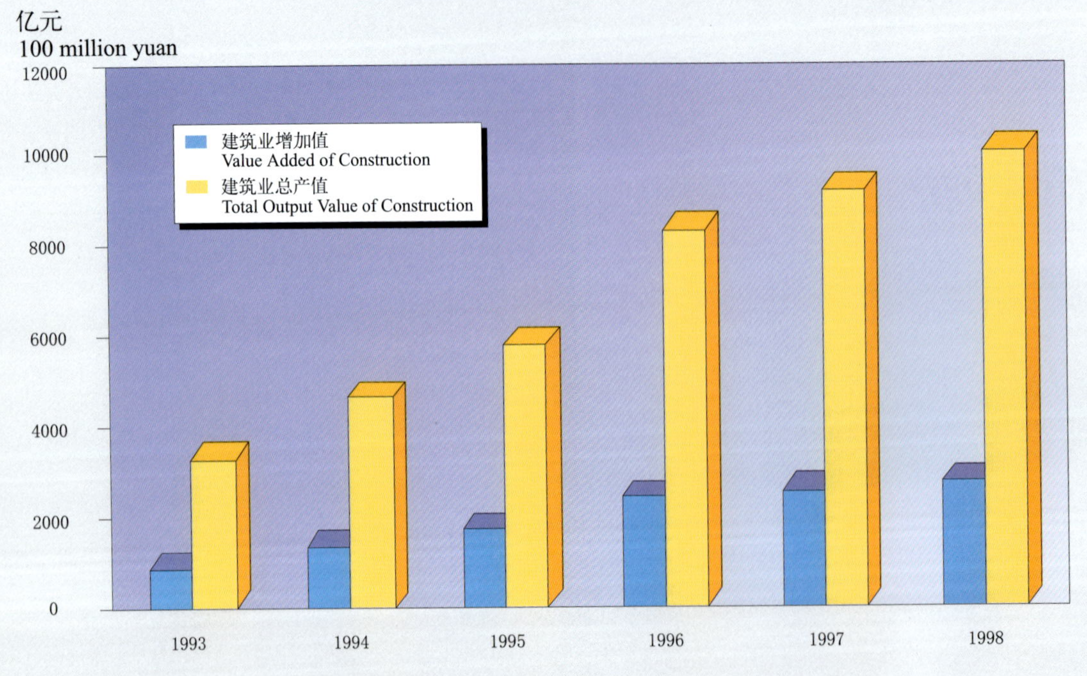

城乡居民家庭人均收入

Per Capita Annual Income of Urban and Rural Households

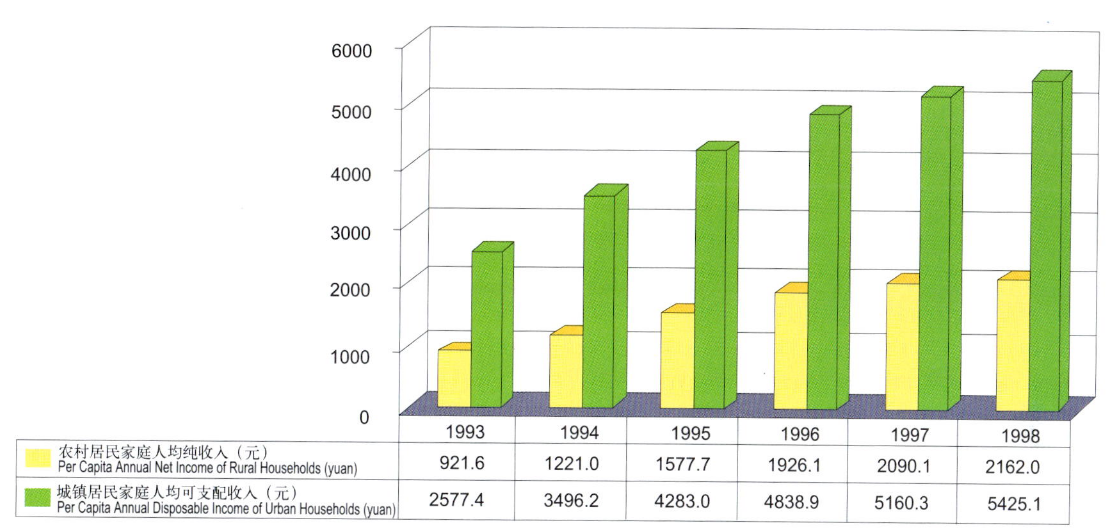

	1993	1994	1995	1996	1997	1998
农村居民家庭人均纯收入（元）Per Capita Annual Net Income of Rural Households (yuan)	921.6	1221.0	1577.7	1926.1	2090.1	2162.0
城镇居民家庭人均可支配收入（元）Per Capita Annual Disposable Income of Urban Households (yuan)	2577.4	3496.2	4283.0	4838.9	5160.3	5425.1

农、林、牧、渔业总产值

Gross Output Value of Farming, Forestry, Animal Husbandry and Fishery

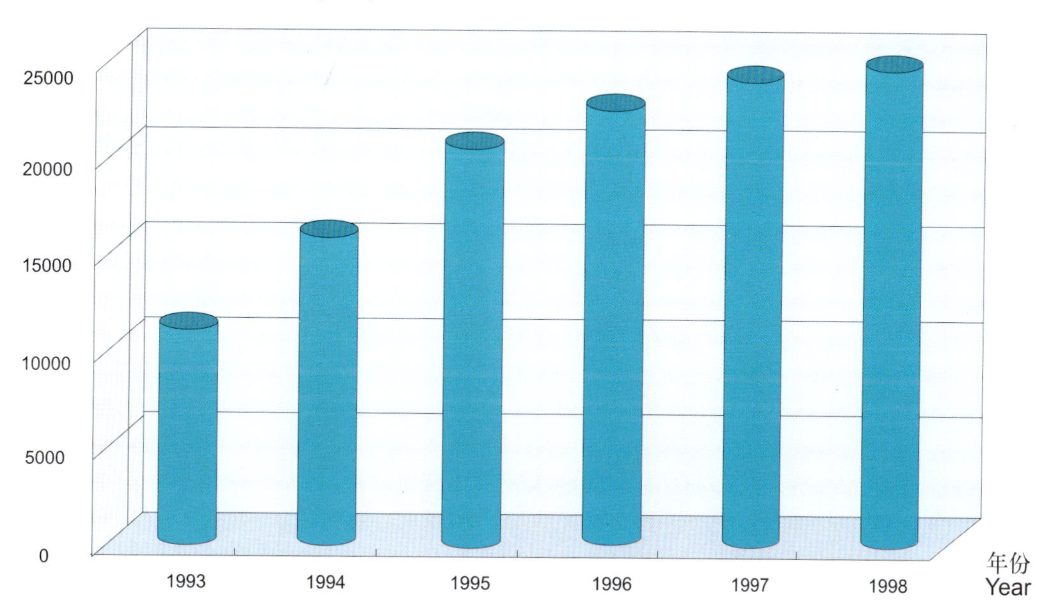

全国城乡居民储蓄存款年底余额和年增加额

Outstanding Amount and Added Amount of Savings Deposit in Urban and Rural Areas (Year-end)

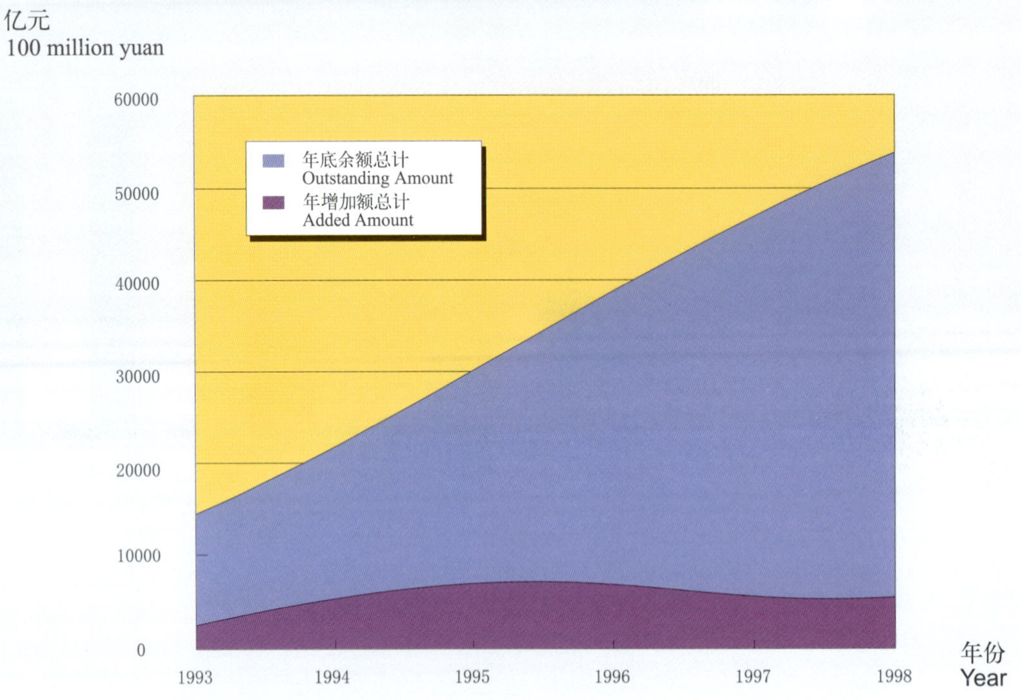

商品零售价格指数和居民消费价格指数

General Retail Price Index and General Consumer Price Index

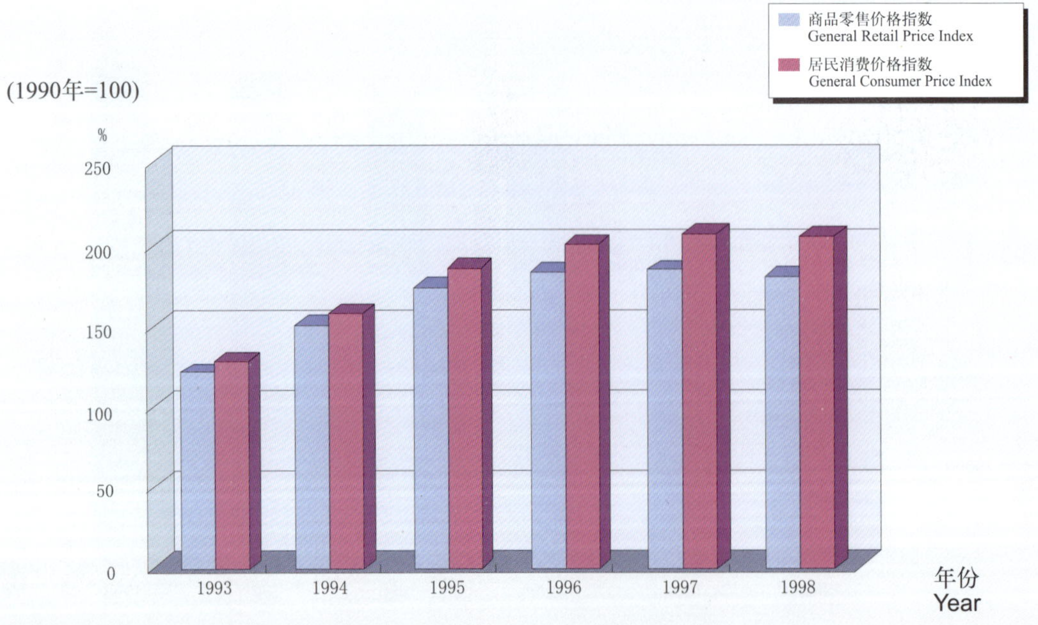

1950~1998年国家财政收支增长图

Growth of Government Financial Revenue and Expenditure Between 1950 and 1998

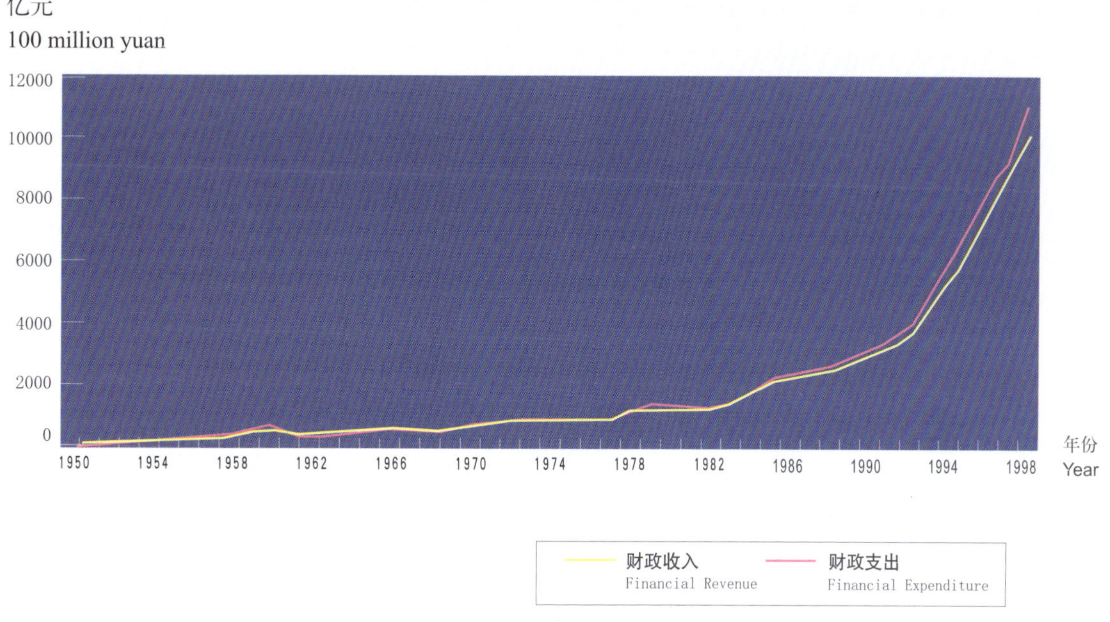

1950~1998年国家财政收支增长速度对比图

Comparison Between the Increase Rates of Government Financial Revenue and Expenditure From 1950 to 1998

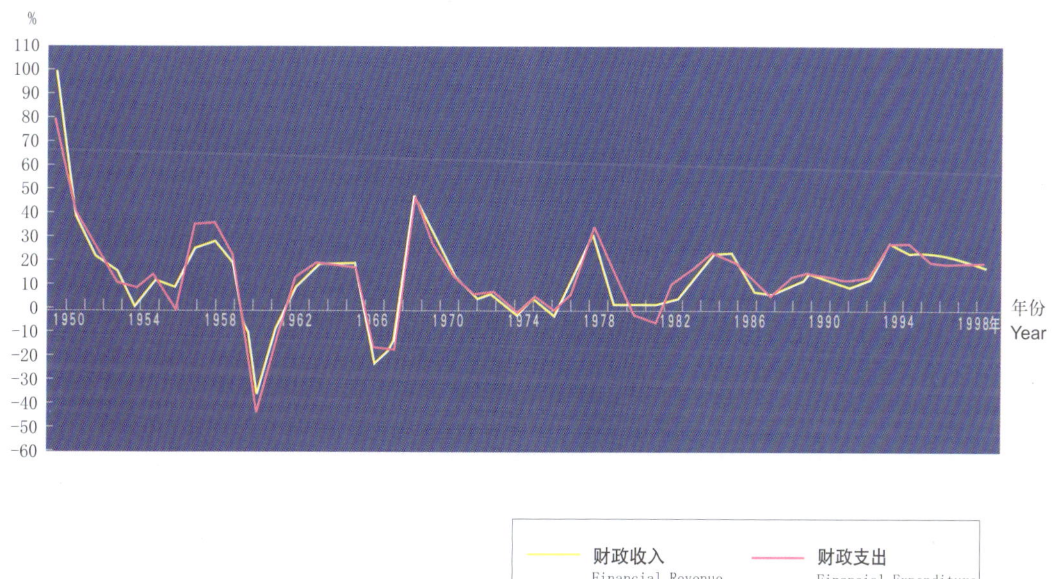

1978~1998年国家财政收支与国内生产总值增长速度对比图

Comparison Between the Increase Rate of the Government Financial Revenue and that of GDP Between 1978-1998

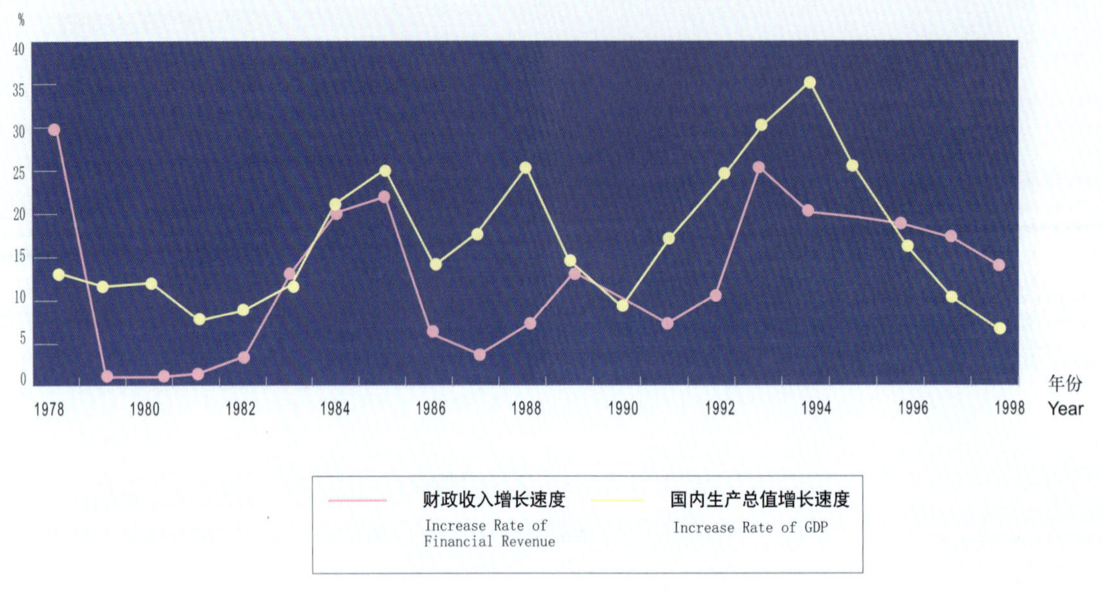

1978~1998年国家财政收入占国内生产总值比重图

The Percentage of Government Financial Revenue in GDP

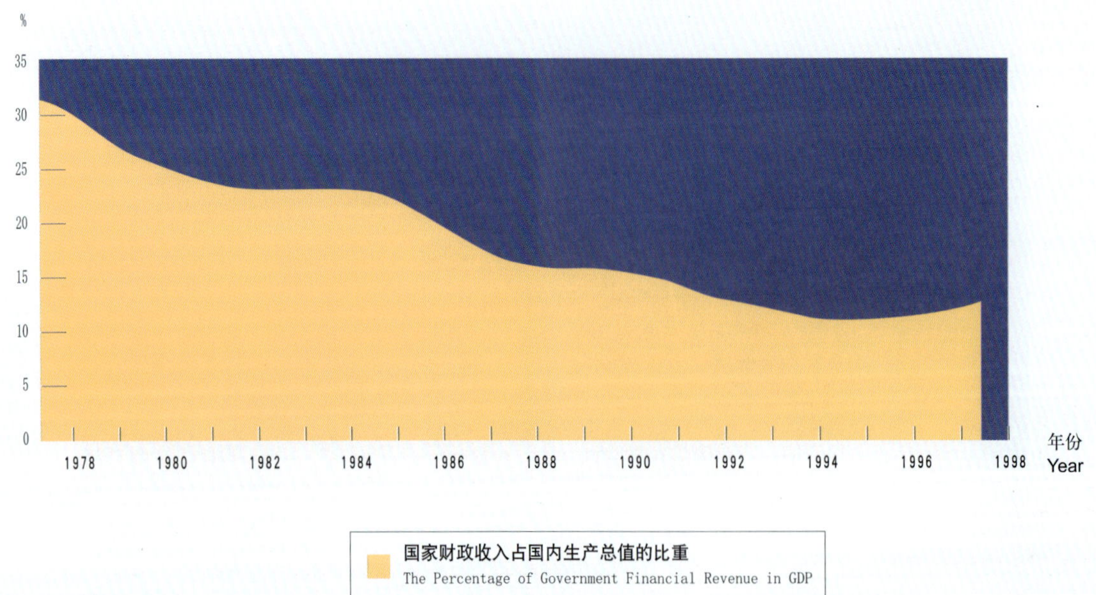

国内生产总值

Gross Domestic Product

本表按当年价格计算。

The data in value terms in this table are calculated at current prices.

单位：亿元 (100 million yuan)

年份 Year	国民生产总值 Gross National Product	国内生产总值 Gross Domestic Product	第一产业 Primary Industry	第二产业 Secondary Industry	工业 Industry	建筑业 Construction	第三产业 Tertiary Industry	交通运输仓储邮电通信业 Transportation, Post and Telecommunications	批发和零售贸易餐饮业 Wholesale, Retail Catering Trade	人均国内生产总值(元) Per Capita GDP (yuan)
1952	679.0	679.0	342.9	141.8	119.8	22.0	194.3	29.0	80.3	119
1953	824.0	824.0	378.0	192.5	163.5	29.0	253.5	35.0	115.5	142
1954	859.0	859.0	392.0	211.7	184.7	27.0	255.3	38.0	120.3	144
1955	910.0	910.0	421.0	222.2	191.2	31.0	266.8	39.0	119.8	150
1956	1028.0	1028.0	443.9	280.7	224.7	56.0	303.4	46.0	131.4	165
1957	1068.0	1068.0	430.0	317.0	271.0	46.0	321.0	49.0	133.0	168
1958	1307.0	1307.0	445.9	483.5	414.5	69.0	377.6	71.0	136.6	200
1959	1439.0	1439.0	383.8	615.5	538.5	77.0	439.7	94.0	145.7	216
1960	1457.0	1457.0	340.7	648.2	568.2	80.0	468.1	104.0	133.1	218
1961	1220.0	1220.0	441.1	388.9	362.1	26.8	390.0	69.2	110.8	185
1962	1149.3	1149.3	453.1	359.3	325.4	33.9	336.9	57.4	80.5	173
1963	1233.3	1233.3	497.5	407.6	365.6	42.0	328.2	55.0	76.1	181
1964	1454.0	1454.0	559.0	513.5	461.1	52.4	381.5	58.4	94.0	208
1965	1716.1	1716.1	651.1	602.2	546.5	55.7	462.8	77.4	118.3	240
1966	1868.0	1868.0	702.2	709.5	648.6	60.9	456.3	85.1	148.1	254
1967	1773.9	1773.9	714.2	602.8	544.9	57.9	456.9	72.3	153.5	235
1968	1723.1	1723.1	726.3	537.3	490.3	47.0	459.5	70.5	138.9	222
1969	1937.9	1937.9	736.2	689.1	626.1	63.0	512.6	84.9	163.6	243
1970	2252.7	2252.7	793.3	912.2	828.1	84.1	547.2	100.2	178.1	275
1971	2426.4	2426.4	826.3	1022.8	926.6	96.2	577.3	108.4	178.3	288
1972	2518.1	2518.1	827.4	1084.2	989.9	94.3	606.5	118.0	194.3	292
1973	2720.9	2720.9	907.5	1173.0	1072.5	100.5	640.4	125.5	211.0	309
1974	2789.9	2789.9	945.2	1192.0	1083.6	108.4	652.7	126.1	206.6	310
1975	2997.3	2997.3	971.1	1370.5	1244.9	125.6	655.7	141.6	175.8	327
1976	2943.7	2943.7	967.0	1337.2	1204.6	132.6	639.5	139.6	147.2	316
1977	3201.9	3201.9	942.1	1509.1	1372.4	136.7	750.7	156.9	213.8	339
1978	3624.1	3624.1	1018.4	1745.2	1607.0	138.2	860.5	172.8	265.5	379
1979	4038.2	4038.2	1258.9	1913.5	1769.7	143.8	865.8	184.2	220.2	417
1980	4517.8	4517.8	1359.4	2192.0	1996.5	195.5	966.4	205.0	213.6	460
1981	4860.3	4862.4	1545.6	2255.5	2048.4	207.1	1061.3	211.1	255.7	489
1982	5301.8	5294.7	1761.6	2383.0	2162.3	220.7	1150.1	236.7	198.6	525
1983	5957.4	5934.5	1960.8	2646.2	2375.6	270.6	1327.5	264.9	231.4	580
1984	7206.7	7171.0	2295.5	3105.7	2789.0	316.7	1769.8	327.1	412.4	692
1985	8989.1	8964.4	2541.6	3866.6	3448.7	417.9	2556.2	406.9	878.4	853
1986	10201.4	10202.2	2763.9	4492.7	3967.0	525.7	2945.6	475.6	943.2	956
1987	11954.5	11962.5	3204.3	5251.6	4585.8	665.8	3506.6	544.9	1159.3	1104
1988	14922.3	14928.3	3831.0	6587.2	5777.2	810.0	4510.1	661.0	1618.0	1355
1989	16917.8	16909.2	4228.0	7278.0	6484.0	794.0	5403.2	786.0	1687.0	1512
1990	18598.4	18547.9	5017.0	7717.4	6858.0	859.4	5813.5	1147.5	1419.7	1634
1991	21662.5	21617.8	5288.6	9102.2	8087.1	1015.1	7227.0	1409.7	2087.0	1879
1992	26651.9	26638.1	5800.0	11699.5	10284.5	1415.0	9138.6	1681.8	2735.0	2287
1993	34560.5	34634.4	6882.1	16428.5	14143.8	2284.7	11323.8	2123.2	3090.7	2939
1994	46670.0	46759.4	9457.2	22372.2	19359.6	3012.6	14930.0	2685.9	4050.4	3923
1995	57494.9	58478.1	11993.0	28537.9	24718.3	3819.6	17947.2	3054.7	4932.3	4854
1996	66850.5	67884.6	13844.2	33612.9	29082.6	4530.5	20427.5	3494.0	5560.3	5576
1997	73142.7	74462.6	14211.2	37222.7	32412.1	4810.6	23028.7	3797.2	6159.9	6053
1998	78017.8	79395.7	14599.6	38691.8	33429.8	5262.0	26104.3	5029.3	6609.6	6392

注:1980 年以后一、二、三产业之和与国民生产总值的差额为国外净要素收入。

Since 1980, the difference between the total of primary, secondary & tertiary industries and the Gross National Prcduct has been the net factor income from abroad.

国家财政收支总额及增长速度

Total Government Revenue and Expenditures and Their Increase Rate

年份 Year	财政收入 (亿元) Total Revenue (100 million yuan)	财政支出 (亿元) Total Expenditures (100 million yuan)	收支差额 (亿元) Balance (100 million yuan)	增长速度(%) Increase Rate(%) 财 政 收 入 Total Revenue	财 政 支 出 Total Expenditures
1970	662.90	649.41	13.49	25.8	23.5
1971-1975	3919.71	3917.94	1.77	4.2	4.8
1971	744.73	732.17	12.56	12.3	12.7
1972	766.56	765.86	0.70	2.9	4.6
1973	809.67	808.78	0.89	5.6	5.6
1974	783.14	790.25	-7.11	-3.3	-2.3
1975	815.61	820.88	-5.27	4.1	3.8
1976-1980	5089.61	5282.44	-192.83	7.3	8.4
1976	776.58	806.20	-29.62	-4.8	-1.8
1977	874.46	843.53	30.93	12.6	4.6
1978	1132.26	1122.09	10.17	29.5	33.0
1979	1146.38	1281.79	-135.41	1.2	14.2
1980	1159.93	1228.83	-68.90	1.2	-4.1
1981-1985	7402.75	7483.18	-80.43	11.6	10.3
1981	1175.79	1138.41	37.38	1.4	-7.5
1982	1212.33	1229.98	-17.65	3.1	8.0
1983	1366.95	1409.52	-42.57	12.8	14.6
1984	1642.86	1701.02	-58.16	20.2	20.7
1985	2004.82	2004.25	0.57	22.0	17.8
1986-1990	12280.60	12865.67	-585.07	7.9	9.0
1986	2122.01	2204.91	-82.90	5.8	10.0
1987	2199.35	2262.18	-62.83	3.6	2.6
1988	2357.24	2491.21	-133.97	7.2	10.1
1989	2664.90	2823.78	-158.88	13.1	13.3
1990	2937.10	3083.59	-146.49	10.2	9.2
1991-1995	22442.10	24387.46	-1945.36	16.3	17.2
1991	3149.48	3386.62	-237.14	7.2	9.8
1992	3483.37	3742.20	-258.83	10.6	10.5
1993	4348.95	4642.30	-293.35	24.8	24.1
1994	5218.10	5792.62	-574.52	20.0	24.8
1995	6242.20	6823.72	-581.52	19.6	17.8
1996	7407.99	7937.55	-529.56	18.7	16.3
1997	8651.14	9233.56	-582.42	16.8	16.3
1998	9875.95	10798.18	-922.23	14.2	16.9

注:1.1985年及以前，价格补贴冲减财政收入,1985年以后改列财政支出。为统一口径,本表对1985年及以前数字做了调整。

2.本表不包括国内外债务部分。

a)Government price subsidies were listed as negative revenue items prior to 1986, but they have been listed as expenditure items in government accounts since 1986. For comparison purpose, figures before 1985 were adjusted accordingly.

b)Domestic and foreign debts are excluded in this table.

人口数及构成

Population and its Composition

本表各年人口包括中国人民解放军现役军人数据，未包括港澳台人口数据。

Data in this table include the military personnel, but exclude the population of Hong Kong, Macao and Taiwan.

单位：万人 (10 000 persons)

年份 Year	年底总人口 Total Population (year-end)	按性别分 By Sex				按城乡分 By Residence			
		男 Male		女 Female		市镇总人口 Urban		乡村总人口 Rural	
		人口数 Population	比重（%） Proportion	人口数 Population	比重（%） Proportion	人口数 Population	比重（%） Proportion	人口数 Population	比重（%） Proportion
1952	57482	29833	51.90	27649	48.10	7163	12.46	50319	87.54
1957	64653	33469	51.77	31184	48.23	9949	15.39	54704	84.61
1962	67295	34517	51.29	32778	48.71	11659	17.33	55636	82.67
1965	72538	37128	51.18	35410	48.82	13045	17.98	59493	82.02
1970	82992	42686	51.43	40306	48.57	14424	17.38	68568	82.62
1975	92420	47564	51.47	44856	48.53	16030	17.34	76390	82.66
1978	96259	49567	51.49	46692	48.51	17245	17.92	79014	82.08
1980	98705	50785	51.45	47920	48.55	19140	19.39	79565	80.61
1985	105851	54725	51.70	51126	48.30	25094	23.71	80757	76.29
1986	107507	55581	51.70	51926	48.30	26366	24.52	81141	75.48
1987	109300	56290	51.50	53010	48.50	27674	25.32	81626	74.68
1988	111026	57201	51.52	53825	48.48	28661	25.81	82365	74.19
1989	112704	58099	51.55	54605	48.45	29540	26.21	83164	73.79
1990	114333	58904	51.52	55429	48.48	30191	26.41	84142	73.59
1991	115823	59466	51.34	56357	48.66	30543	26.37	85280	73.63
1992	117171	59811	51.05	57360	48.95	32372	27.63	84799	72.37
1993	110517	60472	51.02	58045	48.98	33351	28.14	85166	71.86
1994	119850	61246	51.10	58604	48.90	34301	28.62	85549	71.38
1995	121121	61808	51.03	59313	48.97	35174	29.04	85947	70.96
1996	122389	62200	50.82	60189	49.18	35950	29.37	86439	70.63
1997	123626	63131	51.07	60495	48.93	36989	29.92	86637	70.08
1998	124810	63629	50.98	61181	49.02	37942	30.40	86868	69.60

注：1985-1989年数据是根据1982年、1990年两次人口普查数据调整的，1990年以后数据是人口变动抽样调查调整数，其余年份数据为户籍统计数。

Data in 1985-1989 were adjusted on the basis of the 1982 and 1990 National Population Censuses. Since 1990, data have been estimated on the basis of the annual National Sample Surveys on Population Changes. Data of other years were taken from the annual reports of the Ministry of Public Security.

全社会固定资产投资
Total Investment in Fixed Assets

指　　标	Item	1997	1998	1998年比上年增长% Increase Rate in 1998 over 1997(%)
投资总额（亿元）	**Total Investment (100 million yuan)**	**24941.11**	**28406.17**	**13.9**
按经济类型分	Grouped by Ownership			
国有经济	State-Owned Units	13091.72	15369.30	17.4
集体经济	Collective-Owned Units	3850.87	4192.24	8.9
#农村	# Rural	3055.64	3233.31	5.8
个体经济	Individuals	3429.42	3744.37	9.2
#农村	# Rural	2691.16	2681.52	-0.4
联营经济	Joint Owned Economic Units	123.12	60.49	-50.9
股份制经济	Share Holding Economic Units	1387.21	1947.01	40.4
外商投资经济	Foreign Funded Economic Units	1955.94	1639.61	-16.2
港澳台投资经济	Economic Units Funded by Entrepreneurs from Hong Kong, Macao and Taiwan	937.14	1334.20	42.4
其他经济	Others	165.68	118.95	-28.2
按管理渠道分	Grouped by Channel of Management			
基本建设	Capital Construction	9917.02	11916.42	20.2
更新改造	Innovation	3921.94	4516.75	15.2
房地产开发	Real Estate Development	3178.37	3614.23	13.7
按资金来源分	Grouped by Source of Funds			
国家预算内资金	State Budgetary Appropriation	696.74	1197.39	71.9
国内贷款	Domestic Loans	4782.55	5542.89	15.9
利用外资	Foreign Investment	2683.89	2617.03	-2.5
自筹投资	Fundraising	13879.65	14864.19	7.1
其他投资	Others	3216.84	4495.42	39.7
按构成分	Grouped by Use of Funds			
建筑安装工程	Construction and Installation	15614.03	17874.53	14.5
设备工具器具购置	Purchase of Equipment and Instruments	6044.84	6528.53	8.0
其他费用	Others	3282.25	4003.10	22.0
屋建筑面积（万平方米）	**Floor Space of Buildings (10 000 sq.m)**			
施工面积	Floor Space Under Construction	230490.98	245755.73	6.6
竣工面积	Floor Space Completed	166057.13	170904.75	2.9
#住宅	# Residential Buildings	121100.96	127571.61	5.3

注：按资金来源分组为财务拨款数，各项相加不等于投资总额。
Total investment grouped by sources of finance refers to financial appropriation, and the broken-down figures do not add up to the total.

能源生产总量及构成

Total Production of Energy and its Composition

年份 Year	能源生产总量（万吨标准煤） Total Energy Production (10 000 tons of SCE)	占能源生产总量的比重（%） As Percentage of Total Energy Production			
		原煤 Coal	原油 Crude Oil	天然气 Natural Gas	水电 Hydro-power
1952	4871	96.7	1.3	...	2.0
1957	9861	94.9	2.1	0.1	2.9
1962	17185	91.4	4.8	0.9	2.9
1965	18824	88.0	8.6	0.8	2.6
1970	30990	81.6	14.1	1.2	3.1
1975	48754	70.6	22.6	2.4	4.4
1978	62770	70.3	23.7	2.9	3.1
1980	63735	69.4	23.8	3.0	3.8
1985	85546	72.8	20.9	2.0	4.3
1986	88124	72.4	21.2	2.1	4.3
1987	91266	72.6	21.0	2.0	4.4
1988	95801	73.1	20.4	2.0	4.5
1989	101639	74.1	19.3	2.0	4.6
1990	103922	74.2	19.0	2.0	4.8
1991	104844	74.1	19.2	2.0	4.7
1992	107256	74.3	18.9	2.0	4.8
1993	111059	74.0	18.7	2.0	5.3
1994	118729	74.6	17.6	1.9	5.9
1995	129034	75.3	16.6	1.9	6.2
1996	132616	75.2	17.0	2.0	5.8
1997	132410	74.1	17.3	2.1	6.5
1998	124000	72.0	18.5	2.4	7.1

注: 电力折算标准煤的系数采用当年平均发电煤耗计算。

The coefficient for conversion of electric power into SCE (standard coal equivalent) is calculated on the basic of the data on the average coal consumption in generating electric power in the same year.

能源消费总量及构成

Total Consumption of Energy and its Composition

年份 Year	能源消费总量 (万吨标准煤) Total Energy Consumption (10 000 tons of SCE)	占能源消费总量的比重（%） As Percentage of Total Energy Consumption			
		煤炭 Coal	石油 Petroleum	天然气 Natural Gas	水电 Hydro-power
1957	9644	92.3	4.6	0.1	3.0
1962	16540	89.2	6.6	0.9	3.2
1965	18901	86.5	10.3	0.9	2.7
1970	29291	80.9	14.7	0.9	3.5
1975	45425	71.9	21.1	2.5	4.6
1978	57144	70.7	22.7	3.2	3.4
1980	60275	72.2	20.7	3.1	4.0
1985	76682	75.8	17.1	2.2	4.9
1986	80850	75.8	17.2	2.3	4.7
1987	86632	76.2	17.0	2.1	4.7
1988	92997	76.2	17.0	2.1	4.7
1989	96934	76.0	17.1	2.0	4.9
1990	98703	76.2	16.6	2.1	5.1
1991	103783	76.1	17.1	2.0	4.8
1992	109170	75.7	17.5	1.9	4.9
1993	115993	74.7	18.2	1.9	5.2
1994	122737	75.0	17.4	1.9	5.7
1995	131176	74.6	17.5	1.8	6.1
1996	138948	74.7	18.0	1.8	5.5
1997	138173	71.5	20.4	1.7	6.2
1998	136000	71.6	19.8	2.1	6.5

注:1998年能源消费量为估算数。

Data on energy consumption in 1998 were estimated figures.

农、林、牧、渔业总产值及指数

Gross Output Value of Farming, Forestry, Animal Husbandry, and Fishery and the Related Indices

本表绝对数按当年价格计算，指数按可比价格计算。

Data in value terms in this table are calculated at current prices, while the indices are calculated at comparable prices.

年份 地区 Year Region	绝对数(亿元) Gross Output Value of Farming, Forestry, Animal Husbandry, and Fishery (100 million yuan)					指数（上年=100） Indices of Gross Output of Farming, Foresry,Animal Husbandry, and Fishery (preceding year=100)				
	农林牧渔业总产值 Total	农业 Farming	林业 Forestry	牧业 Animal Husbandry	渔业 Fishery	农林牧渔业总产值 Total	农业 Farming	林业 Forestry	牧业 Animal Husbandry	渔业 Fishery
1978	1397.0	1117.5	48.1	209.3	22.1					
1980	1922.6	1454.1	81.4	354.2	32.9	101.4	99.7	112.2	107.0	107.7
1985	3619.5	2506.4	188.7	798.3	126.1	103.4	99.8	104.5	117.2	118.9
1990	7662.1	4954.3	330.3	1967.0	410.6	107.6	108.0	103.1	107.0	110.0
1991	8157.0	5146.4	367.9	2159.2	483.5	103.7	100.9	108.0	108.8	107.6
1992	9084.7	5588.0	422.6	2460.5	613.6	106.4	104.2	107.7	108.8	115.3
1993	10995.5	6605.1	494.0	3014.4	882.0	107.8	105.2	108.0	110.8	118.4
1994	15750.5	9169.2	611.1	4672.0	1298.2	108.6	103.2	108.9	116.7	120.0
1995	20340.9	11884.6	709.9	6045.0	1701.3	110.9	107.9	105.0	114.8	119.4
1996	22358.2	13539.8	778.0	6020.0	2020.4	109.4	107.8	105.7	111.4	114.0
1997	23764.0	13852.5	817.8	6811.0	2282.7	106.6	104.5	103.3	109.5	111.5
1998	24516.7	14241.9	851.3	7000.7	2422.9	106.0	104.9	102.9	107.4	108.8
北京 Beijing	176.6	89.2	3.2	76.6	7.6	103.4	102.3	89.2	104.5	113.0
天津 Tianjin	156.2	98.8	1.2	38.1	18.1	112.6	108.2	140.1	115.5	127.6
河北 Hebei	1505.9	885.9	27.4	547.6	45.1	107.8	107.4	102.1	108.5	110.4
山西 Shanxi	359.2	249.5	13.3	94.8	1.6	111.5	116.5	89.6	105.2	105.4
内蒙古 Inner Mongolia	534.4	335.3	16.9	177.4	4.8	108.1	110.3	104.9	104.6	122.3
辽宁 Liaoning	969.8	534.7	17.4	269.6	148.1	116.0	124.0	111.2	109.7	109.8
吉林 Jilin	666.5	394.9	8.1	254.1	9.4	117.9	125.7	104.0	108.5	107.3
黑龙江 Heilongjiang	736.3	517.6	17.7	184.5	16.6	100.1	96.1	97.8	109.9	110.3
上海 Shanghai	206.8	89.1	0.8	87.3	29.5	102.4	105.1	139.3	101.9	96.7
江苏 Jiangsu	1849.2	1096.9	24.2	435.5	292.7	104.0	103.0	109.9	104.2	107.2
浙江 Zhejiang	1003.7	523.0	59.5	165.9	255.4	103.8	100.4	96.5	103.6	112.3
安徽 Anhui	1202.3	679.6	58.5	335.7	128.4	102.7	97.2	108.4	109.3	114.3
福建 Fujian	973.4	411.0	78.4	200.2	283.9	106.0	103.4	103.0	108.3	109.6
江西 Jiangxi	734.9	361.5	47.6	238.3	87.4	98.2	92.1	101.0	104.4	105.8
山东 Shandong	2174.5	1219.9	45.9	583.4	325.4	109.9	111.3	96.0	111.6	104.9
河南 Henan	1823.0	1159.6	50.2	597.1	16.1	106.9	105.3	104.7	109.7	114.7
湖北 Hubei	1147.5	688.1	41.3	296.3	121.9	101.1	98.0	114.2	101.7	107.8
湖南 Hunan	1232.8	628.7	48.2	476.3	79.6	102.9	98.6	102.4	108.7	107.1
广东 Guangdong	1614.6	862.0	54.7	350.8	347.2	104.8	103.4	103.6	105.2	108.4
广西 Guangxi	865.9	476.2	37.8	264.0	88.0	105.2	106.5	95.5	102.9	110.1
海南 Hainan	242.5	117.7	42.7	37.7	44.5	108.5	109.2	104.3	107.6	113.5
重庆 Chongqing	434.4	254.9	15.1	150.0	14.4	102.5	101.5	117.2	101.7	112.4
四川 Sichuan	1394.1	823.7	45.9	493.1	31.5	104.4	102.7	103.0	106.6	111.7
贵州 Guizhou	402.3	274.6	15.5	108.1	4.2	100.3	97.3	102.2	107.0	118.9
云南 Yunnan	614.5	381.3	41.8	179.3	12.2	104.5	100.6	105.2	112.6	124.2
西藏 Tibet	42.3	22.4	0.9	19.0	0.0	102.3	104.5	103.2	100.7	188.0
陕西 Shaanxi	479.4	340.9	19.2	115.9	3.4	108.9	109.2	109.8	107.7	105.1
甘肃 Gansu	335.8	252.6	8.8	73.3	1.2	115.9	119.1	98.9	108.9	119.0
青海 Qinghai	60.8	31.4	1.0	28.3	0.1	104.7	103.4	101.8	106.4	83.0
宁夏 Ningxia	78.8	53.8	1.0	22.4	1.6	109.3	109.9	66.8	111.6	119.6
新疆 Xinjiang	498.4	387.4	7.4	100.1	3.5	110.8	111.5	105.7	109.0	101.8

工业总产值指数

Indices of Gross Industrial Output Value

本表按可比价格计算。

Data in this table are calculated at comparable prices.

(上年 =100) (preceding year=100)

年份 Year	工业总产值 Total	# 国有及国有控股企业 State-owned or Controlling Share Hold Industry	# 集体企业 Collective-owned Industry	# 个体企业 Individual-owned Industry	# 其他经济类型企业 Industry of Other Types of Ownership
1978	113.55	114.44	110.58		
1979	108.81	108.88	108.57		
1980	109.27	105.61	119.24		
1981	104.29	102.53	109.01	234.57	131.60
1982	107.82	107.05	109.54	178.95	127.73
1983	111.19	109.39	115.53	220.59	133.90
1984	116.28	108.92	134.85	197.47	156.81
1985	121.39	112.94	132.69	189.60	139.54
1986	111.67	106.18	117.97	167.57	134.16
1987	117.69	111.30	123.24	156.59	166.39
1988	120.79	112.61	128.16	147.34	161.53
1989	108.54	103.86	110.48	123.77	142.68
1990	107.76	102.96	109.02	121.11	139.33
1991	114.77	108.62	118.40	125.29	150.11
1992	124.70	112.40	133.30	147.00	164.80
1993	127.30	105.70	135.00	166.20	192.50
1994	124.20	106.50	124.90	156.30	174.30
1995	120.30	108.20	115.20	151.50	137.20
1996	116.59	105.13	120.88	120.00	123.77
1997	113.10	101.03	110.21	115.38	130.18
1998	110.75	100.10	109.10	114.70	125.29

各地区历年建筑业增加值

Value-Added of Construction in Various Years by Region

单位: 万元 (10 000 yuan)

地 区	Region	1994	1995	1996	1997	1998
全 国	**National Total**	**13221143**	**16686358**	**24056186**	**25405426**	**27837909**
北 京	Beijing	880241	1071808	1348018	1424872	1787588
天 津	Tianjin	364477	463342	510525	508102	580644
河 北	Hebei	622007	753626	1004433	1058799	1026622
山 西	Shanxi	388467	457235	533155	571361	619820
内蒙古	Inner Mongolia	267967	274225	321049	309691	352602
辽 宁	Liaoning	1150259	1257086	1352915	1331824	1271822
吉 林	Jilin	358850	390506	451124	428432	410049
黑龙江	Heilongjiang	553728	642264	675666	720763	796891
上 海	Shanghai	682109	874100	995145	1209914	1311338
江 苏	Jiangsu	905461	1275984	2540378	2620881	2915897
浙 江	Zhejiang	530486	843427	2099332	2212090	2431151
安 徽	Anhui	339063	441310	731606	680801	703797
福 建	Fujian	326032	422848	561023	618988	738348
江 西	Jiangxi	186018	216570	260372	256353	262760
山 东	Shandong	630366	783307	1770885	1894007	2020712
河 南	Henan	408568	585294	849905	795700	875188
湖 北	Hubei	553597	776716	941654	951010	1063379
湖 南	Hunan	340530	430640	804491	836320	876333
广 东	Guangdong	1321791	1853664	1854934	1964243	2230076
广 西	Guangxi	237820	283733	365971	378210	436240
海 南	Hainan	47803	47202	35148	73788	67747
重 庆	Chongqing				677742	783224
四 川	Sichuan	886370	1117663	1985461	1593421	1776678
贵 州	Guizhou	154018	170791	207235	230913	244071
云 南	Yunnan	222159	295731	496463	613405	678146
西 藏	Tibet	9695	13947	31016	33468	41089
陕 西	Shaanxi	312102	339780	440665	508819	509819
甘 肃	Gansu	181481	219400	382693	347624	380112
青 海	Qinghai	61751	75236	92589	97950	117884
宁 夏	Ningxia	58404	64952	89034	110707	120438
新 疆	Xinjiang	239525	283882	323300	345229	407445

交通运输业基本情况

Basic Conditions of Transportation

指标	Item	1995	1996	1997	1998
运输线路长度(万公里)	**Length of Transportation Routes (10 000 km)**				
铁路营业里程	Railways in Operation	5.46	5.67	5.76	5.76
#电气化里程	#Electrified Railways	0.97	1.01	1.20	1.30
公路	Highways	115.70	118.58	122.64	127.85
内河	Navigable Inland Waterways	11.06	11.08	10.98	11.0
民航	Total Civil Aviation Routes	112.90	116.65	142.50	150.58
#国际航线	#International Routes	34.82	38.63	50.44	50.44
管道	Petroleum and Gas Pipelines	1.72	1.93	2.04	2.31
客运量总计(万人)	**Total Passenger Traffic (10 000 persons)**	**1172596**	**1244722**	**1325364**	**1377252**
铁路	Railways	102745	94162	92578	93620
国家	National Railways	102081	93550	91919	92991
地方	Local Railways	664	612	659	629
公路	Highways	1040810	1122110	1204583	1257332
水运	Waterways	23924	22895	22573	20545
民用航空	Civil Aviation	5117	5555	5630	5755
旅客周转量总计(亿人公里)	**Total Passenger-Kilometers (100 million passenger-km)**	**9002**	**9143**	**10019**	**10559**
铁路	Railways	3546	3325	3548	3696
国家	National Railways	3543	3322	3544	369
地方	Local Railways	3.09	3.36	4.72	5.01
公路	Highways	4603	4909	5541	5943
水运	Waterways	172	161	156	120
民用航空	Civil Aviation	681	748	774	800
货运量总计(万吨)	**Total Freight Traffic (10 000 tons)**	**1234810**	**1296200**	**1275802**	**1264361**
铁路	Railways	165855	168803	169734	161243
国家	National Railways	159346	161678	161880	153208
地方	Local Railways	6509	7125	7854	8035
公路	Highways	940387	983860	976536	976004
水运	Waterways	113194	127430	113406	109555
民用航空	Civil Aviation	101.1	115	124.7	140.1
管道	Petroleum and Gas Pipelines	15274	15992	16002	17419
货物周转量总计(亿吨公里)	**Total Freight Ton-kilometers (100 million ton-km)**	**35730**	**36454**	**38212**	**37841**
铁路	Railways	12870	12971	13097	12312
国家	National Railways	12836	12922	13046	12261
地方	Local Railways	34	49	51	51
公路	Highways	4695	5011	5272	5483
水运	Waterways	17552	17863	19235	19406
民用航空	Civil Aviation	22.3	24.9	29.1	33.5
管道	Petroleum and Gas Pipelines	590	585	579	606
民用汽车拥有量(万辆)	Number of Civil Motor Vehicles Owned (10 000 units)	1040.00	1100.08	1219.09	1319.30
载客汽车辆数(万辆)	Number of Buses and Cars (10 000 units)	417.90	488.02	580.56	654.83
载客汽车客位(万客位)	Number of Seats in Buses and Cars (10 000 units)	5213.27	6191.82	7269.93	7621.47
载货汽车辆数(万辆)	Number of Trucks (10 000 units)	585.43	575.03	601.23	627.89
#普通载货汽车	#Ordinary Trucks	568.58	558.16	582.45	609.31
载货汽车吨位(万吨)	Trucks Capacity (10 000 tons)	2370.93	2280.62	2287.51	2408.94
#普通载货汽车	#Ordinary Trucks	2257.07	2167.10	2167.87	2280.74
其他机动车(万辆)	Number of Other Motor Vehicles (10000 units)	1494.62	1773.13	2214.83	2770.72
公路部门营运车辆(万辆)	Number of Motor Vehicles Owned by Highway Departments (10 000 units)	27.49	28.81	29.89	31.88
私人汽车拥有量(万辆)	Number of Motor Vehicles Owned by Individuals (10 000 units)	249.96	289.67	358.36	423.65
民用运输船舶拥有量(艘)	Number of Civil Transport Vessels (unit)				
机动船	Motor Vessels	299717	269879	215814	212093
驳船	Barges	57998	56128	49983	48115
帆船	Sailing Boats	7253	4946	6059	3368
私人运输船舶拥有量(艘)	Number of Private-Owned Transport Vessels (unit)				
机动船	Motor Vessels	182060	157370	147415	127130
驳船	Barges	7964	6533	9944	7290
帆船	Sailing Boats	6712	4556	3217	2934
沿海主要港口货物吞吐量(万吨)	Volume of Freight Handled in Major Coastal Ports (10 000 tons)	80166	85152	90822	92237

邮电业务基本情况

Basic Conditions of Post and Telecommuncations Services

指标	Item	1995	1996	1997	1998
邮电业务总量(亿元)	**Business Volume of Post and Telecommunications Service (100 million yuan)**	**988.85**	**1342.04**	**1773.29**	**2431.21**
函件 (亿件)	Number of Letters(100 million pcs)	79.55	78.68	68.55	65.51
包件(万件)	Number of Parcels(10 000 pcs)	15641.2	14920	9715.3	9726.5
邮政快件 (万件)	Pieces of Courier Services(10 000 pcs)	45057	44437.5	33247.8	16438.3
特快专递(万件)	Pieces of Express Mail Services (10 000 pcs)	5562.7	7096.6	6878.9	7331.8
刊期发数(万份)	Number of Newspapers and Magazines Circulation (10 000 copies)	21688.6	21157.4	21875.2	22989.3
电报(万份)	Number of Telegrams(10 000 pcs)	13287.6	9610.7	6580.6	
传真(份)	Number of Faxes	4423080	5650000	7118000	
长途电话(万次)	Number of Long-distance Calls	1013966	1273951	1554026	1825941
本地电话年末用户(万户)	Local Telephone Subscribers of at Year-end (10 000 subscribers)	4070.6	5494.7	7031.0	8742.1
年末市内电话(万户)	Local(Urban) Telephone Subscribers at Year-end (10 000 subscribers)	3263.6	4277.8	5244.4	6259.8
#住宅电话	#Residencial Telephone Subscribers	2358.4	3224.6	4057.2	4911.1
年末无线寻呼电话用户(万户)	Number of Subscribers of Pageing Service at Year-end (10 000 subscribers)	1739.2	2536.2	2969	3908.2
年末移动电话用户(户)	Number of Mobile Telephones Subscribers at Year-end (subscribers)	3629416	6852752	13232876	23862874
年末农村电话(户)	Number of Rural Telephones Subscribers at Year-end (subscribers)	8070047	12169172	17866341	24822816
邮电局所	Number of Post & Telecommunications Offices	61898	72496	79273	102225
邮路及农村投递路线总长度(公里)	Length of Postal Routes and Rural Delivery Routes (km)	5231930	5476991	5766054	6215426
#汽车邮路	#Highway Routes	819412	917151	873688	930622
铁路邮路	Railway Routes	183036	183884	186382	189652
长话电路(路)	Number of Long-distance Telephone Lines (line)	735545	998287	1146121	1576483
电报电路 (路)	Number of Telegraph Lines (line)	12250	11569	12624	11715
邮电通信工具拥有量	Telecommunications Facilites				
局用交换机容量(万门)	Capacity of Office Telephone Exchanges (10 000 lines)	7203.59	9291.23	11269.17	13823.66
中央国有	Central State-owned	5456.35	6923.67	8406.8	9951.35
地方国有	Local State-owned	1747.24	2367.56	2862.37	3872.31
电话机(含移动电话)(万部)	Number of Telephone Sets (including hand phone) (10 000 units)	5762.26	7732.03	10111.12	13123.43
中央国有	Central State-owned	4346.32	5537.78	6745.23	7963.28
地方国有	Local State-owned	1152.06	1508.97	2042.61	2773.86

注:1.邮电业务总量按1990年不变价格计算。

2.从1997年起市内电话用户数为城市电话用户, 农村电话用户数为乡村电话用户。

a) The business volume of post and telecommunications is calculated at 1990 constant prices.

b) Since 1997 figure of local telephone subscribers refers to telephone subscribers in urban areas, and rural telephone subscribers refers to subscribers of townships and village.

国内贸易基本情况

Basic Conditions of Domestic Trade

单位: 亿元 (100 million yuan)

指　　标	Item	1994	1995	1996	1997	1998
法人机构(个)	**Number of Corporation Units**					
批发零售贸易业	Engaged in Wholesale and Retail Trades	511757	548487	592487		
餐饮业	Engaged in Catering Trade	47578	45201	48240		
从业人员(人)	**Persons Engaged (person)**					
批发零售贸易业	In Wholesale and Retail Trades	37000908	41515693	44991244		
餐饮业	In Catering Trade	6350650	7100962	7753108		
批发零售贸易业	**Wholesale and Retail Trades**					
商品购进总额(亿元)	Total Purchases (100 million yuan)	32433.0	36983.6	38549.7	39788.3	24297.4
商品销售总额(亿元)	Total Sales (100 million yuan)	35161.0	40545.3	42546.9	55168.7	56437.7
商品库存总额(亿元)	Total Inventory (100 million yuan)	6100.9	6705.5	7227.3	7544.8	3789.7
社会消费品零售总额(亿元)	**Total Retail sales of Consumer Goods (100 million yuan)**	**16264.7**	**20620.0**	**24774.1**	**27298.9**	**29152.5**
按销售单位所在地分	By Location of Establishments					
市	City	9661.2	12376.7	14951.2	16650.4	17825.2
县	County	2407.2	2919.6	3280.0	3500.1	3681.9
县以下	Under County Level	4196.3	5323.7	6542.9	7148.4	7645.4
按行业分	By Sector					
批发零售贸易业	Wholesale and Retail Trades	11039.7	13801.3	16205.1	18108.3	19185.8
餐饮业	Catering Trade	1175.1	1579.2	2024.9	2433.3	2816.4
制造业	Manufacturing	1272.8	1540.7	1775.3	1987.9	2037.6
农业生产者	Farm Producers	2143.7	2777.6	3261.9	3744.9	4088.7
其他	Others	633.4	921.2	1506.9	1024.5	1024.0

注:1.1998年批发零售贸易业商品购、销、存总额为限额以上批发零售贸易业数据。
2.1997年以后社会消费品零售总额不含居民购买住房。
a) Figures of 1998 on purchase, sales and inventory by wholesale and retail trade refer to units above designated size.
b) Data on total retail sales of consumer goods since 1997 exclude purchase of commodity housing by households.

对外经济贸易

Foreign Trade and Economic Cooperation

指标	Item	1994	1995	1996	1997	1998
进出口总额(人民币亿元)	**Total Imports and Exports (RMB 100 million yuan)**	**20381.9**	**23499.9**	**24133.8**	**26967.2**	**26854.1**
出口总额	Total Exports	10421.8	12451.8	12576.4	15160.7	15231.7
进口总额	Total Imports	9960.1	11048.1	11557.4	11806.5	11622.4
进出口差额	Balance	461.7	1403.7	1019.0	3354.2	3609.3
进出口总额 (亿美元)	**Total Imports and Exports (USD 100 million)**	**2366.2**	**2808.6**	**2898.8**	**3251.6**	**3239.3**
出口总额	Total Exports	1210.1	1487.8	1510.5	1827.9	1837.6
初级产品	Primary Goods	197.1	214.8	219.3	239.5	206.0
工业制成品	Manufactured Goods	1013.0	1273.0	1291.2	1588.4	1631.6
进口总额	Total Imports	1156.1	1320.8	1388.3	1423.7	1401.7
初级产品	Primary Goods	164.8	244.1	254.4	286.2	229.5
工业制成品	Manufactured Goods	991.3	1076.7	1133.9	1137.5	1172.2
进出口差额	Balance	54.0	167.0	122.2	404.2	435.9
对外签订利用外资协议(合同)项目(个)	**Number of Projects for Utilization of Foreign Capital in the Signed Agreements & Contracts**	**47646**	**37184**	**24673**	**21138**	**19850**
对外借款	Foreign Loans	97	173	117	137	51
外商直接投资	Foreign Direct Investments	47549	37011	24556	21001	19799
对外签订利用外资协议(合同)金额 (亿美元)	**Total Amount of Foreign Capital to be Utilized in the Signed Agreements & Contracts (USD 100 million)**	**937.56**	**1032.05**	**816.10**	**610.58**	**632.01**
对外借款	Foreign Loans	106.68	112.88	79.62	58.72	83.85
外商直接投资	Foreign Direct Investments	826.80	912.82	732.77	510.04	521.02
外商其他投资	Other Foreign Investments	4.08	6.35	3.71	41.82	27.14
实际利用外资额(亿美元)	**Total Amount of Foreign Capital Actually Used (USD 100 million)**	**432.13**	**481.33**	**548.04**	**644.08**	**585.57**
对外借款	Foreign Loans	92.67	103.27	126.69	120.21	110.00
外商直接投资	Foreign Direct Investments	337.67	375.21	417.26	452.57	454.63
外商其他投资	Other Foreign Investments	1.79	2.85	4.09	71.30	20.94
外商投资企业基本情况	**Registered Foreign-funded Enterprises**					
年底登记户数(户)	Number of Registered Enterprises	206096	233564	240447	235681	227807
投资总额(亿美元)	Total Investment (USD 100 million)	4907.24	6390.09	7153.22	7534.70	7742.29
注册资本(亿美元)	Registered Capital(USD 100 million)	3122.75	3991.23	4414.85	4598.14	4672.87
# 外方	#Capital from Foreign Partners	1963.15	2568.84	2897.96	3029.87	3137.12
对外经济合作(亿美元)	**Economic Cooperation with Foreign Countries & Territories (USD 100 million)**					
合同金额	Contracted Value	79.88	96.72	102.73	113.56	117.73
# 对外承包工程	#Contracted Projects	60.28	74.84	77.28	85.16	92.43
对外劳务合作	Labor Services	19.60	21.88	25.45	28.40	23.90
完成营业额	Value of Business Fulfilled	59.78	65.88	76.96	83.83	101.34
# 对外承包工程	#Contracted Projects	48.83	51.08	58.20	60.36	77.69
对外劳务合作	Labor Services	10.95	14.80	18.76	23.47	22.76

中国利用外资概况

Utilization of Foreign Capital

项目单位：个；金额单位：亿美元 (USD 100 million)

年份 Year	总计 Total		对外借款 Foreign Loans		外商直接投资 Direct Foreign Investments		外商其他投资额 Other Foreign Investments
	项目 Number of Projects	金额 Value	项目 Number of Projects	金额 Value	项目 Number of Projects	金额 Value	
签订利用外资协议(合同)额 Total Amount of Foreign Capital to Be Utilized Through the Signed Agreements and Contracts							
1979-1983	1471	239.78	79	150.62	1392	77.42	11.74
1984	1894	47.91	38	19.16	1856	26.51	2.24
1985	3145	98.67	72	35.34	3073	59.32	4.01
1986	1551	117.37	53	84.07	1498	28.34	4.96
1987	2289	121.36	56	78.17	2233	37.09	6.10
1988	6063	160.04	118	98.13	5945	52.97	8.94
1989	5909	114.79	130	51.85	5779	56.00	6.94
1990	7371	120.86	98	50.99	7273	65.96	3.91
1991	13086	195.83	108	71.61	12978	119.77	4.45
1992	48858	694.39	94	107.03	48764	581.24	6.12
1993	83595	1232.73	158	113.06	83437	1114.36	5.31
1994	47646	937.56	97	106.68	47549	826.80	4.08
1995	37184	1032.05	173	112.88	37011	912.82	6.35
1996	24673	816.10	117	79.62	24556	732.77	3.71
1997	21138	610.58	137	58.72	21001	510.04	41.82
1998	19850	632.01	51	83.85	19749	521.02	27.14
实际利用外资额 Total Amount of Foreign Capital Actually Used							
1979-1983		144.38		117.55		18.02	8.81
1984		27.05		12.86		12.58	1.61
1985		46.47		26.88		16.61	2.98
1986		72.58		50.14		18.74	3.70
1987		84.52		58.05		23.14	3.33
1988		102.26		64.87		31.94	5.45
1989		100.59		62.86		33.92	3.81
1990		102.89		65.34		34.87	2.68
1991		115.54		68.88		43.66	3.00
1992		192.02		79.11		110.07	2.84
1993		389.60		111.89		275.15	2.56
1994		432.13		92.67		337.67	1.79
1995		481.33		103.27		375.21	2.85
1996		548.04		126.69		417.25	4.10
1997		644.08		120.21		452.57	71.30
1998		585.57		110.00		454.63	20.94

城市公用事业基本情况

Basic Statistics on Urban Public Utilities

本表 1990 年以后各项指标按全社会范围计算，1985 年按城建部门管理的范围计算。

Data since 1990 have covered the public utilities of all urban units, whereas data in the preceding years only covered the urban units under the city construction department.

项目	Item	1985	1990	1995	1997	1998
自来水年供水量(亿吨)	**Annual Supply of Tap Water (100 million tons)**	**128**	**382.3**	**496.6**	**476.8**	**470.5**
#生活用水量	#Water Consumption for Residential use	51.9	100.1	158.1	175.7	181
平均每人生活用水（吨）	**Per Capita Water Consumption for Residential Use (ton)**	**55.1**	**67.9**	**71.3**	**90.2**	**91.1**
用水普及率(%)	**Percentage of Population with Access to Tap Water (%)**	**81**	**89.2**	**93**	**95.2**	**96**
公共汽(电)车总数（辆）	**Number of Public Transportation Vehicles (Buses and Trolley Buses etc.) (unit)**	**45155**	**62215**	**136821**	**169121**	**189002**
平均每万人拥有(辆)	Number of Public Transportation Vehicles per 10 000 Population (unit)	3.9	4.8	7.3	8.6	8.6
铺装道路长度(公里)	**Length of Paved Roads (km)**	**38282**	**94820**	**130308**	**138610**	**145163**
平均每万人拥有(公里)	Length of Paved Roads per 10 000 Population (km)	3.3	6.4	7	7.1	7.3
铺装道路面积(万平方米)	**Area of Paved Roads (10 000 sq.m)**	**35872**	**89160**	**135810**	**152664**	**163993**
每万人拥有(万平方米)	Area of Paved Roads per 10 000 Population (10 000 sq.m)	3.1	6	7.3	7.8	8.3
下水道长度(公里)	**Length of Sewer Pipelines (km)**	**31556**	**57787**	**110293**	**119739**	**125943**
平均每万人拥有(公里)	Length of Sewer Pipelines per 10 000 Population (km)	2.7	3.9	6	6.1	6.3
人工煤气供气量(万立方米)	**Coal Gas Supply (10 000 cu.m)**	**249754**	**1747065**	**1266894**	**1268944**	**1675571**
#家庭用量	Consumption of Coal Gas and for Residential Use	107060	274127	456585	535412	480734
煤气管道长度(公里)	**Length of Gas Pipelines (km)**	**10567**	**16312**	**33890**	**41475**	**42725**
天然气供气量(万立方米)	**Natural Gas Supply (10 000 cu.m)**	**162099**	**642289**	**673354**	**663001**	**688255**
液化气家庭用量(万吨)	**Consumption of Liquefied Gas for Residential Use (10 000 ton)**	**54.7**	**142.8**	**370.2**	**437.1**	**547.8**
用气普及率(%)	**Percentage of Population with Access to Gas (%)**	**22.4**	**42.2**	**70**	**75.7**	**78.8**
城市绿化	**Afforestation in Cities**					
绿地面积(公顷)	Public Green Areas (hectare)	159291	474613	678310	682238	745654
每万人绿地面积（公顷）	Public Green Areas per 10 000 Population (hectare)	13.7	32.2	36.7	35	37.5
公园动物园个数(个)	**Number of Parks and Zoos**	**1026**	**1970**	**3619**	**3813**	**3990**
公园动物园面积（公顷）	**Area of Parks and Zoos (hectare)**	**21896**	**40081**	**72857**	**68933**	**73198**
环境卫生	**Environmental Sanitation**					
清运垃圾(万吨)	Volume of Garbage Disposal (10 000 tons)	4477	6767	10748	10982	11302
清运粪便（万吨）	Volume of Disposal of Excrement and Urine (10 000 tons)	1731	2385	3071	2845	2915
每万人有公厕(座)	Number of Public Lavatories per 10 000 Population	5.8	6.6	6.1	5.6	5.4

注：人均拥有指标按城市人口中非农业人口计算。

Data on the public utilities per 10 000 population are based on the non-agricultural population in urban areas.

教育事业基本情况

Basic Statistics on Education

指标	Item	1985	1990	1995	1997	1998
学校数（所）	**Number of Schools**					
普通高等学校	Regular Institutions of Higher Education	1016	1075	1054	1020	1022
中等学校	Secondary Schools	104848	100777	95216	92832	92071
#专业学校	# Specialized Secondary Schools	3557	3982	4049	4143	4109
普通中学	Regular Secondary Schools	93221	87631	81020	78642	77888
小学	Primary Schools	832309	766072	668685	628840	609626
专任教师(万人)	**Number of Full-time Teachers (10 000 persons)**					
普通高等学校	Regular Institutions of Higher Education	34.4	39.5	40.1	40.5	40.7
中等学校	Secondary Schools	296.7	349.2	388.3	418.6	431.2
#专业学校	# Specialized Secondary Schools	17.4	23.4	25.7	27.6	27.9
普通中学	Regular Secondary Schools	265.2	303.3	333.4	358.7	369.7
小学	Primary Schools	537.7	558.2	566.4	579.4	581.9
招生数（万人）	**New Student Enrollment (10 000 persons)**					
普通高等学校	Regular Institutions of Higher Education	61.9	60.9	92.6	100.0	108.4
中等学校	Secondary Schools	1789.8	1815.8	2354.1	2501.5	2705.4
#专业学校	# Specialized Secondary Schools	66.8	73.0	138.1	162.1	166.8
普通中学	Regular Secondary Schools	1606.9	1619.6	2025.9	2128.2	2321.0
小学	Primary Schools	2298.2	2064.0	2531.8	2462.0	2201.4
在校学生(万人)	**Student Enrollment (10 000 persons)**					
普通高等学校	Regular Institutions of Higher Education	170.3	206.3	290.6	317.4	340.9
中等学校	Secondary Schools	5092.6	5105.4	6191.5	6995.2	7340.7
#专业学校	# Specialized Secondary Schools	157.1	224.4	372.2	465.4	498.1
普通中学	Regular Secondary Schools	4706.0	4586.0	5371.0	6017.9	6301.0
小学	Primary Schools	13370.2	12241.4	13195.2	13995.4	13953.8
毕业生数(万人)	**Graduates (10 000 persons)**					
普通高等学校	Regular Institutions of Higher Education	31.6	61.4	80.5	82.9	83.0
中等学校	Secondary Schools	1279.1	1497.5	1636.9	1929.8	2124.1
#专业学校	# Specialized Secondary Schools	42.9	66.1	83.9	115.7	129.3
普通中学	Regular Secondary Schools	1194.9	1342.1	1429.0	1664.0	1832.0
小学	Primary Schools	1999.9	1863.1	1961.5	1960.1	2117.4
每一教师负担学生数(人)	**Student-teacher Ratio**					
普通高等学校	Regular Institutions of Higher Education	5.0	5.2	7.2	7.8	8.4
中等学校	Secondary Schools	17.2	14.6	15.9	16.7	17.0
小学	Primary Schools	24.9	21.9	23.3	24.2	24.0
全国教育经费支出（亿元）	**Total Expenditures for Education (100 million yuan)**			**1878.0**	**2531.7**	
# 国家财政性教育经费	# Government Expenditures for Education			1411.5	1862.5	
#预算内教育经费	# Budgetary Expenditures for Education			1028.4	1357.7	

全国各种物价总指数
General Price Indices

(上年=100)

(preceding year=100)

年份 Year	商品零售价格指数 General Retail Price Index	居民消费价格指数 General Consumer Price Index	城市居民消费价格指数 Urban Areas	农村居民消费价格指数 Rural Areas	农产品收购价格指数 General Purchasing Price Index of Farm Products	农村工业品零售价格指数 General Rural Retail Price Index of Industrial Products	工农业商品综合比价指数 General Price Parity Index of Industrial and Farm Products
1978	100.7		100.7		103.9	100.0	96.2
1979	102.0		101.9		122.1	100.1	82.0
1980	106.0		107.5		107.1	100.8	94.1
1981	102.4		102.5		105.9	101.0	95.4
1982	101.9		102.0		102.2	101.6	99.4
1983	101.5		102.0		104.4	101.0	96.7
1984	102.8		102.7		104.0	103.1	99.1
1985	108.8	109.3	111.9	107.6	108.6	103.2	95.0
1986	106.0	106.5	107.0	106.1	106.4	103.2	97.0
1987	107.3	107.3	108.8	106.2	112.0	104.8	93.6
1988	118.5	118.8	120.7	117.5	123.0	115.2	93.7
1989	117.8	118.0	116.3	119.3	115.0	118.7	103.2
1990	102.1	103.1	101.3	104.5	97.4	104.6	107.4
1991	102.9	103.4	105.1	102.3	98.0	103.0	105.1
1992	105.4	106.4	108.6	104.7	103.4	103.1	99.7
1993	113.2	114.7	116.1	113.7	113.4	111.8	98.6
1994	121.7	124.1	125.0	123.4	139.9	117.2	83.8
1995	114.8	117.1	116.8	117.5	119.9	114.7	95.7
1996	106.1	108.3	108.8	107.9	104.2	106.2	101.9
1997	100.8	102.8	103.1	102.5	95.5	101.1	105.9
1998	97.4	99.2	99.4	99.0	92.0	97.8	106.3

注: 工农业商品综合比价指数是以农产品收购价格指数为100。
The general purchasing price index of farm products is taken as 100 in calculating the general price parity index of industrial and farm products.